NOW THEY FLY WITH ANGELS

Edward J. Thorne

Now They Fly with Angels ©2009 by Edward J. Thorne

Publisher:
Folio Bookworks
Minneapolis, MN 55407 USA
www.folio-bookworks.com
612-827-2552
liz@folio-bookworks.com

ISBN: 0-9744986-2-9

The illustration of a P-51 airplane on chapter opener pages, and the photo of P-51s on the book cover, are royalty-free. Used with permission from the Air Force Image Gallery and the U.S.A.A.F. Resource Center. Over 3,700 P-51 Mustangs were produced during the war years. The P-51 was prototyped in October of 1940. The Mustang was built as a high speed fighter and was used early on as an escort plane for bombing raids in Europe. It also saw action in North Africa and against the V-1 rocket in Britain. Near the end of the war, the Mustang was used as a fighter escort to B-29 in raids against the Japanese mainland.

"May he fly with angels," a toast by Squadron Commander Irvine to the first combat casualty of one of Ed's friends, was repeated thousands of times during the Air War over Europe.

This book is dedicated to the 50,000 of the author's fellow combat fliers who gave their lives serving in the Eighth and Ninth Air Forces, European Theatre of Operations, WWII. They were members of the great brotherhood of combat fliers. They died too young. The book was written with profound respect, fond memories, and love, by an Eighth Air Force P-51 pilot who came within an eyelash of being one of that 50,000. His story is the story of thousands of young men who went from civilian life into training, then into combat. By the narrowest of margins, he ended his combat career as a POW, instead of as a casualty. In combat, that slight margin, almost always a matter of luck, is the difference between life and death.

E.J.T.

ACKNOWLEDGMENTS

Lois Jeanne (Pat) Thorne, my wife and mother of my four children, gets credit for the existence of this book. When I came home after we had won WWII, she did as she had told me she would before I left to join the war: She waited for me so we could marry, which we did less than a year after my return. Shortly after our honeymoon, over dinners she begged me to tell her about my part in the war. When she heard some, she said, "Ed, you've got to write this down, or you will forget it."

After thinking about it, I decided to do it. She was delighted, and when I finished a page, she would pick it up and read it. Each time she would tell me how good it was, and hug and kiss me.

As time went on, we had children. As they grew old enough to read, I began to type what I had written, then make copies, which I mailed to the children who were then living away, working, and getting married. They always read what I sent to them, and they would call or write about what I had sent. So my children were important in pushing to finish the book.

Various people read early parts of the book. There was, at that time, only one copy—it wasn't typed very well, but all who read it said, "you should get this published!" My children and their children and wives and husbands said the same. All that you read in the book, then, is a product not only of the writer but of those who encouraged the writer, and worked to get it printed and sold.

Of all the readers of the book not related to the writer, one stands out: Sally Barton and her husband.

I thank all of you, and all who read the book.

— Edward Thorne
August 8, 2008

PRODUCTION NOTE

Like many WWII veterans, my father rarely spoke of the war while we four children were growing up. He said he had sealed it in a box and pushed it aside in order to build his family and career. Right after the war he told much of it to our mother Pat, but about twenty years ago, at her prompting, he realized that he wanted to write it all down while he could still bring up the memories. He believed that a detailed account of this part of our family heritage would benefit his own children and grandchildren.

Now They Fly With Angels was typed out in full by Ed Thorne from 1987–89. The remarkable level of detail will be a treasure trove for WWII buffs and all who enjoy military, aviation or cultural history. Dad wanted minimal editing, and we honored that wish. This means that it is a long story, and we know that not every reader will want to read every word of it. We encourage all readers to use the book section headings in the table of contents to dive into topics of greatest interest to them. The writing lends itself to episodic reading, and there are riveting story pieces in each section.

Each of Ed and Pat's four children assisted in production of this book. Jamie and Joe Thorne scanned and converted Dad's massive word-processed manuscript into electronic files. Debra Rose Barry researched and helped figure out printing and publicity options. Erika Thorne coordinated and helped with proofreading and hand-holding. Her spouse, Liz Tufte, brought her professional expertise, sensitivity, and a growing love of our entire family to design the book and tenderly shepherd all aspects of production.

—Erika Thorne

CONTENTS

INTRODUCTION

My father was certainly a hero, and a true representative of the Greatest Generation. This book chronicles his journey from factory worker in Pittsburgh in 1941, to prisoner of war in Nazi Germany in 1944, to liberation by General Patton in May of 1945.

The story includes two clearly deadly moments when no rational reason can be assigned to why he lived:

1. When his P-51 Mustang was shot down and crashed into German territory.
2. In the forced POW march of 300 miles across Poland and Germany in the bitterest winter, with his injuries not yet healed.

Less-stark dances with death abound in my father's story, as they do for every surviving veteran of every war throughout all of time.

Yet it is not heroism, nor his gut-it-out survival instinct, which ultimately makes Ed Thorne's story worth telling. It is the response of this thoughtful, artistic 25-year-old to combat and war. His decision to enlist, taken before Pearl Harbor, was the result of German workers at his factory recounting what the Nazis were doing to European Jews. When the discipline, ritual and pomp of his training in the Army Air Corps contrasted with the slaughter of GIs at Normandy—where he was *not* allowed to dive and strafe the German gun emplacements on the cliffs above Omaha Beach—he wept, vomited, and vowed to devote his life to teaching communication as a better way.

On December 25, 1944, he sang a rag-tag performance of "Messiah" in Stalag Luft III to an entranced and exhausted audience of POWs and Nazi guards. As he describes it in the book: ". . . a great surge of emotion flooded through him . . . as he started 'Comfort Ye.' Ed looked out on the eager faces and saw eyes glittering. . . . . he poured himself into the music . . . feeling his soul emptying itself of anger, frustration and fear. He sensed the listeners giving back everything he gave. . . . Even the commandant and the other Germans stood. No one applauded, as if they all were afraid it would break the spell."

Ed Thorne came to war as a principled young man with an artist's soul. This story is about the trials, tempering, and in the end the triumph of that soul.

—Erika Thorne
October 22, 2008

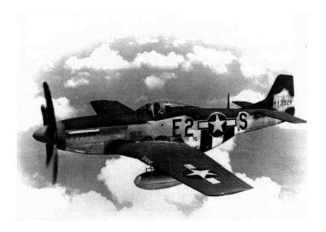

NOVEMBER 4, 1944

The P-51 bucked with the violence of an unbroken mustang. Its pilot's head, bent forward checking cockpit instruments, snapped up. In quick, practiced motion his eyes swept the sky, now suddenly peppered with black puffs of smoke, each with its deadly red core. Simultaneously he jammed the stick forward and left, kicking left rudder, while he shoved the throttle full forward, starting violent evasive moves. In the same instant, he pushed the mike button on the throttle and yelled, "Let's get out of this flak!"

As he did a right wing-over to look earthward to determine where they were to bring on such a barrage of anti-aircraft fire, he had a brief glimpse of his wingman disappearing through the smoke puffs. Disgusted with himself, he noted that they had invaded the airspace over a huge Nazi airdrome, the dispersed enemy planes, 17,000 feet below, looking like toys.

With all the skill acquired on many missions, he changed speed, altitude and direction continuously to confuse the gunners below. From the locations of the puffs around him, he knew that they had bracketed him and were successfully following his changes.

Two puffs, much too close, burst in front of his prop. He felt a jolt. The nose of his ship jerked upward. The engine stopped cold. He drove the stick forward to drop the nose to avoid stalling out, jamming the throttle forward again to restart the engine. It was useless. There was no life in the twelve-cylinder beauty.

Keeping the nose down and circling to the left, he pushed the mike button once more and said, his voice thick with resignation, "I guess I've had it."

Quickly now, he unbuckled his seatbelt and shoulder harness, lowered his goggles, disconnected his oxygen tube, and rolled back the canopy. Reluctantly, for this was his favorite plane, the first one assigned to him months earlier, the one he had flown on most of his combat missions, he started to roll the plane over to pop himself out of the cockpit. He hoped to float down unobserved in his parachute, then make his way to Allied lines.

Halfway over, right wing pointing to the sky, left to earth, earth's details much clearer now, he felt a stabbing pain in his left shoulder. A blow to the chin snapped his head back, and all went black.

DECIDING TO ENLIST

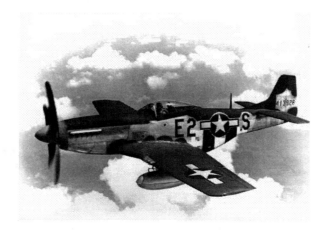

1

The quiet of Sunday afternoon was intensified by the sound of "The Harvest of Stars" orchestra playing softly on the radio, as Ed came down the stairs and into the living room. Only his father was there, reading the "Pittsburgh Press." His mother was resting upstairs, his brothers and sister were all out for the afternoon. Snow had fallen during the night, and it reflected the November sun through the front windows.

"Dad. Do you have a minute to talk?" Ed felt awkward because, although he loved and admired his father, lately they hadn't talked much.

John closed the section of paper he had been reading, folded it carefully, and placed it on the side table with the other sections. He liked to keep the paper neat and orderly for the next reader. "You bet. If you want to turn the radio down a little, I wouldn't care. Oh, James Melton's going to sing. I think you like him."

"I do, Dad. But I've got some things on my mind that make listening to a singer, even a Met tenor, seem sort of unimportant."

"Must be serious for you to say that. What's it all about? I'm listening."

"Okay if I turn it off?" Ed asked. John nodded, looking puzzled. "Dad, what do you know about what's happening in Europe?" Ed had learned years before that with his father it was best to go straight to the point.

"Well, you know, I read the papers and my 'Literary Digest.' And I rarely miss the news on the radio. I guess I know as much as the next fellow." He was a little put out by the question.

"Right, Dad, I know you keep up. The news is scary enough, all right. The Nazis just don't seem stoppable. The war is really going badly for the Allied countries. I'm not sure we can stay out. I think FDR thinks we should be in. What do you think?"

"Not a day passes that I don't pray that we can stay out. That you and John and Bob won't have to go, that any Americans won't. But, if things get worse over there, or something happens with Japan, well, I don't know. You might be right."

"Well, Dad, I think that's the picture, all right. FDR and Churchill are real chummy; Germany is rolling over everybody, and Japan is making more and more threatening noises. But there is something else."

"I think that's enough, son. What do you mean? What else?"

"I mean . . . well. Some of the guys and I have been talking a lot. We don't think we're being told everything about what's happening. We've been hearing stories—rumors—and it sounds really awful."

"Ed, I . . ."

"No, Dad! Let me finish. I know what you've always told us about rumors. And I remember what you told us about rumors during the World War, and how Germans were treated in this country, partly because of those rumors. But, listen, there are reports, printed reports, circulating around—at work, among friends, even in some churches—everywhere. They say things that are so awful that if they are even half, even one-tenth true, then some kind of insanity is loose over there. Dad, it turns my stomach. Gives me nightmares!"

"You mean the rumors about what some of the Nazis are doing? I've heard some of that and, to be honest, I doubt them very much. They're humans, you know, not animals. They've produced great scientists, writers, musicians. How can we believe these stories?"

"I know you've heard some of this, you'd have to. But Bill, Hoot, Joe, and I have been making a sort of collection of these reports. Some of them claim to be from actual witnesses, people who have left Germany and are now in England, Canada, or right here in this country. Dad, it's unbelievable! But for the last couple of months, I've read and heard so much that I'm believing it. The work camps where people are worked on a starvation diet until they die. No medical care, no doctors, inadequate sanitation. Even worse, there are experiments on living people without anaesthetics of any kind. People kept alive and purposely caused pain, by drilling their teeth, putting needles under their fingernails, and worse. Sometimes I'm so horrified I nearly vomit. Other times I'm so mad I think I'm going to blow up."

"Now, Ed, this is . . ."

"Wait! It's no good telling me anymore that it can't be true, that these are old atrocity stories that always go on. I don't believe that any more. Look, there are two tool-and-die makers at work, both Germans. They left with their families just before Hitler moved on France. They got out just in time. I've been talking to them. Not everybody does. One of them knows a lot about music, so we have a common interest. A couple of times, all three of us have gone to a bar in East Pittsburgh after work and we've talked. They're very careful about who's around when they talk. But they confirmed a lot of what I've heard and read. They saw some of it. They think their country has gone crazy. That's why they got out."

"I still don't know, Ed. Just a couple of men. Who knows why they left?"

"True, but that's not all. Have you noticed how many writers, scientists, musicians have left Germany the last few years? We have. Hundreds. Even Einstein! And Fritz Reiner, our Pittsburgh Symphony conductor. You know the Lohners. I talked to Henrietta. They're from Austria. They got out. They couldn't stand what they were seeing happen. There's too much here for me not to believe something very wrong is going on over there."

"All right, Ed. Let's say some of what you've heard is true. Where does all this lead? Aren't you giving yourself nightmares over something beyond your control? If you can't change something, don't you just frustrate yourself by dwelling on it? Can't you put it out of your mind? It's wearing you down. I knew something was. I've been worried about you. Some mornings you look as if you hadn't slept all night."

"It's true. I haven't been sleeping. The images are awful. I can hear the screams, just as if I were there."

"Son, listen to me." On his feet now, his hands on Ed's shoulders. "You can't carry the burdens of the world. Torturing yourself won't help them, and it can only hurt you."

"I've got to do something!"

"Don't do something foolish, now, it's out of your hands."

"Dad, what if it turned out to be true! How will I live with myself, if the war ends, and we learn that the rumors were right? That what I thought was going on WAS going on! And I did nothing. I can't face that."

"It's not yours to do anything about. I understand what you're saying, and I think I can see what you're going through. But it isn't your problem to solve."

"I can't just do nothing. This is eating at me all the time, I've got to do something."

"There's nothing you can do."

"I know I can't influence our national policy. I've written to our congressmen asking for information, and urging more action—at least an investigation. They don't even answer. But—sit down, Dad." His father had moved over to the window. Now, he seated himself in his chair. "There is something I can do." Ed paused, not sure how to say what he had in mind. Again, he decided that the straightforward approach would be best. "Dad, the RCAF, Royal Canadian Air Force, has a training program for volunteers from this country."

This brought his father to his feet again. Shaking his head, he took three steps away, then snapped around to face Ed, "No! No, not when we aren't even in it . . ."

"I've been waiting. We may never get in, I want to sign up with the RCAF. If I'm good enough, I'll be a fighter pilot. If not, I'll be a navigator or bombardier, or a gunner. *Something*. I can do this."

"Dear God!"

"Dad! Dad, listen to me, I can't live with what's inside of me, I've got to do something! This is what I can do. This is what I want to do."

"I won't sign any authorization."

"You've forgotten. I'm of age. I just turned twenty-one last year. I grew up. I know if you could stop me you would. You are a man of peace. But, I want to do this. I'd like to have your blessing, if not your approval. It would grieve me not to have it, but it wouldn't stop me."

Some moments passed, as his dad gazed out the window at the fresh snow, then up at the ceiling, as though searching for something he could say that might change Ed's mind. At last, he spoke. "Let's both calm down and talk quietly for a while. What about your singing career? What will it mean if you leave that for three or four or more years? Those years will be essential. A long interruption at this point in your development could end your career."

"Well, Dad, let's face it. I'm a pretty good second-rate singer. I've tried a lot, but I haven't set the world on fire. Remember, I auditioned for the Radio City Chorus. I didn't even make that! 'Your voice is good,' they said, 'But you're not a choral singer. You are a solo voice, and you don't dance well at all.' End of that story. I tried to get on with one of the famous voice teachers in New York, they all had full schedules and waiting lists, No luck there. And, thanks to what I now recognize as exploitation by my good old voice teacher, 'Prof,' I've never said this to anyone else, my voice is showing serious signs of wear. I'm too young for that to be happening, but it is happening."

"What do you mean? What exploitation?"

"Well, since I seemed to be able to sing anything, and please listeners doing it, and since I guess I'm sort of attractive to girls, he had me sing all kinds of things, under all kinds of conditions and places—often things I should not have been singing at my age, and at my still-developing stage of voice. I was a good showpiece, and a good advertisement for him, I brought in the pupils. I'm not bitter. I must say I enjoyed it. But, now I'm paying for it vocally, and I probably always will. It's time to face facts. I'm not going anywhere with my singing."

"I'm really distressed to hear this. It's news to me, and sad news. I knew he had you singing a lot. You've been gone almost every evening, and nearly always on Saturdays and Sundays. I felt good about it, thought your career was going well."

"That's what everybody thought. I did, too, until the last few months. I got thinking about what was going on, I tried to forget about the fun I was having doing all that singing. I began to see that I was marking time, that I had been for about three years—vocally, I mean. I wasn't making any progress in vocal technique, none at all. Then I began to think about all the voice students he had, many a lot longer than he'd had me. And it really shook me to realize the same was true of them. They'd reached a plateau, not progressing.

"Then I asked myself, 'With all the voice pupils he's had, some of them with real talent, why haven't any of them made careers as singers?' My stomach tightened into a hard knot when I faced the truth: He had only so much he could teach us. But when we reached that level, instead of sending us on to someone qualified to take us beyond that point, he just held on to us, letting us think we were still growing. Actually we were standing still, and as we got older, lacking competent guidance, our voices began to wear out. Remember Marie Tagliani, that beautiful little Italian girl? Remember the first time we ever heard her sing?"

"Yes, I remember that. She sang 'Caro Nome,' really sang it beautifully. What was she? Not very old, I remember."

"She was eight. And, if I ever heard a talent, that was it. But five years later, she was still singing 'Caro Nome' exactly the same way. It was beautiful for an eight year old, but not what a thirteen year old should have done with it."

"What happened to her?"

"She's studying with an excellent voice teacher from Carnegie Tech's music department. Her father—you met him at one of those picnics we used to have—is a no-nonsense Italian when it comes to his daughter's voice. After that recital last spring, when she sang, he came storming backstage, told Prof off, and took his crying daughter out of there. That's when I really began to open my eyes to what was going on."

"This is very sad news for me to hear. You've always shown such promise, always pleased your audiences. You've been in demand, too, and it's what you've always wanted to do."

"It is what I want to do, but it's time to be realistic. I can limp along singing here and there, doing other work to support myself, until I'm old and gray. But if I can't be the best—or one of the best—I'd rather not keep hammering at it. Let's drop this and get back to what we were talking about before. It's much more important than my no-longer-promising career. You were going to bring up something else. Want to go on with that?"

"Yes, but I'm not happy with what you just told me. I'm the one who first took you to Prof for voice lessons. He thought you had a great future as a singer. Anyway, I was about to ask you about that young lady you've been so crazy about ever since high school. What happens to that situation if you sign up with the RCAF?"

"Right. That's another thing. I think I really do love her, but it's hard to know any more. I haven't seen her for about a year now, mainly because I've been afraid to let the relationship go too far. I have nothing to offer her, or any other girl, for that matter. I have no real profession or trade, just barely a start of some college courses, night courses. When defense work is over, I doubt that I'll get anywhere at Westinghouse, even if they keep me. And even if my singing career were really going great guns, it would be years with no real security, just hit-or-miss income. How can I expect a girl to go for that? I remember the Depression well enough to know you can't live on love."

"If she cared enough for you, she'd be willing to take her chances."

"Maybe so, but I'm not willing to ask anyone to do that. But I'm glad you brought it up, I met another girl up at Canadohta Lake when I was up there summer before last, I think I'm in love with her too. Can a guy be in love with two girls at the same time?"

"At your age, I guess you can. In a year or so, though, things will come into better focus;

then you'll know. It might be someone entirely different. You haven't—umm—gotten some young lady in trouble, have you? I'm beginning to wonder if you aren't trying to run away from things, Ed. "

This was a new thought to Ed, one he had to wrestle with for several moments before he could answer, "No, Dad, no one's father is after me with a shotgun. But I don't think I'm running away from anything. I can see how you might think so, but no, it isn't so. None of the other things in my life can mean anything until I face up to doing something about what is eating my guts. I'm going to sign up with the RCAF. I'd like you to say that it's okay."

"Have you told your mother?"

"No, I'd like to have you with me when I do that."

"It'll be hard for her."

"I know. But harder if you aren't willing for me to do it."

"I think it's a waste, Ed. But you will go with or without my approval. So, go with my love and blessing."

"Thanks, Dad, and thank God." For the first time in many years, they embraced.

Ed and his father went into the bedroom where his mother was resting. "Mom, I have something to tell you." She looked up, then got up at the side of the bed. He told her about his intention to join the RCAF. To his surprise, she accepted his decision without hysteria, even without tears. She listened, looked at John, then kissed Ed on the forehead.

"I knew you'd be going." She said it matter-of-factly, dry-eyed. Then she returned to the bed and turned her face to the wall.

As they left the bedroom, Ed remembered how withdrawn his mother had been for the last few months. Had she known? He wondered.

"Mothers have the toughest time of anyone in war-time, Son. She says very little, but I know she's worried; I've heard her crying quietly at night. One night, just last week, I asked her what was wrong. She was quiet for a long time, choking off sobs. I said, 'Tell me.' She turned to me, moved against me, and said, 'They're going to go, John. All the boys. Our three, all of them.' I held her, trying to make her believe it wouldn't happen, that we weren't even in it. But she knew. I guess after that, I did too. It's very hard on mothers, Son."

"You don't think I should go, do you?"

"I'm proud of you for your feelings about what you believe is happening. I've been denying to myself that these things can really be happening. But, in my soul I know they are. I can see why, with your belief, you feel you have to do what you can. I think it's a terrible waste. I don't want you to go; I surely don't. But I think you have to; I respect that. I wish it didn't have to be, but I'll support you all the way."

"God, Dad, that's great! What a load off my mind! Try to make Mom see it too, will you?"

"I think she sees it—and where it will lead—better than any of us. It's troubling her. But she'll be all right, I know it."

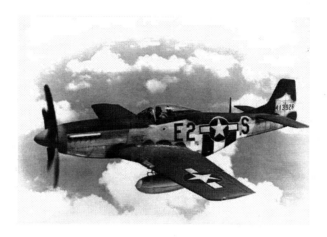

2

Ed came down the stairs two at a time and leaped from the bottom step across the hall into the living room. "Dad, I'm glad we talked . . ." He stopped as his father raised his hand, gesturing silence. Ed saw that John was standing close to the radio, straining to hear words that were indistinct, garbled by interference. ". . . bombing . . . Japanese . . . Pacific Fleet destroyed . . . sneak attack . . . hundreds of Americans dead. Robert Downy . . . from Honolulu."

Ed looked at his father's gray, stricken face. "What . . . ?" Again he was waved to silence.

Now a voice came clearly from the radio. "This is Herbert Kane in New York again. The preceding shortwave transmission from Hawaii was poor due to circumstances beyond our control. We repeat what we have been able to learn: In a sudden, unprovoked attack, completely without warning, and without a declaration of war, Imperial Japanese aircraft attacked several of our bases in the Pacific. The largest forces were concentrated at Pearl Harbor, Hawaii. The surprise attack on the unalerted American forces has, apparently, been devastating to our Pacific Fleet, at anchorage there, and to our Air Corps installations. Details are scant at this point. We are doing all we can to get further information. We now switch you to our Washington facilities, where Douglas Trent is standing by."

"This is Douglas Trent, NBC, Washington. We have only the stories from overseas that you have in New York. We have learned that President Roosevelt has called an emergency

Cabinet meeting. Secretary of State Hull and Secretary of War Stimson were both seen racing toward the White House, police escorts accompanying each. We understand there will be official announcements issued soon. Several senators and government officials have appeared at Government buildings, asking everyone to remain calm. All information will be made available as fully and as quickly as possible.

"We are certain that the President will speak to the nation, likely following the emergency Cabinet meeting. We will, of course, carry that address on this network. Now, our diplomatic correspondent, William Hart, at the State Department. Are you there, William?"

"Yes, I'm here." The voice was breathless and strained. "I just ran into the Radio Room from the office of the Undersecretary of State; he was clearly distraught. He reminded us that Japanese envoys were in Washington at the very time of the attack. They were here ostensibly to continue peace talks with our representatives. What a violation of civilized international conduct! Not only attacking with no declaration of war, no warning, but attacking while their envoys were actually in the capitol of the nation to be attacked! What can we say, what can we think about this? What will President Roosevelt be able to say? This is an outrage! William Hart at the State Department."

"This is Herbert Kane in New York again. Reports and many rumors are coming in. NBC will stay on the air to bring you as much information as possible. I want to assure our listeners that there is no threat—I repeat, NO THREAT—to any part of our mainland. All of our armed forces have been placed on alert, and patrol boats and aircraft are out to detect any threat to any part of the nation. We are not officially at war, but all forces are on a war-footing right now. There is no reason for panic. All citizens are asked to remain calm and to listen for further information and instructions as it is broadcast. This just in! The White House has announced that President Roosevelt will certainly address the nation. Time to be announced later. Please stay tuned. This is Herbert Kane, speaking for NBC, and returning you to your local NBC station."

Ed's father turned the radio down, then sat heavily in his chair. His face held incredulity and horror. Mother came in and stood swaying and moaning softly. In a choked voice, she said, "I knew it! I knew it! What next? What will come of this? What will we do?"

"Mom! Mom, sit down. It may not be as bad as it sounds. Nobody really knows yet. What the President has to say will be important to hear. Sit down, please. Take it easy," Ed said.

John's voice, a little unsteady, husky, as though his throat were constricted, said, "You wanted to tell me something, Son? I shushed you. What was it? Lord help us, we can't stay out of it now. That's what the President will have to say."

"I know, Dad. We can be thankful that he got our industry going earlier, almost on an emergency footing. And Selective Service is operating. Reserve units and the National Guard have stepped up the last couple of years. We aren't really ready, but we've made a start. Oh no! I wonder what's left of the Pacific Fleet? I hope it isn't as bad as it sounded on the radio. Damn! Sorry, we're all shaken by this. What I wanted to tell you doesn't matter now, but I'll tell you anyway. I just wanted to tell you how glad I am that we talked last Sunday, and that I got the papers for the RCAF. I felt a lot better after we talked. The RCAF doesn't matter now. Our own Air Corps will need lots of us now. There'll have to be crash training programs now. They'll have to drop some requirements for pilot training, like four years of college. I'd already heard, even before this attack on Hawaii, that they were planning to substitute some comprehensive tests for the college requirement. I hope so—I'm going downtown tomorrow and see if I can apply."

"You'd better plan on going early," his dad said. "With what's happening today, every recruiting office will be mobbed. I'm glad you told me what was on your mind last week. The whole picture is different now. We've been attacked! We have to respond. I still wish you didn't have to go. But at least now you'll be in our own Air Corps."

"Not so fast, Dad, I'm not in yet. I may not even have a chance."

"You'll make it, Son. You'll get in, and you'll make a good pilot. And . . . well . . . I'll envy you the flying part."

"Okay, Mom? You okay?"

Ed's mother had straightened in her chair. She held her head up. "Of course I'm all right. The waiting for it to happen is over. We know, now. I'll be fine. And so will you, Son. Give it your best and, God willing, come back to us."

"Come on, Mom, I'm not going anywhere yet. It may be a long wait. Things will be in a mess everywhere for a while. I doubt if any of the forces can handle all the volunteers they're going to get now. Where will they put them? Where will they get supplies? I'll bet there aren't even enough uniforms in the warehouses for everyone who will need one. This is going to be a wild time for a while."

"I know, I know. But we have to say things to each other at times like this, or we'll never say them. You will go with my blessing and my love." This said, she looked embarrassed for a moment. Then, "Well, war or no war, it's Sunday and we'll all want something to eat. So back to the kitchen for me."

"Isn't that something, Ed?" said his dad. "It was the uncertainty she couldn't handle. Now we're in it, and she feels all right again. I have a feeling that that will be true of the whole country, too. I hope FDR finds the right words to say it. I think he will; he usually does."

It had been like waiting for a threatening storm to break. When it finally came, it brought a relief of tension, energizing everyone.

The Pearl Harbor attack had been made at a few minutes after 7:30 a.m. Hawaii time, or just after 1:30 p.m. Washington time. At 2:00 p.m., Secretary of the Navy Knox received a flash from Hawaii: AIR RAID PEARL HARBOR—THIS IS NO DRILL. Knox called the President, saying that the message must be in error, that the Japanese would not have attacked Hawaii. The President replied that it was probably true, just the kind of unexpected thing the Japanese would do. At 2:00, the President called Secretary of State Hull, who was about to receive the two Japanese envoys, Nomuro and Kurusu, who would present a note from their government. Just as the President finished his call, the Japanese envoys were ushered into Secretary Hull's office.

The Japanese envoys handed Secretary Hull their government's note. They did not know that Mr. Hull already knew the contents of the note, due to the Americans having broken the Japanese code, and having intercepted and translated the note as it was transmitted from Tokyo to their Embassy in Washington. Mr. Hull left the envoys standing. They did not know, either, that the Secretary knew that the Japanese had attacked Pearl Harbor.

Mr. Hull pretended to read the note. Then he said, "In all my fifty years of public service I have never seen a document that was more crowded with infamous falsehoods and distortions—infamous falsehoods and distortions on a scale so huge that I never imagined until today that any government on this planet was capable of uttering them."

Nomura seemed to be struggling to find something to say. Mr. Hull dismissed both envoys with a nod toward the door.

President Roosevelt met through the day with Cabinet members, advisers and members of Congress, and received phone calls from foreign leaders. Included was an important call from Prime Minister Winston Churchill of Great Britain.

The next day, December 8, the President addressed the House and the Senate in the Representatives' chamber:

> Yesterday, December 7th, 1941—a date which will live in infamy —the United States of America was suddenly and deliberately attacked by naval and air forces of the Empire of Japan.
>
> The United States was at peace with that nation and, at the solicitation of Japan, was still in conversation with its government and its emperor looking toward the maintenance of peace in the Pacific.
>
> Indeed, one hour after Japanese air squadrons had commenced bombing in the American island of Oahu, the Japanese ambassador to the United States and his colleague delivered to our Secretary of State a formal reply to a recent American message. And while this reply stated that it seemed useless to continue the existing diplomatic negotiations, it contained no threat or hint of war or of armed attack.
>
> It will be recorded that the distance of Hawaii from Japan makes it obvious that the attack was deliberately planned many days or even weeks ago. During the intervening time, the Japanese government has deliberately sought to deceive the United States by false statements and expressions of hope for continued peace.
>
> The attack yesterday on the Hawaiian islands has caused severe damage to American naval and military forces. I regret to tell you that very many American lives have been lost. In addition, American ships have been reported torpedoed on the high seas between San Francisco and Honolulu.
>
> Yesterday, the Japanese government also launched an attack against Malaya.
>
> Last night, Japanese forces attacked Hong Kong.
>
> Last night, Japanese forces attacked Guam.
>
> Last night, Japanese forces attacked the Philippine Islands.
>
> Last night, the Japanese attacked Wake Island.

And this morning, the Japanese attacked Midway Island.

Japan has, therefore, undertaken a surprise offensive extending throughout the Pacific area. The facts of yesterday and today speak for themselves. The people of the United States have already formed their opinions and well understand the implications to the very life and safety of our nation.

As commander in chief of the Army and Navy, I have directed that all measures be taken for our defense. But always will our whole nation remember the character of the onslaught against us.

No matter how long it may take us to overcome this premeditated invasion, the American people in their righteous might will win through to absolute victory. (Cheers and applause exploded. The cheers subsided, and the President continued.)

I believe that I interpret the will of the Congress and of the people when I assert that we will not only defend ourselves to the uttermost, but will make it very certain that this form of treachery shall never again endanger us.

Hostilities exist. There is no blinking at the fact that our people, our territory, and our interests are in grave danger.

With confidence in our armed forces, with the unbounding determination of our people, we will gain the inevitable triumph — so help us God.

I ask that the Congress declare that since the unprovoked and dastardly attack by Japan on Sunday, December 7th, 1941, a state of war has existed between the United States and the Japanese empire.

Every newspaper, evening and morning editions, carried the entire text of the speech, accompanied by enthusiastic editorials and commentaries. All regular news programs on radio played recordings of the speech many times over. President Franklin Roosevelt had, as Ed's father had predicted, found the right words. As he so often did, the President had sensed the mood of the nation and expressed that mood in a speech which was to become one of his most notable.

On December 9, the President held his regular news conference, confirming for the reporters much of what he had said to the Congress.

That evening the President spoke to the nation in one of his radio "Fireside Chats." He did not attempt to soften the nature of what they were facing:

We are now in this war. We are all in it — all the way. Every single man, woman and child is a partner in the most tremendous undertaking of our American history. We must share together the bad news and the good news, the defeats and the victories — the changing fortunes of war.

So far, the news has been all bad. We have suffered a serious setback in Hawaii. Our forces in the Philippines, which include the brave people of that Commonwealth, are taking punishment, but are defending themselves vigorously. The reports from Guam and Wake and Midway Islands are still confused, but we must be prepared for the announcement that all three outposts have been seized.

The casualty lists of these first few days will undoubtedly be large. . . . It will not only be a long war, it will be a hard war.

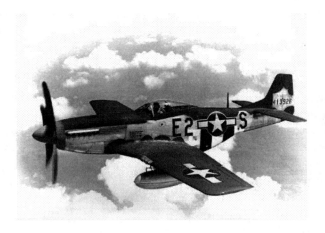

3

The Saturday night following the attack on Pearl Harbor, Ed appeared as soloist with the McKeesport Chamber Orchestra. Originally the program had been made up of French and German songs. After the events of the week following Pearl Harbor, including a declaration of war on Germany and Italy as well as on Japan, the German part of the program was abandoned. In a frenzied series of hastily arranged rehearsals, American and English songs were substituted. Those for which no orchestral arrangements were available were sung with piano accompaniment. The program was completed with only three minor miscues. At the end of the performance, the "Star Spangled Banner" was sung with full-throated, lusty patriotic fervor by the audience, soloist, and orchestra.

A formal reception followed. As is usually the case, boredom set in soon, and guests began to say their goodnights at about 11:45. Half a dozen members of the orchestra invited Ed to a much less formal get-together at the home of a bass player and his wife, one of the violinists. As soon as he could decently do so, Ed thanked the hosts of the reception and escaped.

The informal party was great fun, tinged with the kind of hysteria that was taking hold of the country. "This may be our last party, let's make it a real one!" As a consequence, it was four in the morning when Ed got home, swallowed two aspirins with a glass of milk, and collapsed on his bed.

He seemed barely to have fallen asleep when his mother's screams cut through the blackness of unconsciousness. "Edward! Edward!" The shrieking urgency lifted him out of bed and propelled him down the stairs.

His father was lying face down on the living room floor, fully dressed for church, except for his shoes, held in his right hand. He was lying beside the piano bench, which had been angled partially under the piano by his fall. He was lying very still, ominously still.

Ed kneeled. Gently taking his father by the shoulder, he turned him over onto his back. His dark suit coat was open, his vest buttoned, his tie neatly tied and inside his vest, the orange Parker pen, as always, showed in the inside left pocket as the coat fell farther open. John's freshly shaved face showed good color, but there was no movement, not the slightest tremor, even of the closed eyelids. No rising or falling of his strong chest.

Ed's own chest felt a terrible restriction as he looked at the face, so animated the day before as he had told him about a piece of work he had done at the Evans's mansion that week, matching and replacing a piece of carved wood mantlepiece that had originally been installed nearly one hundred years before. And now his face itself looked wooden in its immobility. While he looked down into his father's face, the color was draining from it.

Certain of what he would find, reluctantly, wanting to avoid confirmation of what he already knew, dreading it, Ed forced his fingers to his father's wrist, probing deliberately for even the faintest flutter of pulse. Tears ached behind his eyes, and as his fingers searched for a sign of life and found none, the tears broke through, running down his face and onto the floor.

Jessie, Ed's younger sister, awakened by their mother's screams and Ed's running down the stairs, now hurried into the room. "Here, Jessie," Ed barked, trying to control his feelings, "rub his wrists. Mother! Get the ammonia bottle; I'll see if I can get Dr. Pyle from across the street." He went to the phone in the hall.

After getting Dr. Pyle's assurance that he would come right over, Ed returned to his father's side. "Come on, Dad! Breathe! Don't leave us!" he said, as he raised John's head and held the ammonia bottle under his nose. "Come on!" shouting now. "You aren't finished living yet!" More quietly, then, sensing the futility of their efforts, "We have too many things to say to you. How can we say them if you aren't here? Please, Dad. Don't go."

Heavy steps sounded on the porch, and the door swung open. Rugged-faced, white-haired, Dr. Pyle stepped into the hall. "I'm afraid it's all over for him," he said brusquely, not pausing in his stride. This announcement brought racking sobs from Mother, and an "Oh no!" from Jessie, followed by a long, moaning sigh.

"Please, Doctor, an injection? Can't you do something?" Ed pleaded.

Dr. Pyle, already kneeling beside John's still form, unsnapped his medicine case and removed a syringe and a vial of colorless liquid. Swiftly and smoothly he filled the syringe and plunged the needle into John's chest. As he depressed the plunger with his left hand, he reached over with his right hand, raised each eyelid in turn, and looked for a moment into each eye. He then held his fingers on the side of John's neck, and slowly shook his head. "It's no use, he's gone. I'm sorry. What happened?"

Ed spoke first. "I was in bed. Mother's screams woke me, Dad was lying right there—on his face. I turned him over. He wasn't breathing, and I couldn't feel any pulse. Then I called you. Mother, can you tell the doctor what happened?"

Hesitantly, her voice tight and trembling, she said, "Daddy—John, I mean—was all ready for church. He . . . he bathed last night, then got up early this morning—he never has been able to sleep late—and he shaved. While he was shaving, I got up and came down to fix his . . . oh, do you want me to tell you all this?"

"Yes, Mother, go on," Jessie said. Dr. Pyle nodded in agreement.

"Well, I fixed his breakfast. Grapefruit and corn flakes. I could hear him singing in the bathroom. He almost always . . ." She broke off with a sob. Wiping her eyes, she continued. "He liked to sing in the morning. I thought I should tell him he'd wake up Jessie and Ed, but I didn't. He came down quickly, seemed to be feeling very good. He had his white shirt and suit trousers on, and his slippers. He hurried into the dining room, put his coat and tie over the back of a chair, saying, 'That looks good, Jess,' and sat down. It was the same breakfast he'd had for years, and he always said the same thing. But he seemed especially happy. I suppose it was because work had picked up and it seemed the Depression was over." Again, she paused, trying to keep from crying.

"It's okay, Mother. Take your time," Ed said.

"Well, I said, 'What church are you going to?' 'The one I always attend,' he replied. 'Why don't you come along? We're going to have some special music.' 'You know I'm not comfortable in that church. I'll walk down and take the streetcar over to Edgewood. I feel more at home there,' I said. 'That's a long walk to the 64 line, Jess, I can go that way and drop you off,' he said. 'What would I do getting there that early? Thanks, I'll just take the streetcar. Or maybe Ed will be up early enough to drive me over in his little Studebaker.'

"He finished eating and wiped his hands and mouth, then stood up and put on his tie, looking in the mirror over the sideboard. He slipped on his suit coat. Then he said, 'Pshaw, I left my shoes in the bedroom.' 'I'll get them while you get your overcoat and hat,' I offered. 'No thanks,' he said, 'I'll have them in a jiffy,' and he ran up the stairs. I remember thinking that he was acting like a fifteen-year-old, running up like that, but I didn't say it. He came down just as fast, still wearing his slippers, and carrying his shoes. He stepped in here and . . . and . . ." She faltered, covering her face for a moment with both hands. Then she raised her head and, as if seeing it all again, she spoke in a low, unsteady voice. "He looked as if he wanted to say something, but all that came out was 'Oh,' and he fell face down, hitting his head on the piano bench. He didn't move. I said, 'John! John, what's wrong?' He didn't answer. I knelt down and shook his shoulder. Nothing happened. 'Dear God, help us,' I remember saying. Then I screamed for Ed." Now she sobbed quietly, deep in her chest. "That's all, that's all that happened, just that fast."

All was quiet for a moment, then Dr. Pyle said, "You will have to call a mortician. If you have a preference, tell me, and I'll call for you."

"Thanks, Doctor," Ed said. "We had no plans for this, of course. Mother, would McKinley's be best?"

"For what? What McKinley?"

"I'm sorry, Mother, Dr. Pyle wants to call a funeral director for us. Would Mr. McKinley be the one you want?"

"Oh, dear, it's true, then? John is gone?"

"I'm afraid so. It's hard, but we have to make arrangements. Unless you want someone else, Dr. Pyle will call Mr. McKinley." His mother made no response, so Ed asked Dr. Pyle to call.

"All right, I'll take care of it as soon as I get to my house. There's one other thing. If your father hasn't been seen by a physician within twenty-four hours of his death, the coroner will require an autopsy to determine the cause of death."

"Will that be necessary, Doctor? You heard what my mother said."

"The law requires it, son," replied the doctor. "You have no choice."

"Will you call him, Doctor?"

"The undertaker will do that, it's routine." The doctor took Mother gently by the arm and led her to a chair in the dining room. "Are you all right, Mrs. Thorne?" She nodded, and he returned to Ed. "Let's lift your father off the floor, Ed, and place him on the sofa. You lift at the shoulders. He'll be heavy, but we can do it."

Ed went to his father's head, but Dr. Pyle said, "Not that way. Come to his side and slide both hands under his shoulders."

Ed moved and knelt beside his father's body. As he started to push his hands under his father's shoulders, his chest felt suddenly compressed, and the pressure of tears behind his eyes was too great to resist. He bent forward, resting his head on his father's chest, and wept. After a moment, he raised his head and looked into his father's face, then reached up and caressed the still cheek, saying, "Dad, I'm sorry, you went too quickly. I didn't have a chance to say 'I love you.' But I did, and I do. All these years, and I never said it. There always seemed to be plenty of time. I'm sorry, I'll always cherish the good talk we had two weeks ago."

Unable to hold back any longer, Jessie knelt on the other side and, between sobs, said, "Yes, Daddy. You were a wonderful father, we all love you."

Now Mother spoke, dry-eyed at last. "He was a good man. We never showed him enough love, but he never failed to show us his—in everything he did. Life is going to be very different for all of us now. We'll have to help each other."

Ed and Jessie were surprised and touched by this simple but eloquent tribute by their usually taciturn mother. They both got to their feet and went to her, embracing her and saying that they would be with her.

"Uh, Ed, we were about to lift your father onto the couch."

"Sorry, Doctor. Of course." Ed knelt again at his father's shoulders, and together he and Dr. Pyle lifted the lifeless body onto the sofa. Ed rebuttoned the shirt that Dr. Pyle had undone, and straightened his father's tie.

"Thank you, Doctor. We appreciate your coming over so quickly. We'll take care of any charges. Just send us your bill," Ed said.

"That won't be necessary; I never charge in cases of this kind. Sorry I couldn't do anything to revive him. It appears that he died instantly, probably before his head struck the piano bench. I must get back; Mrs. Pyle will want to know about your father. You may take comfort in knowing that he didn't suffer. As a physician, I say that I'd rather go like that than linger and suffer, as some do. Good day."

"Goodbye, Doctor. And thanks again."

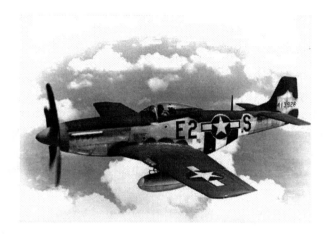

4

"I've talked with Mr. McKinley and Reverend Aiken." Ed's older brother, John, was speaking to Bob, Ed's younger brother, Jessie and Ed, all seated at the dining room table. "The service is all arranged. Dad's choir will sing some of his favorite hymns, and Reverend Aiken will conduct the service. Mr. McKinley thinks Mother, Jessie and I should be in the limousine right behind the hearse, with Ed and Bob, plus Grace and Carl (Dad's two children from a previous marriage), and Harry (Grace's husband) in the second one. Okay?"

"Fine with me," Ed said. "Bob?"

"Okay. Will there be a graveside service, too?"

"A brief one, yes," replied John. "A few words, a prayer and benediction by Reverend Aiken. Then each family member can have a moment beside the grave, after the casket is lowered. Each one who wants to can drop flowers in. Then we return home in the limousines."

Jessie asked, "Is everything worked out about—I mean, Mr. McKinley's bill, and everything?"

"Yes," John answered. "Grace and Harry, Carl and Margaret, and Bob, Ed and I, we're working, so we'll share the expenses. You're still in school, Jessie, so you don't have to help."

"I want to, though, I've saved some money, I want to help. Probably not as much as the rest, but some."

"It isn't necessary, Jessie, we'll take care of it."

"But I want to! I won't feel right if I can't take part in it, the last thing we can do for Dad, I want to."

"We understand. Whatever you can," answered John.

"Is there anything else?" Bob asked. "I have to pick up Ruth. She wants to be with me this evening when people come to pay their respects."

"Hold on a minute, Bob," John said. "There is one other thing. Reverend Aiken would like it if one of us would say a few words at the service, you know, sort of speak for the family." As he spoke, John looked directly at Ed, and soon Bob and Jessie were doing the same.

Reading their looks, Ed asked, "Why me? It would be an honor, but John, you're the oldest. Shouldn't you do it?"

"Well, Ed, since I'm married and not living here any more, and you and Dad were especially close in the last couple of months, I think it should be you. In fact, Jessie and Bob and I talked this over yesterday, and we agreed that you have more experience before the public, and you're the best speaker in the bunch, so you should do it."

"Is that right, Bob? Jessie?" Both nodded, and Ed continued, "Sounds like a plot. Okay, but I'll need your help. I'll want to say what characteristics we'll remember most about Dad, and maybe some anecdotes to illustrate them. Also, I'd rather speak at the graveside service—a last goodbye, you know, just before the final benediction. Bob, before you go, what do you want me to include?"

"Every one of us could give you twenty or thirty things right off. But, you know what keeps coming up in my mind? His sense of joy when he would get away from the day-to-day struggle to feed and clothe us; how he loved to pitch horseshoes, how far he could hit a softball, the fun when he would sing folk songs, and his special humor. Do you remember how he caught us every doggone April Fool's day? How he'd gaze out the front window, then quietly exclaim, 'Well, I'll be switched! Would you look at that!' And we'd all rush to the window to see nothing but an empty street? Then, we'd all get the joke and break up laughing."

"Right," replied Ed, "We bit on that every time, I'll use that. We'll see you and Ruth later, okay?"

"Yes, so long. See you all later," Bob answered as he went to put on his coat.

"John?"

"I'll remember his fun times too. But what I'll remember even more is how he always seemed to know what to do in every situation. I remember when Carl had the Haller's Bakery route, driving a horse-drawn wagon. One really icy day, right in front of the Spahr Street house in East Liberty, the horse slipped and went down, then couldn't get up. Some men passing by stopped to help. They and Carl tried everything, pulling and pushing on that horse, but he couldn't get any footing. The horse was working up a sweat, close to panic. Someone told Dad. He came out with some burlap bags and a bucket of ashes. He told the men to step back and stop yelling. Then, very quietly, he talked to the horse, stroking him gently all the time, until he was calm. Next, he spread the ashes, and put the sacks on top of them. He took the horse by the halter strap, talking and stroking him all the time, and gently got him to move so his forefeet were in front of him. Next, he pulled firmly on the halter, and the horse came up, first with his forefeet, then, feeling good footing from the ashes and sacks, he got his hind feet under him, and he was up. Dad kept hold of him, talking and stroking, meanwhile telling Carl to hitch him up again, and cover him with the sacks so he wouldn't be chilled from the cold air on his sweaty body."

"That's good, John, I remember that, too. You're right! When everyone else seemed to run around in circles, Dad always remained calm, and seemed in control," Ed said. "Remember when the man down the street went crazy and was chasing his wife with a gun? I'll never forget it! I was sitting on the porch swing. The woman ran up on our porch. Dad looked out, took in the situation, and came out the front door just as the man stopped on the sidewalk right in front of our house, aiming his rifle at the woman. Dad never hesitated. He stepped in front of the woman, and with that wonderful voice of his, started quietly talking to the man. The gun remained pointed right at Dad, and the man's finger was on the trigger. I was so scared I couldn't move. I don't know what words Dad said, but his voice was calm, steady, soothing. Slowly the rage and frustration drained from the man's face, and soon he lowered the gun. Very deliberately, still talking quietly, Dad went down the steps and over to the man. He didn't reach for the gun at all. Instead, he put his arm around the man's shoulders and gently guided him up the steps and into the house, taking the woman by the hand as they passed, leading her in too.

"They were in the house for quite a while. I was too scared to leave the porch swing. Finally they came out. Dad had an arm around each of them. They both thanked Dad, and walked together toward their house. Dad called after them, 'God bless you. Go in peace.'" Ed finished this narrative, then turned to Jessie, and said, "I think I know what you'll want me to tell about."

"You're right, if you mean about the hospital."

"You were four years old, Jessie. You were playing with some neighborhood kids at the back of a house half a block away and on a dare you climbed a pear tree to throw down some of the fruit for the kids. As you reached for a pear, the branch you were standing on snapped, and you fell onto a rotting picket fence. One of the pickets tore deeply into the inner side of your thigh, tearing it open and leaving pieces of rotten wood embedded there. The kids ran screaming to our house, and Dad raced to you, gathered you into his arms, and ran home. While Mother called the doctor, Dad applied pressure to stop the gushing blood, and doused the wound with turpentine. Later, the doctor said the turpentine acted as an antiseptic, and probably saved your life."

Jessie took up the story. "I only know this from what the Sisters, a priest, and the doctors told me later, because I was unconscious when it happened. It was a Catholic hospital, even though we were Protestants. The doctor cleaned the wound and removed all the wood he could find. Then he sewed the wound closed. They gave me painkillers so it wouldn't hurt when I came to. The doctor went to tell Dad and Mom that I'd have a scar, but that I should be all right. He was sure that he'd gotten all the foreign stuff out, no internal damage was done, and in a few days I could go home.

"For a few days I did improve. Then I started getting worse. Fever, chills, aching in my leg, then hurting all over. Dad told me later I became unconscious and began wasting away. Dad confronted the doctor and asked him to re-open the wound, that he must not have gotten everything out. The doctor refused, saying that he was certain he'd cleansed the wound thoroughly.

"I got worse, tetanus set in, my whole body began to contract and curve into the fetal position, Dad got angry. He rarely did that, as you know. He told the doctor that if he didn't re-open the wound, he'd get a court order and get another doctor to do it.

"Faced with this threat, with its implication of a malpractice suit, the doctor backed down. I was taken to surgery, the wound was opened, and two more pieces of rotten wood were found and removed. They said that the doctor turned pale and almost cried when he saw them. This time, he probed the entire wound, applied powerful antiseptics, and kept the wound open, with new antiseptics and dressings every few hours.

"The doctor went to Dad and Mom, took Dad's hand, and said, 'I was wrong and stubborn. Your determination may have saved your child's life. She is still in very grave danger. She has tetanus. We are doing all we can to counter that. If she goes into convulsions, especially weak as she is, I don't see how she can survive.'

"I was returned to my room unconscious. Cold compresses were kept on me continuously to try to keep the fever down. Dad and Mom stayed in my room all night, praying and hoping.

"The next morning I went into convulsions. Since the hospital was Catholic, when the Sisters called the doctor, they also called a priest. They all gathered around my bed with Dad and Mom. The doctor held my wrist, shaking his head sadly, and the priest prayed. They told me I looked dead. All the Sisters, the doctor, had no hope. Then, Dad reached out and put his hand on my head. His voice, rich with that faith we all know was a part of him, spoke, 'In the name of the Father, and the Son, and the Holy Ghost, *come out!*'

"There was a moment of absolute silence. Then, startled, the doctor looked up. He felt my muscles start to relax and my pulse get stronger. Color started to come back into my face. I opened my eyes and saw them all standing there. I saw Dad and said, 'Daddy, what's wrong?' He bent over, hugged and kissed me, saying, 'Nothing now, everything's fine now, you got hurt, but you're going to be all right.'

"The priest said, 'Thank God!' Then, to the Sisters and the doctor he said, 'We have witnessed an act of immeasurable faith. We have been blessed. Mr. Thorne's faith moved him to speak directly to God, and God answered. We are blessed to have been here, to have witnessed this.'

"Later, the Sisters told me all of this, and as I got better each day, the priest kept coming in to see me, to touch me, to bless me, and the Sisters treated me like someone very special.

"That's how I will always remember Dad, a man of unchanging belief in God and His goodness, and of limitless faith. And never afraid to show that faith, whatever the circumstances."

". . . This, then, is the man we lay to rest here, a man of strength, of honesty, of integrity, and a man of profound faith. He lives on in our hearts. We are better for having known him. I do not expect to know another like him. We—his wife and his children—will never forget him."

This ended Ed's graveside tribute. Reverend Aiken said a final benediction. Everybody but the immediate family left. The family joined hands at the side of the grave and stood silent, each with his own thoughts and memories, then they went quietly to the limousines and were driven home.

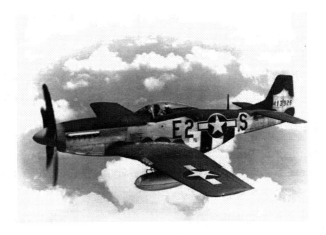

5

Mr. Calahan, chairman of the Draft Board, spoke to the members of the Board. "Edward and Charles Thorne have asked to appear before the Board. I'm sure all members know Ed. He seems to be singing somewhere in our area several times a week. Of course, just about everybody knew him when he was in our high school. Every program they had seemed to include him and his singing. His classmates, including my daughter Mary, elected him senior class president in 1938. No doubt some of you remember him from the time he worked in Bards, down on Noble Street, during his last two years in school. Well, Ed and his younger brother Charles are here now. Hello, boys. Come on up and sit at the table.

"Now boys, you are both properly registered with the Selective Service. I assume you want to talk to us about something related to that?"

"Yes, sir," Ed and Bob replied together.

"All right. Ed, we know that you've enlisted in the Army Air Corps. You notified us of that, and everything's in order there. By the way, Ed, since you're working at Westinghouse Electric, you could have a deferment, since that is a defense industry. Did you know that?"

"Yes, sir."

"Is that why you wanted to see us?" asked Board member Mrs. Carlson.

"No, ma'am. Bob and I are . . ."

"Just a minute," Mr. Calahan interrupted. "You refer to 'Bob,' but we have 'Charles' as your brother's name. Are our records wrong?"

"No, sir. My name is Charles Robert, but the family has always called me Bob."

"Oh. All right, then. What do others call you?" Mrs. Carlson asked.

"The teachers always call me Charles, and the bosses at work do the same. All my friends call me Bob."

"Which do you prefer?" Mrs. Carlson continued.

"It doesn't matter. I guess I prefer Bob."

"Okay, Bob-Chuck. Sorry, I couldn't resist that. Would you continue, please, Ed," said Mr. Calahan.

"Yes, sir. What I started to say is that Bob and I are here to let you know that our father died not too long ago."

Mrs. Johnson interrupted this time, saying, "Yes, Ed, we heard about it. Terribly sudden, wasn't it? We're sorry."

"Thank you, Mrs. Johnson. Yes, it was sudden. No warning at all. Well, Dad died. Our older brother, John, is married and has a son. He no longer lives with us. Jessie, our sister, is still in school. This means that when I leave for the Air Corps, Bob will be the only one left at home who can support our mother and keep the house going. We just want to ask—and this is my idea, not Bob's—that since I've volunteered to go, if you can give Bob a deferment?"

"Seems like a reasonable request," said Mrs. Carlson. "What do you think, Mr. Calahan?"

"Strikes me that way, too. Probably a hardship deferment. We'll have to check it out with the County Board. We'll make a notation of your request, give it full consideration, then make a recommendation. My guess is that it will be granted. Is there anything else, boys?" asked Mr. Calahan. "By the way, if manpower needs get really heavy, many deferments will be taken away. You should keep that in mind."

"Thank you," Ed replied. "That was all we wanted to talk to you about."

Mr. Calahan inquired, "Ed, any word about when the Air Corps will be calling you?"

"No, sir. I've passed all the tests. The physical was pretty thorough, but I made it. The Air Corps sponsored a special evening course in math and physics at Fifth Avenue High for Aviation Cadet applicants. I took the course and, with a lot of help from Park Finney, I passed. Those aren't my strong subjects. I guess enough rubbed off on me, because I passed all phases of the exams the Air Corps required. Did some sweating, though. That was three weeks ago. Captain Florio told us that we could expect a call-up any time, maybe a week, maybe a month. So, I expect it to come any time. I've notified Westinghouse that I may have to leave suddenly. It can't be too soon for me. I'm ready!"

"That's the spirit, Ed!" exclaimed Mr. Calahan. "Let me shake your hand and wish you luck. We probably won't see you again before you go. Take care of yourself. If I were younger, I'd like to be going with you." Mr. Calahan enveloped Ed's hand in his enormous paw. The other Board members shook hands with him, too, each wishing him luck. Mrs. Carlson added, "Don't hesitate to drop us a line to let us know how you're doing. We'll miss you around here, just as we do all our boys."

"I won't, Ma'am. Come on, Bob, let's go home," Ed said. Outside he added, "I'm sorry, Bob. I hated that in there. They were all over me, ignoring you."

"Don't worry about it. They were just doing their job. It's a tough one, deciding who goes and who stays. I didn't mind. Besides, I'm feeling I'll be going eventually, anyway."

"You better not! You heard what they said."

"Yeah, I heard what they said. All of it. I wasn't too impressed. When they start feeling the pinch and have to meet a quota, I think they'll nail me. To tell you the truth, I won't mind. Most of my friends have gone, or are about to. In fact, if I thought I could pass the physical, I'd try for the Air Corps, too. We could each send an allotment home for Mom and Jessie. Might be better than waiting to be drafted and taking whatever they give me."

"Hmmm. You been thinking about this?"

"Yep."

"Might be better in the long run. Especially if you think you'll be drafted anyway. Why wouldn't you pass the physical?" They pulled up at the curb in front of their house, and Ed shut off the engine. "We'd better finish this conversation before we go in. Mom is counting on your staying home. I tried to tell her that you might have to go, no matter what."

"Remember the pneumonia I had when I was six or so? Well, I think that left some scarring or something—something in my chest. Damaged something, maybe the heart, maybe the lungs. Anyway, when I was given a physical for a job, the doctor said that there was something there. He didn't elaborate, and I didn't ask."

"Ouch! I never knew that!"

"Neither did I. I've never felt anything, and he didn't tell me anything more."

"Maybe if the Draft Board does you wrong, you'll flunk the physical and be 4-F. A lot of guys are—football injuries and that kind of stuff."

"Thanks a lot! It'll be just my luck not to be able to pass the Air Corps physical, if I try, and sail right through the Army one. Well, we'll see."

"Listen, Bob, I hope I didn't put you in a bind on this. I really need to go. But I didn't know you wanted to."

"I'm not sure whether I do or not. I think things are going to be a lot different when this is over. Veterans will probably have a lot of influence. It might be that guys who aren't veterans will be at a disadvantage. There will be millions of veterans."

"Yeah, I think you're right. Well, keep on thinking about it, and let's talk some more. Man! I'm starving. Let's see what's to eat inside."

"What did the Board have to say?" Mother asked from the living room as Bob and Ed paused to hang their coats on the hall tree.

Bob replied, "They accepted our request. They'll check it with the county, then make a recommendation. They thought it should be approved. Is there anything to eat?"

"There's some of that ground-meat gravy out there. You can heat it up and put it on bread. There's no milk, though, until it comes in the morning," answered Mother.

"Not sure I want that," Bob said. "Any cheese?"

"You'll find a little in the refrigerator. American cheese."

Ed laughed. "American! No German? No Japanese, if there is such a thing? Ja! Ve haf no Deutsch case today."

"Boy! I could go for some Limburger or Liederkrantz. How about you?" Bob said.

"Jahwohl, mein bruder. Ich liebe der Liederkrantz!" replied Ed.

Mother spoke sharply, "You'd better be careful where you say things like that! You know how touchy some people around here are these days."

"Don't worry, Mother. Only in the bosom of my family," Ed responded. "Come on, Bob. Let's get that grub."

TRAINING
AS AN
AVIATION CADET

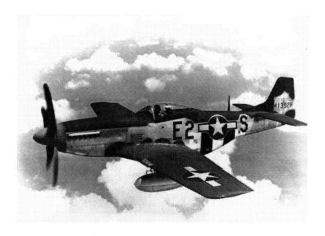

6

The steam locomotive and its train of antiquated, delapidated coaches had barely lumbered out of Pennsylvania station, with families and friends waving and cheering from the platform, before the crap and poker games were under way. Most of the young, newly-sworn-in Army Air Corps aviation cadets, still in civilian clothing, sat on the worn, sooty coach seats. Ed had rubbed some of the grime from his window with a piece of newspaper and was watching the Western Pennsylvania countryside slide by.

After a brief struggle to get the moveable seat-back opposite Ed to shift, Red Hunt sat down facing Ed. Ed knew him from the special preparatory course they had taken at Fifth Avenue High School. "How you doing?" asked the tall redhead. He was one of the few in the contingent with any military experience, having been in R.O.T.C. in college, and having spent several weeks during summers at Army Reserve camps. "Welcome to the kind of transportation the good ol' Army provides for its elite troops. Get used to it. You sleep whatever way you can, you rarely get in the latrine, and you never get a bath. Shaving is impossible. The 'dining service' will be sandwiches and coffee, plus an apple, if we're lucky. Even if you're being shipped all the way to California, it's the same. Before half the day's over, the toilets will be a stinking mess, and the floors will be so dirty you'll have trouble walking from one end of the car to the other. Some of the guys will get stinking drunk with hooch they brought with them, and a couple will be sick. At least one won't be able to get into the toilet in time, so he'll upchuck on the floor. Just hope it isn't near you. Welcome to the wonderful world of the flying corps. If you live through trips like this, some day you might get to see an airplane. Maybe even fly one."

"You trying to discourage me, or what? It won't work, Red. I can handle anything that comes up, as long as I know that sooner or later I'll get to fly, and as long as I can get into combat," Ed said.

"Are you kidding? You sound like an eager beaver. Wow! The Air Corps will be glad to have you. I'll bet you'll be a perfect aviation cadet, too."

"If that's what it takes to do what I want to do, that's what I'll be." Ed would have been angry at Red's needling, except that he knew from talking with him when they took the classes together that Red felt the same way about flying and fighting the Nazis as he did. "Don't try that cynical stuff on me. We both want the same thing."

"Don't be stupid! If you work things right, you can ride out the war and never get anywhere near combat."

"Not interested!" Ed was feeling anger now, thinking he might have misjudged Red. "You can shove that!"

"Okay, okay. Don't get hot! I'm just needling you. I feel the same way you do, but you have to know there are some guys on this train who don't. They joined this outfit because the training would be longer than in other branches. Then they plan to wash out of pilot training just before they finish. Then they'll do the same in navigation school, then bombardier school. They'll just keep it up until the war is over."

"Just keep bastards like that away from me. They're poison, as far as I'm concerned."

"Yeah, I don't want them around me either. But I know from ROTC and Reserve camps that we'll be thrown in with all kinds. They won't all feel the same way we do. If you're smart, you won't start anything with anyone you disagree with; it'll just get you in trouble. You'll get demerits and a reputation as a troublemaker. Suddenly, you'll find yourself washed out. There goes your hopes of being a pilot. Take out your anger in the gym and outside workouts. Punch the punching bag, not your fellow cadets. You can't do anything about those operators. They'll only make you look bad, take my word for it."

"Okay, Red, I'll try. Thanks for the advice. But I hate the guts of guys like that. They want all the good they can get, and let everybody else take all the risks."

"They're everywhere, Ed. Look at the crooked defense contractors. They're opportunists who don't give a damn about anything but making a profit out of this war. God! How can they do it? Kids are dying, and these guys are only interested in getting rich."

"They ought to be shot!"

"Right. But they won't be. They know how to work the system. And they always cover their tracks. Same with the guys who know how to work the army system. A lot of them not only know how to avoid combat action, they'll come out of this rich, too. Damn! Let's change the subject. It's making me sick."

"Good idea. Where do you think they're shipping us?'

"God knows. We might be shuttling around in this claptrap train for a couple of weeks. I've heard talk about Florida, Texas and Kansas, but who knows? The army moves in mysterious ways. Hey! Here come the sandwiches and coffee. I'm ready, how about you?"

"Sure am! Breakfast was a long time ago. All I've had since is a Hershey bar. Hope the coffee's hot—it sure is cold in this car."

"The coffee'll be hot. The army always gives you hot coffee. It might taste like dishwater or lye, but it'll be hot. And when they turn on the heat in this car, it'll get so hot you'll wish it was cold again."

"We can open a window. Ouch! Man, you're right, that coffee *is* hot! I burned my tongue."

"I told you. We'll be lucky if there's one window in this car that will open. So, enjoy the heat—I smell it coming on right now."

"Yeah, I smell it too. What kind of sandwich did you get? This one used to be ham and cheese, I think. I don't care if it's cardboard; I took two. Man, I'm starving."

"Me too. You got ham and cheese, eh? Well, I got cheese and ham. Like that better. The only kinds the army knows how to make: ham and cheese, and cheese and ham. Usually wait until you're so hungry it doesn't matter, just like now. The apples look good. Let's grab a couple. Where do you think we are?"

"I've been trying to watch. I think we're in West Virginia; looks like that kind of country."

"Guess we're headed south, then. Hope we don't wind up in the Deep South when summer comes. Ever been down there?"

"Nope."

"Well, you've got a treat coming. Heat, humidity and mosquitoes. Can't sleep without a mosquito bar. And bugs! Roaches as big as mice!"

"Yeah, sure. What's a mosquito bar?"

"That's army for mosquito netting. Have to have it around your bunk and keep it closed tight. Otherwise, you don't sleep. Those little suckers won't let you."

Evening turned to night. After finishing his sandwiches, Ed got as comfortable as he could. It seemed he had just dozed off when, "Hey Ed! Look alive! Here comes our deluxe breakfast." Red's voice ended Ed's uncomfortable sleep. He looked out at the gray sky of early morning.

"What's that music?" Ed asked, stretching, trying to ease the aches of his body from sleeping slumped in his seat. "Oh, my aching back!"

"Join the group. All backs are aching. Government Issue, GI. You call that music? Some idiot is trying to play 'reveille' on a mouth organ. Looks like the army is providing coffee and rolls."

"Oh, brother! Grab me a couple of rolls and a coffee, will you? I've got to take a leak before I can even look at coffee!" Ed yelled, as he started up the aisle.

"Good luck," called Red. "The line is a half-mile long. Your coffee will be cold before you get back."

"Can't help it. Got to go," Ed replied, as he made his way up the aisle toward the end of a line of twelve men. "This the latrine line?" he asked as he stopped behind the last one in line.

The young man in front of him turned around to look at Ed, then, his eyes crinkling humorously, said, "I don't know for sure, I'll find out." He turned back, bawling out, "There's a Ayviashun Kay-det back here wants to know is this the lay-trine line?" The next one in line repeated the words, followed by each one in line doing the same in turn, each one loud enough for everyone in the car to hear. A ripple of laughter started, and by the time the man at the head of the line repeated the words, the whole car was laughing and repeating the "lay-trine" line.

At the first several repetitions, Ed felt the heat of embarrassment creeping up his face. Then, realizing how ridiculous his question had been, joined in the laughter.

The young man at the head of the line turned, yelling above the general laughter, "Ain't no lay-trine line here. This be a piss-line!" This was shouted out by each one in line back to the man in front of Ed.

By this time, Ed was laughing so hard he could hardly get the words out as he yelled, "Sure figured I was in the wrong line when I saw all the shit-heads ahead of me!"

This brought more laughter and a few cheers. Then someone in the middle of the line yelled, "Whoever's in the can now must have thought this was the shit-line! What're you doing in there?" Another bawled, "Hey! Nobody shits 'til everybody's pissed." "Nobody can piss that long. He's got to be shittin'—come on!" "I think he's jackin' off. Drop it, and get out of there!" "If I piss in my pants, I'm tearin' yours off when you get out of there." "Let's break the door down."

The man in front of Ed turned again and said, "Hi. I'm Bill McKinley. Put 'er there."

Ed shook the offered hand, saying, "Ed Thorne. You had me going there for a minute."

"Yeah, I figured. I half expected a knee in the butt. I couldn't resist doing it, though. Your question just hit me funny."

"It really *was* funny the way it took off. I laughed so hard I nearly wet my pants. Man, I have to go! This line hasn't moved a foot."

"Yeah. Somebody's been in there a good five minutes. Must think nobody else has to go."

"Listen," Ed said, "My kidneys are floating up in my throat. I'm going out on the platform and see if I can let it go out the side of the train."

"You might get court-martialed for indecent exposure," replied Bill.

"When you gotta go, you gotta go, court-martial be damned!"

"I'll be right behind you—this qualifies as an emergency. Lead on."

Ed, followed by Bill, shoved his way to the end of the car and pulled the door open. They stepped out onto the platform, each moving to one side, and relieved themselves as the train lumbered along. "Here's to you, friends and neighbors," Ed yelled, as he finished.

"God, that felt good," Bill sighed, and they turned to go back inside, hampered by a line which had formed behind them when other cadets saw what they were doing.

"Piss across America!" someone called out, and everybody laughed.

"Be sure you aim toward the back of the train, and one at a time on each side, or the wind will blow it right back on you," Ed suggested to the men in line.

Back in the car, Ed said, "Red, meet Bill McKinley. We just had a piss-out."

"Yeah, I know. Better hope nobody gets pissed off. You guys started something. Sit down, Bill. Where're you from? Here's your coffee and rolls, Ed."

"Thanks. Yes, where do you hail from, Bill?" Ed asked. "South Hills, Pittsburgh. Mt. Lebanon, actually," responded Bill. "Red, any word of where we are?"

"Someone said he saw a sign about Tennessee. I don't know where in Tennessee, if that's where we stop. Maybe Nashville. There's a large Army base there."

Bill answered, "I sort of thought we'd go to an Air base, not an Army base."

"Might want to fit us with Army clothes and do a little indoctrination before we go to an Air base," Red said. "But who knows, nobody's ever accused the Army of doing what's logical."

"Yeah," Bill replied. "Hey! I better get back to my buddies, they probably want to get back to playing blackjack. And I need to win back what I lost. See you later. Good to know you."

"Right," Ed said, "later." Then to Red, "Nice guy."

"Yeah, seems like it. By the way, you had me worried when you were in line there."

"Worried? How come?"

"Saw you start to get hot under the collar. Good thing you joined in the fun. If you hadn't, they'd really get on you, never let up. Word would get around that you couldn't take it. That would follow you from there on. Everybody'd be picking on you. That's tough to take. I've seen guys come all apart when that happens. It's tough enough in the army without that. Lucky you got into it the way you did."

"I did start to get mad. Then I saw how funny it was, and joined in."

"You don't usually talk that way, I've noticed."

"Yeah, well, I know all the words, and can use them, they don't bother me. But my family never used them, so I just never got in the habit."

"You're a sojer, now. You got to talk like a sojer. If you don't, guys'll start thinking you're different, stuck-up, or something. We're all guys together, and you have to be one of the boys. That means talking like everyone else, and about the same stuff. It's the same in all military outfits. Part of the way it works is for everybody to be a part of the unit. Anyone who isn't is an outsider, and outsiders can't function in the army. It's a part of belonging together and functioning together. It gets to be like a family, everybody takes care of everybody else. No outsiders. So, don't let yourself get branded as one. If you do, you'll wind up being one. Nothing is lonelier, and nothing is worse in the army. If you're an outsider, nobody gives a damn whether you live or die. It's not a good thing to be in the military."

37

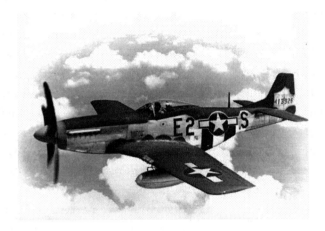

7

"Look! Look at that! D'you see that son of a bitch!"

"Where'd he come from?"

"Oh shit!"

Wakened by voices the length of the car, Ed realized that the train was no longer moving. Sitting up abruptly, he quickly saw what was causing the exclamations. Standing erect and motionless, just inside the front doorway of the car was a sergeant, looking as if he had just stepped out of a "Life" magazine picture of the perfect soldier. Light brown hair neatly trimmed, tanned face clean-shaven, shirt and trousers perfectly pressed and fitted to his trim, muscular body, as though they were an extension of his skin; belt buckle gleaming in the morning light, shoes reflecting that light almost as brilliantly as the "U.S." on one side of his collar and the metal Air Corps insignia on the other; necktie neatly tucked into his shirt-front; three inverted cloth vees with three rockers under them, indicating his rank of master sergeant, and four cloth bars lower on his sleeve, indicating four four-year hitches in the Army.

He stood quietly erect as the voices subsided, and then quieted completely. Then he spoke, his resonant voice carrying easily the length of the car.

"Misters, I'm Sergeant Stuart. I'm in charge of all the Misters in this car. The train is on a siding not far from Nashville. Shortly, several GI trucks will arrive here. At that time I will dispatch you in an orderly way, single file, to exit this car by the door behind me, and load into the trucks. Take all of your belongings with you. Anything you leave behind will become the property of the train crew. You will need your overcoats or jackets. There is no heat in the backs of GI trucks. When all of you are loaded into the trucks, we will depart for a nearby Army Post, where you will be assigned to barracks. You are now under military control, and under my command. Anyone not boarding the truck to which he is assigned, or not present in his assigned barracks when I come to call the roll, will be AWOL, and will be a candidate for immediate transfer out of the Air Corps and the aviation cadet program and into the infantry.

"You will be assigned a bunk. That will be your bunk while at this post. There is to be no swapping or changing bunks. When you enter your assigned barracks, place your belongings on, under, or at the foot of your bunk. You may use the latrine at the end of the barracks, but do not attempt to take a shower or to shave, though God knows you all need both!

"Shortly after you are in the barracks, I will come in. At that time you are each to stand at the end of your bunk. I will then check the roll. After that, I will say 'Fall out.' At that point you are to exit the barracks and line up four deep in front of and facing the barracks. You will get your first experience in making a formation and marching. We will march to the mess hall for breakfast. After breakfast, we will form up again and march back to the barracks. There will be a time to ask questions after breakfast. Until further notice, you are to remain in your barracks, until and unless I tell you otherwise. There will be a time later to get out and look around. Your training as military men and potential fliers starts here and now.

"Now, get your belongings together. Keep your seats until I call your name, then pick up your things and move out the door to the truck. Corporal Johnson will be there to get you aboard."

With that, he opened an envelope and, taking out a list, started calling off the cadet's names in alphabetical order.

Once on board the trucks, the expected expressions of anger and frustration began.

"What the hell is this!"

"What the fuck are we going to an Army base for?"

"There's no godammed Air Corps training base at Nashville."

"We been had!"

"We got sucked in, and now we're gonna be son-a-bitchin' foot soldiers. I knew it!"

"It'll be a cold day in hell before we see an airplane."

"This shit stinks!"

Red Hunt spoke up. "Hold on now, wait a minute. You know the Air Corps isn't ready for us. I'll bet this is a temporary assignment. We have to be sent somewhere to be issued uniforms and equipment, and get physicals. And most of us don't know left from right in drill. My guess is this is where we'll get that, and at least make a start on acting and looking like cadets."

"Hey, redhead, what the hell makes you so smart? What do you know that we don't know?"

"I don't know anything, I'm just guessing. But the Air Corps is short of pilots, navigators, and bombardiers. We all know that. So we can be sure they didn't test us and sign us up just to dump us out of the program before we even start training. So why don't we . . ."

"Okay, Red, you're probably right. Anyway, we can ask the sergeant when we have the question time after breakfast." He started to sing 'Into the Air, Army Air Corps.' Everybody joined him in the song, and they sang their way to the Army base.

Soon after that, the truck turned off the highway and stopped briefly at a guard hut, then proceeded, sliding, skidding, kicking up red mud on a mucky, rutted dirt road, finally sliding to a stop in front of a row of one-story wooden barracks buildings. The barracks looked totally unlike those pictured in recruiting posters. Each one stood on concrete block pilings, and was surrounded by the same red mud the trucks had just plowed their way through. None of the grass, shrubs or trees that appeared around recruitment-picture barracks, and none of the clean white paint they usually showed. Rather, the entire area was barren of plant life, the paint on the barracks was weathered to a dull gray, and peeling in places. The wooden steps up to the doors were dilapidated with weeds growing under them. The windows were caked with dirt.

Sergeant Stuart and the driver, Corporal Johnson, appeared simultaneously, Stuart on the right, Johnson on the left of the rear opening of the truck. The corporal lowered the tailgate, and the sergeant said, "All right, Misters, welcome to your home away from home. Bring your belongings and, one at a time, jump down. Watch your step, this gumbo is slippery."

Before the sergeant got that out, the first cadet, Bob Mitchell, grabbed his suitcase and jumped. His feet went out from under him as he landed, and he fell flat on his back. "Son of a bitch!" he yelled, getting up, red mud sticking to his back from his shoes to his hair.

The others couldn't help laughing. After that, each one dropped his bag out first, then put his hand on the floor of the truck to steady himself as he landed. Each one after Bob landed and stayed upright. But each one found his shoes stuck in the mud. The mud gripped them like red glue. Several found their shoes stayed in the mud when they tried to step forward.

"All right, Misters. As I read off your names, pick up your stuff and go in. Scrape the mud off your shoes on the mud scraper at the top of the steps. First man called takes the first bunk on the left. Second man the first one on the right, third takes the second on the left, and so on. I'll be right in after the last one in to check that everyone has the correct bunk. Then we'll go for chow. First Mister, Anderson, George."

The inside of the barracks was worse than the ouside. The reactions were immediate as the men stepped in. "What the hell is this? A prison!" "Look, no mattresses or pillows, no bedding on the goddam bunks!" "The fucking toilets are filthy, and they don't flush!" "Situation's normal, all fucked up!" "We've been screwed!" "Man, I'll never believe a recruitment poster again!" "So this is the way the Air Corps treats us elite?" Each man voiced his disgust as he entered.

As the bitching crescendoed with the last man entering, everyone yelling at once, Sergeant Stuart appeared in the doorway. In a voice that topped the hubbub, he roared, "AttenHUT!" Red Hunt, reacting to his Reserve training, leaped to his feet and into the attention stance. Ed, who had been sitting on a bunk near Red, followed suit. Others slowly did the same. As some remained seated or slouching, the sergeant roared, "Move it Misters! On your feet, eyes straight ahead, chin and gut in, hands and arms at your sides, heels together, let's go! When you hear 'Attenhut!' move, drop what you are doing, shut up, and pop-to."

When all the cadets were standing in a reasonable imitation of "attention," Sergeant Stuart called out, "At ease." Various men slouched or slumped, some starting to sit down, and half-a-dozen began to yell, all at the same time. "What kind of bunks are these? Where are the mattresses? How come this place is so filthy?"

The sergeant roared again, "AttenHUT!" Every cadet popped to. "Now then," Stuart said. "*At Ease* does not mean fall down or take a rest. It means put your hands behind your back, spread your feet, and keep quiet. Let me demonstrate for all of you how you should look when at *Attention,* and at *At Ease.* This is *At Ease,*" and he took the stance he had described. "Now I'll give the command *Attention* for myself. You ignore it this time, but never again! AttenHUT!" His heels came together with a resounding click, as he popped into what they would learn as the perfect "attention" position.

"Now," he continued, "I'm going to call you to attention. Then I will order you to assume your assigned positions. At that point, each of you is to stand at the foot of your assigned bunk, as I am doing at the foot of this one, at attention. "AttenHUT!" he barked. All of the cadets snapped to attention.

"Not bad," said the sergeant. "You will improve. Assume your assigned positions!" Each cadet went to his bunk, taking his place at the foot, standing at attention.

"Good!" called the sergeant. "Now, remain at attention as I check the roll, and respond with 'present' when I call your name. He proceeded to call each cadet's name, making sure that each one stood in front of the proper bunk. Having finished that, he returned to the doorway, where he said, "Stand at ease. Now, this time as I call each name, you are to go outside where you will form up as follows: First man out will go into the street and turn right, line up with the corner of this barracks, facing the barracks, remaining there at ease, until I come out after the last man is called. The second man will line up one step behind the first man; third man behind him, fourth man behind him, fifth man will line up to the right of the first man, sixth man behind the fifth man, and so on to make up a formation of four lines. Each of these lines will be called a 'flight,' and all four flights will be a 'squadron.'" With that, Sergeant Stuart called "Attenhut!" and started down the roll again, each man going out the door as his name was called.

As the last cadet came out, Sergeant Stuart followed him, stopping in front of the center of the formation. "Attenhut!" he called. "This is a raunchy formation, We have to dress it up. To do that, I'll give you the order, 'Right Dress,' which means you do this." He demonstrated, placing his left hand on his left hip and turning his head to the right. "When I give the order, do just as I showed you. The order will be 'Right Dress!' On the word 'dress,' your left hand goes to your hip, and your head snaps to your right. You then space yourselves so your left elbow is just touching the arm of the man on your left, and you form a straight line by centering yourself on the man to your right. When you have done that, I will say 'Eyes Front!' On 'front' you will snap your heads back to the front, and drop your left arms to your sides, remaining at attention. Ready! Right Dress!" After considerable shuffling back and forth, and from side to side, the columns were fairly straight, and the sergeant seemed reasonably satisfied. "Eyes Front! Well, not bad. You'll get better. Now, I'll give the order, 'Rest.' This is more relaxed than 'At Ease.' Your hands need not remain behind you, and you may talk quietly, but still remain in formation. At that time, I want the cadet at the right end of flights 2, 3, and 4 to raise his arms straight from the shoulders with the hands open, and the fingers just touching the man in front of him. That will be the proper spacing between the flights. When you have done that, drop your arms and the rest of the men in each flight are to line up on the four anchor men.

"I will call you to 'Attention,' order 'Right Dress,' 'Front,' then 'Left Face,' and we will be on our way to chow. All right, line up now. Squadron, Attenhut! Good. Right Dress! Eyes Front! Left face! Settle down, get your columns straight. Okay, Forward Harch! Left, left, left right left. Hup, hup, hup, hup. Look proud. Uniforms don't make men. Look proud in your dirty civvies. You are in the Army Air Corps."

In reasonable order, the squadron slogged through the mud to the mess hall, where the sergeant halted them. There he ordered, "Right Face!" Following that, he said, "Now I will give the order, 'Fall Out' to each of the flights in order. When given that order, the named flight will leave the formation and form a single line inside the mess hall. You will see a long counter. Go to the end nearest the door, pick up a tray, silverware, and a cup. Move down the counter to get your tray filled with food. Take all you can eat, and eat all you take. You will be free to talk in the line and while you are eating, until I call you to Attention. Flight One is the front line, facing me; Two, Three, and Four behind in order. Ready, Flight One, fall out."

The hungry cadets, with many exclamations of approval and audible sighs of satisfaction, finished eating. Sergeant Stuart called them to attention, formed them up outside the mess hall, and marched them back to the barracks. There he dismissed them, and followed them in. After all who needed to relieve themselves returned from the latrine, the sergeant sat on one of the bunks, and all the cadets gathered around him.

"All right, men, relax. Smoke, if you have them. Sit or stand, as you wish. You did all right in your first formation and march. You'll get better, a lot better. Some of you, being smart-asses, probably wonder why you, as potential fly-boys, should drill. It's basic to your training. You'll be doing it every day from now on, wherever you are sent during your training. You will learn to respond immediately and with precision to every order, no hesitation, no questions. Do it! You will learn to function as a unit. This will be drilled into you every step of the way. Your lives will depend on this kind of response when you finish training and go into combat as pilots, navigators, bombardiers. In fact, long before you are ready for combat, your lives will depend on immediate and appropriate responses to orders, or to situations. When your flight instructors give you an order, do it RIGHT NOW! For instance, you may be taking off. You pull back on the stick too soon. The ship starts to stall. He will sense that. You probably won't, early in your training. He'll yell, 'Give it more throttle, and put the stick forward!' Do it! You won't be far enough off the ground to waste any time. You must react immediately to his command, or you crash. That's what drilling is all about—immediate response with absolute precision.

"You will always function as members of a unit. The integrity and efficiency of the unit depends on each member knowing his function and carrying it out. That must become second nature to each of you. Making that happen starts here, with the orders I give you, with the drills I will put you through. You won't always like it, but do it. You'll do it here, you'll do it at Maxwell Field, you'll do it at Primary Flight School, in Basic and Advanced. Kids like you who can't, or won't, get good at it, wash out of the program. It's tough, and your goddammed bones will ache, but you've got to do it to make it.

"Some people even learn to like it. The feeling of being part of something bigger than yourself, of functioning as part of an efficient unit, can be a good feeling, and a necessary one in combat situations. My advice to you is to get as good at it as you can, as fast as you can. You can still be an individual while you are a part of a unit, but you can't go your own merry way when the unit is functioning.

"You will be part of a flight; the flight will be part of a squadron; the squadron a part of a group; the group part of an air force; the air force part of the whole Air Corps; the Air Corps part of the Army. Every part depends on the others. If any individual fails to carry out his function, not only does he endanger himself, he endangers the entire unit. Your training includes not only teaching you the skills of your job, but making you an efficient, functioning part of your unit. You will learn that without your unit you are worthless. The entire military system depends on you, not as an individual, but as a functioning part of a unit. That is why you will drill throughout your training, and why you will march to and from the mess hall, to and from classes, P.E., the flight line, to stand retreat, and so on."

Listening to the sergeant, Ed felt his respect for this man, who was articulating a concept of military organization and functioning clearly and without loud declamation, growing. He glanced at other cadets near him, and saw that they were as rapt as he was.

Sergeant Stuart continued, "Now, before you start asking questions, let me tell you that you, if you don't wash out, will become fliers and officers. Every one of us non-coms here envys you the fact that you will fly. We all wish we could. We are all career Army men. When the cadet program was established, we requested assigment to it. Those of us who met the qualifications were assigned. We are too old, not by much, but too old to be cadets. We are all devoted to the Air Corps, and to the cadet program. Most of you have college. It may surprise you to know that every sergeant here either has, or is near, a master's degree. We have earned our degrees in night school, Saturday classes, and by getting furloughs or leaves to go to school. Don't sell us short. If we were eligible, we'd be right with you in the program. We'd like that. We can't be, so we are doing the next best thing—helping in the training program. Some of us do fly, by the way. We've taken flight training at our own expense, and on our own time. But you will get much better and more extensive training than we can get. And you get it free, you lucky bastards!" With that he gave a big laugh, and the cadets joined in. Along with Ed, they were all clearly impressed by this articulate and knowledgeable man. He was some ten years older, but clearly he shared their dreams of flying. He had acted on his dream, in the limited way he could. What he had said strengthened their determination to succeed in the cadet program, whatever it took.

"Okay, now. That's enough of that for now. I know you want to know what's happening here, so shoot your questions."

"What about showers? I stink."

"Right. It's cold-only today. Tonight and tomorrow morning, too. We've been promised the boilers will be operational by 15:00 tomorrow. Cold ones aren't so bad after the first thirty seconds. Besides, they say it helps keep down hard-ons." He said this with a laugh, and he was joined by hoots and yells from the cadets.

"We expected to sleep on these bunks without mattresses? Will that keep our peckers down too?"

"I doubt that would help. It might keep you from sleeping enough to have wet dreams, though. Mattresses and pillows will be here right after noon chow. When we get back, the truck should be here. I'll hold you in formation in front of the barracks. Flight One will go to the truck first, two men to each mattress. Carry, do not drag, into the barracks, placing the mattresses on bunks as you come to them. Flight One will exit and re-form. Flight Two will then do the same. We will continue until every bunk has a mattress. Then pillows will be handed out, one to each man.

"After that, we will form up and march to the equipment depot where blankets, sheets and pillowcases will be issued. We will then march back here and have a drill on military bed-making. You'll have to learn this. Every day you will have to stand inspection, as long as you are cadets. Learn how to make your bed fast, and do it right. You'll be sorry if you don't. You'll be going to Maxwell Field from here, and they are tough there. Learn it here, and save your ass there."

"What about uniforms? And heat?"

"Heat will be on tonight, guaranteed. Uniforms? It'll be another day or two. Make do with your civvies until then."

"This place is filthy. We supposed to clean it?"

"There is good and bad on that. The good is that a crew of civilians will come in here after we finish our bunk-making drill. The bad is that you have to be out of here while they work. When they show up, I'll call you for formation.

"We'll do some drilling, then I'll march you around the base to get you oriented. Don't leave watches or wallets or rings lying around, or those silver I.D. bracelets your girlfriends gave you. Other stuff will be safe. Corporal Johnson will be here overseeing the work. He'll watch for sticky fingers."

"What the hell went wrong with this place that it isn't ready for us?"

"SNAFU. Situation all fucked up. When with your parents, it's situation all fouled up."

"Looks like that's what we've got here."

Stuart said, "The SNAFU is a little thing called Pearl Harbor. President Roosevelt and the brass have been trying to get us mobilized, but this country wasn't ready for it. They barely got the Draft set up after a tough struggle. Pearl Harbor happened, and suddenly people were screaming for an overnight miracle. The Southeast Training Command, which is what we're in, has been trying to do in a few months what should take two years. Everything is getting done, but not everything can be done at once. Suddenly millions of uniforms and shoes and gear have to be made and shipped to bases. Bases that haven't been used for years, like this one, have to be activated. We'll get it done, but it's a hassle. It'll get better. This country will be one huge, well-oiled war production machine. For now, we all have some inconveniences. While you're going through this, the airplane companies are working twenty-four-hour days, seven days a week, to build the ships you'll train in and then fly in combat; gun-makers are turning out the weapons you will use; ship-builders are turning out ships that will carry your asses into theaters of operation; food-processers are getting the food out to feed us. The SNAFU is the result of isolationists, America-firsters, pacificists, and just plain head-in-the-sand voters who kept saying, 'It's not our war,' and 'Let's stay out of it.' That all came to a screeching halt when the Japs did their sneak attack last December 7. Sorry, I got a little preachy there, but it burns my ass! Anybody who wasn't blind could see that we couldn't just isolate ourselves and stay out, not with the things that were going on. And plenty of people tried to tell everyone. Now, the same people who were yelling, 'Stay out of it!' are bitching because we aren't totally ready right now. Well, what the hell, let them bitch, we'll get there."

Suddenly pandemonium broke loose, as every cadet jumped up and started to yell, "Yay, Sarge! Tell 'em, Sarge!" and applauded.

"Okay, okay. Settle down. Thanks. Now, you're on your own until chow time. Take a cold shower, shoot the shit, do what you want. But be here at 11:45 hours, ready to fallout."

With that, Sergeant Stuart left. High morale had been restored for the cadets.

For the next two weeks, as things fell into place, heat came on, hot water flowed, uniforms arrived and were issued, the cadets drilled in the mud, perfected their bed-making speed and skill, were issued footlockers and learned to pack them and keep them in order for inspection, learned military terminology, both official and unofficial, saw training films and some feature films, got hardened to and by physical training every day, played pick-up softball, talked endlessly and eagerly about what Maxwell Field would be like and, more importantly, Primary Flight Training after Maxwell. Each one already seeing himself as a super pilot, flying unscathed through endless hours of combat, returning home a hero, ready to volunteer to return to combat in a different theater. Flying was their objective and the end-all of their existence. The horror of washing out of the program was out there, but no one thought it would happen to him. As to the other, greater horror—war—it never interfered with their dreams of glory, or, in Ed's case, and a few others', of ending what they knew to be the horrors of the Nazi regime.

On the morning of the cadets' scheduled departure, Sergeant Stuart stepped into the barracks, called them to attention, and conducted the inspection that had become routine. The only difference being that each cadet, as instructed, instead of making his bunk, had removed the sheets and pillowcase, folded them and the blankets, and stacked them neatly on the end of his bunk.

After the inspection, the sergeant called, "At ease." The cadets snapped to the proper position. Sergeant Stuart moved down the two rows of cadets, shaking each one's hand and wishing him luck. Then, standing near the door, he said, "Misters, you've shaped up into pretty respectable-looking military men. You look healthy, sharp and alert—different from the raunchy bunch that came here just two weeks ago. You're the first to be processed through here. You're going on to bigger things. Remember the basics you've learned here, and build on them. You'll do fine. Finally, I wish to God I were going with you. Rest!"

Red yelled, "Let's hear it for Sarge. Hip, hip, hurray!"

All the cadets joined in with wild enthusiasm.

The last they saw of Sergeant Stuart, their first Army Air Corps mentor and friend, was him standing alone in front of their barracks, looking exactly as he had when they first saw him on the train. He did not move as the buses carrying them pulled away.

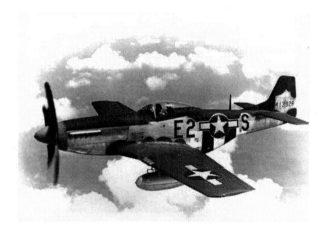

8

"Hey! This is more like it!"

"Yeah. This looks more like recruitment pictures."

The bus had just pulled up to the neat, freshly-painted guard hut, where perfectly uni-formed, white-gloved military policemen were checking the orders handed out the driver's window. Stretching in a straight line ahead of the bus was an immmaculate, smoothly-paved road with manicured lawns neatly trimmed at its edge. Some one-hundred yards down the road was a huge banked flower bed spelling out MAXWELL FIELD.

The M.P. sergeant said to the bus driver, "Proceed straight ahead to the first intersection. Turn right to the reception area. Cadet officers will take over there."

As the bus turned at the intersection, the cadets could see neat rows of single-story, light-brown stuccoed buildings, each with well-tended grass and shrubbery, and a screened ver-anda running its entire length. In front of the grass area was a perfectly straight, clean, paved sidewalk edged by another strip of grass, fronting on a wide, immaculately clean street.

Except for fatigue-wearing men trimming shrubs and grass, there were no people in sight, no cadets loitering or lounging about. Then, as the bus moved toward the recep-tion area beyond the grouped barracks, singing was heard. A squadron of cadets, in perfect formation and lustily singing "Alouette," came out of one of the streets, executed a perfect "Column Right," and passed the bus in the opposite direction, without one marching cadet so much as glancing at the bus. One cadet, a chevron on his sleeve — indicating that he was a cadet officer — marched at the side of the column, clearly in command.

The bus pulled up and stopped in front of four spit-and-polish turned out cadet officers, shoes, belt buckles and insignia sparkling; shirts and trousers perfectly fitted and pressed, the trousers showing razor-sharp creases; their hair neatly trimmed and faces cleanly shaved. The taller of the four, the one with four chevrons on his sleeves, stepped to the bus door and called out, "All right, Misters. Get your handbags, debark, and form up facing the three officers standing there."

The cadets, glad to be out of the bus, rushed out and formed up as Sergeant Stuart had taught them to do. When the cadets were in position, but not at attention, the tall cadet officer stepped in front of them and said, "Put your bags on the ground to your right. Now, Attenhut!" The cadets popped to. "Dress it up! You look too sloppy to be cadets. The cadets shifted about to straighten the formation, after which the officer said, "Not good, but better. Parade Rest," and the cadets snapped to that stance, "Not too bad for a bunch of zombies. I'm Cadet Major Brubaker. I'm commander of I Squadron, to which you are now assigned. I find you a raunchy gaggle of zombies. As raunchy as I've ever seen. You will shape up, or you will ship out. This squadron tolerates no sloppiness, no unmilitary appearance or behavior, and no insubordination. Orders given by any cadet officer are to be obeyed instantly, and without hesitation or challenge. In addition, since you are underclassmen, known as rats and zombies, orders given to you by upperclassmen, who are in every way superior to you, are to be obeyed. No question, no hesitation. Instant obedience! You will understand, and don't forget it for a second, that we operate strictly on the honor system here. Any lying, stealing, cheating on tests, shirking responsibilities, missing formations, copping out on physical training, or any other hint of less-than-honorable behavior, will result in your being drummed out of the Corps. That would be the end of your career in the Army Air Corps. Now, Misters, I find your uniforms, your unshaven faces, your unshined shoes, your generally slovenly appearance, unacceptable."

Major Brubaker then stepped up to the front rank of cadets, and stopped directly in front of Ed. Looking straight into his eyes, he said, "Mister, how do you account for your sloppy appearance?"

Ed started, "Well, we . . ."

"At ease, Mister," ordered the major. "Pop to! When an officer or upperclassman speaks to you, you pop to, understand?"

Ed popped to attention and said, "Yes, Sir." "Now," said Major Brubaker, "How do you answer my question?" "Well, Sir, we've been . . ." He got no further. "At ease!" barked the major. "I'm losing patience with you, Mister. The only acceptable response is 'No excuse, Sir.' Now, you pop to! Zombie! Do you call that popping to? I want to see you in a 'brace.'

That's what 'pop-to' means around here. Especially for zombies, suck in your gut until it rubs against your spine! Make your chin disappear! Get your shoulders back so they touch behind you! Tighten your butt muscles so you get red in the face! Come on, Zombie, you aren't trying. Show some strain! Do it!"

Ed sucked and squeezed and strained every muscle and part of his body, and his face turned red, sweat broke out on his forehead. He held his breath so no muscles would move.

"Better, Zombie. You'll learn. Now, do you understand me?"

"Yes, Sir," Ed replied in a half-strangled voice.

"All right, Mister. Now, ease into attention, before you bust. What's your name, Mister?"

"Edward Th–"

"At ease! Your response is 'Aviation Cadet, last name, first name, middle initial, and serial number.' Always, and every time an officer or upperclassman asks your name. Now, what's your name, Mister?"

"Aviation Cadet Thorne, Edward J., 13129304, Sir."

"That's better. Resume Parade Rest. Every one of you rats remember what I just taught Mr. Thorne. If you don't, you'll spend a lot of hours walking tours, carrying a full field pack, in the hot sun. And it will be on Saturday afternoons, when you could be in town, or playing cards, or relaxing. Some other lessons you are to learn right now. You won't be told again. Any time you are in your room and an Army officer, a cadet officer, or an upperclassman, steps through your door, the first rat to see him immediately calls 'Attention!' and every mister in the room is to pop-to, remaining in that position until given the order, 'At ease,' or 'As you were.'

"Next, as long as you are underclassmen, you never step out of your rooms unless you are in the uniform of the day, and in perfect order. The moment you step out of your door, you are to be at attention, walking 160 paces per minute, and on the ratline. The ratline is the outer edge of the stoop right next to the screen, and the outer edge of the sidewalk. Your eyes must be straight ahead at all times, and every corner you turn must be perfectly squared. You are to stop only if ordered to do so by an officer or upperclassman. Under no circumstances is an underclassman to address another underclassman outside your rooms. You are to be silent unless spoken to by an officer or upperclassman. Even then, you are limited to 'Yes, Sir, No, Sir, No excuse, Sir,' or to identify yourself as indicated earlier. If you have something else to say to an upperclassman, you must request his permission to speak, as follows: 'Aviation Cadet Thorne, Edward J., 13129304 requests permission to speak, Sir.' Then, if permission is granted, you may speak.

"Further instruction in proper conduct for underclassmen will be given to you for the rest of today and tomorrow. It is now 08:00 hours. You will be marched in formation to your barracks and dispatched to your assigned rooms. Your foot lockers are already there. At 1000 hours you and your rooms will be inspected. Your rooms will be in perfect condition, foot lockers open and in proper order, bunks properly made, your equipment and uniforms in proper condition and in their designated places. You will be showered, shaved, and in the uniform of the day, which is GI shoes and khakis. Your shoes and brass will be flawlessly shined, and you will be at attention at your bunks when the inspecting officers step in.

"When inspection is over, and all corrections made, you will hear 'Mess Call' on the P.A. speakers. You will fall out on the street beside the barracks, using the ratline to get there, and immediately fall into your formation to the right of I Squadron upperclassmen.

"The upperclassmen will be at 'Rest' until the squadron is called to Attention. You will fall in at Attention, and remain so until ordered otherwise. At the mess hall you will file in after the upperclassmen. You will be at ease as you go through the chow line—no talking. As you follow the upperclassmen to I Squadron's tables, you will see the upperclassmen standing at every other chair. You will file in order to the empty chairs, and place your plate and salad bowl on the table. You will then stand at Attention behind your chairs until given the order to take seats. You will sit at Attention, moving only to take the beverage pitcher as it comes to you, fill your glass, and pass the pitcher on. No one touches his food until all have received the beverage, and the order is given, 'I Squadron, Fall to.'

"Still sitting at Attention, you will eat as instructed by the upperclassman to your right. You will eat a 'square meal.' The meaning of that will be made clear by your upperclassmen. When you hear, 'I Squadron, Attention,' you will immediately cease eating, and place your utensils on your plate as instructed.

"The order 'Fall out' will then be given. You will rise, push your chair in to the table, and, at attention, file out and form up." With that, Major Brubaker stepped back and ordered, "Squadron, Attenhut!" Then, with many "Dress-it-ups," "Look-prouds," "Eyes-aheads" from the cadet officers, they were marched to their assigned barracks, where they were introduced to the ratline and to upperclassmen's harrassment, which would be a dominant part of their lives for the following weeks.

Ed and his four roommates found that their foot lockers and duffel bags had been placed in their room. Conscious of the short time they had to dig out their suntan uniforms, shine their shoes and brass, shower and shave, plus get the room ready for inspection, they set to work immediately. Soon the air was heavy with the smell of Palmolive, Sweetheart and Lifebuoy soap, shaving cream and toothpaste, shoe polish and blitz cloths. Clean bodies, shining shaved faces, and neatly combed hair transformed the scroungy-looking cadets who, forty-five minutes earlier, had emerged from the bus.

Knowing the time for inspection was near, they made their beds, thankful that Sergeant Stuart had taught them thoroughly, holding them to high standards. They organized their foot lockers as they had been taught, made sure the room was in perfect order, then carefully inspected each other, knowing that this first inspection would be tough. It was.

George Stock, one of Ed's new roomates, was the first to see the inspection team at the door. In his best imitation of Sergeant Stuart, he blasted out "Attenhut!" All six cadets popped to at the bottom ends of their bunks.

In jumping to his place, Jim Smith accidentally bumped the lid of his foot locker, and it slammed down. He reached to open it, but the cadet captain leading the three-man inspection team commanded, "Pop to, Mister! Get your chin in, it's sticking out like Pat O'Brien's. Squeeze your butt muscles, it looks loose as a goose. Now, then, Mister, why did you slam your foot locker closed?"

"I didn't . . ." Jim started to say.

"At ease, Mister," barked the captain. "What is your proper response?"

"No excuse, Sir."

"That's better. Now, is there something you don't want us to see?"

"No, Sir."

"Then, why did you close it when we came in?"

"No excuse, Sir."

"What shall we do about it?"

"I'll open–"

"Mister! You're begging for some gigs. What is the proper procedure here?"

"Aviation Cadet Smith, James C., 12934132, requests permission to open his foot locker for inspection, Sir."

"Granted, Mr. Smith." Jim reached down and opened the foot locker.

All three inspectors then moved around the room, bracing each of the remaining five cadets in turn, examining each one carefully, mentioning a smudge here, a less than perfectly shined buckle there, a small wrinkle in a shirt, a collar stay not quite right, but finding no major violations.

The captain, followed by the lieutenants, stopped near the door. "Stand at ease, Misters. Not bad. Take care of the items we've mentioned for tomorrow's inspection. I'm Captain Tom Wilson, second in command of I Squadron. This is Lieutenant Gordon Thompson, executive officer, and Lieutenant Art McKenzie, supply officer. Welcome to the squadron. Remember what Major Brubaker said to you this morning and keep sharp. You'll do okay. We're tough, but we're fair. And we're the best damn squadron in the Corps. You'll hear chow call in a few minutes. I suggest you go over your shoes and buckles before you fall out for formation. Lieutenant McKenzie will tell you about laundry services. Art."

"Laundry is picked up once a week, Thursday morning right after 'reveille.' Be sure you have your names on your clothing, including socks and underwear. You'll find tags and indelible pens in your desk drawers. You'll find six khaki barracks bags on the shelf by the shower. Put your marked laundry in those, and put a name tag on the bag. On Thursday morning, put your laundry bags in a neat row on the stoop to the left of your door. They will be returned, everything washed and ironed, Saturday morning. Your OD (olive-drab) uniforms do not go to the laundry. They go to the Post Dry Cleaners. After classes on Tuesday morning there will be a 'drycleaning call.' Be sure to put your names on everything you want cleaned. When you hear 'Fall out for dry cleaning,' have the things you want cleaned over your left arms, and hit the ratline to the street where the detail will form to march to the cleaners. Friday mornings, after classes, there will be another dry cleaning call, and the detail will march to pick up the things you had cleaned."

"All right, Misters. We'll see you at chow. As you were." The captain and the lieutenants left the room.

"I think they're serious about all this," whispered Jim, afraid the inspectors might hear him.

"You damn well better believe it," growled George Stock. "Just like at West Point. Only theirs goes on a lot longer. We have to absorb all this crap in a few weeks."

"Hey, you guys, this is good stuff. I like it. I can see the reason for it," said Ed. "It's like when I was studying singing. I had to do a lot of exercises that I thought were stupid. Then, when I started really singing, I could see the use of the exercises and discipline. Just like this."

"You a singer?" asked George. "Hey, guys, we got a singer in our midst."

Ed quickly saw where this could lead. "Wait a minute!" he yelled. "I didn't mean to say that; I'm here to learn to fly. So, do me a favor, okay? Don't let this go beyond this room. I don't want some stupid upperclassman ordering me to sing every time I hit the ratline, okay? What do you say?"

Jim spoke up. "I don't know, Ed. We'll all be on the ratline together a lot. If they get on you to sing, they'll leave the rest of us alone."

"Yeah, that's right," agreed George.

"Come on, you guys. Don't screw me up. It'll be bad enough on the line without that. What do you say?" Ed asked again.

"Well, Ah don't know," drawled Billy Dalton. "We might just."

"Fall out for chow," blared the speakers on the veranda, followed by "Mess Call" on a bugle. The six cadets grabbed their overseas caps and, giving their shoes a last wipe on the backs of their trousers, raced out the door to the ratline, each making a right-angle turn to the left as he reached the screened wall of the veranda. Eyes straight ahead, shoulders squared, stomachs sucked in, they quick-stepped to the end of the veranda, where each made a squared-off left turn, then a right, exiting the screen door, straight out to the curb side of the sidewalk, where they turned left, proceeded to the rear of the upperclassmen — already formed up — turned left past the upperclassmen's formation, and stepped into their own formation, standing at attention.

"All right, Zombies," snapped a cadet sergeant, standing in front of the underclassmen's formation. "This formation is raunchy! Line up with the formation to your left. Now! All right. Eyes Front. Dress Right, Dress! Front. That's better."

Major Brubaker, standing on the sidewalk, now called out, "I Squadron." The sergeant repeated, "Squadron." Brubaker, "Left Face." Both formations turned. "Forward Harch." The entire squadron marched toward the front street. As the leading men of the upperclass formation entered the intersection, Brubaker ordered, "Column Left . . . Harch."

As the squadron turned into the front street, the underclassmen could see other squadrons ahead of them and behind them, all marching in precise formation, all in identical uniforms. One of the underclassmen, curious to see how many squadrons were marching behind, turned his head to look. Immediately, the sergeant barked out, "Eyes Front! No gawking. We'll let that one go. One more and it's a gig. Heads up, shoulders back. Suck it in. Hands swing six inches to the front, three to the rear, elbows straight. Look proud, Misters, you're in I Squadron."

Someone in the upperclass formation started to sing "Alouette," and soon everyone in the squadron was joining in, and they sang all the way to the mess hall. There Major Brubaker halted them. The upperclassmen entered first, in columns of two, followed by the underclassmen. The new cadets were astonished at the array of food before them as they arrived at the serving counter. They were to find that the food was excellent at every training base to which they were assigned, but none would outdo Maxwell Field. Each cadet's plate was loaded with a large New York strip steak, potatoes, fresh peas and tomato slices, and his salad bowl was heaped full of fresh garden salad, for which he selected his preferred dressing from the six offered.

The new cadets followed the upperclassmen to the I Squadron table, where they were directed to the empty places, each one between two upperclassmen. They were directed to place their plates on the table with printed wings precisely at 12:00, and their salad bowls at 11:00.

Out of force of habit, Bill started to pull his chair out to sit down. Every upperclassman at the table yelled, "Mister!" Bill popped to behind his chair, standing at rigid attention as all the others were.

When the last cadets had taken their places, Major Brubaker called, "I Squadron, be seated," and all the cadets pulled out their chairs and seated themselves. Several underclassmen, famished, immediately reached for knives and forks, only to be roared at by the upperclassmen seated beside them.

The upperclassman to Ed's right began to instruct him, as did all the others with underclassmen next to them. "You will sit at attention, with your eyes fixed on the wings at the top of your plate. When Major Brubaker gives the order, 'Fall to,' you may pick up the appropriate utensil and eat. Except when cutting meat, you will have one utensil in your hands at any time, When you cut meat, you will cut one bite-sized piece, then place your knife across the top of the plate, exactly parallel to the edge of the table. Once you lift a utensil, it is not to touch the table again. When you take a bite of food on your fork or spoon, you are to raise it straight up until it is mouth level, then straight to your mouth. Return the utensil to your plate, following the same pattern in reverse. When you want bread, which will be passed at the table, break the slice or roll in half, spread it with butter, and raise it straight up, then straight to your mouth, always squaring the corner. After taking a bite, return the half-slice to the bread plate at 1:00. The same thing with water, milk, or coffee. The square movement applies to everything you eat or drink.

"You will have ample time to eat, and you are to clean your plate. When you have finished, place your knife precisely straight across the top of your plate, your fork below that, and the spoon below that. Then sit at attention, with your hands on your thighs, palms down. Do not speak, unless asked a question by an upperclassman. Waiters will remove your plate, salad bowl and bread plate, and serve dessert, with spoon or fork, as appropriate. If you want coffee, leave your cup as it is; if not, invert it. The 'gunner,' the cadet at the foot of the table, will dispatch pitchers of water and milk. Coffee will be served with dessert."

Just as the instructions were concluded, Major Brubaker, at the head of the table, called, "Fall to." Free of the square meal restrictions, the upperclassmen set to, while the underclassmen struggled with the new way of eating.

Inevitably, some underclassmen's eyes wandered from their plates, bringing equally inevitable reprimands from upperclassmen. "Mister! You want to buy the place? Eyes on your wings."

Inevitably, too, small mishaps occurred, resulting in insulting comments, such as, "What a slob. You'd better have a clean tie, because you can't wear that one 'til it's cleaned." "Can't you find your mouth, Rat? It's too big to miss. It isn't in your pants, is it? Why is that piece of tomato down there? There's no hope for this bunch of Zombies." "You're right, there goes I Squadron, down the drain." "Are you too feeble-minded to know straight up? You'll never be a flier," and so on until, to the relief of the underclassmen, Brubaker called the squadron to attention, and they fell out for the march back to the barracks. Before dismissing them, the major informed them that they had ten minutes until they'd be called out for ground school — barely enough time for those who had food stains on their clothes to put on clean ones.

After classes in Aircraft Engines, Theory of Flight, Math, Physics and aircraft recognition, the cadets marched back to their barracks, with ten minutes to change into shorts, tee shirts, sweat socks and tennis shoes, and get back on the ratline to return to the street and form up for physical training. In formation, they went at double-time to the exercise area where they were put through a half-hour of vigorous calisthenics, followed by a two-mile run. In formation again, they double-timed back to their barracks.

This time, after the formation was dismissed and the underclassmen hit the ratline back to their rooms, they were given a taste of heckling by the upperclassmen. "Get that chin in, Mister!" "Suck it in, Rat!" "Halt, Zombie. One step to your right. Do you know what a brace is?"

"No, Sir."

"Well, you're about to find out. Pop to. You call that 'Attention?' Suck it in! More! Chin

IN! Don't you know what that means? Did I tell you to breathe, Mister? You blinked! Do that again, and you'll spend all day Saturday walking off gigs. Now, hold it just like that until I dismiss you." The upperclassman had picked out Ed to be braced. It was only a minute that he had to remain braced, but to Ed it seemed endless. "Back on the line, Mister." Ed's held breath exploded, and he gulped air, blinking his eyes, which hurt from being held without blinking for so long.

Back in his room, where the others were either already in the showers, or stripped and waiting their turns, Ed said, "That's one mean son-of-a-bitch! When he braces you, you're braced! I hope I don't run into him often." Unfortunately, Ed was to discover that that upperclassman, Joe McGrane, decided to be Ed's chief tormentor. From then on, every time Ed hit the ratline, Joe seemed to be there.

The third evening at Maxwell, during the short break between retreat and Study Period, Ed and his roomies were discussing what they were going through, ribbing each other, and having a few laughs. Suddenly George got serious, and said, "Hey, Ed. You're a hell of a cadet. You really like this stuff, don't you?"

"Yeah, I do," Ed replied. "Thanks. So are you. Every guy in this room is. We're super cadets."

"Yeah," Bill added. "Isn't that funny? We bitch a lot, but we're good. Come to think of it, every cadet I've seen is good. I wonder why?"

"Same here," Ed put in, "How come? You can't just take eight hundred or a thousand red-blooded American boys and stick them in a program like this, and get eight hundred or so guys to be as good as every cadet here is. How come?"

George said, "Sure couldn't. But you know, they didn't just take a bunch of guys at random, right off the street. Remember all the screening we went through? Remember those Air Corps officers, and men in civvies, snooping around asking questions about us in our home towns, our schools, our jobs, even checking out our friends, and any clubs we belonged to? They even checked up on our parents and brothers and sisters. They checked to see if we had police records, even traffic fines, or parking tickets."

"That's right," Jim said. "I forgot all about it. So, that was a serious investigation. I bet you're right."

"Yeah, I remember some guys who applied when I did. They seemed as qualified as me, but for some reason they were turned down." This came from George. "In fact, there were about thirty of us from my town who applied. As far as I know, I'm the only one who got into the program."

"Man! That's pretty fine screening," Ed exclaimed. "No wonder every guy you see here is so sharp. God, I'm glad I made it!"

"Me too," the others chorused.

"Guess that makes us the creme de la creme," George boasted, standing up and strutting. "See me! I'm creme de la creme, and the creamiest cadet of all."

"Crummiest, you mean!" Ed yelled.

"Yeah, and your French is crummy, too," Jim said. "Watch it, cadet, or I'll cream you," George responded.

"You got an army outside to back you up?" Jim asked. "If you don't, don't talk about creaming me."

George laughed, and faked a punch at Jim. "Don't need no army, cause I'm a very special person. I'm a Ayviashun Cay-det, and I've been screened."

"Man! What bullshit! They should've screened you *out*. I didn't think they'd take somebody with his finger up his ass and his thumb in his mouth," Jim said. They were all laughing as Study Hour was announced.

On Monday of the second week at Maxwell, Ed was on the ratline back to his room after a visit to Red Hunt's room in the next barracks. Major Brubaker stopped him as he was about to cross the street between the barracks.

"Halt, Mister." Ed stopped, standing at Attention. "What's your name, Mister?"

"Aviation Cadet Thorne, Edward J., 13129304, Sir."

"Ah, Mister Thorne, I thought so. I'm told that you're a singer. Is that right?"

"I didn't want . . ." Ed started.

"Mister, I asked you a question!"

"Yes, Sir, but . . ."

"I didn't ask for any buts. Are you a singer?"

"Yes, Sir."

"Do you know 'The Lord's Prayer'?"

"Yes, Sir."

"Sing it."

"Request permission to speak, Sir."

"Refused. Sing!"

Standing at attention, seeing no choice, Ed began to sing. Looking straight ahead, he saw cadets coming out of their rooms, among them his roommates, one or more of whom must have betrayed him, telling someone that he was a singer. The cadets stood on the stoop listening. Then he saw Lieutenant Hamill step out of his tactical officer's office.

Ed finished the climactic, "And the glory forever and ever, amen."

Major Brubaker said, "God, that's beautiful. At ease, Mr. Thorne."

All the cadets broke into applause. Lieutenant Hamill came across the street. "One of the upperclassmen told me you were a singer, but I had no idea you were that good. What do you think about being our squadron song leader? When we march, you start and lead the songs?" asked the Lieutenant.

"What can I say, Sir? I didn't want anybody to know that I was a singer. That's behind me. I'm here to become a pilot," Ed replied.

"Talent like that should be used. It won't interfere with your training. Once word gets around, you'll be asked to sing a lot—chapel, churches, weddings. You'll have to watch that you don't let it take you away from studying. You can always say 'no.' But I would like you to sing in our formations. That won't take any time away from your training, since you'll have to be in the formations anyway."

"Yes, Sir. Thank you, Sir." Ed saw no way out.

From then on, each time I Squadron marched, Ed would lead the singing. The favorite marching song was "Alouette," but, for variety, Ed would start "I've Got Sixpence," "Stout Hearted Men," or "Old MacDonald Had a Farm," and the squadron became known as "The Singing Squadron."

Later, Lieutenant Hamill had another idea. Each day at retreat, when the colors would be lowered at the main flagpole, all the cadet squadrons would march to the parade ground, where they would move into parade formation, officers wearing Sam Brown belts and sabres, they and all the cadets in garrison caps and white gloves, each squadron penant mounted on a guidon, would wheel with precision into position in front of the stand on which the base commander and his staff stood at attention.

The squadron commanders reported to the group commanders, "I Squadron present and accounted for." "J Squadron . . ." and so forth. Following this, each group commander reported his group present and accounted for to the corps commander, who would then give the order, "Present Arms!" and each cadet officer would snap his sabre up vertically in front of his nose. With a precise about-face, the corps commander would face the base commander, make his sabre salute and hold it, as he said "Cadet corps present and accounted for, Sir." The base commander would snap a salute, and the cadet commander would lower his sabre to his shoulder, do another about-face and order, "Shoulder arms!" Every cadet officer would snap his sabre to his right shoulder. The base bugler would play "To the Colors." This would be followed by the order, "Present arms," and again, the sabres would flash up in front of the cadet officers' faces.

The base commander and all members of his staff would do an about-face and snap into a salute as the bugler played "Taps," and as the colors were lowered. Led by the base commander, all the officers on the stand would lower their hands and do an about-face, to face the cadet corps. The cadet commander would then shoulder his sabre, face about, and command, "Shoulder arms. March your squadrons to their quarters." Under the practiced orders of the cadet officers, the block formations would break up into standard columns of four for the march back to their barracks.

Lieutenant Hamill's idea was to place Ed at a strategic location which all squadrons would pass on their way to the Parade Ground, and have him lead all squadrons in singing "Alouette," picking it up from Ed as they passed his location. After getting approval from the tactical officers of all the other squadrons, Lieutenant Hamill presented the idea to the base commander, who liked the idea. Until this plan was put into effect, each squadron would be singing "Alouette," but each would be at a different part at any given time, and each in its own key, leading to often unpleasant sonic clashes.

The first time the plan was tried, the various squadrons were already singing when they arrived at Ed's position, and not all broke off where they were to coordinate with Ed. Things were chaotic. More squadrons got the idea the second time, and by the third time, all went smoothly, resulting in the entire corps singing the same part of the song as they entered the Parade Ground. The base commander commended Lieutenant Hamill and, through him, sent his commendation to Ed.

As the daily physical training sessions continued, each cadet was encouraged to participate in a particular sport after the calisthenics half-hour was over. Some chose baseball, basketball, touch football, soccer or tumbling. Ed chose boxing. He felt a growing anger at the increasingly personal and petty hazing Joe McGrane subjected him to every time he stepped out of his room. Knowing he had a bad temper, particularly when he felt he was unfairly or unreasonably treated, he decided to take Red Hunt's advice to "take it out in the gym, not on another cadet." Boxing—either punching the bag or sparring with other cadets while wearing large-sized gloves—seemed an excellent way to vent his anger and frustration.

On the third day of Ed's participation in boxing, the instructor said to him, "You seem to be going after that bag with a lot of intensity. Is something wrong?"

"No, Sir, just letting off steam," Ed replied.

"Okay, that's good. This is a good place to do that. You seem to move pretty good. Let's see how you do sparring. Come here, Mister." The instructor called to a cadet who was shadow boxing. "I want to see you two sparring. Okay, touch gloves, and go!"

Ed and Jack, the other cadet, moved around each other, mostly missing each other with poorly timed swings. Suddenly, Ed lowered his left while swinging hard with his right. He missed Jack's jaw, but Jack countered over Ed's lowered left, landing hard on Ed's chin.

"Keep that left up, Mister, and keep moving. Don't try to end the fight with one big punch. Box, move, jab with your left. That's it," came directions from the instructor.

Both Ed and Jack were aiming at each other's head, mostly missing, but occasionally landing a punch. Ed noticed that every time Jack shot a right at his head, he raised his left, exposing his mid-section. He timed his next punch to take advantage of this opening. He slipped the right Jack shot at his left jaw, and pounded his own right into Jack's unprotected midsection. The punch was so unexpected that Jack took two steps backward, gulping for air, and said, "Hey! This is a friendly sparring match. Don't try to kill me."

"Sorry," responded Ed. "For a second there I thought you were someone else."

"Time," called the instructor. He then told Jack to work out on the bag, and took Ed to the side. "You've got ability, Mister. What's your name?"

"Aviation Cadet Thorne, Edward J., 13129304, Sir," answered Ed.

"Okay, Ed. Now, if you're interested in getting better at this, I'll work with you, along with a couple others I've picked out. Are you interested?"

"Yes, Sir," Ed replied with enthusiasm.

"Okay. Right after calisthenics every day, you report to me here. There'll be six of you. I'll work with you in pairs."

"Yes, Sir. Request permission to ask a question, Sir."

"Shoot."

"Why, Sir?"

"Mainly because I like to work with young men who have ability, especially when they seem to be motivated, as you do. I think you have anger in you. Boxing is a good way to get that out in a controlled way. You'll be a better pilot if you learn to use that anger—and a better man, too."

"You saw all that in those couple of minutes, Sir?"

"I've been working with young fellows like you for twenty years. I know a lot about a man the minute I see him boxing. We'll see how you do the next couple of days. If you shape up all right, there's an extra bonus in it."

"What's that, Sir?"

"Let's see how you come along over the next few days, then I'll tell you. Okay?"

"Yes, Sir."

"All right, the period is nearly over. Go over and watch yourself in that mirror. See what you do with your left when you punch with your right."

The session ended, and Ed ran back to the barracks double-time in the formation, feeling as if there was air under his feet. He'd been enjoying the discipline, the square meals, the drilling and the parades, the camaraderie with the other underclassmen, the two, three and four-mile runs, the feeling that he was growing mentally, emotionally, and physically. Now, in addition to being singled out for his singing, he had found a new interest and he had been told that he might be good at it. There was still Joe McGrane to contend with, but he felt relieved of some of his anger at Joe through the boxing. And the instructor's approval made that seem especially good.

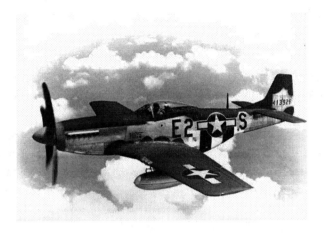

9

Meeting what had seemed, at first, impossible deadlines had become routine for Ed and his fellow underclass cadets. The formations, the inspections, the parades, the square meals, even the heckling by upperclassmen—everything—had become an accepted part of their way of life. As the days passed, fewer and fewer demerits were issued for being late for a formation, inspection infractions, or improper uniforms.

In spite of plenty of help from classmates, and his own determination to master it, Ed continued to have trouble with math. He kept plugging away at it, but it was discouraging. Joe McGrane continued to be a pain, but it helped some to hear from other underclassmen that Joe was on them too.

Five days into guidance by the boxing instructor, Lieutenant George, Ed began to feel confident that his skills were improving, including his ability to put his whole body into his punches, not just his arms. He was more alert and quicker in his defensive moves as well. Rarely did a sparring partner tag him with a good punch, and never without a solid counterpunch from Ed. He was becoming especially proficient at getting his whole body into what Lieutenant George called the "six-inch-jolt," a short, sharp punch that was never telegraphed, therefore taking the opponent by surprise. As Lieutenant George said, it wasn't usually a knockout punch, but a shot into the solar plexus followed up with a left and a right to the head, that would win a fight.

At the end of the boxing session on the fifth day, Lieutenant George called Ed and the other five selected cadets aside. "You fellows are doing fine," he said. "You will need more work, but you're coming along. Now, I want to tell you what the extra bonus will be. In a couple of weeks, President Roosevelt will be touring this base. We'll have the usual parades and review. But he especially asked that we have some cadets demonstrate physical training. We've set it up so some will play basketball, some soccer, some touch football, and you—if you get good enough—will be boxing each other. The ring will be set up right along the side of the tour route. Before he got polio, the President was quite an athlete, and he was especially fond of boxing. Pretty good, I understand. So you can be sure he'll be paying attention to what you're doing. We'll alternate pairs in the ring. We don't know exactly when his car will drive past that spot. But, when one pair is in the ring, the other two pairs will be sparring on the grass on the two sides of the ring. That's why I want you to work hard and get good. What do you say?"

Their excitement had been growing as the Lieutenant spoke, but they had held it in. Now, all six of the cadets started yelling at once, while pounding each other on the back. "Wow! Boxing for the President!" "That's great, Lieutenant. Thanks. We'll work twice as hard as before."

"Okay, I thought you'd like it. It's a once-in-a-lifetime event. I know you'll make me proud. Better get to your formations. See you tomorrow, tigers."

"Yay, Lieutenant!" the cadets shouted, as they raced to the formations.

Several days later, Ed was summoned to the room of an upperclassman named Sean Riley. Evening chow was over, and required study time hadn't yet started. Ed hit the ratline and, to his surprise, made it to Riley's room without being stopped by Joe McGrane. Arriving at Riley's room, he stopped in the doorway to say, standing at attention, "Aviation Cadet Thorne, Edward J., 13129304 reports as ordered, Sir."

"Come in, Mr. Thorne. Stand at ease," said Riley. "You're quite a singer, Mr. Thorne."

"Thank you, Sir. Glad you like it."

"Do you know 'Trees'?"

"Sir?"

"Do you know the song 'Trees'?"

"Yes, Sir."

"Sing it."

Reluctantly, because he didn't care much for the song, Ed mentally found a pitch, and started, "I think that I shall never see, a poem lovely as a tree." Amused at the rapt look on Riley's face as he went on, Ed almost broke, but caught himself, as he realized that Cadet Riley was utterly sincere in listening to the song. Reponding to this, Ed got into the song. He finished, "But only God can make a tree."

"God, I love that song," Riley said, as the other cadets applauded. "My dad used to sing it."

Relieved that he hadn't shown his amusement, Ed said, "I could see that it had an emotional meaning for you, Sir. I'd better get back to my room, Sir, it's almost study time."

"Okay, take off," replied Riley. "And thanks."

It was twilight as Ed hit the ratline to return to his own room. He had just stepped inside the screen door of his own barracks when Joe McGrane's voice grated out, "Halt, Mister! Take one step forward and pop to!"

Ed obeyed.

"Suck it in, Zombie. Get that chin in. Squeeze your ass! All right, now hold it." Putting his face close to Ed's, McGrane growled, "You think you're hot shit, don't you, Mister?"

"No, Sir."

"The hell you don't! I've watched you, acting hot shit singing, and now boxing. You sure as hell think you're hot shit. I've seen the shit-eating look on your face. You think you're hot shit."

"No, Sir."

"What do you mean, 'No, Sir'? You calling an upperclassman a liar?"

"No, Sir."

"Then, you do think you're hot shit."

"No, Sir."

"The hell you don't. Now, listen, hot shit. Do you have a cock?"

"Sir?"

"Do you have a cock? A prick? A pecker? Whatever you call it in your singing circle?"

"Yes, Sir."

"What size is it?"

"Sir?"

"Are you hard of hearing? How did you pass the physical? What size is it?"

"I don't know, Sir."

"You don't know? Didn't you ever see it? Or is it so small that you can't see it? Is that your problem?"

"No, Sir. Normal size, I guess."

"Well, we're going to find out about that. Next time I catch you out, and I will, we're going to find out. Now, Hot Shit, get to your room, or I'll report you for being late for Study Hour."

Relieved but angry, Ed got back on the ratline and to his room. "That son-of-a-bitch!" he yelled, as he shot into the room. "Who the hell does he think he is? I came close to punching him out there."

"Who you talking about, Ed? Calm down," said Jim, looking up from the book he was studying.

"That gross bastard, McGrane. I don't know how much more I can take. He wanted to know how big my cock is! Where does he get off? Says he's going to find out how big it is next time he catches me out of the room."

"He can't do that," Jim said.

"I tell you, he better not try. I'll deck him."

"God, you could wash out for that."

"If he gets me mad enough, I won't even think about that. I'm taking a shower to try to calm down. I've got to study my math before lights out."

The next day was routine, with Ed taking out his frustration on the punching bag, feeling better about things for having done so. By the time retreat and evening chow were over, he had pretty well put McGrane out of his mind.

Dusk began to settle down during the brief relaxation time before Study Period. Ed was checking over his foot locker to make sure it would be right for the next day's early inspection when a message came down ordering him to report to Lieutenant Hamill. He quickly put on the tie he had taken off only minutes before, gave his shoes a quick wipe, grabbed his hat and sped out the door to the ratline, turning right, and heading for the screen door at the far end of the barracks. Squaring corners, eyes straight ahead, and walking 160 paces per minute, he followed the ratline into the next barracks, where the Lieutenant's office was the first room inside the screen door. He stopped in front of the open door and knocked on the door frame.

"Enter," called Lieutenant Hamill.

Stopping in front of the Lieutenant's desk, Ed stood at attention and snapped his hand to his forehead in a salute. The Lieutenant returned the salute, and Ed lowered his hand to his side and said, "Aviation Cadet Thorne, Edward J., 13129304 reports as ordered, Sir."

"At ease, Mr. Thorne. Have a seat," responded the lieutenant. "How's everything going?"

"All right, Sir. I'm really into the routine, and I like it. And the food is great."

"It's a tradition here to have a good mess. Any problems?" asked the lieutenant.

"No, Sir. Everything is fine. Well—I'm having a little problem with math. It's coming at us so fast, and my background is weak in it. But I think I'm doing okay."

"It'll come, keep at it. I want to thank you again for the singing. It seems to be good for morale. Has it been a problem?"

"No, Sir. I enjoy it. No problem at all."

"Good. Now, I'm going to ask you to do something else, but understand, you don't have to do it. It has nothing to do with cadet training or the Air Corps." He paused, seemingly uncertain how to proceed. "Well, Mr. Thorne, Mrs. Hamill and I go to church in Montgomery every Sunday. Now remember, you can say 'no,' and no harm done. We'd like it if you would come in with us some Sunday and sing at our church. What do you say?"

"I'd like that, Sir. I don't have any music with me, though."

"I mentioned that to our choir director. He said that he has plenty of things in the choir library. I could take you down the Saturday before you sing. You could find something then, and practice with the organist. That okay?"

"That would be fine, Sir. Do you want it to be this weekend?"

"I'd like that. By the way, Mrs. Hamill said to ask you for lunch after church, okay?"

"Thanks. It isn't necessary, Sir."

"No, we want to do it. Let's see, Saturdays you have two hours of classes, then a two-hour P.T. period, right?"

"That's right, Sir. Then we have free time after chow, if we don't have gigs to walk off."

"Do you have any this week?"

"Not so far, Sir."

"You report to me here at 13:30 Saturday. Okay?"

"13:30, right. I'll be here, Sir. It's almost study time, Sir." Ed stood up and popped to attention. "Request permission to leave, Sir."

"Granted." Ed saluted, did an about face, and darted out the door to the ratline.

Dusk had deepened as Ed, feeling happy, opened the screen door of his barracks, and squared his turn to the left, then right, to continue on the ratline. Then the feeling of happiness was destroyed as the hated voice spat out, "Halt, Mister. Two steps to your right, and pop to."

Ed obeyed, and stood in a brace, his forgotten anger starting to boil up all over again.

"Been down brown-nosing the Lieutenant, haven't you, Hot Shit?" sneered McGrane.

"No, Sir."

"Don't lie to me, Hot Shit, I saw you come out of his office. Had that shit-eating grin on your face. Trying to make some points with him, huh?"

"No, Sir."

"What other excuse would a hot-shit underclassman like you have for going to the Lieutenant's office?"

"No excuse, Sir."

"Oh ho! 'No excuse, Sir.' Well, aren't we wising up, Mr. Hot Shit! Well, that's not what this meeting's about, is it Mister?"

"I don't know, Sir."

"The hell you don't! I told you last night. We're going to check and see if your cock is up to standard. Now, do you see this?" McGrane was holding a ruler in front of Ed's face.

"Yes, Sir."

"What is it?"

"A ruler, Sir."

"Wrong, Mister. It's a peter meter. Do you see that red line there?"

"Yes, Sir."

"Well, that's the standard which all cadet cocks have to meet. How was that standard established? That's the measurement of mine. That's how it was established for the entire corps. Do I make myself clear?"

"Yes, Sir."

"Now, we have to check to see if your cock meets cadet standards. Open your trousers, Zombie, and get it out."

"No, Sir."

"What did you say, Mister?"

"'No, Sir,' Sir."

If there had been more light, McGrane might have noticed that Ed's neck was red, and a vein on his forehead was pulsing. His eyes had narrowed to slits.

"That's an order, Mister."

"It's an improper order, Sir." This came out through Ed's clenched teeth.

"Listen, Hot Shit. underclassmen don't tell upperclassmen what's an improper order. Do it!"

"No, Sir," Ed said in a tense, tight voice. "I will not obey an improper order."

"You pussy-eating bastard! I gave you an order. Obey it!"

Both of Ed's fists were clenched. Every muscle of his body was tensed. Through his teeth, he said, "No, Sir."

"You son of a whore mother, I'll . . ." He got no farther. Ed's right fist shot out, and his entire body was behind the punch as he drove a six-inch jolt into McGrane's gut. Then, he returned to his rigid stance at attention. McGrane's breath was expelled with a whoosh, and he doubled over, gagging and choking. He struggled to get his breath. He gasped in a strangled voice, "You butt-fucking, cunt-licking son-of-a-bitch, you just washed yourself out. No underclassman strikes an upperclassman. You just bought it! Your Air Corps career is over."

"You go to hell! I don't want to be in an outfit that has you in it!" Ed stepped back on the ratline and hurried to his room.

"I just did it! I'm done for. But, by God, it felt good! That jerk's been asking for it," Ed spat out as he stepped into the room.

"You did what? Not McGrane! You didn't punch McGrane! You did, didn't you? That damn temper of yours! He'll crucify you. There'll be a hearing, sure as shit! He'll report you. You're a dead duck. What a rotten way to go!"

"I had to do it. No one has to take what he was saying to me. If I've had it, I've had it. There goes my dream of flying!"

"Well, at least you won't be drummed out; that's the worst thing. But that's for serious infractions, usually for breaking the Honor Code. You might have busted McGrane, but you didn't bust the Honor Code."

"Either way, I guess I'm done for. I'm not even going to study tonight. What's the use? I'm going to shower and hit the sack." In spite of knowing that he was in trouble, he felt surprisingly good. Weeks of frustration and anger had finally been ended.

It was an hour past lights out, and Ed was still awake. His feeling of euphoria had been replaced by tension and worry. He was not sorry; McGrane had it coming. He did what he had to do. The nights were warm, so the cadets had left the door open while they slept. In the darkness, from the direction of the door, Ed heard, "Psst, Ed."

Ed sat up. "Who is it?" he whispered.

"Bill Malone. Come over by the door," came the answering whisper.

As quietly as possible, Ed got off his bunk and slipped over to the door. "Bill, you aren't supposed to be out after lights out. You can get five demerits."

"I know that. But I had to tell you. You know, my room is the first one at the end of the veranda. All six of us in my room heard everything between you and McGrane. We almost cheered when you slugged him. He's been pulling that stuff on two of the guys in my room. I just wanted to tell you that, if he reports you and there's a hearing, we'll testify for you, okay?"

"Thanks, Bill. Do you think it'll help?"

"We think there's a chance it will. Tomorrow we're going to scout around and see if we can find any other underclassmen willing to speak out against McGrane. A lot of guys don't think what he does is right. I've even seen upperclassmen look disgusted when he gets going on some poor rat. He has a couple of buddies who laugh and egg him on, but I don't think he has many friends. Okay?"

"Tell your roommates I really appreciate this. And thanks again, Bill. You better get back to your room. I'll see if the coast is clear." With just the top of his head barely out the door, Ed looked up and down the veranda and the street beyond. "Looks all clear, Bill. Stay close to the wall and go."

Ed watched until Bill's shadowy figure disappeared into his own doorway. Then he stepped into the latrine, relieving himself, and flushed the toilet, just in case sharp ears had heard anything going on. They would, hopefully, assume someone had had to go. Feeling much better, and grateful to Bill and his roommates, he fell asleep.

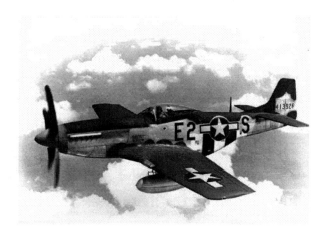

10

After classes, P.T., and noon chow on Saturday, Ed reported to Lieutenant Hamill promptly at 13:30. They drove to the Baptist Church, which the Hamills attended in Montgomery. The choir director/organist showed Ed a number of sacred songs. Then he said, "A favorite of the congregation is 'Hear The Bells.' Want to try it?"

Ed agreed, and it went well. After several run-throughs, it felt good, and the organist was satisfied. He picked up a church bulletin and showed Ed where in the service he was scheduled to sing. "It sounds great. They'll love it," he enthused. "Thanks very much."

On the way back to Maxwell, the lieutenant and Ed talked about church, music and the cadet program. "By the way," said the lieutenant, "I think you would make a good cadet officer when you're an upperclassman, but I don't want you shouting orders and hurting that voice of yours. For that reason, I'm not going to recommend you."

Ed was disappointed, but said only, "Yes, Sir. I understand." When they reached the main gate, Lieutenant Hamill said, "Ed, I've got to get right back to pick up my wife's parents at the train station. Do you mind if I drop you here?"

"Fine, Sir."

"Okay. Mrs. Hamill and I will pick you up at 09:30 hours tomorrow. Don't forget, you're invited to lunch."

"I won't, Sir. Thanks." Ed got out of the car and enjoyed the walk back to the cadet area without worrying about the ratline.

All his roommates were either in Montgomery, or walking off gigs, so he returned to an empty room. He picked up a note from his desk and his heart dropped to his stomach as he read, "Ed, report immediately to Captain Hendricks." There couldn't be any doubt about why he was summoned there. Captain Hendricks was the base disciplinary officer. He brushed his shoes, tucked in his shirt, and rinsed his face before hitting the ratline to the captain's office. He saluted and identified himself in the prescribed manner.

"Stand at ease, Mister." The captain spoke in a brusque, clip-toned manner. "You are aware, are you not, Mister, that you have been reported for a serious infraction of the Cadet Rules of Behavior?"

"Sir, I was not aware that I had been reported, but I am not surprised."

"All right, Mister. In a few minutes yon will be called into the adjoining room. A cadet hearing board is assembled there. It is comprised of the cadet corps commander, Colonel Billings, and three squadron commanders, including yours, and your squadron executive officer, who will take minutes. They will question you, and then send you back out here while they deliberate your case. Disposition of your case will be entirely in their hands. Understood?"

"Yes, Sir."

"All right. Sit down over there until you are called."

Ed had barely seated himself before the door opened and I Squadron Executive Officer Lieutenant Gordon Thompson stepped out and said, "Mr. Thorne."

"Yes, Sir," Ed replied, snapping to attention.

"Step in here, Mr. Thorne," Lieutenant Thompson ordered.

Ed entered the room and stood at attention in front of the long conference table, behind which sat Colonel Billings, with Major Brubaker and Captain Tom Wilson, second in command of I Squadron, to his right, and two other cadet majors to his left.

No one else was in the room. "Aviation Cadet Thorne, Edward J., 13129304 reports as ordered, Sir," Ed said, remaining at attention.

"Mr. Thorne," Colonel Billings began, looking stern and staring directly into Ed's eyes, "a very serious charge has been brought against you. You are charged with striking an upperclassman."

"Yes, Sir."

"Are you aware of what the consequences of that act may be?"

"Yes, Sir."

"What?"

"Wash-out, Sir."

"Right. It is a severe punishment because the cadet training program is based upon strict discipline, as applied to underclassmen by upperclassmen. If underclassmen are allowed to disobey, or strike back at upperclassmen, the system will disintegrate. Understood?"

"Yes, Sir."

"What, then, do you have to say for yourself?"

"No excuse, Sir."

"No excuse! You have no explanation, no justification to offer?"

"No, Sir."

"Sir," Major Brubaker spoke, "May I address Mr. Thorne?" Billings nodded.

"Mr. Thorne, this is a very grave matter," Brubaker said, looking straight at Ed. "You have an excellent record as a cadet. You haven't had a single demerit since coming here. Your future in the Air Corps is at stake. Is 'no excuse' all you wish to say?"

"Yes, Sir."

The members of the Board looked at each other. Then Majot Brubaker leaned over and whispered in Billings's ear. The colonel nodded, then addressed Ed. "Mr. Thorne, Major Brubaker tells me he has some information relating to your case. Step back out to Captain Hendricks's office until we call you again."

Ed took his seat again in the captain's office, feeling dejected, for all the members of the Board had stared fixedly at him, with stern looks on their faces. He knew he'd broken the rules, and he knew what the probable punishment would be. He felt the end of his dream of flying was just in front of him. He felt caught between two conflicting obligations: one to himself and his personal code of honor, which refused to allow him to obey a clearly improper order, and one to the "No Excuse" requirement of the Cadet Honor Code, which permitted no other response when asked about an infraction. Or so he believed. His only hope had been Bill Malone and his roommates, and there had been no sign of them anywhere.

After thirty-five minutes of worry and tension, Ed was called again into the hearing room. Colonel Billings addressed him. "Mr. Thorne, Major Brubaker has presented testimony that clearly indicates extenuating circumstances in your case. We cannot, however, condone the kind of breech of discipline of which you are guilty." Ed's spirits, which had started to rise from the low point they had reached as he sat in the waiting room, plummeted again. "Therefore, on the basis of extenuating circumstances, and in consideration of your good record, which Majot Brubaker has told us about, the Board has concluded that your punishment will be five demerits, to be walked off next Saturday afternoon. Furthermore, we have concluded that only demerits will be placed on your record, not your infraction, Do you understand and accept this?"

"Yes, Sir," Ed responded, his relief clearly showing in his face. "Thank you, Sir."

"No thanks are called for, Mr. Thorne. It's a relief not to have to wash out a promising cadet. Dismissed."

Fearful that they might change their minds, Ed wasted no time doing an about-face and getting outside. He exceeded 160 paces per minute all the way back to his room, where he let out a whoop, used the toilet, then headed to the gate where he got a cab for a ride into Montgomery. There, he sought out Bill Malone and his roommates for a celebration.

Ed had just stepped into the third of the cadets' favorite restaurants he had checked when he heard Bill's voice calling, "Over here, Ed." Shouldering his way through the crowd of cadets waiting to be seated, he made his way to a table where Bill sat with two of his room-mates, along with two other cadets Ed didn't know.

"Hey, Ed, let's get you a drink, even though you look mighty happy for a washed-out cadet. What'll it be?" Bill asked, pulling out a chair beside him.

"I'm singing in church tomorrow," replied Ed. "I'll just have a Coke. Man-oh-man! I can't get over it! I was sure I'd get washed out."

"They didn't wash you? That's great! What'd they give you?" asked Bill.

"Five gigs! Can you believe it? That's almost a reward!"

"I can believe it, since I know what these two guys told Brubaker when we took them to him. Meet Jim Stillson and Andy Downy. These guys saved your ass."

"Boy! Am I glad to meet you guys. I don't know what you told Brubaker, but it worked. Thanks," Ed said, shaking hands with the two cadets from G Squadron.

Bill said, "Here's your Coke, Ed. Don't you want something else? Anyway, here's what happened. My roommates and I went to Brubaker's room night before last and asked if we could speak to him in private. He wanted to know what about. When we told him it was about the charges against you, right away he said, 'Hell yes,' and took us outside away from everyone. We told him everything we'd heard between you and McGrane. He said that he was glad we told him, but he doubted that was enough to save your ass. Then we told him that McGrane had pulled the same stuff on two of us. He thought that would help, but he wasn't sure it would be enough. We told him we were going around all the barracks to ask underclassmen if they'd had any trouble with McGrane. He told us that that was good, but we'd need something pretty solid to get you off. If we got anything, we should come to him right away. He was really hoping for a break for you."

Jim Stillson broke in, "Andy and I heard about these guys running around asking about McGrane, so we looked them up. He had been giving us the same shit. Then the other night, it must have been the night you punched him, he caught us ducking back to our room dur-ing study hour. We had our work done, so we snuck out to B.S. with some friends a couple of rooms down from us."

Andy took up the story. "Man, that son-of-a-bitch was mad. He braced us and chewed us out. Threatened to report us for being out of our room. Then he said, 'All right, Misters. The time has come. Time to see if you measure up!' 'Sir,' we both said. 'Get 'em out!' he said. We didn't want to, but he had us for being out of our rooms illegally. 'Unzip and get 'em out,' he growled. So we did, and he measured us. Then he said, 'Put 'em away, Misters. Don't stand around with your pricks hanging out!' We zipped up and he let us go."

Jim continued, "Bill here took us to Brubaker. We told him our story. He really got mad. We thought he was mad at us and would chew us out. Then he calmed down. 'Did McGrane actually touch your penises?' he asked. Well, we told him that he did when he

Pants had buttons Then!

measured them. 'Okay, that's it,' he said. 'Thank you. I'll give this information to the Board at the appropriate time. I think that will do it. If not, will you appear before the Board to testify?' We said yes. 'Okay,' he said. McGrane'll be lucky if he doesn't wash out. Any kind of sexual contact between cadets is a serious offense. Thanks again.' And he dismissed us."

"God! I never thought about that," Ed said. "What a twist that would be, if McGrane washed out! I think I'll have a beer after all. Drink up, I'm buying all of you a drink. Let's order. I'm starved."

Sunday was a beautiful day. Ed felt good and sang well, his happiness at the resolution of the McGrane incident buoying him. Lunch with the Hamills was fun, especially since they had invited a neighbor couple and their daughter, an attractive blond a year or so younger than Ed. She was quite taken with this aviation cadet, and complimented him on his singing.

After lunch, Mrs. Hamill asked Ed if he would sing something for them. Ed felt a lot like singing, so he went to the upright piano and sang "0 Sole Mio," accompanying himself. They wanted more, so he sang "Because." Then he excused himself, saying that he had fallen behind in his studies, and that he couldn't stand that.

Lieutenant Hamill said, "I'll drive you out to the base, Ed." When Ed declined, saying that he'd get a ride, the Lieutenant took him aside. "I've heard about the hearing. I'm glad it turned out all right. We'd hate to lose a promising cadet like you."

"Thanks, Lieutenant, I'm sure relieved." Then he noticed Belinda, the neighbors' daughter looking at him. "Would it be improper for me to ask Belinda to walk a little way with me? At least a couple of blocks?"

"I don't see why not. Ask her," the Lieutenant said.

Ed did, and she turned to her father. "May I, Poppa?" she asked.

"Yes, but not far," her mother said.

Everybody shook hands, and they all thanked Ed for the singing. Ed thanked Mrs. Hamill again for the lunch.

Belinda walked with Ed as far as the stop where he could get a bus back to Maxwell. She was interested in what he had to say about the cadet program, and he enjoyed telling her all about it. As the bus came around the corner, he asked her if he could see her the next Saturday night. She agreed, and waved goodbye as he rode off in the bus.

The bus was loaded with cadets, and they began to rag Ed about the cute blond. Since off the base the upperclass–lowerclass rules did not apply, Ed gave back as good as he got. They arrived at the base singing "Alouette" at the top of their lungs. Ed's world was back to its pre-McGrane order.

Had it not been for the ratline, Ed felt so good he would have run and jumped all the way to his room. The memo on his desk was like a dash of cold water in his face. "Report to Captain Hendricks immediately after morning chow tomorrow, Monday."

"Now what?" Ed said, deflated. "Don't tell me there's more on the McGrane situation!"

He was talking to himself, since no one else was there. He told himself to put it out of his mind, and get on the books. He'd lost ground in math and physics. He had fair success studying, but concentration was hard. He wondered if he could walk off his gigs early enough next Saturday not to be late picking up Belinda. He decided he'd better skip noon chow — permissible on Saturdays and Sundays. That way he'd have time to shower and shave, and take Belinda some place for a snack before going to a movie. He'd probably be too pooped after walking five hour-long gigs in the hot sun, with a full field-pack on his back, to do much more than go to a movie.

He drifted off to sleep, his head on his arm on the desktop. His roommates exploded into the room, everybody pounding him on the back and yelling how great it was that he'd escaped washing out. The hubbub stopped abruptly, as lights out sounded, and everybody rushed to brush teeth, use the toilet, get out of their clothes, and into their bunks. Ed fell asleep immediately.

Reveille brought him back to consciousness. He and his roommates fell into the morning routine of showering, shaving, shining shoes and brass, and donning the uniform of the day, while making sure the room was ready for inspection.

Chow call sounded and they hit the ratline, formed up, and marched to breakfast. They then marched back, as usual, to their barracks. After dismissal, instead of returning to his room, Ed hit the ratline to Captain Hendricks's office. The captain told him to take a seat. In a moment, Bill Malone came in, followed by his roommates and Jim Stillson and Andy Downy. Each wanted to ask the others what was up, but as underclassmen, they were forbidden to talk outside their rooms unless addressed by an officer or an upperclassman.

After a few moments, Cadet Captain Tom Wilson opened the door and said, "Mr. Thorne, step in here, please."

Surprised at the "please," Ed snapped to attention and walked into the hearing room. His heart sank as he saw the entire Hearing Board seated behind the table looking just as stern as previously. "I think I've had it," he thought. "They must have changed their minds."

"Stand at ease, Mr. Thorne," Colonel Billings said, again surprising Ed. "Cadet McGrane has been charged with a washable offense, as you were. In your case there were extenuating circumstances. In his case, there are none. This Board wants to get the opinion of each cadet involved in the case. We put this question to you: Do you think Cadet McGrane should be washed out? If you need it, take a moment to think about it."

"I don't need any time to think about it, Sir. I don't want to see anybody wash out. My answer is 'No,' Sir."

For the first time the stern faces relaxed, with Major Brubaker actually smiling. "Thank you, Mr, Thorne. Do not discuss this with anyone. Go out the side door here, and return to your room. You are dismissed," Colonel Billings said.

"Thanks, Sir," Ed said as he snapped to attention, then happily escaped through the door indicated. He walked the ratline to his room.

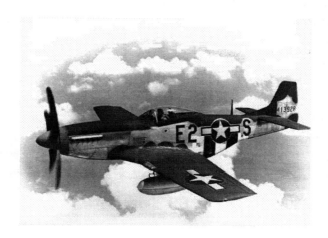

11

Except for that early-morning hearing on Monday, the week passed without incident until Thursday. Classes seemed to be getting easier, the members of the boxing team were sharpening their skills and enjoying the anticipation of the Presidential visit, and Ed saw no more of Joe McGrane, although he understood that he had not washed out. He, too, had been given demerits.

It was pitch dark Thursday when reveille sounded. "Oh God, that time already," groaned George.

"Like hell it is," snapped Jim. "What's going on? It's only 04:00."

"Listen. Shut up a minute," Ed said, sitting up. "What's that sound?" He went to the door. "It's drums! Hear them?"

"You're crazy! What drums? They never play drums at 04:00. Why would they?" George said.

They all crowded to the door. Out of the darkness came the slow, steady cadence of drums, much slower than the usual beat for marching. "What's going on . . ." Jim started to ask. An announcement on the P.A. interrupted him: "All cadets fall out at 04:30 for special formation. Dress shoes, khakis, garrison caps, white gloves. Cadet officers sabres."

"In twenty-five minutes! What the hell! Let's get on it."

With the distant sound of drums as background, the cadets dressed and formed up on the street. No stars showed through the clouds, and the nearest street lights glowed as dull yellow balls in the low-lying mist. Major Brubaker called the squadron to attention. Then, instead of ordering "Left Face," he said,"Misters, this is a very solemn and sad occasion. You are about to take part in a ceremony which you will never forget. And one I hope you never see again. We will march to the Parade Ground as usual, with two changes. First, there will be no singing. For that matter, you are to be as quiet as possible. Commands will be spoken, not shouted. Second, we will march to the slow cadence of the drums you hear in the distance." Then, in a speaking voice, he said, "Squadron, Left Face, Forward March." To the slow beat of the drums, Brubaker sounded out, "Left, left, left right left," then fell silent. Ed thought, "I wonder if somebody died. Not FDR, I hope."

Silently, eerily, the cadets marched to that extremely slow beat. Slowly they moved into parade formation with the other squadrons, slowly moving up and halting in block formations, just as they usually did at retreat.

The drumbeat continued as the squadron commanders, using a conversational voice level, ordered "Guidons, post!" After the banner-bearers had come to the right-hand corners of each of the block formations, the squadron commanders reported their squadrons present and accounted for. Colonel Billings returned their salutes and gave the order, "Squadrons, Parade Rest." This was followed by an unusual order: "Guards, bring the prisoner front and center." Two cadet officers came forward with a cadet between them. They stopped at the center in front of the formation, facing the massed cadets. There was an audible gasp, as Ed and his friends recognized the prisoner. It was Joe McGrane.

On Colonel Billings's order, the two guards stepped two paces behind McGrane, leaving him a lone figure facing the Corps. As the drums continued their doleful beatings, Billings increased the volume of his voice, saying, "Joseph McGrane, you have been found guilty of gross violations of the Cadet Honor Code. It is the decision of the Honor Board that you be drummed out of the Cadet Corps, and dismissed from the Air Corps. Your name has been stricken from the records of the Cadet Corps, making you a nonentity. From this day forward, it will be as if you had never been in the Corps. To all of us, you will be no more. The honor of the Corps and the integrity of the Honor Code must be preserved. At the conclusion of this ceremony, you will report to Base Headquarters, where you will be issued orders directing you to report to an infantry base for basic training."

Billings ordered the guards to strip all Air Corps and cadet insignia from McGrane's uniform, including the emblem on his garrison cap, the Air Corps insignia from one side of his shirt collar, and the "U.S." from the other, and his white gloves.

Billings paused for sixty seconds, during which there was no sound but the slow, steady drum beat. Then he ordered, "Squadrons, Attenhut!" The entire Corps snapped to attention. Deeply affected by this sad ceremony, the cadets stood in absolute silence as a lone bugle sounded "Taps" from the far perimeter of the Parade Ground, signifying the death of Cadet McGrane.

McGrane was led away by the guards. He would be escorted directly to Headquarters. He would be given no opportunity to mingle with the cadets, no chance to say goodbye, no chance to shake hands.

Orders were given and, again to the doleful cadence of the drums, the cadets returned to their barracks, were dismissed, and hurried to their rooms.

Back in their room, Ed and his roommates got to work getting themselves and the room ready for inspection. "Sure makes you think pretty hard about the Honor System," remarked Jim.

"Scared the shit out of me," added George.

"Glad it wasn't because of me," put in Ed. "Anybody hear what he did?"

"I heard an upperclassman say he heard that the aircraft recognition instructor caught him cheating on a test. Then another instructor reported that he had seen him using a crib on an exam. Guess that nailed him," answered George.

They had just finished getting the room in order when the Inspection Team came. Jim yelled, "Attenhut!" and they popped to.

Cadet Captain Wilson, leading the team, said, "You Misters remember what you saw this morning. The Honor System is vital to the cadet program. We have to be able to trust everyone in the program now, and, more importantly, when we are flying. If you can't trust your fellow cadets, or your fellow fliers, the entire operation comes apart. All right, stand at ease." The three inspectors checked each bunk, desk and foot locker. One checked the latrine, and came out carrying a tube of toothpaste.

"Attenhut!" he ordered. "Whose toothpaste is this?" "Mine, Sir," George answered. "Why is its cap off? Why was it not in its proper place?" "No excuse, Sir."

"Put him down for one gig. There's no room for such carelessness. Every detail is important. You must learn that before you start to fly."

Captain Wilson had just run his white-gloved finger around the top of Jim's desk-lamp shade. Holding his finger out, he said, "Did you ever see such filth? Look at it." All the roommates looked. None could see any dirt. "Whose desk is this?"

Jim spoke. "Mine, Sir."

The captain stepped in front of him. "Look at my glove," he ordered. "What do you see?"

"Nothing, Sir."

"What! Look closer, see that speck there?"

"Yes, Sir."

"Is it yours?"

"Yes, Sir."

"What is your explanation for this gross untidiness? Do you realize that I will be unable to use this finger to continue my inspection?"

"Yes, Sir."

"How do you explain this filth?"

"No excuse, Sir."

"Two gigs, Mister. This place is supposed to be clean. Every detail is important. Nothing is to be overlooked." With that, the captain said, "As you were," and the inspectors left the room.

"Whew!" Ed's breath exploded. "I lucked out. If they'd given me one more gig on top of the five I have already to walk off on Saturday, I'd never make it for my date."

"You have a date, huh? What's going on here?" questioned Bill Malone, who had just come on the ratline from his room.

Blowing on his fingernails, Ed answered, "Just a neat Montgomery blond I met last Sunday after church."

"After church! I'll bet. You haven't been to chapel since we've been here, except that time you sang. Where'd you pick up this babe? She come from that 'Royal Escort Service,' or what?"

"You think I have to pay some dame to go out with me, like you? You're full of it. This is a nice girl. Lay off her."

"How can I lay off her, when I haven't laid on her?"

This broke up the whole room, partly in release of emotions built up during the drumming-out ceremony. The more they laughed, the harder they laughed.

"Watch what you say, or I'll give you a 'McGrane,' and you won't be able to talk at all." This new name for a six-inch jolt set them laughing again.

Mess call interrupted their laughter, and they hit the ratline for breakfast formation.

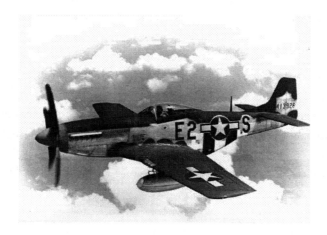

12

After the turmoil of the hearing and the emotion of the drumming-out ceremony, the days passed routinely. Ed continued to struggle with math and physics, just scraping through. He saw Belinda once more, and found her to be pretty, but shallow. Her interests seemed to be limited to hair-dos and pretty clothes—and flirting. Ed noticed that when he was with her, her eyes were continuously flitting around, rarely on him. This was especially annoying when he was trying to make a serious point of any sort. Her attention was so fleeting that she seemed always to be saying, "I'm sorry, Ed. What were you saying?" He did not ask her for a third date and, of course, the guys got on him, saying, "She finally wised up and dumped you, huh?" or, "What's the matter, Ed? Couldn't you make it with her?" It didn't matter to him, so he let it roll off without reply.

The big announcement about the President's visit was finally made. It was to be Friday of the weekend when the upperclassmen would leave for Primary, and the underclassmen would finally be upperclassmen. No more ratline! No more square meals! No more braces!

Excitement built during the week preceding the visit, and demands on the cadets increased each day. More drilling on the Parade Ground, so when the Corps passed in review for the President, everything would go perfectly. Lieutenant George had the boxing squad polishing their moves and intensifying their workouts, just as the coaches for the other sports to be on display had their teams doing. Shrubs and lawns were tended with special care, and cleaning squads were extra busy. There seemed to be a special erectness in the carriage and brisk purposefulness in everybody's actions as they moved about the base. A squadron of P-40s practiced precision passes over the base several times a day, to the awe and delight of the cadets. A pleasant anticipatory tension pervaded the base.

The big day came, bright and sunny, with a slight breeze rustling the leaves of the trees. Until P.T. time, the daily routine was followed. Then, instead of the usual calisthenics, the cadets reported to their sports instructors, who had them warm up under their direction.

Ed and the other boxers did deep breathing, stretching and limbering, then sparring. Their shorts and white tennis shoes—they had not been issued boxing shoes—were, as ordered, spotlessly clean, After warm-ups, Lieutenant George had them remove their tee-shirts and spar on the grass without gloves—easy open-handed thrusts and parries.

When all the boxers began to show some sweat, the Lieutenant issued each one a large towel to put over his shoulders. Next, they drew straws to see which pair would be in the ring first. Then the Lieutenant had all six sit on a bench, and he put their gloves on, double-checking everything as he did so, and telling them over and over, "Don't grandstand. Just box as you've been doing every day. That's what he'll want to see. Okay?"

"Now," he said, after finishing with the last pair of gloves, "I'll give a signal when the President's motorcade is a few minutes from here. I'll say, 'Take your places,' and you get in the ring, or on the grass at the side, as assigned. Take off the towels, and when I blow the whistle, start boxing. Until then, keep the towels on and move around the area, flexing your arms and legs to keep warmed up. All clear? Okay, move around until I call you."

The cadets did as instructed, occasionally feinting a swing at each other, or running a few steps in place. They were both excited and on edge. Would the great man like what he saw? Would they ever know? Would they even get a good look at him?

At last the Lieutenant gave a quick tweet on his whistle and said, "Places, men."

Ed had not pulled the right straw to be in the ring first, so he and his partner squared off in a ring marked out on the grass with whitewash, and the others took their places.

"Now, just start slowly. Move around, keep your left up. Don't let your excitement make you forget what you've learned. Spar, box, move around, keep your guard up," the Lieutenant said. Then he blew his whistle, and the cadets started doing as instructed.

Ed could hear the motorcade coming, and the occasional breaking out of applause. Then as he and his partner, Bob, moved around each other, he caught a glimpse of a large open car with an American flag on one front fender, and the Presidential flag on the other. To get a better look, he glanced away from his partner and leaned toward the street. In doing so, he lowered his left. He left himself open, and a little off balance. Bob saw this, and tagged him with a hard right. Ed immediately countered with a left of his own. But as he and Bob continued to box, he heard a hearty laugh from the direction of the Presidential car, and out of the corner of his eye he could see that the car had stopped.

In a moment a man in a dark suit, who had been riding on the rear bumper of the car, came over and spoke to the Lieutenant, who called, "Mr. Thorne, come over here."

Ed went over and said, "Yes, Sir."

"The President would like to speak to you," the lieutenant said.

"What!" Ed exclaimed. "Oh, yes Sir."

The man in the dark suit said, "You should put on a shirt."

Before Ed could respond, an easily recognizable voice boomed from the car, "It's all right. Come as you are." The man, one of several Secret Service men on and around the car, led Ed to the side of the car. Not knowing what else to do, Ed stood at rigid attention.

The President, showing the famous grin, said, "Relax, son. What's your name?"

"Aviation Cadet Thorne, Edward J., 13129304, Sir." At this point in his training this response was automatic, so it came out without hesitation.

The President laughed softly at the mechanical, obviously practiced response, then said, "Relax, my boy. You fellows all look good. I used to do some boxing. Not for a long time, though." For a moment it seemed to Ed that a shadow of sadness crossed the President's face. Then the grin came back, lighting up his large face. He chuckled, "I saw you get tagged there. Let your guard down, didn't you?"

"Yes, Sir."

"You can't do that, son, no matter what the distraction. Keep your left up. We let our guard down, and the result was Pearl Harbor. You have to protect yourself at all times. Now, shake hands and get back over there and get on with your boxing. Good luck to you, young man. Keep safe." Still holding Ed's hand, he added, as though to himself, "All of you keep safe." His face looked solemn. "God bring all of you back safe." The smile came back, the cigarette holder came up, and he released Ed's hand and waved in acknowledgement of the applause and cheers, as the car moved ahead.

"Yes, Sir. Thank you, Sir," Ed called to the car, as he turned back to the grass ring. Thinking to himself, "Wow! How lucky can a guy get? I actually spoke to President Roosevelt!"

"Way to go, Ed," Bob said. "Lucky stiff."

"It could have been any of us," replied Ed. "It just happened to be me. He got a laugh out of you tagging me with that right. If you hadn't done that, I don't think he'd have called me over. I almost told him it was his fault, but I think he knew that I tried to sneak a look at him when you hit me. Anyway, that's what did it, not because I'm the best looking cadet on the base, even if I am."

"Keep up with that talk, and I'll tag you again. This time I'll mean it."

"Any time, Buddy, any time, but you'll have to catch me off guard again—which you won't."

They continued sparring for a few more minutes, until the Lieutenant blew his whistle and called, "Time. Okay, good work. You all looked good; I heard the President say so. You'd all better hustle, you have to get showered and dressed for the big parade in the President's honor. I'm proud of all of you. On your way. See you Monday."

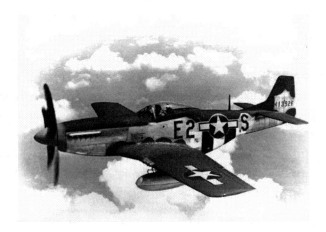

13

Sunday morning the upperclassmen would leave, and Monday the new class would come in. Saturday, Ed and his roommates assumed, would be business as usual. They got up at the sound of reveille, showered, shaved, dressed and shined, and prepared the room for inspection, as they did every day. At mess call, they hit the ratline and formed up to march to the mess hall. Instead of calling the squadron to attention and marching them off to breakfast, Major Brubaker stepped in front of the underclassmen and said, "Stand at ease, Gentlemen. I am now Bill to you. You are not upperclassmen until we leave tomorrow, but all restrictions are off as of now. No more ratline or square meals. No more bracing. We will march as equals, and eat as human beings, hopefully as friends. Ed, I hope you'll lead us in 'Alouette' as we march to the mess hall. We will not be eating together tomorrow morning, and many of us will skip lunch and dinner today, so this will be the last time we will all march together, and eat together. The way you fellows looked when you arrived here, I never thought I'd say it, but you shaped up real well. You're a good bunch."

Red Hunt yelled, "Three cheers for Bill," and the underclassmen gave him a rousing cheer.

"Well, thanks. We'll be around to say goodbye later today. I want to announce who your I Squadron officers will be now. As squadron commander, Red Hunt. Front and center, Red."

Red stepped forward, and Bill placed his sabre and Sam Browne belt in Red's hands. "Put it on, Red. And wear it proudly. Second in command is Daniel Hellrod. Front and center, Dan." Dan stepped forward, and Tom Wilson gave him his sabre and belt, and shook his hand. Sam Simpson was named executive officer, and Don Harberg supply officer. Each was given a sabre and belt. They would get their chevrons later.

The new officers, proudly wearing their belts and sabres, returned to their places in the formation, and Bill Brubaker called the squadron to attention. With a special feeling of oneness, the squadron marched and sang, then sat down to the noisiest and most enjoyable meal they had had since arriving at Maxwell. Every cadet, upper and lowerclass, had a thousand things to say, and they all tried to say them at once.

After marching back to the barracks and being dismissed, there were many handshakes, back-slappings, and a few embraces. Then, for the first time, the underclassmen could walk about freely, not on the ratline, no concern for the dreaded words, "Halt, Mister." They visited from room to room, saying goodbye to upperclassmen, and made plans to "discipline" the new underclassmen.

Ed and his roommates spent Saturday evening in Montgomery, celebrating their release from underclassmanship. They returned to the base much later than they should have, expecting to be reprimanded for getting in so late, but not even that expectation could mute the happiness they felt at having successfully completed the first real test of their fitness as cadets. Having come through trials, difficulties and mishaps together drew them into a sense of oneness, the strength of which they had not realized while they were in subjugation. Now, as upperclassmen, they felt the beginning of a true kinship, a readiness to go on together to meet the challenges before them.

To their relief, there was no reprimand. As quietly as possible, they walked to their rooms, undressed, and fell into as comfortable a sleep as they had had since coming to Maxwell.

There was no reveille Sunday morning. Suddenly George came to. He leaped out of bed and yelled, "Hey! If we're going to see the upperclassmen off, we better . . ." He stopped abruptly as he looked at his watch. "Forget it, guys. It's 09:30. They left long ago."

"Yeah, 'forget it' he says. Man, I was so sound asleep I could have stayed in bed all day. But eager beaver George had to ruin it. What a jerk," grumbled Bill from his bunk.

"I was in the middle of a really great dream, Georgie. You ruined it," came from Jim.

"You know that kind of dream isn't good for little fellers like you," retorted George. "Anyway, they're so messy. I saved you from that. You should thank me."

"Up your butt with your thanks. Hey, let's go see if we can still get some chow," replied Jim.

"Yeah," added Ed. "I heard they do that sometimes on Sundays. They fix a lot of food and not many show up, so they serve it until about eleven hundred. Let's give it a try," and he headed for the shower.

With groans and yawns, interspersed with complaints as befitted upperclassmen, all six were finally cleaned up and dressed. When they arrived at the mess hall, they found the serving tables loaded with fruit, bacon, ham, hashbrown potatoes, cereal, juice, rolls, jam, honey, and a cook taking orders for eggs, any style. Pitchers of coffee were ready to be taken to a table.

The six happily loaded their plates and carried a pitcher of coffee to one end of the table usually used by I Squadron. Only a few other cadets were scattered about the large hall.

"What a crime," Bill said. "All this food, and nobody to eat it."

"Yeah," answered George. "But it looks like you're going to get rid of a lot of it."

"Up yours, Georgie Porgie. You're the one with the weight problem. Good thing you're going to heavy bombers. You'd never get into a fighter. How come you gained weight while the rest of us lost? You must have goofed off, and we were all so busy we didn't notice," retorted Bill.

"Natural talent, old chap. Where I come from we learn from the bears. Store up all the fat so we can hibernate later. When we get done here, that's what I'm gonna do. Back to my bunk and hibernate," replied George between bites.

Jim broke in with, "Yeah, Georgie. The only bears you had where you lived are bare, as in asses. You can hibernate if you want to." Turning to the others, he said, "How about taking a hike through the married officers' area? I hear some of their wives are really good lookers."

"I heard that too," Bill responded. "And some of them are hot for sharp looking cadets, I heard, too."

"That lets you out, you ugly bastard," came from George. "But, I'm a candidate, I can hibernate later. Let's go."

"You'd be scared shitless if one of them looked your way," retorted Bill. "You wouldn't know what to do with it if somebody offered it to you."

"Might be worth a look," Ed said. "Nice day like this, there might be some sunbathing going on. But I wouldn't mess with any officer's wife. That's a sure road to washing out. Might get a court-martial, too. Throw your ass in the brig."

"Might be worth it," said Bill. "I saw some of them watching the dress parade when FDR was here. They looked like manna to a starving man."

This went on until they had eaten their fill. Ed said, "I think I'll go to town, wander around, see what's going on, then eat lunch in a restaurant." All five of the others decided to go along. They wandered away from downtown, saw some fine old homes, had lunch, then walked up and down the main streets of the city, each one hoping to catch the eye of a Southern Belle. None had any luck.

Boredom began to come over them. George said, "Let's go see a movie." Everyone agreed, so they headed for the nearest movie house, where a new James Stewart film was showing. George tried to get the box office girl, a fairly attractive redhead, to give him a date. She gave him a cold stare and said, "Cadets! Forget it, Mister."

After the show, they stopped in a drugstore for milkshakes, then boarded the bus to return to the base. Back in their room, George decided to sack out. Ed and Jim said they needed to study. Bill had letters to write, and the other two walked to the PX to get toothpaste, razor blades, and magazines.

On Monday, the new underclassmen arrived, and Red Hunt and his fellow cadet officers greeted them, much as Brubaker and his officers had done their underclassmen.

For a few days the new upperclassmen had fun harassing the new underclassmen. But they soon began to feel it as a continuing responsibility—a training program, to be taken seriously. It ceased to be just for fun.

Everything else went on much as before. Ed continued to have trouble with math and physics, falling farther and farther behind, but continuing to plug away at it. He continued to enjoy all other aspects of the cadet Program, and the bonding with the other members of his class. Bonding with his roommates, especially, continued to grow, as well as with those, like Red Hunt, who had come with him from Pennsylvania, and had been with him through Nashville, and now at Maxwell. This relationship was especially strong.

His boxing skills also developed well, and he spent all of his P.T. time working out in the boxing area, except for the long cross-country runs, which he found invigorating, even though they were required. Not everyone enjoyed the runs, and some could not complete them. A few washed out because they could not meet that requirement. Each such wash-out seemed like a personal loss to every one of his classmates.

No one had come along to take his place, so Ed continued to lead the squadron in sing-ing, and the entire corps at retreat, as well as singing several times at the Hamills' church, and at cadet weddings at the base.

As the time for his class to go on to Primary Flight Training (where, for the first time they would fly) grew near, Ed felt more and more that math and physics were impossible for him. His roommates were worried, and did all they could to help him. Since he had never had anything beyond long division and general science in school, the math theories and physics principles seemed incomprehensible to him. He had a growing sense of despair, but he never let down in his efforts to master the material. He was doing better in physics, but each time he had to apply math theory to a problem, it all seemed to slip away from him.

Ed and his friends planned to go to Montgomery to celebrate on the Friday preceding the Sunday of their scheduled departure for Primary. The day had been a good one, as all the upperclassmen, anticipating the underclassmen's becoming the new upperclassmen, eased up on their discipline. The last boxing session with Lieutenant George had been enjoyable, as the members of the squad expressed their appreciation and affection for the lieutenant.

Ed and the others were getting ready for their last retreat at Maxwell when word came down that Ed was to report to Captain Morrison's office immediately. "Uh, oh," Ed said. Captain Morrison was director of the Cadet Academic Program.

All his roommates knew what he was thinking. Bill threw an arm over Ed's shoulder, say-ing, "Maybe it isn't what you think. Lots of guys get called in to see him."

"Yeah," George said. "I was in two days ago. He just told me I'd need to work harder on my aircraft recognition in Primary."

"Thanks, guys. Hope you're right, but I doubt it," Ed said, as he left the room and headed for Captain Morrison's office. Not since he'd been called before the Board on the McGrane case had he felt so depressed. What he had sensed all along was going to happen, he now felt was about to take place.

"At ease, Mr. Thorne," Captain Morrison said, after Ed had reported. "Sit down, please."

Ed sat in the chair in front of the captain's desk, feeling unhappy in spite of the captain's friendly attitude.

The captain's next words belied his friendly attitude and plunged Ed deeper into gloom. "It isn't easy, you know, to wash a cadet out of the program. This is especially true when the cadet's overall record is excellent, as yours is. Lieutenant Hamill, your squadron Tactical officer, speaks very highly of you, saying you have great potential as a cadet, an officer, and as a leader. All of your instructors commend you highly, reporting that you are diligent, attentive, prompt, and responsive to instruction in a positive way. Even your math instructor speaks highly of your effort and determination, saying that if you had more time, he's sure you'd come out all right. All of your squadron cadet officers have been in to see me, speaking very favorably of you. What do you think of that?"

"That's very pleasing, Sir. My buddies have been very kind," replied Ed.

"Everything is so positive, we'd hate to lose a young man with your qualities and potential," continued the captain. "Still, there is the matter of your math. This has been a tough one to decide about."

"Yes, Sir," Ed said. "Sir, you've mentioned math. What about physics?"

"Oh, you squeaked by with a Satisfactory in physics. In fact, if you hadn't, there wouldn't be any question. Really bad marks in two basic subjects and we'd have no choice. We'd have to wash you out."

Ed felt a stirring of excitement as he sensed that the captain seemed to be saying that there was some choice. That meant some hope. Unable to help himself, he blurted out, "Sir! Are you telling me there's a choice?"

"That's what I'm saying, Mr. Thorne," the captain replied. "The Air Corps has invested quite a bit in you, and if all those who have spoken to me about you are right, that investment has the potential of paying off in an excellent flier and officer. We have decided that you are worth a gamble."

Ed broke in, "Excuse me, Sir. Does that mean that I can go on to Primary?"

The captain paused, rubbing his forehead, then replied, "I'm sure you will be going to Primary, Mr. Thorne, but not yet. It is highly irregular, but everyone has agreed that we want to find a way to keep you in the program. What we are going to do is hold you back a class. What do you think of that?" He actually smiled for the first time.

"I think that's great," Ed enthused, then added, "Sir, a thousand times better than washing out. Thank you, Sir. This is the best news I've had since the McGrane affair."

"Yes, I know about that. The way you handled yourself at that time is one of the considerations at this time. You will remain here as an upperclassman. Your duties will be the same as they would be if you were just moving up to upperclassman, with one exception."

"What is that, Sir?" Ed could hardly sit still, his excitement was so intense.

"The only class you will be required to take is math. Lieutenant Hamill will give you some other reponsibilities during those class hours. Otherwise, you will function as a regular upperclassman, just not with your regular class," answered the captain.

"Sir," Ed asked, "would it be all right if I took physics over, too? I'm just beginning to understand things there. Another term ought to be a good thing."

"Excellent! Your friends and instructors must be right about you. I believe we've made the right decision in your case. I know you'll dig in, and I won't regret this," the captain said.

"I will, Sir, I'll make you proud of me. Thank you, Sir. It's been my dream to be a flier. Now, I believe it's really going to happen. Thank you for this second chance," Ed said, as he stood up.

"Glad we could work something out. Our thanks will be in seeing you complete the program and get your wings."

"Yes, Sir," Ed said, saluting. "Request permission to leave, Sir."

"Granted, Mr. Thorne. Good luck," and the captain returned the salute.

"Thank you, Sir." Ed did an about-face and headed back to his room, running in his happiness. Then it hit him. His roommates and his entire class would be leaving without him. "Oh, God!" he thought. "All these guys I've gotten so close to. I'll miss them, but thank God, I'm still in the program. I'm going to be a pilot!"

He missed retreat. The squadron had just returned and been dismissed. He ran down the veranda and into his room so fast that he bumped into George who was bending over to brush his shoes. The brush flew across the room and George went down, with Ed on top of him.

"Damnit, man! What're you doing?" yelled George.

Without getting up, Ed yelled back, "I didn't wash out! Did you hear me, guys? I didn't wash out!"

Now all the others jumped on him, yelling and pounding him on the back. George, on the bottom of the pile, roared, "That's great, but you're killing me! Let me up!" They untangled themselves and got up.

"What'd he say? How come you aren't washing?" Jim asked. "They think I'm so great they can't let me go. I'm staying in the program." This set off more yelling and pounding.

Then Ed added the bad news. "But I have to stay here one more hitch. I won't be going to Primary with you." This quieted everyone down.

"God! That's tough, Ed," came from Bill. "We'll miss you."

"Yeah. I know. Me too. But what a break, I'm not washing out. True, I have to be with this crummy lot of underclassmen, but I get to go on and fly."

Chow call sounded and they all headed for the formation. This would be their last chance to "discipline" the underclassmen at mealtime, so they were especially tough on them, chewing them out, bracing them, reprimanding them.

Suddenly the I Squadron table fell silent as Red Hunt called out, "Hey, Ed! What the hell are you doing?" All eyes turned to Ed, who was sitting at rigid attention and eating a square meal.

"You jerk," Jim shouted. "You're no underclassman. You're still in the program. You'll always be a part of our class. We'll miss you, Buddy."

"What's going on?" demanded Red.

Bill quickly told him, and the entire table, what had happened.

"I see," said Red. "That's tough, Ed. But you're still a cadet. And a damn good one, too. I second what Jim just said. You're still a part of our class. We'll miss you. You've been — no, *are* — a good friend."

"Right you are, Red," the rest of the squadron upperclassmen chorused.

Red said, "Ed, you're sure to catch up with some of us at one of the Primary bases. So you'll see some of us. And maybe most of us somewhere down the road. Now, Mister, let's see a real brace. You look sloppy — out of practice."

"Up yours, Mister!" and Ed slouched in his chair. With this, the feeling of tension that had been growing broke, and all the upperclassmen began to laugh. Several underclassmen attempted to take advantage of the situation by stealing a few bites in the normal manner, only to be caught and braced by the upperclassmen.

Soon Red called the squadron to attention, and they marched back to their area, singing "Alouette" with unusual enthusiasm. Ed and his roommates headed for Montgomery, both to celebrate and to grieve their parting from one of their close buddies.

Saturday was a day of relaxation. The six roommates had too much time on their hands, and this led to gloom setting in over losing Ed from their class. Each of his roommates had said all he could to cheer Ed up, and he tried to act happy, but it was a failing effort.

Finally, feeling more depressed the longer he stayed in the room, Ed said, "I think I'll put on my shorts and tee-shirt and take a long run." Nobody objected, and nobody else felt like doing the same, so Ed headed out on his own. As he passed the gym, a familiar voice called out, "Hey, Ed, come here for a minute." It was Lieutenant George. Ed changed directions and trotted to the gym door, where the lieutenant was standing. "Yes, Sir?" he asked, as he saluted.

"Relax, Ed. We know each other pretty well now, so, at least when no one is around, we can drop the formalities."

"Yes, S . . ." Ed started, then said "Okay," instead.

"That's better," the lieutenant said. "You got a tough break. I heard about you having to stay back a term. I have some idea of how you feel, but you're still in the program. I've never heard of them doing that before. That's something, isn't it?"

"It sure is," Ed replied. "I'm grateful. Also, I understand you had some good words to say to Captain Hendricks about me. Thanks a lot."

"Nothing to it, I had to lie a little bit. Anyway, I'm sorry you aren't going on with your buddies, but I'm really glad you didn't wash out. You're too good a young man for that."

"Thank you, Sir."

"Listen, since you're going to be here, how about assisting me in the boxing program?"

"You're kidding, aren't you, Sir?"

"No, I'm not. If you want to do it, you've come along far enough that you could coach the beginners. That'll give me more time to work with the advanced guys. What do you say?"

"That'd be great. If you think I'm good enough, I'd really like that, Sir."

"Okay, we'll set it up. Have to get you a whistle, so you can act like a coach. I think you'll be a great help to me. Did Captain Hendricks tell you whether you have to take all the ground school classes?"

"No, Sir, just math, but I said that I'd like to take physics over too,"

"What about P.T.?"

"I'm not sure. I'll have to ask Lieutenant Hamill. Do you mean if I don't have to take that, you have something in mind?"

"Yep. You could keep up with exercising. You'll have to take P.T. in Primary and everywhere else. But if you don't have to do calisthenics with the other cadets, you can report to the gym. I'll give you some warm-up exercises, then I can continue to coach you in boxing. Then I can tell you what I want you to do with the beginning boxers each day."

"Boy! That sounds good to me. I've already liked being in your boxing program. When I get back to our area, I'll go ask Lieutenant Hamill. Can he say no to a cadet who boxed for the President?" Ed said with a laugh, and the lieutenant joined in. "Thanks a lot, Lieutenant. This'll give me something special to do. Help me get over missing my buddies quicker."

"Good. We'll do it, then. Let me know what Lieutenant Hamill says. If he okays it, you can come straight to the gym when you come over for P.T."

"Yes, Sir. Thank you, Sir." Ed saluted and continued his run.

"See you Monday," the lieutenant called after him.

After running about two miles, Ed returned to his room, feeling much better. All his roommates but Bill had gone out to take care of various personal matters. "You seem to be a little happier than when you left. What's up?" Bill asked.

Ed told him, and Bill congratulated him, adding, "Lieutenant George is a good guy."

"Sure is," responded Ed, sitting at his desk to write some long overdue letters. Every few minutes he was interrupted by classmates from other rooms stopping by to say how sorry they were, and how much they would miss him. As this continued, his earlier feeling of loss returned, intensifying with each handshake and goodbye.

At mid-afternoon Red Hunt, Bill Malone, and four other cadets who had been on the train ride from Pittsburgh to Nashville came in. As the handshakes, embraces and expressions of regret continued, Ed felt his emotions growing stronger. When Bill and then Red each put his arms around him, he broke away and ducked into the bathroom, as tears welled up and spilled out of his eyes. He spent a few moments leaning on the lavatory trying to suppress the sobs that kept shaking him. The bonding that had started in those days on the train had now become so strong that parting with these buddies was suddenly overwhelming. He rinsed his face, then flushed the toilet, to disguise his reason for going in there, and forced a smile as he returned to the room.

Red said, "Hey! Me too." Ed flashed him a grateful smile. "By the way, Ed," Red went on, "Lieutenant Hamill said to tell you to move into the room next to his office. You know, my room, where the squadron commander and his roommates are always assigned. You'll be assigned there. The lieutenant will have some special jobs for you, and he'll need you there."

They spent an hour in banter and reminiscences. Then, the others left, and Ed and Bill decided to go into town. Everywhere they went, someone would come up to Ed and shake his hand, or throw his arms around him. Some were high enough on celebratory drinks that they openly cried as they gave him their goodbyes. Ed was tempted to get high himself, but he knew this would only make the next day more miserable, so he drank Cokes instead.

Final goodbyes and good-lucks were said that evening back at the base. Ed read until late, but even so, he had trouble getting to sleep. Wake-up call for his departing roommates seemed to come just as he finally got to sleep. There was nothing left to say, so Ed pretended to be asleep until his roommates had left.

He got up feeling lonely and abandoned in the empty room. The others, thinking him asleep, had left quietly, not even taking sheets and pillowcases off of their bunks, for fear of waking him. As a last favor to five of the best friends he'd ever had, Ed removed their sheets and pillow covers, putting them into a laundry bag and placing the bag outside the door.

By the time he had showered and shaved, he was certain his class had left the base, so he decided to see if he could get late chow at the mess hall, after which he'd take his personal things to the room next to Lieutenant Hamill's office.

Not eager to see anybody, he sat sideways on his desk chair and visualized his roommates and all the times—good and bad—they'd had together. After a few minutes of this, he said aloud to himself, "This is stupid. You keep this up, you'll just make yourself miserable. It could be a lot worse—you could have washed out. You're still in the cadet program. So come on, snap out of it. You can't do anything about what's over. So get going and make the best you can of the situation."

Moving to get up, his elbow knocked a business-size envelope to the floor. Picking it up, he read, "To Ed, a great guy." He opened the envelope and pulled out several sheets stapled together, headed in capital letters, GOODBYE AND GOOD LUCK, GOOD BUDDY." This was followed by the signatures of all members of his squadron, each one followed by a short message; a humorous, sentimental, or straightforward expression of regret at his staying behind. Ed could see the face of each of them as he read. For a few moments he was overwhelmed by sharp visions of all of them, each a functioning and supporting part of the total squadron, drilling, marching, parading, five-mile-running, eating square meals, hitting the ratline, in the dress parade for the President, doing calisthenics together, bitching about classes, or about drilling in the rain, talking about futures, or about flying. With a sigh, Ed said goodbye to all of them and all of that, folded the pages, returned them to the envelope, and slipped it into his foot locker. That part of it was over. He put on his garrison cap and walked through the brilliant Alabama sunshine to the mess hall for breakfast.

After breakfast, he moved his belongings into the room adjacent to Lieutenant Hamill's office, where he got to know the newly appointed I Squadron cadet officers. They were a good bunch, and he became friends with them, but they weren't, and could not be, his old buddies.

On Monday, Lieutenant Hamill appointed Ed a cadet corporal, saying, "I still don't want you risking your voice shouting commands to an entire squadron. But this will go on your record, and give you status as a cadet officer."

The edge of Ed's hurt at losing his classmates dulled as he threw himself into his new duties for Lieutenants Hamill and George, and into math and physics. The courses were still tough for him, but they proved to be manageable the second time through. Although he never felt the bonding with his new classmates that he had had with the old ones, he did make a number of good friends, and they remained close through their training, and some as far as into combat flying. He also discovered a handful of other classmates who had been held back, due to illness forcing them to miss too much of the required work to allow them to go on. Among these were Larry Sutton and Frank Stillwell. Their paths crossed several times over the next few months.

Time passed much more swiftly than he had thought possible. His new duties, along with his concentrated study for his two classes, and his pleasure in working with Lieutenant George in the boxing program kept him so busy that he had little time to dwell on his sadness. He continued to be asked to sing for various functions. Incredibly quickly, he and his new classmates were finished at Maxwell Field Preflight School, and on their way to Primary Flight School.

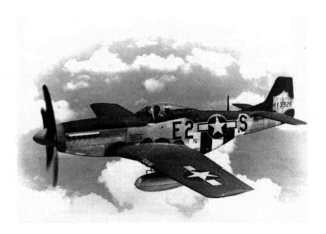

14

Ed and his new friends departed Maxwell Field before dawn on a Sunday. They were not told to which Primary Flight School they were going, but since the entire class was divided into groups of twenty-four, with each group assigned to a specific bus, they guessed that they were not all going to the same place.

Not all of Ed's new friends were assigned to his bus. In fact, only two of his roommates were with him as the bus left Maxwell. One was Bill Schmidt. Ed and he were to remain together until after Advanced Flight Training, when Bill would go to heavy bombers and Ed to fighters, each getting the assignment he wanted. The other was George Standel, a happy-go-lucky Ohioan.

The three took seats together, Ed and Bill side by side, and George across the aisle. They bantered with each other, then did some speculating about Primary, and about where they were going. Soon, however, weariness resulting from the extra activity of the last several days of preparation for departure, coupled with a wake-up call at 03:00 hours, caught up with them, as it did with the others on the bus. Bill's eyes closed as he was talking, and he left a sentence unfinished. Ed laughed a little bit, then closed his own eyes and dropped off to sleep. Less than an hour from Maxwell, and only the driver was awake.

A sudden slowing and a sharp turn to the right awakened everyone at once. Questions were called out, "Where are we?" "Are we there?" "Where's there?" Dawn had come, and the bus had pulled into a gas station.

"Pit stop," called the driver. "Fifteen minutes, no more." He opened the door. Yawning, stretching, and complaining, the cadets got off the bus. Five headed straight for the restrooms. Most went into the small store to buy candy, pop or cigarettes. After five minutes, the driver had the gas tank filled and the water and oil checked. He came into the store and yelled, "Only ten minutes left to departure! Another two hours before we stop again, so be sure you use the toilet. No pop on the bus, so finish them off or throw them away."

Nineteen cadets surged out of the store and around to the restrooms. Since there was only one "Mens," they started using the "Womens" too. Exactly fifteen minutes from the time the bus door opened, it closed, and the bus pulled out. "Anybody know where we are?" yelled Bill.

"The guy in the store said 'Atlanta,'" called someone farther back in the bus.

"My state," said George.

"What are you talking about?" responded Ed. "You're from Ho-hi-ho."

"Don't you get it? GEORG-i-a," George said.

This brought groans from everyone. When the groans subsided, Bill got up and went to the driver. "Where will the next stop be?" he asked.

"Greenville," the driver replied.

"That in Georgia?"

"Nah, South Carolina. We'll pick up sandwiches and coffee there," the driver said.

"Great. Thanks, I'll sure be ready," Bill said, and returned to his seat, where he told the others what he had learned.

"Greenville, South Carolina. Seems to me I heard someone say there's a primary base near there somewhere," a cadet from the seat behind Ed offered.

"Wonder if that's where we'll be going," Ed said.

"Don't think so," replied Bill. "The driver said we'd pick up sandwiches there. We wouldn't do that if we were near where we're going."

Some of the cadets went back to sleep. Others wrote letters to mail when they reached their primary school. Ed and his friends continued to talk. "You're quite a singer, Ed," Bill said. "Where'd you sing before?"

"Oh, around. Lots of places."

"You go to college to learn to sing like that?" asked George.

"Nope. I didn't go to college; I studied privately."

"The hell you say! You don't have any college?" George was all interest now. "How the hell did you get in the cadets? Thought you had to have college."

"Yeah. That was the easy way. I got in by taking comprehensive tests. Lucky the math questions weren't too hard. Special night classes were offered in Pittsburgh for guys who wanted to be cadets. Some other guys in my class at Maxwell were in that class with me, but they had all had some college. I think I was the only one who hadn't. Guess I was lucky to get in."

"Sure were," Bill said. "Then you nearly flunked out, didn't you? Bet that scared you shitless."

"Sure did. Luck stayed with me, though, and here I am going somewhere to learn to fly."

"By the way," Bill asked, "Did you ever sing in New York?"

"Nah, are you kidding? That's the top place. I wish I could, even now." Ed paused, then went on, "Wait a minute! Yeah, I sang at Radio City Music Hall."

"The hell you did!" Bill exclaimed. "I've been there a lot of times. What shows they put on! You never sang there, you're shittin' us."

"Yeah I did, couple years ago."

"Come on! What was the show?"

"No show. I just sang a couple of solos right on the stage."

"Bullshit! Why would they have you sing solos if it wasn't part of a show?"

"Well, I'll tell you, it was sort of a show, called the Great Auditions of 1939."

"You son-of-a-bitch! I knew you were crapping us. Auditions, eh. What happened? Weren't you good enough?"

"Guess not, not for what they wanted. I was auditioning for the chorus, I wanted that so I could stay in New York and study voice. They paid fifty bucks a week. I think you'd be on two weeks, then off one or two weeks. Would have been perfect. Plenty of time to study voice, and more money than I was making back home."

"What happened? How come you didn't make it? Or did you?"

"Nope, I didn't. They were auditioning hundreds of people. They liked my voice, but it was better for solos than for choral singing. They already had great soloists, like Jan Peerce and Robert Weede. I wasn't in their class as a soloist. I needed much more and much better training than I had. I might have made it for the chorus anyway, but they wanted us to dance, too, and I was a lousy dancer. Some of the other guys were really good. Better dancers than singers. I just didn't make it."

"That's okay, Ed," George said. "We think you're great. Just as good as that Jan what's-his-name."

"Thanks, but you don't pay too well." Ignoring their derisive comebacks, Ed went on, "That's all behind me now. We, my friends, are going to be fliers! Can you believe it? I hope the three of us get the same instructor and room together. I also hope you slugs can keep up with me, I'm a natural-born flier!"

"Right. You're going to just naturally fly right up your own ass and never be heard from again."

"Rave on, my boy, rave on. But, you'll see—from your spot on the ground, while I'm up there really living!"

Bill said, "Hey, wouldn't it be great. Maybe we'll get to choose our roommies and instructor."

"Fat chance. The only thing we've been able to choose yet is what kind of soap to buy," George put in, "but it would be great."

With banter, speculation about what kinds of training planes they would fly in Primary, and a few heated arguments about the merits of flying medium bombers, heavy bombers, or fighters, time passed swiftly as the bus rolled through the hills of South Carolina. Suddenly George bellowed, "There's the sign! 'Greenville, S.C., Pop. 40,000.'"

"Great, I'm ready for a sandwich. Hunger pains are getting me down," Bill declared.

Ed agreed, adding, "Bet they'll be ham and cheese. I'm ready for some coffee too."

The bus pulled into a roadside park and stopped beside an Army jeep. A corporal and a private were unloading a carton and a large coffee container, which they placed on a picnic table. As the cadets rushed off the bus and to the table, the two Army men handed out sandwiches—ham and American cheese on white bread—and paper cups of coffee.

The cadets had sat long enough, so they stood around the tables with sandwiches in one hand and coffee in the other. There were enough sandwiches so everyone who wanted to could have two, and several, including George, had three. The coffee was abundant and hot, with milk and sugar available for those who wanted it.

After eating their fill, the cadets stretched their legs walking around the little park, taking turns in the outhouses at the edge of the park. Then the corporal and the private opened another carton and starting pitching apples to the cadets as they walked by.

Thirty minutes after the bus had pulled into the park, the two enlisted men put the cartons and coffee container back in their jeep and, yelling, "Good flying, Misters!" drove out of the park. The driver announced fifteen more minutes until departure, and that it would be another couple of hours before another rest stop, so everybody be sure to relieve themselves of some of that coffee. Fifteen minutes later, the bus was loaded and pulling out of the park.

"Hey, Sarge," Ed called to the driver, "Where will we be for the next stop?"

"Columbia, South Carolina," was the reply.

"Is that our destination?"

"Nope. Two or three hours after that."

"Where will we be then?" a dozen voices yelled.

"Can't tell you. You'll know when we get there."

"Come on, Sarge. You can tell us, we won't tell any Nazi spies."

"Sorry, I have my orders."

"Ah nuts!"

The two-and-one-half hours to Columbia were passed in sleeping, talking, and singing "Alouette," of course, but also "I've got Sixpence," "Into the Air Army Air Corps," and "Night and Day," as it had never been sung before. After Columbia, they continued to Florence for a brief stop to get gas and use the toilets. Out of Florence, they went northeast on U.S. 95 for about twenty miles, and then turned north on a secondary road.

"Okay, Misters. We're moving in on it," the sergeant said. "About twenty-five miles and you'll see where you'll get your first flying training. I really envy you. Wish I could qualify. I'd go with you."

More songs were sung as the cadets stared out the windows for some sign of where they were going to be. Each time a town sign was spotted, someone would call out, "This it?" They passed little crossroads places like Brownsville and Blenheim. Each time the sergeant said, "Nope. But we're gaining on it."

Finally half-a-dozen cadets saw "Bennettsville, S.C., Pop. 8000," and all six yelled, "That's it, isn't it?"

"You got it this time," answered the sergeant. "Only about five miles out of town, now, and we're there."

"Yahoo! Bennettsville, here we come. Get ready to see some real flying!"

"Yeah? I doubt if you ever get off the ground. No guts!"

"Up your giggy! I'll do loops around you any day."

"Sure you will, on the ground!"

Conscious of their reception at Maxwell, under the critical inspection of the cadet officers, the cadets used handkerchiefs and paper knapkins to wipe their shoes, straighten their ties,and tuck in their shirts.

At last the bus passed a sign that read "Bennettsville Airport, elev. 2400 ft.," and pulled up to a gate. A guard examined the papers handed to him by the driver, then waved the bus on. About two hundred yards from the gate, a lone cadet waved the bus to a stop, and stepped to the door as the driver opened it. "Welcome to Bennettsville Primary Flight School. Fall out and form up in front of the barracks behind me."

"Bet he starts that upperclassman shit as soon as we get off the bus," George murmured as all the cadets stepped down and lined up in two ranks, twelve to a rank, each popping to attention as he took his place.

As soon as the last cadet had taken his place, the cadet greeter said, "Stand at ease, Misters. You can forget that upperclass/underclass business here. That was good at Preflight, but we have more serious work to do here. The main distinction between classes is that we are on the flight line half the day, while you are in ground school, then change places for the other half. It's true! We do fly here. You'll get your first flights tomorrow morning, while we are in school. The other big distinction is that we fly solo, and you'll be flying with an instructor for a while.

"Some things will be the same as at Maxwell. We still drill daily, march to chow, to the flight line and to classes, and we have daily P.T. We don't have big parades, like Maxwell. There aren't enough of us. But we all stand retreat every day. But you'll be happy to know, there is no ratline, and no bracing or popping-to by upperclassmen. Socializing is fine, when we have free time.

"Uniform of the day will be announced right after reveille. It will almost always be flight suit, overseas cap, and GI shoes for the flight line, and usually khakis and overseas caps for classes. If you're like my class, you've probably formed little groups who'd like to room together and, if possible, have the same flight instructor. Right?"

"Right," came from all the cadets.

"Okay, we'll need four groups of six. So break up into your preferred groups now."

Ed, Bill, and George got together, and George called out, "Hey, Merv, how about you?"

"Okay, if I can bring these two with me," answered a gangly cadet standing with a short pudgy one, and a thin, medium-height brown-haired one.

"What do you say?" George asked Bill and Ed. "Fine," replied Ed.

"Okay with me," said Bill.

"Okay, Merv," George called, leading Bill and Ed toward the other three. "Merv Schwartz, meet Bill Schmidt and Ed Thorne. Who are your friends?"

"Dick Chenard and Chuck Sparks," replied Merv. Bill and Ed shook hands with the others, and they went to the cadet in charge.

"We're all set," Ed said.

"Okay. You take the first room in the barracks. I'll be in in a minute to get your names."

They picked up their handbags and went into their room. The layout was about the same as the rooms at Maxwell: three sets of double bunks, the desks, chairs, study lamps, location of latrine and showers, all the same. The major difference was that the barracks was wooden, painted white, and the floor in the room was wooden, instead of the composition tile they had at Maxwell. And there was a feeling of being temporary, in contrast to Maxwell's feeling of permanence. There were screens on the windows and a screen door, but no screen on the veranda that stretched the length of the building, with steps leading up to the veranda at every door. They heard the other cadets entering the next three rooms, and then the cadet in charge came in. "By the way, I'm John Rigden, and I'm from Philadelphia. I need your names and serial numbers on this roll sheet. While you're doing that, I'll tell you a few things about this place. It's a civilian airport, taken over by the Air Corps. All the instructors are civilians, and they are good! There are eight of them, plus a chief pilot. Treat them with respect; your lives and your Air Corps futures are in their hands. They will only chew you out if you need it—and you *will* need it. The chief pilot will check-flight all of you at least once, maybe twice or more, if you need it. Usually it will be an unannounced spot check. That is, he'll take the place of your regular instructor, and tell you what to do. He'll only check you on things you should already have learned, so you better do them right. He's sharp, and he demands the best from you, and he's fair. Sometimes, if you make a little mistake, he'll correct you and show you how to do it, then have you do it again. You'd better do it right that time, or goodbye birdy. Of course, if you screw up big on something you should know, it's so long pal. Don't let this worry you, just know about it. The instructors are all business when it comes to flying, but really nice guys. They just won't fool around, and they won't let you either.

"There's also an Army Air Corps pilot who gives all of us the final check, after your

Instructor has you ready to graduate from here, and the chief pilot has checked and okay'd you. Then the Army guy goes up with you for what's called the Army Check. He's supposed to make sure you fly the way the Army Air Corps wants you to. But if your instructor and the chief pilot say you're ready, you won't have any trouble with the Army guy.

"That's about it. Your foot lockers and other stuff will be brought to your room shortly. You'll probably want to shower and shave before evening chow. Oh, by the way, this is a much smaller and friendlier place than Maxwell. You'll really get the feeling of being a part of it in a day or two. There are just twenty-four of you guys, and twenty-four—no, we're down to twenty-one—of us now. So it's easier to get a family feeling here. See you at chow time." With that, he moved on to the next room.

"Hey! This sounds okay," Merv called from the latrine.

"My kind of place," agreed Ed. "Let's decide who sleeps where, okay?"

"Okay," Chuck said. "I'm afraid of heights, of course, but otherwise, I don't care what bunk I have."

"Oh, great," George said. "We have a would-be pilot who's afraid of heights! Good story, Chuck. Guess that means you have to have a lower bunk?"

"No, don't worry about me. I'll be all right, even way up there on a top bunk," and he pressed the top of his wrist to his forehead, making a martyr-face.

"Who recommended him as a roommate?" Merv asked. "Let's dump him."

"Oh, dear," Chuck said. "I really wish you wouldn't; I'll be brave."

Ed said, "You do that pretty well, Chuck. I think you had George fooled."

"Not me! I knew he was kidding," George protested. "I got it right away."

"Sure you did, Georgie-boy," Bill said. "What say we draw lots?"

"Okay," George said, "Or we could flip a coin."

"How you going to do that with six people, knucklehead?" Bill asked.

"Easy, Birdbrain. Process of elimination. Two guys flip. The one who wins flips with another guy, and so on. The one who wins the last flip, picks first. Then the other five do it all over again, see?" George explained.

"You're nuts. That'll take all day! Let's draw lots, and get it over with. Tear up some paper and put a number on each piece, a number for each bunk. Each guy gets the bunk he draws. Okay," said Dick.

"Got them all ready," Bill answered, holding out six slips of paper with numbers on them. "This bunk is Number One, this is Number Two," and he pointed to each bunk in turn. He then folded the slips of paper, and mixed them up. Holding the slips in his cupped hands, he passed them around, each cadet taking one.

They had just finished when a truck pulled up at the end of the barracks, and two privates began unloading foot lockers and barracks bags. All the cadets crowded around, spotting their belongings, and then helped each other carry their foot lockers into their rooms, each one carrying his own barracks bag.

"Ah, now it feels like home," Chuck sighed, as he put his bag under his bunk and his foot locker at the end of his bunk.

"Don't give us that crap," Merv said, "You never had it this good in Buffalo!"

"Yeah, yeah. I'm getting more luxury here in this here man's Flea Corpse than is good for me," responded Chuck.

That started bantering among all six. A couple of minutes later, Ed said, "Hey! It's going to be chow time. I'm taking a shower right now." He grabbed clean underwear from his barracks bag and went into the shower. "Hey, Bill!" he shouted. "There's no soap in here. Hand me that soap dish from my foot locker, will you?"

Bill handed Ed the soap, then started doing what the others were doing, digging out clean clothes, toothbrushes and paste, razors and shaving cream, shoe polish and brushes. There were two showers and two sinks, so it wasn't long before they were all dressed and ready for chow. They all went out on the veranda and soon the cadets from the other rooms joined them.

The usual friendly digs and jabs were going on. Then Merv yelled, "Hey! Someone's flying over there!" Everybody quieted down and looked where Merv was pointing, just as upperclassman John Rigden came from the street and up on to the veranda.

"That's probably one of the instructors. He may be checking out an airplane that just had some work done on it," John said.

"Hey! That's a biplane!" one cadet yelled.

"That's right. What did you expect? A fighter?" asked John. "That's what we train in. She's a PT-17 Stearman. It's all the airplane you'll be able to handle, and is she sweet to fly! You do anything in it. Watch this guy, he might put on a little show."

Just as John said that, the biplane's nose headed for the ground, picking up speed, then, in a long, graceful curve, it pulled up, climbing, then continued over on its back, and headed down again, completing a vertical circle.

"That's a loop," John said.

Now the plane's nose come up slightly and suddenly did a rapid rotation, as if on a spit. "Snap-roll," John announced. "You'll be doing both of those yourselves before long."

"Can you do them, John?"

"Not as cleanly as that, but, yeah, I do them. It's really fun."

"Man! I can hardly wait."

"I know how it is, but you have to learn how to take off and land first. Those are the first things you have to be able to do. When you satisfy the instructor that you can do those, he'll let you solo. Then you learn emergency maneuvers, like getting out of a spin, recovering from a stall, finding and fake-landing dead-stick in a field somewhere, when the instructor turns off the engine without warning. Hey, look! He's doing a barrel roll. Now he's diving to pick up speed. Wow! A beautiful Immelman. Man, that's flying! Here he goes into a slow roll! He's good."

Just then, chow call sounded, and John led the cadets out to the street, where the twenty-one upperclassmen were already forming up. "All right, you Misters. Move it! Fall in right here, and let's go." This from a cadet who was obviously in charge.

When all the cadets were in formation, the cadet giving the orders said, "Squadron, Atten-hut! Left face, Forward Harch!" John had taken his place with the upperclassmen, and the cadet in charge marched to the right side of the column, so there were two columns of twenty-plus marching. In a few minutes they were halted in front of the mess hall, where they were given a Right Face, and a Fall Out.

The upperclassmen led the way, entering the mess hall two-by-two, and the underclassmen followed suit. Compared to Maxwell's, this mess hall was small. There were a dozen tables, each with chairs for six. One was already taken by Air Corps officers. Soon three tables were filled with six upperclassamen each, and one had only three, one of whom was John Rigden, another the one who had been in command as they marched to the mess hall, and one other. Clearly, these were the squadron's cadet officers.

As soon as the underclassmen were seated at four other tables, the cadet officer who had marched them there stood at his place, and tapped a spoon on his glass for attention. "I'm Cadet Major Carl Chapman," he said. "I'm the squadron commander. You've already met Lieutenant John Rigden. The other cadet officer is Captain Jim Ormond—he's second in command. Welcome to Bennettsville, I think you'll like it here. Happy flying. Now, enjoy your chow." He sat down, and all the cadets fell to. The food was excellent and abundant.

When all of the cadets had had their fill of roast chicken, biscuits, mashed potatoes and gravy, fresh peas, tossed salad, lemon meringue pie, milk and coffee, Major Chapman stood and ordered, "Squadron, Attenhut! Fall out."

After marching back to the barracks and being dismissed, the cadets returned to their rooms. Ed and his mates congratulated each other on getting to a place where everyone was friendly, when a voice called from the veranda, "Ed! Ed Thorne! Where are you?"

Ed ran out yelling, "Here!" It turned out to be Bill Malone, and they threw their arms around each other.

"God! It's good to see you," Bill exclaimed.

"Yeah. Me too! Anybody else here?"

"Afraid not. Our gang really got split up. I think George and Red both went to the same place, but I'm the only one here. This place is great—wait'll you get going in that Stearman! It's beautiful. After a week, I began to feel like a veteran pilot. Of course, that's mostly because of my instructor. If you're lucky, you'll get him. He's the best."

"What's his name?"

"Mr. Boone."

"Mr. Boone! You're kidding. Don't tell me his first name is Dan'l."

"No, but that's what we call him behind his back. He's Mr. Boone when we're with him; hope you get him. He can teach anybody to fly. But they're all good."

"Come on in and meet my roomies. Good guys."

"Okay, but I can't stay more than a minute; I've got studying to do."

"Don't tell me about it. I'll be doing that starting tomorrow. But, God! You're flying! You're a flier. Wish I'd come with you from Maxwell. Well, I'll make up for it. And it's great that you're here!"

They went into the room, and Ed introduced Bill. When the other cadets learned that Bill was an upperclassman, had soloed several weeks ago, and now flew alone almost every day, they began throwing questions at him. He answered a few, then said, "I really have to go and hit the books. See you around."

Ed walked down the veranda with him, then they said goodnight and promised to get together the next day.

Retreat sounded, and the cadets formed up and marched to the flagpole for the day's-end ceremony. After retreat, as dusk settled down, Ed and his roommates read or wrote letters, with Merv bringing his daily diary up to date. One by one, they yawned, stretched, brushed their teeth, and went to bed.

No one woke up until reveille sounded. As they climbed out of their bunks, the uniform of the day was announced. They showered and shaved, then donned their flight suits. For the first time they would be worn for the reason they had them. In their excitement, they were ready twenty minutes before chow call. "Man, am I excited! We're going to fly today!" exclaimed Ed, as they stepped out onto the veranda.

"Yeah, me too," echoed Chuck. "Hope there's a latrine on the flight line. With all the excitement, I'll be sure to wet my pants if there isn't."

"Why don't you wear a diaper, little guy?" asked Bill, who stood some four inches shorter than Chuck.

"I guess being nervous and excited at the same time never bother you, eh? Horseshit," shot back Chuck. "And talk about 'little'! You'll be lucky if you can reach the pedals!"

"Hey! I was just kidding, Chuck. Come on, relax," Bill said.

"Sorry, I'm really tense about flying," responded Chuck.

"Yeah, we all are," put in Ed. "Think I'll skip coffee this morning."

"Not me, Buddy! The day doesn't start 'til I have coffee," Bill said.

George spoke up. "Aha! Another caffeine addict! I should have known, you being from New York."

"Yeah. Our big town runs on coffee and Danish. Just what I wish I had right now."

Chow call sounded, and the squadron formed up and marched to the mess hall. "There you go, Billy boy," Merv said, as they reached the serving tables. "There's your Danish to go with your coffee," pointing to a tray loaded with a variety of sweet rolls, including several kinds of Danish. This, along with the usual bacon, sausage, eggs, fruit juice, milk, cereal and coffee, was their breakfast.

"Ah! I finally made it to heaven. Danish, coffee, and my first flight all in one day. After I fly, I can die happy," sighed Bill.

"After your flight, hell!" Dick said, "You'll probably die of fright the first time your instructor banks into a turn."

"What a group we have here. Chuck's going to piss his pants; Bill's going to die. What about you, Dick? You going to shit?" came from George. "And Ed? You going to fall out?"

George was first of the six in the chow line, with Bill second. When George turned to see what effect his crack had, Bill stepped between him and the counter, forcing him out. The other four moved up tight behind Bill, and the rest of the cadets in line followed suit. No one would let George in. "You bastards," George muttered, as he went to the end of the line. When he finally got to the table, the others were nearly finished eating. They immediately got on George to "Hurry it up, let's go." "Quit dragging ass." "Come on, we want to fly some time today."

"Okay, okay, so I made a bad joke. I apologize, okay?" George said.

Bill Malone, sitting at a nearby table, broke in with "I heard some of that. One thing we don't ever joke about is anybody dying, crashing, or getting hurt flying."

"Okay, I'm sorry," George repeated.

"Okay, Buddy," Bill and Chuck said at the same time, and it was over.

After breakfast, the squadron fell in, but instead of the underclassmen following the upperclassmen, John Rigden marched them to the flight line. The first thing they saw as they rounded the hangar was an expanse of level grass field. The second was a row of twenty-four PT-17s, all with chocks in front of their wheels, and tie-down ropes running from eye-bolts under their wings to fasteners in the ground. The cadets' excitement was apparent as they stared at what were to be their classrooms in the air.

Rigden halted the cadets, then gave the order, "Left Face," followed by "Parade Rest." Rigden sensed the disappointment that the "Left Face" order had turned them away from the planes. "Don't worry," he said. "In a little bit your instructors will take you out and introduce you to Mr. Stearman. He'll show and tell you all about it. Now, you see the four gentlemen standing in front of the hangar there?" The cadets saw the four, dressed in semi-military uniforms, light blue, with epalettes on the shirts, and wings embroidered above the left shirt pockets. "Those are your instructors. I'll call your room numbers, and then the name of the instructor for each. The instructor you're assigned to will be yours the entire time you're here, so treat him with respect. Room Number One." Ed and his roomies stepped forward. "You are assigned to Mr. Boone." Ed grinned, and grabbed Bill's arm. Mr. Boone was the one Bill Malone had hoped he'd get.

"Over here," called one of the instructors. Mr. Boone was about 5'9" tall, medium build, dark hair, heavy eyebrows above blue eyes, with deep laugh lines at the corners, and a deeply tanned face.

When the six got to him, Mr. Boone said to them, "Now, I'm going to walk back here into the hangar. When I stop and face you, I want you to walk up to me one at a time, not marching, just walking in your normal, civilian way. Each one wait until the one before him has reached me and I've shaken his hand. Then the next one, and so on, until all six have come to me." He said this in a deep drawl, then turned and walked about fifty feet, just inside the hangar doors, where he stopped and turned toward them.

The cadets did as he had instructed them, and Mr. Boone watched each one intently as he walked up to him. Ed led off, a half-step ahead of the others, all eager to get going. Merv was last, and when he had shaken Mr. Boone's hand, Mr. Boone said, "Welcome to Primary Flight Training. In a couple of minutes we'll go and inspect one of the airplanes out there. First, I want to say one or two things. I'm a civilian pilot. I'm qualified to fly many different types and models of aircraft, but the one you will be flying is my favorite. It's a great little ship, and if you respect it, it'll take care of you. But you have to FLY it. You have to be alert at all times when in her, in the air or on the ground, with me, or solo.

"Second, when I tell you to do something, do it immediately. And any time you feel me take hold of the stick and put my feet on the rudder bars, you let go. Then if I want you to take hold again, I'll tell you.

"Third, you all are going to be eager to solo; I want you to as soon as you're ready. But not until! I'll know when that time comes, and then you'll know. Don't bug me about it. When you're ready, you're ready, and you'll solo.

"Finally, although I'm a civilian, I'm proud to be attached to the Army Air Corps. I tried to enlist, but they looked at my age, and my pilot's qualifications, and they said that I could make an important contribution doing what I'm doing now. So I signed up, and teaching you to fly is my contribution to the war effort. All of us here are serious about our jobs. I expect no less from you. Any questions?"

"Yes, Sir," Ed said. "Why did you want us to walk up to you like that, one at a time?"

Mr. Boone boomed a hearty laugh. "I knew one of you would ask that. Well, I have taught enough people to fly that I can tell certain things about a person by the way he walks. In fact, I can pretty accurately predict how tough a time each one is going to have. Once in a while, I'm sorry to say, I'm even right when I predict that someone isn't going to make it. And I don't like that, because I take pride in having all my students make it."

"How did we measure up—are you going to tell us?" Dick asked.

With another laugh, Mr. Boone said, "Of course I'm not going to tell you this. I didn't see anything that should keep any of you from learning to fly. Any more questions?"

"Sir," said George. "Could you tell us how long it takes most cadets to solo?"

"I could, but I won't. That makes it seem like competition, and it isn't that. It doesn't matter how soon anyone solos; it only matters that everyone solos when he is ready."

Bill asked, "Do any cadets ever wash out because they can't solo in Primary?"

"Yes, it happens. We do our best, but once in a while, a cadet just doesn't have what it takes. It is no shame, it just happens that way. If there are no more questions, let's go look at an airplane."

Led by the instructor, the cadets walked to the third airplane in the row. "Gentlemen," said Mr. Boone, "This is the PT-17 Stearman. 'PT' means Primary Trainer. Stearman is the manufacturer. It is a two-place, radial-engined, wooden-propped biplane, with two open cockpits." He looked at it with what could only be described affection. "The deadliest thing about it is the prop. More people have been killed or badly injured by walking into a rotating prop than anything else around airplanes. Stay well clear of it.

"This little beauty doesn't have an electric starter, so she has to be cranked. You will learn how to do that, and you will crank for each other. Cranking is done with a crank on the side of the cowl, behind the engine. The crank winds up an inertial starter. We'll get back to that. We will also have each of you start her once with the prop, the old fashioned way. But for everyday starting, we'll use the crank.

"Now, come to the left, or port, side of the plane. That's the left side as you look toward the front of the plane, from the cockpit. I'll show you how to climb up and into the cockpit. This is a fabric-covered plane, wings and fuselage, so you step only on designated places. You watch where I step as I climb up and stand beside the cockpit. Then one at a time, you climb up and stand beside the cockpit, and I'll show you each what's inside there, and tell you what it's for. While each one is up with me, the rest of you can continue to examine the outside of the plane. Feel the surfaces, but don't pound or poke, or force anything to move."

Each one in turn climbed up, and Mr. Boone pointed out each item in the cockpit, and explained its use. Ed wound up last. "Now, Mr. Thorne, this is the magneto switch. It's the one you turn on and off to start, run, or stop the engine. This is the gas switch. As part of the starting procedure, which you will learn, there is a time to turn it on. On the instrument panel, there is the magnetic compass, the tachometer, the air speed indicator, the artificial horizon and the turn-and-bank indicator. Also, very important, the altimeter. Up here, above, is the gas gauge." The instructor pointed to each item he named, and briefly described its function.

"Next is the seat adjustment, the seatbelt, the control column, or stick, the rudder bars and brakes on top of them, which work only when the wheels are on the ground," chuckling as he said it. "And the throttle. In a car you have a gas pedal. In airplanes, the throttle is controlled by your hand, leaving your feet free to work the rudder bars. There is no radio in this airplane, so we use this, which is called a 'gosport.' Through this, I can talk to you, but you can't talk back—the way it should be between teacher and student, don't you think?"

Thoroughly overwhelmed by the amount of new information and new experiences he was having, Ed could only respond with a "Yes, Sir."

"Don't ever forget it, Mr. Thorne. LISTEN to your instructor. That's the way to learn. You put these into your ear holes in the flight hat, and I talk into this end. It isn't easy to hear in an open cockpit, but it works. You have to listen, and you will get used to it.

"Now, Mr. Thorne, since you were the last up here, you get to be the first one to fly with me. You climb down and go over to the hangar and get two parachutes. I'll climb out and get the others to untie the wings and operate the crank. Then you'll get your first ride to get you oriented to this kind of flying, and to see how you like it."

Ed's heart was beating fast, and his legs felt so weak that he thought he'd fall as he climbed down. His legs still felt rubbery as he ran, unsteadily, to the hangar. There a man in coveralls asked what he needed.

"Two parachutes for Mr. Boone," Ed replied, breathless in his excitement.

"Does he want them for demonstration, or for flying?" the man asked, laughing.

"Flying, flying! I'm going flying!" Ed blurted.

"Okay, okay," the attendant said, as he showed Ed how to put on the parachute and fasten it. Then he demonstrated how to carry the second one. "Don't try to run. The one you're wearing will beat on your legs, and carrying one of these is awkward. Here's the rip cord handle, if you need it. Don't run; Mr. Boone won't go without you."

"Okay, thanks," Ed called over his shoulder, as he walked awkwardly back toward Mr. Boone and the airplane. He shivered, as he thought about the attendant mentioning the rip cord.

"Right," called the attendant after him. "Keep your wings straight and level."

"All right," Mr. Boone said. "Mr. Schwartz, you and Mr. Schmidt, the long one and the short one, take those 'chutes up. Mr. Schmidt, you climb up. Mr. Schwartz, hand them up to him. Put one in each cockpit."

When Bill and Merv had come down from the wing, Mr. Boone continued, "You five follow around while I take Mr. Thorne through the ground check. You ALWAYS do this before you mount the aircraft." He led Ed around, checking the prop, wheels, wing surfaces, ailerons, rudder and the elevators. He removed the cover from the pitot tube, which fed air to the air speed indicator to measure speed through the air.

"All set," said the instructor. "Mr. Thorne, you climb up and get in the rear cockpit." Ed did, nearly losing his footing in his nervousness and excitement. "Now, you're sitting on the parachute. It fits in the bucket seat, and makes a seat about the right height. Snap the parachute straps on, just like the attendant showed you. Now, all of you listen better than you've ever listened in your life. This is the only time I'm going to tell you this. As soon as you seat yourself in the cockpit, FASTEN YOUR SEAT BELT. Don't ever forget! Don't think, 'Well, I'll buckle up after I do this or that . . . Buckle that seatbelt first thing! Make it a habit you never break. Mr. Thorne will tell you why when we get back." Mr. Boone climbed into the front cockpit, fastened his 'chute and seatbelt, removed the starting crank from its bracket, and said, "Who wants to crank her?" Five hands went up. "You'll all get a chance, don't worry. Mr. Sparks, here, you take the crank this time. But don't do anything with it until I tell you to. Mr. Thorne, take hold of the stick. Can you move it?"

"No, Sir."

"Why not?"

"It's locked."

"Right. See how to unlock the controls?" "Yes, Sir, you showed us earlier." "Good. Unlock the controls."

"Unlocked, Sir."

"Now, hold the stick easy, and put your feet on the rudder bars. Let the stick and the rudder bars move wherever I move them." Ed followed the stick forward, backward, to each side, then in a circle. Then his feet followed the left, then the right rudder bars forward and back. "What am I doing, Mr. Thorne?"

"Checking the controls, Sir."

"That's right. Now, are these controls attached to anything?"

"Yes, Sir, to the ailerons, elevators and the rudder."

"Well then, shouldn't your eyes be looking at those control surfaces as I move the controls?"

"Yes, Sir." Ed was crestfallen.

"Okay, we'll forget it this time. Never again. That goes for all of you. Don't just wiggle the stick and kick the rudder bars. Look at the control surfaces, see if they are free and move as far as they should. The controls are no good to you if they don't move the control surfaces. Now, Mr. Thorne, you check the controls. I'll keep my hands off."

Ed's chagrin vanished instantly as he grasped the stick and put his feet on the rudder bars. He moved the stick to the left and watched the left aileron rise, and the right one go down. His fingers tingled. He repeated, this time to the right, and watched as the right aileron rose and the left went down. He pulled the stick back, looking at the tail of the airplane to see the elevators rise, then, pushing the stick forward, the elevators go down. Still looking backward, he pushed the left rudder bar, and the rudder swung left, then did the same as he pushed the right bar.

"Good," said Mr. Boone. "From now until I tell you otherwise, keep your hands and feet off the controls. Mr. Sparks, you get ready to crank her up. Mr. Stendel and Mr. Chenardou will be in charge of pulling the chocks when I give you the signal. All of you keep away from the prop.

Now, listen to what I'm saying, all of you," and he called out so all could hear, "Gas on, switch off, throttle cracked, seat down, controls unlocked, seatbelt fastened. Now, wind her up, Mr. Sparks, then hand in the crank and get down, away from the prop."

Chuck cranked until Mr. Boone said, "Okay," and then handed the crank to him and got away from the prop area. "Contact," Mr. Boone said, as he turned on the switch. The propellor, driven by the inertial starter, was turning. When the magneto switch was turned on, sparks were sent to the spark plugs, and the engine coughed, then started. Mr. Boone pressed the brakes at the tops of the rudder pedals, and signalled for George and Dick to pull the chocks away. When they were clear, Mr. Boone released the brakes and advanced the throttle. The plane moved forward out of the line of planes, turned right, and taxied along the edge of the field to the western end. A left turn, then Mr. Boone stopped, and into the gosport said, "See the windsock on top of the hangar?"

Ed looked and nodded. Mr. Boone could see him in the mirror mounted on top of the windscreen. "Which way is it blowing?"

Ed pointed to the right. "Good. Which way will we take off?" Ed pointed to the left. "Good," Mr. Boone said. He continued holding the plane with the brakes, and ran the throttle up, while he turned the switch to right, then left mags, than back to both. Pulling the throttle back, he released the right brake, and the plane turned so it was headed down the field, and into the wind. Ed saw that the brakes had to be used to steer the plane on the ground. Holding the stick slightly back, Mr. Boone eased the throttle all the way forward, and the plane moved down the field, picking up speed.

Ed was feeling a continuous thrill as the speed increased. Then Mr. Boone eased the stick forward, and the tail came off the ground. More speed, and the trees at the end of the field seemed to be rushing toward them. Mr. Boone pulled the stick back, and Ed laughed as the ground and the trees fell away below them.

Mr. Boone spoke into the gosport as he made a 90-degree turn to the left. "We fly a standard rectangle pattern here. When you're airborne and reach the edge of the field, you make a 90-degree turn, as we just did." Now, at the side edge of the field, he made another 90-degree turn to the left. "If you're just taking off and landing, you do just as I did. We are now on the downwind leg. If we were going to land, we'd go past the edge of the field where we started our take-off run, then make another left, and line up to the left of the Direction Tee. See it in the middle of the field?" Ed nodded, and he continued, "Turn left again, and be on the approach, cut the throttle back, and ease her in. But instead of that, we'll make a right turn and leave the pattern."

Mr. Boone had eased the throttle back after turning onto the downwind leg. Now he increased the throttle setting and started climbing toward the fluffy clouds to the north of the field. Mr. Boone hadn't mentioned it, but Ed had noticed the numbers in the small window left of the center of the altimeter turning as the instructor set the altimeter before they took off. He'd made a mental note to ask Mr. Boone how he knew where to set it. Now, the two hands on the clock-like face of the altimeter were moving—one, the longer one, moving rapidly, the shorter one more slowly—as they climbed. This reminded him to be sure to ask when they landed.

Now, as 3,000 feet approached on the altimeter, the planes on the field looking like toys, the people like ants, Mr. Boone spoke into the gosport again. "We never do maneuvers or aerobatics below 3,000 feet altitude. Why?" He cut the throttle all the way back, dropping the nose to avoid stalling, so he could hear Ed's reply.

"So if anything goes wrong, you have a chance to recover?" Ed shouted.

"Excellent," and he advanced the throttle to regain the little altitude they had lost. "Now, Mr. Thorne, would you like to fly this baby?"

"Yes, Sir!" Ed yelled, grinning and nodding his head.

"Okay. Do just as I tell you, and only what I tell you. Left hand on the throttle, right on the stick, and feet on the rudder bars. Loosen up! I can feel your tension through the stick. Just relax. Now, see where the nose is relative to the horizon?" Ed nodded. "I'm going to let go of the stick. Keep the nose just the way it is! Okay? All right, not bad. Now, no sudden big moves. Everything you do with the stick will change the attitude of the aircraft. Steady. Now, ease the stick forward to lower the nose. Good. Level off. Not too far back on the stick. Ease off. Okay, keep the nose like that. Now, ease the stick to the left. Enough. Now, we're banking. Keep the nose up. Up! Okay. Now, ease the stick a little more to the left, and slowly push the left rudder bar. Easy. Keep the nose up. Bring us around to a heading of 90 degrees on the compass. Easy. Keep the nose up. Don't increase the bank. Okay, straighten her up. Nose down! You'll stall her if you pull the nose up like that. Everything has to work together. You have to be in control and guide the craft to do what you want her to do.

"Okay, get your wings level. Good. Are you scared or excited?"

"Excited!" Ed yelled.

"Your eyes were so big I couldn't tell. Okay, now do the same thing to the right, back to zero degrees on the compass. Easy, not so jerky. Smooth, easy. Okay, keep your nose down now, as you straighten her out. Good. I'll take over now."

"Whew!" Ed blew his breath out. He had been holding it almost the whole time. Now, beginning to relax, it began to dawn on him: he had actually flown an airplane, and on his first ever flight!

"How do you feel?" asked Mr. Boone. "Great! Unbelievable!" Ed yelled. "I flew it! I flew!" "See? Flying is simple, right?"

Not knowing how to answer, Ed nodded and smiled. Mr. Boone answered for him. Suddenly the nose came up and Ed's head snapped on his neck as the airplane whipped around on its nose-to-tail axis, and stopped abruptly in the straight-and-level attitude it had had before. He reached down to make sure he had fastened his safety belt. He saw Mr. Boone looking at him in the mirror, so he grinned and gave the "Okay" sign.

Mr. Boone nodded, and the nose went far down, putting them into a vertical dive, gaining speed. At the bottom of the dive, the nose came sharply up. Ed's stomach sank, and he seemed to be pressed into his seat. The nose now pointed straight up toward the sky. A moment later he was hanging by his seatbelt, and he had to grab his flight hat, which he had not snapped, to keep it from falling off. He looked up, out of the top of the cockpit, and saw the ground above him. Then the nose was on the horizon again, as they finished the loop.

"Great," he thought. "First a snap-roll, then a loop. Wonder what's next?"

He got his answer as the nose came up slightly, and they went into a barrel roll. This was followed by another dive, a pull up to make a half-loop, then half of a slow roll back to straight-and-level, completing an Immelman turn. Now they went into a series of graceful chandelles. Next, Mr. Boone pulled the nose up until the plane seemed almost to stop;

then, as he pulled the throttle all the way back, the nose dropped quickly, and as the craft stalled out, Mr. Boone let them fall into a spin. After several turns to the left, with the horizon turning around them in a clockwise direction, Ed felt the left rudder bar go in. This surprised him, because this was the direction of their spin. Abruptly he felt the right rudder bar go all the way in. This stopped the spinning motion; the instructor popped the stick forward and at the same instant shoved the throttle full forward. This put them into a controlled power dive. In another moment, the recovery was complete and they were again flying straight-and-level.

"Okay?" asked Mr. Boone.

"Great!" Ed yelled.

"See where the field is?"

"Yes, Sir," Ed responded, as he spotted it to their left.

"All right, take the controls and fly us toward it."

Excitedly, Ed yelled, "Yes, Sir!" He made an uneven but successful turn toward the airport.

"Okay, keep the wings level, and lower the nose. Not so much, just a little; you're over-correcting. Okay, now keep the nose down just like that, and reduce your throttle. We need to lose altitude. Steady. Not too much, just a slow, even power glide. Hold her like that. Keep those wings level."

Doing his best to keep the wings straight, Ed kept the plane headed toward the airport, slowly losing altitude. About a quarter-mile from the field, Ed felt Mr. Boone take the stick, and he said, "I'll take over now."

Ed relaxed back in his seat, glowing, when Mr. Boone said, "You did all right."

With the sure-handed ease that comes with long experience, Mr. Boone turned as they approached the field and, precisely at 500 feet altitude, he turned into the pattern, and did a perfect, three-point landing, smoothly and easily. He turned left halfway down the field and stopped, nowhere near where the others were waiting. "Want to make the others turn green?" he asked.

"Okay, I mean, yes, Sir."

Mr, Boone smiled, then said, "All right. You can taxi us back to our parking place. Hold the stick back in your stomach, just as it is now. You always need to zigzag as you taxi, so you can see what's ahead of you. You steer with the brakes, using the pedals on top of the rudder pedals. Just a touch with your toes. I'll take over to turn into the parking place. You just have to keep zig-zagging up the edge of the field."

Hardly able to believe what was happening, Ed carefully eased off the brakes; then, after an uneven start on the first zig, he began to get the feel of it, and, fairly smoothly, took them to their parking place and stopped. As they approached their spot, Mr. Boone, seeing the other five cadets watching, put his hands behind his head and leaned back, as if he were a totally relaxed passenger.

The instructor took over, pressed the right brake, releasing the left, and gunned the engine. Neatly and cleanly, the plane slipped into its parking place. "Shut her down, Mr. Thorne!" shouted Mr. Boone so all could hear. Ed reached down and turned the magneto switch to off, then did the same to the gas switch.

"Any questions, Mr. Thorne?"

"Yes, Sir. When will I fly again? This was great!"

"Be patient. You'll do so much flying you'll get fed up with it."

"Never!"

"We'll see. In any case, the other five get their turns now, so let's climb out."

When they were both on the ground, Ed a little unsteady on his feet, the other cadets rushed him. "How was it, Ed?" "Were you flying?" "Was it scary?"

Ed, feeling pride and elation, replied, "It's just as great as I dreamed it would be. You won't believe it until you're up there. It's fantastic! I did a little flying. Mr. Boone let me. Lordy me! It made my fingers tingle and my heart race, but what a sensation! Now I know why Mr. Boone emphasized fastening my seatbelt; I'll never forget that."

"What do you mean?"

"I mean, if I hadn't, I'd have had an unplanned parachute jump. I'd have fallen out. There's nothing else to keep you in. That's what I mean."

"Were you really taxiing her? Was he, Mr. Boone?"

"You bet. He did all right. You all have to learn to taxi, all of you. And do it safely. You have to keep your head and eyes moving, whether flying or taxiing. We've had more accidents on the ground than in the air, because people tend to relax when they're on the ground. That can be fatal! When everyone in your class is flying, there'll be lots of traffic down here, and up there. Watch it!"

"I have a question, Mr. Boone," said Ed, remembering the altimeter.

"Shoot. Then I've got to get these other men up."

"I saw you setting the altimeter. How did you know where to set it?"

Merv spoke up, "I know, Sir." "Good, you tell him," Mr. Boone said. "Look at the Tower, Ed."

"Got it," Ed said, as he looked up and saw the barometer reading in the window of the Control Tower. He felt sheepish for not having seen it before.

"Very good, Mr, Schwartz. There are two other ways, also. Later, when you file flight plans, you will get the setting in the Flight Control Office. When in flight, since we have no radios, you can look down at the field, near the directional tee, and the numbers will be there, big enough to be read up to about 3000 feet. The altimeter setting is extremely important, and so is the weather report. Get in the habit of checking both of them before you take off tomorrow, and always. Now, who's next?"

"Thanks, Mr. Boone. It was terrific up there," Ed said, "Will I ever be able to do the things you did?"

"Sure you will. But it's one step at a time. Before long most things'll be like second nature. But it will take time and effort on your part. Okay?"

"Yes, Sir."

"Okay, Mr. Schwartz, climb aboard." "Oh, God!" exclaimed Merv. "No, I'm just your instructor. Get up there, Mr. Schwartz."

Merv shook hands with Ed, saying, "I hope to see you soon," and climbed into the cockpit.

"Hey, Merv, you'll love it!" Ed called.

"Mr. Thorne, you crank for us," said Mr. Boone, climbing into the front cockpit. "A couple of you take care of the chocks."

The same routine as before was followed, but Ed noticed that Merv's hands remained on the sides of the cockpit. "Hey, Merv," he called, then pantomimed fastening his seatbelt.

"Oh, God!" Merv shouted. "Thanks. Oh, God! What am I doing here?" as he buckled his seatbelt.

The Stearman taxied out and down the field, pausing just as it had with Ed before turning to take off.

"Good you noticed that," Bill said to Ed. "He's so excited and scared he really forgot about buckling up. All the time you were up he kept saying, 'God, look what they're doing. I don't know if I can take that!' But I think he'll be okay."

"Once they get in the air and he feels the perfect control Mr. Boone has of the ship, he'll be fine, I'll bet," Ed responded. "What a ride, though! A couple of times I thought those flimsy looking wings would come right off! It was a thrill a minute. You guys'll love it."

"What was going on before all those stunts?" George asked. "The airplane began wiggling around—nose up, nose down, wings rocking! What was going on?"

"Oh, that," Ed replied, assuming an air of casualness. "That was Aviation Cadet Thorne, getting the feel of the aircraft before undertaking the succeeding aerobatics."

"You're full of shit! Were you handling the controls that soon?" Chuck asked.

"Sure was. And man, when he let go of the controls, it was like electricity going through me, coming from the stick and rudder bars! It was about as good as sex! Wait'll your turn. Mr. Boone talks you through everything, and he catches you before you do anything stupid. But it was beautiful; I didn't care how it looked. I was flying!"

"It can't be that great," said Chuck.

"It was for me," Ed replied. "I've been dreaming about flying ever since Lindy flew the Atlantic. Six or eight of us used to walk out to Wilkinsburg Airport, about a five-mile walk each way, and watch the flying going on there. It was a grass field, about like this. Always something going on. Right then I knew I wanted to fly, but until now, I couldn't afford to do anything about it. Now, I'm getting it, thanks to Uncle Sam."

"How'd you feel in all those stunts?" asked Bill.

"The first one really took me by surprise," Ed replied. "He never said a word, just glanced at me in the mirror, and wham! We were doing it! And it didn't stop for about fifteen minutes. One thing after another, unbelievable! And I felt confident every minute. Mr. Boone can make the ship do anything he wants it to do."

"What was that first thing?" Chuck asked.

"That was a snap roll. He said we'd learn to do all those things. I don't know how it looked from here, but up there, it was fantastic. I want to do that stuff."

"I can't wait for my turn," put in George. "Did he let you fly any more, or did he give up on you?"

"Yeah. After the spin, which gave me a sort of sick feeling, he asked me if I knew where the field was. Luckily I pointed to it, so he said, 'Okay, take over and fly to the field.' I couldn't believe it! I took the controls, and he let me go, except when I'd do something dumb, then he'd set me right. Same thrilling feeling, though. We were too high to enter the pattern, so he showed me how to let down as we headed toward the field. Then, just as we were getting near the edge of the field, he said, 'I've got it.' He took over, and right at 500 feet, we entered the downwind leg and went in for a perfect landing. I want to fly more than ever now!"

The five cadets watched the little Stearman climb, with Ed now an expert, explaining what was going on, starting with the climb to 3000 feet, before doing any stunts. It was obvious when Merv took the controls, and Ed saw what Chuck had asked about when he was flying. The little ship seemed to rock and pitch erratically, like a canoe in a rough lake. "Hey! It never looked that bad when I was flying it," he said.

"Just about," said Chuck.

Soon they saw the Stearman turn toward the field, and soon after that Merv, looking like an entirely different person from the shaky cadet who had climbed into the cockpit a half-hour earlier, climbed out, grinning broadly.

They all yelled, "Way to go, Merv! How'd you do?"

"Ed wasn't kidding. It was incredible! But, you bastard, you didn't tell me how hard it is to keep the nose on the horizon and the wings level at the same time!" Merv exclaimed, laughing with relief and exhiliration.

"You looked like a sick cow, Buddy-boy," Ed replied. "You wouldn't have heard me anyway. You barely heard me when I saved your ass about the seatbelt."

"Right! Thanks again. After that ride, I'll never forget it again," responded Merv.

The next two hours passed as the remaining four cadets got their rides, each one returning glowing with excitement and enthusiasm. By the end of the session, each cadet had cranked the starter, and pulled and replaced the chocks. George was the last to fly. When he and Mr. Boone taxied up, parked and climbed out, George had his few minutes of glory, expressing how fantastic it had been. Then Mr. Boone sent him to return the two parachutes to the attendant at the hangar.

Meanwhile, Mr. Boone instructed the others in securing the airplane with the wing ties and wheel chocks. "We don't want her to blow away if a sudden wind comes up," he explained. "We never leave them untied and unattended."

George had returned, so Mr. Boone gathered the six around him. "All right, fellows. I put you through a lot of basics today, and you did all right. Then I showed you some of what you can do in this little beauty. Do you like her?"

"You bet, we sure do!" they chorused.

"So," he continued, "you can see why I praise her so much. You'll see more and more as we go on. Don't get cocky; you did okay, but you have a lot to learn. I was glad nobody got sick, because if you get sick and mess up the airplane, you have to clean it up. That's the rule. Any questions?"

Ed had had more time to think, so he asked the first question. "How do you know when you're about to stall, Sir?"

"You'll develop a feeling about that. It's one of the first things you need to learn. It's part of what is called 'flying-by-the-seat-of-your-pants.' It gets to be instinctive. No matter what attitude the craft is in, you feel what it's about to do, not just what it's doing. We'll practice stalls a lot, every day. And that's always a part of your checkflights, so you have to master it. You know, landing is a matter of stalling at the right moment; so, one moment you're flying with the wheels just off the ground, the next moment you're stalled, and the wheels and tail skid are on the ground in a three-point landing."

"Will we be practicing spins, Sir?" Chuck asked,

"You bet. You'll learn how to put the ship into a spin on purpose, get it under control and bring her out, just as I did. If you don't learn that, you won't know what to do if the ship falls into a spin when you don't intend for it to. That can happen any time you get into a stall. After I've taught you how to handle a spin, you can expect me — or the chief instructor — to put you into a spin when you least expect it, and then tell you to get us out of it. You have to learn it."

After a few more questions, Mr. Boone said, "I see your class forming up to march back to your quarters, so tomorrow each of you will do the preflight check, the cockpit check, and the starting procedure. Then you'll taxi to the proper take-off spot. I'll have the controls for take-off, and you'll keep your hands and feet in touch with the controls and follow me through as I get us airborne and out of the pattern. Then, you'll take over and climb to 3,000 feet. We'll practice stalls and landings in the air. After that, we'll each do a couple of practice touch-and-go landings, with you following me on the controls. Okay, take off. See you in the morning." As he said these final words, he took a pack of Chesterfields out of his shirt pocket and lit up, leaning against the lower wing of the Stearman.

All talking at once, the six hurried to join the other eighteen cadets of their class who, equally excited and enthusiastic, were also all talking, like kindergarteners after their first day at school.

John Rigden hurried to them and called them to attention. "Misters, there is no reason for you to have an upperclassman march you down here and back every day. One of you can do it. Any of you officers at Maxwell?" Half-a-dozen pointed at Ed.

"I was just a corporal, Sir," Ed protested. "I didn't do much commanding. Dick Chenard would be better."

"Okay, Mr. Chenard. Step up here. You walk with me so you'll get the directions. Then tomorrow you get the class down here on time! Okay?"

"Right," Dick replied.

When they got to the barracks, John didn't dismiss them immediately. Instead, he said, "You'll need to change for chow and ground school. The entire squadron marches to chow together, so fall out at chow call, ready to go. Then Dick and I will march you to ground school. After that, he'll be in charge of getting you to and from the flight line and ground school. We all go to P.T. together, so Dick won't be in charge for that. Same for retreat. Dismissed."

Picking up where they left off talking about the day's flying, the cadets rushed to their rooms, washed up, used the latrine, and dressed in khakis. Chow call came just as they all had finished wiping their shoes.

"Mr. Thorne! Start a song," called Major Chapman, and Ed started "I've Got Sixpence." The entire squadron joined in as they marched to the mess hall. Still excited, the underclassmen gulped down their food between words and phrases, expressing their feelings about their first flights and about their expectations for the next day.

Chow over, John Rigden marched them to the classroom building, with Dick Chenard walking beside him. Compared to the morning, the afternoon was dull, but in addition to more aircraft recognition, they were introduced to two new courses: aerial navigation and weather. The same instructor taught both of the new courses. In navigation class, he introduced maps and how to read them. In weather class, he introduced terms like fronts, inversions, cumulonimbus and cirrus clouds, and what they mean. He spent a great deal of time on wind shifts, stressing that in that part of South Carolina, and throughout most of the Southeast, sudden thunderclouds with their accompanying changes in wind direction would make almost magical appearances on clear, sunny days. He stressed over and over the importance of fliers being alert and sensitive to weather changes when on the ground and especially when in the air. "Make it a constant factor in your lives," he said. "As fliers, your lives will depend on your knowing about weather."

He also emphasized that any change in the weather would likely change barometric pressure, so fliers should never be too confident that their altimeters were perfectly accurate. He would stress these matters over and over as the course continued. At times, he illustrated these critical matters with stories of pilots trusting their altimeters and confidently letting down through clouds and crashing, because they had had much less actual altitude than their instruments showed, due to changes in atmospheric pressure.

Ed felt a chill of apprehension, as the possible consequences of what the instructor was saying became apparent to him. He glanced at several of his classmates and saw them looking as uneasy as he felt.

Back in their room, changing for P.T., the cadets talked about the implications of pressure changes while in flight, and not knowing about them. "Yeah," Dick said. "Some of those overcast days we had at Maxwell. Remember the fogs? Those were clouds right down to the ground."

"Right. What if you're flying above that and you have to let down through it," put in Ed, "and you don't have the right setting?"

"You're a dead duck," Chuck replied.

"Let's ask Dan'l tomorrow," George suggested, using the affectionate nickname they had already adopted for Mr. Boone when he wasn't around.

"Yeah. He'll know. Man, that's the scariest thing I've heard yet," Bill said.

P.T., evening chow, retreat, study time, lights out, taps, and sleep. The next day arrived. All six were up before reveille, hardly able to wait for morning chow to be over so they could get to the flight line.

At last they were there, and Mr. Boone gathered his students around him. "Good morning, Gentlemen. I trust you slept well, and are ready for today's work-outs?" Everyone replied affirmatively and eagerly. "Right. We'll be doing what I told you about yesterday. Any questions before we begin?"

Ed said, "We do have one, Sir. Our weather instructor was talking about quick weather changes, and how they bring changes in barometric pressure. We were wondering what you do if you're flying above solid cloud cover, and you don't know how close the clouds are to the ground, and you aren't sure your altimeter setting is right, but you have to let down through the cloud cover."

"That's a good question—one of the tough things that fliers have to deal with. When you get to Basic, and from then on, you'll have radios. You call the Tower and ask for the altimeter setting. When you get into cross-country flying there, you'll learn how to get the setting en route. But here, we have no radio. We do our best here to keep you out of that situation. You may have noticed a plane taking off earlier, and there it is coming in now. That's the morning weather check. He flies up and all around to see if anything threatening is headed this way. That, plus regular weather reports, gives us a good picture of what the weather is likely to be. If it is threatening, you don't fly!

"Now, sometimes things change fast. You will never be far from the field when you are up solo. Keep a visual check on the field. If bad weather is coming, there will be a red flag up on the Tower, and a red panel out by the landing tee. That means come home and land. If really dangerous weather is coming in fast, a red rocket will be fired every few minutes. You'll be able to see that wherever you are—hightail it home! Be careful entering the pattern, because every aircraft in the air will be coming in.

"Because we take every precaution we can, we haven't lost anyone to weather yet. Don't ever take a chance on weather. If it looks bad, come home. I'll never chew you out for that, okay?"

"Okay," the cadets responded.

"Right. Let's get started, then. Mr. Stendel, you were last yesterday. You'll be first today. Get two 'chutes." George ran to the hangar. "The rest of you go through ground check, as we did yesterday."

The five cadets walked around the airplane, checking everything. When they were finished, George had returned with the 'chutes. "Now, Misters, when it isn't your turn to fly, don't waste your time. Watch every take-off and landing, and watch every plane in the air. You can learn a lot by observation. If you see a bad landing or take-off, try to figure out why it was bad. Watch planes maneuvering in the air, and try to understand what the pilot is doing to make the plane behave like that. All right, we'll be going the reverse order of yesterday, so each man be ready when it's his turn. We won't be parking, and I won't be getting out after each turn. As soon as the one in the plane climbs out, the next one climbs in, okay?"

After George and Mr. Boone walked through the ground check, they climbed in, each one fastening his seatbelt and parachute. Three of the other cadets manned the chocks and the crank. The engine caught on the first try, and Mr. Boone and George were off.

By the time Ed's turn came, he knew pretty much what the drill was going to be. He was ready and eager as he took his place in the cockpit and fastened his belt and 'chute harness.

"All right, Mr. Thorne, let's go. Taxi to take-off position and stop." Fortunately, Ed remembered to look up at the Tower and check the altimeter setting. At the same time, he saw that the windsock, which had been pointing west — indicating the wind was coming from the east — was now pointing south. The altimeter setting had been changed, too. As soon as he had his hands and feet on the controls, Mr. Boone released the brakes. Ed taxied at the edge of the field toward the west end; as he made the turn toward where the others had started their take-off runs, he saw Mr. Boone looking at him in the mirror. He sensed that the instructor expected him to turn to a take-off position heading east. Knowing that the wind had changed directions, he taxied on across the field to the south edge, where he made another turn. Mr. Boone's voice came through the gosport, "Aren't you the smart one, Mr. Thorne? That's good. You checked the wind direction. Did you also check the altimeter setting?"

Ed nodded, and Mr. Boone smiled. Before turning into take-off position, Ed used the brakes, with the stick back in his stomach, and came to a stop. He reached forward and re-set the altimeter, noticing that Mr. Boone leaned forward to reset his as well. The instructor held up his hand in the "okay" sign, and released the right brake, easing the throttle forward to swing the nose of the plane into the wind for take-off. "I'll take over now," Mr. Boone said. "You follow with a light touch on the controls." Ed relaxed his hands and feet on the controls.

Mr. Boone gunned the engine and they accelerated down the field. Ed felt the stick move forward, and the tail come up. In a moment they were airborne and making a climbing turn to the left, followed by another left turn. Halfway down the downwind leg, they made a right turn out of the traffic pattern, and continued their climb toward a cluster of clouds to the west of the field.

Ed felt the throttle being eased back, and he looked at the altimeter: 3,000 feet. They were flying straight-and-level. "Okay, Mr. Thorne, keep the same light touch, but pay attention to what I do. I'll pull her up into a power-off stall. I don't want you to watch the instruments. Watch the nose, and be alert to how it feels just before the stall. Okay? Here we go."

The throttle went all the way back in Ed's hand, the stick moved back, and the nose came up. In a moment Ed thought there was a perceptible shudder, then the nose dropped as the plane lost lift, stalling out. He felt the rudder bars move as Mr. Boone kept the plane from falling into a spin, then the throttle and stick both eased forward, and they were flying straight-and-level again.

"Did you feel anything?"

"Yes, Sir!" yelled Ed. Mr. Boone lowered the nose and cut the throttle so he could hear. "What did you feel?"

"A little shudder just before she stalled."

"Good," and Mr. Boone pushed the throttle forward and brought up the nose. They climbed to 3,000 feet again.

Again the nose came up, and the throttle back. Again Ed felt the little shudder, and they stalled and recovered. Mr. Boone looked questioningly in the mirror and Ed nodded.

Mr. Boone's voice came through the gosport, "Mr. Thorne, you aren't looking around enough. Keep your head and eyes moving—you need to know what else is in the air. Your head should be on a swivel, in constant motion. Look front, both sides, to the rear, and up and down." Ed did so and, to his horror, saw another Stearman about a hundred feet to their right and slightly above them. He hadn't even been aware of it. He looked so crestfallen that Mr. Boone laughed and said, "Don't let it happen again. It can be a deadly mistake. Keep your head and eyes moving. Okay, take us back to 3,000." Ed did, doing his best to keep the wings level, and to handle the plane as smoothly as he could. He missed 3,000 feet, levelling off at 3,050. This brought a sharp jerk on the stick, letting him know that Mr. Boone had noticed, and that that was not good enough.

"Now," said Mr. Boone, "I'll put her in a stall, then let go of the controls. You bring her out." He pulled up and into a stall.

In his effort to get out of the stall, Ed was so anxious to get the nose down that he unconsciously pulled the stick to the left, as he pushed it and the throttle forward. The left wing dropped and he tried to bring it up with the stick. It was too late. They fell into a spin, and to make matters worse, the throttle was still forward. They were in a power spin. He tried to pull the throttle back, but Mr. Boone had a tight grip on it, and it wouldn't move. They made three turns in the power spin, then he felt Mr. Boone pull the throttle back, and push in the left rudder in the direction of the spin, making it a normal, power-off spin. A moment later he felt the right rudder bar go all the way forward. The spinning stopped for a moment, and in that moment, Mr. Boone popped the stick forward and put on full power. The spin was over, and they came back to straight-and-level.

"Do you know what you did wrong, Mr. Thorne?"

"Yes, Sir!" Ed yelled.

"Okay, back up to 3,000." Ed succeeded in leveling off at 3,000. "Now, we'll do it again," Mr. Boone said.

This time, while not smooth, Ed succeeded in getting them out of the stall and back to straight-and-level. After a half-dozen more, each one a little better, Mr. Boone said, "Okay, you're getting it. This time, *you* put her in a stall and get her out."

Ed did so, and he found that when he made the ship stall, it was easier to control it and get them out of the stall. Mr. Boone had him do three more of the same exercise. "Okay, you're getting the hang of it. Remember, that's what you do when you land. You stall out, with the wheels just off the ground. Now, take us down and back to the field, into the pattern, and line up for landing. When you're lined up right, I'll take over. You stay on the controls, but let me handle them. We're going to do some touch-and-goes."

Ed pulled the throttle halfway back, and lowered the nose for a long power-glide toward the field. "Keep your left wing up, Mr. Thorne, and keep your head and eyes moving."

Ed got the plane down to 500 feet, but they were too far away from the field, so he levelled off and added more throttle to hold the altitude as they approached the downwind leg. As they got closer, and he was thinking about making the turn into the pattern, he caught sight of another Stearman just turning on to the downwind leg at the far end of the field. Mr. Boone didn't say anything, but Ed saw him watching him in the mirror. He decided it would be best to turn out and circle until the pattern was clear, so he fed in right rudder, and moved the stick to the right and slightly back. He made a reasonably steady turn to the right. He flew a little distance back the way they had come. He kept looking around, and saw the other plane start to turn into the base leg.

Ed continued the turn, and seeing no other craft in the pattern, he eased into the downwind leg. Mr. Boone gave him the "okay" sign, and Ed felt better. A little bit steadier, he made the turn on to the base leg, and another to line up for the landing.

"Not bad, Mr. Thorne. I've got it, follow me." Ed felt Mr. Boone take control of the airplane. The throttle eased back, then farther back, all the way back, then the nose came up and he felt the wheels and the tail-skid hit the ground. Mr. Boone grinned in the mirror, and Ed smiled back.

The instructor gunned the engine, brought the tail up, and they were airborne again. They came around to do the same exercise again, then once again. The next time around, Mr. Boone said, "This time you land her. I'll have my hands and feet on the controls, but you'll be flying her in. You've got her."

Ed felt a great thrill, and thought, "This is it," as he took a tight grip on the stick and throttle, with his feet solidly on the rudder bars. He made a good turn at the base line, but Mr. Boone said, "You need to put your base leg farther from the field. Go around and come in again." Ed did so, noticing another Stearman lining up to take off.

This time, on the downwind leg, they passed the end of the field, then flew on about a hundred yards. Mr. Boone said, "Okay, here," and Ed made his turn. He looked to his left at the field, and saw the other Stearman clearing the far end of the field. No other planes were moving, so he took a quick look at the tee, and turned for his approach. He eased back on the throttle, put the nose down, and then pulled the throttle all the way back because he was too high as he approached the edge of the field. Still about twenty feet up as he crossed the border of the field, but losing speed, he put the nose down. Now, very close to the ground, he eased the stick back, bringing up the nose. They hit the ground with a jolt, and Ed realized they weren't as close to the surface as he had thought. Ed stole a glance in the mirror at Mr. Boone and was relieved to see that he was laughing. Using the brakes, Ed turned to the edge of the field and taxied to the parking place. Following Mr. Boone's instructions, he succeeded in turning the plane into its parking place, and then shut off the engine.

"You landed too high, Mr. Thorne. That's a little hard on an old man's guts, but not too bad for a first try." They climbed out, and Ed carried the 'chutes to the hangar. When he got back, the Stearman was tied down and the controls locked.

Mr. Boone gathered the cadets around him and from memory gave each of them a surprisingly detailed critique of what each had done. He ended saying, "We're coming along fine. More of the same tomorrow. Better get to your formation. See you tomorrow."

For the remainder of the week, the routine was the same. All twenty-four cadets in the class were practicing stalls, learning how to correct for cross-winds when in flight, called "crabbing," spotting fields for emergency landings, and shooting practice landings. Since all were eager students, anxious to get to the next great event—soloing—they learned rapidly. By Friday, Ed and all five of his roommates were making good take-offs and landings.

With twenty-four student pilots all doing the same things, the runways and the air space around the field were busy. This kept all the cadets alert. Every cadet, and every instructor, kept his head and eyes moving at all times. Because of this there were no collisions, either on the ground or in the air.

One cadet, not one of Mr. Boone's, did have an accident in landing. He was doing a "wheel" landing, not a three-point one. In a wheel landing, the pilot comes in faster, essentially flying right into the ground, and touches both wheels down, keeping the tail up, then cuts the throttle and drops the tail as he slows down. It is an easier landing than a three-point one, and many pilots prefer it. All of the cadets had to learn to do it, but not as thoroughly as they learned the three-point.

In this case, the cadet was just on the verge of having his wheels touch down when, apparently, he moved the stick to the left, bringing his right wing up. Just at that moment, a strong gust of wind came from his right. The wind lifted his right wing, and the tip of his left wing hit the ground, throwing the plane into a "ground loop." Only minor damage was done, and no one was hurt. His instructor explained to everyone that it was not his student's fault, that it could happen to anyone.

With that exception, Friday and the entire week preceding it passed without mishap. Fridays were the last days of classes and flight instruction each week. Saturdays and Sundays were always off days for the cadets. Ed's six explored the small town of Bennettsville, eating lunch at a cafe, taking in a movie, and having dinner in the town's best restaurant.

Following dinner, they strolled down the main street and came to a drive-in soft ice cream eatery, which appeared to be the favorite hang-out of the local young folks. There they spotted a group of eight giggly girls, evidently of high school age. They sauntered over to the girls and started chatting with them. Soon, being older and knowing that these girls were too young for them, they began teasing them about their drawls, and their "hick town." The girls gave as good as they got, and everybody was having a good time.

Suddenly two car-loads of local boys screeched into the parking area. The boys got out and headed toward the high school girls and the cadets. Apparently resenting the outsider cadets talking to the local girls, they sounded off in pretty nasty and belligerent terms. Ed and George started to bristle, and were about to give back the same to the boys, when Chuck said, "Hold it, guys. You know we've been told what will happen if we get into any trouble with local people. It's goodbye to the cadet program for us. So, back off. Let's just walk away."

George and Ed saw that Chuck was right, so they and the other four called, "Good night, girls," and walked back to the sidewalk.

"Nothing to do here," said Chuck. "What do you say we get back to the base? There's a Rec Room there. We can play some ping-pong, shoot some pool, or play cards. What say?" They all agreed, so they went to the bus stop and soon were back at the base.

Sunday seemed endless. Ed did some aimless walking about the base, and a mile or so down a country road and back, he found Bill Malone. They threw a softball back and forth, then played several games of ping-pong in the Rec Hall. Then each went to his room to write letters or read.

Sunday meals were informal, with cadets making their way to the mess hall individually or in small groups. No marching. Ed, Bill, Chuck, and George wandered over to dinner together. They talked mostly about what Mr. Boone would probably do with them the next day. Ed said he hoped he could shoot some more landings. He felt that he was doing all right, but each one seemed like a big adventure to him. Conditions were different for each landing: some other plane or planes in the pattern, changes in wind direction or velocity, the angle of the sun making seeing difficult, light rain falling. The others said that it was the same with them. Chuck hoped for more practice getting out of spins, and Bill said that he needed the same thing. George felt pretty satisfied with everything he was doing. They returned to the room and talked until lights out.

Reveille sounded, and nobody protested. They were eager to get breakfast over and get to the flight line. There, Mr. Boone greeted them with his usual cheery, "Good morning, Gentlemen," then he went on to say, "We'll continue shooting touch-and-go landings, then we'll go up to 3,000 feet, where I'll put you in unusual positions for you to get us out of. Okay, Mr. Schwartz, I believe it's your turn to be first. Go get the 'chutes."

The other five went through the routine ground check and untied the plane. When Merv came back with the 'chutes, and he and Mr. Boone were in the cockpits, Chuck cranked the starter, and they were off.

Ed was second to fly, so when Merv taxied in and climbed out, he climbed in. At Mr. Boone's say-so, Ed taxied down the field and into take-off position. Mr. Boone nodded, and Ed took off confidently and smoothly. "Man," Ed thought, "Just a week since I had my first airplane ride, and here I am taking off!" He turned out of the pattern and began to climb as directed by Mr. Boone. They had just reached 1,000 feet when the engine went dead. Ed put the nose down as Mr. Boone said, "Find a pasture and take us in."

Mr. Boone had taught his students to determine the direction of the wind by observing grass, weeds and tree leaves below. Ed saw that they would have to turn left to be headed into the wind. He spotted a short open field in that direction, and keeping the nose down, he headed for it. He was lucky. By slipping, another technique Mr. Boone had taught them, he was able to lose enough altitude to be able to line up and come over the edge of the field just above the treetops.

Just then, the engine caught as Mr. Boone turned the switch back on. "Give her the gun and take us back up, Mr. Thorne," came through the gosport. "The field was too short. Even if we could have landed, I doubt that we could have taken off from there. But it was the only field we could have reached. Good. Take us up to 4,000 now."

Ed put them into a wide, circling climb, and levelled off at 4,000 on the altimeter. "I've got her," Mr. Boone said. In a moment they were upside down. "She's yours," he said. Not too steadily, but without losing control, Ed rolled the airplane back to normal flying position.

Next, Mr. Boone put them in a spin and turned it over to Ed to bring them out. Calmly, as Mr. Boone had taught him, Ed stopped the spin with the rudder, popped the stick, shoved the throttle forward, and brought it out in the best spin recovery he had done to that time.

After several more position exercises, Mr. Boone said, "All right, let's go down and shoot some landings." Ed put the ship into a shallow dive. Suddenly Ed felt Mr. Boone take the stick. He pulled the nose up and over, until they were upside down again. Instead of having Ed roll them out, though, Mr. Boone pulled back on the stick and put them into a vertical power dive, straight at the ground. With the wind screaming through the wing struts, and the earth racing toward them, he grinned at Ed in the mirror, and yelled through the gosport, "Pull her out, Mr. Thorne!"

Ed cut the throttle back, held his feet firmly on the rudder bars, and started to pull back on the stick. The Stearman responded immediately, bringing her nose up, as the pull of gravity made Ed feel heavy, pressing him down in his seat, and light-headed, as the blood drained from his head. He began to yell, leaning forward to lower his head as he had been taught, to keep the blood up so he wouldn't black out. He glanced at Mr. Boone in the mirror and saw that the flesh on his face was sagging and the lower lids of his eyes were pulling down. Ed felt the same pull on his face.

When Ed got them back to straight-and-level, the altimeter read 700 feet, and the airspeed indicator said 150.

Mr. Boone, looking normal again, said, "That's the quick way to come back downstairs, but don't let me catch you doing it that way. How'd you like it?"

"Great! Can we do it some more?"

"Not now. Take her into the pattern and let's see if you can do three decent landings."

Ed shot three touch-and-go landings: two good, and one the best he'd ever done.

"Okay, Mr. Thorne. You're beginning to look pretty good. Take us home."

After stopping and climbing out, Ed joined the others. "Wow!" Bill said to him, "I thought you were in trouble in that dive. What'd Dan'l say when you did that?"

"He got us into the dive, man! Then, when I thought the wings were coming off, he calmly says, 'Pull her out, Mr. Thorne.'"

Merv came over and Ed asked him if Mr. Boone had done that with him. "Hell, no," Merv replied. "We just did the normal stuff. Then he said, 'Okay, take us in.'"

"I guess he just had an impulse or something," Ed commented. "Or maybe he was trying to scare me. Well, it *was* getting scary there, before he told me to pull out. I didn't know if he'd gone off his rocker or what."

Dick asked, "What the hell air speed were you doing?"

"I don't know in the dive. When we were straight-and-level again, it was 150," Ed answered.

"I didn't think she'd do that much without blowing apart," Bill put in.

"I was pretty worried about that myself," Ed said. "You should have heard those struts screaming. And I don't know how many Gs we pulled when I brought her out, but Mr. Boone looked funny in the mirror, and I was being pulled down hard in my seat."

"Guess we have to learn to handle that," came from Chuck.

"Yeah," Ed replied, "But I didn't need so much all at once."

High School

Before Performing a Concert

Ed as Faust

121

Ed, Cadet Buddies, PT-17

Bill Schmidt, Ed, PT-17

Ed, Cadet Buddies, PT-17

Ed, Cadet Buddies, PT-17

PT-17 Stearman (Primary Trainer)

BT-13A (Basic Trainer)

Ed, Cadet Buddies, PT-17

AT-6 (Advanced Trainer)

Red Hunt, Ed

Ed, P-40

Ed, P-40

Bill Schmidt, Red Hunt, Ed

Buddies, Ed, Wrecked P-40

Ed in PT-17, Bill Schmidt on Wing

Ed in Princess, in full flight gear, ready to take off on a mission

Ed with his Crew Chief & Gunnery Chief

Ed's P-51, Princess Pat

POW

Ed & Pat
Summer 1945

1945 or 1946

Summer 1945

Former Fighter Pilot
Gets Philosophy Degree

Ed with Joe & Jamie

126

August 18, 1945

Ed & Pat 2003

Ed with Son Jamie & Daughter Erika
National Air & Space Museum – The Red Mustang
January 2008

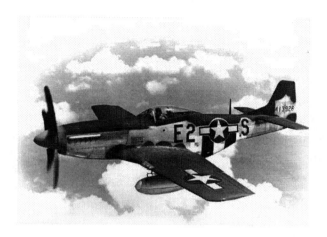

15

The next day, Tuesday, started with an overcast sky, the first since the cadets had arrived at Bennettsville. As the six got ready to march to the flight line, they wondered if the weather would prevent their flying that day.

"Guess we won't know 'til we get down there," said Dick. Chuck came back with, "Doesn't look too bad to me. What do you guess the height of that cloud cover is?"

Bill looked up and replied, "My expert weather eye says 3,500 to 4,000 feet."

"Well, if you're right, we should be able to fly. It's not raining, and the wind doesn't seem too strong," Chuck responded.

Glancing at his watch, Ed yelled, "Time to go! Let's hit it. It's my turn to fly first, so whatever we do, I'll do it first. You guys can watch and learn." Accompanied by hoots and Bronx cheers, Ed raced the other five to where the rest of the class was forming up to march to the flight line. He began "I've Got Sixpence," and the others joined in singing on the short march to the Line.

They reported to Mr. Boone, who greeted them with, "I see you're all feeling good this morning, eh? Probably because you think the weather will keep you from flying today, hm?"

"Are you kidding, Sir?"

Ed asked, "What about the weather, Sir? I'm scheduled to be first, if we fly. Will we be flying?"

"The weather check plane just came in a few minutes ago. The overcast is no problem; it's at 4,500 feet. There is a fast-moving front coming in from the west, but it's several miles away. We'll have to watch for it, and the shifting winds ahead of it. We should get some time in before it gets here. We'll have to quit when it gets close, though. It's bringing a line of thunderstorms, and that can be dangerous. Usually means increased wind velocity, and shifing winds, too. You know we don't fly in that stuff. Okay, Mr. Thorne, get the 'chutes; let's get whatever time in we can. We'll stay in the pattern and shoot landings, keeping an eye on weather changes."

Ed went for the two 'chutes, and the others untied the plane and did the ground check. When Ed got back, he and Mr. Boone climbed into the cockpits and buckled up. "Okay, Mr. Thorne, get her going and take off. Stay in the pattern and land, then take off again. Continue until I say otherwise."

Ed went through the now automatic starting procedure and pre-flight sequence. "Gas on, switch off, throttle cracked," and so on and, checking the windsock, which indicated wind out of the east, and the altimeter setting, he taxied out, looking carefully around, and seeing no other ships on the runway, turned east and took off. Making two left turns as he climbed to 500 feet, he continued on the downwind leg, turning on to the base leg, then into his approach, getting the wheels and tail-skid on the ground shortly after crossing the western edge of the field. He felt proud of the landing, his best to that time, and even prouder as Mr. Boone gave him the "Okay" sign. The instructor then indicated that he should gun it and take off, then come around for another landing.

Two more good landings, finding each time that he had to keep more power on for a longer time to get past the edge of the field to land. He glanced at the windsock, and saw that it was standing straight out from its mast, meaning that the wind had picked up in velocity. He was glad that Mr. Boone drummed into all of them that they had to keep enough power on to keep the plane a little above flying speed, until exactly in landing position. This was in case anything changed, they would still have control, and could add power to go around again.

After the third successful landing, Ed waited for the signal to go around again. Instead, Mr. Boone said through the gosport, "Take us in, Mr. Thorne."

"Rats," Ed thought. "Is this all I get today?" He tried to look his disappointment through the mirror to the instructor, but Mr. Boone seemed to be avoiding looking at him. "What did I do wrong?" Ed asked himself. "My landings were okay. I checked wind and altimeter settings. Everything seemed all right. Why are we going in so soon?"

They pulled up in front of the five waiting cadets, all of whom looked as perplexed as Ed felt. Mr. Boone snapped off his seatbelt and started to climb out. Ed started to follow suit, but Mr. Boone, already on the wing, said, "Stay there, Mr. Thorne."

"Now what?" Ed wondered. "Does he have to take a leak, or what?"

At the instructor's next words, Ed felt a tingle in the seat of his pants. "Take her around once, and bring her back to me."

"Yes, Sir," Ed blurted out, feeling the tingle climbing up his spine growing stronger. Gripping the stick tighter, Ed released the brakes and started taxiing to the west end of the field. By the time he got there, the tingle had grown to a full-blown thrill, surging up to his shoulders. He felt the hairs on the back of his neck rising. Through his shoulders and to his finger tips, the thrill traveled. He felt energized, vitalized, as though suddenly he were more alive, more charged. "It feels like opening night, the first time I sang in an opera," he thought.

He stopped to look again at the windsock and the altimeter setting before turning east for his take-off run. The windsock was still rigid, even a bit more so than when he had looked a few minutes before, still horizontal and pointing west. The altimeter setting had been changed to a lower number, indicating a drop in atmospheric pressure. He re-set his altimeter. After checking the mags, he turned so the nose pointed to the east, advanced the throttle, picked up speed, moved the stick forward to raise the tail, then eased it back, and he was airborne.

Both tense and excited at once, thinking, "This is it! This is what I've wanted all this time, and now it's actually happening! I'm flying!" He made a good climbing turn left, then another left, putting him on the downwind leg. With the tension and excitement, he paid no attention to anything but the airplane, and doing as perfect a flight around the pattern and landing as he could. Keeping his head and eyes moving had become automatic. Otherwise, his attention was entirely on his altimeter and his air speed indicator.

Levelling off at 500 feet, he made the left turn on to the base leg, finding that he had to crab a little to the right to stay parallel to the edge of the field. If he had been less caught up in the excitement of what he was doing, it would have occurred to him that it was odd that he had to correct to his right, since the windsock had indicated that the wind would be coming from his left.

For a moment, there in the isolation of the cockpit, with no one able to see him, tears welled in his eyes. After twice coming close to washing out in Pre-Flight, his dream of becoming a pilot was being realized. He pulled the throttle back and lowered the nose, intending to ease the craft down for the landing.

Everything seemed to be going all right until he realized that he was running out of field. That is, he was flying past the tee, and his wheels were still well above the ground. He glanced at the air speed indicator, seeing that it was just a little above landing speed, as it should be. But he was much too far down the field, so he gunned the engine and pulled up to go around again. "Well, I misjudged," he said to himself. "It happens to pilots all the time. I wish it hadn't happened to me on my first solo, but it did. So go around again and put her down again." He wasn't happy about it, but he didn't think he'd be in any trouble for having to go around a second time.

He pulled up, made his turns, and headed down the downwind leg again. This time, partly out of embarrassment, he looked down at his classmates, and saw that they were waving their arms. "Good guys," he thought. "They're telling me that it's all right, not to worry." He was tempted to rock his wings in acknowledgement, but he didn't want to appear to be acting the hotshot on his first solo flight. Instead, he waved at them with his left hand. Again, he came around and lined up for his approach and landing. Again, unaccountably, he sailed down the field, unable to get down. "Well," he thought, "must be that not having Mr. Boone aboard makes the ship a lot lighter. I'll go farther past the field before I start my approach, and get this baby on the ground." He was getting worried now. What would Mr. Boone think? Going around two times wasn't good, but it would be acceptable on a first solo. But three times! Would that wash him out?

This time, as he flew by his classmates, they were pointing westward as they waved. "Okay, guys. I know. You're telling me to go farther west and make a longer approach. Just what I've decided I have to do." Allowing what he thought had to be more than enough extra distance to get the plane down, he started his approach. Nose down, keeping the air speed just above stalling speed, he tried to get on the ground, passing over the field's edge at twenty-five feet above the ground. "Should be okay now," he thought. But it wasn't okay. Again, he sailed past mid-field, where the tee was, and wasn't able to get on the ground.

Really concerned now, he came around again. Again, his classmates, and this time, Mr. Boone, too, were all pointing to the west, and not waving. This time Ed knew he had misunderstood what they were trying to tell him, so he looked in the direction they were pointing. What he saw shook him. A line of thunderclouds was clearly visible, not far from the field, He remembered how much the weather instructor had emphasized how dangerous such clouds could be, especially for a light airplane. Waving to the men on the ground to let them know that he understood, Ed made a right turn out of the pattern, and headed north, then east, away from the line of thunderheads, climbing.

He checked the fuel gauge, seeing that he had plenty of gas. Not far from the field, he could see an opening in the overcast. Believing that the best thing to do would be to get above the overcast and wait until the storm front had passed, he climbed in a spiral toward, then up through the opening.

The cloud cover was not very thick, so at 4,700 feet he was well above the clouds. He looked to the west and could see the boiling tops of the thunderheads. Maintaining his altitude, he started circling, waiting for the storm clouds to pass. He pushed his worry about what would happen to him when he finally landed to the back of his mind. He gloried in the vast blue sky above the white cottony clouds below him, and the utter solitude of this space, stretching from horizon to horizon. It was, for the moment, a world all his, and he laughed at the pure wonder of it.

The solitude was not his to enjoy for long. As he completed his second circle, another Stearman broke through the clouds and immediately turned toward him. Ed's first thought was, "Oh-oh! Another cadet had trouble landing and climbed up here, just as I did." His next thought was, "Why is he heading right at me? We aren't supposed to get close to any other plane." Ed just started to turn away, when he noticed that someone was in each cockpit of the other Stearman. "Can't be a cadet in trouble if there's an instructor with him," Ed reasoned.

By that time, the other plane was rocking its wings, and the two in the plane were signalling to Ed to get close to them. Ed turned so the planes were flying in the same direction, and then he throttled back to slow down. The other plane came level with him, about twenty-five feet to his left. Now he recognized the person in the front cockpit. It was the Chief Civilian Pilot.

The other plane suddenly dropped back, and Ed realized that the pilot must have cut his throttle all the way back. This is what Mr. Boone had done when he wanted to say something and hear Ed's answer, so Ed cut his throttle all the way back. Now he heard Mr. Crane, the Chief Pilot, yell, "Stay beside me and do what I do!"

Ed yelled back, nodding, "Yes, Sir!" and advanced the throttle. Mr. Crane brought his ship a little closer, and matched Ed's air speed. Then he began a slight turn to the right, and Ed did the same, trying to keep the same relationship to the other ship. Slowly Mr. Crane put his nose down, and Ed followed suit. In a moment Ed saw that they were heading toward an opening in the clouds. Soon they were descending through the opening, coming out headed east, with the landing field to their left. Continuing to lose altitude, they made a wide turn to the north. At 1,100 feet, they turned back toward the field. At 500 feet, they entered the pattern on the downwind leg. But Ed realized they were setting up to land east to west, instead of west to east, as he had been trying to do.

"Oh, God!" Ed thought. "Now I know what happened. And I, like a klutz, didn't pick it up. The wind changed 180 degrees between the time I took off and the time I tried to land! Just like the weather instructor said it sometimes does. No wonder I couldn't get down! All I needed to do was look at the windsock, and I'd have known. Oh, man! I'm looking right at wash-out now, for sure." Totally embarrassed, Ed continued on the downwind leg as Mr. Crane turned out of the pattern. With a normal turn onto the base leg, Ed pulled the throttle back as he turned for his approach. This time, heading into the strong wind, he had no trouble getting down in a neat three-point landing.

Because he had landed on the opposite side of the field from the side they had been using for all his previous flights, Ed had ample time to stew about what kind of greeting he'd get from Mr. Boone and the other cadets, and what would happen to him for his stupidity.

He taxied to where the others were waiting, cut the engine, and climbed out. Head down, he walked toward Mr. Boone and the others. He stopped in front of them, waiting. No one said anything. He looked at them, and with no emotion in their faces, they stared back. His heart sank.

After several moments of agonizing silence, Mr. Boone spoke. "Glad to see you back, Mr. Thorne. Nice landing." Then Ed's roommates broke the silence.

"We never thought we'd see you again!"

"Who do you think you are? Charles Lindbergh?"

"What a dirty trick, logging all that solo time!"

"What a dumb ass! Can't even tell when the wind changes!"

"What's wrong with looking at the windsock?"

Now Mr. Boone spoke again. Holding out his hand, and shaking Ed's, he said, "Congratulations, Mr. Thorne. You're the first one to solo. You owe me a pack of Chesterfields. Now, what the hell were you doing? I ought to chew you out, but I'm so glad to see you safe, I can't. You just set a record for longest first solo flight at this Primary School. But what the hell did you think we were waving and pointing for each time you came down this side of the field?"

Ed didn't know whether to laugh or cry. "First time around I didn't even see you. I knew I'd blown the first landing, and I was determined to make the second one good. My attention was all on the plane. Second time, I saw you all waving, and I thought you were encouraging me, so I waved back. The third time I thought you meant for me to go farther from the edge of the field before I started my approach. Since I had already thought of that, that's what I did.

"Next time you were all pointing west again, so I looked that way and saw the thunderclouds coming. I thought that was what you wanted me to see. I remembered how dangerous we were taught they could be, so that's when I decided to get out of their way, up above the overcast."

"Well," said Mr. Boone, "that was a good move if that's what we were trying to tell you. But it wasn't, was it?"

"No, Sir, you were trying to tell me to land in the opposite direction, from east to west. I'm ashamed of myself, Mr. Boone. I should have been aware that the wind had changed."

"Yes, you should have been. But it could have happened to anyone. You were too excited at first, then too frustrated to be aware of the change. You'll never forget this lesson," Mr. Boone said, kindly.

"No, Sir, I sure won't. It was scary, but fun. I liked being up there alone."

"Yes, I know that feeling. That's probably why your record shows you want to be a fighter pilot. In bombers, you never get that sense of aloneness. It's one of the reasons some of us are flying. By the way, I don't know what Mr. Crane is going to say, but you did a good job of flying, and used good judgment as to what to do, given the situation as you saw it. Here comes Mr. Crane now."

"What's your name, Mister?" snapped Mr. Crane.

"Aviation Cadet Thorne, Edward J., 13129304, Sir," responded Ed.

"By damn, Mr. Thorne! I've never seen anything like it! That wind shifted a full 180 degrees in about a minute. Usually a shift like that takes longer. Was this your first solo?" asked Mr. Crane.

"Yes, Sir."

"A neat job of flying for a first solo, but by God, you gave us a scare. You didn't lose your head, though. That's good. I think you learned a lesson, an important one that every pilot has to learn. You learned it the hard way, but I think you'll remember it, right?" Mr. Crane said.

"I'll never forget it, Sir," Ed replied.

"What do you think, Mr. Boone?" asked Mr. Crane, sending an apprehensive shudder through Ed.

Mr. Boone answered, "I think he showed he can fly under tough conditions, Mr. Crane. And he made a damned good landing."

"Well, Mr. Thorne," Mr. Crane said, looking into Ed's eyes, "You did a pretty good job of formation flying, too." Here, he looked at all the cadets. "Don't let me catch any of you trying formation flying on your own. That is strictly forbidden." Turning again to Ed, he put out his hand and shook Ed's. "Glad you made it, son. Congratulations on your first solo." With that, he winked at Mr. Boone and strode away.

Overwhelmed, Ed stood there as his friends crowded around him, shaking his hand and pounding him on the back. All he could think was, "I'm the luckiest guy in the world. I missed washing again!"

Mr. Boone interrupted the congratulations to say, in a very serious tone, "Mr. Thorne, if I thought you did that just to get extra solo time, we'd bust your butt out of here so fast you wouldn't know what hit you. The rest of you hear what I'm saying, and don't any of you try anything like that!"

"Yes, Sir. No, Sir," they responded in chorus.

Since the thunderclouds were now over the field, and rain was imminent, all flying was cancelled for the rest of the morning. Mr. Boone dismissed them, and the cadets marched back to their barracks. Ed spent the rest of the time until noon chow answering his friends' questions and enjoying the knowledge that he could fly, and more than anything else, the fact that he miraculously had not washed out.

During the next two days, Wednesday and Thursday, Ed's five roommates soloed, each going around only once and making an acceptable landing. For the remainder of Thursday, and all morning on Friday, they took turns practicing landings. Each would shoot three, then come in, and while the next cadet shot his three, Mr. Boone would critique the one who had just finished, with the other four listening.

Because the other instructors were doing the same thing with their students, and although they were using patterns on both sides of the field, the patterns were busy, and every flier had to wait his turn for every take-off and landing. In spite of this, all six of Mr. Boone's students got in two series of three landings. By the end of Friday's session, all six felt comfortable and confident taking off and landing. Mr. Boone was pleased, and told them so.

Again, the weekend was boring, They wanted to fly, but the six spent time on Saturday in the Rec Hall, which was more crowded than the flight pattern had been the day before. An old John Wayne movie was shown at 03:00, but the sound track was bad, so they left. They went to the PX to buy supplies and milkshakes, then to their room. Until evening chow, they talked and joked with each other, getting on Ed again about his first solo. After chow, they read and wrote letters, then slept.

Ed had been asked to sing at a Methodist church in town, so Sunday morning the others, all but Merv, went in with him. He sang "If With All Your Hearts," from Mendelssohn's "Elijah." On the way to a restaurant after church, the others complimented him on his singing. He thanked them, but he knew that he hadn't sung well. He'd had to force his voice on the high notes. "But," he thought, "that's not what I'm here for."

Merv met them at the restaurant for lunch, then they took the bus back to the base. Ed, Bill, and Dick put on shorts, tee-shirts amd tennis shoes, and ran around the airfield. After they showered, all six went to the Rec Hall where they played some ping-pong and billiards. After evening chow, Ed went to Bill Malone's room and spent the evening with him and his roommates. Word had gotten around about Ed's record-setting solo, so he had to recount the whole story for them. He naturally embellished the story, but they all thought it was great.

On Monday morning, the six found a different routine at the flight line. Two more airplanes had been assigned to Mr. Boone. The instructor would take a cadet up in one plane, teach him to do a maneuver—the first was the snap roll—have him do it until he was doing it reasonably proficiently, then have him land. Mr. Boone would then climb out, and the cadet would take off and practice snap rolls on his own. Meanwhile, Mr. Boone would take the next student up and repeat the procedure. The same with the third. By the time he was back with the third, the first would have completed his time, and the instructor would take the fourth one up. And so on, until all six finished instruction and practice of that maneuver. This completed the morning's flying. Following Mr. Boone's critique, the cadets marched off for chow, then to change and go to ground school.

This procedure was followed for several weeks. Some maneuvers required several days for everyone to master. The slow roll was especially tough, because it took carefully coordinated use of stick and rudder to keep the nose of the ship on a point on the horizon as the plane was rolled slowly on its axis. It was four days before Mr. Boone was satisfied.

When all six cadets could do snap rolls, barrel rolls, slow rolls, loops, Immelmans, and chandelles one after the other with acceptable accuracy, Mr. Boone gave them turns flying around doing them at will. This went on right into the time when they were upperclassmen. That transition was so unmarked that they would not have noticed it, except for saying so long to their friends among the upperclassmen as they left. They grew in proficiency and confidence. Mr. Boone had only to say, "Mr. Schmidt, take Number Six and do some aero-batics for an hour," and he'd be off.

A few days before they became upperclassmen, Mr. Crane took each one up for a check ride. They all passed, although Ed suffered bruised knees during his check ride. He had got-ten proficient at stalling and getting out of the stall quickly and without getting into a spin. He, like the others, had learned to tell by the "seat-of-his-pants" when the plane was going to stall, and properly anticipating the stall, start recovery procedures. While practicing stalls one day, Ed had found that he could anticipate the stall even more certainly by watching the air speed indicator. This was not acceptable, for all the fledgling pilots were expected to "feel" what the plane was doing, and about to do, at all times. But Ed had gotten so he enjoyed the feeling of beating the "feeling" of about-to-stall by just a split second, by watching the speed indicator.

As Mr. Crane checked him on stalls, Ed made the mistake of "pre-anticipating" the stall. The second time, Mr. Crane saw what he was doing. Suddenly, the stick rapped hard back and forth on Ed's knees, and Mr. Crane was yelling, "If I wanted you to do this on instru-ments, I'd put you in the Link Trainer! Get your eyes off the instruments, and FEEL what's going on!" During the entire time, the stick was unmercifully beating on Ed's knees. "Now do six more stalls, Mister, and they'd better be good!"

Ed did as he was told, and he was lucky enough to catch every one as it started, and correct it. "Okay, Mr. Thorne, but you were close to being in deep trouble." The rest of the check flight went well, and when they were on the ground and parked, Mr. Crane was affable again, even saying, "Except for that stupidity on stalls, you did all right. I trust you haven't taken any more unauthorized trips above storm clouds."

"No, Sir," Ed replied, relieved. But he thought, "I wonder why I'm always doing these damn fool things to get me in trouble?"

In the last two weeks of their stay at Bennettsville, Mr. Boone started them on formation flying. He would fly one plane and two cadets would fly two others, making a simple "V" formation. They learned to take off with all three abreast, and instead of following the pat-tern after take-off, they would fly straight ahead, climbing. At 2,000 feet, Mr. Boone would rock his wings and, as instructed on the ground, the two cadets would move in close to Mr. Boone with their wings just behind his. At first, the instructor had to keep signalling the cadets in closer. "Tuck it in," he would mouth at them. "Make it a tight formation."

When the students got used to being so close to another plane in the air, Mr. Boone would start a gentle turn—first to the left, then to the right. The cadets were expected to maintain their positions through the turns. After getting acceptably competent at taking off and making turns in formation, Mr. Boone would wave the cadets out slightly away from him, and they would do chandelles in formation. As their confidence grew, they did loops in formation, and finally Immelmans.

In their last few days at Bennettsville, all the cadets were given Army Check Flights by Lieutenant Browning. All the remaining twenty-one in the class passed. Two had washed out, and one had killed himself in a crash. Mr. Boone said, "I know when my pupils are good enough; I knew you'd pass."

The night before they were scheduled to leave Bennettsville, the six took Mr. Boone and his wife to dinner in town. After that, he wished them all good luck and they said goodbye. They had gone a few steps away from Mr. and Mrs. Boone when they heard Mr. Boone call, "I'll never forget that solo of yours, Mr. Thorne. But you didn't have to give me a whole carton of Chesterfields. A single pack would have been enough," and he laughed. The cadets laughed too as they walked to the bus stop. They were all elated because they had successfully completed another major step toward getting their wings. Although they had a few moments of sorrow and regret about the three who hadn't made it, they weren't close to those classmates and it wasn't enough to dampen their spirits. This was a time for joy and celebration.

16

Unlike the departure from Maxwell, this time the entire class went together to the same Basic Flight Training School. It was Shaw Field at Sumter, South Carolina. They arrived shortly before noon, at about the same time as three buses from other Primary Schools.

They piled out of the bus carrying their hand satchels, and milled around for a few minutes until a U.S. Army Air Corps captain came toward them. Someone shouted "Attenhut!" and they all popped to. "As you were," the captain said. As he stood in front of them, they saw that he wore pilot's wings and a row of ribbons over the left pocket of his blouse. "My name is Johnson, and I'm your tac officer. This is a military base, and we do recognize upper and lower classes. But there is no ratline, and no hazing. There are formations, drills, parades and regular physical training. We have a formal parade each evening at retreat, and military discipline and courtesy are observed at all times.

"You will be housed four to a room in Barracks Twelve, just down this street. I will meet you immediately after noon chow for orientation. You will find your names posted on the doors of your assigned rooms. You are already dressed in the uniform of the day, so you don't have to change, even if you do look a bit crumpled from the bus ride. You'll just have enough time to relieve yourselves before chow call.

"Are there any former cadet officers in this group?"

On an impulse, Ed raised his hand. Dick did not raise his. "All right, Mister, step forward," the captain said to Ed.

Ed stepped in front of the captain and saluted. The captain returned the salute and asked, "What's your name, Mister?"

"Aviation Cadet Thorne, Edward J., 13129304, Sir," Ed replied.

"Right, Mr. Thorne. Form up this group and march them to Barracks Twelve, down this street. Then dismiss them to find their rooms."

"Yes, Sir," Ed said, snapping a salute, which the captain returned. Ed formed his classmates in four ranks, called them to attention, ordered Right Dress, Front, Right Face, Forward Harch, and counted out hup, two, three, four, as they marched the short distance to Barracks Twelve. There he halted them, had them face left, and dismissed them. They rushed to the screened veranda and to the doors to find their rooms.

Ed, Bill, Chuck, and Merv were roommates again. Three S's and a T, so they concluded that the rooms were assigned alphabetically. They quickly used the latrine, and rinsed their faces. They wiped their shoes with toilet paper.

All the cadets rushed out at mess call. Ed was forming up his classmates when a cadet wearing the chevrons of a cadet captain walked up to him. Ed popped to.

"Mr. Thorne?" the cadet officer asked.

"Yes, Sir."

"I'm Jerry Smolens, cadet commander of this squadron. I'll give the commands; you repeat them for your class. That is, when we march together. You will give the commands when just your class is marching to flight line, classes, etc."

"Yes, Sir," Ed responded.

"Squadron, Attenhut!" Smolens called. With Ed repeating each command, they marched to the mess hall. They found the only distinction between upper and lowerclassmen was that they sat at different tables.

With the large exceptions of no ratline and no upperclass disciplining of lowerclass cadets, Ed and his classmates found the military aspects of Shaw Field very similar to those they had experienced at Maxwell: dress codes, grooming, military courtesy, proper saluting, formations and marching required. They had enjoyed the more relaxed atmosphere of Bennettsville, but Ed welcomed the stricter military discipline at Shaw. It renewed his sense of being a part of something much larger than himself. During his time at Bennettsville, he had lost much of that sense, although flying so captivated him that he had not been conscious of the loss. The certainty that he would continue to fly excited him now, and the challenge of flying the larger, more powerful and complex Basic Trainer stimulated him. And he was happy to re-acquire the sense of oneness with a vast number of other fliers in a precisely disciplined organization having a serious mission to accomplish.

Noon chow over, the squadron fell out and formed up on the street. Captain Smolens called the squadron to attention. He then gave Ed the directions to the flight line, and told him to march his men there. The route was direct and clear, so the class arrived at the flight line without difficulty. Ed put his formation at ease while he looked for Captain Johnson. Finding him, he reported as he had been instructed.

The captain returned Ed's salute, and told him to stand at ease. "Here are the instructor assignments for your class, Mr. Thorne. The five instructors for your people are standing over there," he said, pointing to a group of four lieutenants and a captain, all with pilot's wings, and the captain with a double row of ribbons under his wings. "Four of the instructors — the lieutenants — will have four of each of you, and the captain will have five, since there are twenty-one of you. Take this typed sheet. It has the names of the instructors and the cadets assigned to them. Return to your people, proceed to where the instructors are, and call off each instructor's name, and the names of his pupils. Have the cadets report to their instructors. Any questions?"

"No, Sir."

"Good. Dismissed."

Ed came to attention and saluted, then returned to his group of cadets. After calling them to attention, Ed told them what he had been told, and then marched them to where the instructors were waiting. "Allen, Arthur, Barnes, and Carlson," he called out, "report to Lieutenant James." On through the list arranged alphabetically, ending with "Schmidt, Schultz, Sparks, and Thorne, report to Lieutenant Bellows."

The four double-timed to the only instructor not yet talking to cadets, and popped to. "Lieutenant Bellows?" Ed asked.

"You got me," the lieutenant replied, as he returned Ed's salute. "Stand at ease, men. I've just returned from a rotten tour in the Aleutians. It's good to be back where it's warm. I expect to be ordered to the European Theatre soon. The sooner the better! All we did in the Aleutians was patrol. Never saw anything to fire my guns at. It'll be better in the E.T.O. (European Theatre of Operations). My request for re-assignment is in, but knowing how slow paperwork is in the service, I'm sure I'll finish with you before my new orders come through.

"I'm due for captain's bars soon, so watch for these single silver bars to become railroad tracks, and address me properly, or I'll put you in an outside spin you'll never recover from. Anybody know what an outside spin is?"

"Yes, Sir," Chuck spoke up.

"Tell me."

"In a normal spin, the pilot is in the center, and the rest of the plane turns around him. In an outside spin, the landing gear of the plane points to the inside of the spin, and the pilot is turning on the outside," Chuck explained.

"Very good. You must be a college man."

"Yes, Sir, but I didn't learn that there. Mr. Boone told us about outside spins and how dangerous they are."

"Oh, so you had ol' Dan'l in Primary! Good. The rest of you?"

"Yes, Sir," they replied in unison.

"You couldn't have had a better instructor. Did he tell you why such a spin is especially dangerous?"

"Yes, Sir," Merv replied. "If it's a fast spin, the centrifugal force on the pilot is very strong. He may get disoriented quickly, or not be able to work the controls well enough to get control of the airplane."

"Good. You misters are pretty sharp. But Dan'l's students always are. By the way, he taught me to fly as a civilian. I know how well he trains his pilots, so I'll expect the best from you. Any questions?"

"Will we be flying today?" Ed asked.

"Don't be impatient. Yes, you will. You'll be flying the BT-13A. Quite a step up from the PT-17s you flew for Mr. Boone. Let's walk to the Line, and I'll introduce you to the aircraft. Relax and talk, if you wish."

Chatting among themselves, and with the lieutenant, they walked between two hangars and out to the flight line. There the cadets stopped and let out a collective gasp. Glowing in the afternoon sun, parked on a wide concrete strip, was a row of seventy-five low-winged, aluminum covered, monoplanes, each with a cowled radial engine and a birdcage-like canopy.

"God! They look like fighter planes!" yelled Chuck.

"Sure do," agreed Ed. "Flying these babies ought to be something!"

"All right, men," Lieutenant Bellows said, "let's stop here. You've already noticed some differences from the Stearman. Aluminum skin, cowled engine, monoplane, canopy. Also, notice the tail-wheel, instead of the Stearman's skid. Do you see the flat pole sticking up behind the canopy, with the wire running from it toward the tail? What is it?"

"Looks like an antenna," replied Bill.

"Right. That's a big difference between this and the PT. These are equipped with radios. That means I can talk to you on the intercom while we are flying, so you'll be able to hear and understand me. Big difference from the gosport, right?"

"Right, Sir," they all replied.

"It also means some other things. For one, you can talk back to me, but you'd better not! You will talk to the Control Tower, and they will talk to you. You will learn radio procedure, and every move you make must be cleared with the Tower. You can't even taxi without being cleared. Keep that in mind. Notice this is a huge airport with well-marked concrete taxi strips and three major runways. It is also a very busy airport, so the Control Tower means just that: it is the control center for every pilot on or near the airport.

"A second thing it means is that these ships are equipped with radio compasses, as well as magnetic ones. Finally, having radio means you can 'fly the beam.' You will learn how to do that in the Link Trainer, and then I'll introduce you to it in flight."

Chuck broke in, "We get Link here, Sir?"

"You sure do. You will all be scheduled regularly; make the most of it. You can learn a lot in simulated flight. Take advantage of it. Now, there are other differences from the PT. I've mentioned the radio compass. There's also a rate-of-climb indicator, and a gas switch so you can keep a balance in the fuel between the right and left wing tanks. Finally, on these we have electric starters, so no more cranking. Okay, let's climb up on the wings, two on each side. Step only where indicated."

Lieutenant Bellows climbed up and into the rear cockpit, and the cadets took places on the wings. The lieutenant pointed out the items that were new to the cadets. Then he unhooked the headset and put it on, and pulled the microphone to his mouth. "Tower, this is E24, over. Now," he said to the cadets, "the Tower will say, 'Roger, E24, read you loud and clear.' I will say, 'E24 to Tower, request clearance to start engine and taxi to runway for take-off on training flight.' 'Roger, E24, clear to start engine and taxi to runway 90. Stop on strip at edge of runway and call for take-off clearance. Over,' 'Roger, Tower, Wilco, out.' That's the procedure for getting clearance to start and taxi. 'Wilco' means 'will comply.' Okay, whoever is on the left wing and closest to the front cockpit, climb in and get ready to fly."

Merv and Bill were on the left wing, with Merv nearest to the front seat. Bill, being shorter, tried to squeeze past Merv, but Merv blocked him and climbed in.

"All right, Mr. Schwartz, what's the first thing you do?"

"Seatbelt, Sir."

"Right. Now, put on the earphones. You won't need the microphone. E24 to Tower, over."

"Tower to E24. Loud and clear, over."

"Request clearance to start engine and taxi for take-off on training flight, over."

"Roger, E24, runway 90 clear to start and taxi. Call before entering runway, out."

Lieutenant Bellows now switched to intercom, and said to Merv, "Mr. Schwartz, reach down and turn the gas switch to 'Left On,' then turn the mag switch to 'Both On.' No! Don't close the canopy. We taxi with the canopy open. You three get off the wings now, and stand clear. All right, Mr. Schwartz, crack the throttle about one-half inch. Good. Now, press the starter button."

Merv did as he was told. The engine coughed twice and came to life with a steady, staccato firing.

The three cadets watched as the lieutenant taxied to the end of runway 90, stopping before moving on to the end of the runway.

"Man! That's one neat airplane. It sure looks like a fighter!" Chuck exclaimed.

"Sounds like one, too," Ed said. "Radio, intercom, radio compass, rate-of-climb indicator, canopy! We're going big-time!"

"Lot of new stuff to learn," Bill said. "Hey, Ed. What trick are you going to pull on your first BT solo?"

"Watch it, little shot. I haven't forgotten how to do a six-inch jolt. Just because I broke the time record for soloing in Primary doesn't mean I have to do something spectacular with every new plane we fly. Maybe it's your turn," Ed shot back. "Of course, I'm not sure a pygmy like you can handle a great big airplane like this."

"You watch it! I can deliver a pretty good jolt, too. And I have a height advantage. Mine will land well below the belt and cripple you for life."

"You jerks are a couple of pains in the asses," Chuck said. "How many asses do you have, Chucky baby?" Ed asked. "What the hell do you mean?" Chuck said, bristling. "Take it easy," Ed answered, "You said we were pains in the asses. That must mean you have more than one ass to get a pain in."

The three laughed, then watched Lieutenant Bellows and Merv as they swung on to the runway, gunning the engine as they turned into their take-off run. The silver BT gained speed, then gracefully lifted off and turned left at the end of the field.

"Mmm, pretty," Bill commented. "Wonder if the lieutenant will let Merv handle her?"

The answer came shortly after the plane left the traffic pattern. They saw the nose dip, then jerk up suddenly, but too high, then back down again. "That's got to be Merv doing that. Bet it feels a lot different from a Stearman," Ed remarked. As they watched, the BT did a smooth slow roll, then headed down, picking up speed, and pulled up into a loop. Each maneuver was done with smooth precision.

"No way that's Merv," Chuck said.

Next, the airplane began a series of choppy, erratic figure-eights, losing altitude, being jerked up several times in the first ones, but smoothing out as the maneuver was repeated.

"That's Merv," Bill said. "He's getting better. Must feel a lot different. He was having trouble keeping the nose up at first, but now he looks pretty good. Come on back, Lieutenant, I'm eager to try that baby."

"Hey, Ed," Chuck said. "Let's lock Bill in that locker in the hangar. Then we'll get our turns sooner."

"Okay, let's do it."

"Stand back, you guys. Remember my height advantage! I'll jolt you both where it hurts the most. Neither of you will ever father a child!"

"I'm not going to touch him. How about you, Chuck?"

"Not with a ten-foot pole."

"Yeah. You got the message," Bill said, sticking out his chest. "I'm short, but I pack a big punch."

The BT-13 was on its landing approach. It came in, hit the runway hard and bounced. At the top of the bounce, the left wing dipped, but was snapped level again before it hit the ground.

"That's Merv, sure enough," Bill remarked. "Good he had Lieutenant Bellows there to straighten him out."

The BT pulled into its parking place and stopped. Merv leaned forward and turned the engine off. He unbuckled his seatbelt and started to climb out. Lieutenant Bellows snapped, "You're forgetting something, Mister!"

Looking embarrassed, Merv took off the earphones, then started to climb out again. "Mister! Get on the ball. You forgot something else. You always turn the gas switch off when you park. You should have learned that in Primary."

"Sorry, Sir,"

"Okay, but don't forget again."

The other three cadets looked at each other. The exchange with Merv showed them that Lieutenant Bellows would not tolerate slip-ups on things they had already learned, or that were simple and obvious. Lieutenant Bellows confirmed this, speaking to them from the cockpit. "Gentlemen, flying is a demanding profession. It demands precision and good judgernent. Every detail is important. Your training is aimed at teaching you what to do, and how and when to do it. And it is cumulative. What you learned in Primary applies here, and what you learn here will apply in Advanced, and it will all apply to fighters or bombers. Every detail is important. Small mistakes can kill you and endanger others. Some detail overlooked can destroy a mission, or put an entire squadron at risk in combat. You are being trained not to make mistakes, and to use good judgement. Learn your procedures and apply them every step of the way. Mr. Schwartz, you did fine except for those goofs at the end. All of you, remember that when you are in an airplane, it isn't the same as being in your bunk. You must be keenly aware of where you are and what you are doing every second, on the ground or in the air. If not, you don't belong in a military plane." The lieutenant's face relaxed, and he said, "Who's next?"

Bill, not to be denied, beat the others up onto the wing, and said, "I am, Sir," as he climbed in.

"Okay. Tomorrow we'll use a schedule." With Bill strapped in, Lieutenant Bellows went through the same procedure he had with Merv. The cadets noticed that this time he asked for an altimeter setting when he asked the Tower for clearance. The engine roared to life, and Bill and the lieutenant were off.

"How was it, Merv?" Chuck and Ed asked almost in unison. "Great. But it's a different feeling bird than the Stearman. And a lot less forgiving. It doesn't respond as quickly, but it reacts to everything you do, and the reaction is pretty definite. I'm going to like flying her."

Ed said, "We noticed you didn't do any snap rolls. How come?"

"I asked the lieutenant that. He said that in this plane, and every military plane we fly from now on, we won't do snap rolls. Too much stress on the plane. These aluminum ones aren't as flexible as the fabric-covered Stearman. So snap rolls are out. He warned me not to even try one."

"You looked pretty ragged in those figure eights. How come?"

"You'll see when you fly her. It's a whole different feeling. Harder to keep the nose on the horizon. But I began to get the feel of it as we went on. Part of it, the lieutenant says, is the effect of torque from the bigger engine. And, anyway, it's a lot heavier than the PT."

"What happened on the landing?"

"You mean the bounce?"

"No. When your left wing dipped."

"Well, as I told you, she doesn't respond as fast as the PT, and we were just about at stalling speed, so she was even slower to respond. Anyway, my right wing dropped a little bit. You know how in the Stearman just a little movement of the stick would bring the wing up. That's what I tried. She didn't respond, so I moved the stick farther to the left. Then she responded more than I wanted, and the left wing went too far down. The lieutenant jammed the throttle forward to give us a little more air speed, and snapped the wings level just in time. Otherwise, we'd have ground-looped. Not a good start with a new instructor."

The three friends watched as Lieutenant Bellows took Bill through the same routines as he had Merv. They landed without trouble, and Chuck was next. When Chuck returned, it was Ed's turn. Having the advantage of the comments of the other two, as well as having watched them in the air, Ed felt confident and exhilirated as he climbed into the cockpit and strapped himself in. He no sooner had the earphones on than Lieutenant Bellows surprised him by saying, "Do you think you know how to call the Tower, Mr. Thorne?"

Startled, Ed responded automatically. "Yes, Sir."

"Go ahead, then. Push the radio button marked 'T' and call in."

Ed pushed the button and lifted the mike to his lips. Just as he was about to make his request, another voice came on, requesting clearance to land. The Tower responded, and that exchange ended, clearing the channel. In what he thought was his most experienced-sounding pilot's voice, Ed said, "E24 to Tower, over." No response. "E24 to Tower, over," he repeated. No response.

Since the engine wasn't running, the lieutenant spoke through the canopy. "Push the mike button, Mr. Thorne. Push the mike button."

Red-faced, Ed pushed the button on the mike and called, "E24 to Tower, over."

"Tower to E24, loud and clear, over."

"E24 to Tower, request clearance to taxi to runway for take-off on a training mission, over."

"Roger, E24, clear to taxi." Ed was feeling less embarrassed when the Tower continued, "But shouldn't you start your engine first?"

Ed felt the red deepening in his face as he called again, "Roger, Tower. Request clearance to start engine, and taxi to runway for take-off on a training flight."

"Roger, E24. Clear to start engine and taxi to runway 90 for a training flight. Altimeter setting 3,020. Repeat, altimeter setting three zero two zero."

"Roger, Tower. Runway nine zero, altimeter setting three zero two zero, E24 out."

"It's okay, Mr. Thorne," Lieutenant Bellows said, chuckling, easing Ed's embarrassment. "We all have a little trouble the first time we use the radio; you'll get used to it. Crank her up. Let's get in the air."

The engine was warm, so it caught the first try. Ed remembered to switch the radio back to intercom. Immediately, the lieutenant's voice said, "Okay, Mr. Thorne, you can get some feel of this aircraft by taxiing. Make sure you are all clear, and taxi out to the end of the runway. Stop before you go on the runway."

"Yes, Sir!" Ed said, feeling his morale leap upward, since the lieutenant had enough confidence in him to let him handle the taxiing. He looked carefully right, left, and straight ahead. Easing the throttle ahead, he took pressure off the brakes with his toes, and the plane started forward. Then, with a slight pressure on the right brake, he got the BT turned, and slowly zigzagged down the taxi strip toward the runway, then stopped at the edge of the runway, where he set the altimeter to 3,020.

"Not bad, Mr. Thorne," came the lieutenant's voice through the earphones. "Now, before we take the runway, one of the characteristics of this airplane is that it has a lot more torque than what you flew in Primary. When adding throttle going down the runway for take-off, in order not to go off the runway, you'll have to feed in some right rudder. Understand?"

"Yes, Sir," Ed replied, wondering why the lieutenant was telling him this.

"Okay. Now, do you know how to check the mags?"

"Yes, Sir."

"Do it."

Ed pressed the brakes with his toes and switched to left, then ran the engine up to 1500 rpm on the tachometer. The engine sounded steady and clear. He switched to right mag, and did the same. Both sounded good, so he switched to both, and eased the throttle back.

"Good. Now, call the Tower for clearance to take off."

Remembering to press the mike button, Ed called for, and got, clearance. The next thing the lieutenant said took Ed completely by surprise and sent a thrill up his spine, very much like the one he felt the first time he took the controls of the PT. "Now, Mr. Thorne, remember what I said about correcting for torque. You'll need to keep the nose headed straight down the center of the runway. You'll feel when the tail-wheel is ready to come up. Let it. Don't push the stick forward. Get up to full throttle in the first couple of seconds, and stay there. Let the plane fly itself off the ground. Stay straight and keep the throttle on full until I say otherwise. Can you do that?"

"Yes, Sir!"

"All right. Make sure the runway and the approach are clear, then go when ready."

Feeling goose bumps up his arms, across his shoulders, and up the back of his neck, Ed said, "Yes, Sir" once more, and looked to his left and his right. A twin engine aircraft was on the approach, so he waited for it to land and clear the runway. Since it had been too long since he got clearance, he pushed the mike button after switching from intercom to Tower, and re-confirmed his clearance. The Tower voice added, "There's a P-40 practicing maneuvers about a half-mile east of the field. Keep an eye out for him, over."

"Roger, Tower, thank you. Over and out." Ed checked and saw that the approach and the runway were clear, so he released the brakes, advanced the throttle, moved to the center of the runway, and turned left into the wind, pushing the throttle farther forward as he turned. He continued advancing the throttle, feeling the torque increase as he did so, and pushing the right rudder pedal in to compensate. For the first half of the run down the runway, with the throttle wide open, he didn't manage to keep the plane perfectly straight, but it never came close to veering off the runway. By the second half, he had gotten the feel of it, and as he felt the tail come up, he eased the stick back slightly so the nose wouldn't go too far down. Now he had better control and kept the nose aimed straight down the center of the runway. A moment later, he felt the airplane lift off the ground, and he felt the thrill of the take-off that he'd had every time he flew the Stearman, and sensed that he would always feel, as long as he flew.

As they cleared the edge of the field, Ed pushed the intercom button, and the lieutenant said, "Good job, Mr. Thorne. Ease the throttle back and close your canopy." Ed did so, cutting off the wind and much of the noise. "Do you see the P-40, about one o'clock high?"

Ed looked and saw the P-40 streaking earthward in a dive. "Yes, Sir," he said.

"Okay, we'll make a 90-degree left turn here. We don't want to tangle with that fellow. Ease your throttle back to about three-quarters; keep the nose up. We want to keep climbing. Not that much! You'll stall her out. Just a little above the horizon. That's good. Now, ease her into a gradual turn, one needle-width. Keep the nose up. Go to a heading of zero. Good, straighten her out, wings level! Don't over-correct. This is a good stable aircraft, but not as forgiving as the Stearman. You need to be smooth and easy. Good. Keep her like that up to 3,500 feet."

Ed's confidence grew as he adjusted to the greater size and weight, and the more powerful engine of the BT. He kept his head and eyes moving, as Mr. Boone had taught him, as it became easier to keep the wings level and the rate of climb steady. He resisted the temptation to watch the P-40, and kept his mind on flying the BT.

As 3,500 feet showed on the altimeter, Ed expected Lieutenant Bellows to take over. Instead, the lieutenant said, "All right, Mr. Thorne, you're getting the feel of it. Now, let's see you try a hard turn to the right. Keep the nose on the horizon, use the stick to put your wings vertical to the ground, and pull back on the stick to make the turn. Use the rudder as needed to keep the nose up. Do a 180-degree turn." Ed remembered doing this often in the Stearman. He automatically added a little throttle, and rolled half over, then pulled the stick back into his stomach, using the left rudder to keep the nose up.

"Not so far back on the stick, Mr. Thorne. That's it. Pull the turn too tight, and we'll stall out into a spin. That comes later. Okay, back to straight-and-level. Now give me some figure-eights. Smooth and easy. Make it flow. Keep the nose on the horizon all the time. Good, you're getting it. Do you have a feeling of being part of the aircraft?"

"Yes, Sir."

"Good. Every good pilot gets that feeling, especially fighter pilots. It makes all actions seem automatic, as if you and the machine were part of each other. Then all movements become natural, man and machine together, like a single organism."

Ed recognized immediately what the lieutenant meant. He had begun to feel some of that as he flew the Stearman; in fact, his first sense of it had been on his first solo. He hadn't mentioned it to anyone else, thinking they might laugh. He was pleased to hear the lieutenant, an experienced fighter pilot, talk about it. He was feeling good, beginning to relax and enjoy flying, as he had in Primary. Everything seemed to be coming easily to him.

"Good work, Mr. Thorne. You have a good feel for it. I think you are going to make a good flier. I'll take her now," the lieutenant said. At the unexpected compliment, Ed's heart leaped as he let go of the stick and took his feet off the rudder bars, and his hand off the throttle.

The lieutenant put the nose down and shoved the throttle forward, picking up speed. He then pulled back on the stick, climbing up and over, in a smooth, tight loop. Next, he continued up after completing the first loop, but this time, when they reached the top of the loop, he pushed the stick forward so they flew inverted for a couple of seconds, then did a half-roll, so they were straight-and-level, completing the Immelman. This was followed by a barrel roll, then a perfect eight-point slow roll, the nose held perfectly on a point on the horizon, and the roll stopped momentarily at each of eight points on its way around its axis. "Not bad," the lieutenant said, obviously pleased with himself. "Okay, you take it back now. Want to try a loop?"

"Yes, Sir," Ed answered, his excitement evident in his voice.

"Okay, put the nose down in a shallow dive, giving about half throttle, to about 200 air speed. Then, pull her up, giving full throttle, and over on her back."

Ed followed instructions, but was a little slow pulling the stick back at the top of the climb, and he felt the lieutenant pull the stick back. "Have to be a little quicker pulling her over in this one. It's heavier than the Stearman, and loses its speed quicker in a vertical climb. She'll stall out before you get her upside down if you're too slow on the stick. Take her on down, and get up your speed for another try."

Ed did, and was successful. "Good," the lieutenant said. "Time to go home. Know where the field is?"

"Yes, Sir."

"Take us home."

Ed headed south toward the field, letting down slowly. "Take her down to 1,500 and level off. We'll pass over the field and check the tee, instead of asking the Tower."

Ed did as he was directed, and they saw that the tee was still set for using runway 90. With the lieutenant instructing him, Ed flew on over the field past the south border, then he called the Tower for clearance to land. Cleared, they let down to 500 feet, and entered the pattern on the south edge of the field, turned right on the base leg, and right again for their approach. Just as they crossed the west edge of the field and lined up with the runway to land, the Tower came on. "Tower to E24, pull up and go around. Repeat, pull up and go around. Acknowledge." Ed gunned the engine, then spoke into the mike, while he pulled the nose up. "Roger, Tower, pulling up and going around. E24 out."

As they flew over the runway, they saw the reason for the Tower's call. Taxiing to the end of the runway was the P-40 they had seen in the air. As they cleared the field and turned right, the P-40 swung on to the runway and sped into its take-off. Ed was thrilled at the sight, as it climbed faster than any plane he'd ever seen. Lieutenant Bellow's voice came over the intercom. "Do you know why the P-40 had priority?"

"No, Sir."

"Because it, like most of the world's fighters, has an inline engine. It's liquid-cooled, not air-cooled, like this one and all radial engines. Inline engines can't sit on the ground long, or they overheat. As long as we were still in the air, even though the Tower had cleared us to land, he had priority. Understand?"

"Yes, Sir."

Ed switched back to "T" on the radio. "Tower to E24, clear to land, over."

"Roger, Tower. We're on the downwind leg, south side of the field. Understand, clear to land, over."

"All right, Mr. Thorne," the lieutenant said. "You did pretty well, so let's see if you can land her, okay?"

"Yes, Sir!" Excited by his chance to fly, and the compliments from his instructor, as well as seeing the P-40, Ed came in a little bit fast, and did a wheel landing, letting the tail come down as they slowed.

The lieutenant's voice bit through the earphones, "Oh huh! A smart-ass, eh!" For a moment Joe McGrane's face flashed in Ed's mind. The lieutenant continued, "When I want a wheel landing, I'll tell you so. Next time, I want a three-point landing, and it better be good." Obviously upset, Lieutenant Bellows shouted to him as they taxied toward their parking place, "Crank your canopy open!"

Ed knew he'd made a mistake, and was crestfallen after having had such a good flight up until then. He pushed the mike button and said, "I'm sorry, Lieutenant I didn't mean to do that. I was excited."

"Okay, Mr. Thorne, this time. I'll tell you when I want a wheel landing. Don't forget it!

You do not deviate from routine procedure unless I tell you to. I let you do some extra things because Mr. Boone sent a very strong recommendation for you. Don't blow it! A good pilot does his job no matter how he feels. Learn that, and learn it good. Your potential is excellent. But you have to realize it!"

"Yes, Sir. I will."

"Okay, let's park this thing."

After parking the aircraft and shutting her off, Ed climbed out and started to lift the parachute out. Lieutenant Bellows said, "Leave the 'chute in, Mr. Thorne. I have another class before chow."

Ed knew from the tone of his voice that the lieutenant was unhappy with him, and he felt bad. He joined the other cadets walking to their assembly point to march to the barracks.

"What happened, Ed?" Bill asked. "The lieutenant seemed pissed."

"He was. At me. I had a good flight. He let me take off and land. Also, I got to do a loop. I got too excited, and came in hot. Had to do a wheel landing. He didn't like it."

"What the hell!" Chuck exclaimed. "You took off and landed, plus getting to do a loop!"

"Guess I did all right taking off, and doing easy turns in the air. Anyway, he had me do a tight turn, with the wings perpendicular to the ground, and it was okay. After he did a few things, he let me try a loop. Not too good on the first try, so he let me try again. Worked out okay. Maybe he was tired or something. Anyway, after that he told me to take it in. We had to go around because of the P-40 taking off. He was okay, but I don't think he liked the delay. I goofed, and I think I got myself on his shit list."

"Maybe not. Maybe he just had a bad night, or something," Merv suggested.

"Yeah, Maybe. Did he get mad at you guys?" Ed asked.

"No," Merv said. "How about you?" Chuck and Bill shook their heads.

"Oh, God," Ed said. "He had confidence enough in me to let me do some things up there, and take off and land. And I blew it! Up 'til then he was in a good mood. We both had a good time up there. I know this is going to hurt me; I wonder what he'll do."

"Damn it, man," Bill said, "This was your first time to fly the BT. He can't hold it against you that you made a little mistake like that. If so, we'll all be in trouble."

Ed said, "1 don't know. He seems to be a stickler for procedure. He wants precision from us." They reached their assembly area, and Ed formed them up and marched them back to the barracks. He dismissed them, saying, "Fifteen minutes 'til P.T. formation. Dismissed."

After P.T. and evening chow, the cadets had fifteen minutes to get ready for retreat parade. The retreat routine was identical to that at Maxwell, only on a smaller scale. When they got back to their room, Captain Johnson, their tactical officer, stepped into the barracks. "You men are scheduled for Link Trainer day after tomorrow afternoon. You'll get a half-hour each, during your time on the flight line. You'll go in alphabetical order, the first two while the other two are flying, then the second two while the others are flying. You'll be practicing take-offs and landings."

Chuck asked, "Sir, what is Link like? We've never even seen one."

"You'll find it's just like flying, but it's simulated. You'll be closed in a cockpit, set up just like a BT-13 you fly on the field. You'll do everything on instruments; no visual reference to anything outside the cockpit. You won't believe how real it seems. You'll swear you're really in the air. And that's what your instruments will tell you. So will the Link instructor. He'll be giving you instructions and information all the time. He will also control things like wind and the attitude of the machine. Later on, you'll learn to fly the beam in the Link. Some people find themselves near panic as they work in the Link. But most adjust to it after a time or two. If you hope to fly in the Army Air Corps, you have to do it. You have to pass an instrument-flying test before you get your wings. After the first few minutes, you'll enjoy it. Good night, gentlemen."

Since the four had no studies, they spent some time showering and straightening up the room. Those who had them put pictures of girlfriends or family members on their desks.

"Hey, Ed," Bill called. "Where'd you get that picture? That's a different girl from the one you had at Bennettsville. How come? I liked the other one you had, what was her name? Henrietta? Yeah, she was neat."

"That she was," Ed replied. "But this one is neater. Her name is Pat. Henrietta was fun, but I have a feeling that I'm going to see a lot of Pat in the future. I haven't seen her for a couple of years, but I think I'm in love with her. I got this picture just before we left Primary. Knew you guys'd be jealous, so I kept it out of sight 'til we got here, then I put Henrietta away, and got out Pat."

"Yeah. How do you rate two good-looking gals like that? You in school together, or what?" Merv asked.

"No, there were some great-looking, neat ones in my high school, and I was crazy about one of them. No, Henrietta studied voice with my teacher. That's how I met her."

"Sure bet you two made beautiful music together."

"Matter of fact, we never sang together, except in groups."

"Sure, sure. Bet you made something else together, away from groups."

"Take it easy, Buddy. She isn't that kind of gal. She and Pat are both good girls, and I like them that way. So don't smart off."

"Okay, so you and Henrietta met at singing school. How about Pat? You pick her up in a bar or something?"

"Cut the crap! I told you she's a nice girl. Right now she's in college in Tennessee. It's a long story, and I don't think I want to waste it on you jerks."

"Come on, brother jerk. What's the story? Give us the straight dope, dope. We have about an hour before lights out."

"It won't take an hour. And if I tell my story, you guys have to tell one too."

"Okay," they responded.

Ed sat on the edge of his bunk and started, "It was the summer of 1939, a year after I graduated. I was still working in a dairy store for thirty cents an hour, just as I had the last two years of high school. And still studying singing, and doing quite a bit of paid singing, too. I didn't see any way I could go to college, and jobs were hard to find. But I was fed up with the dairy store job, and wanted to get away somewhere. Three other guys and I decided to go up to Canadohta Lake and camp for a few weeks."

"Canadohta! I know where that is," Chuck broke in. "We stopped there once on our way to Lake Erie. Near Oil City, isn't it?"

"Right, not far from Oil City. Anyway, we got some food together, along with our swimming trunks, some blankets and a frying pan, plus half a pup tent."

"What were four guys going to do in half a tent?"

"Well, we thought we could make a lean-to with it. It was all we could find, and we really wanted to go. So we did. One of the guys had an older brother with a car, a thirty-six Studebaker, four-door sedan. He offered to drive us up and spend a couple of days with us so we didn't have to hitchhike. He was going to sleep in his car.

"Well, we got there and found a spot in the woods, just off a path. We unloaded our gear and started trying to figure out the best way to rig up our shelter, when we heard a laugh on the path. We all turned at once, and saw a man in jeans and a work shirt, about twenty-five years old, looking at us and laughing his head off."

"What's so damned funny?" we yelled at him.

"You all going to try to sleep under that little piece of canvas?" he asked, still laughing.

"Sure, what of it?" Jim asked.

"Well, it won't keep the mosquitoes away from you, but I guess it'll be okay until it rains," the laugher said.

"You have a better idea?" I asked.

"Matter of fact, I do. By the way, my name's Jim Hayes. Mind if I come in?" This set him laughing again, since there was no place to come in to.

"By this time, we could see how funny we must have looked, and we started to laugh too."

"Okay, come on in, Jim," I said, holding out my hand and introducing myself, Jim, Bob, and Jack, as well as Ned, Jim's older brother.

"Well, gentlemen, I don't think you can make it with that dinky piece of canvas. If you're interested in a deal, I can help you, and you can help me," Jim said, leaning against a tree.

"What do you have in mind?" Jim asked, a bit suspiciously.

"Well, I own a couple acres right over there. See where that half-cabin is, with the tent top?" Jim said.

We all said that we saw it.

"Okay. You need a place to sleep, and I need help in clearing my land. You interested?"

We looked at each other and nodded.

"Good. You help me with the clearing, say a couple of hours a day, and you can sleep in my cabin."

"Sounds good to me," Bob said. "Can we all sleep in there?"

"Bigger than it looks. I've got six bunks, a sofa, and a couple of chairs in there. Also, a table and benches for eating. And a kerosene heater for chilly nights. Grab your stuff and come have a look—I think you'll find you're a lot better off there than here. Besides, I can't be here all the time, I'll feel better with somebody looking out for my place, and my tools. Come on over."

We gathered up our stuff and walked the fifty yards or so to his cabin. He was right; it was much bigger than it looked from where we had seen it.

"Well, what do you say?" Jim asked.

Ned said, "Looks like you'd be better off out of the mosquitoes and rain. I'd go for it if I were you guys."

We all agreed, and Bob wanted to know when we could start working.

"Plenty of time for that," Jim said. "Get your stuff in here. We can do a little work tomorrow. Let's have some coffee," and he took a large pot off the stove and filled six cups. We all went outside and sat on logs and stumps around his fireplace.

"We settled in, working our two hours most days, clearing brush and cutting trees, then we were free to swim, or canoe, or explore, or just hang around looking at girls from around the lake for the rest of the day. We used the showers and toilets in the bath-house at the swimming area. We all got good, healthy tans. All but Jim; he burned beet red.

"The fifth day, we finished our work and showered, then had some lunch. The other guys decided to go swimming. I didn't feel like it, so I hung around camp a while, then put on my red plaid shirt and walked down the path to the area where the store, bathouse, and swimming area were. This is where people would hang out when they had nothing else to do, and, sometimes, there'd be some good-looking girls around. I'd gotten to know a couple of them, so I guess I was hoping to see one of them.

"As it turned out, neither of them was around, and very few others. So I sort of loafed around, waiting for something to happen. And something did.

"I was leaning against a pine tree, gazing out over the placid lake, when a shiny, black 1936 Dodge sedan came along the road toward me. As the car got closer, I saw that it was being driven by an elderly man—about fifty, I guessed—and with him were four girls, about sixteen, all with that bright, excited, energetic look of joyous youth on their faces, and all of them looking in my direction—just as I was looking in theirs.

"All four of the faces were pretty, but one stood out from the rest, as if it were illuminated by a flash bulb, and it imprinted itself on my mind, like a clear photograph. The other faces faded into the background, At the same time, I felt a jolt, as if an electric charge had leaped from that face to me. I was instantaneously enthralled.

"The car moved on, but awestruck as I was, I watched to see to which cottage it would go."

"Man, it's piling up fast and deep here," cracked Bill. Merv said, "Don't interrupt him, this is getting interesting."

"You don't want to hear all this," Ed said, standing and stretching.

"The hell we don't," Chuck said. "You can't leave us hanging there. What happened?"

"Well, okay." Ed was leaning against the latrine doorjamb, and he continued, "I raced back to the camp, where I found Jim making a pot of coffee. 'Hey, Jim,' I said, 'Something crazy just happened."

"What? Did you see a girl in a bathing suit and get a hard on?"

"No, you jerk. A carload of four neat-looking girls just drove in and stopped at Cottage Eighteen."

"Wow! That should make the news. We better listen to Walter Winchell's program tonight. He'll probably make that his lead story."

"Why do I even try to talk to a smart-ass like you? Well, anyway, one of them hit me like a ton of bricks."

"Come on, Ed, cut the bullshit! A girl driving past in a car! You're really hard up, my boy."

"Listen, I'm telling you. It was like sparks flew from her to me."

"You're serious, aren't you? Well, Pal, looks like you're a goner. Guess you've been bitten by the ol' love bug. Here—have a cup of coffee."

"Huh-uh. You have coffee; I've got to go over and see her. Maybe get a chance to talk to her. See you later."

"I walked back to the road, and started toward Number Eighteen, where I could see the black Dodge. I thought I needed an excuse for knocking on their door, so my idea was to ask if there was a stepladder at the cottage, and if I could borrow it. I didn't have to knock. When I got to the front door, I saw the four girls from the car, four more girls of the same age, two older women, and the man who had been driving the car, all crowded around inside the screendoor, all looking out at me. My eyes went straight to the face that had struck me so forcefully as the car drove by. Our eyes locked, and I had the feeling that she had felt something like I had felt. While our eyes remained locked, I managed to stammer out, 'I wonder if there's a ladder under your cottage that I could borrow?'"

"The man said, 'I don't know, we'll have to look.' With that, he came out to the stoop, and all the others poured out after him. He put his hand out and said, 'Hello, I'm John Stauffar.' 'Ed Thorne,' I replied, shaking his hand. Then he introduced me to the others, and only one name stuck in my mind. It was hers, 'Pat Howarth.'

"She was tall and slender, long-legged. She had a lovely open face, framed in dark hair. Her brown eyes shone, and when she smiled, they crinkled and her whole face lit up. Her wide mouth opened, revealing even white teeth, with a small chip out of each of her two front teeth, which seemed to emphasize the perfection of the rest of her. By this time, I knew that Jim was right. I was, indeed, a 'goner.' I felt exhilarated, walking on air.

"There was no ladder under the cottage, but it didn't matter. We fell into the kind of easy chit-chat that comes so uninhibitedly to young people in groups, but is usually so difficult when there is no group, and two find themselves alone together.

"I learned that they were from Ambridge, Pennsylvania, and that they had just finished their junior year in high school. Mr. Stauffer would be returning home the next day, but the girls and the two teachers who were their chaperones would be remaining for two weeks.

"On a sudden impulse, I asked if any of them would like to go for a canoe ride. Laughing and giggling, they all responded, 'Yes, I would!'

"I said I'd be back in a little while with a canoe and a friend, and offered to take them two at a time. Although I was talking to all the girls, I couldn't resist looking right into Pat's shining eyes. Her smile was radiant, and I felt myself grinning broadly back at her.

"I rushed back to our camp. When I got there, I found the other guys were all back, discussing dinner. I told them what had happened, and they hooted and hollered, calling me 'Romeo' and 'Smooth Operator.' Then they asked me how I was going to get a canoe, since they knew I didn't have much money—none of us did. Good old Ned spoke up. He would rent the canoe if he could go with us. I was eager, and he would be leaving the next day, so we changed into swimming trunks, ran down to the beach, and rented a canoe.

"By now it was six o'clock, and we hadn't eaten since lunchtime. Ned bought a sandwich and Coke at the concession stand, and asked if I wanted anything, but I said I wasn't hungry, and thanked him.

"I paddled the canoe while Ned ate his sandwich and finished his Coke. We pulled up on a little sandy area in front of the girls' cottage, where all eight of them were waiting for us.

"I introduced Ned and stepped out of the canoe. The girls had drawn straws to choose the order in which they would ride. I was disappointed that Pat wasn't one of the first two. As we shoved off, one of the chaperones called, 'Don't be too long. There're six more to go, and it's getting late.' I agreed, and paddled out onto the smooth lake.

"As it turned out, Pat and the girl named Nancy were the last two for us to take out. By the time we finished paddling the other six out and back, it was twilight, and an early-rising three-quarter moon was beginning to reflect on the lake.

"I held the canoe as Nancy got in and sat near Ned. My heart was beating rapidly as I took Pat's hand to help her aboard. I shoved off, climbed in, and took my seat in the stern of the canoe. We paddled out on the darkening lake.

"Pat had seated herself so she was facing me, and this gave me an additional thrill, since I thought this meant that she felt toward me some of what I felt toward her."

Ed's story was interrupted by lights out. He and the other cadets got ready for bed in the dark. "Guess I'll knock this off," Ed said, as he settled into his bunk.

"Good idea," Bill cracked.

Chuck said, "Oh no you don't. This is just getting interesting. You can go on in the dark. Anybody who wants to go to sleep can go ahead; I want to hear the rest of the story."

"Okay," Ed said, "but you'll all probably fall asleep," and he continued.

"We paddled well out onto the lake. It was now dusk, and the moon was getting brighter and brighter. Ned and Nancy were talking a lot at the front of the canoe, mostly about Ned's college experiences and Nancy's college plans. Pat and I said little, just enjoying being together, and looking into each other's eyes.

"The evening was mild, and the water lapped gently against the sides of the canoe. We stopped paddling and just drifted on the quiet lake. A canoe is not a good place for necking, but I wanted some physical contact with Pat. Even holding hands was awkward, facing each other as we were, but I reached out toward her, and she put her hand in mine. An electric thrill went through me. Then, holding my hand, she carefully got up from her seat, turned around, and sat down on the bottom of the canoe, leaning back against my knees. I couldn't believe it! She seemed to want contact, just as I did. After a few moments, Pat turned half around and rested her head on my knee. I thought I'd died and gone to heaven. I reached down, ran my fingers through her hair, and carressed her cheek. I felt her shiver, just as I did.

"I said, 'You're the most beautiful girl I've ever seen,' and I meant it. Then she surprised me by saying, 'You know, when we drove past you in the car, I felt something I'd never felt before, as our eyes met.' I said, 'So did I. What a wonderful feeling!' She smiled up at me, and her face in the moonlight was gorgeous. It was a moment I'll never forget. 'Do you know what I said to the other girls in the car?' she asked. I shook my head. 'That one's mine!' I was really stunned at this—what happens in movies and books had happened to us! We were meant for each other.

"We sat there just enjoying being together as several minutes went by. A tiny fragment of Lifebuoy soap drifted by on the surface of the water. I reached out and caught it. I dampened Pat's cheek and gently rubbed it with the soap. Then, wetting my hand again, I rinsed the soap off. This simple, meaningless bit of intimacy thrilled me like nothing ever had before. She was utterly motionless. Her eyes shone up at me, and I knew she felt the same thing that I did. We were enchanted with each other, there in the beauty of the evening.

"Nancy broke the spell. 'It's getting pretty late. We'd better get back, or we'll be in trouble.' Pat straighened up and said, 'You're right, Nancy. We're going to get grounded, for sure.' She squeezed my hand as she turned around and got back on her seat.

"Ned and I paddled fast and hard toward the girls' cottage. But in spite of our furious paddling, by the time we beached the canoe, total darkness had fallen. The two chaperones were standing at the water's edge, hands on hips, hard looks on their faces. Nancy's father stood several yards behind them, arms folded, looking bemused. The other girls were all standing on the cottage porch, doing their best to suppress giggles.

"We knew we were in trouble when one of the stern chaperones ordered Pat and Nancy into the cottage. 'We'll deal with you later. First, these young men.'

"Pat started to say, 'But, Miss McNees, don't blame the boys. We just lost track of the time, it was so beautiful . . .' That's as far as she got. 'Into the cottage at once!' Miss McNees spat out.

"As the two girls headed toward the cottage, Pat turned around, smiled at me, and soundlessly mouthed, 'Thanks, Ed.' The other chaperone spoke sharply, 'Right now! Go!'

"The girls hurried up the path and into the cottage. The other girls crowded in after them, asking questions as they went.

"Miss McNees said, 'Now, you two young men, we trusted you, and you failed.'

"'It's our fault,' I spoke up. 'Please don't blame the girls. We should have watched the time. We just . . .'"

"Enough!' interrupted Miss Frederick. 'You two are barred from this property and from further contact with these girls. We are responsible for them, and you and they have broken the rules!'

"Ned broke in, 'Ma'am, nothing happened out there. It was all just fun, We're sorry—'

"'Never mind all that! Just get into your canoe and go. And don't come back!'

"'Yes, Ma'am,' Ned and I said. As we turned toward the canoe, I glanced at Nancy's dad, and saw that he was smirking, trying not to laugh. This made me feel better. If one of the girls' fathers wasn't upset, things couldn't be too bad.

"Ned and I paddled away, returned the canoe, and made our way to our camp. Pat and I were able to surreptitiously see each other quite a few times after her two days of grounding were over. We exchanged addresses and promised to keep in touch. We sent each other occasional letters. The more I saw of her, and the more we talked, the more certain I was that she was the one for me.

"Believe it or not, we haven't seen each other since, but we will, you can bet on that."

"Some story," Bill said. "Are you giving us the business?"

Chuck said, "Sounds like a fairytale to me. Sure you didn't make it up?"

"Go to sleep, you jerks," Ed responded. "You wanted to hear it, so I told you."

Merv, half asleep, yawned and said, "I doubt that this girl, Pat, even exists. You're just dreaming."

"Think what you want. It's all true," Ed asserted.

"You want us to believe you're really in love with someone you saw a half-dozen times nearly three years ago, and haven't seen since? That's bullshit. I agree with Merv. I don't think this girl exists. You probably had your sister or brother find a picture and send it to you," Bill said.

"How you going to prove this?" Merv asked.

"I don't have to prove it. I know what I know. It's obvious none of you damn fools ever met someone you know is right for you," Ed replied.

"It's a damn good story, Ed," Chuck called from the latrine. "I think I believe it. I know you're a real romantic; I'd sure like to meet this wonder girl."

"So would I," Ed responded. "I should have seen her before now, but I was afraid we'd do something stupid, like get married, and I didn't even have a decent job—not a permanent one, anyway—so I couldn't support a wife. I sure wish I had gone to see her, though." Ed took a turn in the latrine before getting back into bed.

"Hey, I know what. We'll be having a graduation dance when we finish Advanced. We'll get our wings and our commissions. And I hear there's a big party and dance. I'll write to Pat and ask her to come down. Then if you guys haven't washed out—and that's a big 'if'—you'll get to meet her."

Bill yawned and said, "Good idea. Bet I can take her away from you."

"Fat chance, little man. She's about a foot taller than you," Ed replied.

"I like 'em tall. I'll bet I can charm . . ." and Bill's voice trailed off as he fell asleep.

Silence fell as all four cadets drifted into sleep, each with his own dreams.

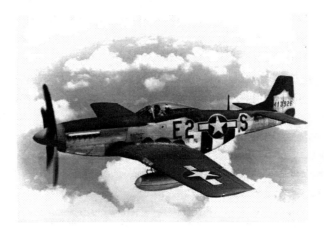

17

Reveille sounded, and the four cadets hurried to shower, shave, make their beds, make sure the room was ready for inspection, and fall out in the uniform of the day for morning chow. Upper and lowerclass cadets marched together under Captain Smolens' command to the mess hall. After chowing down, the squadron assembled in front of the mess hall, and Captain Smolens turned over the underclassmen to Ed, giving him directions to the ground school buildings. Ed marched his men to ground school, and they entered their assigned classroom.

Most of the time was spent reviewing what they had learned in Primary, with a few extra aircraft introduced in aircraft recognition. One of the new ones was the P-38, a twin-boom, twin-engine fighter plane, which was just being activated for combat in both the E.T.O. (European Theatre of Operations) and the P.T.O. (Pacific Theatre of Operations). The cadets had heard of this, but this was the first time they had had it in aircraft recognition.

The second new American-built Allied aircraft to be introduced in the course was a sleek-looking fighter-type, single-engine craft, with squared-off wing tips, a squared-off vertical stabilizer, two fifty-calibre machine guns in each wing, and a four-blade propellor. Ed really liked the looks of this, so he asked the instructor if it would be used by the Air Corps as a fighter. The instructor disappointed him.

"Afraid not. This is the A-36. The 'A' means Attack. In other words, it is meant for low-level attacks, mainly as tactical support for ground troops, strafing and dive-bombing. It was designed and built by North American Aviation for the British. It's excellent for ground support, except for one thing. You notice it has an inline engine, so it is liquid-cooled, unlike radial engines such as the P-47 has, which are air-cooled. The trouble is, when an inline engine is hit by enemy fire, it loses its coolant, and it's done for. The enemy knows this, and aims at the engine. The A-36 is very vulnerable, and lots have been lost in combat. Too many."

"Sir," Ed asked, "if it's vulnerable as a low-level attack plane, why not use it as a fighter, like the ME-109 the Germans have, or the British Spitfire? They both have inline engines, and they seem to do all right."

"Good question, Mister," replied the instructor. "I understand they're working on that. The big trouble is the engine. When it gets to about 10,000 feet in altitude, it loses its power. That's no good against ME-109s and FW-190s, or even Japanese Zeroes, all of which have power much higher than that. A plane that falters at 10,000 is a sitting duck for enemy fighters, and for anti-aircraft fire too. Anyway, the last I heard, they're working on it, because it seems to have everything else we want in a fighter. There's talk of modifying it and putting in a Rolls-Royce engine, the same one as in the Spitfire."

"Wow!" Ed exclaimed. "Excuse me, Sir, but I've always hoped I'd get to fly a Spit. Since I'm in the U.S. Air Corps, I've pretty much given up that hope, but I really like the way the A-36 looks. Hope they get the problems solved, and we get to fly it when we get ready for combat."

"Okay, let's get back to aircraft recognition. Remember the A-36, and watch for future developments," said the instructor, as he flashed more pictures on the screen.

Ed said to himself, "I sure will remember her. She's the neatest looking thing I've seen since the Spit." He hadn't felt so excited about an airplane he couldn't fly since he'd seen a Spitfire in a flying demonstration at Maxwell.

Ground school over, the four had chow, and reported to Lieutenant Bellows on the flight line. Chuck was scheduled first, so the others watched as the lieutenant had him clear with the Tower, start the engine, taxi out and take off, just as he had had Ed do the day before. They continued to watch as Chuck flew away from the field, did a series of stalls and recoveries, then a spin and recovery, and landed.

Ed was next, so he climbed in expecting the same as Chuck had done. The lieutenant had him taxi and take off, but instead of having him leave the pattern for air exercises, he told him to go around again, and clear with the Tower to land. Ed did so, thinking, "Oh man! I think I've had it, he's ending my instruction right now." He continued around the pattern and, luckily, did an excellent three-point landing.

The lieutenant's voice came over the earphones, "Not bad, Mr. Thorne. Take her around again." Five more times he had Ed shoot landings. Ed was extremely careful, and luck was with him as each landing was on the button.

After the sixth landing, the lieutenant instructed him to return to their parking place. On the way he said, "Mr. Thorne, that was well done. I want you to know, we can now get back to where we were yesterday. That hot-shot landing is now forgotten. But if you had messed up today, you'd have been in deep trouble. Let's go park."

Ed could tell that the edge of irritation was gone from the lieutenant's voice, and he was relieved. Now he felt the sweat running down his back. He hadn't been aware of how tense he had been until then.

After P.T., chow, and retreat, the four cadets settled down to studying and letter-writing until lights out.

The next morning, ground school and noon chow over, Ed and Chuck reported to the Link Trainer hangar, right off the flight line. There they found a row of odd-looking machines, each one with a control console in front of it, and a sergeant seated at the console. One sergeant called Ed's name, another one Chuck's.

"I'm Cadet Thorne," Ed said, and the sergeant said, "Okay, Mister, have you ever been in a Link Trainer?"

"No, Sergeant."

"All right. You'll find this one just like the cockpit of a BT-13. Except when you get in and close the canopy, you will be cut off from any visual contact with anything outside the cockpit. I'll be in voice contact with you through the earphones. Put them on as soon as you are seated, and I'll give you instructions from then on. This time, you'll do just ordinary maneuvers: take-offs, climbs, turns, a few figure-eights, as I tell you. I control wind, barometric pressure, and other variables, but we won't go into any unusual positions or heavy crosswinds today. That will come later. Before you land, I'll put you in one or two stalls, and you will recover. Any questions?"

"No, Sir," Ed responded automatically. "You don't 'Sir' me; I'm a non-com, just a sergeant." "Okay, sorry."

"You do everything on instruments in the Link. You'll have to trust your instruments—learn to depend on them. You'll need to learn that for when you fly in fog or bad weather, or on night missions, okay?

"Climb in and close the canopy. Then put on the headset. Further instructions will come through the earphones. Keep in mind that you'll think you're flying, but you'll never leave the ground."

Ed climbed into the trainer, fastened the seatbelt, and closed the canopy. Immediately, he had a sense of total isolation, of being cut off from everything but the instruments, glowing in a soft, phosphorescent light, and the controls. He put on the headset, and the sergeant's voice immediately spoke. "All set, Mr. Thorne?"

"All set, Sergeant."

"Okay, start your engine." Ed went through the start-up procedure, and had the sensation of the engine taking hold, and running steadily. "Holy smokes," he thought. "This is spooky."

The sergeant's voice continued, "You're clear to taxi. Release your brakes and let the airplane move forward. Now, turn right. Far enough, straighten out. Add a little throttle and taxi straight ahead." Ed did as he was told, and had an instant of panic, as the sensation of movement was real, and he tried to look out to see where he was going. He saw nothing, and felt foolish, as he realized that this was all part of the simulation.

"Now, watch your compass and make a 90-degree turn to your left. Straighten out. Now stop. You are at the edge of the runway. Set your altimeter to 29.50, then check your mags." Ed did so.

"Okay, release the brakes and move forward. Now, make a 90-degree left turn. Good. You're headed down the middle of runway 90, so give it full throttle. More right rudder, you're edging left. Good. Hold it like that."

Again, the sensation of speeding forward and not seeing where he was going came over him, and he felt little prickles on his scalp and down his back, as sweat started through his pores. "My God, this is scary," he thought. He didn't realize that he had said it out loud until the sergeant said, "It's okay, Mr. Thorne. It's supposed to seem real. But, believe me, you're still bolted to the floor. You haven't moved an inch."

"Phew!" Ed responded. "I've got to keep remembering that. But it sure seems real."

"All right, you're passing over the east edge of the field. Do a single needle-width turn to the left, to zero on your compass. Fine, straighten out. Now, another left turn to 360 on the compass. Fine, straighten out. Keep your nose up. You're too close to the ground to lose altitude. Okay, throttle back to three-quarter and turn forty-five degrees right. Keep climbing. Nose is too high now, just a gradual climb. Watch your artificial horizon, your rate-of-climb, and your air speed. They're your best friends when you're flying on instruments. All right, You're at 2,000 feet, right?"

"Right."

"Okay, you're clear of the field. I want you to get the feel of stalling on instruments. Throttle back to about half. Now, pull the nose up, watching the artificial horizon. Pull up above the horizon. A little more. Feel it? Okay, you're in a stall. Get out of it."

Ed popped the stick forward and gave full throttle. The nose came down, and he used the rudder bars to keep the plane from falling into a spin. He wiped the sweat from his forehead as he regained flying speed, and resumed straight-and-level flight. He longed to be able to see his surroundings, but he had to look only at his intruments.

"Good! You didn't let her get away from you. If you'd fallen into a spin, you'd really know what scary is. Getting out of a spin on instruments is hell!"

"I believe you, Sergeant. Does this ever get to be fun?"

With a laugh, the sergeant said, "Yeah, most cadets get to like it. I think you will, too, once you find you can do almost anything on instruments, with no visual contact outside the cockpit. Take her back up to 2,000 feet."

Ed added throttle and climbed, levelling off at 2,000 feet on the altimeter.

"You're getting too far from the field. Do a 180-degree double needle-width turn. Keep the nose up, more right rudder and pull back on the stick to tighten the turn. Okay, you're headed right at the field, about five miles out. Make a 90-degree right turn. Okay, now do another stall and recovery."

Ed did, and he felt much more in control this time. "Hey, Sarge, I'm starting to get the hang of it."

"Yeah, I think you are. Let's see if you can do a figure eight. Remember to keep the nose on the horizon and the air speed up. Go."

Ed did a rough figure-eight, losing and gaining altitude several times, but getting better. He ended the figure-eight heading due west.

"Okay, Mr. Thorne. Do you know where the field is?"

"Let's see, we took off east, turned north, then west, then north away from the field. When you had me turn around, you said we were about five miles from the field. Then you had me turn west, about two miles from the field. I did a figure-eight, ending back on a west heading. I'd say I'm about two miles north of the field, and headed to the west edge of the field."

"Pretty good. Actually, you're about a half-mile beyond the west edge. Otherwise, right on the money. Do a 180 right turn to a heading of 90. Stay on that heading and let down to 1,000 feet."

Ed followed the instructions. "Now, do a 90-degree to the right. In a few seconds you'll be at the downwind leg of the pattern. Now! 90-degree right, to a heading of 180. Let down to 500 feet. Now a 90-degree left. You're on the base leg. Turn 90 left again. You're on the approach. Watch your altimeter. Throttle back, nose down. Not so much. Okay, you just passed the edge of the field. You're over the runway. Cut the throttle." Ed felt, or thought he felt, the wheels touch, with a big sigh of relief. "Turn left, good. Straighten out. Now, left again. You're turning to your parking spot. Left. Straight. Stop now! Shut her off and come on out. Nice job for a first time."

Ed opened the canopy and could hardly believe that he'd never moved an inch. "Man! That's some kind of experience. It really feels as if you're flying!"

"You bet it is. Your imagination plays a big part in it. See you next time."

"Roger. Thanks, Sarge. Hey, Chuck," he called, seeing Chuck climbing out of his trainer.

"Yeah, Ed. Is that sensational!"

"Sure is. I see your flight suit is as wet as mine. Makes you sweat, doesn't it?"

"Man, I couldn't believe I wasn't flying. Like to wet my pants."

"Let's go. We don't want to be late for Lieutenant Bellows."

"Right." They both took off at a run. The lieutenant greeted them with, "Well, gentlemen. I see you've been in the tension machine. If that's anything but sweat soaking your suits, I don't want you in my airplane."

"No, Sir, it's all sweat," Ed replied. "But there's plenty of that."

"Yeah," the lieutenant said, "the Link is a real sweat machine. Believe me, flying for real on instruments is no picnic either. We had lots of fog in the Aleutians. You men ready to fly?"

"Yes, Sir," they replied.

"Okay, Mr. Sparks, let's go."

Bill and Merv had already left for their Link session, so Ed didn't have a chance to tell them what it was like. He found a water fountain and had a long drink, then relieved himself in the latrine. He sat on the wheel of a parked BT, in the shade of a wing, and thought about how real the illusion of flight was in the Link Trainer. He thought how easily you could be misled when your normal visual and audial reference points are taken away. He imagined how disoriented a person could become when locked in a completely closed room — like in solitary confinement. And he thought about what Lieutenant Bellows had said about flying on instruments. He began to understand how it must have been for Lindbergh during part of his solo flight across the Atlantic. He'd always admired him for that feat, but now his admiration grew even greater.

"Hey, Ed! You're up." He had been so deep in thought that he hadn't noticed that Chuck and the lieutenant had landed and parked.

He raced to the airplane, remembering how Lieutenant Bellows wanted everyone to be on time. He thought, "Rats! I screwed up again." But the lieutenant said, "Thinking about the Link Trainer, Mr. Thorne?"

"Yes, Sir. I was thinking about how disoriented you can be when you're cut off from the rest of the world."

"You're right. Makes you think how important learning to read your instruments is. And to trust them. Ready to fly?"

"Yes, Sir."

"Okay. Get clearance and let's go."

Ed got clearance from the Tower, and in a few minutes they were airborne and clear of the field.

"Take it up to 4,000 feet, Mr. Thorne."

Ed pulled the nose above the horizon and started to climb. He felt a great sense of relief to see the sky. This kind of flying, contact flying, beat instrument flying by a long shot.

When 3,000 showed on the altimeter, the lieutenant said, "Now do the rest in a spiral climb."

At 4,000 feet, Ed levelled off, and the lieutenant said, "Do me a barrel roll."

Ed was surprised at the order, but he rolled to the left and came back to straight-and-level.

"A little sloppy, Mr. Thorne, but not bad for your first one in the BT. Do one to the right." Ed did so.

"Better, but notice that it's easier to the left than to the right. Now, let's see how you do a series of barrel rolls, three to the left, three to the right. Make them a little tighter. Pick out a reference point on the horizon. Keep your eye on that point, and make a circle around it with the nose of the airplane."

Ed did so, and found that he had much better control of the roll with this technique.

"Okay, Mr. Thorne, good enough. Now, I want you to do a slow roll. Not stopping on points, but a steady roll, holding the nose right on your point on the horizon, as if the airplane was a drill and you're drilling a hole right in that point."

Ed followed the instructor's directions and held the nose on the point until he was coming around from the inverted position, when he didn't coordinate the stick and rudder smoothly enough, and slipped off the point, getting back on as he returned to the upright position.

"Okay, you've got the idea. Practice is what you need. These maneuvers have to become as natural as breathing. In combat you have to just do them, you can't take time to think of this step, then the next one. They have to be automatic. Do another one in the opposite direction, then put the nose down, add throttle and get up speed, pull up and do an Immelman."

Ed did so, and felt proud that he came out almost exactly opposite to the compass heading on which he started.

"Good enough, Mr. Thorne. It's time to go back. I'm going to put us in a spin, and I want you to let it spin down to about 2,500 feet, then get us out of the spin and take us home. I've got it."

Ed let go of the controls, and the lieutenant pulled the nose up, stalled and cut the throttle, then let the plane fall into a spin to the right. At 2,500 feet, Ed took the controls, and pushed the right rudder all the way in, so they were in a controlled spin. Next, he shoved in full left rudder to stop the spin, and as soon as they stopped spinning, and before they started to fall off to the left, he popped the stick forward and shoved the throttle full forward. This put them in a dive, and he pulled out at 1,500 feet.

"Good job, Mr, Thorne. Dan'l Boone was right about you. You have a good feel for this game. I'm going to have to turn you loose in this crate pretty soon."

"Thank you, Sir. You mean you're going to let me solo?"

"Think you can handle it?"

"Yes, Sir."

"Okay, we'll see. Shouldn't be long. Take us in."

"Yes, Sir." Ed was excited, but he remembered to concentrate on precision in entering the pattern and landing. He didn't want to screw up again and get in trouble with the lieutenant. He parked the plane, turned off all switches, unbuckled his seatbelt, and climbed out. The lieutenant got out at the same time, since Ed was the last of his students for the day. Ed popped to and snapped a salute, but the lieutenant said, "Never mind that. We're a little late. Your gang is ready. Take off, or you'll be late for P.T. See you tomorrow."

"Yes, Sir." Ed ran to the formation and marched the cadets double-time to the barracks to change for P.T.

"Hey, Ed, Did you get a letter from Pat, or what? You seem excited. What's up?" Bill asked.

"Weren't you watching?" Ed replied. "I flew the rivets off that machine today."

"Hell no, I was in Link. What'd you do up there?"

"Oh, nothing much. Just a couple of barrel rolls, a dynamite Immelman, and some unbelievable slow rolls," Ed responded.

"The hell you did!" Bill said.

"Enough shit," Chuck put in from the latrine, "you're so full of it you have to let some out."

Merv shot out, "Are you serious? We're still doing stalls and figure-eights. The next bullshit we'll hear from you will be that you're about to solo."

"Could be. Hey! Time to fall out for P.T.," Ed replied. At P.T., Ed did everything from push-ups to wind sprints to three innings of softball with an enthusiasm he hadn't felt since he was on the boxing team at Maxwell.

Through chow, retreat and study time, Ed's head remained in the clouds, as he imagined heading into the sky alone in the BT. Since they all had studies to take care of, and everybody wanted to talk about Link Trainer, nobody pressed Ed about what had him so excited.

In ground school the next morning, an instructor introduced "The Beam" to the cadets. This was a guidance system for airplanes based on radio signals. There were installations at airports across the country, so in bad weather or at night, radio-equipped aircraft could fly across the entire country "on the beam." Each installation had its own radio frequency assigned to it. Each was indicated on aerial maps, with its radio frequency shown, and the name of the airport, as well as the call letters that that beam led to.

This was so interesting to Ed that he forgot about his excitement while he listened to the instructor and looked at the charts and other visual material.

"The Beam is based on the Morse Code signals for *A* and *N*. So *A* is dot-dash, and *N* is dash-dot: dit-dah, and dah-dit." He moved to the chalkboard and picked up a piece of chalk. "If I make a sketch of this, I think it may be clearer than if I just try to tell you about it. Now, a Beam installation, using its assigned frequency, sends out two directional radio signals. One is • — and one is — •

"Let's say this indicates Shaw Field, right where we are," and he drew a small circle on the board. "Now, the Shaw installation transmits the • — continuously in two fan-shaped directions. At the same time, the — • goes out in two different fan-shaped directions." He drew a sketch on the board.

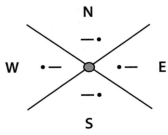

"Now," he said, "the —• and the •— overlap where the fans meet. These signals are perfectly timed so that they pulse in such a way that —• and •— fit together perfectly, resulting in a solid, continuous tone, where the borders of the fan-shaped segments meet and overlap. That solid tone is the 'beam,' like this," and he drew another sketch on the board.

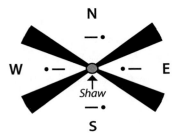

"The solid-colored parts represent the beam—the continuous tone, and the clear areas represent the A and the N, dot-dash, and dash-dot. Notice that one of the N's is in the quadrant that has the magnetic north in it. This is a further help to the pilot trying not only to get on the Beam, and follow it to an identified location, but also to help him determine which quadrant he is in, either north or south, east or west.

"Now, once he is on the Beam, he can check his compass and see which direction he is flying. At the same time, he can tell whether he is going toward the station or away. If he is going toward, the solid signal gets louder; going away, it gets dimmer. He knows whose Beam it is because, intermittently, the station identification is transmitted.

"Now, let's say a pilot is flying in or above heavy cloud cover. He knows he is somewhere in the general area of Sumter, South Carolina, and on a heading of 90 degrees. He dials the frequency of the Shaw Field Beam, found on his chart. He gets a faint dit-dah. He holds his course for about one minute, and the dit-dah fades. He turns around to a heading of 270 degrees, and holds it. After a minute, he picks up the dit-dah again, and it gets stronger. His destination is Atlanta, which he knows is south of Sumter, so he continues his 270 heading, with the dit-dah getting louder.

He knows he is in the eastern quadrant, because the signal faded when he headed east

(90 degrees), and got stronger when he headed west (270 degrees). But he doesn't know whether Shaw lies directly ahead, or to the north or south of his line of flight.

"He has to be patient. He looks at his chart and sees how the Beams go out from Shaw. He knows that if he holds his heading, he will intersect the Beam, either the NE–SW, or the NW–SE one. When he hears the solid sound of the Beam, since he wants to go in a southerly direction, he will begin to turn south. Shortly, he loses the solid sound, and starts getting dah-dit. Now, he knows he needs to continue turning more to the southeast. Soon he gets the solid Beam sound again. He now turns more south, but still generally southeast. He has the solid sound longer this time, but he does lose it, getting the dit-dah sound. Now, he knows he is in the eastern quadrant, so he turns more to the south, and gets the solid Beam sound again. Now, he establishes a definite S–SE heading, and stays on the Beam.

"Before long, the Shaw Beam begins to fade. As it gets quite dim, he looks at his chart and dials the Atlanta Beam, or one between Sumter and Atlanta. That Beam grows louder and stronger. With a few directional adjustments, he is able to follow the Atlanta Beam to his destination.

"That, gentlemen, is the way the Beam works, and how you will learn to use it. It sounds complicated, but after you work it a few times in the Link, it will become clear to you. Your flight instructors will probably tune in the Shaw Beam for you, so you will know what it sounds like. In Link, you will actually learn how to get on the Beam and stay on it.

"Here's how our pilot's flight would look on our sketch," and he turned again to the chalk board.

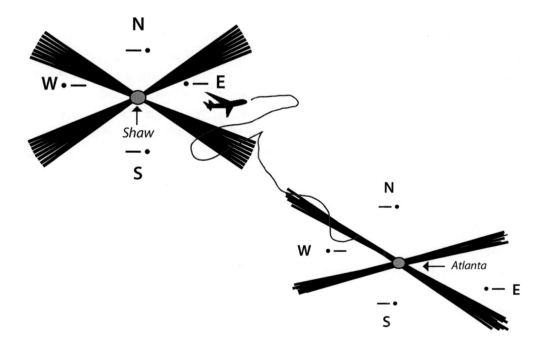

After answering several questions, and clarifying some points, the instructor looked at his watch and dismissed the class, saying, "That's a lot to absorb at once. Study it together with your roommates, using your notes. We'll handle any questions tomorrow."

"Boy, is that interesting," Merv exclaimed, as they formed up to march to the mess hall.

"Yeah," Bill agreed. "I'm anxious to work on that in Link."

With noon chow behind them, the cadets reported to Lieutenant Bellows on the flight line. Bill and Merv then went to Link, while Ed and Chuck went to their BT-13. "Okay, Mr. Thorne, you're first today. Let's get this thing in the air."

The lieutenant was now letting all four of the cadets do the entire procedure of taking off and landing. Ed quickly went through the ground check, then climbed in, fastened his seatbelt, unlocked and checked the controls, called the Tower, and cranked the engine. As he taxied to the runway, the lieutenant said, "Use the right side pattern today. A few miles south, climb to 2,500 feet. When we get there, I'll tune in the Shaw Beam, and you can play with it for a while."

Ed stopped beside the runway, called for clearance, set the altimeter, checked the mags, and did a smooth take-off, turned right to the south side of the field, left the pattern and climbed to 2,500 feet, about three miles south of the field.

"All right, Mr. Thorne, Shaw Beam's frequency is 125. When I say to, switch from intercom to radio, and use the little crank to turn to 125 on the pointer. Then you can play around to get the feel of the Beam. Give yourself five minutes, then switch back to the intercom so I can give you further instructions, okay?"

"Yes, Sir,"

"Okay, switch over."

Ed pushed the radio button and turned the crank until 125 was at the pointer. He immediately heard dah-dit in his earphones. He checked his watch, and saw it was 13:17. Since he had gone south from the field, he was sure he was in the south quadrant. He turned eastward, to a heading of 130. Soon he heard the steady signal indicating he was at the Beam. He turned more south, and in a few moments was back at dah-dit. He made a small correction to the east, and was able to stay on the Beam for two minutes. His watch now showed 13:21. This meant he had a minute left, so he did a fast, tight turn to 340 on his compass, and followed the Beam back toward the field for 45 seconds, finishing his five minutes.

"Good enough," Lieutenant Bellows said when Ed switched back to intercom. "Take us in and do a touch-and-go landing."

Ed entered the pattern after calling the Tower for clearance, and did a touch-and-go. It went well.

"Okay, Mr. Thorne, take her down again and land, then taxi back to the end of the runway."

Ed felt a thrill, thinking he knew what was coming, as he did a clean three-point landing, and taxied down the taxi strip to the West end of runway 90.

"All right, Mr. Thorne," the lieutenant said, "She's yours for fifteen minutes. Take her up and out of the pattern, don't do anything radical, no hot stuff. Just fly around a bit, and come back, land and park her. I'll walk back to our parking area. Got it?"

"Yes, Sir!" Ed responded with enthusiasm. It was happening! As the lieutenant climbed out and went well out on the grass beside the runway, Ed called the Tower for clearance and the altimeter setting. He was given clearance, and tingling with excitement, he checked the mags, rolled out onto the runway, pushed the throttle forward, felt the tail come up, and he was off the ground and on his own. His watch indicated 13:40. By the time he closed the canopy, he was at the east border of the field, and he made a 90-degree turn left, then another, then a right out of the pattern.

All the feeling of freedom and joy he'd felt as he mastered the PT-17 began to come back to him. He climbed to 1,500 feet, did some gentle turns, two stalls, then a tight turn back toward the field. "Fifteen minutes," he thought. "Man, I could fly this baby for fifteen hours and never get tired."

After getting cleared to land, he turned onto the downwind leg of the pattern. Another BT was landing as he turned onto the base leg, so he backed off on the throttle to allow the other plane time to clear the runway. He turned toward the runway, and made an easy three-point landing. He felt confident and fully in control of the plane, thrilled to be flying solo again.

The thrill never stopped as he taxied to the parking area, parked, shut off the switches, and climbed out. Then his spirits dropped as he saw the lieutenant frowning and looking at his watch. "Oh no," Ed thought. His watch said 13:55:30. "I'm in trouble."

As he approached, the lieutenant barked, "Pop to, Mister!" and Ed snapped into a brace. "What time is it, Mister?"

Ed looked at his watch. "13:55:45, Sir." "What time should you have been here?" "13:55, Sir." Ed felt sick. "Were you late?"

"Yes, Sir."

"Why?"

"No excuse, Sir."

"At ease, Mr. Thorne."

To his astonishment, Ed saw that the lieutenant was smiling.

"I was pulling your leg, Mr. Thorne. You did a good job. I knew why you were late: you had to throttle back to let the other plane clear the runway. You were almost right on the tick in spite of that. Relax, everything is fine. Congratulations."

Chuck, who had been trying to keep from laughing, finally burst into a loud guffaw as he shook Ed's hand. "Had you going, didn't he? Made you sweat a little bit, right? How come you didn't go play around in the clouds like you did in Primary?"

"You mean he planned to do that, and let you in on it?"

"You bet. If it hadn't been the time, it would have been something else. He really liked what you were doing with the plane."

"I'll be damned!" Ed said, so relieved he felt like letting out a whoop. Instead, he grinned and felt great.

"Let's go, Mr. Sparks," Lieutenant Bellows called. "Do you want to talk or fly?"

"Chuck ran over to the plane and climbed in, saying, "Fly, Sir."

Ed leaned against the wing of the BT in the next parking spot and enjoyed the feeling of delight at what had just happened. "I flew her by myself. I did it! That's two different airplanes I've learned to fly. Wow! A few months ago I'd never even sat in an airplane. I don't believe this is happening to me!"

He daydreamed for a few minutes, seeing himself in a fighter, hopefully a redesigned A-36, or a Spitfire. Then he snapped out of it to see what would happen with Chuck. It turned out that the lieutenant didn't think Chuck was quite ready yet, so he didn't solo.

After a disappointed Chuck climbed out of the airplane, he and Ed headed to the Link Trainer hangar. Ed tried to cheer up his buddy, telling him he'd probably go the next day. But Chuck was not happy.

The rest of the day was uneventful. Chuck felt better when he learned that neither Bill nor Merv had soloed either. lights out brought immediate sleep to all four cadets.

After reveille, the usual morning routine was followed, until Cadet Captain Smolens was about to march the entire squadron to breakfast. Tactical Officer Captain Johnson strode up to Smolens just after the squadron had been called to attention. Smolens saluted and Captain Johnson returned the salute. Johnson said a few words to Smolens, then Smolens called Ed over. Following instructions from Smolens, Ed kept the underclassmen of J Squadron at attention as the upperclassmen marched off to breakfast.

"Put your men at ease, Mr. Thorne," Captain Johnson said.

"At ease!" Ed commanded his classmates. "Sir?" he asked, turning to the captain.

"Nothing wrong, Mr. Thorne. This will take only a few minutes, then you'll be off to breakfast." Turning toward the standing cadets, he said, "I know you all had gunnery training at Maxwell, and you had to qualify with the colt .45 automatic, and the M1. You had to do that to continue in the cadet program. I see from the records that some of you qualified on the Thompson submachine gun. But have any of you ever shot skeet?"

The cadets looked at each other, shaking their heads. None seemed to know what the captain was talking about. Then Chuck put his hand up. "Is that anything like trap shooting, Sir?"

"Yes, it's the same thing, basically. But in trap, the clay pigs are released in front of you and fly away from you. You shoot at them from behind. In skeet shooting, the pigeons come from the left and right, and you shoot at them from different stands, as they cross in front of you in the air. The pigeons are released from wooden towers, one on each side of the range. You use a two-barrel shotgun and scatter-shot. The idea is to learn to 'lead' the target—shoot enough in front of it that your shot and the target meet, and the target breaks up. I think you can all see the relevance to military flying and shooting at targets moving in the air. The Air Corps requires each cadet to fire a minimum number of rounds on the skeet range as a part of aerial gunnery training.

"Starting today, each of you will be scheduled twice a week on the skeet range. You will report there instead of to P.T. on your scheduled days."

Turning back to Ed, he said, "Mr. Thorne, here is the roster with scheduled dates for each of your men. I suggest you go over it with the men before you go to chow. Okay?"

"Yes, Sir. Attenhut!" Ed called to the cadets, before he snapped a salute to the captain, who returned it and walked away.

It took only a minute to locate the names for this day, then Ed said that he'd post the schedule on the squadron bulletin board. With that, they marched off to chow and the day's work.

The main excitement of the day for the four buddies was that Bill and Chuck soloed. The main disappointment was that Merv did not. The other three sympathized with Merv, and comforted him as well as they could. But Merv was beyond comfort. "Every time things are going okay, I screw up some little thing, and the lieutenant says, 'You're not ready yet, Mister.' I can fly that damned bird! But I always seem to slip up on some little detail."

They all had Cokes in the PX, and tried to encourage Merv, before time to clean up for retreat Parade. Merv continued to brood, and during study time he was very quiet and despondent.

Four more days passed, and still the lieutenant did not let Merv solo. Merv no longer took part in the joshing and joking as he always had before. He was embarrassed and ashamed, as if he weren't as good as the rest of them. Nothing anyone said seemed to console him. He no longer eagerly anticipated going to the flight line, or to Link. His ground school work fell off, and he ate very little at mealtimes. Ed suggested that he see the chaplain. After two days of fighting it, Merv did finally go. He returned just as down as when he went.

When the other three got up on the fifth day, Merv was already up and gone. He did not report to formation for chow. The three were worried, so they went to Captain Johnson, who called the major in charge of the military police detachment. They immediately began a search. The gate guards were questioned and they indicated that no cadet had attempted to leave the base.

Captain Johnson told the others to go on with their day's assignments and that he would stay on top of the situation, letting them know what he found out.

After ground school and flight line, Chuck and Ed were scheduled for Skeet Range instead of P.T. They were introduced to the Skeet Range procedure and rules by the instructor, who emphasized safety, stressing especially the need not to follow a bird almost to one of the towers before firing. The reason, he explained, is that there is a serviceman in the tower, loading and firing the pigeon release. If the person shooting at the pigeon fires too late, some of the buckshot may enter the tower at the pigeon release opening, hitting the man in the tower, injuring him, perhaps blinding him. This was an absolute rule.

The instructor also checked them out on the pump-action shotgun, how to load, cock, aim and fire; how to proceed around the stands, arranged in a semi-circle from one tower to the other; how to call "pull" when ready to aim and fire, and gave them some instruction in leading the target. He also cautioned them to hold the butt of the shot gun firmly against the shoulder, indicating that most people forget this on their first day, in the excitement of aiming and firing. The result is always a painful and ugly bruise.

Both Chuck and Ed found this to be true. By the time they had each fired 25 to 30 rounds, they both had aching bruises on their right shoulders.

They had some success in hitting the pigeons. The instructor told them that they had done well for first-timers, and that they would get better with practice. He also warned Ed about shooting toward the tower, since once in tracking a target from stand 4, he had actually fired so late that he heard the buckshot hit the tower, and the serviceman jumped out of the tower, saying that he wasn't going in there again if Ed was going to do that again. Ed apologized, and said that he wouldn't.

In spite of their painful shoulder bruises, Ed and Chuck really enjoyed the skeet shooting, and they talked excitedly about it as they walked to the P.E. area to join their classmates to march to the barracks.

Just after Chuck, Ed, and Bill got into their room, Captain Johnson stepped in. His face was sober as he said "As you were" when the three cadets popped to attention. "Please sit down," he said, as he sat on one of the chairs. "I'm afraid I have some bad news for you."

"What is it, Sir? Is something wrong with Merv?"

"Yes. The worst possible thing," and he paused, seemingly too emotional to go on.

"Sir," Ed said, "Please tell us. What is it?"

"Well, I know how close you all were. But you have to know. When you told me about Merv's depression, I was concerned. But since I've seen lots of cadets down because of one difficulty or another, I didn't think too much about this one. They all shaped up later. We did what we could, and Chaplain Kinney felt that Merv would be all right. Sadly, it didn't turn out that way." The captain's face grew pale, his eyes moistened, and he lowered them. Then, taking a deep breath, he raised his head, looked directly at the cadets, and said, "Fellows, your friend is dead."

Shocked, the three leaped to their feet. "No." "He can't be!" "You must be mistaken!" "How could he be?"

"Easy, men," the captain said, putting a hand on Bill's shoulder. "Somehow he got his hands on an automatic. We found him in one of the skeet towers, covered with burlap sacks, with a bullet through his head, the gun in his hand. We think he used the sacks to muffle the sound of the shot."

Stunned, the three cadets stared at the captain. At last, Chuck spoke. "Damn! God-damn it! He was a great guy, and would have been a good flier. It's what he lived for. Ah, Goddamn it!"

"I know you cared for him," the captain said. "These things happen. It's done. Life goes on. As your friend, he would want you to go on with your lives."

His voice thick with emotion, Ed choked out, "Yes, Sir. He would. But, damn! It's hard! He loved flying. He loved the cadet program. We wanted to go to combat together. God! I'll miss him."

"Yeh. Me too," Hill said. "We were practically neighbors growing up, but we didn't know it. It'll be hard without Merv. He was our buddy."

"It'll be tough on Lieutenant Bellows, too. He'll think it's his fault," Ed remarked.

"He already knows," said Captain Johnson. "He took it like a hard punch in the gut. For a minute I thought he was going to break down. But he was just doing his job. Since he didn't think Merv was quite ready to solo, he couldn't let him go up alone. What if he had, and Merv had crashed? That would have been terrible too."

"That's true, Captain," Chuck said. "We know how much Lieutenant Bellows thinks of all of his students. It wasn't his fault. But dammit, Merv. Why? You would have soloed in another day or so. Why couldn't you just relax and wait?"

"There's no way Merv could do that. He wanted to be first and best. Being last in any-thing was not something he could accept." Bill's affection and respect for Merv were evident as he said this.

"Well, men, the best thing for all of us to do is to get on with our duties. It's no favor to the memory of your pal to let down, or bail out. For him, keep on giving your best. The time will come when you can shoot down an enemy in Merv's name. I must get back and contact his family. Carry on." With that, the captain left.

For a few moments the three cadets stood silent, then they spontaneously put their arms around each other. Chuck began "Our Father," and the others joined in, each fighting back tears until Ed let his go, then Bill and Chuck did too. Although a little bit embarrassed by their emotion, all three felt better for it.

Bill said, after blowing his nose noisily in his handkerchief, "Let's ask the captain for Merv's parents' name and address and write to them. What do you say?"

"Good idea, Bill," Ed agreed.

"Right," Chuck said.

Having released some of their feelings, and decided on something they could do, they were ready to get on with their scheduled activities. They knew that Merv was likely to be only the first of many friends they would lose in the course of the war.

All three of the cadets had soloed, so for the remainder of their time at Shaw, most of their flying was aimed at refining their skills, developing ever greater precision and accuracy in handling the aircraft, and dealing with traffic and radio procedures so all of their moves would become automatic. Lieutenant Bellows would spot-check them twice a week until they became upperclassmen; then he checked them only once a week.

They became proficient in instrument flying through work in the Link Trainer, and, although Bill did not like Skeet, Ed and Chuck continued to enjoy it. When Bill and others did not want to fire all of their rounds, Chuck and Ed would gladly take them. Bill had his heart set on getting into heavy bombers, the B-17 or B-24, so he did not think that learning to lead a flying target was as important for him as it was for Ed and Chuck, who were determined to get into fighters. Bill shot the minimum required number of rounds, with Ed and Chuck happily doing the rest.

Flying the Beam became routine in the Link, and often, when up practicing maneuvers solo, they would steal fifteen minutes to fly the real Beam, pretending they were in heavy fog, or night flying. Air traffic was too heavy around Shaw Field for them to risk just concentrating on instrument flying, without someone else to watch for other nearby aircraft. So they tried to fly a few seconds at a time staring at the instrument panel, but that was not very satisfactory.

In response to their letter to Merv's parents, the three cadets received a heartfelt note from Mr. and Mrs. Schwartz. The note expressed no bitterness and made no accusations. It simply said that they missed their son terribly, but, though not in combat, he had given his life because he was not satisfied with his own efforts to serve his country. The parents also said that Merv had often written about his three friends in his letters, and that they hoped the three of them would keep in touch. Perhaps, they suggested, it would be possible for them to visit them when the war was over.

After receiving the letter, the three spent time talking about Merv, and how wonderful his parents must be. It was a quiet tribute to their lost buddy, and it helped them to put Merv's death behind them.

When they had moved to upperclass status, Ed was delighted to be appointed cadet captain and squadron commander, succeeding Smolens. They said goodbye to their friends in the former upperclass, and went on as though nothing had changed.

"All right, Mr. Thorne," Lieutenant Bellows said, appearing suddenly and unexpectedly beside the BT assigned to Ed for the day's practice. "Take me up to 3,000 feet."

"Yes, Sir," Ed replied, and he completed his ground check, then climbed into the front cockpit. There he did the radio clearance, followed by his cockpit check. He started up and taxied to runway 90 as directed by the Tower. Getting clearance and altimeter setting from the Tower, he set the altimeter, checked the mags, and took off. He left the pattern and, about five miles from the field, he started a spiral climb to 3,000 feet.

When he switched to intercom, Lieutenant Bellows said, "I know you and the others have been playing around with instrument flying when you've been up solo, supposed to be practicing maneuvres."

"Oh, oh," Ed thought, "am I in trouble again?" He glanced in the mirror at the lieutenant's face.

"It's okay, Mr. Thorne. That's better than horsing around, showing off, or sneaking above clouds to have a pretend dogfight, which, by the way, could get you grounded. That, of course, would mean washing out. You can't stay in the program if you can't fly."

Consternation set in as Ed thought about the half-dozen times he and Chuck had done just that. "No more," he thought. "Too risky."

They had reached 3,000 feet, so Ed levelled off. "All right, Mr. Thorne. Now I'll be your lookout. You keep your head down and fly by your instruments. I'll give you a demerit every time I see your head come up. Okay? Go."

After all the time he had spent in Link, Ed found the actual instrument flying easy. What was hard was not looking up and around, as had been drilled into him since his first flight. He did fairly well, raising his head only once or twice. Each time the lieutenant would say, "Gotcha!" and mark it down on his clipboard.

"Okay, Mr. Thorne. Not bad, but you owe me a couple of drinks for these demerits. Now, I want you to switch back to radio, and dial the Shaw Beam. Then, keep your head down, find the Beam, get on it and fly away from the field for five minutes, turn around, and fly the Beam back to Shaw. Every time you raise your head it'll cost you another drink. Okay, now, switch over and let's see how you do."

Ed switched over, dialed the Shaw Beam frequency, and immediately heard a strong dit-dah. His compass heading was 350, so he guessed he was in the east quadrant. He held his course for a half-minute, and the signal grew louder. This meant he was going toward the field. He turned 90 degrees left, to a heading of 340, and in a few moments he heard the solid tone of the Beam. But he needed to fly away from the field, so he did a single needle-width turn to the right, coming around to a heading of 170. He did not get the solid tone immediately, but he knew he was close to the field, where the Beam is narrow, so he held his course. In a minute he got the solid signal. He adjusted his course slightly to the left, checked his watch, and held the heading for five minutes.

As the last second of the five minutes ticked off, Ed started an easy turn to the left, to a compass heading of 340. Soon he intercepted the Beam again, made a slight correction to the right, and had the satisfaction of hearing the solid tone get louder and louder. In a few minutes the sound stopped, then started again. He knew that he had passed over the dead spot, directly above the transmitter. He was at the field. He looked in the mirror, and the lieutenant nodded, smiling.

Ed switched back to intercom, and the lieutenant said, "Nice work. You didn't look up once."

"I guess I was so fascinated by what I was doing that I never even thought of looking up," Ed replied.

"That's good and bad. The ability to concentrate is good. But any time you're in the air, even on instruments, you must check around now and then. Sometimes there's a clear spot, and you can see the ground, or the sky, and this can help to keep you oriented. It might also save your life, if you see a shape or some wing lights through the fog. You'll know there's another craft in your air space and get out of there. But you didn't add any more drinks to what you owe me, and you did what I told you to do, so good. Let's get into the pattern and land."

Chuck and Bill got the same treatment from Lieutenant Bellows, and they did fine too. Bill grew less and less interested in Skeet, so Chuck and Ed got lots of extra rounds. The instructor told them that they were among the best Skeet shooters on the base. Lieutenant Bellows heard about it, and told them that that was good. "But," he added, "you'll find aiming your fighter plane at a flying target is a lot different from standing still and firing at a clay pigeon. But skeet is great to learn how leading the target works."

Bill turned out to be a whiz at flying on instruments. He loved Link practice, and Lieutenant Bellows said that he did the best job flying on instruments when he checked him. This all fitted into Bill's plan to fly heavy bombers, in which instrument flying was a much larger factor than it was in fighters.

Captain Johnson commended Ed for his excellent work as squadron commander, adding that he intended to put that in his record, and pass it on to the people in charge wherever Ed went for advanced training.

All three felt good about things, although they often had twinges of regret that Merv was not with them to share in it. Ed's enjoyment of military protocol, and the sense of being a functioning part of a large, generally smoothly operating machine, with occasional inevitable glitches and examples of incompetence, continued. He did not engage in the general bitching that seemed to be a part of military life at all levels.

Two weeks before the end of their upperclass term at Shaw, Captain Johnson informed the squadron, through Ed, that there would be a field trip to the historic city of Charleston, South Carolina. It was not to be required, but the captain urged all cadets to take advantage of the opportunity. He indicated that the city had many beautiful old homes built before the Civil War, as well as important historical sites. He added, with a slight chuckle, that the city was famous, also, for its beautiful southern belles. He correctly thought that this would encourage some cadets to go who might not go just to view the historic sites. The base would provide free bus transportation and box lunches for all who wanted to go.

Bill, Chuck, and Ed all signed up. They had enjoyed weekend visits to Sumter, an interesting southern historical city in its own right. But Charleston was much larger, and it sounded exciting.

The trip turned out to be great. The city was everything they had been told it was, including the houses, the sites, and the southern belles. When the buses unloaded in the heart of town, the tac officer of each squadron announced the time for departure to return to Shaw, and until then, the cadets would be on their own. They must be back at the bus area promptly at 19:00, or make their own way back to the base. Anyone not in his room by lights out, 24:00, would receive five demerits.

The three found Charleston to be big and beautiful, as they had been told. What they had not been told was that, on Saturday night Charleston was crowded with servicemen of every rank and from every service: Marine, Navy, Merchant Marine, Army — every branch — and, of course, Army Air Corps.

Most of J Squadron stayed together for the first hour. The cadets were all dressed in spanking clean, fitted suntan uniforms, with regulation ties neatly tucked into their shirt-fronts, collar stays, garrison caps with the cadet insignia big and bold on the front, and their collar insignia, U.S. one side, and the Air Corps insignia on the other, both in highly polished brass, matching their shining belt buckles. Everything about them bespoke good health, intelligence, and vigor. Their tanned faces, shining eyes, energetic movements, animated conversation, all seemed to say just what they thought they were: the best of American youth. Compared to many of the other servicemen, they looked very impressive.

Apparently many of the other servicemen thought so, too, because the cadets hadn't walked a half-block before approaching servicemen started saluting them. This was not proper, since the cadets were not officers, but regulations required that salutes must be returned. The cadets tried to wave off the first few salutes, but they kept coming so fast that they gave up and simply returned the salutes. Ed, Bill, and Chuck were hurrying on ahead of the other squadron members because Bill said that his parents had brought him to Charleston when he was ten or twelve years old, and he remembered being impressed with the area that fronted on the ocean. Their being ahead of the others meant that they got all the salutes before the others did, resulting in an almost continuous raising and lowering of their right arms.

The entire trip was a great success. The box lunches were excellent, the sightseeing rewarding, and the break from the Shaw routine welcome. The only sour note came when the three decided to try one of the excellent-looking restaurants they saw, to have an early dinner before heading back to the buses. They tried three restaurants, only to find a long line of servicemen waiting to be seated in each one. They gave up, and started a leisurely return to the bus area. Suddenly Bill exclaimed, "Hey! Look. There's a diner that has some empty seats. Let's try it."

Chuck and Ed agreed. They went in and found that the diner specialized in southern fried chicken, fried clams, and lobster. Each was served with a salad, a vegetable, choice of fried, mashed or baked potato, and, of course, grits. Each chose a different entree, and found the food super. Another house specialty was pecan pie, baked daily in their own kitchen. None of the three had ever had pecan pie, and they became devotees of it for the rest of their lives.

Dinner took longer than they expected, so they had to hurry to make the bus. As a matter of fact, when they got in sight of the bus, they saw Captain Johnson standing on the sidewalk signalling them to hurry. They made it, barely, and settled in their seats for a happy return to Shaw field.

Time passed quickly for the remainder of their stay at Shaw. They flew almost at will, during their scheduled flight-line hours, practicing whatever they wanted to, each feeling very comfortable and secure flying the BT-13. Every move had become automatic, which was, of course, the objective of the training program. But flying never became routine or tiresome. All three of the friends were in love with flying, and just being up there, free of earth and its restraints, continued to thrill them. It had become so much a part of their lives that if for any reason they had to give it up, their feeling of loss would have been enormous.

Ground school, on the other hand, had become so routine as to be boring. The instructors seemed to be struggling to find new things to teach and, in the main, failing. The last week of classes became largely bull sessions, as welcome to the instructors as to the cadets.

At last they stood their last retreat at Shaw, after which they sought out Lieutenant Bellows and Captain Johnson to thank them and to say goodbye. From each they got warm handshakes, wishes for good luck in Advanced and, eventually, in combat, and a final salute.

Much harder was saying goodbye to Bill. Ed and Chuck, as future fighter pilots, were assigned to Spence Field in Moultrie, Georgia. Bill would be going to Bainbridge, also in Georgia. The three had been together since Maxwell Field, good friends from the time Ed had been held back a class because he had failed math.

They went into Sumter for a final meal and some drinks together, periodically saying to each other how much they would miss one another, and raising their glasses to wish each other good flying. Others from the squadron wandered in, and before long they had put six tables together and had a fine party going.

The next morning Chuck and Ed shook hands with Bill, and embraced him. Then, with a final "good luck," they went their separate ways.

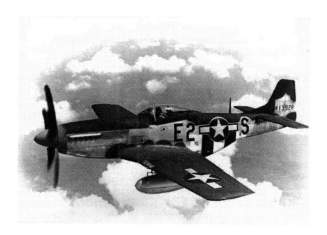

18

Spence Field turned out to be even larger and more active than Shaw had been. The air traffic flow was enormous, and radio transmission between the Tower and planes in the air and on the ground was nearly continuous. Ed and Chuck would find, when they began to fly out of Spence, that just getting through to the Tower would be a chore.

Captain Albertson, their squadron tactical officer, met the bus and greeted the new underclassmen of J Squadron. He congratulated them on completing Basic, and welcomed them to Advanced. He informed them that, just as at Maxwell and Shaw, strict military discipline, courtesy and protocol would be followed at all times. He also indicated that, since graduation ceremonies were held here for each class, with commissions and pilots wings awarded to each cadet who completed the program, retreat parades had to be even more precise than had been the case at either Shaw or Maxwell. Graduation involved a parade to the Parade Ground, the ceremony there, with several bigwig Air Corps officers in attendance. "Where is Cadet Thorne?" he asked.

"Here, Sir," Ed said, surprised.

"Mr. Thorne, form the men up and march them to Barracks 14A. That will be your quarters until you graduate. Then you will be relocated to B.O.Q. (Bachelor Officer's Quarters) until orders arrive for your assignments for fighter training."

"Yes, Sir," Ed said, and formed up his men.

"Mr. Thorne, you will be responsible for getting these underclassmen to classes, flight line, chow, P.T., Link, everything but retreat and other major formations. For them, Cadet Colonel Bernard Hunt will be in command."

"Yes, Sir," Ed said, excited to know that Red Hunt, his friend from Pennsylvania, was here.

"Your ground school, flight line, P.T. schedules will begin tomorrow. For the rest of today, you are free to get settled and familiarize yourselves with the layout here. You will form up here for evening chow and for retreat."

Ed saluted and marched the cadets to Avenue 14, where the first barracks on the corner of Avenue 14 and Spence Street, the main road through the cadet quarters, was 14A. Ed dismissed the cadets, and they all consulted the roster posted on the bulletin board inside the stoop, beside the tac officer's room/office.

Chuck and Ed found that they had a whole room to themselves, and welcomed the extra space and freer access to the latrine and shower, although they missed having Merv and Bill with them.

Since they had over two hours until evening chow, they showered and put on clean uniforms, then walked around the base to locate the PX, ground school, P.T. area, Parade Ground and Skeet Range. The last place they went was the flight line.

Their first view of the AT-6s was a disappointment, At first glance these airplanes looked a lot like DT-13s. As they got closer, however, they could see major differences. Although the AT-6 was also a low-winged monoplane with a radial engine and a bird-cage canopy, when they got closer they saw that the engine was larger, that the wingtips were squared off, the wings shorter and narrower, and the vertical stabilizer was squared off too. Ed remembered that the squared-off wingtips and stabilizer were shared with the A-36 he had been impressed with.

"Bet these are made by the same company that developed the A-36," he said to Chuck. "I remember that was North American Aviation."

"That thing's still stuck in your mind, hm?" Chuck responded "Better give it up. I haven't heard anything about what they might be doing with it."

"It's too good an airplane for them to dump it. I still expect it to become a first-line fighter. If it does, man, I'll ask to be assigned to it right away."

"Okay, okay. We all have to have something to aim for. Hope you get it," Chuck responded.

They soon discovered that Ed was right. The AT-6 was, indeed, a product of North American Aviation. They also heard a much more powerful engine than they were accustomed to hearing on the BT as various ATs started up, taxied, checked mags and took off, gaining much more speed on the runway than the BTs, getting off the ground quicker and climbing faster.

Their excitement grew as they watched other ATs doing aerobatics in the distance, hanging on their props much longer and attaining greater speed on the straight-and-level than the planes they had flown in Basic and Primary.

"It's another big step closer to fighters!" Chuck exclaimed. "Man, this is going to be great!"

"Sure is!" Ed replied, with equal enthusiasm.

They were just about to leave the flight line when they saw an AT-6 taxiing on the strip, with the pilot waving furiously at them. "That guy better watch where he's taxiing, or he'll get in trouble," Ed said. Then he recognized the pilot as Red Hunt, and waved back. He attempted to follow the plane to its parking place. A lieutenant, a stub of a cigar stuck in the side of his mouth, and a crushed, grommet-less garrison cap tilted to one side of his head, yelled, "Get off the flight line if you aren't scheduled here!"

"Yes, Sir," Ed responded, snapping a salute. He and Chuck returned to their room, both happy to have seen Red. Until chow call, they speculated together about flying the AT-6, and wondered if the cigar-chewing lieutenant was an instructor, and if he was as mean as he sounded.

Just before chow call sounded, a loud voice shouted outside their door. "Pop to, you miserable rats! And it better be perfect."

Ed and Chuck jumped up, startled. Then Ed, recognizing the voice, yelled, "Stuff it, General," as Red bounded into the room.

"Son of a bitch!" he enthused, "I was sure you'd both wash out and I wouldn't be bothered by you anymore. But here you are, sniffing along behind me." With that, he gave Ed and Chuck each a hug. "I'm just a colonel, you miserable shave-tail. I see you've kissed ass enough to be appointed a cadet lieutenant, eh Ed?"

"Yeah, Red. And you've done enough brownnosing to reach the highest cadet rank, hm?"

"Roger. If I'd known you were being considered for a cadet officer of any rank, I'd have squashed it."

"I guess you would have. You always were jealous of how good I was at military stuff, and you tried to stymie me every chance you got. But here I am in spite of your puny efforts."

"God, it's good to see you, Ed. And you seem in fine form."

"Great to see you, too, Red. How's it going?"

"Just great. By the way, that was 'Mean Joe Murphy' with the cigar. He's the best instructor here, but don't mess with him. He's frustrated because he can't get a combat assignment. He's a true hot pilot. You'll be lucky if you get him as an instructor. He'll teach you everything you need to know and more, but he'll burn your ass if you screw up. If you have him and he recommends you for graduation, you're in."

Chow call sounded. "All right, you low-lifes, fall in!" Red spat out.

"No thanks, Sir," Ed replied. "We have our own formation. And I'll bet you a beer we look better than any other squadron in this raunchy outfit you command." All three ran out to take their places, with Ed in front of his fellow underclassmen, and Red in front of all the squadron commanders.

Retreat was indeed done with more precision and gusto than it had been at Maxwell, giving Ed a sense of pride in the Air Corps. Red came to their room afterwards and said, "Let's go. I owe you a beer. I have to admit, your outfit looked sharp out there. You, too, Chuck. Come on, I'm buying." They went to the PX, found seats on benches outside, sat, drank and talked.

Chuck and Ed told Red how things had gone in Primary and Basic, and Red filled them in on what to expect at Spence. Then he said, "By the way, Mr. Thorne, I hear you had quite a solo for Ol' Dan'l Boone."

"Don't tell me you heard about that. Are there no secrets in the cadet corps?"

"Heard about it! It was all over Basic when I was there. Surprised you didn't run out of gas, being up above the clouds for two hours."

"Two hours? Where'd you get that crazy story? It wasn't anything like that, was it Chuck? Man, stories sure get blown up in this service."

"No," Chuck said. "I think it was more like two hours and fifteen minutes."

"Some friend!" Ed shot back. "I tell you, Red, it was great. Never felt freer in my life. But it was only about twenty-five minutes for the whole thing. Not even a half-hour. But it was beautiful while it lasted. Except I figured I'd be washed for sure."

"Lucky you weren't. In fact, you've been lucky all along, haven't you?"

"Sure have. Hope it lasts."

Red looked at his watch. "Almost Study Hour. We'd better get back to our rooms."

"Right. Let's go," Chuck said.

They hurried back. Red said goodnight when they reached his barracks. Ed and Chuck spent the time until lights out writing and reading.

Reveille, room inspection, breakfast, and then Captain Albertson gave the roster of flight instructor assignments to Ed, who assembled his J squadron classmates and read out the assignments. Chuck and Ed were pleased and disappointed at the same time that they did not get Lieutenant Murphy. Pleased because he sounded mean, disappointed because Red had said that he was the best. Ed looked over the roster again, and said, "Hey, Chuck, nobody got Murphy. Maybe he only teaches upperclassmen."

"Bet that's right," Chuck answered.

Ed marched his cadets to the flight line, where each found his instructor.

Chuck and Ed were assigned to First Lieutenant Simpson, who had a long, broad mustache, waxed and curled at the ends, and who walked with a limp. He also had several combat ribbons over his left shirt pocket, one a Purple Heart. It seemed the lieutenant was wounded when the Japanese attacked Pearl Harbor. He was one of the pilots who had been strafed when they tried to get to their planes to get into the air during the attack. He said that they were caught completely by surprise. He had jumped out of his bunk and tried to make it to his plane barefooted and in his shorts. He didn't make it. He had just been released from the hospital a few weeks ago. He'd asked for another combat assignment, but the doctors had said, "No." He was assigned to this post as an instructor until he was fully recovered. Then his request for combat was to be considered.

After introducing Chuck and Ed and two other cadets, Bob Watson and George Jorgensen, to the AT-6, the lieutenant said, "Men, the first thing I want you to learn is where every contol in the cockpit is, and learn it so well that you can put your hand on it blindfolded. So first, I want each of you to take turns getting into the cockpit and studying the location of each control. Put your hand on it and say what it is out loud. When you've done that, and practiced doing it with your eyes shut, I'll put this hood over your head, and when I call out a control, you put your hand on it. Okay, you're first," pointing to Bob.

After all four had passed that test, Lieutenant Simpson took each one for an introductory ride like they'd had in the BT-13. Each got to call the Tower for clearance and take-off. Then the lieutenant let each one get the feel of handling the airplane in the air, and follow in his movements on stick, throttle, and rudder bars as he landed and taxied to the parking area.

They all found this airplane sweet and responsive, and they could feel the extra power.

All four soloed the fourth day, after doing stalls and practice landings to the lieutenant's satisfaction. Entirely new to them was the retractible landing gear and the flaps. Both of these had to become fully integrated into their take-off and landing procedures. It was easy to forget to get the wheels up after take-off, and, worse, to forget to put them down for landing. The flaps gave an entirely different feeling to the plane for landing, and they had to learn to compensate for them when they put them down. In fact, they learned, landing this airplane without flaps was virtually impossible without running out of runway. They had to practice until landing gear and flaps became automatic.

From then on, each cadet had an AT-6 assigned to him. The lieutenant would give them flying exercises to do on their own, occasionally spot-checking them, just as Lieutenant Bellows had done with Ed and Chuck during their last days at Shaw.

Link Trainer and Skeet continued, and Ed had gotten to be an expert at commanding his classmates, being sure they met every formation promptly and arrived on time for assignments. retreat Parades continued to be rewarding for all of them. Among other flying assignments, Lieutenant Simpson would occasionally tell them to work out on the Beam, but not to bury their heads in the cockpit.

Ed, Red, and Chuck spent much of their free time together, but sometimes Chuck would get bored with talk about Western Pennsylvania and Pittsburgh, and go off with some other classmates. Red gave them both clues about what various officers and instructors liked and didn't like, and what really angered some of them. He also gave them ideas about what not to try to get away with when flying. "Two guys in my class thought it would be neat to fly under a low bridge a few miles away from the field. They might have gotten away with it, but one of them caught a telephone line with his tail-wheel when he was pulling up on the other side of the bridge. They are no longer in the pilot program."

Another new requirement to the cadets in flight training was learning to file a Flight

Plan. This meant filling out a form indicating Take Off Time (TOT), Estimated Time of Arrival (ETA), Destination, Route, Weather and Wind conditions along the way, and Altitude. When they got wind directions and speeds, they calculated Ground Speed for each leg of the flight. The Flight Plans were then filed at the Flight Control Office, and each pilot would make a chart of his flight with compass headings, check-points, wind direction and velocity, as well as an ETA for each check point. This he kept in the thigh pocket of his flight suit to guide him in his flights.

Until a few days before the cadets became upperclassmen, the Flight Plans were just paper exercises, since all of their flying practice was done within sight of the field. Then one day when they reported to flight line, Lieutenant Simpson said, "All right, fellows, you're all doing fine. Now, I want you to do your first cross-country exercise. Each one prepare a Flight Plan, destination to be twenty miles from the field. Ed, you go north; Bob south; Chuck east; and George, fly west. Check your maps and find a checkpoint: a city, or a major highway intersection, an air field, a river fork—some visible item you can use as a checkpoint. It should be about twenty miles from our field in the direction I have assigned you. Get wind direction, velocity, weather conditions along your routes, then file a complete Flight Plan. Let me check them before you file them. Any questions? Okay, get started. And don't forget to make your flying copy."

Full of excitement at this new experience, they got to work and soon had their Plans ready. Lieutenant Simpson okayed them, pointing out a few things to watch out for along the way, and telling Bob that he'd forgotten to include a heading for his return. "Keep in mind, you have to correct for wind when you're flying, not just on paper, whether it's headwind, tailwind, or right or left crosswind, and what its velocity is. I don't think you will, but if you have any trouble, get lost or disoriented, call the Tower, okay? File your plans, then, and get going."

Ed had picked a little town just over twenty miles north and a couple of miles east of Spence Field. He'd indicated that his altitude would be 3,000 feet, and the weather people had said there would be strong winds from the east, about 30 MPH at that altitude.

Excited about really flying to some place and back, not just within sight of the field, he filed his Plan, did his ground check, strapped himself in, got clearance, started up, checked everything, especially the fuel gauge, and took off. He felt proud of having progressed so far, and enormous excitement at being on his own, heading for an area new to him, and not near enough to the home field to be seen from the Tower. "I'm beginning to think of myself as a pilot," he said aloud.

After leaving the pattern, he did a circling climb out of local air traffic. When he reached 3,000 feet, he set his course at 100 east of north. The little town, Bakerstown, was actually 30 east of north from Spence, but he allowed an additional 7 degrees for the east wind.

The day was beautiful and sunny, with a few harmless clouds floating below him. The engine was throbbing steadily, and Ed was enjoying himself. Twenty miles did not take long, so as the ETA for his checkpoint, 09:17, approached on his watch, he began to watch for Bakerstown. It should be dead ahead, but it wasn't there. He put the plane up on its right wing and looked below. Not there. Now he was worried. His ETA had passed, and no checkpoint. "Maybe the wind was stronger than I figured," he thought, and strained his eyes to the east. At first he saw only fields and a solitary country road. He squinted against the morning sun, and then put on his Ray-Ban pilot's sunglasses.

Now he could see a tall chimney almost due east. He turned toward it, and found the little town he was looking for. Piles of coal surrounded the tall chimney. There was a small grass airfield just north of the town, and Ed flew over it. On the roof of the single small hangar was painted in large letters, "Bakerstown." With a sigh of relief, he said to himself, "The wind velocity must be a lot greater than 30 MPH. I must have been 5 or 6 miles off course."

He lined up with the airport, rocking his wings in greeting to the two men who came out of the hangar to look up at him. He set his southerly course for the return to Spence, but he corrected to 15 degrees east of south. In a few minutes he saw Spence Field dead ahead. "Man, that's a good lesson to learn," he said. "Five miles off course in just 20 miles of flying! I'm going to have a lot of intermediate checkpoints from now on."

By the time Ed landed, the others were already talking to Lieutenant Simpson. "What happened to you?" the lieutenant asked.

Ed told him what he had learned. "Good point," the lieutenant said. "The weather people do a good job, but wind is so variable that they can't be absolutely accurate about it. All of you, learn to have good checkpoints in between your major ones. Okay, everyone, see you tomorrow."

"Boy," Ed said to Chuck, as they walked toward their formation point, "I thought just flying around the field was a great feeling, But crosscountry is even better. You're really on your own and free then!"

"Sensational," Chuck agreed. "But you were five minutes past your ETA. The lieutenant was really worried. He kept looking at his watch while we reported."

"But he didn't say anything."

"Yeah. Guess he was so relieved that you made it that he didn't think of that. He'll probably burn your ass tomorrow."

"Sure he will. What instructor could pass up a chance like that, to chew out his best pupil!"

"Oh no! Here comes the bullshit. By the way, Buddy, I was getting worried too."

"Yeah, talk about bullshit."

"No, I mean it, I don't want to lose another pal."

"Right. Thanks Chuck." Both were thinking of Merv.

Problems given to them in Link grew increasingly difficult: zero visibility, strong winds, unusual positions, sudden stalls, spins, engine failures, mountainous terrain, rapidly changing barometric pressure, and emergency landings in the ocean, including simulated inflation of Mae Wests and dinghies. Chuck and Ed and their two new flying partners enjoyed the challenges and mastered the required techniques.

Ed remarked, after an especially grueling session of water drills, "No matter what combat theater we get, we'll have to fly over water. Good we're getting this training."

"Yeah," Chuck responded. "Too bad they can't let me have a dip in some real water to get cooled off after sweating out these drills."

"You don't mean to tell me you still sweat buckets in Link! Come on!"

"I guess you don't, huh? That must be piss then, soaking you all the way up to your neck," Chuck shot back.

"Okay, okay, so I still sweat, too. But it's good to have these drills so you'll know what to do if you get shot down over the North Sea. I hear that's water that'll cool you off real fast."

"Yeah. Guess it's close to freezing all the time."

"Right now that wouldn't feel too bad."

"Time for us to fly. Let's cool off in the air."

"Right," Ed replied, and they sprinted to their planes.

Graduation for Red Hunt's class came, and Ed and Chuck, along with all the other cadets, marched in the big parade, giving a mass salute to the newly commissioned second lieutenants, now wings-wearing Army Air Corps pilots. Ed felt special pride as he watched Red functioning with the group of cadet command officers. He thought, "Good for you, Red. It won't be long now until I may be doing something like that too."

The Graduation Parade was impressive. All cadet officers, including Ed, wore sabres and white gloves. Shoes and brass of all the cadets were buffed until they sparkled in the sun, and every maneuver was performed with snap and precision. General "Hap" Arnold, Army Air Force commanding general, took the salutes as the cadets paraded past the reviewing stand. When all the cadets were set in block formations, the cadet wing commander presented the wing to the colonel who commanded the Post. He, in turn, introduced General Arnold, who spoke briefly of the need for pilots in all theaters, of his pride in the air power the U.S. was building, of the bombing runs being made—especially over Europe—and of the growing superiority of our fighter groups, with P-38s, P-47s, P-40s, and what might turn out to be the best of them all, the newly introduced P-51, named the Mustang, the previous A-36.

A thrill went up Ed's spine. So they had done it! Made a competitive fighter—maybe the best of them all. He made a vow to himself, "I'm going to fly that baby. That's mine!"

General Arnold went on to congratulate all the graduating cadets, expressing his pride in the program which was providing increasing numbers of qualified pilots for the war that had been forced upon us.

The general concluded and took his seat. The colonel gave a command, and the entire wing of cadets snapped to parade rest. Next the long process began of having each cadet who had made it mount the stairs to the platform, salute, have his wings pinned on, receive his printed, rolled-up commission, and receive a handshake from General Arnold.

When it was over, instead of parading back to their barracks area, the cadets were dismissed right there. A tremendous noisy melee ensued, with cheers, hat-tossing, embraces, congratulations, and hundreds of cadets milling around, trying to get to their special friends, parents, wives or other relatives, even some girlfriends. Ed and Chuck got to Red and threw their arms around him. "Best day of my life," he yelled. "Let's get somewhere and celebrate. It's on me!"

They made their way through the throng, got to the main gate and there, to their surprise found half-a-dozen cabs lined up, waiting for cadets and others who wanted to go to town. They grabbed the first one and were on their way to Moultrie.

Well ahead of the crowd, Ed and his two friends had no trouble finding a restaurant with a bar. They sat in a booth, ordered beer and studied the menu. "Anything you want, men. Lieutenant and fighter pilot Hunt speaking. Anything you want," Red said, sticking out his chest.

At Red's elbow a voice snarled, "You're out of uniform, Lieutenant! On your feet!"

Red jumped up. "Sir?"

"What do you mean coming into town dressed like a bloody cadet when you're an officer in the Army Air Corps?" It was Lieutenant Murphy, but he couldn't help laughing. "Sit down, Red, I won't report you. You beat all the others in here because they all went to put on their new officer's uniforms and get all gussied up. Move over. Let me buy you a beer. Jesus God! Is this Sparks and Thorne? Do I have to put up with you two heads-up-and-locked, lousy fliers come Monday?"

"What do you mean, Sir?" Ed asked.

"I have the misfortune of having you two boneheads to try to make fliers out of when you are promoted to upperclassmen next week. If you get promoted."

"What do you mean? Did Lieutenant Simpson get transferred?" Chuck asked.

"Hell no. God help us! Don't you jerks know anything? Why do I get all the knuckleheads? What made you think you'd keep the same instructor? Everybody gets a new one when he gets to the exalted status of upperclassman. And I got stuck with you. God help us all to survive this latest calamity."

"Sorry, Sir," Ed said.

"Sorry hell! Just don't fuck up. If you do, I'll burn your ass like it's never been burned before." Ed saw him wink at Red, and felt better.

The lieutenant continued. "Come on, Lieutenant Hunt, Let's find some other place to sit. I don't want to be seen with these loose-assed beginners."

"No thanks, Lieutenant. I'll stick with my buddies. See you later in B.O.Q."

"Hell you will! I don't live in that rat trap. Got an apartment in town. Much better. Well, okay, I'll take off then. Try to shape up these sad sacks. By the way, Red, you can call me Joe, But don't you pissantes try it. He saluted Red and wandered off.

"I'm glad he's gone," Chuck said. "He makes me uneasy."

"It's all talk," Red said. "He likes to make noise like that. But he's okay. Just can't get assigned to combat. He's too good as an instructor, so he's frustrated. I like him; you're lucky to have him as your final instructor. He'll see to it that you make it unless you really goof up. Just listen to him, laugh at his weird jokes, and do what he tells you."

"Okay, Red, thanks for the advice," Ed said. "Why should you buy for us? You make the same ninety bucks a month we do."

"You forgot already, Mister. I'm about to become a high-paid officer. I'll get flight pay, and pretty soon, combat pay too. Tomorrow I'll have my new officers' clothes on, and you guys better not forget to salute."

"Okay, okay, big shot."

"Let's order, Garçon!" Red shouted, and a waiter came over. They all ordered prime rib, vegetables, potatoes, salad, and a bottle of red wine. Red ordered another round of beer while they waited.

"Where do you go from here?" Ed asked. "Did you get an assignment for fighter check-out?"

"Not yet. We all go to Tallahassee, down in Florida. We'll probably spend a couple of weeks there, then be assigned to some base to be checked out in some kind of fighters."

"Sure wish I were ready for that. I'm anxious to get going in fighters," Ed said. "I really liked what Hap Arnold said about the P-51. They should be ready for us when we get into combat."

Red said, "I've heard they're already shipping them over. I'm hoping for P-38s. I really like that airplane; it can do anything other fighters can do, and it has two engines. If one gets knocked out, you can get back home on the remaining one."

Chuck broke in, "I'm for the P-47. That's an airplane! I like that thick body and stubby nose, and it has a radial engine, not as vulnerable as inline ones."

"You guys are real conservative, aren't you? I want to fly the newest one; I'll bet it'll turn out to be the best. To me, it already looks the best, although I agree the 38 is a slick looking plane too. And Chuck's right about the radial Pratt and Whitney engine bringing you home," Ed said.

After dinner, Red won the argument about paying the bill. They walked around town for a while and returned to the base. Sadness about saying goodbye again to Red began to build in Ed, as he and Chuck helped him move his things to his B.O.Q. room.

Red showed them his new pinks, greens and suntans, bought during the last few weeks with his officer's uniform allowance. Next they helped put Red's gold bars, wings, and Air Corps insignia on the shirts and blouses. Red put on one complete uniform, showing that it fit perfectly. Ed and Chuck saluted. Red returned the salute. It was nearly time for lights out. This no longer applied to Red, but Chuck and Ed had to return to their room. Ed and Red embraced, and Red and Chuck shook hands. The cadets wished the new lieutenant good flying and good luck, then went out into the evening feeling a real sense of loss.

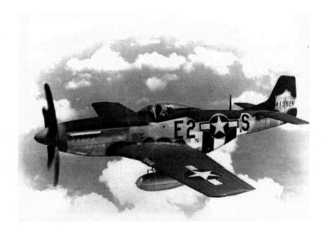

19

"All right, you clods, which one of you wants to be first to show me how little he has learned about flying," Lieutenant Murphy growled, his cigar wagging up and down as he talked.

Ed beat out the others saying, "I do, Sir." All of them had done well with Lieutenant Simpson, so they were confident.

"Okay, Mr. Thorne, let's do it."

Ed did his ground check, strapped himself in, called the Tower for clearance, and taxied out to runway 260 as directed. There he checked his mags and called for altimeter setting and clearance to take off. He took the runway, gradually advanced the throttle to full, then took off smoothly and easily, raising the landing gear as he reached the edge of the field. He felt good about it.

The lieutenant's gravelly voice came over the intercom. "Go around and land her, then come to the edge of the runway for another take-off." Ed wondered what was wrong; everything had seemed fine to him.

After he had again stopped at the edge of the runway, Lieutenant Murphy said, "That was okay, Mr. Thorne, but you're going to fly fighters. That was a *bomber* take-off! In fighters, sometimes you will be flying off of short fields, and possibly with enemy fighters nearby. They'll have a good chance to kill you if you take off like that. From now on, when you take off for me, get on the runway, put on the brakes, hold the stick back in your gut and run the engine up to full take-off RPMs. Then release the brakes and you'll get up to take-off speed in a hurry. Get the wheels up as soon as you feel them off the ground. Keep the nose down until you have all the air speed you can get, then pull the nose up and climb as steeply as you can, and and as high as you can without stalling out. Okay, go."

Ed had always wanted to do just what the lieutenant was telling him to do, so he was excited to be instructed to do it. Holding the stick firmly back, he ran the throttle forward until the plane began to quiver as if it wanted to go. Then he pushed the throttle the remaining inch of its travel, and released the brakes. The plane leaped forward like a throughbred out of the gate. Speed increased faster than ever before, and he moved the stick forward. The tail came up, and, in another instant, he felt the wheels leave the runway. He pulled up the wheel retracter lever while holding the nose down so they were just skimming above the runway.

"Not too low, Mr. Thorne," the lieutenant cautioned. "If your prop hits the runway, we're both finished."

As they reached the edge of the field, Ed felt that they had as much speed as they could get, so, leaving the throttle full forward, he hauled the stick back, hanging the plane on its prop. After a few seconds, air speed began to drop off rapidly, so he moved the stick forward to keep climbing, but at a reduced angle. Although far from the speed and rate-of-climb he would achieve later in P-40s and P-51s, this was by far the most exhilarating take-off he had ever experienced.

"What the hell are you grinning about, Mr. Thorne?" the lieutenant growled.

Ed hadn't realized he was grinning, but he was elated. "Because that was so great, Sir. You want me to do that every take-off?"

"That's what I want. Make it a habit. Next time I'll have you hold her on the deck instead of climbing, then when you're up solo, you can do it whichever way you want, just see it isn't like a civilian take-off. Take us up to 3,000 feet and put us through some rolls, loops, Immelmans and anything else you can do. Wring it out if you can, and don't be afraid to use the throttle. That's what it's there for. Wring this baby out; see if you can surprise me."

"Now, that's an invitation!" Ed thought. He went through every move he knew, the lieutenant giving him suggestions now and again, but seemed in general satisfied.

Before they returned to the field, Lieutenant Murphy said, "Let me show you how fighters land in combat zones." He took over the controls and, finding an open pasture, flew directly over it into the wind, did a quarter roll to the left, pulled back on the stick, cut the throttle all the way back, and began a spiral descent, taking him just beyond the downwind edge of the field. Before making his final turn into the wind, he raced the engine to clear it, then did a simulated power-off landing. He gunned the engine and pulled up over a row of trees at the far edge of the field. "There's another one I'll show you on another day. You cannot do this at the main field, so don't even think about it. A good way to wash out! Okay, now, take us home," Ed took over and returned to the field, thoroughly pleased with his first flight with "Mean Joe."

Lieutenant Murphy went through the same procedure with Chuck, Bob, and George. Then the four cadets left for chow and ground school, loudly expressing their enthusiasm with their tough-talking instructor.

As everyone expected, Ed was appointed squadron commander with a cadet rank of captain. He had observed what cadet commanders did through Preflight and Basic, had experience as a commander there, and had been functioning as a junior squadron commander in charge of his fellow underclasssmen here at Spence. As a result, he had no trouble handling his new assignment.

Just a week after his appointment as squadron commander, Captain Johnson sent for him to come to his office. "What did I do now?" Ed thought, as he hurried to the tactical officer's office.

"At ease, Mr. Thorne. Sit down," the captain said, after returning Ed's salute. "There is, suddenly, a vacancy at Cadet Wing Command. You have been nominated to fill the vacancy. Are you interested?"

"Yes, Sir," Ed replied.

"I thought you would be. The position has the title, 'Executive Officer,' and carries the second highest rank a cadet can achieve: 'Lieutenant Colonel.'"

"I'm honored, Sir. What does the executive officer do?"

The captain explained, "In the actual military structure, the executive officer takes care of the administration of the unit, relieving the CO of most of the routine paperwork. In the case of the cadet set-up, the executive officer is second in command, and functions as backup to the cadet commander, marching just to his left and a pace behind him. The wing commander is Colonel Smiley. You probably know him."

"I do, Sir. A good man."

"Yes, we think so too. Well, what do you say? Will you accept the appointment?"

"Certainly, Sir."

"Good. You already have your saber and white gloves. You will be issued the chevrons of your rank. Any questions?"

"No, Sir."

"All right. That will be all. You are dismissed." Ed saluted and left the office, feeling elated but surprised. "Oh, man! I almost washed out in Preflight, and here I am one rank below top dog in the cadet wing! Beats me how all this happens."

Ed didn't say anything to Chuck until he stepped away from his squadron and joined the the cadre of wing officers at retreat time. Meanwhile, Bob Watson had been named their squadron commander to replace Ed.

When they got back to the room, Chuck started in on him immediately. "Boy, you've really been brown-nosing, haven't you? I think I'd better move out and find another room-mate. This room isn't big enough for both of us."

"What brown-nosing? Everybody just recognizes superior quality when they're exposed to it. You're kidding about moving, right?"

"Yeah, but if your head gets too big, I'm getting out."

"Good. I want you to stay. My head will stay just the size it is. Keep in mind, what we do here, in addition to learning to fly and related subjects, is preparation. Our real job comes later, in combat."

"Yeah. I know, Buddy, just pulling your leg. You deserve the appointment."

"Thanks."

Ed's functioning as executive officer was routine, and he carried out his duties efficiently and with enthusiasm. One day, not long after his appointment, as he was cleaning up for retreat, a messenger came to tell him that Captain Johnson wanted to see him immediately. He left what he was doing and reported to the captain.

"Mr. Thorne, did you know that Mr. Smiley is sick?"

"No, Sir. He did look a little pale this morning, and he mixed up some of his commands, but he said he was okay."

"Well, he is not okay. He's in the infirmary, and we have a call in to his parents. The doctors don't know what the problem is. We need to speak to his parents to see if anything in his background could account for his sudden weakness, high fever, and disorientation."

"Sounds bad, Sir."

"It does. We are going to put him in quarantine."

"That's really too bad, Sir."

"Meanwhile, Mr. Thorne, as second in command, you will take over as acting wing commander until we see what happens to Mr. Smiley. Okay?"

"Yes, Sir."

"All right, then. You will be in charge starting with today's retreat."

"Yes, Sir." Ed saluted and left.

After returning to the room, he told Chuck about it while they got ready for retreat.

"Wonder what it could be. It sure had to happen fast, because he was on the Skeet Range yesterday and seemed okay," Chuck said.

"Yeah, I know. But I heard he had a really bad headache last night, and didn't feel like eating this morning."

"Hope it isn't contagious."

"Yeah. They have him in quarantine. Whatever it is, it could sweep right through a place like this. Maybe we better keep this to ourselves. Don't want to start a panic."

"Right," Chuck agreed.

Ed's first experience as wing commander got off to a slightly shaky start, but the cadets were so disciplined, and so accustomed to the procedure, that the entire operation had become almost automatic. Ed saw this, and his confidence grew. He also sensed that the entire wing was behind him, and that they took pride in their parading. So after the first several minutes, everything went smoothly.

After a few more days of disciplined work with Lieutenant Murphy, the four cadets were doing things his way, and he seemed pleased with their progress. "Now," he announced one day, after each had been up with him, "This next week is going to put extra demands on you. First of all, you're going to start aerial gunnery. You'll fly one of the AT-6s, as usual, but it will have a single .30 caliber machine gun mounted on its nose. It will be synchronized with the prop, so it will fire through the prop and not hit it. Just like World War I fighters did. You will find an "Arm" switch on the instrument panel, and the trigger will be built into the hand grip on the stick. You will arm the gun only when you approach the target, and fire only at the target. We don't want any AT-6s shot down, and we don't want .30 caliber slugs falling on us, or on anyone else. All your shooting will be done over a designated firing area; over a swampy area west of the field.

"All four of you will be firing in turn at the same target. Each one of you will have bullets coated with a different color chalk, so we'll have a record of hits and misses. The target will be towed by an instructor in an AT-6. All four of you will be in the air at once. All of your shots will be deflection shots, and you will be coming in at the target from the side. This means you will be leading the target, just as you do in skeet. If you lead the target too much, you'll shoot down the tow plane and the instructor flying it. We do not take kindly to that. So, better not fire if there is any chance of hitting him.

"DO NOT ATTEMPT TO FOLLOW THE TARGET AND SHOOT AT IT FROM BEHIND. If you do, you'll risk shooting down the tow plane. We can't afford to have that happen. Also, he'll damn well burn your ass if you shoot anywhere near him. You may be excused for coming close once, but not twice. You'll get the bum's rush out of here for certain if you hit the plane, or if you come close more than once. Pay attention to what you're doing. Stay on the ball.

"Aerial Gunnery starts tomorrow. You'll get more instruction from a gunnery instructor who will meet with you and tell you when to rendezvous with your tow plane.

"The second new thing starts day after tomorrow. Instead of reporting to the flight line at your usual time, you will report after dark. The time will be given to you by your tactical officer. I'll be checking you out on night flying. You'll all be briefed in a general meeting of your squadron before take-off time. Then I'll go up with each of you in turn. Later, after I've checked you out, you'll do night-time solos. It's a whole new ballgame at night. You'll like it.

"Then, in a week or so, you'll do a night cross-country solo. Maybe I'll get rid of a couple of you on that one." With that, he stuck his cigar back into his mouth and headed for the Officers' Club.

"Hey, guys!" Bob yelled. "We're getting near to the real thing!"

"Yeah. Guns, night-flying and night cross-country! He must think we're okay," Chuck said.

Ed put in, "Naw. He doesn't think that at all. These are required of every cadet in the pilot program."

"You know, Buddy, sometimes you're a real pain in the ass," Chuck said. "Can't you just let us think that Murph thinks we're okay?'"

"Not good for you," Ed said. "Give you big heads."

The next day the four reported as instructed by Captain Albertson to the gunnery instructor, about 50 yards down the parking strip from where they usually met Lieutenant Murphy. The gunnery instructor, a hard-bitten regular Army man, gave each of them a cockpit check, pointing out the arming switch and the trigger. After that, he spent five minutes lecturing them on safety, emphasizing the need to be aware of where the other planes flying in the same target pattern were, and how deadly a .30 caliber slug was. "You're just as dead when a .30 hits you as when a .50 hits you. Matter of fact, the British, the Germans and the French use .30s in their aircraft. These are not playthings. If you shoot someone, your butt is gone from here. Come in from the side, lead the target, but not so much that you endanger the target plane. When you squeeze that trigger, be sure you know where those slugs are going to go. Better to miss the target than to hit the tow plane. If you aren't sure, don't fire. Come around again, and be sure. Nobody will get on you for a dry run, but everybody will sure as hell be on you if you hit the tow plane. Hit the target! Nothing else! Understood?"

With that, the instructor told them the order in which they would fly in the shooting pattern, and that the range was 10 miles west of the field. Each was told what color was his. Ed's was green.

They climbed into their AT-6s, got clearance, and took off in the order the instructor had given them. Chuck led off, followed by Bob, Ed, and George. It was a clear day, and they spotted the tow plane with its target almost as soon as they turned west.

Each cadet flew an oval pattern at the target, then, after firing a burst, went under the target and turned right immediately, circling around in front of the tow plane to get into position for another run.

On his first run Ed misjudged the speed of the tow plane, winding up well behind it. He wanted to fire his gun, so, thinking he was at enough of an angle, he fired away. Looking at the tow plane, he saw the pilot shaking his fist at him, "Oh no," he thought. "Did I come that close?"

His next run was better, and the third and fourth were excellent. The other three had four good runs each, so when they were shown the target, there were Ed's first shots showing up as long slashes with green chalk around them.

"Who the hell had green?" the tow pilot asked through clenched teeth.

"I did, Sir," Ed said.

"You came too close to me, Mister. Get your ass on the ball. One more like that and you're in real trouble! Got it?"

"Yes, Sir." Ed felt rotten. Not only had he been too close directly behind the target when he fired, he also had fewer total hits than the other three. "I think I'm starting my run too far back," he said to Chuck on the way to their room. "I need to cut my last turn into the target tighter, and head toward the tow plane, then fire as the target starts to cross my sights, turning a little to the right to lead the target."

The next aerial gunnery session, Ed tried that and had a much better score. He never forgot how those long, green-circled tears in the target looked, nor how close he had come to causing an unnecessary tragedy. He also never forgot how much easier it is to hit a target being towed or an enemy plane when you get on its tail than it is to shoot from the side. Deflection shots are great, but when you're coming in fast, and the target plane is moving in a direction perpendicular to yours, you have a second or less to fire your guns while within range and the target is in your sights. That lesson would serve him well later, in combat.

Night flying was a new and exciting experience for the cadets. Lieutenant Murphy was nervous and tense, as were the other instructors. The entire squadron was on the line, and all would be taking off and landing on the same runway. Fortunately, the base administration had closed that runway to all other traffic, and the Tower routed every non-cadet pilot to an alternative runway. Still, all the the students and instructors had to be extra careful both on the ground and in the air. All the planes had their flying lights on, but everything looked different in the dark. Distances were deceptive. Even the instruments looked different, with an eerie, phosphorescent glow.

In the briefing made by the chief instructor, each student pilot was given an order of take-off and landing. Each instructor would make sure that his students used their assigned orders, along with the usual things he would say to the Tower when getting clearance.

The chief instructor stressed again and again how alert everybody had to be, and forcefully said, several times, "To expedite the flow of traffic, no one—that's NO ONE is to go to the END of the runway for his take-off run. ALL TAKE-OFFS ARE TO BE FROM WHERE THE TAXI STRIP INTERSECTS THE RUNWAY."

He repeated this, then said it again at the end of his briefing. He then wished everyone good luck and good flying.

Bob was the first of Lieutenant Murphy's students, number eight in the overall order of take-offs by the squadron. Chewing furiously on the cold stub of his cigar, the lieutenant said, "All right, you chumps, you have an order of flying. If you screw up in your first try, you have to wait through all the rest of the squadron before you get another shot. So keep your heads out of your asses and do it right the first time. Then, thank God, I won't have to go up with you the second time. I love night flying, but I hate it when everybody and his goddam brother is up at the same time. Okay, Mr. Watson, let's do it."

The first seven were safely off, and Bob and the lieutenant turned on to the runway and took off, smoothly and firmly. The take-off was perfect. They circled the field, did a good landing, and taxied back into the parking area. The other two shook Bob's hand as Ed climbed into the plane. He was number sixteen in the order. He got clearance, and started out on the runway off the taxi strip. He was just turning into the wind for his take-off when simultaneously Lieutenant Murphy yelled, "You're going to get your ass chewed," grabbed the stick and throttle, gunned the engine, and kicked the right rudder all the way forward. The plane spun to the right and headed for the grass. Just then an AT-6 roared out of the dark from the end of the runway behind them. Its pilot yanked back on the stick when he saw Ed's plane in front of him. Between the lieutenant's quick action and the other pilot's use of the stick and throttle, a real collision was avoided. As it was, the right wheel of the other plane rolled across the top of Ed's left wing.

Lieutenant Murphy stopped the plane on the grass, then called the Tower to report what had happened. The Tower immediately came on, stopping all take-offs and instructing all planes in the air to circle the field, maintaining the order in which they were flying.

Ed and the lieutenant returned to their parking place. Chief Instructor Parker was waiting for them. The two saluted, and Major Parker said, "As you were." Then he inquired of Lieutenant Murphy what had happened.

"We had just left the taxi strip to go to the center of the runway. We were number sixteen in the order, and as far as we knew, number fifteen had already taken off. There was nobody in front of us on the taxi strip.

"Mr. Thorne got clearance from the Tower. He was just about to give it full throttle for take-off when I saw lights approaching at the end of the runway. I didn't even think; I just grabbed the controls and got us out of the way. The other ship pulled up, even though it didn't have enough speed to get airborne. Lucky he did. His right wheel ran up our left wing. Then he dropped down to the runway, bounced once, and continued his take-off run. That's about it." His hand shook as he put a match to a new cigar, and drew in heavily.

"What about you, Mr. Thorne? Anything to add?"

"No, Sir. I didn't know what was happening until I saw an AT-6 right on top of us. Lieutenant Murphy's quick action saved my life. Thank you, Sir," Ed replied.

"Yeah, yeah. You owe me a beer," Murphy said, acting as if what he did was routine.

Major Parker then asked, "Were my instructions about not using the end of the runway not clear?"

"We understood them, Sir," Lieutenant Murphy replied.

"Some son-of-a-bitch is going to get burned for this. We haven't had a crash since I was appointed Chief Pilot. Thank God this was a minor incident. You two go see the flight surgeon, then get back in the rotation. Our schedule won't allow us to lose this night's flying. Somebody had his head up his ass, and I'm going to find out who. Okay, get going."

Ed and the lieutenant headed for the flight surgeon's office. "We aren't hurt," Ed said. "How come we have to see the flight surgeon?"

"Regulations, Mr. Thorne, regulations. Any time an accident happens, no matter how small, everybody involved has to be checked over before he can fly again. Let's get moving. I have a date tonight, if we ever get through flying. God, what a way to start!"

They double-timed to the flight surgeons's office, where the doctor gave them a quick checkup: pulse, blood pressure, and a look into their eyes. All he said was, "Murph, cut down on the salt. Your pressure is too high. Ought to cut out the cigars too." Then he gave them both an okay to fly, and they went back to their plane. While they were gone, the flight engineer and his crew had gone over their plane and released it for flying.

Nothing interfered this time, and Ed had an excellent take-off, flight around the pattern, and landing. He taxied back to the parking area. "Okay, Mr. Thorne. Do you feel okay?"

"Yes, Sir."

"All right, you're ready for night solo. So take it up. But watch out for meatheads who might screw you up. Take off."

"Yes, Sir," Ed said, and called the Tower for clearance. Since all take-offs and landings had been stopped, he fit right into the sequence. When number sixteen was called, he was already at the edge of the runway. With a long look toward the end of the runway, he taxied out, gunned her, and headed into the black sky. He did four take-offs and landings, feeling better about it with each one. Shortly after he got back and parked his AT-6, the others finished up and parked. Walking away from his plane to join the others and the lieutenant, suddenly his legs felt weak, and he felt his hands trembling. "Just a delayed reaction," he thought. It had passed by the time he joined the others.

"Okay, Men. You did all right. Mr. Thorne and I had a little bit of extra fun, but it was okay. Right, Mr. Thorne?"

"Yes, Sir," Ed replied. "Not an experience I want to have again. But I'll never forget again to look even where no one is supposed to be."

Lieutenant Murphy agreed. "Me either. Say, men, I have time for a beer, and Mr. Thorne owes me one. Can't stay long, I have a date. What say, Mr. Thorne?"

"Roger, Lieutenant. Any time you want a beer, I'll buy it," Ed replied. "You saved my life out there."

"Bullshit! Any more of that and I'll see you never graduate. I want one beer from you, then let's forget about it."

"Yes, Sir, one beer. But I won't forget about it."

"Let's go," and the lieutenant stuck a new cigar into his mouth as he led the way to the PX.

The other three wanted to know what had happened, but every time Ed started to tell them, the lieutenant would order, "At ease, Mister. You're asking for it! And I can give it to you!"

"All right, Sir. By the way, are you going to be late for your date?"

Murphy looked at his watch, gulped the last of his beer and said, "Yeah. Got to go. Keep your heads out, men," and left them.

With the lieutenant gone, Ed was able to tell the others all about the incident, repeating several times how lucky he was to have had Murphy for his instructor. He stressed that the lieutenant's quick action had probably saved both their lives, as well as those of the two in the other plane.

Ed never did learn who the cadet in the other plane was, nor who the instructor was. He didn't know if there was any connection betwen the accident and the fact that Captain Johnson called him into the office two days later.

"Sit down, Mr. Thorne," the captain said. "There has been a major change in the Cadet Wing Command. Colonel Smiley is unable to function any longer as wing commander. Since you are second in command, you are, as of this date, permanent wing commander. Since you will be going to Eglin field in a day or so for dive-bombing and strafing training, and since your graduation isn't far off, we might not get the paperwork done to get your promotion to cadet colonel finished, but you are it anyway."

"Thank you, Sir. What is the problem with Smiley?"

"I'm not at liberty to say, Mr. Thorne. That's it; you are dismissed."

Ed saluted and left, feeling uneasy, but not knowing any more than what the captain had told him. He was never to find out any more. None of the other cadets knew anything, and if Lieutenant Murphy knew anything, he wasn't telling them.

After two more sessions of night flying with assigned take-off numbers, the cadets alternated night flying and day flying, as assigned by their instructors. They were free to leave the pattern and return at will, but Lieutenant Murphy cautioned them to stay near enough to see the lights of the field. This allowed them plenty of space for flying, getting on the Beam and off, getting accustomed to spotting landmarks in the dark, and getting a feel for how close or far other aircraft were by the way their lights looked. Ed grew to like nighttime flying almost more than daytime flying because of the intensified feeling of being alone in a vast universe of space, with brilliant stars arching over him and the world. At times the stars were so clear that they seemed almost reachable if he put his hand outside the cockpit.

Landing at night became as routine as daytime landing had become. All the cadets felt that they had grown enormously in competence and confidence in their ability as pilots.

Three days before Ed and the other three were scheduled to fly AT-6s to an auxiliary field at Eglin Air Force base, Lieutenant Murphy told them that the next night the entire squadron would be taking a night cross-country flight. "Each one is to work up a complete Flight Plan. The flight everybody will fly is Spence, Valdosta, Thomasville, then back to Spence. It is a triangular course, with both turning points well lighted. Easy to see. Get predicted weather and wind conditions now, and update your plans with the latest weather information before take-off time. Take-offs for the entire squadron will be at five-minute intervals. Order of flight numbers will be assigned at a briefing before take-offs begin at 20:00 tomorrow. After this, if you make it, all you have left before you graduate is dive-bombing and strafing, and a final instrument-flying check after you get back from Eglin. You guys are doing okay, so don't screw up on this. That's it. Get out of my sight."

"Hey, Ed," Chuck said as they walked to their room, "we must be okay, must be going to make it. What do you say?"

"You're right, old Buddy. Mean Joe, that fake grouch, must think we're ready, or he'd never have said that. By the way, remember my picture of Pat and the story I told you, Bill, and Merv about how we met?"

"Yeah, I remember all that crap, 'Moonlight Eddie.'"

"Well, remember I said I'd invite her to our graduation and dance, at which, I now know, as wing commander and a natural-born leader of men, I will lead the Grand March?"

"It never stops flowing out of you does it? You must be Irish, you're so full of Malarkey."

"Only part."

"Thank God! Think what I'd have to listen to if you were all Irish."

"Well, anyway, I wrote to Pat last week, and I got the answer today. She's coming! You'll see everything I said about her is true."

"That's great, Buddy. Too bad Bill and Merv can't be here to meet her. God! I miss them."

"Me too. Bill's okay, doing fine, wrapping up his bomber training. I just got a letter from him. He loves it. But good old Merv. He never got to do what he most wanted to do, just what we're doing. I can't forget that day. And I can't forget him."

"Yeah," Chuck said. They walked in silence to their room, each with his own thoughts and feelings.

The next night at 19:30, the squadron's instructors and cadets met in the Briefing Room. Using a pointer, the chief pilot indicated the cross-country route on a large wall map, pointing out the turning points as well as major features the fliers could use as intermediate checkpoints. After his briefing, he wished them all good luck and good flying, then called on the chief meteorologist for an update on weather and wind. Each cadet made minor changes in his Flight Plan. As they left the Briefing Room, each one was handed a card with an order number and a time for take-off on it.

Ed was scheduled for a 20:30 take-off, the first of Murphy's students. The other three had times spaced out through the list. Ed went over his Flight Plan with the lieutenant, then checked his AT-6 carefully, made sure his route map was in his thigh pocket, got clearance from the Tower, and took off.

After clearing the pattern and climbing to 3,000 feet, Ed took his heading for Valdosta, southeast, and settled back to enjoy the night. Clear sky, brilliant stars, headlights of cars travelling below, and an occasional sighting of another aircraft flying by. One was a Lockheed passenger airline.

He could see the lights in the passenger compartment through the row of windows on the side.

Still keeping alert, he allowed himself to dream a little bit about Pat. What would she be like? Would he even recognize her? How neat it was that she had agreed to come.

Abruptly he snapped out of his reverie, as he glanced at his Flight Plan and his watch, realizing that it was past his due time at Valdosta. He peered out in all directions, but the lights of Valdosta were not in view. "How could I miss Valdosta?" he asked himself. "I must have figured the heading wrong to be so far away that I didn't see any lights."

He decided tbe best course of action would be to turn west toward Thomasville and cor-rect a little north, on the assumption that he was south of Valdosta. He did so, and flew the time indicated on his Flight Plan. When the time had elapsed, he saw no lights indicating Thomasville was below him. Looking down he realized that he was flying over solid overcast. "Okay, take it easy," he said to himself, as he turned N–NE for what should be his homeward leg. "The weather people never mentioned any chance of overcast!" He knew that he had spent more time on his Spence-Valdosta leg than his Flight Plan called for, so he knew he'd not make it by his Estimated Time of Arrival (ETA).

Soon he was free of the overcast, and thinking he was close enough to Spence to recog-nize some landmark, he kept looking down. The terrain did not look familiar. "I guess I'm lost. Am I going to blow it all this close to finishing pilot training?"

He knew that Spence's Beam was off the air for repair, so he looked on his aerial chart for a field with a beam that would be in line with Spence. He found Tifton. He quickly tuned in the frequency indicated on the chart, and got the solid tone right away. He stayed on the Beam which, according to his chart, passed almost directly over Spence Field. Slowly out of the dark, he saw airfield lights emerging. Now, well away from the overcast, visibility was excellent. The lights were close enough that he recognized them as those of Spence. With enormous relief, he switched from the Beam frequency to Spence Tower, and requested clearance to land. The Tower cleared him immediately, and he landed.

"Where the hell have you been, Mister?" Lieutenant Murphy exploded. "You're ten min-utes over your ETA. The others are all in. What have you been doing?"

"No excuse, Sir. I miscalculated my heading for Valdosta. That threw me off for my Thomasville heading. I was over solid overcast in the Thomasville area."

"Yeah, others reported that too, but it didn't bother them. What did you do then?"

"I took a heading of 30 degrees and flew a while looking for terrain I'd recognize. When I didn't see anything that looked right to be around Spence, I tuned in to Tifton Beam and flew that until I saw our lights. Then I came in."

"Son of a bitch! Why do I get them all? Good thinking to use the Tifton Beam. I don't like to admit it, but I was worried about you. How in hell could you get lost in a simple triangular cross-country?"

Ed was chagrined. Everything had been going extremely well, and then a simple miscal-culation seemed to have put him in the doghouse. After letting him stew for a few minutes, the lieutenant came over, put his hand on Ed's shoulder, and said, "It's okay, Mr. Thorne. You must have overestimated the effects of the headwind on your air speed, and your head-ing must have been off a couple of degrees. Either error wouldn't have been a problem, but both together must have made you miss Valdosta. Probably got there sooner than you expected, and those few degrees wrong on your heading could add up to several miles in that distance. I have to share the blame, because I checked your Flight Plan before you took off. It was heads up to use the Tifton Beam. No problem. Forget about it."

Ed gave a deep sigh of relief and said, "Thanks, Lieutenant."

"For nothing," the lieutenant said. "Anybody for a beer?" All but Bob said, "Yes, Sir." Bob said that he had some bookwork to do for tomorrow's ground school, and he headed for the barracks. The other three went to the PX with the lieutenant.

Beer glasses in hand, they sat at a table outside in the pleasantly cool evening. "Chuck tells me you have a girl coming for the big graduation dance, Ed," the lieutenant said.

"Yes, Sir. She wrote and said she's coming. It's been a few years since I've seen her, so I'm pretty excited," Ed responded.

"What's her name?"

"Pat."

"A good Irish name. Is she Irish?"

"Don't think so. I think she told me German and English."

"Well, that's okay. I was hoping to meet an Irish beauty."

"Well, Sir, she's a beauty, but not Irish. I'll settle for her kind of beauty."

"Good man. If she's pretty and a nice gal, grab her. Most of them are walking down the aisle with somebody else while we're away."

"She might do that, but I hope not. Anyway, I have no strings on her, and she's really popular. I hope she hasn't got somebody else, but I wouldn't be surprised if she has."

"Well, it's a good sign if she's willing to come all the way here from Pennsylvania just for your graduation, even if you are a big cadet mucketymuck."

"She won't be coming from Pennsylvania, Sir. She's in college in Tennessee."

"College! She's pretty and popular, and going to college too! You'd better tie on to this gal real fast."

"We'll see, Sir. First she has to get here, and we have to get to know each other all over again. We might not even hit it off now, the way we did a few years ago."

"Good luck, Ed. Let's drink to Ed and non-Irish Pat."

They all raised their glasses. After finishing their drinks, the cadets went to their rooms, and the lieutenant went to get his '36 Nash to drive into town.

Final instructions were given for the flight to Eglin Air Force Base, and the auxiliary field in a remote part of the Okeefenokee Swamp, where they would practice strafing with live ammunition, and dive-bombing with flour bombs. Lieutenant Murphy would lead them to the field, see them landed, then return to Spence. Each of the cadets was given a copy of the lieutenant's Flight Plan, in case anyone got separated from the others. The take-off, flight and landing were all routine, and Lieutenant Murphy rocked his wings in farewell as he headed back to Spence.

Two instructors were in charge of the little rough grass field, surrounded by jungle. Everywhere the cadets looked they saw swamp water, palm trees, cypress trees, and a profusion of vines, shrubs and occasional scrubby pine trees. Captain Miller was in charge, and First Lieutenant Jerome was the other instructor.

After showing the cadets their barracks—no rooms, just a line of bunks, a latrine at one end, the lieutenant's office and quarters at the other—Lieutenant Jerome warned them about sleeping without the mosquito bar closed and tucked under their mattresses. He also warned them about walking out into the swamp. This warning he underscored by saying, "Hear that godawful roar? That's what the natives call a 'gator. We call them alligators. Mostly they leave us alone, but now and then one is hungry enough to climb out of the water and up on to the field. Stay away from them! Some are enormous, and all are potentially danger-ous, especially in mating season. And they are frighteningly fast on land; much more so in the water."

"The target areas are near enough to the field that you can always see the field. If anything happens—the engine cuts out, loss of fuel, anything—you must make it back to this field. Dead-stick in here any way you can. Survival in the swamp alone and without proper equip-ment is very, very chancy.

"There are two other buildings here, besides storage ones. One is Captain Miller's head-quarters and living quarters. It also houses the radio equipment, our only contact with the outside world. The other is our chow hall. We have a good mess sergeant, and one corporal to assist him. They also work as supply people. The chow is good, but not as good as you get at Spence. The sarge and Corporal Jones are pretty creative.

"There are twelve cadets here at a time. Four are in the air right now, and you can hear their .30 caliber guns popping if you listen. Four others are getting ready for their bomb-ing runs. You four won't fly until this afternoon. We work in sequence here: four on gun-nery, four on bombs, four on ground briefing and instruction. Each cadet gets four flights a day—two strafing and two bombing.

"Safety is our number one requisite. I'll be instructing you on that this morning. Any questions?"

Chuck spoke up. "Do we fly alone, or do we have instructors with us?"

"Good question," the lieutenant replied. "We don't have enough instructors to assign one to fly with each of you; there's only the captain and me. You fly alone—I'll instruct you on target locations. You already know about the arming switch and trigger for the guns; I'll instruct you on releasing the bombs. Anything else?"

"When do we eat, Sir?" Bob wanted to know.

"About an hour from now. Anything else?"

With no further questions, Lieutenant Jerome led the cadets out to one of the AT-6s already equipped with the .30 caliber gun, the same as they had used in aerial gunnery at Spence. He pointed out a button on top of the stick and explained that they would release the bombs by depressing that button.

Next he described the pattern they would fly when firing at the gunnery target. It amounted to a circular pattern, each plane at a safe distance from the one in front of him, so that one would have pulled up and turned away before the one following him came in on the target. They would circle at 750 feet, then dive toward the target to ten feet above the ground, fire a burst of 6, pull up to 100 feet, then do a climbing turn back to 750 feet. The swamp growth and trees had been cleared out of an alley leading to the target.

Finally, he stressed, "Guard against getting hypnotized by the target. We've lost a few cadets who, for some reason, didn't pull up, flying right into the target and crashing. He underscored this by leading them to a crumbled plane parked at the fringe of the field. Each cadet was told to climb up on the wing and look in to see bits of bone embedded in parts of the cockpit trim, and bloodstains everywhere. Each cadet turned pale and felt sick, as the lieutenant pointed out to them that those were deposited there by a cadet just the preceding week. Ed and Chuck rushed to the grassy area at the side of the parking area and upchucked. "I'm sorry, men. But this seems the most effective way to impress you with the danger in not staying alert to where you are when shooting at ground targets. In combat, you'll be flying much faster than these ATs can go, so learn now to stay alert. Only one cadet has crashed into the target here and survived. Better to pull up too soon than too late."

Having said that, the lieutenant handed out charts that indicated the field, and locations and compass headings to the targets. Gunnery was east, bombing west. He then dismissed them to follow the smell of food to the chow hall.

Talking excitedly about the new experiences they would have starting that afternoon, they suppressed their nauseous feelings about what they had seen in the demolished plane, and gulped down their food, barely chewing it, interrupting their talking only to swallow. At 13:30 they reported to Lieutenant Jerome.

The lieutenant reviewed his earlier instructions, then said, "You keep flying the target pattern, making passes at the target until you've exhausted your ammunition. Then return here, and your plane will be reloaded with ammunition. You won't need radio clearance to land. Just make sure the runway is clear and come on in. Keep your head and eyes moving, and don't forget what I said about getting hypnotized by the target!"

"Sir," Ed said.

"Mr. Thorne, what is it?" the lieutenant replied.

"Lieutenant Murphy taught us fighter take-offs and landings. Would it be okay if we did that here?"

"Good old Joe. His students always ask that. It's okay if you want to do that. Good experience for you. You don't have much space after you're airborne, so you can't hold your ship down too long on take-off, but if you keep your heads out you should be okay."

"Yahoo!" Chuck exploded. "Sorry, Lieutenant."

"Okay. Any questions?"

There were no more questions, so the cadets went through their ground and cockpit checks, started up, checked mags, and rolled out onto the runway in the order they'd been given for take-off: Ed first, Bob second, Chuck third, and George fourth.

Ed taxied as far as he could to the end of the runway, checked his mags a final time, depressed the brake pedals, and ran his engine up to the point where it seemed the airplane would take off without any run at all. Then he released the brakes and felt the satisfying feeling of his head and back pressing against the headrest and seat back. He barely got his wheels up before he saw the jungle growth at the end of the runway. He pulled back on the stick and began his climb, but with such a short take-off run, and practically no space for building up speed, the climb had to be gradual.

When he reached 750 feet, he levelled off and saw the gunnery range dead ahead. He circled and began his dive, fired his first burst, and had the satisfaction of seeing new holes appear in the target. Pulling back on the stick, he waited until the other three got into the pattern and fired their rounds, then he went in again. This time he started his dive farther back, and came in at ground level, firing when he guessed he was in range. He'd guessed right, and again saw little puffs as his slugs hit the target. He pulled up and saw Bob coming in on the target.

All four were excited and enjoying themselves. They all ran out of ammunition at the same time, and returned to the field, maintaining their sequence.

Ed led off with a spiral fighter landing. He misjudged a little, so, after clearing his mags before the final turn, he had to feed in more throttle to get beyond the edge of the field; otherwise he would have run out of field before he got the plane stopped. The other three saw this, and they started their spirals just at the edge of the field, instead of at the center, as Ed had done. All made successful landings.

As they waited for the armorer to reload their guns, the other three got on Ed about his landing. "Well," he responded, "you guys got educated by watching me. It wasn't too bad for a first try. Hell of a short field!"

Just then Lieutenant Jerome walked up to them and said, "Not bad men, but remember how short the field is, as Mr. Thorne found out."

"Yes, Sir," all four said.

George, number four in the sequence, said, "Sir, the target is pretty well shredded."

"Not a problem. By the time you get back there, there'll be a new cover on it. They're expendable."

"Who puts them on, Sir? The 'gators?" Chuck wanted to know.

"Nice try, Mr. Sparks. You probably didn't notice the bunker off to the left of the target. It's rotten duty, but we have to assign a man out there every day. When a group finishes its run, as you just did, he puts a new cover on for you to shred. It's a lonely job, so keep an eye out for him. He'll appreciate a wave or a wing rocking once in a while, so he knows we know he's there."

Their second run at ground-level gunnery went well, and all four made excellent fighter landings. Chuck, in exuberance, added a slow roll as he passed over the field to check the windsock. When all four had landed, Lieutenant Jerome asked them how everything went. They all said it was fine and lots of fun. He instructed them to change their pattern the next day by circling at 1,000 feet, and diving on the target at a steeper angle; again, allowing plenty of time to pull out. He suggested that each one make a trial run without firing their guns. This way, they could get the feel of when to start pulling out of the dive.

Before they left to change out of their flying suits and clean up for evening chow, Lieutenant Jerome said, "Congratulations, Sparks."

"For what, Sir?" Chuck asked.

"For being the first American to shoot down an enemy plane while flying a training plane in the States."

"I don't understand, Sir." Chuck was puzzled.

"Okay," the lieutenant said. "You did a slow roll over the field before you landed. Don't you know what that means?"

"No, Sir."

"Any of you know?"

"No, Sir."

"When a fighter pilot shoots down an enemy plane on a mission, if his plane isn't too crippled, he does a slow roll, just as you did, Mr. Sparks, right over his home field before he lands."

"I didn't know, Sir. Sorry." Chuck was crestfallen.

"It's okay; how could you know? Okay, get going. Tomorrow morning you start bombing."

"Damn," Chuck said as they walked to the barracks. "Somebody ought to tell us things like that."

"You're right, old Buddy," Ed said. "You claimed a victory you didn't have. What was it? ME-109? FW-190? Jap Zero?"

"You're a zero, old friend. I'll hold that roll in reserve. Bet I'll need it before you need one."

"We'll see about that. You may never see an enemy plane. Bet you suck around to find a cushy job in the Training Command when it's nearly time to ship over."

"You son of a bitch! You calling me chicken?"

"Don't get your balls in an uproar. I'm just pulling your leg; didn't mean anything."

"Okay, okay, I guess I'm getting touchy. This gunnery is something, isn't it?"

"Sure is. Let's go. Nearly time to hit the chow line."

Since there was no formal retreat at this outpost in the swamp, the four cadets spent the evening talking, writing letters to be mailed when they returned to Spence, playing cards, and reading while an ancient Philco table radio played big band dance music in the background. Although there were screens on windows and doorways, it wasn't long after sunset that mosquitoes began to hum around their ears. For a while they swatted and slapped, but much earlier than usual, they all used the latrine, checked their mosquito bars, climbed into their bunks and fell asleep. It had been a long but good day.

The next morning, unlike the day before, was solidly overcast. Lieutenant Jerome announced at breakfast that flights would go on, but according to the weather bulletin, there might be heavy rain starting about noon. For that reason, afternoon flights might have to be scratched. All the cadets groaned their disappointment. To be grounded any place was a pain, but in this forsaken place, with no rec hall, PX or movie—no entertainment at all—it would be hell.

"All right, men. The two flights assigned to bombing practice—your planes are ready. The flight assigned to strafing—yours will be ready in thirty minutes. Good flying. Any sign of a severe storm coming up, hightail it home. On your way!"

While the first flight to head for a target area got under way, Lieutenant Jerome instructed Ed and his friends, "Point the nose of your plane a little beyond the target, as you come out of your dive. Then, as you you release the bomb, pull up and away. Your forward momentum should ark your bomb right at the target. As you turn away, look at the target and see how close you came. You can then adjust your technique the next run. As soon as you finish your run, come back for another bomb. Good luck, and keep your heads out and up."

They found the bombing a different kind of fun. It lacked the excitement of the chattering machine gun and seeing holes appear in the target. But it was fun to watch the cloud of flour rise as the bomb exploded. All four missed the target the first run. Ed and Chuck overshot and Bob and George undershot. The second run they all hit within the target area, but no one got near the bull's eye.

As they returned to the field, large raindrops began to splash on their windshields, and they could see lightning flashing in the black clouds roiling overhead. The captain had ordered the landing strip lights turned on, since it was as dark as evening, even though it wasn't quite noon.

"That's all the flying for today, men. You have the afternoon off, but don't try to walk into town," Lieutenant Jerome said with a chuckle. "There'll be a movie shown in the mess hall at 14:00. No, it won't be a training film on venereal disease; it will be 'Gone With The Wind.'"

The rain fell all afternoon, all night, and all the next day. All the cadets were getting jittery, not only because they couldn't enjoy watching the movie over and over, but also because they had to wrap up their training back at Spence. They had to have their final instrument checks to get their instrument flying cards.

The rain let up that night, but started again the next morning. It continued. By the fourth day, Ed was really concerned. If Pat arrived for graduation and the big dance, and there was no Ed to meet her, what would she do? With no phones and no mail, he had no way of getting word to anybody at Spence.

At last, after five days, the rain stopped. The captain announced that everybody would fly as many missions as possible, to wrap up this phase of their training. The next day they would be dispatched in flights of four to return to Spence.

All the cadets flew enough strafing and bombing runs to be qualified, and that evening every cadet made out a Flight Plan for the trip to Spence. When they were done, Lieutenant Jerome checked them, made a few suggestions, but approved all of them. "Keep each other in sight, and talk to each other by radio, if you aren't sure of anything. Breakfast will be at 06:00, take-offs begin at 07:30. Better pack your things tonight. See you at breakfast."

As the four waited for their take-off time, Ed said to Chuck, "Damn! The weather screwed up my plans for Pat. Good thing old Bill Schramm isn't there. Remember, he said he'd take her away from me. I don't have to worry about him, but there are a lot of other wolves among the cadets. You know, graduation is tomorrow and the dance is tomorrow night. I hope she didn't come, then get right back on the bus when I didn't show up."

Chuck said, "Hey, man, she wouldn't do that. She wouldn't come all the way from Tennessee, and then turn around and go back. She'd ask, and they'd tell her at Post Headquarters where you were, and why you couldn't be there to meet her. Relax, Buddy. Take it easy."

Ed could see the logic in what Chuck said, and it eased his mind some. He was still concerned, though. Finally, their turn came and they took off. They got to Spence with no trouble. Ed rushed to his room to change, and there he found a letter from Pat:

> *Dear Ed,*
>
> *I'm crying as I write this. I had everything planned, had all my clothes ready to pack, had the money for my bus ticket, and my parents' permission to come down for your graduation, and then the hammer fell. I was told that I had too many 'cuts' already, and if I took enough cuts to make the trip, I would not be able to graduate! I can't afford not to, I can't afford to give up the degree I've worked so hard for, and I can't get the money to come back for another semester to finish my requirements.*
>
> *"I am absolutely broken-hearted, and I beg you to forgive me. More later, if you want to hear from me again.*
>
> *"With tears in my eyes,*
> *Love, Pat*

Ed sat on his bunk and almost cried from a combination of relief and disappointment. Pat hadn't come, so his worry about not meeting her on arrival was relieved. But she wouldn't be coming at all! That was a deep disappointment. He no longer cared about the dance. He'd ask someone else to lead the Grand March. Graduation would still be wonderful, but neither Pat nor anyone else from the civilian population would be there to share his sense of accomplishment and joy in achieving an important goal. "Well, that's life," he thought. "Maybe we can get together some other time before I ship out. Sure is rotten, though. Don't those professors know there's a war on?"

All the cadets who had been detained at Eglin were scheduled for final instrument checks the afternoon of the day they returned to Spence. Ed and his friends were meeting with Lieutenant Murphy to plan their order of flying, when the same kind of weather that had plagued them at Eglin closed in. A quick call to the weather officer gave them the bad news that the weather system was widespread, with no possibility of relief before noon the next day.

In desperation, the base commander made an unprecedented request: that the cadets be given their final instrument flying check in the Link Trainer, and be issued their instrument flying authorization cards. He argued with Southeast Training Command Headquarters that all of the cadets had had an abundance of in-the-air instrument flying, supervised by their instructors, as well as the required hours in Link. He insisted that they all had excellent records, and that it was not their fault that the weather had delayed their final work. He insisted that not to allow this would be to deny these men their graduation, and he could not agree to that. Finally, permission was granted, and the twelve cadets were hurried to the Link Trainer building, where they all qualified and were issued their instrument cards.

"We just cleared the last hurdle, Buddy-boy," Chuck exulted, clapping Ed on the shoulder.

"Yeah! We're almost there," Ed agreed. "Tomorrow is the day we get our wings and commissions. I sure feel rotten about Pat not coming, though. To hell with the dance, I'm not even going."

"I don't blame you. Maybe I'll sit it out too; we aren't required to go. What say we put on our new officer's uniforms after the ceremony and strut our stuff in Moultrie?" Chuck suggested.

"Great idea; we'll do it. I feel better already. I wrote to Pat as soon as I read her letter. Imagine how disappointed she is! I told her it was okay, and that we'd get together some other time. 'Mean Joe' was sorry too. He thought we should write to her college president, but what good would that do? It's too late now," Ed said.

Lieutenant Murphy treated all four of the cadets to beer at the PX. He said, "If any of you aren't going to the dance, maybe I'll see you in town. But you better not be out of uniform!" With that he took off.

The four showered, shaved, and got dressed for chow, then retreat. Realizing it would be their last retreat as cadets, they, with all the other graduating cadets, were especially energetic and alert. Ed and all the other cadet officers made their orders and reports especially crisp. This was the final rehearsal before the next day's big graduation parade and ceremony.

Tired from the extra tension of completing their final requirements under unusual circumstances, the four sacked out early, and all slept well in spite of their growing excitement.

They were up early the next morning. Ed and Chuck helped each other pack their duffel bags and foot lockers, then fell out in the rain, wearing regulation raincoats and GI shoes, for breakfast formation. Back in their room, they picked out their best suntan cadet uniforms and polished their brass and shoes, and Ed his saber and Sam Brown belt. He practiced Present Arms and Order Arms with his glistening sabre, and reviewed the orders he'd be responsible for during the parade and ceremony. He then located the four cadets who would be in front of the four-rank column, which he would lead to the Parade Ground. He asked them to say to him "move right," or "move left," as he marched in front of them, so he wouldn't have to look back to see if he was centered on the column as they marched.

By noon chow, the rain had stopped, the clouds had blown away and the sun was drying the streets and grass. Almost, but not quite too excited to eat, Chuck and Ed finished their meal, and for the fifth time toasted each other with their coffee cups. All the other cadets were doing the same. At 12:45 hours, Ed stood at the end of the mess hall and called, "Squadron Commanders, move your men out for return to barracks."

Each squadron commander in turn ordered, "Fall out and form up outside." They all formed up and marched back to the barracks area. Ed announced, "Parade formation at 13:30, Oxfords, sun tans, Garrison caps. Officers wear white gloves, Sam Brown belts and sabers. Let's look sharp today, guys. Make this the best Graduation Parade they've ever seen here. Congratulations to all graduating cadets."

Before he could say, "Dismissed," someone shouted "Three cheers for Cadet Colonel Ed Thorne," amd the entire wing shouted, "Hip! Hip! Hurray!"

"Thanks, Buddies. Right back to you. Dismissed," and the formation broke apart.

At 13:15 Ed and all the wing officers, group commanders, and squadron commanders were in place at the side of Main Street 1328, and the band was in place. The rest of the cadets were lined up and their squadron commanders dressed their formations, and then put them at Parade Rest so that precisely at 13:20 Ed commanded, "Squadrons, Attenhut!" and every cadet popped to. The sound of heels clicking together echoed among the empty barracks.

"Squadrons!" Ed shouted, and each commander echoed, "Squadron!" "Right Face," Ed ordered, then moved to the head of the long column of fours, turned to face them and shouted, "Forward HARCH!" On "Harch," the drums began their cadence, and every cadet's left foot stepped forward. Ed was now marching at the head of the column, thrilled, as he was sure every other cadet was. After the first ten paces, the band began to play "Stars and Stripes Forever," and Ed felt his chest swell with pride, and his shoulders straighten. Every cadet did the same, their heads up, backs straight, their arms swinging the prescribed inches forward and back, their fingers curled in a loose clench. Every movement was precise, crisp, energetic, and in perfect time to the music. Even a cynical observer would have to be moved by the sight and feel of these healthy, proud, well-trained young men, ready to fight for their country and their shared beliefs.

As the last four cadets passed through the Parade Ground gate, the band stopped playing, except for the trap drums keeping cadence. Ed called out, "Parade Formation, HO!"

and the column of four merged into the block formation they had become used to. The band began to play again, and the formations were done so smartly and precisely that the spectators—wives, parents, sweethearts—broke into applause.

The block formations made, the most difficult moves of all had still to be accomplished. In block formation, they had to Pass in Review. They did not get much practice at this, since it was not a regular part of retreat Parade.

"Wheel Left!" Ed ordered, as the first rank of the first block reached the marker. Without missing a beat, the proud cadets obeyed, the left pivot man marking time, and those to his right each taking a slightly longer step, so the entire rank was straight for the entire turn. Each succeeding rank of each block did the same.

"Wheel Left!" Ed ordered again, to get the formation moving parallel to the Reviewing Stand. Again, the execution was excellent. "Eyes Right," Ed ordered, and "Present Arms," as he and the first rank passed in front of the reviewing stand. Ed and his fellow officers snapped their sabers up in front of their noses in salute, as all the other cadets, except the one at the right end of each rank, snapped their heads to the right.

When the last rank of the first block had passed the reviewing stand, Ed ordered, "Order Arms!" and all the heads pivoted front and the sabers flashed down, then to the right shoulders of the officers. Each block, made up of three squadrons, repeated this salute.

Meanwhile, Ed was giving the orders for each block to make three more left turns, ending up with the entire formation facing the reviewing stand. When all were in place, he centered himself, facing the blocks of cadets and their officers. "Guidons Post," he called, and the standard-bearers carried their penants to the right front of each block. "Group commanders, have your squadrons report."

Each squadron commander reported to his group commander, the calls resounding around the Parade Ground. "J Squadron present and accounted for," and so on through the squadrons.

"Group Commanders, Report!" Ed commanded. Each group reported present and accounted for. Ed ordered, "Present Harms!" and every cadet officer's saber snapped up in front of his nose. Ed did an about face, snapped his saber to Present Arms, and said, "Cadet Wing III of Southeast Training Command present and accounted for, Sir."

With the cadet wing at Present Arms, the colonel and his party of officers turned toward the flag on the pole behind them and saluted, holding the salute. This was the signal to the band. It struck up "The Star Spangled Banner," and the spectators all stood, placing hands or hats over their hearts. Ed felt the thrill he always felt when he heard the nation's anthem, and he knew that most of his fellow cadets felt the same thrill.

At the end of the band's playing, the colonel turned toward Ed and returned the salute. Ed lowered his saber, did an about-face, and ordered, "Order Arms." He followed this with "Sheath Sabers," then, "Parade Rest."

The ceremony was the same as they had participated in when Red Hunt and his class had graduated, except that instead of General "Hap" Arnold, an Air Force major general from Washington spoke. The message was essentially the same as Arnold's had been.

Once again, the ceremonies over, the celebratory tossing of hats in the air and congratulatory handshakes and hugs took place. As soon as they could, Chuck and Ed extricated themselves from the rest of the excited cadets and headed for their room. They bantered excitedly as they put on their officer's uniforms and pinned on their wings and officer's bars. A final wipe of their shoes, and they were ready to move into B.O.Q. and head for town.

After finding their assigned rooms, hanging up the uniforms they wouldn't be wearing, and stowing their duffel bags, they set out for Moultrie. They were in buoyant spirits, having completed the grueling months fulfilling the requirements to become true, fully-qualified pilots and officers of the Army Air Corps. There were cabs waiting at the main gate, so they were driven to what had become their favorite restaurant and bar, the one where they had said goodbye to Red Hunt.

Instead of beer, they decided that the occasion warranted something more "high falutin'."

"Have you ever had a Baccardi cocktail?" Chuck asked.

"What's in it?" Ed responded.

"Not sure. Rum and something to sweeten it and make it pink."

"Pink!" Ed exploded. "Man, we're about to become fighter pilots, and you want to sit here, wearing new uniforms, bars and wings, and drink a pink lady? You can't be serious," "Try it, Lieutenant, you might like it."

"I don't like rum, and it doesn't like me. But if you're buying, Lieutenant, I'll drink it."

"You've got a deal, Lieutenant. Two Baccardi cocktails coming up."

Ed did like it, but rum usually made him queasy, so he had Scotch and soda for his second.

They had started their second round when a familiar voice sang out, "Well, lookee here. A couple of brand new lieutenants, sittin' here like bigshots. Moosh over, Lieutenant Ed, and let old Joe scoosh in beside you." It was Murphy, of course, more than a little drunk.

"Goddam piss-offs. Here I teach all you bastards how to fly. You go off to combat. Whatta they give me? Another fuckin' class, for me to make combat pilots out of. You buyin', Lieutenant Ed? Gonna buy yer ol' 'structor Joe a dink . . . drrrnk, what the hell! Buy me a dink," and he started laughing hysterically. "What the hell."

"Hey, Lieutenant Joe. Looks like you've had quite a few already," Ed said. "Maybe a cup of coffee would be better."

"You tight-ass sumbich! Don' wan spring for a drink for ol' Joe who can't get assigned to com'at? Shoulda washed you out, you no-good stick jockey." Lieutenant Murphy broke into laughter again. "Yer all right, Lieutenant Ed. You, too, Lieutenant Chuck. Les' have a drink, an' don' try ta shit me, okay?"

Ed asked, "What'll you have, Lieutenant?"

"Same as you, ol' cock," and he roared in laughter again.

Ed went to the bar and got a Scotch for Murphy, who picked up the glass, eyed it with one eye closed, started to raise it to his lips, stopped, spilling a few drops on the table, and said, "Looks like plain water, boy. You pullin' one on ol' Joe? I asked for a drink! Oh well, What the hell!" and he raised the glass and drank it down without a pause. He peered into the glass, set it carefully in the middle of the table, smiled benignly at Ed and Chuck, then pitched forward and was motionless, his forehead between the knife and fork at his place.

Murphy remained there motionless, except for the rise and fall of his back as he breathed. His elbows were on his thighs, and his hands hung down from his limp wrists.

Ed and Chuck, embarrassed that some of his students might come in and see him, tried to arouse him. He remained as he was. Finally, between them, they lifted and pulled until he was lying on the bench-seat on one side of the table, with his face toward the back of the bench so anyone passing would not see who it was. Then Ed and Chuck sat on the other bench.

"Guess he just has to drink off his frustration once in a while," Ed said.

"Yeah, but we've never seen him this far gone," Chuck replied.

"Well, maybe it's because he's losing the best two cadets be ever had," Ed said.

"Fuck you both at once," Murphy mumbled, but did not stir.

"Hey, Joe. How about some coffee," Chuck said.

"Bug off!" Joe responded. "Coffee's for after. Joe's not done yet."

Chuck and Ed decided to go ahead and order dinner. They did not want to just leave Joe there, so they ate, talking about what a great instructor he was, speculating about where they would go for fighter checkout, and more importantly, what they would fly.

They had just started on their favorite dessert—pecan pie—and coffee, when Lieutenant Murphy sat up, clear-eyed and, apparently, stone sober. "How about some of that coffee, men?" he asked.

"You bet," Ed said, filling Murphy's cup. "How do you feel?"

"First rate. Why?"

"We sort of thought you might have a little headache or something," Chuck said.

"Hell, I'm fine. Ready to fly rings around you two, or anybody else. It was the Scotch that did it. I've been sipping rum all afternoon. Couldn't stand to watch another bunch of you guys get your wings and be ready to go to combat when I can't. I always have some reaction to Scotch. Bourbon the same thing. That's why I stick to beer and rum."

"Sorry, Joe," Ed said. "I got you the Scotch."

"Okay. I think I said I wanted whatever you were having, and that's what you got me. Not your fault. I did pass out, didn't I? Yeah. But, you know, it isn't the same as passing out from too much to drink. It never happens if I stay with rum or beer. It's just a reaction I have to Scotch and Bourbon. Thanks for putting me on the bench. Anybody who didn't know would think I was a passed-out drunk. Not a good thing for certain people to see. Well, thanks for the Scotch and the coffee. Good luck and good flying. You'll do all right in fighters." He shook hands, saluted, and left.

"Man is that weird! I've seen a lot of alcoholics, but not one who went out like that, and half-an-hour later is up and ready to go, sober, no sign of a hangover," Chuck said.

"Yeah," Ed responded. "It was a little bit scary. I wonder if that's the real reason he can't get a combat assignment."

"That's a thought. Could be. Probably in his record somewhere. Good thing he isn't teaching in Primary. What if he had a reaction like that when he's taking a kid like we were up for the first time!" Chuck said.

"Yeah. Well, he's a great instructor no matter what," Ed responded. "Here's to Mean Joe Murphy, the best advanced pilot instructor in the Army Air Corps." They downed their drinks and left to find a cab back to the base.

On the way, they reminisced about their experiences and then spoke sadly about Merv, and how much they wished he had made it all the way to share this day with them. At B.O.Q., they said goodnight to each other and went to their rooms to write letters home about the day's events.

After two uneventful days of waiting, Ed and Chuck got their orders, directing them to report to Tallahassee Assignment Center within five days. As officers, they realized that they would have to arrange their own transportation, so they went into town to check at the Greyhound Bus Station to see if they could make the trip by bus. They found that it would be quite simple, not even involving a change of buses. Each one bought a one-way ticket, then they returned to the base to pack, and to say goodbye to friends and instructors. They would leave early the next day, so they paid their B.O.Q. bills ahead of time, then walked out to the main gate to arrange a morning pick-up with one of the ever-present cabs there.

This done, they rounded up Bob and George, and all four went to the PX for a farewell beer. All of the new lieutenants in the graduated class saluted each other, shook hands and wished one another good flying. They also said goodbye to the few underclassmen around, and to the instructors, tactical officers and administrative personnel who were there.

Ed made a special point of saying goodbye to Marie, a local dark-haired, dark-eyed beauty who worked as a cashier. He'd tried, unsuccessfully, to make a date with her. She was always friendly and pleasant, but she said that she no longer dated cadets or new lieutenants. Too hard, she said, to become attached to them, then never see them again.

Chuck and Ed, as well as all the other graduates, left early. Most of them had made bus reservations too. Greyhound had had to put on an extra bus to accomodate them. Those not going by bus had rides with parents, wives, or girlfriends. A few had their own cars. One, Bill Ryan, had had his wife drive their car down from Maryland. He'd offered Ed a ride, but they couldn't take Chuck too, so Ed thanked him and said that he would stick with Chuck.

The two buses left right on time, and all the pilots settled in for the long ride. Ed sat quietly beside Chuck, thinking about the long, rough road they had travelled to arrive where they were. He had special feelings for each place he'd been — Maxwell, Bennettsville, Shaw, Spence. Each name evoked strong memories and reminders of how close he had come to washing out and how fortunate he had been each time. And here he was, commissioned and a fully-qualified Army Air Corps pilot! "I don't believe it!" he said out loud.

"Don't believe what? Did you forget to pack something?" Chuck asked.

"No, I don't believe I made it. It's a dream come true. I'm the luckiest guy in the world," Ed answered.

"Lucky is right. You sure didn't make it on ability!"

"Up your ass with a weekend pass, Lieutenant," Ed answered.

Chuck came back with, "You actually think you made it on ability! You're nuts. You accumulated more brownie points than the rest of the cadet corps put together!"

"Thanks, Pal, you're a great friend. Hope you get assigned to a different place than mine out of Tallahassee. I don't know how much more of you I can take," Ed replied. "Besides, I'm fed up with saving your ass all the time."

"Getting touchy, aren't we? Okay, okay. You're one of the best fliers in the class. But you sure got yourself in some scrapes, you'll have to admit," said Chuck.

"You're right. Yeah, I've been lucky. So, if you promise to stop riding my coattails, I'm willing to have you get the same assignment as I get. Wonder where it'll be?"

"Seems half the cities in Florida have been taken over by the Air Corps. Hard telling where we might go," Chuck responded.

"Hey! Maybe we'll stay in Tallahassee long enough to promote something with those southern beauties at the Florida State College for Women. It's right in the city, I've heard," Ed said.

"Not a chance, Pal. At the rate you go, it'd take you six months, and we sure won't be there that long."

"I've got two beers that say I can get a date before you."

"You're on. You don't have a chance, my friend. I happen to be a fraternity man, and that'll impress them."

"I knew there was something about you that I hated! I doubt these rebel gals even recognize your 'goddam yankee' frat."

"They will; we're national."

"But gals don't join fraternities."

"They join our sister sororities, especially the good-looking ones."

"We'll see, my boy, we'll see." With this, Ed returned to memories of his experiences as a cadet. He drifted off to sleep. He was dreaming of his first solo flight when Chuck shook him awake.

"Rest stop. Want to get some coffee or something?" Chuck asked.

"Yeah, thanks." He stretched and yawned, then followed the others out the door. While he had slept they had reached Thomasville. It was now afternoon. The driver said that in another hour they would cross into Florida, then another hour to Tallahassee.

Ed stood in line for the toilet, and Chuck got in line for sandwiches, coffee and sticky-sweet rolls. After their snack Chuck used the rest room. Refreshed and fully awake, they again loaded into the bus. Settling into his seat and pushing the recline lever, Ed said, "What do you think about this war, Chuck?"

"What is there to think about it? We're in it, and we have to win it," Chuck responded.

"Why do we have to win it?" Ed asked.

"We can't let the Japs and Nazis get away with what they've done, can we? We have to win. We have to give them a real lickin,'" Chuck said.

Ed responded, "Yeah. Looks like the Germans intend to overpower all of Europe, and the Japs want the Far East to themselves. Funny. The Japanese absorbed western ways, including the technology of armaments, even though they seem to despise our culture and want us out. Now they're turning our technology against us. I agree—we need to win. Otherwise, between Germany and Japan, we'll be next, and I'm not sure we can whip them if they have all the resources of Europe and mainland Asia to use against us."

"Right. We're good, but not that good. So we have to stop them now. That's what we've been training to do," Chuck replied.

"I agree," Ed said. "We don't want to live under a dictatorship, German or Japanese. I wish we didn't have to go to war to stop it, though."

"What kind of talk is that?" Chuck burst out. "You some kind of Commie pinko or something? There's no other way to stop it! Hitler attacked everyone in Europe, and the Japs sneak-attacked Pearl Harbor and a lot of other places too. You going anti-war suddenly?"

"No, Chuck. There's no doubt in my mind that we have no choice but to fight and, if possible, to win. I just mean that we, the Allies from World War I, screwed things up after that war, so Germany needed to build up its war machinery to get its economy going again. Too bad a genius like Hitler went about it in the evil way he did. But he did bring Germany back from chaos, revived its industry and economy, produced an unbelievable number of airplanes, ships, submarines, weapons—all the stuff of modern warfare—and took on everybody, beating all of them except England. And if we hadn't gotten in, he might have taken it too. He *is* an evil man. Some of what he instigated is unbelievable. It's part of what made me sign up for the pilot training program."

"Well, so? What's that got to do with the price of cheese?"

"What I'm saying is that we—the Americans, British, and French—imposed impossible terms on Germany at the end of that war. We made Hitler inevitable. Now, you're right. We have to fight him with everything we have. But we created the monster we're trying to stop now," Ed continued.

"Okay, Hotshot. I'm not saying you're right. But maybe part right. What about Japan? We didn't destroy them in WWI, did we?" Chuck asked.

"No, we didn't. But we sure moved into their territory with a vengeance. We exploited them and the Chinese, and all Orientals, trying to destroy their culture and impose ours, all in the name of 'saving' them, to make them like us," Ed replied. "We kicked dirt in their faces. We thought we had a right to do this, because we were 'superior.' Well, they learned our ways, all right, with a vengeance. They showed us they could do our things as well as we could, and faster. At Pearl Harbor they struck back at the 'White Devils' with that devil's own weapons."

"You make a crazy kind of sense, Ed. One of my history professors used to say things like that. If he hadn't retired, I think he would have been fired. So, watch your mouth. You could get in big trouble saying things like that."

"Yeah, I know. I've been told that before. I don't often get on the soap box, but I was just thinking about this a while ago. Whoever created the monsters, we have to beat them. But sometimes it bothers me a lot. Fighting seems like the most stupid possible way of solving problems! I wonder if we'll do things differently when this one is over."

"I don't even want to think about it. We have a war to win first. Then we can worry about what to do when it's over. Can we give this a rest for now?" Chuck asked.

"Sure," Ed replied. "You're right. First we have to win. And that's still up for grabs. Then we can work out what to do to keep it from happening again. Hey! Are we in Florida? I didn't even see a sign when we entered Florida."

Chuck said, "It was there. About a half-hour ago. You were spreading shit as usual, and missed it."

"Okay, okay, okay. I'm only trying to educate stupid college grads like you," Ed responded.

"Why don't you go back to sleep, Pal, and give all of us a rest? You know, you're a real pain in the ass when you talk like that. I don't want to think, I just want to fly and help destroy the enemy."

"Roger, Lieutenant. That's what we're supposed to do. I'll be right there, just like you. But once in a while I catch myself thinking."

"Well, put a lid on it and save it 'til the war is over, will you?"

"Right. The lid's on. Wish we had those beers I'm going to win from you right now."

"Sure would taste good, but you'll never win them."

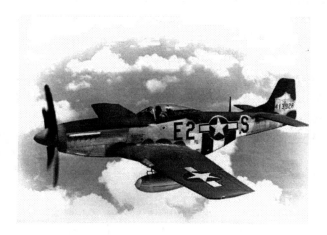

20

The base at Tallahassee was a staging area, with hundreds of Air Corps people awaiting assignment. It was boring. There was no possibility of providing all the pilots with air time, so they did not get flight pay. B.O.Q.s were two-story wooden barracks, no individual rooms and general-use showers and latrines. There were no parades, and no standing retreat, although all military personnel on the base were required to come to attention and salute when retreat was sounded and the colors were lowered. The PX was always jammed full, as was the base theater that showed movies every night. There was a rec hall with a jukebox and a small dance floor, usually crowded with men whose wives or sweethearts had come to Tallahassee to be with them before they shipped out, or who were lucky enough to have dates from town.

Ed and Chuck found Tallahassee to be a delightful town. Even though it was too full of men in uniform, all the civilian population made the men welcome, often buying them drinks or dinner, and giving them lifts to and from the base. They knew, of course, that this would be the last staging area for many of these men before they left for combat areas.

The Women's College was on a beautiful campus on a hill, at the edge of town. Their first trip into town, Chuck and Ed stood at the main gate of the campus. They found that almost all of the coeds would smile and chat with them, but neither had any luck getting a date. After an hour of trying, they went back downtown, neither owing the other a beer yet.

The next day Chuck told Ed that he was going to try something else, and went off to town alone. Ed stayed at the base, wrote letters home, and wandered about the base to see if he recognized anybody.

"Hey, Ed! Is that you?" A voice hailed him.

Turning, Ed recognized Grant Perrin who had been at Maxwell when he was, but in a different squadron. They had met through a mutual friend in Montgomery, and had an occasional drink together. Grant was from Cleveland. Glad to have someone to spend time with, Ed suggested they fight their way into the PX for a beer. Grant agreed, and they pushed their way to the bar to get two semi-cool bottles of Budweiser. There were benches outside, so they went out and found an unoccupied one.

"Well, what have you been up to since Maxwell?" Grant asked.

"Anything and everything. Funny our paths never crossed after Maxwell."

"Not really. We just got on different tracks, Different Primary, Basic and Advanced. I did fine after Primary, but I had a rough go there. Unfortunately, I had done some flying as a civilian. My instructor knew this and was on me all the time. I couldn't do anything right, and I was sure I was going to wash out. But here I am, ready to fly with the big boys. How about you?"

Ed told him briefly about his adventures, from his first solo to being named wing commander at Spence.

"Sounds like you had a great time, right?" Grant said.

"Had some scary moments, and was sure I'd wash out if I didn't kill myself. But yeah, I've had a really great time. Loved almost every minute of it," Ed responded.

Grant asked, "What's the scoop on this place? How long before we get some orders?"

"You know as much as I do. Nobody's telling us anything. All they say is, 'Watch your bulletin board for your orders to be posted. Then you'll know where you're going.' And that's it," Ed replied.

"Thought things'd be different when we got to be officers, but it's the same old bullshit."

"Right. Well, I don't really care what kind of fighter I get for this stage of my training, but I know what I want in combat."

"What's that?"

"General Arnold told us at Spence that they'd re-made the A-36, and now it's a really great all-round fighter. That's the one I want."

"Hey! I just saw something about that in an Air Force magazine. They put a Rolls-Royce Merlin engine in it, and a supercharger that kicks in at 10,000 feet. Sounded like a real honey of an aircraft," Grant said.

"Did they give it a P number?" Ed asked, eager to hear more.

"Yeah. Let me think. It was something in the 50's, Maybe P-50, I'm not sure. But they did give it a P designation."

"Hot dogs! I'll bet that's the one I want. Where's that magazine?"

"Back at my Advanced base. Might be one like it in the rec room here. Let's go look," Grant suggested.

"Let's go!" Ed yelled, heading for the rec hall.

After searching through a pile of well-worn magazines, Grant said, "Here it is! This is the one," and handed Ed a rather mutilated Air Corps magazine.

The table of contents was intact, so they quickly found the page number for the article. The first page of the article had been torn out. Evidently it had had a picture of the new fighter in flight, and someone had ripped it out. Most of the information was in the remaining pages, and Ed excitedly read every word: h.p., armament, rate of climb, fuel consumption at cruising speed, ceiling for effective maneuvering, absolute ceiling, and the rest. Not until he got to the last paragraph which started, "From all tests and trials, it looks as if the P-51 . . ."

"There it is!" Ed burst out, "P-51. That's the one. That's mine." Then he read the remainder of the paragraph, ". . . will out-speed, out-climb, out-maneuver, and out-gun any first-line fighter in the world. North American Aviation is in full production, and the first combat-ready planes are already on their way to England. They will replace aircraft in many groups now flying P-47s and P-38s. Looks like a winner."

"Yippee!" Ed yelled. "I can't believe it! They're going to be there, ready when I get there." It didn't occur to him that he might be assigned to some other theater of war which wouldn't get his plane until later.

Elated, Ed returned to his barracks and did some reading, but mostly he daydreamed of flying P-51s. Later, when he went to the Officers' Mess, he saw Grant. They ate together, talking about fighter planes, and speculating about what they would fly when they got to their fighter-training assignments. After eating, they went to the crowded Post Theatre to see a John Wayne film, in which the star was a Navy fighter pilot. As usual, the film was more about interpersonal relationships than about flying. But there was some flying depicted, and they enjoyed that.

After the film, they sat on a bench in the cool night air and chatted about home, their girl-friends, and their plans for the future. Grant said that he might want to stay in the Air Corps after the war. Ed said that he hadn't even considered that, but the idea wasn't too appealing to him, since the peacetime services tended to be tough on officers who hadn't graduated from the military academies. Soon they said goodnight and went to their barracks.

Shortly after Ed had stretched out on his bunk, Chuck came in and said, "You owe me some beer, Ol' Buddy."

"How come?" Ed wanted to know.

"Because, my friend, you're looking at a man who has a date. Tomorrow night. With a coed from the college. How do you like them onions?"

"Well, well. How'd you work that? Did you offer her money, or what?"

"Don't be a jerk. I went to the inter-sorority office and introduced myself, showing my fraternity card. Why, they welcomed me like a long-lost brother. They told me there was a tea coming up in about a half-hour, and invited me to go. I was introduced like a celebrity. They were all neat, but I hit it off real good with one. She's the one I'm dating tomorrow for dinner and a movie—in town, not at this crummy movie out here. How about that?"

"Man, they must be hard up for men," Ed said, "if it was that easy for the likes of you."

"It's just my natural charm and good looks. Sorry, Ol' Son. You want me to use my influence to fix you up with one of the others?"

"No thanks. I'd be afraid of what you'd find for me. I'll find my own. Just give me time."

"Okay, Pal. We may not have enough time for you to do that, remember. Anyway, I'm hitting the sack. Been a strenuous day. Goodnight."

Ed stripped down to his shorts and went to sleep.

The following day, Saturday, Ed ran into Grant again after noon chow at the Officers' Mess. Chuck had left for town, saying he had some shopping to do and wanted to get a real haircut from a civilian barber before his date at 4:30. Ed and Grant played some ping-pong, then had a beer at the Officers' Club. Ed asked, "You going into town tonight?"

"No, I have to make some calls back home. I promised my mother I'd do that every Saturday evening. Sorry."

"Way the ball bounces," Ed said. "Think I'll head in and have a drink, and then if nothing turns up, guess I'll see a movie. Wish we'd get our orders. This is boring, hanging around, no flying, no duties. Don't they know there's a war on? They need us over there. At least, that's what Hap Arnold says."

"Yeah, I know what you mean. But maybe we'd better just enjoy this. It may be the last real break we get in a long time," Grant replied.

"Guess you're right. I'm just getting frustrated. See you around," Ed said, and headed for his barracks to shower and dress for town.

The town bus was just pulling out as Ed got to the bus stop. He ran alongside and pounded on the door to get the driver's attention. The driver did not see him, and the bus went on its way.

A major, driving a staff car, pulled up to the curb and called out, "Need a lift, Lieutenant? I'm on my way to town."

"Thank you, Sir, I appreciate that," Ed said as he got into the car.

Holding out his hand, the major said, "I'm John Howard, Lieutenant. Who're you?"

"Ed Thorne," Ed said, shaking the major's hand.

"Where're you from, Ed?"

"Pittsburgh, Sir."

"How about that," the major said. "Another Pennsylvanian. I'm from Greensburg."

"Nice town; I've been there a few times," Ed said. "We sure have a lot of Pennsylvanians in the service."

"Seems that way. But then, there're a lot of people in that state. Where'd you go for Advanced?"

"Spence Field, Sir, up at Moultrie."

"Oh yeah. I know where that is. In fact, I helped set up that training center," Major How-ard said. "I'm regular Army. Do you know, we started planning bases like Spence back in the thirties? Then, when it began to look like we'd be in this war one way or another, by the Presi-dent's order, we began setting up some of them even before we got in."

"No, Sir, I didn't know that. Good thing you did, though, the way things turned out."

"Sure was. I've never heard of such incompetence and laxity as was evident in Hawaii and the Phillipines when the Japs attacked. I'll deny it if you ever tell anyone I said it, but if MacArthur weren't who he is, he'd have been strung up for that mess. I don't see how he could have allowed that to happen."

"Do you mean MacArthur was the only one to blame for all the Japanese did in the South Pacific?"

"No, of course not. Everybody out there must have been asleep at his post. But he was the top dog, the one in charge. Others have been reprimanded and censured. But do you know what happened to him?"

"No, Sir."

"He got promoted! Got his fourth star. Made a full general. He protected his ass, no mat-ter who else got blamed. Good P.R. work by him and his people. I shouldn't be saying these things, but it really burns me how all the inquiries and investigations have left him almost untouched."

"Wow! I sure didn't know all that!"

"Well, you still don't know it, as far as I'm concerned. My whole career could be ruined if the wrong people heard me say these things. So just pretend I never said any of this. I don't care what you say; just leave my name out of it. Maybe history will put the blame where it belongs. Well, here we are. I'll drop you here. Good luck and good flying, Ed."

"Thank you, Sir, and thanks for the educational conversation."

The major waved him off, saying, "Just be careful who's around when you talk about such things, and please keep my name out of it."

"I will, Sir. Goodbye, and thanks again." With that, Ed turned and walked toward Farley's restaurant and bar, which he and Chuck had found to be good.

He entered Farley's and looked around, hoping to see Chuck and his date there, or some-one he knew. No luck. Then he looked to see if any tables or booths might be empty. All were occupied. He was about to give up and go to the bar to wait for an opening in the din-ing area, when he spotted a smartly dressed, slightly older, but very attractive woman sitting alone in one of the booths. Thinking, "Can't kill me for trying," he approached her.

"Ma'am," he said. "Every place is taken, and I'm starving. Would you mind if I sat on this other side to have dinner?"

"Not at all, Lieutenant. Please be seated," she said in a soft, cultivated voice.

"I won't be a bother, Ma'am. Thank you," Ed said.

She laughed, displaying white, even teeth. "You'll be no bother, I assure you. It will be nice to have some company."

Ed was thinking, "Boy, is she pretty. I don't care if she is 28, or even 30. I wonder . . ."

She interrupted his thoughts. "What's your name, Lieutenant? I assume you're from the base?"

"Yes Ma'am. Like all the other pilots, I'm waiting for assignment. My name is Thorne, Ed Thorne. I'm so new at being an officer that I'm not used to being called 'Lieutenant' yet."

"You'll get over that. Everybody does. My husband went through that when he was first commissioned a few years back," she said.

Ed, disappointed but not surprised, said, "Your husband is an officer, then? Stationed at the base?"

"Yes. He's a regular Army major, and yes, he's at the base. In fact, he was to meet me here for dinner, but he got called to an emergency meeting of some sort. I could tell by the look on your face that you were hoping he might be located someplace else, right, Lieutenant? Maybe even overseas?"

Ed, embarrassed, said, "Well, yes, Ma'am. You're a mighty good-looking woman. No offense."

She laughed again, a throaty, musical laugh. Ed thought, "She's fantastic. Some guy's sure lucky."

"No offense, Ed. May I call you by your name? These titles make every conversation so stilted. Please call me Jane. I'm Jane Howard, and I'm flattered that you find me attractive, even though I'm obviously too old for you."

Ed laughed, relieved, then said, "Jane Howard. I just had a lift from a Major Howard. I wonder if he's your husband."

"From the base? Yes. As far as I know, he's the only Major Howard out there, but there's one sure sign. Did he talk about the mess at Pearl and all the rest of the South Pacific?" she asked.

"Yes, Ma'am. I mean Jane. He did. Really surprised me. I didn't know any of that," Ed answered.

"Did he caution you about talking about it?"

"Yes, he did, and I will be careful."

"Thank you. He may be too sensitive about that, but since we're in the military as a career, it's best to be careful. But actually, all the old hands know about it. The rest is politics, and most of the top brass are expert politicians, so he could get hurt," Jane said.

"I'll remember that, Jane," Ed said. "Oh, I'm forgetting my manners. I was about to go to the bar and get a drink before dinner. Can I get you something?"

Jane said, "That would be nice. A martini. Ask for Joe, the bartender. Tell him it's for me; knows how I like them. She reached for her purse. Here. Let me give you money for the drinks."

"Oh, no, Jane, I'm buying. Consider it payment for your husband giving me a lift, and you sharing your booth with me."

"We don't want payment for simple friendly acts. But if that's the way you want it, okay," she said.

Ed ordered the drinks and carried them to the booth. Jane lifted her glass and said, "Here's to the Air Corps. Long may you fly." After a sip, she gave Ed a radiant smile. "Joe did it again; thank you."

"Here's to you Ma'am," Ed said, sipping his Scotch and soda.

"Where's your home, Ed?" Jane asked.

"Pittsburgh."

"Oh. Quite a city," Jane said. "Since John is from Greensburg, we get to that area often. Visit friends down in the city. We've always found it quite different from its reputation. What is it? The Oakland area? That's beautiful. The University of Pittsburgh, with its Cathedral of Learning, and its other buildings and stadium all over the area, Carnegie Library, Museum and Art Galleries and Music Hall. And Syria Mosque. We've been to concerts there. We heard the great heldentenor, Lauritz Melchior there, with Fritz Reiner and the Pittsburgh Symphony not too long before John was assigned down here."

"You did!" Ed exclaimed. "I was there for that too. What a coincidence! That was a great concert. Remember how Melchior towered over Reiner, then, when they were taking a bow, Melchior put his arm around Reiner's shoulder, like a father comforting a little boy? The audience laughed and applauded, and the whole orchestra laughed along with Melchior and Reiner. I'll never forget that voice, ringing out over the full orchestra playing full force!"

"Oh yes, I remember that. Well, isn't that something! We were both there, and now we meet here. John will get a kick out of that. That area, with Schenley Park and everything, is excellent. Other parts too. Those wonderful mansions up on Fifth Avenue, the churches, the streetcars, taking you anywhere for a few cents. I find it a wonderful city. I don't think it deserves its reputation."

"You sound like a native. All of us who live there know the city has a lot to offer. People who have only been to the railroad station or the airport never see the real Pittsburgh. If you hadn't mentioned some of its features, I would have. I hope you will visit there again," Ed said.

"I'm sure we will. John has family in the area, and we have many friends there."

Their conversation continued as they finished their drinks and had dinner. Jane was from Baltimore, it turned out. They were just finishing their dessert when Jane's husband came in.

"Well, Lieutenant, we meet again," said Major Howard.

Ed leaped to his feet. "Yes, Sir, Major. Your wife was kind enough to allow me to use one side of her booth. The place was jammed when I came in. Let me get you a drink, Sir."

"No thanks, Lieutenant. We have to go—we have company coming for the evening. Thank you for keeping Jane company," the major said.

"My pleasure, Sir. She's almost as enthusiastic about Pittsburgh as I am," Ed responded.

"It's a city with a lot to offer," responded the Major. "Well, Jane, if you're ready, let's move out. See you again."

"I hope so, Sir. Goodnight, Jane. Thanks again."

"I enjoyed it, Ed. Goodnight," she said, flashing that beautiful smile again.

After they left, Ed paid his bill and carried his drink to the bar, hoping to find someone he knew to talk with. Only one stool was unoccupied, so he took it. On his left was a rather plump, fifty-ish woman, talking energetically to the man to her left. To Ed's right was a young second lieutenant. As soon as Ed had ordered another Scotch, the lieutenant turned toward him and, with a little trouble focusing his eyes, said, "Washername, fly-boy?"

Ed saw that the lieutenant was not wearing wings, and had no ribbons over the breast pocket of his blouse. "My name's Ed; what's yours?"

"Wilsh . . . Wilsh . . ." the lieutenant tried to reply. "Oh, hell. Call me Willy. Washa diff'rence?"

"Okay, Willy. Let's have some coffee."

"Don' wan' coffee, wan' 'nother drink."

"You don't need another drink; you're already smashed!"

"There y' go. You goddam fly-boys are all hoshots. Wanna tell us all wha' t'do. Gripesh my ash!"

"I'm not telling you what to do. You don't want coffee, you don't get coffee. It's your head, not mine. I'll be glad it's yours in the morning."

"Yeah, you son-a-biches. You get all the glory. All we hear 'bout is fly-boys thish, fly-boys thash! Like us guys in Supply didn't deserve shome cred't. How could you fly if we didn't get shtuff for you? We're 'portant too. Don' you forget it."

"Sure you are. Nobody says you aren't. Listen, Willy, if all you want to do is bitch about your bad treatment, find another ear. I don't want to hear about it."

"Goddam fly-boys. Don' wanna lishen to the truth."

"Okay, Willy. I'm moving to another seat."

"Don' go. Won't say any more bout' it, okay?"

"Okay," Ed said, getting back on the stool. "Now, how about that coffee?"

"Right. Coffee."

Ed ordered two cups of coffee, black, and he and his new acquaintance sipped it as it cooled. Ed ordered more, and before long, Willy began to get his brain partially unscrambled.

Ed wasn't ready to return to the base, so for the next hour, he and Willy chatted about their home lives, what they did, and what they hoped to do when the war was over. Ed mentioned his interest in singing, and Willy told him he'd made up a song, or at least part of one. "I didn't know what time it was," he crooned, and several more phrases. It sounded familiar to Ed, but he just said, "Sounds pretty good."

"My name isn't Willy," Willy said. "It's Wilson, Wilson Cummingham. I live in New York City."

"Okay, Wilson," Ed said, shaking his hand.

"Just call me Will," Wilson said.

"Okay, whatever you say."

Once he was half sober, and off his gripes about the glorification of fliers, Wilson was an interesting and entertaining conversationalist. He'd graduated from Columbia and hoped to return for a master's degree in education. He wanted to be a school administrator.

Ed looked at his watch. "Hey, it's 21:30. Time I headed back to the base. Goodnight, Wilson. Nice talking to you," and he started toward the door.

"Goodnight, fly-boy," Wilson said. Then as Ed was about at the door, he called out, "Wait a minute, Ed," and, not quite steady on his feet, he caught up to Ed. "You have to be in at a certain time or something? You have some special duties? Most of you guys stay in later than this. You don't have to go back to the base, fly-boy. You can stay in town."

"What? And pay for a hotel room? Forget it! My bunk is fine, and a lot cheaper. All my stuff is there, and breakfast at the Officers' Mess is great."

"No. You don't have to stay at a hotel. I have an apartment in town, right near here. We can get something to eat, have a couple more drinks, and sack out at my place. What do you say?"

The idea of not having to ride back to the base and then come back in the next day appealed to Ed, as did a late snack. "Well, okay. But no more drinks. I don't want to have to carry you home. So coffee, okay?"

"Okay, let's go."

Wilson led the way to a little lunch counter he said wasn't far from his place, and they had coffee and doughnuts, then walked to the apartment. Small it was: tiny kitchen, bathroom, and bed-sitting room. "All I can afford on a second lieutenant's pay, without flight pay, of course."

"Don't start on that again, or I'm taking off."

"Just needling, just needling."

Ed used the bathroom, stripped down to his shorts, and got into one side of the large, double bed. Wilson put on pajamas and got into the other side.

Ed dozed off quickly. He was almost sound asleep when he felt something across his legs. Startled, he was immediately wide awake. It was one of Wilson's legs. Ed had known homosexuals, had even been approached by one or two during his singing career, but this was the first time he'd ever found himself in bed with one if, in fact, Wilson was one. Not being sure, and not interested in making accusations, he said, "Hey, Wilson! You're on my side of the bed!" No response. Ed moved his legs abruptly and said, "You're drunk, Wilson. I'm not one of your sleep-over girlfriends. Go to sleep."

The response was a mumbled, "Yeah, drunk," and the leg was removed. Ed had trouble getting to sleep again, and spent the rest of the night tossing and turning. No other contact was made. Ed was uneasy about confronting Wilson in the morning, so as soon as dawn began to break, he got up as quietly as he could, put on his uniform and left the apartment.

The air outside was refreshingly cool and clear, so he walked to the center of town, found an early-opening coffee shop, and had some breakfast before returning to the base. He never saw Wilson again, and never could answer the question in his own mind: "Was it a homosexual advance, or was it incidental contact by a man used to having the entire bed to himself?" He decided it was not his business, and that it didn't matter one way or the other. He put it out of his mind; there were more important things to think about.

Back at the base, he showered and sacked out until noon chow, where he met Chuck. He was full of enthusiasm about his date. "Had a great time," he said. "She has a neat roommate. Want a date?"

"Maybe. I haven't had any luck on my own. Met a really beautiful older woman. Had dinner with her, but she's married to a major here at the base. He came on the scene just as we finished dinner," Ed answered.

"Did he chew you out for messing around with his wife?" Chuck asked.

"Naw, it was okay. He had given me a ride in, on his way to a meeting in town. Anyway, the place I went to eat, you know, Foley's, was jammed. I saw this neat-looking lady sitting alone in a booth, so I asked her if I could use the other side. She didn't mind, and I bought her a drink. Then, since her husband seemed to have stood her up, we had dinner together. She told me about her husband, and I realized he was the guy who gave me the ride. We talked about everything. She knows Pittsburgh! Can you beat that?"

"Oh, God! Can't you get that stupid city out of your mind? Nothing else to talk about with a beautiful lady?" Chuck snapped.

"You can take a man out of Pittsburgh, but you can't take Pittsburgh out of the man," Ed asserted. Chuck rolled his eyes up toward the ceiling, and Ed went on, "I'm proud of that city, and it's been given a bad rap by everybody who has never been there."

"Okay, so you had a decent evening on your own, but no date. You picked up a lady, but she was already taken. Nice going. Then you came back here."

"Well, as a matter of fact, no," Ed replied.

"Aha! The husband never showed up, and you went home with the beautiful married woman. Well, that's progress," Chuck said, laughing.

"No such luck! The major showed up and they left right away. Had company coming. I went to the bar and got talking to a lieutenant in Supply. He has an apartment in town, so I slept there," Ed said.

"Oh?" was all Chuck said in response.

"Come on! Nothing like you're thinking. I was about to say that I had to admit I missed you, you no good bastard, but I'm not going to say it now."

"Yeah, yeah. Don't get mushy on me. We've been together a while; we get along pretty well. But who knows what lies ahead. Any orders posted?" Chuck asked.

"Not for you or for me, but lots are posted all right," Ed answered. "Hope ours come soon; I feel rusty. Think it'll all come back when we get to fly again?"

"Probably will for me, but you? Not a chance. You faked your way this far, but this is the end of the line for you. You've had it. Soon as they see you try to handle a fighter, they'll take those wings off of you and give you a desk job," Chuck taunted.

"You're probably right. I think I can fly, but I'm not real sure."

"I know what you mean, I was just kidding. I have the same uncertain feeling. Probably because we've been used to flying every day, and now we've been off for a couple of weeks," Chuck said.

"Yeah, That has to be it. I'm really itching to get going again."

"Me too. Let's go over to the Officers' Club and see if there's any scuttlebutt."

"Good idea. Maybe we can find out who's winning the war."

"Fat chance. But let's go."

They learned only two things at the O.C. One was that all the other new pilots were as frustrated as they were. The other was that a lieutenant colonel on the permanent staff at the base had said that he understood that a new batch of orders would be posted the next day.

Chuck and Ed had a beer, then walked back to B.O.Q. On the way, Chuck said, "Hey, I'm taking Gloria out again tomorrow. If I call her, I think she'll fix you up with her roomie, even though I told her what you were like. What do you say?"

"What's she really like?" Ed wanted to know.

"Neat, Buddy. If I'd seen her first, I'm not sure I'd have made a move on Gloria. You'd really like her—she's sort of quiet, seems to do a lot of thinking. You'd fit together. How about it? Dinner, a little dancing. A walk around the campus, maybe some smooching," Chuck pressed.

"Okay, but if she's not as advertised, you're in big trouble, Ol' Pal o' mine," Ed said. "I'm not too good on dancing, but the rest sounds good."

"Great! I'll call as soon as we get to B.O.Q. If I can get a turn on the phone, that is."

"Okay, I'll be at my bunk reading. Come give me the sordid details," Ed said, as Chuck stopped at the pay phones on the veranda.

Chuck made the call and set up the date. They would pick up the two girls at 17:30. Not an elaborate evening: dinner at a place the girls knew in town, where a little dance combo played evey night. Return to the campus. Walk around, chat, then say goodnight.

It sounded good to Ed, and he said so. The friends said goodnight and went to their bunks. Ed went to sleep, wondering what Elizabeth would be like, and more importantly, whether his name would be on orders posted the next day, where he would be sent, what he would fly.

"Hey, Ed. Wake up. Get dressed—there're new orders posted. Let's get over to headquarters and see if we got lucky."

Ed jumped out of bed and got into his uniform. He and Chuck sprinted to the large bulletin board in front of headquarters. A crowd of eager pilots was milling about, each trying to find the orders with his name on it. Ed and Chuck separated so each could search through different sets of orders for his name. They finally made it to the bulletin board. Ed went through all sets of mimeographed orders tacked to his half of the board and found nothing. He started working through the orders posted on Chuck's half.

"I found it!" Chuck yelled. "Here it is. We're both on the same set." Ed shoved his way to where Chuck was holding his place, his finger on the page. Ed got to a position beside Chuck and, skipping the usual military jargon, read from the page where Chuck was pointing.

"The below named officers will report at the earliest possible date to Sarasota Air Field for fighter plane indoctrination and training," and on the list below was Sparks, Charles M., 0-937221 and Thorne, Edward J., 0-817132.

"Yahoo!" Ed yelled. "Finally! Let's get some breakfast and celebrate."

They made their way through the crowd and to the Officers' Mess. Over eggs, sausage, hashbrown potatoes and grits, plus coffee, they exulted together, both that they had finally been assigned and that, once again, they would be together.

"What should we do about our dates?" Ed asked, as their excitement subsided.

"I don't know. The orders say at earliest possible date," Chuck replied. "I guess that means that we should leave today. It's still early. I'm not sure where Sarasota is, but I think it's about halfway down the west coast of Florida. Let's finish up here and call the Greyhound station, see if we can get a bus this afternoon."

"Right, I'll do that. You'd better call Gloria and tell her what happened, okay?" Ed said.

"Will do," Chuck answered, downing the last of his coffee. "Let's go use the pay phones before there's a long line." They did, surprised to find two of the six booths empty, unusual for a Sunday morning.

Ed found that there would be a bus leaving at 15:05 that afternoon, arriving at Sarasota at 21:00 that evening. Chuck said that Gloria was disappointed, but Elizabeth was not, since she hated blind dates. "How the hell she knew you're blind as a bat beats me, I never told her. Come to think of it, how'd you get to be a pilot when you're blind?"

"You jerk. Too bad we're both going to Sarasota. I hoped I'd finally be rid of you, but I guess they know you can't make it without my help. Let's go pack our stuff. The Air Corps will move our foot lockers; we have to take the rest. So let's get going. We can have lunch in town."

"Right. Let's go."

The bus arrived right on time, and Ed and Chuck stepped off to find Sarasota a lively town, even at 21:00 on a Sunday evening. Many men in uniform, many walking with girls or young ladies, and a few women in uniform, too, seemed to be everywhere. They walked a block and a half from the bus station and stopped in front of a busy restaurant/cocktail lounge.

"Shall we eat, then get a cab and report to the base? Or shall we take our chances on getting something to eat out there?" Chuck asked.

Ed answered, "I don't know about you, but I'm starving. Let's eat."

They stepped into the crowded restaurant and almost immediately a voice called out, "Ed! Ed Thorne! Over here." Ed looked and saw Bill Ryan, who had offered him a ride from Spence to Tallahassee. He was sitting at a table with an attractive young woman.

"Hi, Bill," Ed said, shaking hands. "Do you know Chuck Sparks?"

Bill and Chuck shook hands, and Bill said, "Meet my wife, Mary; Ed and Chuck. Sit down. This is a table for four."

They accepted the invitation. Ed said, "We just got off the bus. When did you get here?"

"About three hours ago. As soon as I saw the orders this morning, I drove in and picked up Mary, and we hit the road," Bill replied.

"We were at Tallahassee all that time, and I never saw you. How come?" Ed asked.

Bill responded, "Everybody's at Tallahassee! But I'm lucky because Mary had a room in town, and we have our car here. I wasn't at the base any more than I had to be. When you're done eating, I'll leave Mary off at the Orange Blossom Hotel, where we have a room, then we can drive out to the field and check in. Okay?"

"Great," Ed said. "Any idea what we'll be flying out there?"

"I hear it'll be P-40s," Bill said.

"P-40s, eh?" Chuck said. "Too bad, Ed."

"Why too bad?" Mary asked.

Ed replied, "I keep dreaming about the P-51. I've got my heart set on that plane. Guess they're too new to be used in training. That still leaves me hoping to be assigned to a group that's flying them in combat. This looks like quite a town, Bill. How is it?"

"Well, we haven't been here long enough to know. Seems like it's just the way it looks tonight. Lots of girls, good restaurants, and too many servicemen. I think most of the guys know this is the last stop before combat, so they're out for a last fling," Bill responded.

"Well, guess we should join them. Who's for a drink?" Ed said. Just then a waiter came and took their drink orders: three Scotch and sodas, and a glass of sherry, and their dinner orders.

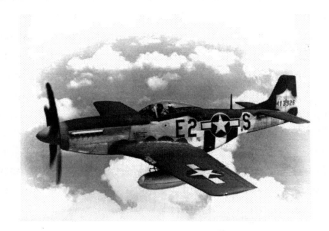

21

Ed, Chuck, and Bill reported to Sarasota Air Base, and were assigned places in the B.O.Q. Unlike at Tallahassee, each had his own small room. Also, unlike officers in the movies, they were not assigned "bat boys" to shine their shoes and look after their clothing and clean their rooms. As Bill observed, "There's a war on, guys, or hadn't you heard?"

They found a bulletin board outside one of the doors, and there was located a list of names, including all three of theirs, indicating that they were to report to a Captain Fillmore on the flight line promptly at 09:00. "Good we didn't wait until tomorrow to leave Tallahassee," Chuck said.

After showering and shaving, all three went to bed to sleep soundly. Ed, at least, dreamt again of the time when he'd be flying P-51s.

Promptly at 06:30, Ed was up. He dressed in suntans and went to get Chuck and Bill out of their sacks. They were both up and ready for breakfast. They headed for Officers' Mess, where they found good food in abundance. "Wonder if we'll get chow like this overseas," Ed said.

"Not likely," Bill responded. "But I guess it depends on where we wind up."

Chuck said, "I don't know. Seems to me in the movies all combat fliers do is fly and drink. Maybe we won't have chow at all."

"You're nuts, Buddy," Ed said. "The movies make everything different from reality. I'll bet there are plenty of guys in combat who don't drink at all."

"Maybe this Captain Fillmore has been in combat. We can ask him," Chuck said.

Bill said, "I have a lot of things I want to ask about, but food isn't one of them."

"Me, too," Ed said. "Wonder if we should put on our flight suits? The posted list didn't say."

"I think we should," Bill replied. "If we're going to fly, then good, we'll be dressed for it. If not, what have we lost?"

"Good," Chuck said, and they returned to their rooms to change.

Three other new pilots joined Chuck, Bill, and Ed reporting to Captain Fillmore. "Gentlemen," the captain said, "I'm going to introduce you to an airplane that is one of the worst and one of the best still flying combat today. One of the worst because she's so hot and unforgiving that some pilots call her 'The Killer.' One of the best because she is hot, and, once you master her, she'll do just about anything you ask her to do. In the right hands, the P-40 is a match for the best the Japs can put up, and she's been known to hold her own with the Germans' 190 and 109. But she's temperamental. She has to be maintained, and when she's been wrung out in combat, like these we have here have been, she gets warped, especially her wings, and that makes her unpredictable.

"She's hot because she has less wing surface for her size and weight than other fighters. If you try to land at an air speed less than 120, without flaps, she may kill you. She stalls without warning. Since she loves the ground, if she stalls near the surface, there's nothing you can do about it. You're going to crash. I recommend wheel landings and full flaps. Anything else is suicide. But when you lower the flaps, she'll balloon like crazy. So, if you have a long—very long—runway, come in low and hot, no flaps, and fly her right down on to the runway. That is, after your first couple of landing attempts. Those had better be with flaps. You'll probably have to pull up and go around a few times until you get the feel of how she behaves with flaps. Make a couple of landings with flaps, then decide on with or without for subsequent landings.

"With the warped wings our 40s have, when you put them into a dive, they'll try to twist themselves away from your control, putting you in a spin. Be sure you have plenty of air under you before you try diving. But give her a workout after you get the feel of her. Remember, though, no snap rolls! Try that, and you'll not only be landing without flaps, you'll be landing without wings.

"She has a great engine. Allison 12-cylinder inline, and once you get her in the air and up to speed, she is very responsive. But give her plenty of throttle for take-off, or you'll run out of runway. She'll vibrate like hell, and you'll think you're giving her too much, but gun the guts out of her, and hold her down as far down the runway as you can.

"These babies have seen lots of action in the Pacific, so treat them with respect. Get the feel of them before you do any aerobatics. She won't forgive you. If you make a mistake, it may be your last mistake.

"That's a lot to swallow in one dose, but I wanted you to have some idea about her before you fly her. Any questions?"

"Yes, Sir. Do we get to fly them today?"

"That's what you're here for; you're pilots aren't you? Soon as I give you each a cockpit check, you'll be off. Any other questions?"

"Where'd you have your combat time?"

"In the Pacific. Okay, let's get started."

The captain took each one of the six, in turn, up on the wing of a P-40, showed him where everything was, then told him to call the Tower and get her in the air.

Ed was third, after Bill and one of the other three. "Use the rudder bars to keep the nose straight down the runway, Ed. She has a hell of a lot of torque. When you get near take-off speed, the warp of the wings starts to fight you too. Don't let anything pass. Correct everything right now. If you don't, she'll mess you up. She'll do what she wants if you aren't on top of everything, keeping her going your way. Okay? Get your clearance, and good flying. Take her up to 1,500 feet and feel her out. About an hour ought to do it."

Ed switched on the radio. This was the first time he'd used a throat mike, so he had to get used to pressing the two small plates to his throat before he could make contact with the Tower. Then he was cleared to start and taxi to runway 180, and to call again before taking the runway.

He strapped himself in, moved the stick and rudder bars, watching the control surfaces move as he did so, then started the engine. Its powerful throb put him in a state of high excitement. Here he was, at last, in a real fighter plane, and one that had been in combat. Controlling his excitement, he released the brakes, made sure he was clear, and increased the throttle. The 40 eagerly responded with a quick move forward. Ed used the right brake and turned right toward the strip that led to runway 180. Everything he did seemed like a new peak experience. All his senses were sharper than ever. He seemed to see more, hear more, feel more.

Zigzagging down the strip, keeping an eye on the engine temperature gauge, he felt on top of the world. "This is almost it," he thought exultantly.

At the edge of the runway, he turned the plane into the wind to keep the inline engine from overheating, and stopped. The Tower gave him the altimeter setting, 33.2, and cleared him to take off. Remembering what he had learned from Lieutenant Murphy, as well as what Captain Fillmore had said, he released the brakes, added throttle, and went to the center of the runway. There, he applied the brakes again, held the stick in his gut and pushed the throttle forward until the roar of the engine and the vibration of the airplane seemed nearly unbearable. Then, releasing the brakes, he felt his back pressing against the seat back and his head pushing against the headrest, as the P-40 leaped forward.

All the way down the runway, Ed fought the powerful torque, pushing hard on the right rudder bar as the plane kept trying to swerve left off the runway. The tail came up quickly as the powerful engine propelled him forward. He eased the stick forward to stay on the runway as long as possible. Then, moving the stick slightly back, he felt the wheels leave the runway, and he retracted them immediately. He cleared the end of the runway, but the countryside ahead looked clear of obstruction, so he kept the plane level, about 15 feet above the ground. Speed was building rapidly. When the air speed indicator reached 240, he pulled back on the stick, and the P-40 screamed upward. When air speed dropped to 180, he pushed the stick forward to hold the ship in a more gradual climb; at the same time, he eased back on the throttle. For the first time he realized that he wasn't fighting torque any more as much as he was fighting the effects of the warped wings. He attempted to adjust the trim tabs, but they had no noticeable effect.

The altimeter showed 10,000 almost before lie realized it. He leveled off and pulled the throttle back to cruising. Feeling the plane out, trying to get used to its characteristics and responses, he tried some gentle turns, then some figure-eights. "Man, this thing may be beat up, but its reponses are quick. Every move of the stick or rudder bars gets an instant response. I can see what the captain meant. She's almost too quick to respond at speed. If I give her too much rudder, she gets into too tight a turn too soon. Got to play the stick and rudders like fine-tuned musical instruments, just enough but not too much. Have to read her every second, stay on top of every move. Let's try a dive, and see how the warped wings act on it," he said to himself, thrilling to every move the plane made.

To be sure he had enough air under him, he advanced the throttle and pulled the nose up. In seconds he was at 15,000 feet. "Can't stay here long without oxygen," he thought, and put the nose down for a dive. At 10,000 feet he was going 320 mph, faster than he had ever gone before, and he couldn't keep from rolling. The warped wings had an increasing effect as his speed increased. For a few scary moments, he wasn't sure he could get full control. He cut the throttle all the way back and, forcing the left rudder bar all the way in to counter the roll to the right, which threatened to become a spin, he hauled back on the stick. The airplane shrieked in protest, and vibrated madly, but the nose slowly came up. When he was straight and level again the altimeter showed 1,500 feet.

"Wow! What a ride!" Ed exclaimed, sweat rolling from under his helmet. "Flying a fighter is everything I dreamed it would be, but this baby needs careful handling. She took control for a while there."

He climbed to 10,000 feet again, then levelled off. Keeping his air speed under 300 mph, he went into a shallow dive. Pulling back on the stick, he went up and over in a loop. No problem, so he did an Immelman. "Sweet," he thought. A barrel roll and three successive slow rolls, and he felt he was getting to know the airplane.

"Better try some stalls," he thought. "Need to know how she feels when she stalls." He climbed to 12,000 feet. There he cut the throttle back and pulled the nose up. No stall at 120 mph, but a fraction of a second later, at 117 mph, the stall came without warning. The nose and the left wing dropped simultaneously, and he was spinning toward earth as if the P-40 was eager to get there.

He jammed the right rudder bar to the floor. It didn't seem to have any effect. All the responsiveness the ship had shown minutes before seemed gone. The airplane was heading to the ground, and he had no control. He kept the rudder pressed to the floor. Then, as suddenly as the plane had stalled, the rudder took effect. It was so quick that Ed almost missed the split-second of time needed to pop the stick full forward and get into a dive. Shoving the stick and throttle forward at the same instant, he found himself in a power-dive and, again, fighting the warped-wing effect. Now, easing the throttle back and bringing the stick slowly back, he levelled off. "Thing falls like a rock; I lost 10,000 feet in a few seconds. That's scary. But I like this airplane; I have a feeling the P-51 will do a lot more than this one does."

Ed glanced at his watch and saw that he had exceeded the hour the captain had suggested, so he headed for the field. Getting clearance, he entered the pattern, and did a wheel landing with flaps, compensating for the ballooning when he lowered the flaps, and got the wheels on the runway at 110 mph.

"Everything you said about her is true," he said to the waiting Captain Fillmore as he climbed out of the cockpit. "I think I tasted all the good and bad characteristics she has."

"Yeah, I guess you did. When you stalled her out up there, I wasn't sure you'd get her out. What altitude were you when you stalled her?" the captain asked.

"Thank God I was at 12,000. Any less, I doubt I'd be talking to you right now."

"Thought so. More time and you'll get a better feel for what she's going to do, but you did fine. How'd you like her?"

"She's something! I really liked flying her—makes all the trainers I've flown seem like something from another century. But, it's a good thing you briefed us on her before we flew her."

"That's why I did it; I'd be sending you all to an early grave if I didn't. And we need *live* pilots, not dead ones. That's it for today. You'll get more air time tomorrow. Got to get you fellows enough air time to qualify for flight pay."

"Yes, Sir. We've all been without flight pay too long," Ed said. "See you tomorrow," and headed for B.O.Q.

Ed walked to his room, elated. Stripping off his flight suit and underclothes, he took a leisurely hot shower, reviewing his flight in the 40 step by step. "Had a few hairy moments there," he thought, "but I whipped them, I'm a pilot! I'm a FIGHTER pilot!" Although he knew that he still had a lot to learn, he was in an exultant mood.

Just as he shut off the water and stepped out to dry off, there was a loud knock on the door, followed by a loud voice calling, "Lieutenant Thorne! Open up, or I'll break it down!"

Ed recognized the voice and yelled back, "Open it yourself, you stupid redhead! Or don't you know how to turn a doorknob?" He pulled on his undershorts just as the door flew open and Red Hunt burst into his room.

"You're out of uniform, my lad," Red said, "Is that any way to greet your superior when he comes to see you?"

Ed responded, "Sit down and shut up. When you want to visit me, send in your card with my manservant, and I'll be properly attired." He finished pulling on his shirt and trousers, then came out of the latrine to grab Red's hand.

"Thought you'd show up here," Red said. "Why can't I ever shake off jerks like you? How many P-40s do you plan to destroy before they get rid of you here? Let me know when you're scheduled to be in the air, and I'll stay on the ground."

"I don't know why I'm asking this," Ed said. "Maybe I'll be lucky and you'll say 'no.' How about cutting the crap and going into town with me for a drink and dinner? Or do you have big plans?"

Red responded, "Sad to say, I have no plans. Get a tie on and let's go! Sarasota is pilots' paradise. I haven't bought myself a drink since I got here. These people love us."

Ed tied his tie, gave his hair a quick brush, and they headed for the gate. The cab dropped them at what Red said was the best restaurant/bar he'd found. They barely got in the door before a white-suited man, sitting with a lady, called out, "Over here, Lieutenants, I'm buying. Come on and sit down, tell me what you want to drink."

They sat, saying Scotch and soda, and the man called a waiter over to take the order. "I'm Roger Rodway, and this is Thelma, my wife." Ed and Red shook hands with each. Mr. Rodway was slim and elegant-looking, like a movie star portraying a Southern gentleman. Mrs. Rodway was a good-looking woman, appeared fiftyish, and slightly plump, but very stylish in dress, make-up and hair. Both Red and Ed liked her immediately, feeling comfortable with her.

Mr. Rodway seemed somewhat self-important. After the introductions, he reached for the slim cigar he had placed in an ashtray. Then he put it down, pulled a packet of cigars from his jacket pocket and offered them to Ed and Red. They both declined with thanks.

Their drinks came, and Mr. Rodway said, "Here's to the Army Air Corps, and especially its fighter pilots." All four touched glasses and tasted their drinks.

Mr. Rodway, it emerged in conversation, was a native of Georgia, where he owned a large steel fabricating factory outside of Atlanta. His business was in deep trouble until he converted part of his factory to aluminum fabrication and landed a lucrative contract with the Air Corps for the manufacture of aircraft components. Actually, the contract was with aircraft manufacturing companies who, in turn, had the contracts with the Air Corps. Either way, Mr. Rodway told them, that conversion and contract saved his business. Now, everything looked better than it had just a year before.

Suddenly he yanked the cigar out of his mouth, and angrily stubbed it out in the ashtray. "I hate these things," he expostulated. "I've been smoking them so I'd seem more like an important executive. But I'm done with that!" He took the remaining cigars out of his pocket and broke each one into the ashtray.

Mrs. Rodway beamed, "Oh Roger! I'm so glad. They smell up the whole house, your clothes, the car, everything. I'm happy that you're giving them up."

"Yes, my dear. I'm happy about it too." She leaned over and kissed his cheek.

Smiling broadly, Mr. Rodway engaged Ed and Red in conversation, and insisted that he would buy their dinners. They protested, but he insisted, saying, "I know you fellows don't get paid anything like you're worth, so let me do this little thing. All right?" They agreed, and they all ordered their dinners.

Conversation was lively, with Mrs. Rodway showing a fine sense of humor. This was a mature couple who obviously loved each other. Both of the young men enjoyed their company, and were sorry when Mrs. Rodway said, "Oh, Roger. We must go. George and Helen are coming to see us at our hotel. If we don't get a move on, they'll arrive and we won't be there."

Ed and Red thanked both of them, and they left after paying the check, with Mr. Rodway leaving word with the waiter that he was to serve the lieutenants anything they wanted. He would then come in and pay up the next day.

Ed and Red had another Scotch each, exchanging news of what had been happening to them in the months since last seeing each other. Finally, Red said, "How do you like these tired, beat-up death planes we're flying here?"

"Important thing is they're fighters. It's a good feeling. Even the danger from the warped wings gives an extra feeling of being almost in combat. I like it. How about you?" Ed replied.

"I guess you're right. I've come close to tearing one up three times; I haven't got the feel of her yet. Too unpredictable for my taste. I think I'd prefer something a little more consistent in response. These things are crazy. No two alike, so it's like learning a whole new plane every time you take a different one up."

"Maybe I'll find that too, but I've only flown one, and it was a thrill even when I got in trouble when it suddenly stalled out and tried to spin on me."

Red responded, "You were lucky to get out of that in your first P-40 flight. Lot of guys haven't been so lucky. That's why the name 'killer planes.' Whatever you do, feel each one out before you try any hot stuff."

"After today's flight, I sure will," Ed replied. "But man, it's a real airplane, not a trainer. A real combat plane. What I've always wanted to fly."

"Right. Just don't fly it so it's your flying coffin, Ol' Pal," Red said. "I know how temperamental they are, believe me. Don't give them a chance to knock you off."

"Okay, Red, I believe you. I'll take care," Ed answered.

"You ready to head back? I fly early tomorrow," Red said. "I only have one more week here, then back to Tallahassee for a week's leave, then an overseas assignment."

"Yeah, let's go." The waiter wouldn't accept any money for their last drinks, so they left a hefty tip and returned to the base.

Ed and his friends flew two or three hours a day at the base. Since this was their only duty, they spent a great deal of time in town. It was lively there. There were several bars with small bands and dance floors, and many restaurants, lounges, and movie theaters.

The civilians were extremely patriotic, and saw it as their duty to treat everyone they met in uniform. The pilots were receiving flight pay for the first time, so none of them had any shortage of money. Patriotic spirit characterized Sarasota's young ladies, too, so getting dates was easy. The whole town seemed to be celebrating.

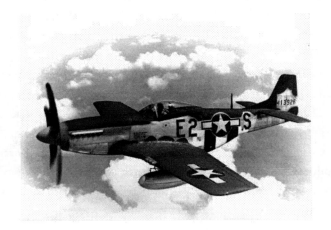

22

For the most part, except for scheduling, they found that they did their flying at will. Captain Fillmore usually made a few suggestions, then left them to themselves. For example, the second day of P-40 flying, he told his four pilots, "Take your ship up to 20,000 feet and wring her out. See what she'll do. You'll need to use oxygen, so put on the mask, and turn on the valve at 10,000. It's a demand system—it feeds oxygen only when you inhale. Get used to it. You'll have to use it in combat. Any military flying 10,000 or above must be done on oxygen. I know some of you guys smoke; not smart in an airplane. But under no circumstances light up when the oxygen is on. Good way to get blown to hell. Okay, do your ground checks, get clearance and take off. Come back when fuel gauges show one-fourth on both wing tanks. Keep the tanks even by switching back and forth. Will help with trim and balance, which is bad enough in these ships anyway."

Ed saw that the P-40 assigned to him was not the same one he'd had the preceding day. He made a more careful ground check than he had the day before, then climbed in and did his cockpit check. Since many flights out of Sarasota were made out over the Gulf of Mexico, all pilots were required to wear Mae Wests as well as the usual parachute. Ed had decided that he would go out over the Gulf, so he made sure that his Mae West was fastened on securely.

Getting clearance from the Tower, Ed started up, taxied to runway 176, checked his mags and took off. About two miles south of the field, he was at 18,000 feet. He turned to a heading of 270 and in moments was over the Gulf. He had turned on his oxygen at just under 10,000 feet, and the plane seemed responsive as he moved the controls. Certainly, the Allison engine was quick to react each time he pushed the throttle forward.

He levelled off at 22,000 feet, cutting back on the throttle. Noticing that the fuel gauge for the left tank was down to three-fourths, he switched to the right tank. To feel the plane out for peculiar reactions, he did a half-roll, stopping with the wings in a vertical position; then, adding throttle, he began to pull back on the stick, slowly tightening his turn, wanting to see if there'd be any warning shudder or tremble before the plane stalled. Just as he was feeling pleasant surprise at how tight he'd been able to pull the turn, without warning, the P-40 flipped as it stalled. Once again, he found himself plunging earthward with no sense of control. He went with what the airplane was trying to do; that is, go into a spin. Then, sensing the right moment, he did just as he had done the day before, getting the spin stopped and the plane into a controlled dive. When speed built up to the point where he could feel the effects of the warped wings, he eased back on the throttle and pulled the stick a little toward himself, then a little more, until he was straight and level again. Since he'd had plenty of altitude, this one was not as hairy as the the day before. Still, he said to himself, "Touchy sucker, aren't you?"

Again adding throttle, he regained the 8,000 feet he'd lost. "Wonder how any of the guys who flew these in combat survived. Flipping out like that, they'd be sitting targets until they regained control. Who needs that?"

Now he put the nose down, picking up air speed, but watching not to gain so much speed that the warped wings would make the ship uncontrollable. He pulled her up into a vertical climb, then over on her back and down, completing the loop. "She does everything for you, but you have to respect her—just fly her. I think I'm getting a feel for her."

Next, he put the nose on a cloud just above the horizon, and pushed the throttle full forward to gain speed again, this time without a dive. At air speed 300, he did a slow roll, having a little trouble keeping the nose on the point due to the wing warp. "But not bad," he thought. Feeling more confident, he did a series of slow rolls, then a sloppy barrel roll. "Man, this is great!" he said to himself. Without diving, he pulled the nose up, added full throttle, hung it on the prop and pulled over, holding the P-40 inverted for a few seconds, until the engine began to run unevenly, then pulled over into a dive to complete the loop.

Seeing the right gas tank needle down to nearly one-half, he switched to the left tank again. Now, he began a series of figure eights, pulling the turns tighter and tighter until again she stalled, he got control, then regained his altitude, and did the same thing over. "I think I'm beginning to sense when she's about to stall," he said, putting the plane into a circle, pulling the turn tighter and tighter. "There it is!" he exclaimed. "It isn't much, but there's a little change in her feel just before the stall." Now he found he could anticipate the stalls, just as he had learned to do in the Stearman, so he did a lot more tight turns, easing up on the stick just in time to prevent the stall. From talking to pilots who had flown fighters in combat, as well as reading about fighter tactics, he knew that the flier who could make the tightest turns in a combat situation was often the one who won out. He also knew that turning so that the plane's torque assisted the turn gave the pilot of that plane an advantage. He schooled himself, in an imagined situation where an enemy fighter attacked him, to turn left if he had a choice. The torque-assisted turns were easier and tighter.

"You're all right baby," he said to the P-40. "A guy just has to learn how much you'll take, and until I get me a P-51, you'll do." From then on, flying the P-40 was fun for him. As he had begun to sense during his earlier training, a fighter pilot's relationship with his plane is very much like an intimate love affair: they get to know each other so completely that they are like a single being. They become one.

As his two gas gauges moved toward one-fourth, Ed pointed the nose east toward the base. On the way, he practiced the spiral fighter landing that Lieutenant Murphy had taught them, using clouds as airfields. "Man, am I glad I made it through the cadet program! Flying this kind of airplane is what it was all for."

He was tempted to do a fighter landing at the base, but traffic in the pattern was too heavy. Besides, he figured he'd be called on the carpet if he did, maybe get grounded. He didn't want that, just when flying was getting to be great. He got clearance and did a normal landing, then taxied to his regular parking place.

The other three were waiting for him. He was the last one in. "I'm really beginning to like this ship," Ed said to the others.

"Forget it," Bill said.

Chuck added, "The son of a bitch tried to kill me up there!"

"Come on. You just have to sense what she's going to do," Ed responded. "We got along great after I began to sense that."

"Bullshit!" Chuck came back. "I saw you flip out twice up there."

"Right! But no more after that; that's how I learned to feel it coming," Ed replied.

"Not me. Sooner I get past this airplane, the better," the other three agreed.

"Guess I'm the only born fighter pilot in the bunch," Ed said.

Captain Fillmore had been standing back, just far enough to hear what was being said, without interfering. Now he came closer and said, "Just don't get cocky, Lieutenant. Maybe you had one of the more stable ones today. It is true, though. You fly a plane and get to know what she's going to do. Rest of you will get it too; don't give up. The plane is out-dated, but she still deserves a lot of respect. Okay, see you tomorrow."

They all went to B.O.Q., showered and dressed, then went to Officers' Mess for noon chow. The base had a skeet shooting range which pilots could use any time, so Ed and Chuck spent three hours there, then looked up Red Hunt, and the three spent some time shooting pool and playing ping-pong in the Officers' Club. They had evening chow together, then each went to his room to write or read.

The next morning, Captain Fillmore said to a larger group of six cadets, "It's time you learned some fighter formation flying. As you already know, the fighter flight is made up of four planes: the flight leader, his wingman, the element leader, and his wingman. The normal formation is like this, and he drew a sketch on his clipboard:

"That is the formation used for getting to a target, or before getting into a combat zone, or getting attacked by bandits. For those of you who don't know, 'bandit' is the term used for enemy fighters, as opposed to 'bogies,' which are unidentified aircraft. It is also the basic formation for cross-country flying or bomber escorting.

"Then there are two other formations. One is all four planes abreast," and he indicated this on the clipboard. This is used on a strafing mission, say across an enemy airdrome. The idea is, if you fly a normal formation, the enemy gunners protecting the target area will aim at the leader, and probably hit the number three or number four man because the fighters will be moving very fast. When in the four-abreast formation, the unbreakable rule is NO ONE gets ahead of the others, NO ONE. If one does, the gunners will aim at him, and hit those behind. The guy who gets out in front is on everybody's shit list forever. Even his pals won't talk to him. One or more of the others in the flight probably won't come back. Don't ever do it!"

"The third formation is the inline one," and he put it on the clipboard. "This is used when the mission is to dive-bomb or skip-bomb a small target, say a bridge, or an oil or fuel storage tank. All four go in one at a time, out of the inline formation.

"The four-abreast is usually referred to as 'battle formation,' and you go into that when bandits, or suspected bandits, are sighted. If you don't have any questions, we'll go up and give some of this a try.

"I'm going to take each one of you up. I'll be in the lead plane, you'll be my wingman, I'll take off first, you'll take off as soon as I'm airborne. I'll turn left, you cut me off and come up on my left wing. Keep your radio on the frequency I give you. I'll tell you if you're too tight, or too far out. We want a tight formation. Your right wing should be inside my left wing. Your job is to keep it there by doing exactly what I do. We'll do single needle-width turns and easy climbs and dives until you get the hang of it. Later on, in a day or so, I'll take two of you up at once, then three. Then each of you will get a turn at flying leader, wingman, and element leader. Okay, Lieutenant Sparks, you're first."

Ed and the other five watched the captain and Chuck take off and make a two-plane formation. From a distance it looked easy and smooth, but they knew it would seem different when they had to do it.

"Crazy, isn't it?" Ed asked. "We've been absolutely forbidden to do any formation flying at all stages of our training. Now, two weeks into learning how to handle the hottest plane we've had to fly, and suddenly we're asked to do formation flying."

"Sure as hell is," Harry replied. "Sounds like it'll be a whole new ballgame now."

Jack said, "Sure does. We've never flown anywhere near another plane. How do you keep your head and eyes moving when you're tucked in tight to another plane?"

"Guess we'll find out. Wonder who's next? Here they come in," Ed said. He decided not to mention that he and Chuck actually had had a little formation flying, thinking maybe the others had not.

Captain Fillmore taxied up and stopped, but kept his engine running, facing into the wind to avoid overheating. He pointed to Ed, and Chuck taxied up, set the brakes and climbed out, leaving the engine running.

Ed climbed in and followed the captain down the taxi strip to the end of the runway. He watched the captain's plane roar down the runway. As soon as his wheels left the runway, Ed began his take-off run. He saw the captain start a climbing left turn and, as soon as he cleared the edge of the field, he started a tighter turn, keeping on full power. By the time the captain reached 2,000 feet, Ed was beside him.

At 5,000 feet the captain called Ed on the radio, saying, "Okay, Number Two, we have enough altitude, so come closer. Closer. Get that wing in here; tighten it up. Okay, that's better. Keep it that way."

Ed found that what looked easy in the movies was hard work. He was constantly working the rudder bars and jockeying the stick to stay close, but not touching. Until he matched the other plane's speed exactly, he found himself advancing and retarding the throttle again and again. He began to sweat. The captain kept telling him to tuck it in, to keep it steady. "Let me do the flying," he repeated. "You just keep your relative position. Don't try to fly independently." After fifteen minutes, Ed began to get the feel of it, and stopped over-correcting. Just as he began to feel confident about holding his position in straight-and-level flight, the captain said, "Okay, Number Two, you hold your position just like that, and I'll do a single needle-width turn to the left. Just keep an eye on me, and let your hands and feet do whatever is necessary to maintain your position."

They started the turn, and Ed held his position fairly well, but not smoothly. He found he had to cut back on the throttle to avoid having his right wing overtake the captain's left wing. Again, he began to get the feel of it, and to anticipate what he had to do. Next was a right turn, and this time he had to add throttle to avoid falling back.

"Okay, Number Two, just keep your position relative to me. Do what I do," the captain's voice said, as he put the nose down in a shallow dive. Now he pulled up, then turned sharply to the right in a climbing turn—a Chandelle. Ed was okay at first, then near the end of the 180-degree turn, he didn't use enough right rudder and got too far out to the left. "Get it in here! Got to do better than that, Number Two," the captain said.

As soon as Ed got his right wing tucked in again, the captain started another Chandelle, this time to the left. Ed sweated a lot, but he held his position.

"Okay, Lieutenant Thorne, good enough. Follow me home," the captain said and broke off toward the field. Ed followed him, and they landed and taxied back to where the other five were waiting. After re-fueling, Harry went up next, followed by Jack and the others.

"How'd it go, Buddy?" Chuck asked.

"Okay, I guess. I sure sweated that out. Seems so close after flying away from all other planes all through training," Ed answered.

"Yeah, I thought so too. Couple times I thought my wing would bump his," Chuck said.

"Mine too. Pretty scary. Haven't sweated so much since first time in Link," Ed said. Jack was looking worried, so Ed said, "Don't worry. You begin to get the hang of it; it's just rough at first. Anyway, the Captain's watching, and if your wing gets too close to his, he'll move his out of the way. He isn't anxious to bump up there either."

"Right, Jack," Chuck added. "It began to get easier even in the short time we were up there. Would've been a good thing, though, if we'd had some of this earlier."

"Probably didn't think we were good enough," Ed said, "and they were probably right. At least about you, Chuck."

"Don't give me that crap. You noticed who he picked first, didn't you?" Chuck shot back.

"Yeah. He wanted to get the slowest learner out of the way first," Ed replied.

When each of the six had had his turn, the captain surprised them by saying, "Okay, men. Take a two-hour break for chow, talk and think about this kind of flying and report back at 14:00 for more of the same."

This was a surprise because up until then they had been scheduled to fly only once a day. Talking excitedly about this new experience, they went to Officers' Mess, where the break time was over quickly. They reported back to the flight line, and spent the afternoon taking turns flying wingman to Captain Fillmore. The next day they followed the same schedule, flying morning and afternoon. But in the afternoon, they took turns flying on the captain's right wing instead of his left. With the experience they had accumulated, they made the adjustment easily.

On the following day, both sessions were taken up with the captain leading each wingman in increasingly difficult maneuvers, and their competence and confidence grew rapidly. They found that they could stay in position no matter what the captain did.

On succeeding days, as Captain Fillmore felt certain that each wingman could handle the position, he first added a second wingman, making one on each side. Later, he had a third join up, so there were the standard two elements, each pilot taking turns with the others in each position. This kept their interest and excitement high—new challenges every day.

Finally, on the Monday of the next week, the captain said, "Today I don't need to fly. Each of you will function as flight leader. Follow the same pattern I have been using to allow the other three to join up, then do easy maneuvers, increasing the difficulty as your time goes on. We'll do this today and tomorrow. Each of you will have two hours as leader. Any questions?" There were none, so he continued, "I drew your names out of a bowl at breakfast, and the order of flying as leader is this: Lieutenant Thorne, Lieutenant Marley, Lieutenant Sparks, Lieutenant Spinks," then he finished the list with the other two names. "Remember, you won't be the only ones in the air, so keep your heads and eyes moving. Don't concentrate so much on formation flying that you aren't aware of what's going on around you. You'll do that every day in combat, so learn to divide your attention in formation. Get a few miles away from the field and fly at about 10,000 feet. Okay, you're on your own. Good flying."

Ed was actually trembling with excitement as he did his ground and cockpit checks, and had trouble keeping his voice steady as he called the Tower for clearance. All set, he taxied out and took off, turning left after clearing the field. He saw Numbers Two and Three take off; then, after a few moments delay, Number Four. The trembling was gone as soon as he started down the runway. He continued a steady climbing turn to the left until Number Two joined him, then a single needle-width climbing turn to the right to give Number Three and especially Number Four a chance to catch up and join the formation. At 10,000 feet all were in place, so he levelled off.

With the thumb and forefinger of his left hand, Ed pressed the throat mike to his Adam's apple and said, "Okay, guys, this is Ed. We will be orange flight. I'll do a few easy turns and climbs and dives, then I'll just start making them harder and faster, without radio contact. Acknowledge." Two, Three, and Four said, "Roger" in turn, and Ed released the mike and returned his hand to the throttle.

Staying aware of the time so he wouldn't exceed the two-hour limit, Ed went through increasingly difficult turns, dives, Immelmans and Chandelles. He was pleased to see all three of the others stay with him without difficulty, although Number Four almost lost it when he pulled one left turn too tight. This was a good lesson for Ed. The guy flying Number Four will be in trouble if the leader makes turns too tight. "Probably be even worse for him if flying inline," he thought. "I guess the leader always has to be conscious of the effect his moves will have on the others."

When his watch showed they'd been up one hour and forty-five minutes, Ed turned toward the field. About a mile out, he signalled the others to get into the inline formation and spread out. Then he went into the pattern after getting clearance, and landed, followed by the others.

Captain Fillmore was waiting for them, binoculars dangling from his neck. "I watched you from the Tower," he said. "You did okay. A little too tight on that one turn, Ed. Almost lost your Number Four man. Got to keep them in mind when you're the leader."

"Yes, Sir, that was a mistake," Ed answered. This was the first time the captain had addressed any of them by his first name. Ed was excited by this, thinking it meant some sort of final acceptance by the captain. Perhaps a stamp of approval.

"Okay, men, take off for chow. Report back here at 13:00."

The afternoon was a repetition of the morning, with Jack leading, and Ed as Number Four, where he got a taste of what his own Number Four had put up with. As Jack tightened his turns, Ed nearly stalled out on one climbing turn as he tried to stay in position. "You can only force an airplane so far," he thought. "Then the airplane rebels, and you could be in trouble. I've learned that before, but this really drives it home."

The day after the last one of the six had his two-hour stint as leader, two more cadets joined the group. The captain said, "You'll probably never have to stay in that two-element formation when you're in a combat situation. Depending on the situation, you will either go into spread formation, abreast formation, or inline. If you encounter enemy fighters, staying in tight, two-element formation will be impossible. You will likely break up into spread formation, and if a real dog-fight develops, probably it will be nearly every man for himself, although you never are relieved of the obligation to watch out for your friends' tails.

"Today we're going to do a couple of new things. First, I've got permission for formation take-off. The runway isn't wide enough for a flight of four to go at once, so it will be elements in simultaneous take-offs. Each of you will have a turn being flight leader and wingman. Follow the same pattern we have been using. First element starts a slow climbing turn to the left as soon as clear of the field. Second element joins up. Circle the field, then come in one at a time, taxi around, and Number Two becomes leader and Number One becomes Number Four for the next take-off. Repeat until all four have flown each position once.

"That will finish this morning's flying. In the afternoon, I will lead all eight of you to the target range, and we will do some strafing. I'll brief you on that before we take off. Okay, get going."

Nobody had any problems with the simple two-plane take-offs. They had plenty to talk about during chow, as they anticipated the afternoon's work. "At last we get to fire real .50 caliber machine guns," Jack said. They all carried on from that, trying to anticipate how it would feel to have four 50s barking out of their wings, how near the ground they would fly as they fired, how fast, and so forth.

"All right, men," Captain Fillmore said when the eight reported back. "I'll take off first, followed by Chuck." Then he pointed to each of the others in turn, indicating the order in which they would take off and join up. "I'll do a slow climbing turn to the right. You cut me off and join up in the abreast formation, first four to my left side, second four to my right side. Allow about ten feet from wingtip to wingtip. When all are in formation, and flying steady, I'll rock my wings. At that signal, the four to my right drop back, keeping the abreast formation, and follow us in. DO NOT FIRE YOUR GUNS UNTIL WE ARE CLEAR OF THE RANGE. Remember, nobody gets ahead, and nobody gets behind.

"The target area is ten miles east of the field. We'll maintain our formations all the way. About a mile from the target, we'll get down to treetop level, then to ground level over the cleared field where the targets are located. Sight on the target in front of you as you sweep across the field.

"We'll go in at 250 air speed. You'll have time for one long burst, then we'll return to treetop level, come around for a second pass at 300 a.s. The third and fourth passes will be at 350. This will be the fastest you have flown at low level, so be extra alert, and don't do anything stupid. Keep tight control of your craft. Mainly, get the feel of the airplane at low level, high speed. Don't be surprised at how these old birds shake when you fire your guns. No questions? Okay, get ready to fly."

And fly they did! For Ed, nothing had been so exhilerating since his first solo flight. At no time in his flying had the sensation of speed and power been so great as it was with first the treetops, and then the ground seeming to rush under him as he made each pass. The firing of his four .50s felt like the climax of an incredibly exciting adventure, sending an icelike thrill up his spine, and raising the hairs on the back of his neck. "Like my first ride on the demon rollercoaster at West View park," he thought. Aloud, he said, "This is as close as it gets to combat, before I'm actually there." Then he yelled, "This is flying! Fantastic!"as he pulled up after his fourth pass.

When they returned to base, all of them excited and elated, the captain said, "Well done, men. Tomorrow we'll simulate dive-bombing. See you then."

Totally pumped up and all talking at once, the eight returned to B.O.Q. to shower and dress for a trip to town to celebrate. As usual, they weren't allowed to buy their own drinks or dinners. Fortunately, the two couples who insisted on paying for everything merely introduced themselves, then left the eight pilots to their own excited talk.

As they said goodnight after returning to the base, Ed said to Chuck, "We're almost there, Ol' Buddy. Another week here and we'll be back at Tallahassee sweating out our overseas assignments. How about that!"

"We sure as hell are. Never thought I'd make it," Chuck replied.

"You're kidding! I never thought you had any doubt, Ol' Boy."

"Yeah? Well I thought the same about you. Did you doubt it too?"

"Did I ever! I seemed to screw up so often, I didn't see how I could get here. Started in Preflight at Maxwell. They sure gave me every break," Ed said.

"No shit!" Chuck said. "I really didn't ever think you had any doubts. Wonder if all the guys went through the same thing?"

"Wouldn't that be funny. All of us thinking everybody else was full of confidence, and we were the only ones with doubts," Ed said.

"Yeah, okay, fellow doubter, my doubts are over. We made it up to here. We're going all the way, right?" Chuck asked.

"You bet. Let's get some sleep. Tomorrow we dive-bomb. Hope we can control these ancient ships in our dives. Goodnight. See you in the morning." They went to their rooms.

"Okay, men," the captain said the next morning. "Here's the drill. We take off and form up same as yesterday. As we approach the target, I'll rock my wings. That's your signal to fall into inline formation, We'll circle the target at 3,000 feet. I'll peel off and go down first, Number Two will follow, then Number Three, and so on. Drop your fake bomb and pull up, climbing back to 3,000. Join up in a "V" formation, four on each side of me. We'll land, get new bombs, and make another run, same as this one, okay? Let's go."

The eight lieutenants were experienced enough with the P-40s that, although each had to fight the warped-wing effect, everything went smoothly. After the second run, the captain called them together to brief them on the next two runs while the simulated bombs were being loaded on the planes.

"The next two runs will be skip-bombing. The target will be a bridge. Our objective will be to 'skip' our bombs under the bridge. To do that, we will approach the target area at 1,000 feet, inline formation. About a mile from the target, I'll start a shallow dive, picking up speed. You will maintain your spacing. We will go in maintaining that spacing, one after another, no counting for intervals on this. Aim your nose right at the target; then, at the last moment, simultaneously release the bomb and pull back on the stick. The bomb should 'skip' once and end up under the bridge. Since there will be no detonation, we can only guess how well we do. I'll circle around after my run and watch you make yours. Okay? Let's get on with it."

They ran to their planes and took off in order. Each one got at least one of his bombs right under the bridge, and the other either under or close enough to damage or destroy the target, for eight successful runs.

The following day would be their last at Sarasota, but they'd be on their own to fly at will, the captain said. When they had finished the day's flying, he said, "Since this is goodbye, the drinks are on me. See you at the O.C. in an hour, okay?"

"Yes, Sir," they all responded eagerly.

"Forget the 'Sir,'" the captain said. "From now on I'm Elliot, or El to you. See you there."

All eight agreed that El was a great guy, and an excellent instructor, as they hurried to B.O.Q. to shower and dress to meet at the Officers' Club. Jack said, "You know, we're about to wrap up our fighter pilot training, and I'm surprised that I made it; I never thought I'd last this long."

Chuck and Ed looked at each other and started to laugh.

"What the hell's so funny?" Harry asked. "I thought the same thing. What's so funny about that?"

"Well, I'll tell you," Ed said, still half laughing. "Just yesterday Chuck and I told each other the same thing. All the way through we each thought the other had no problems, or doubts. But now each of us finds out the others doubted they'd make it."

Now Harry and Jack joined in the laughter, as did the other four. "You mean to tell us that you two guys didn't think you'd make it? I don't believe it! I always thought you two were full of confidence, never having a doubt. God! Wish I'd known this way back at Maxwell. It would have helped if I'd known guys who seemed as good as you weren't any surer of themselves than I was." With that, Jack thumped each one on the back and shook his hand. "Man, you never know what's going on inside the guy next to you. Ed, I used to watch you as a cadet officer and think, 'God! Wish I had that guy's confidence.' Now I see you had as much uncertainty as I did."

Ed replied, "You sure don't. I was so close to washing out, I still don't believe I made it."

Harry joined in, "Sure wish we'd had general bull sessions so we could have let each other know what we thought."

"Might have been good," Jack said.

"Oh, I'm not so sure,"Chuck replied. "If we'd started telling each other about our doubts, we might have encouraged each other to think it was okay not to be confident. I think it was good for us to fight back our doubts and act confident; I didn't want anybody to know when I got down."

"You son-of-a-bitch!" Ed exclaimed. "You mean to tell me that way back when I spilled my guts to you about my doubts, you felt the same thing and never let on?"

"That's right, Buddy. What good would it do to cry on each other's shoulders? I learned in a psych class that you just reinforce another person's attitude or feelings if you tell him you have the same ones. Anyway, it worked out, didn't it?" Chuck replied.

"Yeah, but you're still a son-of-a-bitch. So that's some more of what you learned in college. I guess I'll have to try college when I get home. Let's move our butts, or we'll miss out on those free drinks," Ed said, heading to his room.

The eight had an enjoyable time with El Fillmore as he told them some of his experiences flying P-39s and P-40s in the Pacific. Of greater interest to Ed was his experiences flying P-47s out of England, escorting B-17s and B-24s, and the dive-bombing and strafing missions against German forces on the Continent. Ed was especially happy to hear that it would be only a matter of months until the new P-51s would replace most 47s in England. El seemed to share Ed's enthusiasm for the exciting new fighter, although, like Ed, he had never yet seen one close up. In any case, they had a rollicking good time, and other instructors were treating their students as well. The evening ended with enthusiastic singing of "Into the Air, Army Air Corps," "The Wild Blue Yonder," and a lusty, moist-eyed rendition of "God Bless America." Nobody held back, and everyone in the place had his arms over the shoulders of others.

With shouted "goodnights," "good lucks," and "good flyings," the party broke up. Everybody felt great, and all the fighter pilots who were about to finish the final phase of their training talked enthusiastically about where they hoped to be sent for combat, and what they hoped to fly.

Ed, feeling mellow, fell into a deep, dreamless sleep as soon as his head hit the pillow. He was up early, got his clothes and personal belongings ready to pack for the return to Tallahassee, showered and shaved, and went to breakfast in his flight suit.

Chuck showed up also ready to go directly to the flight line. Together, they bolted their breakfast and eagerly headed for the line. Ed said, as they paid their bills, "I've gotten fond of these old P-40s. I'm sorry this'll be my last flight in one of them."

"Me too," Chuck said. "Scared me shitless the first time I took one up, but as I learned to handle her, I really liked her. Wonder where we'll be going. Wouldn't it be great if we both went to the same assignment? Wonder if we'll have a choice?"

Ed replied, "I doubt it. Wherever they need fighter pilots the most, I'd guess. After listening to El last night, I'm hoping for England. Especially since he said the 51s'd be getting there soon."

"Still hung up on that one, eh? Well, she sounds pretty good. Hope you get what you want."

"Hope you do, too," Ed responded. "Whatever it is, I hope you have good flying."

"Same to you, Ol' Buddy. Let's sign out our 40s and enjoy our last flight for God knows how long."

"Right," Ed said. They signed out two all serviced and fueled, cleared with the Tower, took off and went their separate ways. Ed climbed immediately to 15,000 feet, and spent the next three hours putting his plane through everything he'd ever learned, except, of course, snap rolls. He remembered the first time he'd flown a 40, and how it almost got him, and how he'd gradually learned how to control it and make it do what *he* wanted, not what *it* wanted. This flight, with no assignment of things to accomplish, was pure, uninhibited joy, diving at clouds, breaking off at the last second, or diving on through, pretending to strafe and dive-bomb them, using clouds for landing strips and doing simulated fighter-landings on them, diving at maximum controllable speed, pulling up, hanging on the propellor at full throttle, opening the canopy to feel the cool, crisp air blowing through, and revelling in the great feeling of being part of an airplane, and it a part of him.

Finally, as the fuel gauge needle was moving toward empty, he rolled over and pulled back on the stick to put the 40 into one last, exhilarating, bone-shaking power dive, then pulling out at 1,500 feet, the wings vibrating so hard they were nearly flapping, and the wind screaming around the canopy.

He eased the throttle back and let the plane slow of its own accord. Hating to go back to earth, but impelled by the fuel indicator, he whipped into the pattern and landed. He felt cleansed, free, close to ecstasy, as he taxied to his parking place, and shut the fighter down. "Goodbye, old friend," he said quietly, caressing the cowl. "You've been good to me, once we learned how to deal with each other."

Just as he jumped down from the wing, he caught sight of Chuck coming toward him. "How'd your flight go, Buddy?" he called.

"Okay," Chuck replied.

"That's all? Just okay? Mine was . . ." but looking at Chuck, he knew something was wrong. "What's the matter, Chuck?"

"God! Jack bought it."

"Oh, no! What happened?"

"Nobody's sure, but they say he was having a great time, like all of us. Then he put her into a power dive and they think the warped wings got to be too much for him. He went into a power spin too low to recover. I flew over the plane where he crashed, as I was coming in. Parts were scattered all over, everywhere. He must have gone in at 250–300 mph. No chance of survival. God!"

"Man! What a rotten break. Last day and everything. These damn old crates," Ed said, kicking the tire nearest to him. A chill went through him as he remembered his own power dive just a few minutes earlier. "Could have been any of us. He just got the wrong plane at the wrong time. What an awful way to go. Damn! Damn! Damn!" Memories flooded back. They'd lost too many friends, by death or wash-out.

"Let's round up Harry and the other guys and go to the club. We have to drink one to Jack," Chuck said, no joy in his voice. "He'd do that for us, if we were the ones. God! I can't believe it. We were just getting to know him."

"Right," Ed said. They found Harry just coming out of the B.O.Q. He'd just heard about Jack, and was shattered. He'd known him longer than the others had. Chuck and Ed threw their arms over his shoulders and steered him to the Officers' Club. There Captain Fillmore joined them, and the rest of their group were already there. Everyone had heard the news, and the bar was full of pilots, new and old, for the ritual farewell toast to Jack. The barman filled glasses for them without being asked.

Captain Fillmore raised his glass, and in a commanding voice said, "To Jack. May he fly with angels!" Every officer present raised his glass and chorused, "To Jack."

The captain and the seven lieutenants downed their drinks and left the club in silence. After they had walked a few paces, the captain broke the silence. "He was a good man. He'll be missed. But you're going to have to get used to it. In combat, you'll have to say goodbye this way often. It's always tough. Seems you just start to know somebody, and he's gone. Too bad it had to happen this way. Damn shame!" and he left them.

The seven friends walked about the base in silence, no one knowing what to say, each one feeling a loss and sensing that they were paying silent tribute to a friend. After a half-hour, they said quiet goodnights and went to their rooms. All had final packing to do for tomorrow's trip to Tallahassee, but each was deeply affected by what he saw as an unfortunate loss due to poor equipment. Each one decided to get Jack's parents' address and write to them. All of them did, and the letters were gratefully acknowledged by Jack's parents.

Tallahassee, both the base and the town, was just as it had been before: overcrowded, with nothing to do at the base but wait for orders, or go into town for too much eating and drinking, plus trying to get to know some of the coeds, who seemed to be everywhere all the time, but not very receptive to pilots' overtures. Ed and Chuck had a couple of uninteresting dates with the two they'd had dates with they couldn't keep before, but they began to realize that their own maturity made them seem too old for these young ladies. They gave it up. The girls, after all, were only teenagers who lacked the maturity that their Air Corps experience had given Chuck and Ed. What fun they had was teenage fun, as was right for the innocent young ladies, but soon grew tiresome for the lieutenants.

Ed found Grant Perrin again, and the three friends compared notes on their fighter training. It turned out that Grant had not had the formation flying that Captain Fillmore had given his students, nor the dive- and skip-bombing they'd had, although he did have strafing. He, too, had flown old P-40s, and he had the same complaints about them.

When it came to where they hoped to go, and what planes they hoped to fly in combat, they said that they preferred the ETO to either the PTO or Africa. Ed still held out for the P-51, which he considered the ultimate fighter plane. Grant said that the 51 sounded good, but he was a long-time admirer of Republic Aviation's products. The best military plane they produced was the P-47 Thunderbolt. That's what he hoped to fly.

Chuck and Grant shared an interest in photography, an interest not shared by Ed, and each had a good camera. They began spending time together taking shots of buildings and people in town, especially on the college campus.

Ed found that the base chaplain's office had a good collection of classical records, and that he would be allowed to listen to them in a side room, equipped with a good quality phonograph. While Chuck and Grant wandered around with their cameras, Ed spent time listening to Brahms, Dvorak, Beethoven, Mozart, Verdi and Puccini. He began to be fond of Gustav Mahler, to whose music he had previously paid little attention. His fondness intensified when he attended a concert at the college where Mahler's fourth symphony was given a fine performance.

Unexpectedly, all of the men awaiting overseas assignments were given a week's leave, after which they were to report to various points of embarkation. Ed, Chuck, Grant, and Harry all were to report to Fort Dix, New Jersey, not far from New York City. This, they concluded, meant they were all going to the ETO, and they toasted the European Theatre of Operations at their dinner in town before each left by bus, train, or air for his hometown.

Ed went to his home in Swissvale, a suburb of Pittsburgh, Pennsylvania. There he saw his family and friends, and learned that his brother, Bob, despite the Draft Board's assurances, had been drafted and very likely would also be shipped overseas. When Ed attempted to contact the chairman who had given Bob his deferment, he was informed that he was no longer on the Board, and he could not reach him. "It's no use," his older brother, John, told him. "We've tried, but no one at the Board would tell us anything except that his deferment had been temporary, and that new regulations had forced them to rescind it."

Ed was uncertain whether or not to try to contact Pat. Finally he decided not. Since she was in Tennessee, he wouldn't be able to see her, so he let the few days he had pass with no contact.

The days of his leave passed quickly, and soon, too soon, Ed was on the train to Fort Dix. A regular Pennsylvania Railroad passenger train, its coaches were a far cry from the one in which he had travelled from the same Pennsylvania Railroad Station when he had left for Nashville, many months before. The seats were comfortable, the air clean and pleasantly warm, the toilets in good order, even the water dispenser worked, and paper cups were available from a holder beside the water dispenser. There was a dining car, but a snack vendor came through every hour or so, so Ed contented himself with a sandwich, coffee, an orange, and a package of Oreo cookies. Later on, he had a Clark bar.

When he got off the train, Ed saw an OD-colored bus with "Fort Dix" showing in the destination window above the windshield. Carrying his duffel bag and suitcase, he walked to the bus. The corporal driver said, "Fort Dix, Sir?" When Ed nodded, the corporal said, "Welcome aboard, Sir. Any seat you want." Ed thanked him and got aboard and put his bag and suitcase in the rack above his seat.

"Looks like you're on your way to the ETO, Sir," the driver said.

"Hope so," Ed said. "That's what I've been hoping and training for."

"I hear they need pilots real bad, Sir. High casualty rate."

"I suppose so, Corporal. Guess that's the way it is in combat," Ed said, assuming a nonchalance he did not feel. "But," he thought, "you've always known there'd be risks. People do get hurt and killed. You've got to accept that. It's a price some of us have to pay to combat evil forces in the world. This is what you've wanted, and you're on your way to getting it. Hope you're as lucky in combat as you've been in training." Not wanting to dwell on this morbid subject, he settled down to dream of the P-51 and the adventures he expected to have overseas.

He was dozing when a jeering voice said, "Son-of-a-bitch! I was sure you'd go AWOL."

Ed recognized Chuck's voice and replied, "Not you again. Thought you might fall out of that commercial plane you flew in up from Tallahassee. No such luck. So I guess the U.S. Army Air Corps and I have to put up with you for a while longer. How the hell are you, Ol' Buddy?"

"Great, Ol' Pal," Chuck replied, as he sat opposite Ed. "Leave good? Everything okay at home?"

"Everything normal. Except the Draft Board took my brother when they said they wouldn't. That leaves my mother and sister, who's still in high school, with no man in the house and only a little widow's Social Security to live on."

"That's tough," Chuck sympathized. "Can they make it on that?"

"Not possible. I'll have to increase the amount I've been having the Air Corps send her every month out of my check. I've been doing that ever since I got into the pilot program. That's okay. I won't need all that money. You know, besides flight pay, I understand we'll get overseas pay."

"Yeah. I think that's right. Sorry you have to send money home. I'm lucky. I can save a hell of a lot, and I am, even now. Want to go to graduate school when I get out."

Ed felt a little twinge of envy, but pushed it aside. "It's the breaks," he thought. "Anyway, Dad didn' t choose to die, and Bob didn't choose to be drafted. Can't worry about it. Have to do what I have to do." To Chuck he said, "That's great. Hope it all works out the way you want it to. How was everything at home?"

"Everything's good. Had to see all my relatives. Some I didn't know I had. And friends. Just because I had on a uniform, I was a hero! My mom has arthritis, and it's worse, but otherwise, everybody's okay. Hey! I read an article in 'Life' about your P-51, with pictures. You may have something there. Sounds like a great airplane, and it looks fantastic."

"Welcome aboard. I figured you'd see things my way sooner or later."

"Yeah. I'm beginning to think you might be right for once. If I get a chance, I'll sure as hell try it out."

"Try it out! You think they're going to line up all the active fighters and let us try them, then choose the one we want? You're nuts! We'll be assigned to groups and squadrons and we'll fly whatever they fly. This isn't going to be like registration at school, where you pick and choose from courses and teachers. Sometimes you don't show much smarts, for a college graduate."

"Yeah. You're probably right. Lost my head there for a minute. Forgot this is a war we've been invited to. We'll take what we get, right?"

"Right, and be glad we're pilots, and we can, at last, go after those Nazi supermen."

The bus, which had started while they talked, now passed through the gate at Fort Dix and stopped in front of a building marked "Check In and Assignment." They carried their luggage off the bus and into the building. Two tables—one manned by a lieutenant, the other by a sergeant—faced them. One said "Officers," the other, "Enlisted Personnel." Under the "Officers" sign was a smaller one reading, "Have your orders in hand." They dug their orders out of their suitcases.

The lieutenant at the table said, "Welcome to Dix. You won't be here long. Enjoy yourselves, if you can. Tour orders, please. Okay, Lieutenant Sparks, Lieutenant Thorne," handing back their orders, on which he had stamped, "Reported on Time." "Go out the door you just entered. Cross the street and walk down the street opposite this building. You will see what passes for B.O.Q. here. We're pretty crowded, so you'll have to share a room. You'll see

I wrote A12 on your orders. That's your room assignment. Sign in, then you're on your own until further orders. You'll see the Officers' Club and Officers' Mess on down the same street. That's it for here."

They found B.O.Q. to be a standard two-story Army barracks building divided into small rooms by thin-walled partitions. The latrine and showers were at one end, and an office at the other. At the office they found a corporal behind a desk. He had them sign in, then pointed out a bulletin board saying, "That's where you'll find your orders posted when they come in. Best check every morning. Your names will show up for orientation, physicals, and shots. When your shipping orders come, I'll bring 'em to your room. Okay, Sirs?"

"You bet, Corporal Slanky," Ed said, reading the man's nametag. "Thanks."

"By the way, Sirs, there's a coffee urn right there. I keep it full of hot coffee all the time, an' paper cups. Help yourself any time."

"Thanks again, Corporal," Chuck said. "Think I'll have one right now. You, Ed?"

"You bet." They drew a cup each, Chuck adding milk and sugar, Ed just milk, and carried them to Room A12, down the corridor. The room was small, obviously meant for one, but two bunks, two tables and two chairs had been crowded in. They had to stow their duffel bags and suitcases under their bunks, or they wouldn't have had room to move around. It was cramped, but everything was neat and clean, and they found the latrines and showers to be bright and clean also.

"It ain't the Ritz, but we can manage," Chuck said.

"Right," Ed agreed. "May be better than we'll get in the ETO. Let's go check out the Officers' Club; I'd like a cold beer."

Not far down the street they saw an imposing, large building with a look of permanency and age, as though it had been standing there for a hundred years or more. "That's some building," Ed said. "No chance that's the O.C. — looks too good to be that." Chuck agreed.

As they drew closer to the building, they were shocked to see an elaborate bronze plaque engraved with "Fort Dix Officers Club," and below that, "Est. 1847."

"Good God Almighty!" Chuck exclaimed. "You suppose little ol' lieutenants like us can go in there?"

Getting over his surprise at the contrast between this O.C. building and others they had been in, Ed said, "Only one way to find out." They dusted their shoes on their trousers, straightened their ties, pulled down their tunics, and went up to the heavy wooden doors with brass handles. One door had a sign saying, "All commissioned military officers are welcome to this, the oldest Officers Club still in use in the U.S.A."

Pulling open one door, they stepped into a softly lit, mahogony-panelled, carpeted lobby, with heavy carved chairs, settees and coffee tables placed around the walls. To the left was a reception and information desk, behind which a middle-aged man in a white jacket and black bowtie sat. Straight ahead was what appeared to be a large ballroom. To the right was a room with an elaborate polished wood bar, with heavy crystal chandeliers over it, polished mirrors behind it, and bottles of every imaginable kind of whiskey, brandy, liqueur, and wine, with racks of crystal glasses reflecting light from the chandeliers and making their own reflections in the mirrors.

They stepped to the barroom doors, wondering if such a grand bar would have so mundane a drink as beer. Visible from the doorway, but not from the lobby, was, to their right and behind the bar, a bank of pump handles proclaiming every brand of beer and ale, domestic and imported, that either Chuck or Ed had ever heard of, and some neither had heard of. Behind the bar were two men, one middle-aged and balding, the other younger, with a full head of blonde hair, carefully slicked back and parted in the middle. Both wore white shirts, black bowties, black vests, and armbands around their shirt sleeves on their upper arms.

"Did we die and go to heaven?" Ed wondered.

"Maybe," Chuck replied. "So, this is what an Officers' Club is supposed to look like. Nobody told me. We must have gone to the wrong places on those other bases."

"What'll it be, Gentlemen?" the older of the barkeepers asked.

"Couple of cold beers, please," Chuck said.

The barman waited, obviously wanting a more specific request.

In reading about England, Ed had found that two favorite drinks were, "Half 'n' Half, and Guinness, if you please." Not knowing what to expect, he decided to take a chance, so he said, "Pint of Guinness, please."

"And you, Sir," the man said, looking at Chuck.

"Uh—the same, please," Chuck said.

"It'll take a few moments," the barman said. "Have a seat; I'll bring it to you."

They sat in a booth with leather-covered cushioned seats and a clean, polished mahogany table, and looked around. This was, clearly, an extremely well-designed, antique, but perfectly maintained place. On the walls were plaques commemorating events at Fort Dix over the years of its existence, and many notable officers who had served or spent time there. It was an old Army permanent base, now functioning in part as an embarkation and processing point for service personnel on their way overseas.

Several other officers occupied other booths, but the room was so large, and so solidly built, that only an occasional snatch of a voice laughing, or raised to make a point, could be heard. An air of dignity and reserve prevailed.

Two glasses of the dark-brown liquid with a creamy foam head at the top came to their booth, and with them a crystal bowl of Spanish peanuts.

"Do we pay now?" Ed asked.

"No, Sir. We can start a tab for you, or you can pay as you leave. Whichever suits you."

"Good, thanks. We'll pay as we leave."

"Thank you, Sir," and he was gone.

"Well, Ol' Pal, this is the first time I've felt like an officer and a gentleman since I got my commission," Chuck said.

"And don't forget 'all the privileges attendant thereto,'" Ed added. "This must be one of those privileges, eh, old chap?"

"Rawther," Chuck said in his best British imitation. "Here's to our rights and privileges, or should I just say 'cheers'?" They touched glasses and sipped the Guinness.

"Ugh! What is this stuff? Tastes like they boiled an old boot and poured off the liquid," Chuck exclaimed.

Ed took a second sip. "I kind of like it. Try another sip. I think it grows on you."

"It sure as hell grows on something. Maybe a dank basement wall! But not on me it doesn't. Here, you can have mine. I'm goin' to get a good ol' Bud," Chuck said.

"Wait a minute, Chuck. Give it a chance. You know, with the war on, we probably won't get American beer in England. Might as well try to like it," Ed said.

"Okay, Pal," Chuck said, taking another sip. "Man, I think I'm going to be sick. If this is what I have to drink in England, I might have to give up beer, and that's too much to give up for my country! AWOL might be in order." In spite of his protestations, Chuck continued his sipping. With half of his glass gone, he said, "You're right. It does grow on you. I'm beginning to like it. Let's order another, so it'll be ready when these are done." He caught the barman's eye and said, "Two more, please."

"Yes, Sir," the man said, and began to draw two more.

By the time their seconds were finished, the two lieutenants were feeling very good. Still awed by their plush and dignified surroundings, they restrained themselves, but laughed quietly at just about everything either of them said.

"What'a say to 'nother?" Chuck asked.

Ed looked at his watch. "Nope, better not. Not 'nough to eat today. Let's go eat, okay?'

"Yeah. You're right. Better eat, Hey! This stuff's good, an' it has a real kick, I think you're 'bout drunk. Okay, though, I'll get you to the Off'cers Mess," and he started to laugh, "Mess is right, right? Off'cers Mess."

Ed had enjoyed the Guinness, but it had had less of an effect on him than on Chuck. He paid the check, leaving a tip for the barman, and they left.

The Officers' Mess was almost as big a surprise as the Club. Clearly, it had been done by the same architect and designer as the Club, with similar panelling and chandeliers. The vast dining room was filled with tables, all polished mahogany, as were the chairs. Each table was covered with an immaculate white linen tablecloth, matching napkins, Sterling silverware, and crystal water goblets and wine glasses. At one end of the room was a huge stone fireplace, in which a log fire was burning, since the autumn air was chilly. Instead of a bar directly opposite the door, there was a fourth panelled wall with two sets of swinging doors, in and out of which waiters hurried with trays and dishes serving dinners and removing empty plates and dishes. Although the waiters moved quickly, there was no sense of their being harried. A quiet air of calm, cool efficiency permeated the place. Diners talked quietly as they ate, and the waiters moved quickly and quietly, with the dignity and confidence that comes from long experience.

The maître d' approached Ed and Chuck, and asked, "Dinner?"

"Yes," Chuck answered.

"Will there be others joining you?" he inquired.

"No, just two of us," Ed said.

"Would you care to be near the fire, Gentlemen, or not?"

Ed and Chuck both said, "Near, please," and the maître d' signalled a waiter from that end of the room. He approached, and the maître d' gave him a quiet order. The waiter said, "This way, please, Gentlemen."

The food seemed to them incredibly good, and the service fantastic. The bill was high, but it seemed worth it, since they didn't know how many more meals they would have in the States.

"Almost makes you think of making a career in the military, doesn't it?" Ed asked.

Chuck answered, "Not me. This is an exception. How many military bases do you think there are with facilities like this?"

"Yeah. And how good would your chances be, after the war, of being assigned to some place like this? Besides, I have a hunch that West Point graduates will get the promotions," Ed said.

"By the way," Chuck said, "I read that there are plans to build an academy like West Point and Annapolis for the Air Corps. Have you heard that?"

"No, but it wouldn't surprise me. Air power is really important now; bet we'll be putting more and more money into it," Ed replied. "They'll probably put the cadet program that we went through into the academy, and combine it with college-level courses. That'd be neat, but we'll be too old for that."

"Yeah. Anyway, I'm for graduate school after we win the war," Chuck said.

"I know," Ed said. "You've told me. I don't know what I'll be doing. Have to wait and see what turns up. I read that there's going to be some kind of government program to help veterans go to school. Hope so. I'd like to have a shot at college."

"I've heard that, too," Chuck said. "They ought to do something for us. Millions of us are having big chunks of time taken from us, while others finish college and get on with their careers. But, man! That'd cost billions."

Ed responded, "Sure would. We'll just have to wait and see. First we have to win this war, and it seems we're a long way from that right now. Germany and Japan are sure on the move. And nobody knows what the Soviet Union's going to do."

"Yeah, right," Chuck agreed. "Can you believe a Hitler-Stalin non-aggression pact? Hitler's been screaming his head off about Communists for years. Communists and Jews. Now he signs an agreement with the leading Communist country. I think it'll be a matter of which one destroys the other first."

"Guess you're right. Seems to me Germany gains the most from the pact. Russia would be better off signing with the Allies. If Hitler gets full control of all of Europe, which he seems to be doing, Russia'll be his next target. I don't think he'll pay any attention to the pact," Ed said, as they finished their coffee.

"Probably right. But Russia would be a big bite for Germany to try to swallow. And if Hitler starts an attack, you can bet a month's pay Stalin'll be an ally of ours real fast."

"Bet you're right," Ed said. "What say we go over to the Club and have a Scotch? Then I'm ready to hit the sack, okay?"

"Good. Me too."

The next day, since there were no orders for them, Ed and Chuck found Grant, and they took a bus to New York City. They had lunch in the Automat, a new experience for all three, then went to the matinee at Radio City Music Hall. They enjoyed a spectacular stage show with the Rockettes, and the Radio City Symphony Orchestra and Chorus with soloists, followed by the News of the World and a feature film, "God Is My Co-Pilot."

Returning to Dix, they had another fine dinner at the O.M., then played some billiards, at which none was very good. On the following day they had physical exams, a series of shots, and several training films, loaded with do's and don'ts for England: Words to avoid, like "bloody" and "Limey;" precautions about boisterous and drunken behavior; spending too freely, since British servicemen and women received much lower pay than Americans; hints about what English pubs were like; and precautions about venereal disease, including some resulting from what was, indelicately, referred to as "British Crud," seemingly resulting from a shortage of toilet paper.

The shots made Chuck queasy, so he didn't want to go to dinner. Ed and Grant went and again found the food and service great.

Along with nearly a thousand others, the following day they were scheduled for orientation. They met in a large assembly hall. There they filled out forms for wills, support deductions from their pay and insurance forms, including information on whom to notify in case of injury or death. This served as another reminder that combat would bring about casualties, inevitably including some of the men in the room.

After completing the forms, they listened to a morale-boosting talk by a lieutenant colonel, who spent some time briefing them on the military situation in the ETO. Following that, he spoke of the importance of air power to an Allied victory, concluding that part of his speech with comments on the contributions to that victory each of his listeners would make. He followed this with cautionary comments about loose talk about tactics, missions, assignments, personnel, anything that might conceivably be helpful to the enemy, warning that the Axis powers have agents everywhere. He followed this with the information that their mail would, from now on, be censored; that no information could go out to anyone concerning departure dates or hours, or destinations. Only one letter or card could be sent out by each of the men, and from now on, their return addresses would be A.P.O. numbers. These they would be given at the end of his lecture.

He concluded by instructing them to pack their foot lockers, putting an I.D. tag on each. This would be used to stencil their names and serial numbers on the foot lockers, which would then be picked up for loading on their ship. The men would be taken to the ship by bus, leaving at 08:00 the next day. They were limited to one suitcase and one duffel bag each, and these should have their names and serial numbers on the outside and inside.

The last thing the colonel said was, "You gentlemen will embark on the S.S. Argentina tomorrow morning. I cannot give you a destination, but it will be in the ETO."

This brought forth an enormous cheer from the assembled fliers, with Chuck, Ed, and Grant joining in the general enthusiasm. Calling for quiet, the colonel said, "The buses will deliver you to the embarkation point. You will be assigned quarters as you step off the gangplank on to the deck. The ship will sail into the Atlantic, and then it will join a large convoy. Good luck, good flying, and God bless you. That is all. Dismissed."

Bedlam broke out. Every flier in the room was yelling, "Yahoo! We made it! Finally going to do what we signed up for! Watch out, Nazis, here we come!" Hands were shaken, arms were thrown round shoulders and arms punched as the enthusiastic men, exploding with energy, expressed their joy that, at last, they could contribute to what President Roosevelt had said would be the "inevitable victory."

As the clamor died down, the fliers made their way out of the building and moved toward their B.O.Q. rooms. "By damn!" Chuck said. "1 didn't know there were so many pilots here."

"Why not?" Ed said. "You know how big our cadet class was. Everyone who made it through would be here. They aren't all fighter pilots, though, you know. Some are bomber men; some aren't pilots at all, but bombardiers and navigators. I'll bet ol' Bill Schramm is here somewhere in this mob. I wonder if I can find him."

Grant said, "Hey! I remember him too, from Maxwell. Came from New York, didn't he?"

"Yeah," Ed said. "Nice little guy. He and I went to the same Primary, at Bennettsville. He chose heavy bombers, so I lost track of him. No way I can find him here, not enough time. Maybe I'll find him on the ship." Grant left them to go to his room and pack. Ed and Chuck did the same.

Fort Dix had had years of experience as an embarkation point. As a consequence, the fliers were moved smoothly and efficiently from the base to the busy docks on the East River. None of the snafus and delays that usually plagued large military movements happened. After an early breakfast, the officers were loaded on buses and, precisely at 08:00, the caravan moved out. Led by a jeep, they passed through intersections without slowing down as Military Police stopped all crossing traffic to allow the buses to move through.

At the dock, each bus in turn stopped at the foot of the gangway. As the fliers stepped off, each was handed a paper chit with a stateroom number printed on it. As he stepped off the gangplank on to the gently rising and falling deck of the S.S. Argentina, he was given directions to his stateroom. All were loaded aboard and ordered to remain in their staterooms until loading was completed. Otherwise, all the passengers milling about would have impeded the orderly loading.

Ed was disappointed to find no one he knew among his bunkmates. The Argentina was a luxury liner of medium size; it was under lease to the U.S. as a troop carrier. Ed's stateroom was a beautifully panelled and carpeted room, intended for two passengers. Some of the furniture had been removed to make space for stacked bunks for eight people. The "head," as Ed quickly learned to call the bathroom, had two washstands, a shower, and a stool. Posted in the head was a printed notice which indicated the limited hours per day when fresh water would be available for showering, washing, and shaving. All other hours only saltwater would be available.

After all eight of the men assigned to Ed's room had met each other, they worked up a daily schedule for each to use the facilities during freshwater periods. Posted on the inside of the stateroom door was a timetable for the occupants of the room. They would have their meals in the main dining room, but only at scheduled times, since the room was not large enough to accomodate all the passengers at one time. Diners would be served only at their scheduled times. Each would have to show the chit with his stateroom assignment on it to be seated and served. There was also posted a schedule of hours during which a PX would be open. Snacks, cold drinks, cigarettes, etc., would be available there.

Just as Ed and his seven roommates finished settling in, the P.A. speaker came to life, and a voice thanked all the passengers on A Deck—Ed's deck—for their cooperation, indicating that they were now free to leave their staterooms. They were not, however, to leave their deck. A second voice then came on, "This is the captain speaking. As you know, we will be part of a convoy across the Atlantic. We will rendezvous with the convoy at 17:00 today. The convoy will be protected by destroyers, armed with depth charges to destroy submarines, surface guns and anti-aircraft guns. The threat is real, especially from enemy submarines. You will, at times, hear explosions. These will be from depth charges dropped by the destroyers. You may also see anti-submarine flying boats. These will patrol over and ahead of us as far as their fuel supply will allow them to go.

"Ladies and gentlemen," Ed and his mates exchanged glances, none knowing that there would be any ladies aboard, "When I say that the threat from enemy submarines is real, I mean just that. Your cooperation is required. Any time you are directed to go to your quarters, you are to do so promptly. You will be given instructions concerning abandon-ship stations. When the order is given, move quickly, but without panic, to your assigned stations. Do not attempt to take any belongings with you. You are the important thing. We will have Abandon Ship drills from time to time. You will find flotation equipment stowed in all quarters. You are directed to carry one with you at all times when out of your quarters. You must have it with you when the Abandon Ship order is given.

"Blackout rules will be strictly enforced starting at 17:00 today. There are blackout curtains at every porthole. Close them. There will be no smoking outside your quarters during blackout hours. No flashlights, no matches, no lighters are to be lit outside your quarters. At night, a pinpoint of light can be seen for miles at sea. Violaters will be taken into custody and locked in the brig. We cannot allow a careless or thoughtless person to endanger thousands of people's lives and safety. That is all."

The first voice came on again, "This is Colonel Sampson, in charge of all U.S. troops aboard. Obeying the rules laid down by Captain Spurier is not a matter of choice. You are ordered to obey them. Arrest and punishment will be swift and harsh. The men aboard may not be aware that a large contingent of WAACs is aboard this ship. I'm sure all of the officers are aware of the non-fraternization rule for officers and enlisted personnel. C deck, where the ladies are quartered, is strictly off limits to all male officers. A and B decks are off limits to all female enlisted personnel. These rules, too, will be strictly enforced, and violators will be subject to immediate punishment. With the cooperation of all personnel, we can have an enjoyable trip on this beautiful if crowded ship. Good sailing, everyone. We will be launching in a matter of minutes. That is all."

As soon as the P.A. clicked off, Ed and his mates, as well as all the other fliers, rushed out and up the steps to the deck. The deck was spacious and uncluttered, with lifeboats lashed well above, and life preservers spaced along the rail. Ed found a place at the rail, and looked down to see Merchant Seamen, members of the crew, and longshoremen busy with last-minute tasks, including hauling the gangplank aboard. In a few moments, he heard a piped signal, and the heavy halyards were loosened, hauled aboard, and neatly coiled on the fore and aft decks. The deep-throated voice of the ship sounded, tugboats did their job, and the ship stood proudly and at a stately speed toward the mouth of the river, the Atlantic spreading out beyond. "Goodbye, America!" Ed yelled. All along the rail, men let loose loud cheers. A voice boomed over the P.A., "God bless and keep this ship and every person on board."

Ed turned and put out his hand to the man standing next to him. As they shook hands, Ed looked directly at him for the first time. "Bill! You son-of-a-gun! So we're mates once more!"

"Well, I'll be damned! You look great, Ed. So they let you finish up, eh? What a surprise that must've been."

"So, Little Man, were you able to handle those big clumsy bombers? Hard to believe."

"Watch it, Hot Pilot. Don't forget I'm the guy with the 6-inch jolt to the vitals."

"Can't use that anymore. You're an officer and a gentleman now," Ed replied. They broke up laughing and embraced, then watched as the tugs released their lines, and the ship was headed into the open waters. "Great to see you, Bill. Remember Chuck Sparks? He's aboard, too, but I haven't seen him since we boarded the ship. Grant Perrin, too."

"Thought I saw Chuck moving forward, just as I came on deck. Don't remember Grant, though. Did I know him?"

"Maybe not. He was in your—or rather, our—class at Maxwell. Got to know him when I was held back and forced to be in your lousy class. Nice guy," Ed answered. "Let's go forward and see if he's there." They made their way along the deck, more and more conscious of the rise and fall of the ship the farther forward they went.

"God! Not the Little One again. I was sure you'd been misplaced somewhere in the bowels of a B-24, never to be seen again!" Chuck's voice greeted them from his seat on steps leading from the deck up to the bridge.

"I see nothing but disaster for Fighter Command, if they let the likes of you two fly!" Bill responded. "One of you would be bad enough. Both of you flying fighters makes me glad I'm in bombers." He and Chuck shook hands, and the three friends sat on the steps exchanging stories of their experiences since last seeing each other.

The P.A. came alive to announce first noon chow, and all three checked their chits, finding they were not scheduled until the third seating. Waiting for their turn, they explored all parts of the ship that weren't marked "Crew Only," or "Off Limits." None of them had ever been on an ocean-going ship before, so everything impressed them. Especially impressive were the great diesel engines which they could view from an observation platform, looking through plate glass windows. Oilers and engineers were busy attending to the huge engines. Everything was immaculately clean, even the white coveralls of the workers.

They went forward on the deck to the prow and examined the enormous anchor chains, which they could see by leaning far out over the rail. Every crewman they met was friendly and courteous, willingly answering their questions. Many were civilians, regular members of the ship's peace-time crew, who had been sworn in as temporary members of the Merchant Marine, which offered them insurance and other benefits as part of the leasing arrangement the government had made with the ship's owners. The captain and ship's officers remained civilians, but their salaries were paid by the government as part of the leasing arrangement. All the cabin stewards, waiters, chefs, and other kitchen help were regular employees of the S.S. Argentina, with civilian status.

Hunger pains were starting for the three, and they considered locating the PX to get snacks. Just then, however, third serving was called out over the P.A., and they made their way to the Dining Salon instead. And "Salon" it was, rivaling the Officers' Mess at Dix in elegance and unostentatious decor.

One modification had been made of the civilian routine in the Salon. Instead of waiters presenting individual menus to the diners, a large lighted signboard displayed what was being served. A choice was given of three soups, six salad dressings for two kinds of salad, four hot dishes, all beverages, and a wide variety of desserts. After several minutes of time to allow diners to study the menu, white-coated waiters trooped out of the kitchen doors and moved to the tables to take orders.

Ed, Chuck, and Bill asked for beer, but their waiter said that orders for alcoholic beverages would be taken by different waiters who would be along in a few minutes. Meanwhile, he said, perhaps they would like some coffee or tea. They all opted for coffee, and the waiter signaled an assistant, who hurried over with a pot of coffee for their table, then went to the kitchen (galley, as they learned to call it), to get their orders filled. In a few minutes, another waiter came to their table to take their drink orders. Bill and Chuck ordered Bud, and Ed asked if they had Guinness. Getting a yes from the waiter, Ed ordered a pint, after which the waiter disapeared through another door, off to the side of the galley doors. Five minutes later, he reappeared carrying a large silver tray with all the drinks for their table and one other table nearby. "Sir," he said to Ed, "Yours is the only order for Guiness I've had today." Then to all of them, "If you want the same again, just signal me and I'll bring it right away. Thank you, Sirs," and went on to other tables.

"Man! Talk about great eating," Ed said as they returned to the deck from the Dining Salon. Here we are in what amounts to a combat area on the high seas, and we're fed like high society! I think I'm going to love combat; I've always heard that ships at sea serve great meals, but that was unbelievable."

"Sure was," Bill agreed. "Wonder if it'll continue, or was this just for our first meal?"

"Bet it continues. These ships carry enough provisions to feed a small city," Chuck added. "I've read that the holds are bigger than all the passenger and crew space combined. Probably have an acre of refrigeration. Don't kid yourself, Ed. You won't see this kind of meal anywhere in combat. In fact, I've read that even the restaurants in English cities can't serve decent meals during the war."

"Maybe we can get someone to take us down to the holds," Ed said. "I'd sure like to see that."

Bill yawned, "Not today, Buddy, I'm heading for my stateroom to log some sack time."

"Good idea. How about meeting at the steps up to the bridge at 16:00," Chuck suggested. "Okay?"

The others agreed, and each went to his room. Ed stretched out on his bunk, not expecting to sleep. In a matter of moments, he was sound asleep. The gentle rocking motion of the ship seemed to lull him to sleep. He came awake abruptly and saw by his watch that it was 15:45. He relieved himself in the head, rinsed his face with cold saltwater, and ran up the steps to the deck. The others weren't at the meeting place, so he leaned over the rail, peering forward as far as he could. They had long since lost sight of land behind them, and all he could see was ocean. The swells had increased, so the ship was rising and falling noticeably. With each rise, the visible expanse increased. As he stared ahead, suddenly, at the top of one rising of the ship, he thought that he saw some specks on the horizon. He waited for the next rise, but it was not as high as the previous one, so he could not see the specks. Several rises passed, then, this time more clearly, he saw five larger specks, and thought he saw a thin line of smoke from one of them.

Bill and Chuck joined him, and he told them excitedly, "I saw ships ahead. Must be our convoy."

The others gave him a skeptical look. "Daydreaming again, Ed?" Chuck asked.

"No, no. Keep watching just about one o'clock, when we top another rise." The next two rises came and went, and nobody saw anything. Ed's friends gave him sidelong glances. At the top of the third rise, all three saw them, and at the same time the P.A. came on. "This is the captain. We are about one hour from rendezvous with the convoy. Some of the ships are just coming visible off the starboard bow. We and they are following zigzag courses, so it will take an hour or more for us to close on them. Meanwhile, at 17:00 the blackout rules will be in effect. If you look up at the crow's nest, you will see a seaman signaling with sema-phore flags. We do this to avoid using our signal flasher light, which can be seen for miles, by enemy as well as friendly ships. We are also maintaining radio silence, to avoid attracting enemy submarines. We are, however, using our sonar to detect unidentified vessels in our area. That is all." and the P.A. speakers went silent.

"How about ol' Eagle Eye here," Chuck said.

"Yeah, pretty sharp, Ol' Buddy. You still have that little edge that moved you up to the top position in the cadet program. Yeah, I heard about that, even though I wasn't at Spence with you. Hate to admit it, but I was proud of you. Been wanting to tell you that," Bill said with no trace of envy or animosity, without even his usual jibing tone.

"Thanks, Bill," Ed answered. "Just lucky, I guess. Really surprised me, after coming so close to washing out. Well, that's all behind us now. Here we are, pilots and officers, racing across the Atlantic to take on the Nazis."

Chuck said, "He was a good cadet officer, and he's a good flier. A pain in the ass some-times, but a good buddy."

"All right, all right, lay off the mush. Thanks, but let's leave it at that, before you guys start telling me the truth, which I don't want to hear," Ed said.

"Let's go to the bursar's office and see if we can go down to the hold," Chuck suggested.

"Good, let's go," Ed said, and they did so.

An assistant was on duty at the bursar's office. He was courteous, but he said, "All hands will be busy until we're established in the convoy. Be here at 09:00, and we'll have someone show you the holds. All right?"

"Great," they replied, and thanked him.

Dusk came at 17:00, and with it the warning that blackout was in effect. The P.A. announcement was barely finished when, far forward of where the three stood talking, a match flared, as someone lit a cigarette. "Damn fool! Always has to be someone who's either ignorant or doesn't give a damn!" Chuck exploded. In seconds, they saw two Military Police-men approaching the smoker, one from each side. The first one there grabbed the cigarette from the smoker's mouth and stubbed it out. Then, with one M.P. on each side, he was taken below.

Fifteen mintes later, the P.A. clicked on. "This is Colonel Sampson. Let me remind all personnel, blackout rules will be strictly enforced. One lieutenant who lit a cigarette on deck immediately after the captain announced blackout will be confined to the brig on short rations for one week. That is all," and the speakers clicked off.

"They really are serious," Ed said. "Good thing. A lot of jokers can't seem to get it through their heads that there's a real war on. A jerk like that puts us all at risk."

Their ship, which had been closing on the convoy, now joined it. Ed and his friends could see other transports, shadowy in the dusk, but still visible, spread out around them. Behind their ship, they could make out a destroyer. Just before it got too dark to see much of anything, they heard and briefly glimpsed a PBY-13 Flying Boat, heading westward toward home. "Good to know they're with us, but by morning I bet we'll be too far out for the patrol planes," Bill said.

Chuck responded, "Don't know, Bill, we've been zig-zagging all day. Hard to judge how far we've actually gone as the crow flies."

"Good point," Ed agreed. "We've cut through a lot of water but probably haven't gained much to the east. You know, I read that some fast liners go across without convoys, depending on their speed to outrun and out-maneuver the subs. The Queen Mary is one they mentioned. Boy! If this ship is as nice as it is, imagine what the Queen Mary must be like."

"Yeah," Chuck said. "And don't forget the America, pride of our passenger fleet."

"You bet," Bill said. "I've seen both of them in dock in New York. Overwhelming, but I never got to go aboard."

Since they were in the third dinner group, they weren't finished eating until 20:30. The evening meal was as excellent as the noon one had been. On deck again, they found that the night air had turned cold and sharp with a north wind blowing. "Be back in a couple minutes," Chuck said, "I'm getting my trench coat." The others followed suit.

Back on deck, they found the sky almost totally clear of clouds, and the stars bright, large, and seeming very close. A thin sliver of moon hung low on the horizon. Since none of the ships was showing lights, it was an eerie feeling, knowing they were out there, but unseen and unheard. They felt the increasing size of the swells, as the ship rose much higher than it had before. Leaning over the rail forward, they could see white bubbles washing out and away as the prow cut through the water, the bubbles increasing with each downward plunge, and decreasing as the ship climbed the next swell. Every now and then they could see the ghostly outline of a nearby transport as their ship topped a swell.

"Not as good as flying," Ed said, "but this is great. Thank you, Army Air Corps. I'm having experiences I never dreamed I could have."

Bill said, "Yeah. Too bad it takes a war to let us ordinary folks have some experiences rich people take for granted."

"You some kind of socialist, or something? What do you think? The government ought to give everybody the same experiences?" Chuck asked, a hint of belligerence in his voice.

"Hey, come on, Buddy," Ed said, "I don't think Bill meant anything like that. Did you?"

"I don't know what I meant; I just think it isn't right that a few people can have the means to do just about anything they want, and the rest of us never get a shot at those things," Bill replied.

"Sorry, Bill," Chuck said. "I see what you mean, but what's the answer? Only way everybody can have the same opportunity is if the government controls everything. I, for one, don't want that."

Ed said, "Guess that's right. But ours is supposed to be the land of equal opportunity. Maybe we ought to have a system that would control things better, so there wouldn't be such a gap between, say, Rockefeller and Thorne, or Mellon and Schramm."

"How the hell could we do that, without killing the free enterprise system?" Chuck asked.

"Well, we could increase taxes on the ones with too much money, especially if they didn't earn it, like inherited wealth. And make sure everybody had a guaranteed minimum income. After all, we're the richest country in the world, but sometimes I'm ashamed of the slums and down-and-outers we seem to have everywhere. We ought to be able to do better than that, don't you think?" Ed said.

"Yeah," Bill said, "that's what I meant. FDR did some of that, but he had too many enemies who fought him tooth-and-nail; couldn't get his whole program going. Then the war started, and everything started to go back to normal—the rich getting richer, the rest of us just getting by. What might have been real change got shot down by wartime prosperity."

Ed said, "Good point, Bill, but some of his things are here to stay . . ."

"Like what?" Chuck interrupted.

"Well, Social Security. Better control of the stock market. Slightly better tax structure. Better pension plans, better control of unsafe working conditions like in coal mining, and a system of treatment and compensation for things like black lung disease, control of T.B., and research campaigns to cure or prevent polio. Things that can't be done in an every-man-for-himself society."

"Good points, Buddy. You sure you didn't go to college? Just don't kill private enterprise. That's what makes everything work," Chuck said. "See what I mean, Bill? He can be a real pain in the ass."

"Yeah, I can see that. But this time, he's right. And it doesn't look like FDR's programs have hurt the private enterprisers any," Bill said. "Sure seems to me that those who rake in millions could turn some of it back in to help those who work for them, through higher taxes, if necessary, and still be able to live plenty high on the hog."

"Anybody else cold?" Chuck asked. "I'm going below. We can continue this some other time. See you tomorrow."

All three headed for the comfort of their staterooms, where with blackout curtains closed, they could read or write or play cards. During the night depth charges were heard not far away, and the swells increased as the night wore on.

By norning they were in the midst of a violent Atlantic storm. All the landlubbers were unsteady on their feet, and a few were violently seasick. Everyone had to hold on to his bunk or other furniture to steady himself, or do so by putting his hands on the walls. Making way to the Dining Salon was a challenge, and eating a greater one, with the ship's pitching making it uncertain whether a spoonful of cereal or a sip of coffee would wind up in the mouth or on a cheek, nose, chin, or in the lap. Those who weren't sick, including Bill, Chuck, and Ed, enjoyed the uncertain feeling. The sick ones were beyond enjoying anything.

After laughing their way through breakfast and getting unwanted stains of food on their uniforms, especially shirts and ties, the three got their trench coats and, holding to the handrails, made their way out to the deck. A blast of cold air hit them immediately, but it felt good to them. Trying to time their movements to the movement of the deck, they let go of their hold on the doors and made it to the rail.

Now in daylight, they could see how enormous the waves were. When the ship was up, they could see other ships of the convoy near and far. When the ship fell into a trough, no other vessels could be seen, not even those near at hand, which looked so large when their ship was on top of a swell—not even the tip of the tallest part of the ship closest to them.

"Hang on, you guys!" Bill shouted. "If you get blown or washed off, you're a goner!"

"Yeah, we're the only ones out here. Maybe this isn't smart," Chuck said.

At that moment, a seaman in oilskins came along the deck. "Captain suggests you go below, Sirs. He doesn't want to lose anybody," the seaman said. "We wouldn't be able to stop to help anyone overboard." The three made their way back across the deck and inside.

"Hey, what time are we supposed to be at the bursar's station?" Ed asked.

"09:00," Chuck said. "We've got two minutes to make it. I think we can find a way without going back out on deck."

A steward came around a corner, and when they asked him, he told them how to go. At 09:04 they were there.

The assistant bursar was not there, but a young seaman asked if they were the ones who wanted to be taken to the holds. They answered that they were. He replied, "It can be rough down there in this kind of sea. Noisy as hell, too. But you might find it exciting; I did. First time I had to go down in a storm I got queasy, though, because you can get disoriented. You don't feel much air movement. I'll take you if you want to go."

All three nodded, and trying hard to keep up with the experienced seaman, they went. He was not bothered by the ship's pitching, and he went down the stairways at breakneck speed, waiting at the bottom of each for them to catch up. The descent seemed interminable, down stairway after stairway, and through hatch after hatch. Finally, the seaman stopped. "This is it," he said, standing in a narrow, well-lit corridor, with a row of closed hatches on each side. "Below this is the bilge, and below that the keel."

The air was motionless, the pitching pronounced, but less so than farther up. They could hear the bilge water sloshing below the steel plates beneath their feet. They could also hear the ship groaning and occasionally shrieking—almost as if it would come apart. "Don't worry, that's just the ship's structure flexing. If it didn't do that, she'd have come apart hours ago. Every ship has to flex, or be destroyed."

Under the groaning and sloshing as an audible background was the steady throb of the engines, as they turned the giant screws that moved the ship. And all around them, they could hear the rumble of the seas as they battered the ship's hull.

Opening a hatch and locking it open, their guide said, "This is one compartment of four which contain canned goods." They followed him in and saw what looked like a warehouse full of cartons of canned goods, all secured so they could not break loose. "It would be God's own mess if these could break loose," the seaman said. "Anybody in here would be crushed, and we couldn't clean up until the storm was over."

They stepped out, feeling relieved. The seaman closed and secured the heavy hatch. "The other three are just like that. Now this one is the fresh vegetable compartment." He opened the hatch, and they stepped into a cool compartment, permeated with the smells of onions, beets, potatoes, all the smells to be found in a vegetable market. There they saw row upon row of bins marked potatoes, cabbage, carrots, and so forth.

"Next, up this way, are the refrigerated compartments." He opened the hatch, and they stepped in, glad that they had on their trench coats. "We keep it just a couple of degrees above freezing," the seaman said. "It keeps butter, cheese, eggs, fresh meat, stuff like that fresh. There are three more compartments just like this."

"Last," he said, "we'll take a quick look at one of the freezer compartments." He opened the hatch. "We have hundreds of gallons of every kind and flavor of ice cream and sherbet you could think of, plus frozen Milky Ways, and other frozen candy bars, plus a few other frozen things. Wouldn't want to stay in here too long."

"I saved the best for last," he said, swinging open another hatch. They smelled a wave of air laden with chocolate, mint, and licorice odors. "All kinds of candy bars and sweets in there. We keep it cool in here, too, but above freezing. Care for a bar?"

"Sure," they all said. He unfastened a metal container, opened it, and said, "Help yourself." Ed took a Hershey bar with almonds, Chuck a Mounds, and Bill a Baby Ruth. "Thanks," they said.

"Compliments of the bursar," he said. "This, by the way, is the smallest of our holds."

"My God, the rest must be enormous!" Chuck exclaimed.

"They are. All our stores and supplies are stored in other holds, everything catalogued, listed on inventories, every hold, compartment, bin is listed as to location and content, linens, cleaning, painting supplies, repair materials, electrical supplies, tools, everything we might need for anything on a voyage. Can't get to a hardware store or a grocery in the middle of the Atlantic. We had to stow extra food for this trip, since we're doing troop transport."

After the seaman led them back topside, they thanked him for the tour. Chuck tried to give him a ten dollar bill, but he said, "No thanks, Sir, it's just part of my duty." They thanked him again, and made their way back to their passenger area, hanging on to the handrails as the ship continued to pitch and roll in the enormous seas of the stormy North Atlantic.

Ed said, "Man! Now I know what they mean when they say 'Just the tip of the iceberg.' There's a lot more ship below the water line than there is above."

"Sure is," Bill agreed. "Speaking of water line, I wonder how all those WAACs are doing below. They must be packed in like sardines."

Chuck responded, "You'll never find out, Little Fellow. They have a special guard posted to keep undersized pilots of big airplanes out. We could borrow a rope, though, and lower you over the side. Then you could peek through one of their portholes."

"Good idea, Chuck," Ed added. "Hey, Bill, you could make a change in nautical terminology. From then on, portholes would be called peepholes. What do you say? Shall we look for a rope?"

"Okay with me, Hotshots. Once this storm is over I could probably climb right in and comfort those young ladies," Bill replied.

"I don't think 'comforting' is what you have in mind," Ed said.

"Depends on your definition of comfort," Bill answered.

"Yeah, Bill," Chuck put in, "we know your definition of comfort. We also know how great you think you are as a comforter."

"Just get the rope, and I'll prove how great I am," Bill said.

Stretching and yawning, Chuck said, "This conversation is getting boring. I'm going to the lounge; I saw some books there, Maybe something worth reading."

Ed said, "Good idea! Chuck, I'll go with you. Maybe it isn't so crowded now, with the storm going on. Might even find a place to sit down. How about you, Bill?"

"Nope," Bill replied. "I'm going to my cabin and sack out. Didn't get much sleep last night because of the storm. Maybe I'll dream about going through a porthole into a cabin full of luscious dames."

"Keep your hands outside of the sheets if you do," Chuck said. "See you later."

At midafternoon the storm began to subside, and by evening the sea was calm. With the wind reduced and the rolling of the ship much gentler, the three were comfortable on the deck, as were many others. They walked the deck, talking, as they watched the clouds disperse and the sky clear. Stars and a moon came out, and they could see other ships of the convoy. Now they could feel when the ship changed course as the zig-zagging continued.

At about 22:30 they heard depth charges much closer than any before. Looking aft, they could make out a destroyer closer than normal. It was apparently tracking a submarine that had slipped through the destroyer screen and was moving around inside the convoy. The three were, as were all the others aboard, concerned about this. Two dangers were evident: One was from the sub and its torpedoes; if it could hold a steady course for a couple of minutes, it could target one of the ships and launch its torpedoes. The other danger was from the destroyer; if it had to drop depth charges too close to one of the ships, that ship's hull could be damaged by those charges.

Everyone on deck grew silent as tension built. They could see the destroyer changing course frequently as it followed the submerged submarine. Every time the detroyer's captain thought he had the sub in the right position, he ordered charges dropped. The trouble was that he was getting closer and closer to the Argentina. This meant that the sub was getting closer too.

At less than a quarter-mile astern of the Argentina, the sound of depth charges was nearly continuous, one right after another. "I think he's right on him," someone muttered, and a half-dozen replied, "I hope so."

The destroyer was so close now that in the light of the moon and stars the spectators could make out crewmen moving about on the destroyer. Then the sound of one depth charge was followed immediately by a second, heavier, muffled explosion. Suddenly a small geyser erupted, followed by a slick of oil, clearly visible in the moonlight, spreading out from where the geyser had shot up. A cheer went up from the deck of the Argentina, echoed by the men on the destroyer, who waved as their craft turned to resume its patrolling.

"That was too close," Chuck said as he exhaled a long breath.

"Sure was," Ed agreed. "Sure makes you feel helpless, doesn't it?"

Bill said, "Any closer and I'd have pissed my pants. I've got to go. See you later," and he hurried toward his cabin.

Morning broke clear and crisp, and the three were on deck in time to watch the sun come up off their port bow, its orange glow tinting the tops of waves, making a pathway as far as they could see. Since their breakfast call would be three or so hours later, they had gone to the PX to buy extra large mugs of strong, hot coffee, which they now sipped as they stood at the port rail watching the sun.

"Has anybody seen Grant since we set sail?" Ed asked.

"I think I caught a glimpse of him pretty far down the corridor outside my room. Couldn't tell for sure, but he looked haggard as hell," Chuck responded.

"Hope he's okay. Strange not seeing him around. After breakfast, I think I'll see if I can find where he's bunking and check on him," Ed said.

Feeling the need for exercise, the three walked briskly for several laps around the deck. Bill said, "Let's shed these coats and trot around a few times. I really feel out of shape. What say?"

"Better put our coats in our rooms," Chuck suggested. "This is the only one I have."

"Right," Ed agreed. "We'll need them in jolly ol' wet foggy England."

After stowing their coats, they trotted for two laps, then increased their speed to a run and did two more. Each one felt welcome prickles as inactive sweat glands began to function.

"Feels good," Bill said. "I'm really out of shape. We should do this a couple of times a day."

"Yeah," Ed agreed. "But I'm going to break out a sweatshirt and shorts. I really need a shower, and these clothes are starting to stink."

"Right. And we're too late for fresh water. Guess it'll have to be that lousy saltwater again. I hate that. Always sticky after that," Chuck added.

After showering and putting on clean clothes, they met again for breakfast. Chuck said, "Hey. Did you know we can have our things laundered and dry-cleaned? Won't cost anything. Our steward told me. Be sure your names are on things, and leave them outside your door. They'll be picked up and returned to your room, all done up."

"Great," Ed said. "I've got a lot that need doing. Thanks."

They had just been seated in the Dining Salon when Ed looked up and saw Grant Perrin entering. He did, as Chuck had said, look haggard. Ed stood and called to him. Grant made his unsteady way through tables and chairs, and said with very little energy, "Hi."

"Where have you been hiding, man? You look like hell. What's wrong?" Ed asked. "Here, sit down."

"Okay, but *sitting* down isn't the problem. *Keeping* things down is. I've been sick as hell since the first day. Hardly been out of my cabin," Grant said.

"We were wondering," Chuck said. "Kept watching for you. I thought I got a glimpse of you yesterday, or the day before."

"Yeah. Thought I could make it to the PX and get some tea or something I might keep in my stomach. But that storm was hell for me. I barely made it back to my cabin to upchuck, and I didn't have anything to upchuck. Hell of a feeling. Real misery. Funny thing; I've been out on Lake Michigan in storms and never even felt queasy. But now I've had a really bad case. If I can face eating now, it'll be the first real meal I've had yet."

"You're kidding! That's rough," Ed said. "Hope you can eat; the food is terrific. Whoops! Sorry," he added, as he saw Grant grimace.

"It's okay. I think if I can just get something to stay down, anything, I'll get over this. Right now I feel weak. Think I could get some dry toast and a cup of tea?"

"Sure you can. This looks like our waiter now coming to take our orders. Just tell him what you want."

The waiter took their orders, and a few minutes later he hurried back with Grant's toast and a pot of tea. Grant took a small bite of toast, then a careful sip of tea. After waiting a minute, he gave a weak smile and took another nibble.

Soon he was gobbling up the toast and guzzling the tea. "What a relief," he said. "I want some more to eat, but I guess I'd better take it easy."

Soon the waiter was back with the others' orders: ham and eggs, sausage and eggs, bacon and eggs, toast, marmalade, juice, coffee and pancakes. For a moment Grant felt queasy, seeing all the food, then he smiled and said, "I think I'm okay."

The waiter said to Grant, "More toast, Sir? Or perhaps you'd like to try some cold cereal with skim milk?"

"That sounds good. Corn flakes, please, and more tea."

"Yes, Sir, I'll be right back."

"Goodo, Grant," Ed said, "You're looking better already. But you sure looked awful before. By this afternoon you'll be rarin' to go."

Grant responded, "I hope so. All that junk you guys are stuffing down is beginning to look good. But I'm taking it easy for a while."

"Probably best," Bill agreed. "By the way, I'm Bill Schramm. Don't think we've met before, but Ed tells me you were with us at Maxwell."

"I was. I knew Ed and Chuck there, but I missed you. I was in a different squadron," Grant replied, "then I went to a different Primary when you all went to Bennettesville."

"Way it goes sometimes," Chuck said. "When you feel better, let's compare experiences at your Primary and ours, okay?"

"Sure. I think I might make it now. Feeling a lot better," Grant replied. "Think I better get back to my room, though. I'll hang out there for a while, in case the improvement is temporary."

"Okay. Come up on the deck when you feel better," Ed suggested. "I always feel better up there where the air is better than down here below decks, or even in my cabin. Something about the salt in the air, I think."

"Right. See you all later," Grant said, walking away much steadier than when they'd first seen him.

To the others, Ed said, "He's a good guy. Hope he's over it now; I've never seen a usually healthy guy look worse."

"Yeah," Bill agreed. "He had a bad case of something. Wonder if it was all seasickness, or did he have stomach flu?"

"Hard to tell, but he sure looked drained. You guys about finished? Let's get up on deck and breathe some more of that salt air Ed's talking about," Chuck said.

Ed and Bill gulped the last of their coffee, and the three went up and out onto the deck. The ocean was deep blue and green every way they looked, and calm. All was peaceful. Too peaceful. Time was beginning to weigh heavily on them; too little to do. They had explored every part of the ship they were allowed access to and now, after the often frenetic activity of their training, they were growing bored with nothing to do. They found themselves taking to their bunks early and getting up late. They were eating and drinking too much. They were conscious that these things were happening, and that they were not good, but they continued doing them. They set up a schedule for running on the deck three times a day. Bill tried to interest them in some calesthenics, but they declined. Boredom settled down on them, as on all the other fliers aboard. Some played bridge or poker. Games went on all over their part of the ship. Others read a great deal, Ed among them. A few were chess players, and they indulged themselves in that game incessantly. But none of these activities took the place of the real action for which they were primed.

At length, the captain came on the P.A., announcing that they were leaving the convoy, and that soon they should see Ireland to the east. Then it would not be long before they would be pulling into the London docks. Everybody cheered this news.

Ireland was obscured by fog as they moved past it, too far to the east to see the famous emerald color, even if it had not been cloaked in fog. With the gray blur of Ireland dropping back on the port side, then out of sight, they began a gradual turn eastward, then south again. The coast of Wales came clearly into view, the sun glinting off her mountains. Staying well out, the ship went past the southern tip of the British Isle, then began a slow turn eastward again. At last, taking what seemed an eternity, they made a northward turn into the English Channel.

Now there were many ships, mainly British and U.S., moving about them, as well as tenders and fishing boats, and other small craft. Near the mouth of the River Thames, the engines slowed, and the Argentina seemed to be standing still as a British naval launch came alongside. Uniformed men climbed aboard. They saluted and were piped aboard. Proceeding to the bridge, they exchanged salutes with the captain and Colonel Sampson, exchanged some papers, saluted again, and left. In about fifteen minutes, two sturdy tugs hove to, one on either side of the ship; lines were cast and attached, and, finally, they were moving slowly toward their assigned berth.

Like all major ports, London's waterfront was a busy, rather smelly and dirty place. There appeared to be much random activity both on the water and on shore, but Ed and the others decided that it just appeared random because they, the observers, did not know what was going on. The tugs pulled and nudged the big ship safely and gently into its berth, and they were in England.

From the ship, London, one of the world's great cities, was not impressive. Ugly warehouses and storage tanks were everywhere. Cargo handlers, lifters, cranes, blocks and tackle were scattered over the docks, with no discernible order. Ships of all shapes and sizes, displaying a wide variety of colors, were being moved in and out of berths, or standing still at their moorings for loading or unloading. Visibly oily water lapped at the ships' sides, and an oily pall seemed to hang over the entire area. In the distance, now muted by evening mist and failing sunlight, some of London's buildings could dimly be seen. Darkness came quickly, and no lights could be seen in the blacked-out city.

Fully expecting to go ashore immediately, all the passengers on the Argentina were let down when Colonel Sampson's voice came on the P.A. "We should all thank whatever God we worship for a safe passage. I'm sorry to say that your disembarkation will not start until tomorrow; there is no transportation available for tonight. At 06:00 tomorrow, all members of the WAAC contingent will leave the ship, in the order called out on the P.A. All Air Corps officers are to be prepared to disembark at 09:00. Early breakfast will be served in your established order. The WAACs will be served at their base, not far from here. Coffee and doughnuts will be given to them as they descend the gangway.

"Following breakfast, the Air Corps officers will disembark, load onto buses, and be transported north to Hull-on-Humber. There they will be assigned quarters and await further orders. Your foot lockers will be there when you arrive. As each contingent finishes breakfast, you will move down the gangway as your names are called. Your duffel bags and suitcases will be your own responsibility. This is a combat zone; all military rules and orders are to be observed. In the event of an air raid siren sounding, do what your driver or the nearest air raid warden instructs you to do. Good luck, and God be with all of you. That is all."

Disappointed but not surprised, Ed and his friends went to their cabins to pack up while waiting for their dinnertime.

Ed wondered vaguely what was at Hull, but decided he'd know when he got there. He felt a little shiver when he remembered that, except for two brief drives across the border into Canada, this was his first time in a foreign country. Basically, he thought, I'm still in the States, since this ship is U.S. property. Tomorrow, though, I'll be in a foreign country. Wonder if it will feel different?

Without warning, another feeling rushed over him. "I feel as if I'm really getting close to flying P-51s. I know it's stupid, but I feel it. Wouldn't that be great? Finally doing my little bit to rid the world of Hitler, and doing it in a P-51! Wonder what it's going to be like?"

He packed everything but his uniform for the next day, and his travel kit with wash-up and shaving stuff in it. Then he went to round up his buddies, this time including Grant, who by now was feeling like his old self. All four were ready when their dinnertime came, and they made it a feast of celebration: Four eager pilots ready to do their bit in a cause that they believed was just and right.

COMBAT

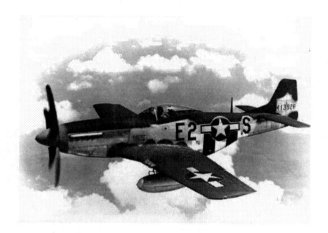

23

Morning came, and after breakfast, the four friends went down the gangway and stepped onto England. Bill, as a bomber pilot, was assigned to a different bus from the other three. All the goodbye they had time for was a "Good flying," and a handshake. "We'll see you over Germany!" they yelled to Bill as he went to his bus.

All they saw of London as their bus headed north was the dock area and the outskirts. This was another disappointment, but knowing they would be based in England, they expected that they would have chances to explore London. On the highway, not far from the Channel coast, they saw hundreds of British and American military vehicles, jeeps, cars, lorries and buses, and a sprinkling of French, along with an occasional Polish one.

They read signposts to villages and towns, and some sixty miles north of London, Ed was excited to see a sign pointing to a village named "Thorne." He said to his friends, "Hey, I knew my background was Norman/English/Irish/Scottish, and I knew my ancestors were famous in Scandinavia, Normandy, and in the Norman conquest of England and Ireland, but I didn't know they were important enough around here to have a village named for them."

"It still flows out of you, doesn't it?" Chuck said.

"Watch it, friend! My heritage is one of great and noble fighters and leaders. Some of my people played major parts in the Norman conquests. They were rewarded with thousands of acres of land. They built many great castles, and gave much to the church, establishing abbeys and monasteries and churches everywhere. Later on, one was knighted by Richard the Lion-Hearted, and one was a guardian of the Magna Carta. So watch what you say. I have conqueror's blood in me."

Chuck continued needling, "Conquerors of what? Shit houses?"

"Yeah," Grant added, "What good is all that crap in a fighter plane?"

"Okay, okay," Ed responded, "just thought it was interesting that my surname is on a village here in England, just as it is on several places in the States, to say nothing of in Ireland too. I can't help it if I'm in the great tradition of heroes."

Grant gave a loud Bronx cheer, and Chuck laughed.

"Okay, I guess I deserved that. Anyway, they rode horses, and I'll ride a P-51 if I'm lucky. In both cases the mission is to destroy the enemy. I hope to do my part," Ed said quietly.

"Right, Ol' Buddy," Chuck said, "we were just needling. We all hope the same."

"Sure," Ed replied. "And I think we're getting pretty close to a chance to do that. Pretty soon we're going to have to take this war seriously."

"You're right about that," Grant said. "We're already in a combat area. Doesn't feel any different yet, but I bet it will."

With that, all three settled down, each quietly thinking his own thoughts.

A few miles up the road they could see a sizeable village off to the right. Suddenly sirens began to moan. The driver immediately pulled over and stopped the bus. "Everyone out and into the ditch beside the road," he ordered. "Take nothing with you." They lost no time doing as the driver ordered, jumping out and down the gravel slope beside the road. The ditch, fortunately, was dry. They huddled low in it.

"Look up there," Chuck said, his voice excited. He pointed eastward. High up against the pale blue of the sky, they saw a dozen condensation trails, and the sun glinting off an airplane at the head of each. Puffs of smoke began to appear as coastal anti-aircraft batteries began to open fire.

"Really unusual," the driver said. "The Germans don't often come over in daylight. Unless they're fighters on a mission to dive-bomb an airfield."

Untouched by the anti-aircraft fire, the planes passed overhead. Then abruptly they moved into inline formation and one after another went into a vertical dive. "That's it!" the driver yelled. "They're dive-bombing something." As they dove, the flak increased around them from an inland battery, probably at the target. The third one in line, halfway down in his dive, exploded. "Good! They got one of the bastards!" someone yelled. "Now they have the range." As his yell ended, another of the German planes exploded, at about the same altitude as the other one had. All the men in the ditch cheered. As they watched, hypnotized by their first sighting of enemy action, a third and a fourth exploded. "Somebody's really good on the Ack-ack," the driver said. "Four out of twelve isn't bad, but the other eight can do a hell of a lot of damage." Just then they saw one of the planes coming right at them. "Get down!" the driver yelled at some of the men who had stood up to cheer. "He's going to strafe us! Get down! Eat dirt!"

Ed and all the others pressed themselves hard against the earth. Any sound of machine guns or of bullets in the air was obscured by the sound of the onrushing airplane. But they were thankful for the ditch when they looked up and saw the bus with shattered windows and small holes in several places. Now they could hear the staccato machine-gun fire from the direction of the village. This was followed by heavier reports as the coastal AA guns opened up again. A booming explosion followed, farther to the east. "I think they got him," the driver said. "Stay down. Some of the others may come over us."

They remained in the ditch until the all-clear sounded from the village. Then the driver said, "Let's go," and they all brushed themselves off and re-boarded the bus.

"Sons-a-bitches," Grant snarled. "They mean business. Without that ditch, some of us would have bought it."

"Hell of a way to go," Chuck spat out, "hiding in a ditch and no way to fight back. Give me an airplane and let me at least have a chance to fight."

Ed and Grant agreed, with Ed adding, "We've had our first taste of combat, and I don't like the taste of it when we're defenseless."

"Hell yeah," Grant agreed. "Give me an airplane. I'm not ready for ground warfare."

Chuck said, "Good thing he didn't have more altitude. He could have put those guns right on us by putting his nose down a little bit. Good break for us."

"Yeah," Ed responded. "We were a target of opportunity all right. Good thing the Nazi blew it. We're here to fly. Hope we get a chance to do it!"

"Man! I've never felt so vulnerable and helpless. Makes you sick to the stomach, doesn't it?" Grant asked.

They all agreed. Chuck called out, "Hey, Driver. Can we have a piss stop pretty soon? That scare made my kidneys work overtime."

Everybody on the bus agreed. The driver said, "There's a fair-sized town just ahead. I'll turn off there. Probably have public latrines. Time for a chow break anyway. There're a couple of pubs right in the town center. What do you say? They usually have some kind of food about this time of day."

All the men yelled, "Yeah! Let's do it."

"Okay," the driver said, turning on to a side road, "but split up. If we all go to the same pub, it'll take forever to get fed."

Ed and his friends, plus fifteen others, went into the King's Arms. As they opened the door, warm, moist air swept over them. It was accompanied by high level conversation noise, punctuated by raucous laughter. Ed, Chuck, and Grant were the first through the door. The conversation sound subsided, then died out, as the pub's regulars saw that the newcomers were Yanks. There were no women customers present. Most of the men wore rough farmers' clothes, with two or three in suits. Half a dozen blue uniformed RAF men were scattered about the room. As the silence continued, all eyes in the pub turned toward the newcomers. While not hostile, the eyes were not friendly either. Ed felt that he was intruding in their domain, and he had the urge to turn around and leave. The rest of his busmates were crowding in, so he was pushed ahead to the bar.

Ed was about to ask if they could get something to eat when one of the blue-uniformed men stepped up behind him. "Hello, Yank. Don't mind the stares. We're not used to seeing so many of you chaps all at once around here. I see by your wings, you're a pilot. My name's Chumley," he said, holding out his hand, "William Chumley. What's yours?"

Ed looked at the broad, red-cheeked face, and at the cloth wings sewed on the blue jacket. The blue eyes were smiling. Relieved, he shook the man's hand, "Ed Thorne," he said.

"Thorne? With an 'e'? We've a town not far from here named 'Thorne.' Any connection?"

"We passed it on the way up here. I don't know about a connection; it's possible somewhere in the past," Ed replied.

"Pilot, are you?" Chumley asked. "Come to help us win the war, eh? We need all the help we can get. I'm a pilot m'self, just learning to handle Lanks—you know, Lancasters."

"Oh, yes. Right. A mighty bomber, I've read," Ed replied. "We're mostly fighter pilots."

"Godamighty! We need 'em. Been getting ours shot to hell out of the skies. Damn Germans have too many fighters. But we'll get 'em," William said. "Well, come on then. Find seats around." Then, to the publican, "Johnny. Got a gaggle o' Yank fliers here. Their money's good as any, can you serve them?"

"Righto, Will'um, are ye lookin' to eat, or is it drinks ye want?"

"Both," the Americans chorused.

Ed said, "How about drinks all around, then some chow?" They all agreed, and the publican asked what they'd have.

Starting the ordering, Ed said, "Pint o' Guiness, please."

"No more of that for me," Chuck said, getting a laugh from the publican and some of the civilians in the crowd.

"Bit 'ard to tyke, eh? It'll grow on ye," the publican said, "Tykes adjustin' to."

Chuck and most of the others ordered lager, and soon they were all seated, sipping contentedly. The conversation level had returned to its previous high, and all of the RAF men, as well as several of the civilians, stepped over to shake hands with the Yanks. William squeezed in between Ed and Chuck. "You blokes will run into some resentment, you know. We've been wanting you in ever since the bloody war started. Nobody over here could quite understand what you were waiting for."

"A lot of us thought the same," Ed said. "That includes FDR. But it was politically impossible for him to bring us in until Pearl Harbor. Then everybody screamed for immediate action. But we were a long way from ready. We were just starting mobilization and training, even just getting a real start on production of war goods when the Japs attacked."

"We know that, but it's been bloody tough going it almost alone. French were done in, with all the rest of the Continent. Then Stalin kept Russia out of it. It's been hell! No matter what you hear, we wanted you in. We're glad you're finally here."

"Hope we can get things going fast enough to make a difference before it's too late," Chuck said.

"You've already made a difference. A great cheer went up all the way from 10 Downing Street to the remotest town in Scotland when the Japs attacked Pearl Harbor. Not cheering for your losses, but because the most potentially powerful nation on earth finally had to jump in. We were hanging on by our fingernails 'til then."

"Beth! Come out here, girl," the publican called through a doorway at the end of the bar. A nice-looking blond girl, about fourteen or fifteen years of age, came out. "Tell the Yanks what we have for eating, and take their orders. There's a good girl."

"Oh, Daddy, please. I . . .

"Now, now, lass, they won't hurt ye, and I need your help. Get along, now."

Eyes on the floor, Beth came toward the Americans. Her face grew pink as she said, barely audibly, "We 'ave meat pie, 'omemade vegetable soup, an' we can make up cheese sandwiches." She had to repeat the menu several times before all the Americans could hear it. They all smiled and said encouraging words to her, and finally she raised her eyes and a radiant smile lit up her face. "You're very nice, you Yanks. We're glad you came here."

All the men cheered and applauded, bringing back the blush. William said, "Good lass, Beth. These chaps have no experience with English food. Why don't you bring out all the meat pies you have, then soup and sandwiches for those who don't care for the pies? All right, chaps?"

All the Americans said that that was a good idea, so Beth did a little curtsy, blushed and smiled again, then hurried back through the doorway.

"She's a killer," Chuck said. "Man-oh-man! What'll she be like in a couple of years!"

"She's a sweet lass, right enough," William said. "If you want to be beaten up and hung out to dry, just try something with one of our really young lasses! We're very touchy about that here. That's another reason why you will encounter some resentment here. Compared to our servicemen, you are all grossly overpaid. With all that money jingling in your pockets, we're at a disadvantage with the lasses. In addition, it's a fantasy of a great many of our finest young ladies to marry a rich American—and we see you all as rich—and live in luxury in the States. Just as they see it in the flicks. I think you can understand why not everybody will be pleasant to you, even some comrades-in-arms. Being allies doesn't necessarily mean giving over all of our most lovely lasses."

Beth served the meat pies, and most of the Yanks liked them. There weren't enough to go around, so those who didn't get pies were served soup, which they found to be excellent, and sandwiches, which were good enough, but dry. Everyone had another beer, and it was time to go.

William held his glass up as he stood, saying, "For the Yanks, hip, hip, hooray," and the entire crowd joined in, repeating it three times. The Yanks called out their thanks, shook hands with William and the publican, waved goodbye to Beth, who was standing near her father, and left to board the bus. They continued north toward Hull.

That city, on the River Humber, turned out to be an active town of some 50,000 inhabitants. As the buses arrived and discharged their passengers, the fliers were assigned sleeping quarters and told to come to an assembly hall as soon as they got rid of their luggage and relieved themselves.

At the hall, they were told that they were there for orientation and briefing sessions, training in the use of Mae Wests and inflatable dinghies, including putting the former on under water, then inflating the dinghies and climbing into them, while floating in the water. This part of the program would be done in a swimming pool in town. They were informed that they would be at Hull for three days. On the fourth day, they would leave for already assigned airfields in England and Scotland, where they would be checked out in fighters. Part of the second day would be their choosing among various fighter squadrons, mostly flying p-47s and P-51s. For each of the squadrons, the fighter currently being used would be indicated. That choice would then determine where they would be sent for checkout.

Ed's spine tingled as he listened to that information. "I get a choice? Wow! I don't care where I go, just so I get 51s. Man! Hope all those slots aren't filled before they get to me. I'm pretty far down the alphabet. Even if I get 47s, I should be able to transfer later, if my outfit doesn't change over to 51s."

Several instructions later, they were dismissed. Ed and his two buddies, talking excitedly, returned to their quarters to shower and change clothes before going for chow. "Well, Ol' Pal, it looks like you have a good chance of getting into Mustangs," Chuck said, using the recently assigned popular name for the P-51.

"Sure does," Ed responded, his enthusiasm showing in his voice and on his face. "Hope all those slots aren't taken before I get to choose."

After dinner, they walked a short distance toward town and found a pub. The local people in the pub had grown accustomed to American fliers, so they felt welcome, and were served drinks promptly. They returned to their quarters and went to bed early, tired after their long and eventful day.

In the morning they were given another orientation lecture, the main point of which was the pervasiveness of enemy spies and agents, and the need for care about where and with whom they talked about their outfits' operations, strengths, number of planes, losses, changes in personnel, major missions planned, and so forth. "The Nazis have eyes and ears everywhere. Their operatives, most of them paid local people, report every little bit of information they pick up to their higher-up contacts. These people then send it on to their higher-ups, and so on, until thousands of tiny, seemingly insignificant bits of what the British call 'gen,' or intelligence information, is relayed to German Intelligence across the channel, where it is all analyzed and collated, so a surprisingly complete picture of our operations is kept, and updated constantly. Loose tongues are the spy's best source of information. They are not distinguishable from other members of the local community. They often buy our guys a drink at the pub, because, 'we're glad you're here, Yank.' It's okay to accept a drink at the pub, but not to talk about anything but the weather." The major concluded by saying, "Of course, we do the same thing, as the British, French, and Russians do. Everybody everywhere has a network of information gatherers. We should always be careful not to make their jobs easier."

This was followed by a demonstration of putting on a Mae West and inflating a dinghy, then by a training film showing how to do these things on and under water. Donning the Mae West was not new to those who, like Ed and Chuck, had had final training in the States near the Gulf of Mexico. It was new to most of the other pilots in the orientation session. The dinghy information was new to all of them.

A special point was made of the frigidity of the North Sea, and how little time one has if he bails out or ditches there before he is immobilized by the cold, and how little chance he has then of surviving. "It is imperative that you get your dinghy opened and inflated quickly, and climb into it," was the final message.

Prior to being dismissed for noon chow, all names were called out, each with a time to board a bus for the swimming pool exercise the next day.

Ed, Grant, arnd Chuck, like all the others, gulped down their food, eager to get to the assembly hall for choosing groups and squadrons. As they expected, the procedure was by alphabetical order. The hall had been rearranged while the fliers ate, now having long tables, each with chairs on two sides. At each place was a large sheet of paper fastened to the table. On each sheet was a list of each group and squadron, where located, and what aircraft they were currently flying.

Each man was handed a form as he entered the hall. The form had a place for name, rank, serial number, and hometown. Below that were spaces marked first, second and third choices. On a large chalkboard, dominating the platform end of the room, the number of each squadron/group was printed as its quota was filled. This information was of no use to the waiting officers until they were seated at one of the tables, and could check the "Filled" numbers with the ones on the large sheet.

The procedure was being carried out efficiently, but to Ed and his two friends, waiting for their turn at the tables, the letters P, S, and T seemed to take forever to be called. Perrin was the third P to be called, and the other two watched as he hurried to a seat, quickly scanned the sheet on the table, looked up at the chalkboard, quickly wrote on his form, and then repeated this twice. Standing up, he grinned at them and gave the "okay" sign, and went out the door, handing in his form as he left.

"Lucky dog," Ed said. "Hope he didn't get the last 51 opening."

Chuck's name was called, and Ed watched him do the same thing. His first look at the chalkboard was followed by a negative shake of his head. The second and third, then a fourth, were followed by an elaborate shrug. Ed translated this as "No 38s. First, second and third choice is P-47s."

Ed heard his name and dashed to the seat just vacated.

He scanned the sheet for 51s. He found lots of them, but each time he looked at the chalkboard, the ones he was checking for were on the board marked "Filled." Finally, he found one that wasn't on the board. He quickly filled out his form, and on an impulse, put that one, the 359th Fighter Group at East Wretham, as first, second and third choice. It was the only 51 outfit left unfilled. He rushed his form to the sergeant who was accepting them, and waited. Sure enough, in a few minutes the corporal at the chalkboard put 359th up. Ed was still standing at the checkout table. The sergeant showed him his form with second and third choices crossed out. "You got the last 51, Sir," he said.

"I got the last 51," Ed thought as he rushed out the door. "I'm going to fly the Mustang!" He rushed up to Chuck and Grant, who were waiting outside the door.

"Damn it!" Chuck exclaimed. "I had to settle for 47s. How'd you do?"

Before Ed could answer, Grant said, "Sorry, Ed. No possibility you got 51s. There were only three 51 outfits left when I signed up."

"Wrong, Ol' Buddy. I got the last one. I'm the last guy for the last 51 group available. Yahoo!"

"What group?" Grant yelled.

"359th!" Ed shouted back.

"Hey! Me too! We're going to the same group!" Grant shouted. "We'll be at East Wretham, wherever the hell that is."

"No 38s left," Chuck moaned again. "I had to go with 47s. The 298th Fighter Group, at some place called Addington."

Ed said, "Hard lines, Ol' Friend. I hate it that we're going to be split up after all this time together."

"Well, I knew there wouldn't be many groups flying 38s, so I'm not surprised. Probably be somebody there I know; if not, it's the breaks. Yeah, I hate it too. We've been through a lot together. But we're on the same team, just at different locations. What say we skip dinner at the base and walk down to that friendly pub? I noticed they serve hot meals there."

"Great," Ed said. "I need a latrine first, though."

"Me too. I think there's one right here. All this excitement makes you have to go."

"Guess I'd better too," Chuck said, and they all went into the latrine, then started for the pub.

They drank toasts to 51s and 47s, with regrets to 38s. They followed this with toasts to Fighter Command, Eisenhower, the Allies, to each other, and joined a group of RAF types in a toast to His Royal Highness, King George.

"Let's get some food," Grant suggested. "This British beer seems to go right to my brain. I don't think it even passes through my stomach; right from mouth to brain."

Seeing his chance, Ed said, "First time I ever knew there was a connection between your mouth and your brain."

Grant said, "If we weren't going to be forced to fly together, Ol' Sock, I'd take offense at that."

They ordered mutton stew, salad, rhubarb pie, and coffee. Although the food was far from what they had had on the Argentina and at the Fort Dix Officers' Mess, it was tasty and they enjoyed it.

After breakfast the next day, buses took contingents of pilots to the building housing the city's swimming pool. They had been instructed to bring an old pair of fatigues, or a flight suit that needed cleaning, with empty pockets. Now they removed their uniforms and dressed in what they had brought. In a real crash situation, they would have on boots or shoes, but it was not practical to require or to supply these, so they were barefoot. Procedures were reviewed; then, six at a time, the fliers were fitted with Mae Wests and parachute harnesses, to which were buckled the folded, deflated dinghies. Then the six would jump, not dive, into seven-foot water. Underwater, they were to disconnect and let drop the harness, hanging on to the dinghy, inflate the Mae West, giving them buoyancy, then with head above water, release the compressed gas from the cylinder attached to the dinghy. The last step was to clamber up and into the now-inflated dinghy.

Ed, not a good swimmer, and very poor at treading water, took a large lungful of air as he jumped, almost losing it when he hit the extremely cold water. He allowed himself to sink as he got rid of the harness, inflated the Mae West, and bobbed to the surface. There he inflated his dinghy and, clumsily, like all the others, climbed in. He and the other five then paddled to the edge of the pool and climbed out. Each one was handed a towel as he stood shivering on the concrete.

"All passed. Get dressed," the officer in charge called, and the six gratefully got out of their dripping clothes, dried off, and got dressed.

The rest of the day was uneventful until late afternoon, when an announcement came over the P.A. that all assignments for fighter checkout had been made and posted on the bulletin board in front of the assembly building. In the mad rush by all the pilots, most missed the rest of the announcement: that orders were being cut for each officer for destination, and how to get there. These could be picked up at headquarters at any time after 17:00, this date.

Ed and Grant were on a list of ten for a base at a place called Larrabee, Scotland. Chuck would be going to a small English town near Cambridge. "We're almost to combat, guys," Ed said. "Chuck, I'm going to miss you. We might not see each other again after chow tomorrow morning. We need some time together. Let's go down to the pub after we get our orders, okay?"

"You bet. Last drinks together. Final toasts, all that," Chuck replied.

Grant said, "Think I'll stay on the base. You guys go without me. I'll see enough of Ed from now on."

Chuck and Ed protested, but Grant was determined, so he and Chuck said their good-byes then and there. Since it was now 17:00, they all went to pick up their orders. Ed's and Grant's were identical. Board bus at headquarters next day, leave bus at ferry crossing in Hull, board ferry for crossing River Humber. Board train for trip to Larrabee station; there Air Corps bus would meet them and transport them to the base for P-51 checkout. Ed shivered as he anticipated P-51s.

A second paragraph instructed them, at the conclusion of their brief checkout period, to proceed by public transportation to East Wretham to join their group. The only variation, aside from their names and serial numbers, was in their squadron assignments. Grant would be in the 368th; Ed in the 369th. Both were elated that they would be flying Mustangs, and in the same group. Chuck would be going to a P-47 base near Nottingham for checkout in the "Thunderbolt."

This settled, Chuck and Ed headed for the pub. Not surprisingly, many of the other pilots had discovered that they were welcome at this friendly, convenient pub, so it was crowded. After a moment's delay, they found seats in a booth and ordered their drinks.

After several pints, Ed and Chuck were as close to tears as was permissible for lean, mean fighter pilots to be, at least in public. They repeatedly drank to their everlasting friendship, to each other, to the Army Air Corps, to the P-51, the P-47, and to Chuck's P-38, which he probably would never get to fly, since they were being phased out in the ETO.

"One more, to the Spitfire," Ed insisted. "I hope to get to fly one of those before I leave Merry ol' England." They drank to the "Spit," and some RAF fliers in the next booth joined in the toast, then reciprocated by toasting the 51.

As the number of Yank pilots increased, most of the locals left, knowing that these young pilots were only days away from active combat flying. Knowing this, they left ungrudgingly. The publican was kept refilling glasses, as "Same again, please," rang out over and over. He had his wife come out to carry glasses to the customers and to wash dishes, as they exhausted their ready supply.

The noise level increased as more fliers had enough to drink to release them from their inhibitions. Toasts, songs, cheers were everywhere. Everyone smiled at the publican's lady, a maturely attractive dark-haired lady, teasing her, getting back from her as good as they gave, but all in good humor. No one said or did anything crude or off-color, so she was enjoying the attention, joining in the fun.

At one point, the evening well along, the publican burst into a funny parody of "God Save the King." All the customers cheered and applauded. The evening was a joyous combination of pride and happiness at what the pilots had accomplished so far, and limitless enthusiasm for what they were about to do. Added to this were fond farewells to buddies from the long training period, with its frustrations, losses, and delays. Now, at last, they were about to arrive at the destinations they had sought. Everybody knew that some of those celebrating would not last out the war, but everybody also refused to let the knowledge dampen his spirits. Each one knew, with the certain invulnerability of youth, that he would make it.

Chuck and Ed ate lots of pub grub to keep the flow of beer from swamping them, and they succeeded. At last, the publican announced, "Time, gentlemen, it's time," and reluctantly all the airmen left, after a rousing chorus of "Into the Air, Army Air Corps." Ed and Chuck, arms around each other's shoulders, each feeling a mixture of joy and sadness, walked to the base. They knew the chips would soon be down, and they were thrilled at the thought. But they also knew that the carefree days of training and easy comradeship were behind them.

Unwilling to end this night of celebration and farewell, and regretting that Grant had not been with them, they went to the Officers' Club. There they found Grant, and they ordered coffee and sweet rolls. Grant had had a good time at the club, where there never was a shortage of companions, but he joined Ed and Chuck for coffee. They all knew that this evening had to end, so after an hour, and with the effects of the beer wearing off, they became more morose. Soon they made their quiet way toward their quarters, where Ed and Grant said many farewells to Chuck, with all three promising to keep in touch. While at the pub, Chuck and Ed had located East Wretham and Cambridge on the large wall map there. They had discovered that the towns were not so far from each other that visits would be out of the question. At last, they shook hands once more, and said goodnight to each other.

Grant and Ed met at the Officers' Mess for an early breakfast, neither feeling quite sound, but neither actually hungover, either. They reported at 08:00 and boarded the bus for the ferry terminal. Chuck had been on ferryboats around New York, and he had told them about them. It was a first time for Ed and Grant, and they were fascinated to see how many people and vehicles could be loaded aboard, to watch some sheep herded on, and then, with what seemed more than necessary clamor and clatter, the boat backed out of the dock, swung around, and headed for the far shore. There it turned about again, backed into the wharf, and unloaded. Ed and Grant saw that the ferry and the train were a part of the same company, so the train depot was right there.

As they had when boarding the ferry boat, they turned over the tickets that had been attached to their orders as they got on the train. "Right," the attendant said. "First-class compartment just there," and he opened the door for them. They had the compartment to themselves, so after placing their suitcases above, they stretched out for a relaxing ride through the beautiful hills of Scotland.

Swiftly and smoothly between stops, the train made its way. Some cows, a few horses, and many sheep were in the rocky pastures. At times, they had glimpses of rugged mountains in the distance. They saw no kilts. All the Scots people they saw were dressed in country work clothes or suits, and once in a while, plus-fours or riding britches. At one point there was a magnificent-looking chestnut horse being ridden up a rocky pass by a young lady in full riding habit. At a rural stop, they watched a fox scurry across the platform, followed a moment later by a group of boys carrying sticks. Some people waved as they watched the train move by. Once, a ruddy-faced gentleman, about fifty, tapped on their door and entered when they said, "Come in." Grant invited him to sit. "Canna stay," he said. "Ye're Yanks, I see. Glad to have ye here. Wi'ou' ye, the war's lost." Opening his briefcase, he produced a bottle labeled "White Horse Scotch." "Would ye care for a tot a' the true liquid?" he asked.

Though it was only 10:00, both Ed and Grant, not wanting to offend, said, "Yes, Sir, please." The man took three small glasses out of the case, and said, "'Tis the liquid that makes the da' bricht." With that, he filled each glass nearly to the brim. Thanking him, they each took a glass as he held them out to them. "To yer verrry guid health," he said, tipping his glass and draining it. Neither Ed nor Grant could do that with this, which from the taste of it, could not be White Horse. It had a powerful bite, and a strong peat aftertaste. Their eyes watered as they swallowed their first too-large gulps.

"Make it m'self," the man said. "I'm Maxwell Campbell," and he extended his hand, shaking with each of them. "The Campbells've always done their own, and I keep the tradition. I use the White Horse bottle to fool the tax man, another grand tradition. Well, lads, drink it down, I must ge' back to m' wife an' m' bairns." He poured and downed another glass of the potent liquid, and the two pilots did their best to gulp theirs down, but they still had to take it easy. At last, both their glasses were empty, but their voices were strange as they thanked the Scot. "'Tis nothin'," he said. "A bit powerful if ye aren't accustomed to it, but the taste will stay wi' ye and grow better. God be wi' ye, lads," and he was gone.

Wondering if they would have to accept more such offerings, and how often, Ed and Grant laughed quietly, knowing that any more such, and they would report drunk. They were spared any such embarrassment as they saw the Ellersbee sign and got off the train.

A small bus was waiting, and all the pilots assigned to Ellersbee boarded it and were whisked away. They stopped at a tiny grass field hidden in a cleft on the side of a mountain. A single airstrip was marked off. At the side was a small hangar housing two fighter planes. Control was from a small ground-level hut, and a set of three quonset buildings marked mess hall, Officers' Quarters, and Enlisted Quarters stood there too.

No one met the bus, so they walked directly to the Officers' Quarters. Stepping in, they found a small office where a first lieutenant in a raunchy uniform, wearing no tie, and with a floppy garrison cap pushed to the back of his head, sat with his feet up on the desk. A curl of smoke rose from a cigarette resting on a saucer, which also held a half-full coffee cup.

"Come in gentlemen, come in," the lieutenant said, and they crowded into the cramped office. His feet remained on the desk as he continued. "I'm Carl Olmstead, Ninth Tactical Air Force. I have the pleasure of being intimately acquainted with the best fighter plane in the world. I was one of the first fliers in this theater to get one, and believe me, she'll outdo anything we or the Brits or the Germans have. I know, because I've flown everything the Brits have, against everything the Nazis have, and the 51's the best."

Ed felt prickles of excitement on the back of his neck, and he nudged Grant, who was standing next to him.

The lieutenant went on. "I'm on detached service with the job of checking you men out in that bird. We'll start on that right after chow. Find yourselves bunks down the hail, stow your stuff, piss if you need to, come back here and we'll chow down."

All ten of the newcomers pushed into the hallway. They found three rooms on each side of the hall, each containing two bunks and little else except two chairs and hooks on the walls. The first room on their right was obviously the lieutenant's, leaving five unoccupied, so they paired off, two to a room. Grant and Ed took the one next to the lieutenant's, and the others claimed the rest. They found the latrine at the far end of the building, and all used it, then they returned to the office. Lieutenant Olmstead said, "Let's go," and led the way to the mess hall.

The mess hall was set up cafeteria-style, and had two long tables — one for officers, one for enlisted personnel. After following the lieutenant down the chow line, where their trays were loaded with mashed potatoes, hamburger gravy, baked tomatoes and rice pudding, they seated themselves, five on a side of the officers' table, with the lieutenant at one end.

During lunch, they learned that Olmstead had joined the RAF in '39, had flown Spitfires and Hurricanes in Africa, and then, during the brief, disastrous campaign on the Continent ending at Dunkirk, he again flew the two famous British fighters. During his time in the RAF, he had also flown the A-36, predecessor to the 51. He and his fellow RAF pilots had learned the good and the bad qualities of that short-lived airplane, and he had followed its conversion to the P-51 with great interest. As soon as the U.S. entered the war, he transferred to the Army Air Corps, flying P-39s and P-38s, until the fully developed 51s started coming over. He requested and got assignment to a squadron in the Ninth, which received some of the first 51s. That was the basis for his judgment on the 51. Then, during a low-level sweep into occupied France, he was hit by anti-aircraft fire, crashed, evaded capture, walked out, and with the help of the French Underground, returned to England on a fishing boat. His superiors decided that he needed a break from combat, and assigned him to his present duty.

"Men," Olmstead said as they finished eating, "You'll be here only today and tomorrow. That means you won't get much time in the 51. You are all in the 8th Air Force, and they're hurting badly for pilots. Not only replacements for casualties, but new planes are arriving faster and faster, at last. This means more and more pilots are needed to fly them. They're no good against Hitler sitting on the ground. Our whole objective here is to knock the Luftwaffe out of the sky and dominate the air space from here to Russia, and from Finland to the southern tip of the Continent, and smash Hitler's forces completely. So by this time next week, you'll be flying 51s in combat.

"We have only two birds here. You will do two things here: This afternoon, each of you will examine one of the birds inside and out. You will be given forty-five minutes each to sit in the cockpit, and get to know where everything is so well that you can put your hand on every instrument and every control blindfolded. At the end of your forty-five minutes, I'll get on the wing. I'll blindfold you. When I say a gauge or control name, you put your hand on it. Nobody flies today.

"Tomorrow everybody flies. Each of you will get one-and-a-half hours in one of our birds. Okay, let's get to it," and he led them out to where the two planes were parked.

Ed's heart was racing as he and the other four assigned to one 51 approached it. He thought, "God, how beautiful she is!" Loving every line, every angle of her. When it was his turn to sit in the cockpit, he climbed in, feeling something akin to awe. He didn't just touch everything in the cockpit, he fondled it, first with his eyes open, then with them shut. By the end of his forty-five minutes, he could unerringly touch every thing, every control, every instrument, the oxygen supply line, the fuel gauges and switches, the throttle, the stick, the radio controls, the instruments, the seat and shoulder harness, the canopy controls, everything. Lieutenant Olmstead's blindfold check was simplicity itself. Ed felt as if he and the P-51 belonged together. Regretfully, he climbed out, his fingers tingling.

While the others finished their cockpit checks, Ed continued examining every part of the exterior of the airplane. All the others wandered around talking, joking with each other. Ed could not get enough of being near, of touching, caressing this beautiful aircraft.

"All right, men," Olmstead said when the last cockpit checks were over, "you all did okay on that. When we get back to our quarters, I'll draw your names out of a hat for the order of flying tomorrow. It will be a full day. Early breakfast at 06:30, and be here ready to fly at 08:00. A word of advice about what to wear for combat flying. It's up to you, but I recommend that you forget about fancy shoes or cowboy boots. The best thing is GI shoes. They're rugged, and if you have to walk out, or are taken prisoner, they will serve you better than anything else you can put on your feet. Same goes for shirts and pants. OD pants and shirts are the best things; they wear longer and are warmer than anything else you can wear. You all have flight jackets, so wear them. You will be issued the new flying helmet tomorrow morning. This has the earphones built into the ear flaps, and oxygen mask attached, with microphone built into it. These go with you when you join your squadron. The helmet is made of chamois, with two liners, one of which is nylon; the Air Corps is trying to make sure you stay warm, but I'll tell you right now, you are going to be cold a lot of the time, with the altitudes you're going to have to fly. The only thing that isn't very good in the five-one is the heater. Just when you need it most, it stops giving enough heat to help much. You will also be issued gauntlets, with double liners. Wear them, you'll need them. The chamois of the helmet will absorb sweat, so, every now and then, on a day when you aren't scheduled to fly, take all the attachments off it and wash it in warm water and soap, rinse it, and let it dry. Otherwise, it'll start to stink. Okay, that's it."

Ed and Grant walked together, Ed's euphoria so strong that he felt as if his feet weren't touching the ground. "What a beauty she is!" he exulted. "I wanted to crank her up and take off. Goose flesh all over me!"

"You're nuts, Pal! Sound like you've just found the girl of your dreams." Then, more matter-of-factly, "She looks good and feels good on the ground. The real test will be how she flies. Ask me how I feel tomorrow."

"She'll be perfect, I feel it in my bones," Ed said.

They had just started to get ready for the showers back in their room, when Lieutenant Olmstead stuck his head in. "The drawing's over. Here's the order of flying: Thorne first, in plane Number One. Perrin third in plane Number Two. See you at chow."

"Yahoo!" Ed yelled, his enthusiasm now almost uncontrollable. "Can you believe it? I'm first!"

"Easy, man. You'll pop a gasket! Take it easy. I don't want a basket case on my hands," Grant said.

"Okay, okay, you're right. Got to calm down. Shower'll help," Ed said, grabbing a towel and heading to the latrine and into one of the showers. There, he broke into song with, "Off we go, into the wild blue yonder." The men in the other showers, and those waiting for a turn, joined in.

Olmstead came in for a shower, too, and he joined in, then said, "That's the spirit, men. The kind you'll fly tomorrow, and at your squadrons, deserve all the enthusiasm you have." He and they sang again, rocking the small, tiled room with their boisterous sounds.

Ed finished off with as cold a shower as he could stand, and this did calm him some. But the excitement was still there. Back in the room, he dug out his OD shirt and trousers, as well as his GI shoes, which needed but didn't get shining. He hung the shirt and trousers on hooks to air out, and to lose some of their wrinkles.

Needling each other, he and Grant went to chow. After eating, they walked out into the gorgeous Scottish countryside, where they sat by a swift stream and talked about their beliefs, hopes and dreams. Grant knew some of what was going on in Germany, but not as much as Ed. He was as appalled as Ed had been by what Ed told him now. He shared Ed's belief that the man who was responsible for this must be stopped, whatever the cost. "Gives you a different perspective on the war, doesn't it," he said, "Makes it a cause, not just a military operation. Gives me a greater sense of dedication."

"Right," Ed said. "I've felt that dedication ever since I heard about what they're doing over there. Guess that's what motivated me to be the best cadet I could be, and made me nearly crack when I thought I'd wash out."

"I can see that. I used to wonder what made you tick. You always seemed to be trying to excell at everything. So now I know what was driving you."

They walked back, a new, stronger, bond starting to grow between them.

Sleep did not come quickly, nor last long for Ed. No matter what he tried to think of—home, music, Pat—the prospect of taking the P-51 up the next morning kept overwhelming all other thoughts. At long last he did sleep, but at the first hint of dawn, he was awake again. Knowing that further sleep was out of the question, as quietly as he could, he got up, put on his ODs, GI shoes and flight jacket, used the latrine, washed his face in cold water, and went out into the crisp, cold air of the Scottish foothills. Seeing lights on in the mess hall, he decided to see if coffee was available. "Good morning," the mess sergeant said. "Bet you're first on the flying list, right?"

"Right you are, Sergeant. Can't wait to get that bird in the air. Don't suppose you have a little coffee for a red-eyed pilot, do you?"

"Sure do. First thing we do every morning, make plenty of coffee. Cream and sugar?"

"No thanks, just black."

Ed sat at the table with the mug of hot coffee the sergeant had handed him. Sipping the strong brew, he reviewed everything he had learned the day before, sitting in the cockpit and listening to Lieutenant Olmstead. He visualized the instrument panel, moved his hands to where the wheels-up lever and the flaps control lever would be, and recalled what Olmstead had said about getting in and out of the little field, as well as his comments about the torque pull of the big engine.

After finishing his coffee, Ed thanked the sergeant and went out. The sky was getting lighter to the east as he walked down toward the small hangar. To his surprise, the ground crew men were busy pre-flighting the two 51s, and just as he got there, the crew chief fired up Number One, the one he would be flying. Fascinated, he watched and listened as the Rolls Royce Merlin engine coughed, caught, hesitated, then steadied into a regular, powerful-sounding roar. With the canopy open, the chief taxied out of the hangar to the edge of the grass, where he held the plane with the brakes and gradually added throttle as he checked the instruments. Satisfied, he reduced the RPM to idle, listened carefully to the sound of the engine, then shut it off. Looking in Ed's direction, he gave the "okay" sign and climbed out. "Everything's tip-top on this bird, Lieutenant," he said. "This one yours today?" Ed nodded, smiling at the prospect. "She's sweet," the sergeant said. "All ready when you are. Got to get Number Two out now," and he returned to the hangar.

Ed climbed into the cockpit of Number One and went over all instruments and controls. He felt as if he belonged in this airplane, more so than any other he had been in. The entire layout felt right to him, almost as though he'd been in her many times, instead of only once. As the sun peaked over the hills to the east, he climbed out and headed back to the mess hall, ready to get breakfast over with and get Number One up.

"Okay, men," Lieutenant Olmstead said, standing with his back to the sun and in front of the two P-51s. "You'll be taking off west, as you can see by the windsock. Once you clear the field, Number One go north, Number Two south, and keep in sight of the field. It's easy to get lost in these hills, and we have no radio homing equipment to guide you back. Remember what I told you yesterday. It is a short field, so hold her at the last marker at the east end of the field, and run up to about one-half throttle, then release the brakes, and feed in full throttle. Keep her on the ground until the last marker, then pull up and over the hills to the west. Get some altitude and wring her out. An hour-and-a-half from take-off to touchdown. Give her full flaps on your approach. Do one touch-and-go, and get the feel of getting into this field, then come around and land.

"One more thing," he added. "You saw the wire across the throttle guide, about three-fourths inch from the end of the guide. That's for Full Emergency Combat Power. You are not to break through that wire! When you need it in combat, you'll use it. But it's hard on the engine, DO NOT use it here. You won't need it. Okay, get 'em in the air. Here're your new flying helmets on the table here."

Ed and the first one scheduled for the other plane grabbed helmets and raced to their planes, pulling on the helmets as they ran. Ed jumped into the cockpit, plugged in the radio lead from the helmet, connected the oxygen hose dangling from the mask, then looked at the crew chief standing at the tip of his left wing. The chief twirled his finger in the startup sign, and Ed put the gas switch on "Left wing," turned the mag switch to "Both," and pressed the starter button. The powerful engine, already warmed up, kicked over and caught at once. His hand trembled with excitement until he released the brakes and pushed the throttle slightly forward and turned the nose toward the east end of the field. Now his hands were steady as he zig-zagged past Olmstead, Grant, and the other pilots, all giving him the thumbs-up sign. He saw Number Two in his rearview mirror, following him. At the easternmost marker on the runway, he swung to the middle of the runway, stopped facing west into the wind, put on the brakes, and ran the throttle forward, with the stick in his stomach. At one-half throttle, he switched to left, then right mags, seeing no significant drop of the tachometer. Returning the mag switch to both, he released the brakes and pushed the throttle to the wire, easing the stick forward.

An enormous thrill surged through him as the 51 leaped forward, pressing his back against the parachute pack at his back, and thumping his head against the head pad. "I'm doing it!" he yelled. "At last I've got a 51!" It seemed to him that no time had elapsed when he flashed past the last marker. He was airborne and he pulled the wheel lever up, held the nose down to allow maximum speed to build; then, as the hills rushed toward him, he pulled the stick back and was in a vertical climb. Above the hills now, he lowered the nose and turned right, climbing rapidly, and switching on the oxygen as the altimeter showed 10,000 feet.

Feeling completely at home, and finding the airplane everything he had dreamed her to be, he started with a loop, followed with an Immelman, slow rolls, barrel rolls, Chandelles, pulled turns tighter and tighter, went through every maneuver he'd ever learned, finding the 51 sweetly responsive, with no bad tendencies. "It's glorious!" he exulted. "What a bird! She's everything I hoped and dreamed she would be!"

Starting at 20,000 feet, he put her into a vertical power dive. No sign of rolling or vibration. He felt in complete control. At 450 a.s., he pulled her out of the dive and into a vertical climb, hanging her on her prop. "She's beautiful!" he exclaimed, as he pulled her over on her back, topping the climb, then rolled over and flew straight and level at one-fourth throttle. He'd taken off at 08:30, meaning he had to be on the ground at 10:00. He looked at his watch in disbelief, seeing 09:40 showing. "Better head back to the field," he thought. He felt fully at one with this great airplane, the wonderful feeling he'd had several times before, but much more complete and intense this time.

A moment of concern shook him, as he looked to the south and could not immediately identify the airfield. "Oh no," he thought. "I was so carried away I forgot to keep the field in sight." He put the nose down, heading south, while straining to see their little field, hidden among the other pastures dotting the hills. He was beginning to think he'd gone too far south when he saw the sun glinting off another plane several thousand feet below him and a mile or two ahead, heading north. Still heading downward, he looked between the two—his and Number Two. There he saw the quonset huts and felt enormous relief. Keeping an eye on the other 51, he steepened his dive, aiming right at the field. At 2,000 feet, and 400 mph, he leveled off, made a large circle as Number Two did his touch-and-go, then landed and cleared the field.

Since Olmstead had not specified a landing pattern, and because 10:00 was just nine minutes away, Ed decided to use the fighter landing pattern. He checked the windsock, let down to 1,000 feet, and came over the center of the field heading west, into the wind. He cut the throttle back and went into his descending spiral, cleared the engine just before completing the spiral east of the field boundary, dropped wheels and flaps, and touched down almost exactly at the easternmost marker of the runway. He immediately pulled up flaps and wheels, pushed the throttle to the wire, went up and repeated the same landing pattern, this time staying down, then taxiing over to where the others stood. His watch showed 09:59. Elated with the flight and in love with the 51, he unbuckled and disconnected everything, climbed out and joined the others.

"Where the hell did you learn to land like that?" Grant asked, grinning.

"Good ol' Joe Murphy at Advanced," Ed replied. "Then we practiced it at the gunnery field in the Okeefenokee Swamp."

"Man, was I short-changed! We never got anything but standard, boring, rectangular patterns," Grant complained.

Lieutenant Olmstead came toward them as the other pilots were crowded around Ed. Ed thought, "Oh, oh. Wonder if he'll ream me out."

"Good job, Ed," Olmstead said. "We always use that pattern in the Ninth, but I didn't think any of you guys in the conservative Eighth Air Force ever even heard of it. Any of the rest of you want to try that, it's okay. Just be sure you know what you're doing. Practice on a cloud before you come in that way. Get the feel of how the bird feels with the throttle all the way back. Okay, next two, get 'em up there."

Still excited, and glowing at what Olmstead had said, Ed raved to Grant and the other six pilots about how great the 51 was. Then, beginning to feel the loss of sleep, and drained by the intense, continuous excitement he had felt, he found a bench beside the hangar, sat down and reviewed mentally all that he'd experienced as he watched the others take off and land. Grant was the only one who tried the fighter landing, and he did it perfectly. Ed went over and congratulated him after he climbed out. The ones who were finished flying went for chow. Olmstead, who had to remain at the landing strip, called after them, "Hey, men. Ask Cookie to give you a sandwich for me, and a cup of black coffee. A couple of doughnuts, too, okay? He'll send it over with one of his men. Thanks. See you back here later."

Ed hadn't seen six pilots so excited about an airplane since first solo flights in Primary. His enthusiasm for the Mustang was now shared by all of them. Grant, who had been a reluctant convert from the P-47, now seemed to be echoing Ed's own feelings and comments. None of them could stop talking about how great this plane felt, how responsive it was, how pilot friendly it was, and forgiving. How stable at every speed and position and attitude, and how great the new feeling of power was when the supercharger kicked in at 10,000 feet. All of Ed's fantasies about the airplane had come true, and now seemed to be shared by the other five at the table.

They finished their meal with coffee and ice cream, then returned to the field, where the last two pilots were ready to take off. They watched until they were both off and over the low western hills, then they began to ply Lieutenant Olmstead with questions about the P-51 in combat situations. Patiently, he gave detailed answers to the questions, all of which he'd been asked often before. His enthusiasm for the ship was as strong as theirs, but tempered by his day-to-day experiences with her, which revealed that, although the best all-round fighter he'd ever seen or flown, being a man-made machine, she was not perfect. He had found that at extremely high altitudes, the 51 was outmatched by the FW-190. He was sharply aware, from his own experience, that the coolant system vulnerability was a serious liability. It had, in fact, had tragic consequences for several of his flying mates. "So," he summed up, "She's still just an airplane; not perfect. But, all in all, you're better off in this than in any other fighter. As long, though, as there are enemy aircraft in the air to make you their target, and anti-aircraft gunners whose reason for being is to shoot you down, you will be vulnerable, no matter what you are flying.

"This airplane, good as it is, will only be as good as the guys flying it. If your head is in your ass, she won't save you. In combat, your first mistake is likely to be your last mistake. Be awake. Be alert. Be ready for anything! The enemy fliers rarely do what you expect them to do, except for one thing: they always come at you out of the sun. Expect that any time, anywhere. They'll come, and come at tremendous speed, because they'll be sitting up there waiting for you, with an altitude advantage. Always keep your head and eyes moving, and always cover each others' tails. If you're flying as wingman, and your leader is hit, your vulnerability is immediately increased. Same is true for him, if you are hit. You have to cover and protect each other at all times.

"My last words are this: If anything goes wrong with your airplane in a combat situation, if she coughs or burps, if she spills out smoke, if the temp needle goes up, if a wing tank won't jettison—anything—don't sit up there and hope; hit the deck with all the speed you can get, and stay there high-tailing it home as fast as possible. You don't have a chance with the enemy in an airplane that is even a little bit off, and they love to catch you in that situation. They'll appear out of nowhere, like hyenas after an injured antelope.

"Okay, that's all for you fellows. You can start packing your stuff for tomorrow's early train. I'll talk to the two guys still flying when they get on the ground. See you at chow."

All eight of them, each vowing silently to remember what Olmstead had said, headed for their quarters to shower and pack. Their enthusiasm was still great, but the realization that tomorrow, or at the latest, day after tomorrow, they would be in the very situation Lieutenant Olmstead had been talking about, subdued them. "Won't be fun and games will it, Grant?" Ed asked.

"Nope. They'll be throwing real bullets at us. Our days of playing war are over. From now on it's going to be too real," Grant responded.

"Well, that's what we're here for," Ed said. "It's what we asked for when we volunteered for the cadet program. Seems like a hundred years ago, doesn't it? I remember being afraid the war would be over before I got through my training. No chance of that now!"

They were in their room now. Grant said, "You going to shower or pack first?"

"Shower."

"Guess I will too." They stripped off their GI shoes and ODs, showered, put on their pink trousers and green tunics, put their dirty clothes in their duffel bags and carefully packed their new flying helmets in their suitcases, along with their new gauntlets, leaving the cases open to have their toothbrushes and shaving kits available for the morning. Next they put on their trench coats and overseas caps, and went to the chow hall.

The mess sergeant had outdone himself with roast beef, mashed potatoes and gravy, peas and carrots, tossed salad, biscuits, coffee and strawberry shortcake. Not knowing when they'd have a meal like that again, the young pilots ate all they could hold, including seconds on the shortcake, topped with Devonshire cream.

When the last delicious bite had been swallowed, Lieutenant Olmstead said, "Gentlemen, it has been a pleasure working with you. I wish you good flying and Godspeed. The early train leaves Ellerbee at 09:07 tomorrow. After breakfast the bus will pick you up at your quarters. You will need to take the Humber, then the ferry over to Hull. At Hull, you will need to work out your trains to your various destinations. Don't forget to apply for compensation for your transportation expenses at your bases. Your foot lockers were shipped from Hull to your bases, and they should be there when you arrive. I won't be at breakfast, so let me shake hands with each of you now."

After thanks and farewells to Olmstead and the mess sergeant, the pilots wandered off in twos and threes to stroll around in the mild evening air, or to read or write letters, to talk, and some to play records on the tinny wind-up phonograph in the lieutenant's office. When they tired of the scratchy-sounding records, someone turned on the radio. They heard the BBC news discussing the latest night-time bombings on London, giving casualties and damage reports, and talking of the effectiveness of anti-aircraft fire in bringing down bombers. Mentioned, too, was how effective barrage balloons were in forcing the bombers to stay at high altitude. The news finished, emphasizing that everyone should be alert to spot aliens, since several parachutes had been spotted after the bombers had been hit.

By 22:00 the barracks building was quiet as all the pilots read or wrote, or were deep in their own thoughts about their immediate futures. At 23:00 no lights could be seen in the barracks except the single shaded bulbs in the office and in the latrine. As always, the black-out curtains were closed over all windows.

Breakfast over, carrying their duffel bags and suitcases, the ten pilots boarded the bus for the uneventful trip on train and ferry boat to Hull. Ed and Grant were the only two of the ten who were going to East Wretham, so after learning which train to take, and that it went right to East Wretham station, they said goodbye to the other eight, and sat on a bench on the proper platform for their train. Since they had a forty-five-minute wait, they bought hot tea and scones at the refreshment window, and continued their wait.

Precisely on time, the train puffed up to the platform, giving one quick toot on its shrill whistle, and they boarded. They entered a first-class compartment already occupied by a lovely, slender, blue-eyed blonde young woman, dressed in a tailored gray suit, and her Mom. After putting their luggage in the rack, they removed their trench coats and hats, and took seats opposite the British-looking ladies. After a few moments, the younger lady smiled and said, "American pilots, I see. Where will you be stationed?"

"East Wretham, Ma'am," Ed said, pronouncing it as it was spelled.

"Oh, my," she replied. "East Wret'am is veddy neah wheah we live."

"Where is that, Ma'am?" Ed asked, quite taken by this lovely young woman.

"We have a cottage in Thetford," she replied. "My husband is in service. He's been overseas for two yeahs."

Ed's interest was blunted by this information. "Oh. Where is he?"

"We aren't sure. Security is so teddibly important, you know."

"Hope he's all right. Have you been to our base?"

"Oh, no, not evah." Her response seemed to say, "I wouldn't even consider such a thing."

"Sorry," Ed said. "I guess I asked the wrong question."

"No, no. It's just that civilians aren't evah invited to your base, you see."

"I understand."

"I can tell you that the base is at Wret'am Hall, owned by Lo'd Cantrell. I understand he turned it ovah to your government for your airfield. He has, himself, taken up residence in a cottage on the estate. He's a lovely man. His family's been there for centuries. Shame, actually."

"I'm sorry," Ed heard himself saying, "I guess we have to have bases somewhere, if we're to help win this war."

"No, no!" she replied sharply. "You misunderstood. I don't mean it's a shame you're here. Not a'tall! We want you here; I mean it's a shame the war has to uproot everything, even a fine family like his. No, please. We're veddy happy indeed that you're here."

"I did misunderstand; I beg your pardon. We've been told so much about British resentment of us, I guess I'm too sensitive."

"That's rubbish! Don't you believe a word of it. Why, the entire country cheered when you came in! Theah will always be a few ill-mannered people everywheah who are unappreciative of your help. But certainly not most. Not a'tall. Not a'tall!"

"Thank you. We want to do our part."

They continued chatting, with Grant joining in now and again, but the mother said nothing, though she smiled and nodded occasionally. Close to noon the young lady said, "Yours will be the next station. The best of luck to you, and safe landings."

"Thank you. I hope your husband comes home soon."

The train stoppped smoothly, and Grant and Ed stepped off. A sergeant hurried up to them, "Lieutenants Throne and Perrin?" he asked, snapping a salute. "Major Irvine sent me to meet you. This way."

"That's *Thorne,*" Ed said, "not *Throne.*"

"Sorry, Sir," the sergeant said, leading them to a staff car—a Chevy. He opened the trunk and helped put their luggage in. They got in and the sergeant, knowing exactly where he was going, drove out of the station yard on the left side of the road, making his way through the tiny village of East Wretham and out into the country.

"Who is Major Irvine, Sergeant?" Grant asked.

"He's CO of the 369th Squadron. Lieutenant Thorne is assigned to that squadron, you to the 368th, Sir. I'm the major's clerk and driver. He's great. You'll like him. Good pilot, all the pilots like him, He's a regular guy."

"Who's my CO?" Grant wanted to know.

"He's new, I don't know his name yet, Sir. He just got in yesterday. Been in the Aleutians, I hear, then in Training Command."

This sounded familiar to Ed. After a few minutes, he remembered. It must be his instructor from Shaw Field—Lieutenant Jorgenson, he thought his name was. He said to Grant, "I had an instructor in Basic who'd been in the Aleutians and wanted a combat assignment. Wouldn't it be something if he turned out to be your CO?"

"Was he any good?"

"Yeah, he was okay, but really frustated. Was waiting for his promotion to captain to come through, and really eager to get to a real combat zone."

They were approaching an imposing, red brick, four-story mansion. The sergeant said,

"Sirs, this's your new home. All officers are quartered in there. Wish I was. Our quonset huts are okay, but nothing like you've got."

Just then a P-51 roared over, followed by another, and another. They kept coming, each one going into a spiral fighter-landing pattern about one-fourth mile behind the mansion. The planes kept coming. The sergeant had stopped the car and gotten out. He was standing beside the car, counting the 51s as they came over. When no more came, he got in, saying, "Only thirty-four. Either two came home early, or they're in trouble and limping home late. Or, worst of all, we lost them."

The sergeant reached to turn the ignition key, then paused. "Do you hear something, Sirs?" he asked. He jumped out again, and Ed and Grant got out too. "Yeah," he said. "There's one of them. Hear it?"

Grant and Ed now heard what the sergeant was talking about. Sputtering and popping, taking hold, then sputtering again, a 51 unsteadily and too slowly, flew erratically, limping toward the hall. As it staggered over them, they could see that it was badly shot up, barely staying up. Ed felt his muscles tensing, urging the plane to stay up, trying to help hold it in the air, not wanting it not to make it.

"He'll go straight in. Hope his landing gear works. There's the siren for the fire truck. There's the ambulance one too. They'll go down to where they think he'll stop. Good, his gear's down; he won't have to belly in!"

They watched the limping Mustang drop out of sight behind the trees. Then, faint but clear, cheers came from the direction of the field. "Means the pilot got out and is okay. He isn't hurt, and no fire. Great! Wonder where the other one is?"

His question was answered as the thirty-sixth 51 came in fast, did a slow roll, came around again, and did his spiral landing. "Okay," the sergeant exulted. "He was covering the crippled one. All home now, thank God. The slow roll means he got one enemy plane. Another victory to chalk up to our group." They got back into the car, and the sergeant drove them to the wide steps with the columned veranda at the top. The excitement of what they had just watched, and their relief at the successful landing of the damaged plane, was enormous.

"We can't get any closer to combat than this until we go on our first mission," Grant said, his voice slightly choked.

Ed agreed, saying, "Man! I don't even know who was flying that hurt plane, and I sweat him out like he was my buddy. I guess everybody on your team in combat is a buddy even before you've met. Let's get in and get on the team. That's the place for me, in a 51, and on a combat team."

"There you are, Sirs. Corporal Jergens, 'Jerk' for short, will be in the reception hall right inside the doors. He'll tell you what rooms you'll be in," the sergeant said, then saluted and returned to the car.

Suitcases and duffel bags in hand, the two new members of Fighter Group 359 climbed the stone steps and stepped into an enormous reception hall. A corporal jumped to his feet and saluted, "Welcome to Wretham Hall, Sirs. Some digs, ain't it?"

"Sure is, Corporal," Grant said. "Have we been assigned rooms?"

"Yes, Sir. Let's see," and he consulted a list on the desk. "Lieutenant Perrin, 229, Lieutenant Thorne, 115. The British are all screwed up on floor numbering. This one doesn't count, so 115 is up one flight, and 229 is up two. Numbers are painted on the doors. You'll both be in with other members of your squadrons."

Noticing a room with two long tables set with silverware, glasses, and plates to the left of the wide double doors, and what appeared to be a large barroom to the right, the two lieutenants climbed the stairway. It was a wide double-curved stairway, with the second curve ending at the next floor; then a narrower, but still impressively wide stairway continuing to the story above that.

"Let's chuck our things in our rooms, then check the place out, okay?" Ed said. "Hope there's a toilet near. I need one."

Grant replied, "Okay. I need one too. See you in two minutes," and continued up.

Ed turned left and went down the wide hallway to find 115. He knocked on the door marked 115. No answer. Turning the knob, he entered. Three sets of double-deck bunkbeds, all neatly made, met his gaze. His foot locker was at the foot of the beds set against the left wall. Assuming he'd have the upper bunk, he put his duffel up there, and his suitcase on top of his foot locker. He went out, intercepting Grant coming down the stairs, and together they located two toilets at the end of the hall.

Ed found an old-fashioned wash basin with rather worn spigots, a cloudy mirror over it, a toilet with a tank just above head height, a chain with a heavy porcelain pull attached dangling from the tank, and a large, porcelain-coated cast iron tub, with claw feet.

After relieving themselves, they went downstairs. As they expected, the room with the set tables was the Officers' Mess. The barroom was the Pilots' Lounge. There a sergeant was busy setting bottles and glasses in place, and wiping everything with a clean white bar towel.

"Hello Sergeant," Ed said, "is the bar open?"

"Yes, Sir. Better be. All the pilots will be crowding in here in about five minutes, dying of thirst. What'll it be?"

"Any cold beer?" Grant asked.

"Yes, Sir. It'll have to be British, though. Haven't been able to get American lately."

"Guinness?" Ed asked.

"Sure thing, Sir. That what you want?"

"Please," Ed said. "And do I see sandwiches back there? We haven't eaten since breakfast."

"Yes, Sir. Ham or cheese, or both?"

"Ham and cheese, please."

The sergeant had been drawing the Guinness while he got the sandwich for Ed. Now he said, "You, Sir?" to Grant.

"Any lager, but not Guinness, and a ham and cheese for me too."

Ed and Grant took their sandwiches and drinks to a table in the corner near a window. Both were a little tense, not knowing how they'd be welcomed by the fliers returning from a mission. In a few minutes they heard voices approaching, and the first of the pilots came into the room. Most of them wore ODs and GI shoes, flight jackets open, and overseas caps on their heads. Several wore pink or green trousers, one with the legs tucked into highly decorated cowboy boots. Another contingent came in, and the room was noisy with their talk about what they'd seen and done, and what had happened when a dozen ME-109s hit them, coming out of the sun. No one paid any attention to the newcomers until a wavy-haired, slim, medium tall first lieutenant came over to where they sat. Putting his beer on their table, he said, "Are you the new guys? Which one is Ed Thorne?"

Ed got up, saying, "I am."

"Hi. I'm Charley (Chuck) Kruger. You're assigned to our squadron, and I'll be your flight leader. You'll be my Number Four." Then turning to Grant, he shook his hand too. "You're in the 368th, right? Hey, Bob," he called to a short, dark-haired first lieutenant at the bar, "Come over and meet the new guys. Bob Fisher, Grant Perrin. He'll be in the 368th with you. And this is Ed Thorne—he'll be in my flight. Shall we join you and give you the poop on us?" He and Bob pulled up chairs and sat.

"Did you get checked out in 51s?" Chuck asked.

"Yeah, in Larrabee, Scotland," Grant answered.

"Good," Chuck responded. "We were doing 47s until two weeks ago. We all hated it when we changed over. I think we're all believers now, eh Bob?"

"Oh yeah. We're all convinced the five-one is the best thing that flies. Sure is hard on the ass, though. Damn thing has such long range it kills you sitting on the effing dinghy all those hours," Bob replied.

"Yeah. We've been doing some eight-hour escort jobs. We're nearly paralyzed when we get back on the ground. Whoever designed that folded up dinghy we sit on put in something hard that bulges up at the worst place. Cuts off circulation. We used to sit on the parachute, but the experts came up with the new improved back pack so the dinghys could be put under us. We call it 'dinghy butt' when we come back with dead asses, which is about every day. How much time did you get in 51s?"

"An hour-and-a-half," Ed said. "That's in the air. Plus forty-five minutes in the cockpit on the ground."

"No shit!" Bob exploded. "That's not hardly enough time to learn how to keep the son-abitch in the air. And you guys don't have any combat experience! What the hell's the matter with our leaders?"

Chuck said, "He's not pissed off at you, but at the Air Corps. We were all combat experienced in 47s when we switched over, and they insisted we get at least twelve hours in these babies before we took them on any missions. Doesn't make sense, but we do need replacements, so we're glad you're here."

"Right," Bob agreed. "I just think Fighter Command is nuts to send you out here with almost no time in the plane you have to take into combat!"

"Guess we'll have to get real on-the-job training," Ed said.

"In spades, my friend, in spades!" Bob said.

"There's 'Chicken Shit,'" Chuck said. "I'll bring him over to meet you guys," and he went over to a man in ODs and flight jacket, a little older than the others, his face lined and weathered, short-cropped light brown hair, pale blue eyes. In a moment he accompanied Chuck to the table, carrying a beer mug with "C.S." emblazoned on it in green letters. "Ed, Grant, Major Irvine. C.S., Ed's in our squadron, Grant's in the 368th. His hard luck."

C.S. shook hands and sat down. "My butt's killing me! That was a hell of a long trip. Sure lucked out, though. Almost lost two, but they made it back. Glad to have you with us."

Chuck sipped his beer, then said, "C.S., we were just cussin' out Fighter Command. These guys got only an hour and a half in 51s before being sent down here."

"Jesus H.!" the major yelled. "Don't those desk jockeys know anything? You can't be effective as a combat pilot when you're still learning how to fly the goddam airplane! That puts everybody at extra risk, and we need these men to get up to our full complement. I'm going to collar the colonel. Maybe we can give these guys a few more hours in the air while it's still light. This is like sending infantry into combat without guns! There he is now. Sit tight, I'll see what I can do."

"That's Colonel Macon, our group CO," Bob said, pointing out a six-foot, blonde-gray man, also in ODs, but without his flight jacket. Silver maple leaves were on his open shirt collar, indicating his rank as lieutenant colonel.

C.S. brought the colonel over, and Ed and Grant jumped to their feet. "As you were," Colonel Macon said, taking a seat. "Is what C.S. tells me true? One and a half hours?"

"Yes, Sir," Ed and Grant said together.

"Those asses! They act like this is just part of Training Command! Here's what we can do. I'll call Wing and get an okay for a patrol flight across the Channel and into France. C.S., call Mike and have him get a crew on four crates amd prep them for 17:00 take-off. Chuck, you lead the flight. Bob, you fly Number Three, and you two fly Numbers Two and Four, as wingmen. Make it two hours over and two back. Should be enough light left for you to land back here. Chuck, you brief them right here. I'll get on the phone to Wing, okay?"

"All right." After Macon and Irvine had left the table, Chuck said, "We take off in formation. The field is short and narrow, so hold your positions and do as I do. Grant, you'll be my wingman. Ed you'll be Bob's Number Four. When we're in position at the end of the field,

I'll hold up one finger. That'll mean to hold your brakes and get up to three-quarter throttle, 2,500 RPMs, and check your mags. When I lean forward, that means to release your brakes and give full throttle. Stay in position, and stay with me. We'll maintain the two-plus-two formation for take-off and climb to 20,000 on a heading of 110. When we close on the French coast, I'll rock my wings. That will mean pull up abreast of me, then I'll rock again, and you spread out, still staying abreast. If shore batteries open up on us, don't wait for a signal; take individual evasive action immediately, but keep me in sight. We'll be out of range pretty fast, then return to spread formation. Do not use the radio unless you see a bogey or a bandit, then tell me what and where. Once we're back over the Channel, resume regular two-plus-two formation until I rock my wings as we approach the base. Then get in line and follow me in a fighter landing. You guys know how to do that?"

"Yes, Sir."

"Okay, any questions? None? Good. You guys have time to change to flying clothes and use the latrine. Be out front in ten minutes. A jeep will take us to the line. Bring your flight helmets, and you'll need your jackets. The heater's a joke in the five-ones."

Excited, Ed and Grant rushed to their rooms, changed, grabbed their helmets and jackets, used the latrine, and rushed down and out to the courtyard. Chuck and Bob were already in the jeep. Chuck was in the driver's seat, and Ed and Grant climbed over the rear mudguards and into the small rear seat. It was 16:45 as they raced past the Control Tower and a small cluster of quonset huts, but no airplanes were in sight. Bob turned and yelled over the noise of the wind and of the battered jeep, "All the planes are kept in dispersal areas, not lined up as easy targets for enemy raiders coming in."

Chuck stopped near a 51 parked under the branches of trees and said, "There's your ship, Ed. When you're ready, taxi to the side of the field, right that way, turn into the wind, and wait until we get there, then follow me and get into position. We won't be long."

Ed got to the 51, eager and excited, shook hands with the crew chief, who said his name was "Al," and climbed in. "She's all set, Sir," Al said, climbing up on the left wing and leaning into the cockpit, making sure Ed hooked everything up right. "Checks out fine, full of gas and ready to go. All warmed up, should fire right up."

Ed strapped himself in, coupled the oxygen tube to his mask, plugged in his radio, already tuned to the group's frequency, and as he set the throttle and mixture control to start, he heard Chuck through the earphones clearing with the Tower. Al stayed on the wing until he was sure his baby started and ran smoothly, then got down, holding on to his hat in the prop wash, to guide Ed out of the small dispersal area. Then he gave the "okay" sign, and Ed hurried toward the field, seeing two of the other planes ahead of him. Then he saw the other one coming out of a dispersal spot, and recognized Chuck in the cockpit. Chuck moved ahead of the others just as Ed caught up, and all four taxied to the end of the field, swung into position and, at Chuck's signal, ran their engines up and checked their mags.

Ed closed and latched his bird-cage canopy. He saw Chuck's head move forward and released the brakes, adding throttle, staying just a few feet behind Bob and to his right. He felt the tail come up, but eased the stick forward to keep the wheels on the ground, just as Bob did. When he saw Bob's 51 rise, he rose with it, immediately retracting his wheels. As they cleared the trees and started a climbing left turn, he tucked his left wing in tight behind Bob's right one. At 10,000 feet, he snapped his oxygen mask into position and began to breathe the richer air. At 20,000 feet, they were south of the North Sea and heading southeast for the French coastline. At Chuck's signal, Ed added throttle and came abreast of the other three, then moved to the right, spacing himself away from, but in easy visual contact distance of the others. Looking down, he could see the coast through the mist, and the sun glinting off his rearview mirror. The world appeared peaceful from his altitude. "Doesn't even look like there's a war going on," he thought.

Abruptly the war made its presence known, as shore batteries of anti-aircraft guns began a barrage of shells toward the four planes. All four began evasive action individually, and no one was hit. In moments they were out of range, but Ed had seen the shells exploding, and he knew that potential death and destruction had been all around them.

Resuming the four-abreast spread formation, they continued eastward, watching for troop movements, concentrations of military equipment, storage tanks, or anything they might report on their return to base. Ed's earphones came alive. "Red Leader, this is Number Three. There's a bogey (unidentified object) in the air at nine o'clock, at our altitude, about a mile away, over."

"Roger, Number Three. I see it. Number Four, break off and take a look. Call when you identify it, over."

"Roger, Red Leader, willco. Out," Ed said, as he pulled under the others and to the left. He saw the object, a little distorted in the haze and the sun, and it was gaining altitude. He pushed his throttle forward and climbed toward it. Seeing what it was, he laughed and pushed the send button. "Red Four to Leader. It's a balloon; looks like a weather balloon. What shall I do? Over."

"Roger, Number Four. Arm your guns and shoot it down, we'll give you cover," came the reply in a laughing voice. "After your 'kill,' return to formation, over and out."

"Willco, Leader. Out," Ed said, then leaned forward and clicked the "Arm" switch. He was now above and to the east of the balloon. He made a tight left turn, got the balloon in his sights, and fired a quick burst. The balloon collapsed and fell toward earth. Feeling good, he rejoined the formation.

The rest of the penetration was uneventful, and at 19:00 they turned toward home. The sun was now low on the horizon, hitting them full in the face as they took a westward heading. Ed had to squint to keep the light from blinding him. Then he remembered the goggles on the helmet, and lowered them. They were tinted, and reduced the glare considerably.

Chuck made a turn northward, leading to an area away from shore batteries, and no AA guns were fired at them.

Within sight of the English shoreline, Chuck rocked his wings, and the fliers went into the two-plus-two formation. As they sighted The Wash—a large, squarish inlet on the East Anglian shore, and a handy landmark for locating their base—they took the inline formation and followed Chuck in the spiral fighter landing pattern at their field. All four landed safely in the half-light and taxied to their dispersal areas.

Ed jumped down off the wing, elated that this 51 had felt as responsive and as much a part of him as he had found the one in Scotland to be. "Congratulations, Sir," Al said, throwing Ed a salute. "Your first combat mission."

"Thanks," Ed replied. "Some mission! All we saw was some ack-ack and a balloon. But it was good to get four more hours in this baby. I shot my guns, so please tell the armorer."

"This one's assigned to you, Sir. I'm your crew chief. I could tell by the smell that you'd fired 'em. We'll get 'em taken care of for tomorrow," Al said. "Congratulations! Shall I put a swastika on your fuselage?" he laughed.

"That'd look wonderful, but I'd be embarrassed," Ed replied. "It was just a weather balloon," joining Al in his laughter.

"Well, Sir, it was an enemy balloon. I could put on a real small one," Al said.

"Naw. You and I will know about it. I don't care if the rest of the world doesn't."

"Fat chance, Sir. It'll be all over the base by tomorrow. You'll get some razzing."

"I guess I will. Well, I guess I can handle that. But no swastika, okay?"

"How about a balloon, Sir?" Al persisted.

"You do, and I'll report you for insubordination, and defacing government property," Ed answered, laughing again. "You said this ship is assigned to me?"

"Yes, Sir. She's a 51-C, and in perfect shape. Has two .50 caliber machine guns in each wing. Never been torn up or hit by anything. I've been her crew chief ever since we got her. How do you like her?"

"She's great. Man! My own five-one! I don't believe it!" Ed enthused, looking more closely at the plane, noticing the green prop spinner, and green rudder, and of course the star in a circle on both sides of the fuselage, below and behind the canopy, and on top and underside of each wing. "My own 51," he thought, "unbelievable! Another dream come true."

Interrupting his thoughts, Al said, "Do you have a name for her, Sir? Our armorer, Corporal Tony Salina, is really good with a paint brush. He'll paint it on in a really good-looking way."

Remembering his daydreaming, and the name he'd dreamed of using if he ever had his own fighter, Ed said, "'Princess Pat,' that's her name, Al. Yes, I'd like to have it painted on."

"Okay, Sir. He'll do it the first day you don't take her out, if it isn't raining. From now on, she's Princess Pat to me," Al said, grinning his approval.

"Thanks, Al," Ed said. "I'd better get to the Ready Room. Lieutenant Kruger'll be looking for me."

"Good night, Lieutenant. The jeep ought to be here to pick you up," Al said, and just then Chuck and the other two pulled up in the jeep. They drove to the quonset hut they'd passed on the way out.

Inside, Chuck said, "Okay, you two have logged your first combat mission. It will go in the records, count toward your first completed combat tour of duty. Nice work, Ed—your first 'kill'. An enemy balloon," with a hint of derision.

"Thanks, Chuck. It was nothing," matching Chuck's tone. Then, remembering Al's offer, he added, "Maybe I'll have a balloon painted below my canopy. Every victory counts. Maybe I'll be our first balloon ace!" This got a laugh from the others.

Chuck said, "Find an empty locker for your gear. Then we have to report to the duty officer for debriefing. What we did and saw becomes part of the Intelligence File, and our records."

Captain Burton was the duty officer, and they told him about the mission, pointing out on the large wall-map of Europe where they crossed into the Continental air space, how much flak they encountered, any significant action on the ground or in the air, about the weather balloon, and Ed's firing of his guns. Burton had one or two questions, laughingly congratulated Ed, then excused them with the comment, "We've got a tough one tomorrow morning, so you guys better get some sleep. Good to meet you, Grant and Ed. I'll see you all tomorrow. Goodnight."

The four piled into the jeep and returned to the hall, where they found the bar full of other pilots, but less full than when they had left. "How'd it go, Lieutenant Kruger?" the barman asked.

"Okay, George. No problems. Lieutenant Thorne killed a weather balloon," Chuck answered, "otherwise, we met no resistance."

The pilots at the bar heard this, and all raised their glasses. "Here's to the balloon killer," one shouted, and they all drained their glasses.

"I'm Cranston," one of them said. "What's your name, balloon killer?"

"Ed Thorne. This is my buddy, Grant Perrin. Maybe some day he'll shoot down a vicious balloon, too. He's assigned to the 368th, I'm in the 369th."

The dozen or so pilots all shook hands with Grant and Ed, welcoming them.

Chuck said, "Jesus! You know, they sent these guys to us with only one-and-a-half hours in a 51? I can't believe it. Can't get it out of my mind. Well, now they have six-and-a-half hours. They did all right on their first mission."

George the barman said, "Lieutenant Kruger, Cookie left some dinner here for you all. If you want it, I'll take it in and heat it up."

"Great, I'm starving," Chuck replied. "Heat it up, George, then give us a drink, okay?

"Yes, Sir," George said, and went to the kitchen. A second barman who had been cleaning up got them their drinks, and they sat down to talk while waiting for their dinner. Major Irvine joined them and asked Chuck how it went.

"Fine," Chuck said. "These guys did all right. They took everything in stride, even the landing pattern we use. How about making Ed my wingman, since Robert, my old one, is now an element leader?"

"Can't tomorrow; maybe later. All positions are already set for tomorrow. He'll be in your flight, Blue Number Four. This trip will be hairy. You'll hear the details at briefing, 07:30. I can tell you now that we have to dive-bomb some oil tanks in Northeast France. Intelligence has it that they're heavily protected by flak, so it won't be a picnic. We'll get in and out as fast as we can, but you know we're easy targets for a few seconds while we dive on the target. Just our squadron. The others will give us cover while we go in. Sorry, Ed, it's a hell of a first mission to go on."

"It's okay, Sir. I guess that's what we're here for," Ed answered, feeling a little silly saying it, but he knew he had to say something. "I'll try not to mess up my new bird on the second time I take her out."

"Good. See you all in the morning," the major said as he left the barroom.

"Dive-bombing's scary," Chuck said, "but it's fun too. And if your number comes up, it's a good way to go—quick and total! Hey, here's our grub. Man, I'm hungry!"

"Hey, Caruso!" a familiar voice yelled, just as Ed was about to take a mouthful of food. He looked up, then leaped to his feet, seeing George Stock, a roommate from Maxwell, rush to him. They embraced. "God, it's good to see you, Ed. Finally quit goofing off in the cadet program and had to join us in combat, hey?"

"George, you ol' S.O.B!" Ed replied. "Never thought I'd see you again after you guys left me all alone at Maxwell. Sit down; we're starved."

George talked as Ed shoveled in the food. When the food was finished, Chuck, Bob, and Grant said goodnight and left Ed, exhausted, staying long enough to say, "Let's get together tomorrow, after the mission, okay?"

"Right. See you in the morning; you'll be my wingman. Get some sleep—tomorrow'll be rough. Then we can bring each other up to date. 'Night."

Ed went upstairs, where he found that Chuck was quartered in the same room he was, with four others. They undressed and got into their bunks quietly, since the others were already sleeping. Ed found that his things had been moved from the upper to the lower bunk, so that is where he slept. Before drifting off to sleep, he thought briefly about what Chuck had said about dive-bombing, liking his attitude toward your number coming up. "Seems like a wise acceptance of a potential reality you can't do anything about. Guess you have to develop some such attitude, or go out of your mind." His head hit the pillow. He had only time to glory in the thought, "My own P-51! *Princess Pat.*" Then he was asleep too.

A knock on the door awakened him too soon. He looked up to see a young man in fatigues, who stepped in and said, "Time to get up, Sirs. Time to get up. Chow in fifteen minutes."

Groans, yawns, and sighs followed, mixed with epithets, as Ed's roommates stirred, stretched, scratched, and crawled out of their bunks. Ed was up first, so he made it to the nearest latrine first. There was no time for a bath; just the necessaries and a quick rinse of his face. The others crowded in as he finished.

Canned fruit juice, sausage, scrambled eggs, hashbrown potatoes, toast, and coffee were wolfed down by all the pilots; then they scrambled aboard personnel carriers and jeeps for a race to the Ready/Briefing Room. At precisely 07:30, all the pilots and other officers present popped to attention as Colonel Macon entered, picked up a pointer, and steppeed up to the low platform in front of the giant map mounted on the end wall. "As you were," he said, and everyone sat down. "Welcome, Lieutenants Perrin and Thorne. This puts us back to full complement again." Going straight to the reason for the meeting, he put the end of the pointer on a spot in Northeastern France. "Our objective is to take out an enemy oil dump, consisting of six 5,000-gallon tanks, half-buried in earth. Tinplate [Ed's squadron] will be armed with 500-pound bombs, and will make the actual dive-bomb attack. Red Cross [Grant's squadron], which I will lead, and Blue Cross will take off at 08:00. Tinplate will get airborne three minutes later. Red Cross will give high cover immediately over the target, at 25,000 feet, while Blue Cross patrols at the same altitude, but a half-mile out, dispersed so as to be on all sides of the target.

"When the first two squadrons are airborne, we will fly a heading of 125 degrees in standard formation. At 25,000 over the Channel, we will go into abreast formation, each squadron will make its own line, with Red Cross in front.

"Tinplate will climb to 20,000 and go into abreast formation for penetration to the target area. When C.S. gives the signal, Tinplate will go into three inline formations. Red Flight will hit the target first, with C.S. leading. White will follow, and Blue will be last. The two flights waiting their turn to dive will give close cover to the flight diving."

Following Macon was Major Howell, the base intelligence officer. He gave details of the terrain around the target area, which was hilly, and showed some blown-up photos of the targets. Next he briefed them on where the heaviest concentrations of flak would be on the coast, and especially around the target. "This is an extremely important oil storage emplacement for the enemy, so flak, both medium and light, will be concentrated and intense. Get all the speed you can, and try to put your bomb at the edge of one of the tanks right where the earth stops. Go in with your guns firing. This might discourage some of the enemy gunners."

Next was Captain Smith, weather officer. He told them what winds and clouds to expect en route and at the target site.

C.S. followed. "Not much to say. My flight will go in first, as the colonel said, followed by White, then Blue. Pour on the coal, and go straight down. When you pull out of your dive, keep as low as you can, which can't be too low because of the hills. Take a count of five after the man in front of you starts his dive, then start yours. Blue Flight, you have the shitty end of this. By the time you go in, the AA guys will have worked out the range and speed, so you'll be easier targets. Blue Leader, you meet with your guys right after we dismiss. Look at the pictures of the target, then give each of your guys a quadrant of the target area. White Leader and I will do the same. Obviously, if one of the tanks in your quadrant is demolished, head for another one. Be sure the guy in front of you has cleared before you release your bomb. Blue, maybe you can throw the gunners off a little by using a three-count instead of a five-count, okay? Any questions?" No one had any, so C.S. said, "Attenhut," and they all stood.

The colonel came front again. "It's a tough target, but we'll get it if anyone can. Synchronize watches. The hack will be on one, at 07:46. Five, four, three, two, hack! Good flying. Dismissed."

There was a rush for the latrine past the lockers, where everybody emptied his bladder. Mae Wests were put on and parachutes slung over shoulders, helmets put on, and they loaded up in jeeps. George, Ed, Chuck, and Bob rode in one jeep to their dispersal areas.

Ed and his fellow members of Blue Flight heard the other two squadrons start, taxi, then take off. As they rose above the trees, Ed saw them. In a moment C.S.'s voice came over his earphones. "Okay, Tinplate, crank up." Al was on his left wing as Ed started, jumping off and giving the thumbs up sign as he taxied out. He had no trouble finding his place, since his flight would be last to take off. The take-off was a repeat of the last evening's, and it went well. Ed felt good about everything.

On a southeast heading, Tinplate climbed to 20,000 feet. Above and ahead, they could see the rest of the group. They crossed into France with no sign of AA fire from coastal batteries. Their intell officer had provided good information, so Colonel Macon had been able to find a gap in the Nazi's coastal defenses.

"Red Cross Red Two to leader, Bogies at two o'clock, low," one of the pilots flying high cover said, breaking radio silence. A minute later, "Roger, Red Two, they're friends." Now Ed could see the friends, a flight of P-47s heading west; whatever their mission had been, it was completed.

Before Tinplate had crossed the French coast, C.S. had given the signal, and all three flights had gone into abreast formation. Now, as they approached the target area, he gave his second wing-rocking signal, and his flights went into inline formations. While his White and Blue Flights circled, C.S.'s flight headed in for the attack. Again, the intelligence officer was proven right, as anti-aircraft shells began to explode, filling the air with puffs of smoke. Irvine rolled over and pulled into a vertical dive, followed at intervals by his two, three, and four men. Three of the bombs missed their targets, but one was a perfect hit, sending a geyser of oil a hundred feet into the air, followed by billowing smoke. All four planes passed through the AA barrage, and hugged the earth out of the target area for several miles before starting to regain altitude.

White Flight followed immediately, with better luck, as three bombs took out three more tanks. All four came safely through.

Now it was Ed's flight's turn. Blue Leader was close behind White Number Four. His bomb took out another tank, and he cleared out all right. That left two more to go down before Ed went. A count of three, and Blue Two was on his way, with George, Three, close behind him, followed by Ed. Flak was coming at them fast and furious now. Number Two never released his bomb. Trailing smoke as Ed watched, he crashed into the hillside beyond the tanks. There was a huge flowerpot of fire as the 51 exploded. Suddenly Number Three exploded right in front of Ed, his bomb falling far short of the remaining tank. "My God, George! No, not George!" Chilled by the shock of seeing his friend blow up almost in his face, Ed forced everything out of his mind but the target, as he hurtled toward it, his .50 caliber guns blasting, and his thumb above the bomb release button on top of the stick.

"Got to get that last tank," he thought. Time seemed to stand still, everything seemed to happen in slow motion, and he had an impression of deep silence in spite of the rush of wind and the rattle of his guns firing. The tank was directly in front of him now, its top clearly visible above the dirt piled up around its sides. He waited a fraction of a second longer than he knew he should before pulling back on the stick as he released his bomb. Barely clearing the top of the tank, he came away at treetop level. With enormous satisfaction, he saw a huge eruption of oil and debris behind him. "I got it! I got it!" he exulted. "We got 'em all!"

Now as he started his climb up to rejoin the rest of the squadron, he realized that his teeth were clenched and his hands were clammy inside his gauntlets, as what had happened to Bob and George, especially George, right in front of him overwhelmed him. "I barely met Bob, and found George again, and they're gone. God, what a waste! Two young lives lost for six oil tanks! So this is what war is! What's wrong with us? Why can't we find a better way to solve our problems?"

Remembering why this war had to be, he suppressed those thoughts as he pulled up beside Blue Leader. The entire group headed home.

Following debriefing, Ed joined the others in the bar for the ritual farewell drink to the pilots who died. Major Irvine called for quiet, then raised his glass. "To two good men, Bob and George. May they fly with angels." Quietly, respectfully, all the men raised their glasses, saying, "To Bob, to George," and downed their drinks. Cold fingers pressed on Ed's heart. Burying his feelings, he did his best to join in celebration of the success of the mission. His uneasiness over the price of that success lay like a pall over his spirits.

Chuck, followed by other members of the squadron, congratulated him on his hit.

C.S. came and shook his hand. "Good job, Ed. You laid that egg perfectly. That tank was demolished."

"Just luck," Ed responded. "Tough losing two of our guys, though."

"Yeah, it is. You never get used to it; just have to push it aside. Otherwise, it'll take over, and you stop functioning. It's the price we have to pay to win this war. Could have been any one of us. You have to learn to live with it. That's part of our job, the toughest part," C.S. said, as he returned to the bar.

Grant joined Ed near the window. "What a hotshot! Two missions and you bag a balloon and an oil tank. Nice going, Ol' Friend. What's next? A couple of 190s or 109s?"

"Lay off, Grant," Ed said.

"What's up? I figured you'd be walking on air."

"The two guys right ahead of me bought it, just like that; they were no more. One was George Stock, my buddy you met last night. We got six tanks, but we lost two guys."

"Hey! I knew we lost two, but I didn't know they were in your flight. Or that one was an old buddy. That has to hurt."

"It hurts like hell to lose an old friend, just after finding him again. We planned to meet after today's mission."

"That's got to make it hard to take."

"That only made it harder. The hard thing is that we — they — paid such a price to knock out those stinking tanks. The world's gone crazy! It doesn't make any sense."

"Hey, wait a minute! Where's all that dedication and commitment we talked about?"

"It's still there, Grant. Hitler is evil, and we have to get rid of him; that hasn't changed. But what grinds me is the stupidity of it all. We stood by and let him get away with all kinds of things. And in the Pacific, we actually helped the Japanese get ready for war — we sold them all kinds of stuff. We saw what was happening both places. We could have stopped it without going to war, could have done that even as late as ten years ago, but we didn't. Almost as if we wanted a war. What did our leaders think was going to happen?"

"Come on, Ed, nobody knew what Hitler was up to. He was —"

Ed cut him off, "How could they help knowing? Why did they think he was building up his military? Then, even when he began striking out and taking over, we still did nothing. Now, we have to pay for it. Our buddies today paid for it! Either they were stupid, or they wanted this war."

"Snap out of it, Pal, or you're going to wind up a Section Eight case. We can't win this war without losing some. You knew that when you signed up, and you know it now."

"Yeah, I know that. Don't worry, I'm committed to helping win it. I'm okay, it just gets me, it seems so pointless to have to keep losing good young men."

Grant responded, "You're right, but that's the way it is, and we're stuck with it." He paused, unsure what else to say. Deciding to try to lighten Ed's mood, he said, "By the way, Chuck Sparks was right."

NOW THEY FLY WITH ANGELS

"About what?"

"About you being a pain in the ass when you get on this subject."

"I guess so, but it's always there, just under the surface. I can't always suppress it," Ed replied.

Noon chow was called, and the bar emptied. This time they got ordinary GI food: fried Spam and scrambled eggs, made with powdered eggs, toast, and coffee.

Following lunch, Ed decided to try to get in a bath. He got soap, towel, and clean clothes, then waited in the hallway for five minutes while another pilot finished, then got into the nearest bathroom. He had to run the water ten minutes before it began to get warm, then it was only tepid. Still, it felt good to get clean. He shaved and put on his clean clothes. As he returned to his room, his roommates rushed out. "Get your flying clothes on, briefing in fifteen minutes!" Chuck called to him as he ran down the stairs.

"Be right there!" Ed yelled. "Hold the jeep for me." He pulled on his OD trousers, GI shoes, grabbed his flight jacket, and raced down the stairs. The last jeep was starting to move as he dashed into the courtyard and jumped aboard as the driver slowed.

"We'll be escorting 17s to Munich," Colonel Macon said. "Rendevous will be here," and he pointed to a spot well east of Brussels, Belgium. "We will be high cover, then we bring them back to the Belgian coast," and he pointed to the spot on the map. "We leave them there and head for home. We will weave back and forth above the bombers, then circle outside the target area. We'll be carrying external fuel tanks, but even so, we will nearly exhaust our fuel, so as soon as we leave the 17s, we'll start a long, slow descent directly toward our base. We will throttle back, and adjust our fuel mix, for maximum fuel economy. Exhaust external tanks first, then drop them wherever we are. From then on, use normal tank sequence: fuselage tank until empty, then alternate right and left wing tanks to maintain balance. In case of action from hostiles, of course, drop external tanks immediately, no matter how full. In that case, fuel will be critical, and we will have to leave the big friends earlier than planned.

"Tinplate will lead, with the other two squadrons following. Red Cross second. Because of probable fuel problems, there will be no 'Chattanooga choo-choo' this trip. Take-off will be 14:30."

Intelligence and weather officers followed, then the colonel took over again to synchronize watches and to say, "Good flying, men. Dismissed," and all the officers popped to as the colonel left the room.

Ed's locker was next to Chuck's. As they got out their helmets, Mae Wests and parachutes, he asked Chuck, "What's a Chattanooga choo-choo?"

"Oh, that's our name for 'targets of opportunity.' You know, after a mission's objective is achieved, and you have fuel and ammunition left, everybody hits the deck and shoots anything they can find that might be of value to the enemy. It's fun."

"Do we get to do that often?" Ed asked.

"Every chance we get. Everybody likes it, but Wing Command is getting touchy about it, the colonel says. Too many pilots and planes are being lost on such trips."

"No orders not to do it, though?"

"Not yet. The colonel expects that'll happen, though," Chuck replied as they went out for the ride to the dispersal areas.

Al was waiting for Ed, and he said, "Tony outlined Princess Pat on the left cowl. If you like it, he'll start filling in the colors next time he has a chance, Sir." Ed looked and saw 'Princess Pat' outlined in fancy, flowing script.

"Looks great," he said to Al. "What will I owe Tony when he finishes it?"

"Usually he gets a bottle of Scotch. But he never asks for anything."

"Okay, what's his favorite?" Ed asked, as he strapped himself in.

"White Horse. But any brand is okay."

Ed cranked up and joined Tinplate White Flight, and they started their take-off run, just as Tinplate Red got to the end of the field. Heavy flak hit the bombers as they approached the Belgian coast. Two were hit. One disintegrated in the air, and no one got out. The other had black smoke pouring from it as it began a sharp dive. When it reached about 10,000 feet altitude, parachutes blossomed, and crew members floated downward. "Two down, and not even to the target yet," Ed started to think, then pushed that out of his mind. "You've got to concentrate on what you're doing. Concentrate!"

A large industrial complex on the outskirts of Munich was the target. Looking down as he and his squadron circled around and above the bombers, weaving about, Ed could see that most of the bombs exploded in the industrial area, although some were off target, hitting what appeared to be a residential area.

Flak was intense, and since the bombers flew over the target in formation, and on the bomb-run itself they had to be straight-and-level to allow the bombardier to focus his bomb sight on the target and release the bombs, they were, for that period of time, easy targets for the AA gunners. Ed could not watch and keep count, being busy watching for hostile fighters, and avoiding collisions with his own fellow fliers, so he didn't know how many 17s went down. He did see five go down over the target, and as they headed home, six others were in trouble. Two of those were smoking badly and losing altitude as they approached the Channel.

"This is Tinplate leader," C.S.'s voice came over the radio. "Tinplate White, follow those big friends down, and give them cover as far as you can across the Channel."

"Roger, Tinplate leader. Willco, out," and Ed's flight went into a shallow dive, overtook the two 17s, and zigzagged above them as they limped homeward.

"Hello, little friends," came through Ed's earphones. "Thanks for the help. Glad to see you. We will go straight in. With you with us, we can concentrate more on staying in the air, not worrying about evading hostiles. Out."

"Roger, big friends. Glad we can help. Tinplate White Leader, out."

They stayed with the bombers until they were at the English coast, then, with fuel getting too low, they headed straight to their own base. All the others had landed by the time Ed's flight got there, so they went in immediately and directly. Ed's left tank showed zero fuel, and his right tank needle was hovering just a hair above zero as his wheels touched down and he taxied to his dispersal point.

After debriefing, during which he learned that of the 300 bombers, 16 went down over enemy territory, and four more were hit, all four limping safely home, Ed said to Chuck on the way to the jeep, "Pretty heavy losses."

"Yeah," Chuck replied. "Those poor bastards! They are totally defenseless against ack-ack on the bomb-run. Nothing we can do to help them, and nothing they can do either. Lucky no hostiles came in on them. Nobody spotted any. Unusual that deep into enemy country. They love to hit the big friends when they're lined up for the bomb-run."

"I was surprised no fighters showed up," Ed said.

"Don't worry. You'll get your chance. They'll be hitting us. Just be happy we didn't lose any of our guys," Chuck said. "This was a milk-run for us."

All the vehicles pulled into the courtyard, and a mad rush for the bar was on. Ed and Grant, although only in their second day at the base, felt like veterans already, joining in the general enthusiasm of the pilots. The tension that had built up during the two missions of the day began to ease as they drank and joked, pushing away the knowledge that they were engaged in a deadly game. Ed knew that he had to learn to do so too. Part of that process seemed to be not to talk about it. In all the talk going on, no one mentioned losses or danger. Seemingly, there was an unspoken agreement to act as if those things weren't there. Partly, Ed guessed, it was the sense of invulnerability typical of young, energetic, enthusiastic men, and part of it was each one's realization that if they began to talk about it, they wouldn't talk about anything else. It would become an obsession.

Ed had had a small sample of dinghy-butt after the first mission of the day, but that was nothing compared to the agony he felt after the second one. He had had to raise and lower his legs several times after parking his plane, grimacing in pain with each move, before he could climb out. Both legs were numb from buttocks to toes. As feeling began to return, the pain was intense. Al had caught him as he almost fell jumping down from the wing.

"It's okay, Sir. It happens to everybody," Al said. "Sometimes we have to lift a pilot out of the cockpit because his legs are paralyzed. I guess you aren't really aware of it until you cut your engine at your parking place, huh?"

"I sure wasn't," Ed replied. "I felt some numbness in the last twenty minutes or so before landing, but I was concentrating on my fuel gauges and getting on the ground, so I didn't really pay attention to how numb I was."

Al said, "If you can walk a little bit, it'll help."

With Al's help, Ed lifted one numb foot after the other as he slowly paced back and forth beside Princess. He felt the numbness decrease, painfully, followed by aching. By the time the jeep arrived, his legs were back to normal. The pain in his backside continued, however, so he sat carefully on the hard cushion of the jeep's seat. At debriefing, he chose to stand beside the wall, as quite a few others did, rather than sit on one of the hard folding chairs.

Ed thought about this after the late dinner of roast chicken, mashed potatoes and gravy, and canned corn with a side dish of applesauce. Dessert was apple pie and coffee. "I'm going to have to squirm around in my seat a lot during these long missions," he said to Grant in the bar. "Maybe I can shift my weight from one buttock to the other, alternating every few minutes. I'll try that next time. None of the guys should misunderstand if we ask them, 'How's your ass?' should they?"

All the pilots were bushed after the two missions of the day, so no one stayed at the bar very long. Ed and Grant spent a few minutes telling each other how the day had been for them, then went to their rooms. Looking at his watch just before he fell asleep, Ed saw that it was only 22:00, but he had no trouble joining the others in sleep.

At breakfast, Colonel Macon announced that the group had no missions assigned for the day, adding that Wing Command had sent commendations on the dive-bombing mission's success. Ed and Grant found several bikes at the side of the hall. When they asked whose they were, they were told, "They belong to the group. Anyone who wants to use one can." The two friends decided to ride out into the countryside and see what was out there.

A scattering of clouds dotted the otherwise clear sky and the sun was bright, although the air was chilly, and a fresh breeze was coming from the east. They wore their flight jackets and overseas caps. After passing through the main gate, they turned in the direction opposite the way into town. The road was paved and smooth, although narrow, and there was little traffic. At first riding on the left bothered them, but they soon got used to it.

At the first crossroad, they decided to take a left turn. There they momentarily forgot to stay left, and made a wide swing, starting up a low hill on the right side, riding side by side. A small truck (lorry) came over the crest of the hill and immediately flashed its lights at them. Quickly they swung to the left side, returning the driver's grin and wave, as he passed by. "Good we didn't meet him right at the top," Grant said.

Neat hedgerows divided the countryside into fields where sheep and cattle grazed. The cows near the road gazed placidly at them, but the sheep scurried away as the bikers passed. Here and there they saw a farmer working at some chore, and clothes were drying on lines near some of the cottages scattered in the fields close to the road. The entire scene was rustic and restful, with none of the busy activity they were used to living with at the bases where they had spent so much time, including their present one.

"Can't beat this for forgetting about military activity, can you?" Grant asked.

"Sure can't," Ed agreed. "I needed this. After only three missions, I was beginning to feel pretty tight. Hope this isn't the way it has to be all the time."

"Me, too. But I think it's just beginners' jitters. The other guys seem fairly relaxed," Grant said. "We're just getting our feet wet. A few missions and we'll be as relaxed as they are."

"Hope you're right. I don't think anyone could stand it if the tension keeps on the way it is now. Anyway, it's great to get out here like this," Ed said.

What had been a narrow road now became an even narrower lane. They peddled uphill and down, stopping now and again to rest, and at times chatting with a farmer or housewife. Once, as they went by a thatched cottage, a pretty girl of about fifteen or sixteen smiled and blushed as they called out, "Hi." She ran into the cottage. An older woman appeared in the doorway and called to them, "Pay 'er no mind. She's a silly bashful thing, just at that age. Good day to ye, Yanks," and waved as they rode on.

"I wonder," Grant said, pausing as they were slowed by an extra-steep hill, and had dismounted to walk their bikes to the top, "I wonder if they grow many like her around here. She looked prime to me."

"Sure did," Ed replied. "Pretty, and what a smile! But too young. They'd string you up for messing around with one like that."

"I just meant," Grant explained, "it would be nice to spend some time walking and talking with someone like that. I get tired of all male company. Don't you?"

"I sure do. Maybe we'll get a few days off soon. We can go to London or Cambridge. I've heard there're lots of sharp-looking, eager gals in places like that," Ed answered.

From the top of the hill they could see a crossroads ahead, with a small country village around it. They coasted down the hill and found that the lane intersected a major-looking road, with a fair amount of traffic moving on it. More interesting was a pub called The Crossed Eye. The sign had a picture of one eye, with an X through it.

"Looks like some pub owner has a sense of humor," Ed said. "What say we stop here, get a pint, and see if they serve any food?"

"Okay."

"Hullo, Yanks," greeted them as they stepped in. "Here's to ye," came from a half-dozen patrons who raised their glasses in greeting.

"What'll ye have, mates?" the barman asked.

A man in farmer's clothes and boots said, "Wotever 'tis, Mr. Withers, I'm payin' fer it."

"Two pints of Guinness, please," Ed said, "and what do you have to eat?"

Drawing the brews, the barman said, "It's hot beef and boiled potatoes with carrots."

Before Ed could reply, the farmer called out, "Serve 'em up, Mr. Withers. Wote're they want, it's the Yanks'll pull our chestnuts out 'itler's bludy fire."

The other patrons chorused, "Aye, they will that!"

"Coom, lads, sit ye doon 'ere. Mr. Withers'll take care o' ye," said the farmer.

Ed and Grant took seats at a table. They were followed by the farmer and the others, who all sat at the same table, several pulling up extra chairs. Grant said to the farmer, "Thanks, but there's no need for you to buy for us."

"'Tis only that I want to," was the reply.

"Take it 'fore he changes his mind," another farmer said. "'Tis a rare thing for Jack to do."

"Mind yer tongue, laddy. I buy when I ha' it, as ye well know."

"Oh, aye. Ye do that. I meant no offense."

"Right, then," the first farmer said. Turning to Ed and Grant, he asked, "Where're ye from?"

"Ohio," Grant said. Ed said, "Pennsylvania."

"Oh, aye. That'd be in America. My meaning was, where're ye from here, in our country?"

"Oh. Our base is at East Wretham," Ed said.

"Ye've biked a fair distance, then, have ye not?"

"About three hours," Grant said. "The countryside is so beautiful we didn't notice how far we were coming."

Ed said, "I notice it now, in my legs, since we've stopped."

"Ye don't cycle much, then, at your home?"

"Not at all. Not for years."

"Ye will feel it, then. But it's not so far now to y're base, if ye take the main road here, going eastward. Ye'll see a sign pointing ye a couple miles on."

"That's good news," Ed said. "My legs don't feel up to going back the way we came."

"Ye'll not find so many hills this way, lads. More lorries and motors to contend wi' though."

Ed and Grant finished their food and drink while carrying on a lively conversation with the local men. When they attempted to pay, the men said, "Noo, Noo! 'Tis all taken care of. We're glad you Yanks are in it noow. Good day to ye, and good look."

Grant and Ed thanked them, shaking hands all around. They used the toilet, then put their aching legs to work again, biking down the main road. "Dinghy-butt yesterday, sore legs today," Ed said. "Nobody said it'd be like this. We're really out of shape. Should have done more exercise on the ship."

The road was nearly level with only slight rises, and soon they saw the sign indicating, "E. Wretham 3 Km." and were relieved.

After replacing the bikes in the rack, they forced their aching legs to take them up the stairs and through the entrance hall and into the bar. Coffee seemed more appealing than anything else. Steaming mugs in hand, they settled gratefully on seats next to the window. Only three other fliers were in the bar. A few minutes after they had seated themselves, Chuck came in. "Hi, guys. That coffee? Good idea," and he ordered a cup, then joined them. "Have you heard what's up tomorrow?" he asked.

"Wait a minute," Ed said, "what's that on your shirt collar? Railroad tracks?"

"Yeah," Chuck replied, "it's Captain Kruger now. C.S. surprised me this morning. Just handed them to me and said, 'My God! Standards for promotion have sure been lowered,' and walked away. I got the official papers later."

"Congrats," Ed said, as he and Grant shook his hand. "Now, give us the less important news about tomorrow."

"Rumors have been around for months that the Eighth Air Force was planning a daylight bombing of Berlin. The word today is that it's scheduled for tomorrow. I'm just telling you what's being said; nobody has confirmed it. But I've never heard a rumor as substantial and widespread as this one. When I tried to corner C.S., he just clammed up. But money says we'll be going to Berlin tomorrow."

"Man, Grant! Wouldn't that be something?" Ed said. "Our fourth mission and we go on the first daylight bombing of Berlin. We'd be a part of history!"

"You're right. So you think it's probably true, Chuck?" Grant asked.

Chuck said, "Sure do, but it still hasn't been confirmed. I'm going up to the room. You, Ed?"

"Right, Captain. You, Grant?"

"I guess so, if my legs'll take me."

Entering the room, Ed said, "Boy, I really need a bath after that sweaty bike ride." He took a towel, soap, and clothes, and went to the bathroom. He couldn't bring himself to refer to these ancient and elegant facilities, shabby as they were, as "latrines."

At evening chow every conversation seemed to be centered on the Berlin rumor. When some early finishers started to leave, Colonel Macon stood and called out, "Don't go yet, men. I have something to say." Conversation stopped, and all eyes turned toward the colonel. "Gentlemen, the rumors are true. We go to Berlin tomorrow!"

The dining room erupted in a great cheer, followed by coffee cups and water glasses clinking as the fliers toasted the "Big B," as that and all subsequent trips to the German capital city were dubbed. The noise subsided and the colonel continued, "As you know, the RAF has hit Berlin a few times on nighttime raids. They have never been able to marshal a massive strike, and as you also know, they always go unescorted. Ours will be the first massive, systematic, daytime raid. The plan is for one thousand U.S. bombers to make the trip; about half 17s and half 24s.

"Almost as many of our fighters will be flying escort. Only 51s have the range to cover as far as Berlin and return. 47s will provide the initial escort, penetrating to the limits of their endurance. 51s will then take over, taking the bombers to the target, and as far back as we can. Meanwhile, the 47s will return, refuel, and relieve us as we reach the limit of our endurance.

"This will be an enormous undertaking, requiring careful attention to timing and coordination. Months of planning have gone into it. We're throwing everything we have into it. It is expected that as important as the strategic damage the bombing will do will be the blow we strike at German morale. This will show them that they have no invulnerable sanctuary. Equally important, we will learn whether or not we can execute this kind of big show. You will get details at our briefing tomorrow at 08:00. Get some sleep tonight. This will be the longest mission we have flown to date. We had to stretch our fuel day before yesterday.

Tomorrow, we'll have to do even more, running lean, and milking every drop out of our wing tanks. Thank you for your attention. Goodnight."

Applause and more cheers followed as the colonel sat down. Ed and Grant joined the others crowding into the bar. Ordinary conversation was out of the question. Only one subject interested the excited, enthusiastic pilots. All were talking loudly and all at once. Only a few bothered to get drinks. After an hour of this, the crowd began to thin out. The men were drifting out in twos and threes. Ed left with Grant to climb the stairs to their rooms. Ed joined the quieter discussion going on in his room. Though less noisy, the topic was the same as that in the bar, and the roommates were just as excited and enthusiastic.

The consensus among the older hands was that, leaks being what they were, the Germans already knew all about the planned raid, had known before our own fliers, and that they would have a real rough reception ready. They'd be throwing everything they had at everything we had to deliver our bombs on their city. If we dared to strike their capitol in daylight, they intended to make us pay dearly for it.

"Count on it, guys. There'll be every kind of German fighter coming at us and at the bombers. You new guys, Ed, will see what they can do. We haven't even seen an enemy fighter on any of your three missions. Well, you'll see them tomorrow! You'll see how good they are, too. They know what they're doing, and they have the ships to do it with. We'll be in the target area, so we'll see plenty of action," Chuck said.

"Right you are, CAPTAIN," Bill Carter said, emphasizing the captain mockingly. "I suppose you'll add to the three you already have. Hope you give the rest of us a few chances."

Ed turned to Chuck, "I didn't know you had three victories, Chuck. That's great!"

"Just pure luck. Got 'em all when we had 47s. None yet in a 51. Haven't seen many fighters lately. I think they've been saving them up for tomorrow. I repeat, we're going to see action tomorrow, and I'm hitting the sack right now," and he started to undress. All the others followed suit, excepting Carl Allen, who had rigged a reading lamp above his pillow, and now, as every night, read as the others settled down to sleep.

Between his tired, aching legs, and his excitement about the next day's mission, Ed lay awake for almost an hour before he dropped off to sleep.

The excitement of the previous evening continued in the morning at breakfast, on the way to briefing, and during briefing. Briefing was routine, following the regular pattern. But before dismissal, Colonel Macon said, "Now, Gentlemen, we can expect maximum resistance from the enemy, both fighter and flak. There is no doubt that they know we're coming, and they know how important we consider this to be. For you newer members of the group, this will be your first encounter with the enemy. It is necessary that we all stay together, and that we watch each others' tails. And again, especially for you newer men, don't get lured away on your own. One of the enemy's favorite tactics is to send one of their planes off on his own, hoping one or two of ours will pursue him. Then, when our guys are well away from the pack, whamo! Half a dozen of theirs will come out of nowhere and hit him. He won't have a chance. They're reluctant to come right at us when we're all together. They will hit us then if they have to, but they prefer to come after us when we are single or in pairs.

"Another of their favorite tactics is for one of them, at a safe distance from us, to release a black substance that looks like oil smoke from the engine. It's almost always a trick to lure one of us away for an easy victory. Same thing. Once one of ours thinks he has a sitting duck and goes for him, his buddies hit our guy, often out of the sun. So watch it! We need all of your eyes all the time, and all of your guns when they hit us, or try to get at the heavies. Together we can handle anything they have. But a loner is going to get his ass shot up. Good luck, and good flying. Dismissed."

When Ed jumped off the jeep, Al was grinning as he stood below the cowl of Ed's ship. The completed "Princess Pat" painted on the cowl was beautiful. Outlined in black, on a background of green, the group's color, were the brilliant red letters. "Great job," Ed exclaimed. "Both sides done?"

"Yes, Sir, and both look great."

"They sure do. Tell Tony how happy I am, and he'll have his Scotch as soon as I can get it," Ed said. He felt extra proud as he taxied out and took his place in Tinplate Blue Flight, Number Four. Chuck was flight leader, and when he saw the beautiful job Tony had done, he gave a wide grin and an okay sign with finger and thumb.

Take-off was normal, as was the climb to altitude. No zig-zagging this time. The group flew directly to its rendezvous destination, each squadron in loose combat formation, all heads and eyes moving, everybody scanning the sky above, especially to the east, where the sun was emerging from the clouds, and examining the air space fore and aft, to both sides and all quarters, and below. Nobody could guess when or from where the enemy would strike, but everybody knew that they would.

Looking up and ahead, Ed saw a glint at twelve o'clock, then others near the first one. He was about to call the sighting of "bogeys" to Tinplate leader when he realized that what he saw was the bombers. As they gained on the big friends, Ed was awed by how many there were, and at their excellent formations. "A thousand heavy bombers all at once! What a sight! I'll remember this," he thought.

Getting closer still, he could see smaller planes above, below, to each side, and behind the bombers. Fighters were zigging and zagging around and in and out of the bomber formations. "A little like our convoy on the Atlantic," he said to himself. "But I can see all the ships in this armada."

As his group joined the vast convoy, Ed saw other groups of 51s come into their assigned positions while 47 groups, reaching the limit of their endurance, broke out and headed west toward home. Now the sun broke free of clouds and shone directly through Ed's windshield, hurting his eyes when he looked that way. He lowered his goggles and this reduced the glare, enabling him to look toward, but not directly at, the sun. "I can see why the Germans like to come out of the sun. Sure would be hard to see them there."

The group was now in its assigned position, left of the last flights of bombers, and at their altitude. The colonel was leading them in a zig-zagging course, not following the same pattern over and over, but covering the territory while varying the pattern, so enemy ack-ack or fighters could not easily predict where they would be at any time. Ed glanced at his watch. Still about an hour to the target. A milk-run so far. This continued for another forty-five minutes; then his earphones came alive as someone shouted, "Here they come! Right out of the sun!" For a moment Ed could see nothing, but then he saw black specks, growing larger. In his earphones came "This is Mohair [the group's code name] Leader. Hold positions and stay alert. They'll probably go for the bombers. Top cover will get first chance at them. We stay put and watch for any that slide our way. If you get a chance to get one, take it. Repeat: stay alert! Probably a second wave will come at us from the left or rear. We're here to protect the big friends. Hold positions! Protect the bombers. Cover each other. Out."

Suddenly a voice, almost hysterical, yelled, "From the rear! About fifty of them coming right at us!" A second voice, "More from the sun! God! They're everywhere!"

Macon's voice came on, cool and calm, "All right. Break up into flights and freelance. Choose targets and go for them. But stay near, cover each other, and don't abandon the heavies."

Chuck had his flight in a climbing turn to the left to face the bandits at nine o'clock. In less than fifteen seconds they were mixing it up, and everybody was too busy to talk. Ed saw a pair of 109s coming from his eleven o'clock, on a course that would cross his path. He flicked on his gun switch and started firing. Missed. Not enough lead! They had flashed past so he made a hard right turn as he went into a shallow dive. He got one in his sights, almost directly in front of him. Again he fired and saw sparks as some of his bullets hit the 109 in his sights. He kept firing until he was almost on top of the target plane, then he pulled up and over. He'd lost sight of the other one. Rolling up on his side and looking down, he saw a 109 below him. About to go after it, he realized that it was the one he'd just fired on. A little smoke was trailing behind it, and it was losing altitude. He switched off his guns. He was aware that his stomach muscles were tight and his teeth were clenched. He forced himself to relax.

A quick look around showed him that he was alone, so he made a fast right turn and began to climb back toward the bombers. Fighters were diving, climbing, chasing and being chased all around and among the bombers. Enemy planes were evading American fighters and diving on the big friends. Every heavy was spitting bullets at the attacking enemies. Bombers and friendly and enemy fighters were dropping from the formations by the dozens, it seemed to Ed.

He spotted a lone 190 diving toward the bombers, above and ahead of him. He jammed the throttle full forward, through the wire, felt the surge of full military power, got the 190 in his sights and squeezed the trigger. He scored a direct hit, and the 190 burst into flames and crashed into the 17 it had been attacking. For a moment it seemed to stick there; then it fell free, its nose crushed, tumbling groundward. The bomber was dented, probably torn, but was still flying straight and level, maintaining its position in the formation.

Ed turned sharply left to avoid ramming the 17. He could not identify any more bandits, but he could see lots of the bombers tightening up their formations, closing the gaps left by big friends which had been shot down. "I wonder where they all went," he thought.

"Princess Pat!" came over his earphones, "two 109s right behind you. Break fast!"

Simultaneously, he jammed the throttle to full military power, shoved the stick forward and left, and kicked full left rudder, putting his wings perpendicular to the ground, then pulled hard back on the stick, making a tight turn as he gained speed. He saw tracers go by his wings, and knew he'd had a close call, a near miss. Now the 109s overshot him as they turned left, unable to turn as tightly as Ed. He flipped the stick and right rudder, sliding behind them. Got one in his sights and squeezed. "It's you or me," he thought, and the 109 seemed to shudder and almost stop before flipping over and going into a screaming dive, trailing smoke. He couldn't see the other one. Starting to turn back toward the armada, he saw, off to his left and about 1,000 feet below, a green-tailed 51 racing after the other bandit.

Now the bombers, having stayed on course through the savage attack, were making their bombing runs, all surrounded by flak, and many of them concealed by smoke from the flak. "Good guys," Ed said aloud in admiration. "Doing their job. How do you like that Adolph, you rat?" He watched load after load of bombs drop out of the bombers' bellies.

He spotted green noses and tails and hurried to join them. He recognized Chuck's "Kruger Koo-Koo," and maneuvered toward him. No other members of the flight were in sight, so he became Chuck's wingman. Chuck gave him a grin and an "okay" sign. Feeling relief at being back with his mates, Ed was again aware of how tight his muscles were and how his jaws ached from being tense. Again he forced himself to relax, but he then realized how tired he was. "I feel drained," he thought, "but we aren't done yet."

Like a confirmation of that thought, Macon's voice came on. "Stay alert, Men. They'll be back. I know fatigue is setting in, but we may have more action. If we let down, it could be fatal. Keep alert. Resume group formation, each squadron in abreast formation, but all close to the rest of the group. The sun is higher, and soon will be behind us, as we are making a slow left turn to stay with the bombers. Keep your heads on spindles, looking up and back and all around as much as possible. This is our most dangerous time on a mission like this. They know how many we've lost, and how tired we are. Keep your minds on business. Don't daydream! Out."

They were headed home, but just as the colonel had said, the fighting wasn't over yet.

"Here they come," the colonel's voice said. "Break up into flights again, and good luck." He didn't have to say where they were coming from. Everybody saw them diving straight down at the bombers.

"They have speed and position on us," Macon's voice said, "so we can't do anything to stop the attack. Be set to dive after them when they've passed through the big friends' formations. Out." Ed stayed on Chuck's wing as he positioned himself just under the bombers, then began a full-throttle dive as the first Germans flashed through the bomber formation.

Throttles wide open, wind screaming around their canopies, Chuck and Ed gradually gained on the two 109s ahead of them. Other 51s were doing the same behind other bandits. Ed got one of the 109s in his sights and fired. Too far away. He saw his tracers dropping behind the 109. He pulled his nose up slightly and fired again. Some hits. He was closing in on his target now, so using the sights, he squeezed the trigger. The 109 exploded almost in his face, and he shot the stick forward to get under the debris. What looked like a small wheel bounced off his canopy, but he missed everything else. Chuck was a little above him and ahead, still firing at the 109 he had targeted. Ed pulled up to Chuck's side in time to see smoke pour out of the 109 as it went into a vertical dive.

No other enemy planes were in sight except those already being pursued, so Chuck led Ed on a slow climb back to the group's position, keeping an eye out for other bandits who might get on the tails of their friends below. All the 51s that hadn't been lost formed up and headed toward home. The ones which had been in pursuit finished their attacks and slowly climbed up to join the formation.

No other enemy planes struck. They reached the point where they left the bombers, and began to save all the fuel they could for the completion of the return to base. Nearing the North Sea's east coast, Ed began to unwind. Every part of him ached with weariness. The slight relaxation allowed him to realize how much tension had built up. Once more, he forced himself to ease off, while still staying alert. He began to appreciate how much energy he must have expended in the life-and-death confrontation with the enemy. "Not a lot of fun," he concluded.

Now he became aware of how urgently he needed to relieve himself. The "Pilot Relief" device was a rubber tube, with a wider rubber end attached. It was fastened by a clip under the seat. He had never used one, but now he was in desperate need. He unclipped it and pulled it out and up. He laughed, thinking, "This is impossible. But I have no choice. There's no way I'm getting to the base with wet pants! I have to use it." In a fighter plane cockpit, there is no room to move. The pilot is strapped into a bucket seat sitting on top of a folded, hard, dinghy. It is impossible to cross your legs, or even spread your knees more than an inch or so. Of course, standing up is totally out of the question, as is raising your buttocks from the seat. Tired as he was, in response to his desperate need, Ed made a supreme effort to unzip his fly and complete the maneuver, allowing him to win the relief he had to have.

He sighed with relief, finished, and returned everything to its proper place. He looked over at Chuck, who was looking back at him with an expression that said, "Can't you keep that damned airplane steady?" Ed smiled and nodded at him.

Now that his number one problem was taken care of, Ed realized that his legs were numb and his feet were like blocks of ice. His butt ached, his legs ached, his neck ached, and his back ached. He was relieved when, at last, they flew over the Wash and toward their home field. He was the last to land, and he groaned as he hit the ground hard, feeling the jolt through his weary, sore body. But he was home! He'd made it.

He cut the engine and set the brakes as Al jumped up on the wing. "Okay, Sir." Ed was slumped down, his head resting against the impact pad behind and above the seat.

"I'm okay, Al, I just don't think I can move for a minute."

"How'd it go, Sir?"

"Went all right. They had a welcoming party for us. But it went all right."

"Hey, Tony," Al called, "Come here and give me a hand with the lieutenant."

Tony climbed up on the right wing. Ed put out his hand. "Hi, Tony. Beautiful job on the lettering. Got a lot of jealous looks. You'll get your White Horse for that, and my gratitude. You're an artist," and he shook Tony's hand.

"Naw, I just like doing it, Sir. Glad you like it."

"I love it. How about two bottles?"

"No thanks, Sir, That's too much. Just one, and even that isn't necessary. It's my pleasure."

"Okay, Tony. Now, Al, I think I can get out by myself." He tried to force his legs to raise him, but they wouldn't work.

"Let's go, Tony. Hoist him up, then I'll help him over the side and down," Al said. One on each side of the cockpit, the two crewmen got Ed up, and he swung his legs over and slid to the wing with Al keeping him from falling. Hanging on to the side of the cockpit, he was able to slide to the rear edge of the wing and lower his feet toward the ground. With the help of Tony and Al, he was able to stand and slowly and painfully take a few steps. Soon the pain of returning circulation followed by needles came, then feeling started to come back. His legs now worked, and he let go of his helpers. What was left was a mighty weariness, and the ache of dinghy-butt. By the time the jeep arrived, he was able to climb aboard unassisted.

"Nice work, Ed. You got a couple," Chuck said as they drove to the shack for debriefing.

Ed just grunted. His sore leg muscles were hurting again, and the jeep did nothing for his dinghy-butt. "Oh, man! I could sleep for a week."

"Forget it. You'll be okay tomorrow. It's the intensity of the action that gets you. We all go through that, but it's worse on your first big mission. They'll have coffee for us at debriefing. Have a cup. You'll feel better as you wind down. By the time we eat, you'll be a new man."

"Not a chance," Ed said. "I'm done for!"

Chuck laughed, but it turned out that he was right. The hot coffee helped him relax, and a Guinness before dinner made him ready to eat. Life began to seem worth living again.

To commemorate the historic mission, dinner was a festive occasion. All the fliers had a choice of chicken, beef or pork. Salad was lettuce and tomatoes or cole slaw. Boiled potatoes, fresh peas and carrots and home made biscuits. Several bottles of white and red wine were on each table, as well as milk, water and soda. Coffee and a choice of strawberry or chocolate pie topped off the excellent meal. "A feast for the warriors returning from battle," Ed said to Chuck and Grant. "Haven't seen food like this since we got off the S.S. Argentina."

"You know something," Grant responded. "This tastes better than anything we had on the ship."

Chuck said, "That's because you didn't do anything on the ship to earn your meals. Today we earned a feast."

As pilots began to push back from the tables, Colonel Macon stood. "Gentlemen," he said, raising his glass, "I salute you for a magnificent job today. Here's to you." Everybody raised his glass or cup and drank. "I have two more things to say. First, and most important—all of our birds came home!" Now cheers went up. At debriefing time three had not made it home. "The last three were together, and they landed at Brixton for fuel, then came home. The last thing is this: Colonel Miller, our adjutant, has just told me that he had a call from Wing Headquarters, and the Eighth Air Force is issuing a commendation to all groups involved in today's historic mission." He sat down, and all present applauded.

From dinner the entire group migrated to the bar, where it seemed every pilot was talking at once about the action he'd been involved in. It was loud, boisterous, joyful. Soon, however, weariness set in, and gradually the voices grew less loud and the crowd thinned as the men wandered off to their rooms. Before long the bar was empty, and Wretham Hall grew quiet as sleep came to the group.

Like the others, Ed was exhausted. He slept deeply, but he was troubled by dreams of bombers falling in flames, and of his own bullets hitting enemy fighters. Had anyone been awake in the room, he would have heard an occasional groan from Ed and two or three others, plus some mumbled words, such as "Those poor bastards!"

Morning came with bright sunshine and a sharp cold wind from the west. Most of the pilots skipped breakfast, but they all turned out for noon chow, since word was sent around that a mission was scheduled after noon, with briefing at 12:45. It turned out to be a short, routine escort job for twenty-four B-17s to bomb a concentration of German tanks and other military vehicles and supplies in Belgium.

After briefing was completed, the colonel commented briefly on the previous day's mission, reporting that all objectives had been accomplished, and adding that intelligence reported that even the psychological mission of demoralizing the Germans appeared to have been successful. Then he said, "As you know, such large-scale operations are not carried out without cost. I'm sorry to report that, as of this morning, 311 bombers and 107 fighters did not return. The enemy put up 300 fighters, and we took out half of them. Good luck and good flying today. Dismissed."

For the next two weeks, all but one of the group's daily missions were routine escort trips, none longer than five hours. They encountered very few bandits; those few would make one lightning pass through the bomber formations, then disappear far below. They went through with such speed that there was no real chance of successful pursuit without risking leaving the bombers alone and vulnerable. Nobody in the group got any "victories" on these missions, although alert gunners on the bombers accounted for eight enemy fighters.

The one exceptional mission was a twilight sweep of a Luftwaffe aerodrome. Air Force intelligence chose the time because their information was that the enemy planes would be on the ground then. Any enemy planes destroyed on the ground would be planes that could not attack ours in the air. Each flight would go in in the abreast formation, and all were reminded that no one was to get out in front of the others. The interval between passes was five seconds, and each pilot would fire at whatever was in front of him, then hug the treetops after completing the pass. This would help them to avoid ground fire.

They also were to come in at treetop level, using the enemy flak towers on each side of the field as guides in getting to treetop level three miles away, as well as to ground level as they crossed the boundary of the aerodrome.

Tinplate was the first squadron to go in, and Ed was Number Four in Red Flight. It was a huge aerodrome, with plenty of targets. Red was to stay close to the right side of the field, White would go to their left, and Blue even farther to the left. Of the other two squadrons, one would concentrate on the center, and the other to the left of the field. There was to be just one fast pass, with no cleanup to follow, because by then all the ground guns would be manned and active.

As Red Number Four, Ed would be closest to the right boundary, so he did not expect to find any good targets in his path. Just as he passed the edge of the field and dropped to ground level, he saw a twin-engine Heinkel bomber directly ahead of him. He'd already armed his guns, so he blazed away, then had to pull up to clear the Heinkel. He was sure he'd poured plenty of slugs into the enemy plane, so he was disappointed that it still sat there, seemingly intact. But in his rearview mirror, he saw it burst into flame, and its column of smoke joined the others along the flight path. Nothing else was in front of him now, except one of the flak towers, exactly where he would exit the field. He had to pull up sharply to get over the tower, and as he did so, he squeezed the trigger, raking the tower from bottom to top as he went up. He couldn't tell what effect his shots had, but guns from that tower opened up on him as he went down again on the far side of it. He saw the tracers, but they all passed under and fell behind him, and he breathed again as he got out of range.

About a mile from the airfield, Chuck began to climb, and the rest of the flight did the same. In less than a minute, all three squadrons had made their passes, knocking out some twenty enemy planes, and five minutes later the group was on its way home. Three 51s lost; a costly but successful trip.

Since the three lost pilots, all surely killed, were one from each squadron, Colonel Macon made the toast at dinner, "To three good men. All will be missed. May they fly with angels."

One of the three was Harry Silker, a new friend of Ed's. They had played ping-pong together, shared ideas and feelings in the bar, and walked around the grounds in the evening. Ed resented what seemed almost a perfunctory acknowledgement of the three deaths. "But," he reasoned to himself, "the colonel has been in combat for many months, and has toasted so many lost members of the group that he has to make the salutes impersonal or lose his sanity."

On Thursday of that week, the colonel announced at dinnertime that a massive weather front was moving in, closing all bases in the East Anglia area. No relief was expected until 06:00 that morning. Immediately, plans were underway for trips to Cambridge or London or Nottingham — wherever the pilots knew, from experience or from hearsay, that they could have a good time. Ed and Grant decided to go to Cambridge and visit the campus of the famous university, leaving right after chow and taking the evening train at 20:00. They had been told that there were reasonable sleeping facilities at the Y, or for more deluxe accomodations, at several hotels. They had also been told that the Red Lion was a real focal point for servicemen of all types, as well as college students and local young folks.

Carrying their overnight bags, the two friends stepped off the train and made their way to the town center. It was now 21:30, but as they walked along, the streets became increasingly crowded. At the main part of town, with many pubs and several hotels as well as shops, tea rooms, and restaurants, the sidewalks were jammed to overflowing, with many pedestrians having to walk in the streets as servicemen competed with young civilians for walking room and a chance to get into pubs and eating places. Uniforms dominated the scene—mainly RAF and U.S. Army Air Corps—all ranks, sizes, and shapes. Clearly, the weather that was keeping Ed's group grounded was doing the same to ships at many other bases. "If Cambridge is jammed like this, imagine what downtown London must be like," Ed said, as they fought their way toward one of the hotels.

They made it to a hotel entrance and noticed there were no crowds pressing in or out of the doors. A uniformed doorman looked down his nose at them, hesitated, and then without looking at them—and certainly not making them feel welcome—opened one of the heavy oak doors with exaggerated dignity. The vast reception area was peopled by a dozen or so elderly folk sitting in lounge chairs and talking in hushed tones. The loudest sound was that of Ed's and Grant's rubber-heeled shoes on the polished marble floor as they walked toward an ancient-looking bald man dressed in evening clothes, sitting behind the polished walnut registration desk. Halfway there, Grant stopped and said in a half-whisper that seemed to echo in the room, stopping all conversation as the residents peered at them, as though their presence were as offensive as that of a cockroach crawling across the floor, "I don't think this is the place for us." They turned around to return to the doorway, almost hearing a collective sigh of relief from the loungers in the ornate room. Ed pushed the heavy door open, finding that it moved easily and quietly on its huge brass hinges, and they escaped to the crowded sidewalk.

Walking toward another large hotel, they laughed. Approaching the door, they encountered another uniformed doorman. This one deigned to speak to them. "I think, Sirs, that you would be more comfortable in other accomodations. Perhaps on down this street?" he said, with a suggestion of a smile. They were tempted to go in anyway, but Ed said, "To hell with it. We're here to relax, not to be examined by snooty English doormen."

Further down the street they found two less imposing hotels, but the queues at the registration desks were long and barely moving, so they decided to try the "Y." There they did get a room, shared with two other men. When Ed and Grant stepped into the room, one said, "Hello, Yanks. Hope you don't mind sharing with RAF types," as he finished adjusting his necktie. The other one was putting on his polished black shoes, sitting on one of the metal single beds.

"Suits us fine," Grant said. "Be a nice change, since we spend most of our time with other Americans."

They shook hands and introduced themselves. It turned out that the RAF men were pilots who were flying the new Mosquito, a recently-introduced plywood fighter-bomber with twin engines and a crew of two. It was used primarily for fast strikes at enemy targets, but was fast and agile enough to hold its own in dogfights. "We're about to go find a pint somewhere," the one who'd just put on his shoes said. "Care to join us?"

Grant and Ed looked at each other, then Ed said, "Give us a minute to rinse the grime off our faces and yes, thanks."

"Right. We'll wait in the lobby," and they left.

Hurrying down, the two Americans found Ced and Syd, their new RAF friends, sitting on a bench along one wall. "The proper place to start would be the Red Lion," Syd offered. "It's certain to be crowded, but that's part of the fun. On your first visit to Cambridge, you must go there. All right?"

"Yes, we've heard of the Red Lion. Lead on," Ed said, and they went out to the street. Evening fog was settling in, giving a ghostly appearance to everybody due to dimly-lit, shaded street lamps and blacked-out buildings. The Red Lion was crowded indeed. As they got near to it, they had to elbow through closely-packed crowds of fun-seeking people, mainly in uniform, but with some civilians. There were a surprising number of young women. British WAAFS and American WAACS, each like a queen bee with uniformed young men crowding around them. A scattering of young ladies in civilian clothes—possibly students—were present, and more than a few "women of the night."

Clearly the pub was full to capacity, for many of the people on the street were holding drinks—the men pint glasses, the women smaller glasses of gin-and-orange, a popular lady's drink in England. In spite of the jostling and the effort it took to fight into the pub and then get close enough to the bar to order drinks, everyone was in high spirits; no one was grumbling or cursing. All were out for fun.

Access to the pub was by doors at street level opening on to a corridor; on the left side of the corridor were the inner pub doors, jammed open by people striving to get in against the tide of others coming out. On the opposite side were doors leading into the hotel and into the restaurant and a tea shop. The Red Lion, Ed and Grant discovered, was not just a pub; it was an accomodation complex. Led by their new friends, they fought their way through the happy crowd in the corridor and the more densely packed mob in the pub. Struggling through until close to the bar, they managed to get a pint each, then they started working their way out toward the street.

"Hullo Syd! Hullo Ced! Over here, mates." The two Americans followed their friends and found themselves at a booth seating four more RAF pilots, friends of their friends. "We're ready to leave," the one who had called them over said. "Thought you might like our places. Two 'bob' each is all we want."

"Stuff it," Ced said. "Thank you very much, mates. We'll take over now."

Others nearby saw the four getting up to leave the booth and the crush as they tried to beat Ed's four to the seats nearly prevented the parting ones from getting out. With good-humored aggressiveness, however, the exchange was achieved, and the four friends sat, waving goodbye and thanks to the ones leaving.

Ced was Cedric Lingmann, from a Welsh mining village, who had been a student at a "red-brick" university when he signed on with the RAF, and Syd was Syd George, reading history at Oxford. Both had learned to fly in the Moth (pronounced moath), a famous light bi-plane, then had fighter training in Hurricanes. Both had wanted to join Spitfire squadrons, but they were assigned to Mosquitoes. They liked the Mosquitoes and the lightning-like strikes they were assigned, but they still hoped to get into Spits.

Ed said, "We've only been over here a couple of weeks. I got just what I wanted, a P-51. Grant has been converted now that he's in 51s too. He loves it, as I do."

"P-51," Ced said. "P-51? Oh yes, it's the Mustang, isn't it? Didn't work out for us. Did they fix it then?"

"Sure did," Grant said. "She's the sweetest bird in the sky now. I used to want P-47s, but I'm glad I got 51s."

They exchanged tales about their training and experiences so far in combat. Then Syd asked, "You weren't on the big raid your chaps had the other day, were you?"

Ed replied, "You mean the Big B?"

"Big B! What the devil is that?" Ced wanted to know. "An extra large bomb?"

"It's our name for a raid on Berlin. We just did our first one a couple of days ago," Grant replied.

"Yes, that's the one I meant," Syd said. "Were you on it?"

"We sure were," Ed answered.

"Big show, was it?" Ced asked.

"Big as I want to see," Ed said.

"So many planes in the air we had to watch that we didn't run into each other when the Jerries hit us!"

"Threw a lot at you, did they?" Syd said.

"Looked like everything they had," Grant said. "But they were after the bombers, not us. We had to go after them. They did a lot of damage, all right."

"Sounds like a jolly good shootout, eh?" Syd said.

Ed replied, "Our first real action. And it was quite a 'show,' as you called it. But Grant, we aren't supposed to talk about details, remember? Enemy ears are everywhere."

"Oh, bosh!" Ced said. "We're always being told that, too. I reckon there is some chance of prying ears, but with all this noise, who could hear?"

"Yeah, but Ed's right. We're not supposed to have loose tongues about our operations, so we'll clam up now," Grant said.

"Right," Ced said. "By the way, that wasn't the first air raid on Berlin, y'know. Our lads've been there a few times at night."

"Yes, we know that," Ed said. "Unescorted, too. Takes guts!"

"Well, yes," Syd put in. "Our lads wouldn't care to do what yours do, either. They prefer the cover of darkness. And your formation-bombing scares the hell out of them. Your ships are too totally exposed, so vulnerable, holding a steady course right on the target! They must be perfect dream targets for the Nazi ack-ack gunners! Our lads want none of that."

"I wouldn't either," Grant agreed. "But it makes for more precise bombing. Sets up a controlled pattern. Ours do more patterned bombing in the target area, each formation hitting a particular area."

"Yeah," Ed said, "but if ours are off, they're all off. Yours are dropped by individual bombers, so if one misses, they don't all have to miss."

"True enough," Ced agreed. "But in enemy territory, anything you hit weakens the enemy. So even if you miss the primary target, whatever gets hit is a worthwhile target. I'm for indiscriminate bombing. Especially in a city like Berlin. Dump them on them!" Ced's vehemence surprised the two Americans.

"Don't look so appalled," Ced went on heatedly. "Have you seen London? The Germans don't bother to pick military targets! They come over at night and drop them without a thought about homes, churches, hospitals. Just let them go! We need to give them the same in return."

"Okay, Ced," Grant said. "No, we haven't seen what they've been doing to London. Our cities in the States haven't been touched, thank God, so you're bound to have a different attitude than we have."

"We bloody well do that!" Ced responded. "Let's get off this. We're supposed to be having fun."

"Right," Syd said. "You chaps interested in birds?" Seeing the blank looks on the Americans' faces, he added, "You know, what the Aussies call 'Sheilas'? Girls, friends, girls!"

"Oh yeah, sure," Ed said. "Birds, eh? We usually use that word for airplanes. Sure, do you know any around here? I mean the kind that don't charge."

"Quite," Ced said. "Say, Syd! Isn't that Sally what's-her-name over there?"

"It is, indeed," Syd answered. "Sally and Lizbet," and he stood up waving to get the attention of two young ladies in the crowd. They finally saw his frantic waving and started making their way over.

Ced, who was sitting on the outer edge of the bench he shared with Syd, stood as the ladies got there. "Hullo Sal, Liz," and kissed each one on the cheek. "You know Syd. This is Grant and Ed, a couple of American fliers come to win the war for us."

Ed and Grant stood awkwardly in their places. Ed, seated like Ced on the outer end of his bench, stepped out as Ced did, and Sal slid in beside Grant, and Liz beside Syd. It was cozy, really tight, but all six were able to sit in the booth.

Ced said, "Time for another round, isn't it? Same again, Gentlemen? Right. Four pints Guinness. Ladies? Gin and orange, right? Come on, Ed. I'll need help getting through this crowd." Ed stood and the two of them pushed and elbowed their way to the bar. Ed paid, and Ced got a tray from a barman. He held it over his head as Ed made a path for him back to the booth.

"It's a bloody combat zone!" Ced said, putting the tray on the table. "I took those elbows in my defenseless kidneys on the trip back!"

After half-an-hour of bantering conversation, in which the two attractive young ladies participated freely, Syd said, "The air is heavy in here, isn't it? Shall we get out and walk about a bit?" All agreed, so they fought their way to the door, not without being almost crushed in the stampede to their booth when people nearby saw them getting up to leave. The four men surrounded the ladies, who were not very tall, to protect them.

The corridor was still jammed full, but the crowd on the sidewalk had thinned somewhat. The cool air was refreshing, and Ced proposed a stroll to the Cam River, which ran through both the town and the university campus. After a pleasant walk on the riverbank, Liz said they would be locked out if they weren't back by midnight, so the four men walked the two ladies to the small residential hotel where they had a room. Thanks and goodnights were said, and the four men went on their way to a good night's sleep at the Y.

Just before he fell asleep, Ed said, "I was hoping for a different conclusion to the evening."

Ced said, "Not likely with those two. They're decent girls. I can't say, though, that such thoughts did not cross my mind."

"Will the two of you not shut up?" Syd grumbled. "I've a bit of sleeping to do." Quiet fell over the room.

Ed was the first awake on Saturday morning. As usual, once awake he could not get to sleep again, so he got out of bed. Looking out the window, he saw low-hanging clouds and a drizzling rain. As quietly as he could, he gathered his clothes and overnight bag, slipped out the door and padded down the hall to the latrine/shower room. No one else was there, so he had a leisurely shower and shave. Since he and Grant would be staying a second night, he returned his bag to the room and went downstairs. The cafeteria was not ready to serve breakfast, but coffee was available at five-pence. He bought a cup and carried it into the adjacent lounge. He found a scattering of outdated magazines and newspapers from the day before. He sat in a worn but comfortable lounge chair, sipped his coffee, and read the "Manchester Guardian." The news and commentary columns were dominated by war and war-related stories, including extensive discussions of a forthcoming meeting between President Roosevelt and Prime Minister Churchill.

Just as the cafeteria opened for breakfast, the other three appeared, showered and shaved like Ed. So they all had breakfast. Syd and Grant were puffy-eyed, still sleepy, but Ced, like Ed, was "bright-eyed-and-bushy-tailed." Much to the annoyance of the other two, the wide-awake ones carried on a good-natured conversation of insults and jibes at each other, their countries, and their respective Air Forces' equipment, tactics and abilities. This went on until Syd, exasperated, said, "For God's sake, you two! Give it a rest, will you?"

Agreeing with Syd, Grant said, "Yeah. Let's decide what we're going to do today."

"Righto," Ced said. "Shall we call a truce, old boy?"

"Okay," Ed said. "Anybody have a suggestion for a mission today?"

Syd answered, "I don't know about this morning, but if you're interested in classical music, Dame Myra Hess will be giving a concert at 15:00 this afternoon. I'd like to attend."

Ed recognized Myra Hess as a renowned English pianist, so he quickly agreed. Ced said, "She's a fine performer, and a favorite of mine. Any idea what she'll be playing, Syd?"

"Mostly Mozart, I believe," Syd replied. "But some Beethoven as well."

"I'd like that. Grant?" Ced asked.

"Well," Grant said, "piano recitals, especially played by 'dames,' aren't my favorite kind of entertainment, but I'll go along."

"Bang on! Good fellow," Ced said. "Syd, do you suppose we can get bookings?"

"I'll ring up and find out," Syd said. "You Yanks understand why we have concerts in the afternoon, not at night?"

"The blackout, I guess," Ed said.

"Righto," Syd said. "Damned blackout screws up everything. What would you chaps like to do?"

"I don't know," Grant replied. "What's to do in an English city on a Saturday morning?"

Ced said, "My parents' home is not far from here. Would you care to visit our farm? I can ring them up. They'd be happy to see their darling boy, and they'd make you welcome, even give you lunch. What do you say?"

"Sounds good, but are you sure they wouldn't mind?" Ed asked.

"I'm their favorite and only son. If they haven't anything on, I'm sure they'd be delighted. They've been wanting to meet Syd, and they're fond of Americans. They've been to your country several times," Ced replied. "There's a public phone just down the street; I'll go ring them right away," and he hurried out.

Shortly, Ced returned. "I spoke to my Da, he says to come along and stay for lunch. Longer, if you like, but I told him we would be going to the concert. We can take a bus just at the corner and Da'll meet us in our little village. I'll just do my teeth, and we'll be off. All right?"

Syd said, "Good. I'll go call for our concert bookings. Meet you out front." Pulling on his topcoat, he went out. In a minute Ced returned, smelling of toothpaste, and he and the others went out into the continuing drizzle. Syd came up to them. "All set. We can pick up our tickets when we get to the concert hall. Pound-five each."

Thirty-five minutes after boarding the bus, they arrived in the little picturesque village of Eddington. "Hullo, Da," Ced said to a tall, slender gentleman wearing polished boots, britches, a belted brown tweed jacket, brown shirt and tie, and a tweed hat. His ruddy face broke into a smile, revealing even white teeth beneath a neatly trimmed, graying mustache. He said, "Hullo, Ced. You're looking fit."

"I am fit, Da. Never better. You're looking splendid. Here's my comrade, Syd, and two American friends, Ed and Grant." That Ced was proud of his father, and his father proud of him, was evident in the warmth of their greeting and in the way their eyes embraced each other.

Mr. Hamilton led the way to a beautiful, slate-gray Humber sedan. He insisted that Ced drive, so they all settled in on the leather seats, and they were off. After fifteen minutes of driving through lovely, hilly countryside, Ced turned off the road and passed between two tall stone pillars joined by a stone arch, the keystone of which had a weathered crest carved into it.

After driving along a curving, tree-lined lane, they pulled onto a circular drive and stopped in front of a mansion. Not as large as Wretham Hall, but impressively large, and built entirely of gray stone, with well-tended ivy clinging to its walls and a collonaded vestibule at the large front door. "Welcome to the farm," Ced said as he hurried to embrace a trim, short, gray-tweed-suited lady who rushed out of the door and into his arms. "Lovely to see you, Ma. You look wonderful. Still my favorite girl."

"Oh, hush, Cedric, I wish you were home to stay. I miss you dreadfully. Now, who are your companions?" and she greeted them all with a brilliant smile that radiated from her entire face. "You are most welcome. Let's go in out of this rain," and she led the way through a foyer into a carpeted, panelled sitting room, where a log fire burned brightly in a head-high stone fireplace.

"Just drop your coats there on the window seat, and let's sit here in front of the fire. You'll have coffee, won't you? Don't ask for tea, I abhor tea before noon."

"Of course they'll have coffee, Ma," Ced said. "I see you've put out some scones, too.

Gentlemen, don't be backward, I love Ma's scones, and so will you. And here's my favorite marmalade. You're a darling, Ma. Perfect to take away the chill and the damp."

They all had cups of the rich, steaming coffee, and the scones were delicious—warm and flaky, with the butter melting into them, and marmalade the perfect spread. Ced's parents were full of questions, first for Ced and Syd, and then for Ed and Grant. They were so engaging, so interesting and interested, that all too soon it was time for lunch. They went into the large dining room with its own fireplace, handsome furniture, and impressive china and silver.

After the lunch, which was more a dinner than a lunch, Mr. Hamilton took them through the spotless kitchen and out a back door. The rain had stopped, although the sky remained overcast. They went into the stable to see the thoroughbred horses, each in a clean, roomy, well-lit box stall. "If you had time, we'd have a ride," Mr. Hamilton said, "But I must get you back for the 2:15 bus. Ced, you must bring your friends back for a weekend."

"I'll try, Da. We don't get many weekends, though. This was due to weather, spread all over East Anglia."

After a quick look at the orderly machine shed, the hay barn, and the two cottages where the farm manager and his assistant lived with their families, they said their goodbyes and thanks to Mrs. Hamilton, then loaded into the Humber for the return to Eddington to board the bus.

With goodbyes to Mr. Hamilton, and a fond embrace between him and Ced, they returned to Cambridge. After queuing up for their tickets, they hurried into the concert hall, finding their seats moments before Dame Hess came on stage to enthusiastic applause. She played with great skill and remarkable interpretive insight. At the interval she had to return three times for bows before the audience would let her go.

During the interval the four pilots had sherry in the ornate, marble-floored lobby bar. Madame Hess stunned the audience with her all-Beethoven second half of the program and received wild applause at the end, requiring three more encores. Finally, she spoke to her admiring listeners, "You are most generous, and I love you dearly. However, the program has been most demanding, and blackout time is nearly upon us. I will play one more piece, and then I truly must stop. I'm certain that you will recognize the piece." She sat down, and as soon as the first few notes were played, the audience recognized a piano arrangement of on old Irish melody, "The Last Rose of Summer." Such noisy applause exploded that the great lady stopped playing until the clapping stopped. Then she started again, to the now hushed audience, playing all the way through, seeming to send currents of feeling through her fingers to the piano keys and out to the hypnotized audience. Many eyes were moist as the audience stood applauding. Miss Hess bowed once, then left the stage for the final time.

"Beautiful," Grant said as they left the hall. "I didn't know anyone could get so much feeling out of a piano."

"Isn't she great?" Ed responded. "I've heard most of the great ones, but this was supreme.

She and Paderewski make the same kinds of things happen on the piano. And they get the same response from the audience. It's a rare kind of magic. Glad you suggested this, Syd."

"Not at all, not at all," but the way he said it told them that he was proud of having suggested attending the concert.

After supper at a restaurant suggested by Ced, they found a quiet neighborhood pub where each had two pints before closing time at 23:00. The morning drizzle had returned as light, persistent rain, so they returned to their room and all were soon asleep.

On Sunday morning, early-riser Ed was out of bed before the others were awake; he slipped quietly out, showered and shaved, and returned to the room to find Grant and Syd up, but Ced still asleep. While the others went to the showers, he took his overnight bag down to the lounge. There he looked at several outdated periodicals, and the previous day's *London Times*. He found the "Letters" section interesting, with several witty letters, and one sounding angry and bitter. It said that while the writer was glad that the U.S. had finally come into the war, and that the Yanks were here, he wished that they would stay on their own "reservation," because he and his friends found them "overfed, overpaid, and oversexed."

Joined by the other three, Ed went to the cafeteria. They had a choice of porridge, sausage and eggs, biscuits or toast, and tea or coffee. They all settled on sausage and eggs, toast and coffee. Ced suggested a daylight walk about the university campus, attending a service at King's Chapel, with its renowned choir. Agreed on this, they set out.

Grant and Ed were astonished at the expanse of greensward, all the lawns perfectly trimmed, the flower and shrubbery beds totally free of weeds and undergrowth. Bicycles were everywhere in use, more in racks, inside archways near the entrances to the historic buildings. The Gothic structures were awesome, but the students behaved like students the world over: laughing and joking as they went in and out and around buildings, playing cricket on the lawns, kicking soccer balls back and forth, or hurrying toward the Cam River for rowing up the river in the famous "punts" — small boats propelled by long poles.

Ced was their guide. Although he was an Oxonian, he had frequently been to Cambridge as a member of the Debating Society or for cricket matches. They entered King's Chapel for the 11:00 service. Sitting far back because the Chapel was full almost to capacity, Ed and Grant were surprised at the beauty of this great building: its stained-glass windows through which the morning light bathed the place with a soft glow; the ancient oak woodwork, which centuries had given a muted, golden patina. And especially for Ed, the superbly trained choir's singing seemed perfectly suited to the acoustics of the chapel. Hymns were sung lustily, with the mainly student congregation trying, unsuccessfully, to outdo the choir. The Anglican service, so like Roman Catholic Mass, was nearly identical to those in Episcopal churches in which Ed had sung back home, although the rector's sermon was more earthy and humorous than he expected.

After church, the four walked along the river, watching the skillful punters and the picnicers on the banks. On one straight stretch, they watched the rowing team working out. Grant said that he was getting hungry, so they found a tea shop where they had sandwiches and tea, followed by trifle.

When they came out of the tea shop, Grant said, "Hey, Ed! Look, the sky is clearing to the east. Do you think we should get back to the base?"

"I don't know. The colonel said we were free until early Monday morning," Ed replied. "But he didn't expect the weather to start looking like that; maybe we should head back. Hate to, though. This has been great."

"We'd best return as well," Ced said.

They returned to the Y, retrieved their bags, and promised to be in touch. The two Americans and two Englishmen parted. Ed and Grant walked to the train station; Ced and Syd, whose base was nearer, took a bus.

By the time the two P-51 pilots got to Wretham Hall, evening chow was in progress. They hurried to stow their bags in their rooms, and rushed down to dinner. They were shocked to see only about half the group's pilots there. "Maybe we aren't so smart," Ed said.

Grant agreed, but added, "I don't know. I have a funny feeling that we need to be here."

Just then Chuck spotted them. "Hey guys, I'm glad you're here! C.S. is just about out of his mind. Headquarters wants to mount a raid on Stuttgart, and we're to fly escort. They're afraid our layoff will give the enemy too much time to recuperate, and we'll lose the psychological advantage we gained by our raid on Berlin. They want to keep the pressure on by continuing round-the-clock raids—the British nighttime raids, and our daytime ones. But you can see we're undermanned. Did you see any more of our guys coming in?"

"No I didn't," Ed replied. "Guess your hunch was right, Grant."

"Get your chow, guys. Briefing will be at 08:00. Who knows, Ed, you'll probably have to be an element leader, maybe even a flight leader," Chuck said.

"I'd like a chance to give it a shot," Ed answered.

"We'll see who shows up," and Chuck left for the bar to tell C.S. that one more of his pilots had come in.

Ed and Grant sat down to eat, not especially hungry after their large lunch, but feeling they'd better eat. Major Smith, Grant's squadron CO, came in and told Grant essentially what Chuck had told them. "Hey, maybe we'll both get booted up to leader, not just wingmen," Grant said.

A few more pilots drifted in, but not nearly enough for a full complement. By briefing time in the morning, it was clear that all three squadrons would be shorthanded. Ed was to fly Number Three Blue Flight, which Chuck would lead. "Weather was a question mark," Colonel Macon said, "but Wing wants us to go, so we will. Ceiling is at 1,000 feet, with solid clouds from there to 4,500. There will be lots of aircraft feeling their way in the soup before we can break through. Not only ours, but those from all the other groups in the area—heavies and fighters. I don't like this, but if possible, we need to do this mission."

Tinplate had only eight pilots; the other two squadrons had six and nine. Ed had bought a bottle of White Horse Scotch in Cambridge, and he left this with Al to give to Tony. He climbed in and cranked up Princess. He taxied out to join Chuck and the others. Chuck's plane was acting up as they stopped at the end of the field to check their mags. Chuck broke radio silence. "Tinplate Blue Leader here. My engine's missing badly. I can't go. Blue Number Three, you lead Blue Flight. Number Two will be on your left wing; Number Four on your right. Blue Leader out," and he rolled away from the formation. Ed's heart jumped as he thought, "Had to happen on a lousy day like this!"

He had no time to worry about it, since Tinplate Red was already lifting off the ground, with White right behind. Ed moved out to the center of the runway and his wingmen took their places for take-off. They ran their engines up, holding the eager birds with their brakes; then Ed leaned forward and they hurtled down the runway. Red Flight had disappeared into the overcast and White was just going into it as it cleared the trees at the end of the field. "Weather people sure got this one wrong," ran through Ed's head. "Stuff's really socked in low. This is crazy!"

Now Ed's flight cleared the trees and immediately found itself in the thick fog. It was just possible for him to see his wingmen, so he knew they could see him. He signaled them to move in closer, both to maintain easy visual contact and to make them a smaller target—to minimize their chances of collision with any of the hundreds of other invisible ships speeding through the dense fog, trying to get enough altitude to get in the clear. He glanced down at the mission sketch on his thigh to confirm the course they were to follow after take-off. They were at 110 degrees; as they climbed he turned slowly to the right, praying that all the other planes—in his group and any others with them in the soup—were on that course, not floundering around, increasing the danger of collision. If all were heading in the same general direction, there was some hope that they would miss each other. Unlike aircraft of the future, they had no radar to guide them in fog.

"God help us!" Ed thought. "I don't know how many ships there are mucking around in here. Maybe as many as a thousand, and I can't see anything beyond my prop! Nothing to do but stay on course and hope." He felt, rather than saw, a large form pass above him, going in the opposite direction. "Too close! They say some day we'll have radar. We need it *now!*" A shape loomed ahead and just below him. He eased the stick back. It was a bomber on the same heading he was holding. Now he felt sweat trickling down his neck and back. "If there's one bomber, there are bound to be others. What a mess! This is insane!"

At three o'clock there was a sudden flare of light, then two lights broke apart, falling. "Two collided!" he thought.

A voice came over the earphones, "This is Mohair Leader. All Mohair Flights return to base. Abort! Abort! All Mohair Flights return to base. Mohair Leader, out."

Ed knew that in a moment there'd be a chaos of voices on his group's frequency, so he immediately pushed the send button on the throttle and said, "This is Tinplate Blue Leader.

Stay close to me. I'll make a single needle-width left turn to 360 degrees and descend slowly. We should be close to the field when we break out of this mess. Blue Leader out."

The cacophony he had anticipated erupted in the earphones as all leaders tried to instruct their wingmen. He was gratified to see his wingmen stay closely tucked in as he turned.

Because he knew that the rest of the group would be doing the same thing, the blind descent was agonizingly long. Sweat continued to trickle from under his helmet and down his face and down his back. At last, at 525 feet, they broke out. Dead ahead was the field, and close—too close—on each side of him were flights of green-nosed 51s. "Well, now that I can see you, you're no threat." He pushed the transmit button and said, "Mohair Control, this is Tinplate Blue Leader in sight of the field. Three ships coming straight in, over."

"Roger, Tinplate Blue. Clear to land. Welcome home, out."

They landed, followed closely by the rest of the group. Ed parked in his dispersal spot, shut off the engine, then sat for a few moments waiting for his knees and hands to stop shaking. "I'd rather fly through flak and have enemy planes everywhere than do that again. Hundreds of guys up there, all flying on instruments and nobody seeing anybody else! You can have it," he said to Al, as, still unsteady, he climbed out.

Back in the Briefing Room, Chuck shook his hand. "Sorry to put you in such a spot," he said.

"My God, Chuck," Ed said. "That was really bad! Thick as pea soup. I could barely see my wingmen. Not your fault."

Ed's two wingmen came up to them, one saying, "You were really cool up there, Ed. Seemed like you'd been doing it for years. Scary, wasn't it?"

"Sure was," Ed replied, "Any coffee left, Chuck?"

"Should be. Here, let me get some for you guys. Sit down. It was stupid to send you up, but since Headquarters wanted it, the colonel had no choice," Chuck said, bringing cups of hot coffee for them. "One of our guys bought it. There were some collisions up there."

"Yeah," Ed said. "We saw one off to our right. Big flare. Didn't make us feel any better, did it guys?"

"Sure as hell didn't! Did you feel that big one pass over us, Ed?"

"Couldn't miss it. Chuck, we never saw it, but we felt it. Had to be a bomber, and it was going the opposite way! Shook my ship, and shook me, too," Ed replied. "We knew there were a lot up there, messing around in that muck, all blind as bats, just as we were. I sweat a bucket!"

Debriefing was very short, and soon all the pilots were back in the hall. Chuck suggested a drink, but Ed replied, "No, thanks. Don't feel like it right now. I want another bath to get the sweat off me. See you later."

Clean, refreshed and relaxed, he came down for late chow. After Major Morda, CO of the 368th, toasted the lost pilot, Zeke Horton from Zelionple, Pennsylvania—a new friend Ed liked—the dining room came alive with stories of the experiences of those who had started out on the aborted mission, and the half-relieved, half-envious questions and remarks of those who had returned too late to go.

Far from dissipating as everyone hoped, the cloud cover came lower until the entire area was closed in with dense fog. Lights were turned on early, and though no enemy planes were likely to come over—or see any lights through the clouds if they did—blackout drapes were closed over all windows of the hall. A strong feeling of isolation pervaded the building, adding to the sense of frustration of the fliers, having been unable to fly for four days.

Ed wandered out into the courtyard and around the disused out-buildings, whose outlines were dimmed by the all-enclosing fog. Returning to the room, he read a little, stretched out on his bunk, then dozed. He woke up to the feel of Chuck shaking his shoulder. "What's up?" he asked.

"Everybody's up but you," Chuck said. "C.S. wants to see you. Come on, he's in the bar. Nearly time for chow, anyway."

"That late? I guess I really slept."

"It's 17:15, my friend. Guess you were pooped from your trip to Cambridge."

"Maybe. More likely the strain of that stupid flight this morning."

"Yeah, probably both. Come on. Time to have a drink anyway, and you can see what C.S. wants."

They went down the stairs and into the bar. "What'll you have?" Chuck asked. "I'll get it while you go see C.S."

"Okay, thanks. Pint o' Guinness, I guess," Ed replied. "I'll owe you one."

The bar was crowded, but there was a little space around C.S., who was sitting alone near the black-curtained window. Ed went over. "Hullo, Edward J. Have a seat." Ordinarily, C.S. called him Ed, but he had heard him address Chuck and other old-timers by their first names and middle initials. He felt that he'd been given some new status. He was tempted to say, "Hi, Chicken S.," but he thought better of it.

"Hell of a mission we started this morning, wasn't it?" C.S. said.

"Yes, Sir. That pea soup was nearly impenetrable."

"'Impenetrable'? Fancy word, Edward J. You have trouble with your prop? I wasn't sure mine could cut through it. Hell of a mess."

Catching the major's humor, Ed responded, "Yeah, mine was coated about an inch thick. Crew chief had to scrape it off when I landed. Couldn't reach it while we were up there, or I'd have scraped it off myself."

C.S. laughed, "That's good, Edward J. Like the shit they have to scrape off this floor when guys like you have been in here."

"Like both of us, Sir, wouldn't you say?"

"You're damn betcha, I can put it out as well as anybody. I understand you did a good job this morning, filling in for Charles S., when he couldn't lead Blue Flight?"

"Given the pea soup, it was a challenge. I was lucky. We were all lucky to make it back."

"Lucky, hell! I heard you were real cool. That's not luck, that's the sign of a potential leader. As of now, you're Charles S.'s element leader. He asked for you. I approve."

"Thank you, Sir."

"My pleasure, and forget the 'Sir.' We're comrades-in-arms. I never did hold with the rank and protocol shit. I know, I know! Somebody has to be in charge and give orders. But when we aren't in combat situations, I'd rather forget the crap. My idea of a CO in a fighter squadron is to be first among equals. By the way, did you ever notice the 'In' and 'Out' baskets on my desk?"

"No, Sir."

"Well, that's another of my ideas about a combat fighter squadron CO. The only things he should have in his baskets is an apple and a comic book. That's why we have ground officers — to take care of paperwork. My job is in the air."

"I like that, Sir."

"I told you to lay off the 'Sir.' Okay, as of now, you're Chuck's element leader."

Chuck came with Ed's drink, and one for himself plus a Scotch and soda for C.S. "Here's to my new element leader," he said.

All the next day the foul weather continued. Late that night the skies cleared. The following day was a Wednesday, and they flew the mission to Stuttgart that had been aborted on Monday. It was Ed's first trip as element leader. Everything went well — a few German fighters were sighted, but they were too far away to get to, and they did not approach the bombers. Flak was heavy and, as usual, bombers were lost.

Weeks went by, and missions were flown at least one a day, sometimes two. On some missions very few enemy planes were encountered; on others, fighter sightings were plentiful and dogfights resulted. The group lost members, but overall, they destroyed more of the enemy than they lost. Ed never subdued his sense of loss over the lives that were sacrificed, but he came to terms with it as the price that had to be paid to stop the greater horror of Hitler. Still, his heart hurt for each one.

One rare bright morning, no missions scheduled, Chuck called his flight together. "I have clearance for us to go up and sharpen our skills. We'll take off as usual, climb to 20,000, then get into inline formation. We'll rotate positions, I'll lead for twenty minutes, then Number Two leads, and I get to be Tail-end Charlie. Then, Number Three leads, and so on. The idea will be for the leader to keep turning, climbing, diving — whatever he can do to keep the second man from being right on his tail, lined up so he could get a good shot at him if he were an enemy. Number Two is doing the same with Number Three, and Number Three with Number Four. Each one tries to pull his turns tighter than the one he is following. Get it?"

The other three got it. "Tail-end Charlie has the toughest job because he has to try to cut off Number Three, who is already pulling as tight as he can to get Number Two, who is doing the same to Number One. Let's have fun, but do it seriously. Test ourselves and our ships. Okay, it's 09:01. Let's take off at 09:45."

They took off together as usual, and maintained the standard formation as they climbed. Ed noted the increasing clouds at 2,000 feet, but they were soon above them. At 20,000 feet, Chuck rocked his wings and the others dropped behind him in line. Chuck was a skillful, experienced pilot, so his turns were tight and his maneuvers well-executed and unpredictable. As Number Three, Ed found it impossible to get Number Two in his sights for longer than a split second, and he knew Number Four had to be having an even tougher time. At no time did Chuck fly straight-and-level. He turned and twisted, dove and climbed continuously, and the followers had to do the same, each one losing a little on each move.

After twenty minutes, Chuck leveled off, rocked his wings, and dropped back to Number Four. Now Number Two became Number One, and Ed moved up to Number Two.

The new leader was good, but not as good as Chuck. Ed had some success staying on his tail, but glancing back, he saw that even Chuck, for all his skill, was overshooting on turns and having trouble getting and staying on Number Three's tail.

Soon Ed was leading. As he went through every move he knew, he was pleased to see that Number Two rarely got on his tail. As always, when flying for fun, he was exhilarated. Princess seemed to respond perfectly to his every movement of the controls. On one fast diving turn, he noticed that more clouds had moved in, and that now they were flying over solid overcast, although they were at least 15,000 feet above it.

Too soon, his time as leader was over. He felt pleased with his performance in this tough test of his skills as he dropped back to the toughest position, Tail-end Charlie. The new leader immediately whipped into a sharp diving left turn. Chuck, now Number Two, pulled tight to cut him off. Number Three could not pull tight enough and turned wide of Chuck's turn, giving Ed a chance to get Number Three in his sights. That turned out to be the last time Ed had what would have been a shot at Number Three if they had been in real combat. He sweated as he pulled hard on the stick, making every effort to pull his turn tighter and tighter without forcing Princess to stall out. He did get Number Three in his sights long enough to fire a burst at him if they had been playing for real. He sensed, though, that he had put serious strain on Princess.

With two minutes left, the leader went into a twisting dive, building up speed, then pulling up into a tight climbing turn. Ed followed Number Three, but slid wide on the turn, feeling like the last kid in line in a game of "crack-the-whip." Now determined to regain his position, Ed pushed the throttle all the way to the wire and hauled back hard on the stick. Princess responded mightily, and he saw Number Three come into his sights. Just then, Princess shuddered and flipped over, stalling and tumbling crazily out of control. He cut the throttle and evened the rudder bars, holding the stick centered. The strange tumbling continued. He waited until the nose was pointed down and popped the stick forward after giving full left rudder since, at that moment, the Princess was spinning to the right.

The rudder stopped the spin, and he was in a power-off dive. He pushed the throttle forward to resume normal flight, but instead of the surge of power he expected, he got no forward thrust at all. The engine raced but delivered no power to his flight. The prop was turning, but not as fast as it should have been, with the engine racing as it was. Keeping the nose down, he picked up enough momentum to give him dead-stick control, but he had to continue his descent to maintain controlled flight. He could not gain altitude. He pulled back on the stick to make his dive more shallow and tried the throttle again, watching the manifold pressure indicator. It was low, but still within acceptable range. Still no power available from the racing engine.

He was close to the overcast, having lost nearly 12,000 feet in his crazy fall. He pushed the transmit button and said, "This is Tinplate Blue Number Three. I have no power. I'm in a dead-stick glide at 4,500 feet, close to the solid overcast. I have no choice; I have to go down through and hope there's a field of some kind that I can get into. Out." He was in the clouds as he ended the transmission.

"Roger, Blue Three," Chuck's voice said. "Good luck. We'll come down and see how you made out, then head home and report. Blue Leader out."

Ed kept the nose down, maintaining flying speed of 140. His instruments were working, so he had no trouble staying steady through the overcast. At 1,200 feet, he came out of the clouds. He looked down and to his left, and had trouble believing what he saw! There was a huge RAF bomber base, with a beautiful, long, wide runway which, with a slight adjustment of his rudder, he was paralleling! A windsock on a hangar farther to his left showed the wind was coming from behind him. "I don't believe it!" he said out loud. "I'm on the downwind leg with a clear, beautiful runway waiting for me!"

At 800 feet, he turned left. Another left turn put him in line with the runway. He put his wheels down but not his flaps, since there was plenty of runway to be used. He did a wheel landing, coasted past one taxi strip too fast to turn, and turned at the next one. Princess coasted to a stop. He shut the engine off and climbed out. An RAF jeep was racing toward him. The jeep stopped and an RAF officer jumped out. "What's the trouble, Leftenant?" he asked, using the British pronunciation.

"Damned if I know," Ed replied. "She fell out of a tight climbing turn, then had no power when I gave her throttle. Thank God your field was right here when I broke through the cloud cover!" While saying this, Ed walked to the nose of the plane. He touched the prop, and it moved. It had no resistance at all. With one finger he could spin it.

"That's odd, isn't it?" the RAF man said. "Something's broken, sure as hell."

"You're right about that," Ed agreed. "Either there's no compression at all in the engine, or something snapped in the prop mechanism. Can you arrange to tow her over to the side, and show me a phone so I can call my base?"

"Of course we can. Jump in; we'll go to the Tower. You can call from there, and they'll arrange to tow the Princess. That's a lovely name, and a lovely painting job too. Odd name for a Yank to pick, isn't it?"

"Well, it's true, we don't have real royalty at home. But the girl I hope to marry is named Pat, and she looks like a princess. So it's the right name for my ship."

"Did you know a Canadian pilot used that name for his crate in World War I?"

"No I didn't. Not surprised, though. It seems like a perfect name."

They raced across the field to the Tower, and Ed climbed the stairs to be greeted by Flight Officer Jewell, who seemed to be in charge. "Hullo, Yank. Bloody good dead-stick landing there. Bloody lucky we were here, too, what? Actually, we never move the field; it's always here," and he gave a stiff smile at his own witticism.

"Sure was," Ed answered. "Can I call my base? They'll want to know what happened and where I am."

"Righto. Do you have the number?"

"Sorry, no."

"Good enough. We have all the bases listed. Where is it?"

"East Wretham; I guess you call it 'Wrettam,' don't you?"

"Right you are. I know Wretham Hall—wish we were billeted there. You Yanks get the best of everything, don't you? Here's the number; let me ring them for you."

"Hullo, East Wretham? Fighter Group? Goodo, we've one of your Mustang lads here at Hempstead." He paused, listening. "You know where it is? Good. Yes, yes, quite all right. Yes, the craft is fine, but oddly enough, it seems to have no compression." Another pause. "Yes, of course—we'll take care of him. You'll have someone over, then?" Pause. "Veddy good, then. You'll call our Tower for clearance?" Pause. "Would you care to speak with him?" Pause. "Yes, in a four-place Stinson scout plane? Veddy good. He'll no doubt be in our pilots' lounge. You don't need to speak to him, then?" Pause. "All right. No problem at all. Goodbye."

"They'll be over," he said to Ed. "You'll want a bite no doubt, and a pint?"

"Thanks. That'd be great."

"Righto. Let me just complete this ruddy form, then I'll get one of our lads to take you to our Pilots' Club. You can get something to eat and a drink there."

By the time the form had been completed a young Leftenant had arrived in another jeep. He had cloth RAF pilot's wings sewn on his tunic breast. "John Baxter," he said as he shook Ed's hand.

"Ed Thorne," Ed replied.

Baxter introduced him to several other pilots at the club, and Ed had a Guinness and a cheese sandwich as he answered their questions about America, the P-51, and about what had happened. The conversation was relaxed and pleasant. All agreed he'd been bloody lucky to come out of the overcast exactly right to put down at their field. None felt that luck more than Ed. He was just finishing his second pint when Captain Moore, the group's engineering officer, came in. C.S. followed Moore.

"Jesus H!" C.S. said, "what're you trying to do, Ed? The guys told me what they saw. Said you flipped over in a power stall, then TUMBLED! Nobody ever heard of a 51 tumbling before. You out to prove something?"

"No, Sir, I just pulled her real tight in a climbing turn with full power on, doing my best to cut in on Number Three. She just went haywire. Lucked out where I came down!"

"Sure as hell did. Nobody's that lucky! Glad you're okay. The ship can be fixed, right Tom?" he asked, looking at the engineering officer. "Let's have a drink before we look at the bird."

"No more for me," Ed said. "My feet already feel like they're not touching the ground. I've had enough."

C.S. and Tom Moore had a quick Scotch and soda, then the three, followed by all the RAF men in the club, went to look at the crippled Princess. "Look," Ed said, reaching up and touching the prop with one finger. "Nothing there. No resistance at all."

"You shouldn't be able to turn that at all," Tom said, reaching up and doing the same thing. "Tell me exactly what happened, step-by-step. Never heard of a 51 acting like this."

"Yeah, Ed. I want to hear that, too," C.S. said.

Ed went through the sequence.

"Craziest thing I ever heard of. Sounds more like a runaway prop than anything else. But 51s aren't supposed to do that, with the new prop controls they have," Tom said. "Maybe the prop drive snapped, but I never heard of that either. When it happened—when you got her into a controlled power-off dive—at that point, you gave her full throttle, and the engine sped up, but you got no power? Is that right?"

"Yes. Exactly. I tried a couple of times. RPMs went up, and manifold pressure wasn't bad, but not up to full indication on the gauge. I swept all the instruments, and that just came back to me, low M.P."

"Holy mackerel! That sounds like it could be blown head-gaskets," Tom said. "We'll check it out when we tear it down, but it would have to be both of them, or you'd have had some power and the engine would have been really uneven. But you said it ran smoothly; just didn't deliver any power, right?"

"Right."

"No. It just is too unlikely. It has to be something else. No, both gaskets at once? Huh-uh! Anyway, we haven't had any head gasket problems since we got 51s. I have to think it's something in the prop mechanism. We'll have to check it all over."

"Don't ask me. I just fly them," Ed said. "If it's any help, she's been going real sweet on every mission I've flown. I really like her."

"Good thing it happened here, not over Germany," C.S. said.

"Right," Ed agreed. "That could be fatal."

Tom said, "I brought her maintenance book with me. Time she had a new power plant, anyway. We'll take this one out and put in a rebuilt one. We'll do a complete post-mortem on this one. If something wasn't up to specs, somebody's ass is going to burn!"

"Take it easy, Tom," C.S. said. "These crates take a hell of a beating day after day. You and your guys do a hell of a job of maintenance. Tear it down, and just be glad it didn't happen in a set-to with bandits. Ed wouldn't be here to tell us about it."

Slightly mollified, Tom said, "Yeah. But it shouldn't happen at all! Checking everything is part of routine maintenance."

"One thing you can be sure of," Ed said. "Al and his crew do one hell of a job of maintenance. Don't lay anything on them; they're the best."

"Sure," C.S. said. "Al's one of the best! Anyway, Tom, you said she was due for an engine change. That means she's had a hell of a lot of tough hours on her. Even Rolls-Royce can't make an engine that can hold up under the beating we give them indefinitely."

"Their car engines do, though," Tom said, "they're famous for running forever."

"Yeah," C.S. said, "I've heard that. But they tick over slowly, low RPMs, and get a lot of torque from those six huge cylinders. With good lubrication, they should run on and on. But we're running high RPMs all the time, to get huge torque from our smaller twelve cylinders. Will you see if you can send a crew over here? See if these guys will lend you hangar space. That'd be better than taking her wings off and hauling her home, wouldn't it?"

"Oh, hell yes," Tom answered. "They'll cooperate, I'm sure." They did cooperate, and after getting back to the base, he took a crew in a truck to work on Princess.

With C.S. piloting, the three boarded the Cessna to return to East Wretham, following thanks and goodbyes to the RAF men. During the short flight, C.S. said, "Listen, Edward J., you're getting a lot of combat hours in. You're a veteran now. We're getting some new P-51s in. You can have one in place of the C you're flying now. Fishbowl canopy, and three 50s in each wing—instead of the two you have now—and fitted with a new type of gunsight. What do you think?"

"I don't know, C.S.," Ed responded. "I really like the Princess. Of course I haven't had a chance to fly a D, but I can't imagine it being much better, if at all. Generally, I find that I can turn tighter than the guys in Ds. And I don't see much advantage in six 50s over four. If you are on target, both will do the job. Besides, two extra 50s, plus ammo and the whole machinery to operate them, has to add a lot of extra weight. It'll be the same engine, won't it? No more horsepower?"

"It will. Your C will soon be the only one left in the squadron. All the other guys have jumped at the chance to have a D. But you have a good point. May not be a good trade-off if you like your C. You have to figure in the thicker chord of the wings to accomodate the extra guns, too. What would you say to flying Jack Burton's D while your ship's being refitted? If you like it, you'll get one. If you want to hang on to your Princess Pat after that, okay. Jack's going for a ten-day R&R. What do you say?"

"Okay, C.S., I'll give it a try," Ed replied. "Who knows, I might have to get another bottle of Scotch for Tony to put Princess Pat on a new plane."

They landed and went into the bar, where Ed had to repeat his story half a dozen times and answer endless questions. All the pilots wanted information detail to help them avoid a similar breakdown in a more dangerous situation than a practice flight. They all wanted to buy drinks for him, to indicate their pleasure that he hadn't come to the end of his flying career. But he knew his capacity, and he expected to be flying someone else's plane the next morning, so he stopped drinking after one Scotch.

After dinner, Lieutenant Colonel Morrison, the group adjutant, caught Ed as he started up to his room. "Just a minute, Ed," he said. "I need to make out a report on what happened today. I have the forms here, so let's sit in the bar and fill them out."

"Okay, Sir," and they found seats at a small table in the bar. Ed went over the story again, providing answers to all of Morrison's questions. Finally the forms were all completed, and Ed and the colonel signed them. "How about a drink?" Morrison asked.

"No thanks, Sir, I'm really bushed. I need to get cleaned up and sack out. Probably have a mission tomorrow."

"Right—there is one coming up. Goodnight."

"Goodnight, Sir." Ed trudged out and up to his room, but he wasn't allowed to relax yet. Chuck and the other roommates had to go over everything again. 22:00 came and went, then 23:00. Finally, Ed said, "Come on, guys, give me a break. Can't we talk about this later? I'm really bushed."

"Okay," they said. "Sure is interesting, though."

Ed collapsed on his bunk, forgetting about cleaning up. He slept well, and was ready when wake-up call came.

Another long escort mission was scheduled, this time to Hamburg, in Northern Germany. After the first fifteen minutes, Ed had adjusted to the newer P-51D, although he felt as if something was dragging him to the left during his take-off run, forcing him to push extra hard on the right rudder bar to keep straight down the field. Whatever it was, it was in addition to the usual pull of torque, and as soon as he was airborne, it was gone. The fishbowl canopy did allow better viewing in every direction, but he missed the surrounding feeling of Princess's bird-cage canopy. There was, too, a decidedly heavy feeling in the D. At first he thought he was imagining it, but during the climb to altitude and the turns to get on their assigned heading for the rendezvous with the bombers, he found it necessary to use more throttle and higher RPMs to maintain speed and position. Flak was intense over the target. Some bombers went down. Neil O'Connor's 51 exploded as Ed watched. Neil was on his first combat mission. Ed hardly knew him, but watching him die and attending the farewell toast back at the base hurt.

After four-and-a-half hours, as the group headed homeward, Ed said to himself, "No thanks, I like the feel of Princess, and I don't get that feeling with this airplane. I'm glad this turned out to be a milk-run, so I didn't have to go after bandits in this ship. Hope Tom gets Princess ready soon. She and I belong to each other."

Tinplate was the last squadron to land, and Chuck's flight the last of the squadron. This meant that Ed, Tinplate Blue Number Three, was next-to-last of the entire group to touch down. Chuck led them in a wide circle around the field as the others got safely down; then, as usual, over the center of the field to peel off and come in. Everything went fine, but the extra heaviness Ed thought he felt in the 51-D was more evident when he cut the throttle back. As he started his spiral descent, he had to keep the nose down a little more to maintain speed, with the engine just turning over at idle. This meant that, in order not to come in too low and short of the field on his final turn, he had to keep the throttle forward longer after final clearing of his mags. This was not a serious problem, but it meant that he came in a little hotter than usual.

With wheels and full flaps down, he came over the trees at the edge of the field and held the ship just off the ground until it had lost its speed, then dropped the last few inches to get the wheels on the ground. As the wheels made contact, the aircraft twisted violently to the left, making a complete turnaround—impossible for Ed to stop—then nosed over, digging the tips of the prop into the ground. Because the danger of fire was always present, Ed switched off the ignition, snapped his seatbelt and harness off, disconnected his oxygen mask and earphones, rolled back the canopy and jumped out, running off to the left of the injured plane as the fire truck and ambulance screamed toward him. All this took mere seconds. Fortunately, there was no fire. A thin wisp of smoke rose slowly from the left wheel.

Ed's wingman had gunned his engine when he saw Ed's plane in trouble on the ground. He went around and came into a safe landing off to the right of the field. Meanwhile, Chuck and C.S. raced out in a jeep. "You okay?" Chuck asked as they jumped out of the jeep. C.S. went right over to the airplane. "Smoke coming from the left wheel," he called. "Brake must have been stuck. Jesus, Ed! Give you a practically new airplane and you tear it up! If you didn't like the D, all you had to do was tell me. Guess you'll do anything to keep that old rig of yours." As he said this, he walked over to where Chuck and Ed were standing. "You okay?" he asked. "That's the most important thing."

"Okay, C.S. Lucky again," Ed said. "Guess ol' Princess put a hex on this airplane. She doesn't want me flying anything else."

"You'll have to be checked out by the flight surgeon, and Colonel Morrison will have to do an inquiry. Have to decide if this is pilot error or mechanical failure. It's a pain in the ass, but required." They climbed into the jeep.

After debriefing, Ed was called into Morrison's office, where he detailed the event, mentioning the unusual pull to the left on take-off and the smoke from the left wheel after the crash. C.S. then came in to inform the colonel of the smoke, and of his belief that the brake in that wheel must have grabbed. He was followed by Captain Burton's crew chief, who said that he'd watched Ed's take-off, and that he had seen puffs of smoke coming from the left wheel as the plane ran down the runway. The colonel thanked them all, then said to Ed,

"Okay, Captain Moore will have his crew analyze the plane, and we'll determine the degree of pilot error, if any. Have you been going to church lately? Two accidents in two days, and you walked away from both unhurt. You must be living right." He dismissed them.

C.S. had to stay behind to complete his report of the mission, so Chuck and Ed, with their wingmen, went on to the bar. There the other pilots razzed Ed about destroying the group's airplanes faster than they could be replaced. "You don't seem to understand, man. You're supposed to destroy German planes," was the recurring theme of their remarks. Ed took the friendly jibing in good spirits, often giving as good as he got.

Tom Moore came in, and Ed asked him how Princess was coming. Moore replied, "We pulled everything out—engine, prop, all the machinery—and hauled it back here. Wing wants their top engineer to be here when we take it apart. You're getting a whole re-built assembly. The fellows stayed down there, and will finish up tomorrow morning."

"That's great! Any clues about what went wrong?"

"Nothing. It's still a mystery. May just have been a fluke. Why don't you check with C.S.—if he can give you tomorrow off, you can ride down with me and fly her home when she's ready."

"Okay. He ought to be here any minute; then I'll ask him."

C.S. said, "Yeah. You have to see the flight surgeon tomorrow morning anyway. Can't fly 'til that's done. Anyway, we don't have another ship for you to fly. If we did, I'm not sure we'd want to risk it with you."

"Come on, C.S. None of this was my fault."

"I know, Edward J., just kidding. You're a good flier. How'd you like the D before you tore her up?"

Ed told him his reactions to Burton's D.

C.S. said, "I know what you mean; I had the same feeling when I first flew my D. But the Ds were all we were getting in. As a CO, I was expected to go with it. Like it okay, now. You can stick with Princess as long as she holds up. But there won't be another to replace her when she goes bad. She'll be one of the few Cs still in service. Okay, when the flight surgeon is finished with you, go ahead with Tom and bring her back."

"Thanks, C.S. Can I buy you a drink?"

"No thanks, Ed. I want to see if I can get in a bath before chow. See you later."

Ed thought a bath sounded good, but every bathroom was full, with others waiting ahead of him, so he went to his room to read and relax.

Major Johnson was the flight surgeon. Ed went to his office immediately after breakfast the next morning. "You check out fine," the major said, "Your blood pressure is always a little bit low, and that's good. Have you had many colds since coming to this group?"

"Haven't had any," Ed replied. He knew the reason for the question. The group was participating in a massive experiment to see if a sulfa tablet a day would cut down on the number of colds American fliers seemed to get in England. Half of the men were given placebos, the rest had varied amounts of sulfa in their pills, and careful records were kept of each group.

"That's good. By the way, I see you have a little red bump on your chin. Is it sore?"

"I noticed that this morning when I shaved. It is a little tender when I press on it."

"May be an ingrown hair—keep an eye on it. If there is any change, like getting larger or festering, come in and let me have a look again."

"Okay, will do. Am I clear to fly?"

"You bet, Ed. Everything is fine. I'll send the forms over to the colonel."

"Thanks, Doc," Ed said, and rushed out to find Tom Moore so they could go get Princess.

Ed and Tom rode to the RAF base in a personnel carrier, an oversize station wagon driven by a corporal. Tom and his repair crew would return to the base in it.

Al, Ed's crew chief, was supervising the repair work on the Princess. "Hi, Lieutenant," he greeted Ed. "She's just about ready. She sounds sweet on the ground, but you'll want to test her in the air before you head home, won't you, Sir?"

"I sure will. Be glad to have her back. I flew Captain Burton's D yesterday. Prefer the Princess."

"Yes, Sir, I heard you had a little trouble landing her. Were you trying to get rid of her?"

"Watch it, Sergeant! Something went wrong with the left brake—nothing anybody could do about it."

"Sir," Al said, turning to Moore, "they want you and the lieutenant to report to the Tower. Some forms to sign."

"Okay, Sergeant, thanks. Let's go, Ed. The RAF's as bad as our Air Corps. Always forms to sign. Will you have this wrapped up when we get back, Sergeant?"

"Sure will, Sir. She's ready now; just want to run one more ground check. Have it done when you get back."

"We'll be back as soon as they let us. Have your men load the tools into the back of the personnel carrier, okay?"

"Okay, Sir, will do."

On the way to the Tower, Tom said, "Al's one of the best men we have in maintenance. He knows his stuff, and he loves aircraft mechanics, especially engines."

"I like him a lot," Ed replied. "He's a neat guy, and he keeps Princess in top shape. I think it hurt him more than it did me when she broke down."

They mounted the Tower stairs. A different RAF officer greeted them. "Care for a cup of tea? Coffee?" he asked. "The forms are all ready. Sit here at the desk. Coffee? Righto." He had a man bring two cups of what passed for coffee in England. The Americans found it weak and watery, but it was hot.

Signing the forms was less distasteful than drinking the insipid coffee. The RAF man handed Ed and Tom their copies, and they thanked him for the cooperation and help. He he said to Ed, "The last time one of your blokes was in here, he gave us a real buzz over the Tower when he took off. Good luck to you. Glad we were here to help," and he shook hands with each of them.

Ed interpreted the RAF man's remark about buzzing to mean that he hoped Ed would do the same thing. After all, most of what they had taking off were heavy bombers, and they weren't good at buzzing. He climbed into Princess and felt at home and happy immediately. She was already warm, so she kicked over as soon as he turned her on and touched the starter button. She sounded sweet as he taxied to the appropriate runway, stopped and ran up the engine, checking both mags and his manifold pressure gauge. Everything was good, so he waved to the Tower, and was flashed a green "clear to go" light; he swung on to the runway.

Unlike East Wretham, this base had long runways. Even so, with buzzing the Tower in mind, he held Princess with the brakes as he ran up the engine to full take-off RPMs, then let her go. The Tower was to the left and opposite the middle of the runway he was using. He wanted to get off the ground with enough speed to be able to turn left and head straight for the Tower when he reached the middle point. He gave his full attention to that and timing his turn for that purpose. In doing so, he failed to pull up his wheels, so, instead of the clean and graceful pull-up over the Tower that he envisioned, he lumbered toward the Tower and, unsure he was going to make it, struggled up, barely clearing the top.

He was embarrassed when he realized why Princess felt wrong, and pulled the wheels up. "Nice going, Yank—we've never been buzzed quite like that before!" came over his earphones. "We all hit the floor, not expecting you'd clear. Nice touch, that, leaving your undercarriage down. We're off the floor now. Good luck to you. Don't fail to put them down before you land."

Too embarrassed to respond vocally, Ed rocked his wings as he circled the field, climbing for his test run before heading home. At 15,000 feet, he put Princess through her paces, putting on a little air show for the men in the Tower. Everything seemed fine, and although he put her through very tight turns with full throttle, there was no repetition of what had happened a few days before. He did a final loop, ending in a dive from 10,000 feet right at the Tower, flew across the field, rocking his wings, did a slow roll, and headed home. "Hello, RAF Tower, thanks again for everything. P-51 out."

"Roger, Mustang. Good show, thanks. Best to you. Tower out."

In a few minutes, he saw his base ahead. Since the rest of the group was on a mission, he had a clear field. He checked the windsock and went right in, glad to be home and to have Princess back, seeming as good as new. As he shut down and climbed out, a jeep drove up.

"Saw you coming in, Sir. Want to go to the hall after you leave your chute at the shack?" the driver asked.

"Thanks, but I think I'll wait for the others to come in. I'd appreciate a lift to the hut, though."

"Right, Sir," and they drove to the hut, where Ed put his chute, Mae West, and helmet in his locker and joined the non-flying people gathered in the bright sunshine waiting for the return of their birds. On his way out, he picked up a mug of coffee. "Now, *that's* coffee," he said, sipping the strong brew with gratitude.

"Hi, Ed. How's Princess?" Chuck asked after debriefing.

"Seems okay. What'd you do today? Any action?"

"Pure milk-run — easy escort job. All we did was log time, except for flak, of course. So you'll be ready to go tomorrow?"

"You bet. Back with good old Princess in perfect shape."

Later, when C.S. joined them for chow, the major said, "Colonel Morrison gave me the report, Ed. You got ten percent pilot error."

"What!" Ed exploded. "What error! I did nothing wrong."

"Easy, Ed," C.S. said, "there always has to be some pilot error in these reports. Ten percent is the lowest they ever give, so it won't hurt your record."

"Sounds stupid to me. There was obviously a mechanical failure," Ed said, still angry.

"They have to cover their asses. It's just in case you have something else happen. They figure they'd look bad if they gave you a totally clean report."

"Cover their own fat asses! Fat from sitting behind their desks all day. Do they ever think of covering *our* asses? *We're* the ones doing missions, while they sit back and write reports!" Then it struck him funny, and he started to laugh.

C.S. laughed too. "You're right, Edward J. But nothing we can do about it. They write the reports, and they make the judgments, even if they've never even sat in a cockpit. It's the military setup everywhere."

"Guess you're right. Hell with them. We fight, they write. I'd rather fight."

"Way to go, Ed. Let's eat," C.S. said, and they went to work on the fried chicken dinner.

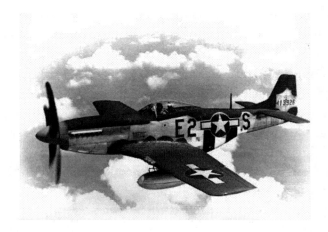

24

E d's first mission in the rebuilt Princess Pat was the next day. They escorted B-24s to Muenster, usually a hotbed of enemy fighters. On their last trip there, though, they had seen bandits, but all were too far away to attack.

When he ran up his engine to check his mags, Ed heard a slight catch in the engine on the right mag, and read a slight drop in manifold pressure. He considered neither significant enough to keep him home, so he took off with Tinplate Blue Flight as usual. As they climbed to their assigned altitude of 22,000 feet, his temperature gauge registered a few degrees higher than normal, but nowhere near the red. When they leveled off, the temp returned to normal. Now flying high cover over the Liberators, all his gauges read normal and Princess felt good; responsive as always.

The concentration of flak over the target area was intense, peppering the bombers unmercifully, as they made their straight-and-level formation bombing runs. He winced as he watched what he now considered to be sacrificial, helpless, bombers being hit and falling toward earth.

"Here they come! Drop your wing tanks. Flights spread out. Let's get the bastards!" Ed heard over his earphones. He saw Blue Leader's plane move slightly ahead of the others in the flight, and he knew he had put on full throttle to get up speed for the onslaught they knew was coming. Ed, like the others, had seen the bandits coming at them — this time not heading for the bombers, but right at his group. He shoved the throttle forward to the wire. Instead of the surge of power he needed to keep up with the others, Princess's response was black smoke pouring from the exhaust pipes on both sides of the engine cowl. He seemed to be standing still as the other three in the flight rushed ahead.

"My God! I'm a sitting duck, and the smoke is a dead giveaway to the bandits!" raced through his mind, He banked left and down, as he worked his throttle back-and-forth, trying to get a positive response. Nothing. No increase in power, although when he reduced throttle to cruising, the smoke abated.

"Two on your tail, Princess!" came through his earphones. Ed put the nose straight down, hoping for more speed. "Okay, Princess, we're on 'em."

"Thank God," Ed said aloud. "But others'll be after me." At 15,000 feet, he tried full-throttle again. The power was there, and no smoke. He tried climbing back to rejoin his group, but every time he got above 15,500 feet, he got smoke and loss of power. "Guess I'll stay down here and watch for strays," he thought.

He didn't have to wait long. From five o'clock he saw two FW-190s hurtling toward him. He turned right toward them, and yanked his throttle back. This slowed him enough that their deflection shots went by him. As the two bandits passed, continuing their dive, he put on full-throttle and went after them. Not gaining on them, he decided that he'd be justified in using full-military power (FMP), so he shoved the throttle forward the last inch of travel, breaking the wire stop. Now he gained on them. They made the mistake of starting a left turn. This was Ed's best turn, so he was able to make a tighter turn than they could. He closed the gap quickly. Getting the right-hand one in his sights, he bored ahead, then pressed the trigger button as he pulled his nose ahead of the target plane. He saw his tracers go directly to the target, then it exploded right ahead.

Realizing he was over-using FMP, he pulled the throttle back. Now he shot past the other 190, who had started a steep right turn, still diving. He did not seem to want to turn back and fight, so Ed turned right too, and worked his way onto the enemy's tail. He'd had to slow down a little bit to get behind his target, but the target was still diving, and he pulled away from Ed. "I'll have to risk using FMP for another half-minute," Ed thought, and poured it on. With added power, Ed gained on the other plane quickly, but they were getting too close to the ground. Just as Ed thought he might have to pull up to avoid following the 190 right into the ground, the other plane started to level off. Ed hauled back on the stick and felt a 5- or 6-G pull. To avoid blacking out, he leaned forward and yelled, forcing blood back up to his head. Now, treetops were racing by him in a green-brown blur. He was overtaking the 190 too fast, so he pulled the throttle back, steadied his plane so the bandit was in his gunsight, squeezed the trigger, and sighed with relief as the enemy plane seemed to vomit smoke, then nose down and into the trees, where it erupted in a flowerpot of flame.

"You okay, Tinplate Blue?" Ed recognized Chuck's voice. "Okay," he replied. "Can't climb all the way back up, though, over."

"Okay, Blue Three. We're above you and have you in sight. Stay on the deck and head home. We'll cover you. It's all over up here."

"Roger, Blue Leader, Wilco," and Ed took a west heading, looking up and feeling secure with the three friends above him. Princess behaved beautifully, never faltering. He altered his course to northwest, crossed out of Germany, over the Netherlands, then saw the Zeuter Zee passing under him, followed by more Netherlands lowlands. Now he skimmed just above the waves of the North Sea. England, and the Wash came in sight. He climbed to 1,000 feet, flew over the home base, and spiraled in for his landing.

"Home early, Sir," Al said, as the prop made its last turn and stopped. "Trouble?"

"Yeah, Al, there's a problem. When I needed power at high altitude, all I got was black smoke. I was a sitting duck up there for a minute or two."

"God, Sir! I'm sorry. She checked out perfect. We ran every test we have on her."

"I know, Al. Not your fault. I test-flew her before I brought her back from the RAF base. Looks like I should have taken her on up to 22,000 feet and given her full throttle."

"That's when it happened, Sir?"

"Yep. Right over the target area, just when the bandits came in on us. Soupy Campbell saved my butt, or I wouldn't be here talking to you. I'll tell Captain Moore about it. He'll be out to talk to you, okay? You and he can figure out what's wrong; I think the rebuilders didn't get it right." The jeep drove up, and Ed stepped up into it. Then, seeing the look on Al's face, he added, "It's okay, Al. Princess did what she had to do, and more. She brought me home. I'll be out to talk to you after chow, okay?" Al gave a half-smile and nodded, but still looked unhappy as the jeep drove away.

When debriefing was over, Ed and C.S. found Tom Moore, and Ed told him in detail how Princess Pat had behaved. He also told him how thoroughly Al had tested everything, and how he himself had tested her before bringing her back from the RAF base.

Moore asked, "Was there anything to indicate a malfunction before you took off this morning? Anything at all? Or in the flight before your failure at high altitude?"

Ed remembered then, and told him about the little miss when he checked the mags before take-off, and the slight rise in temperature as they were climbing.

The captain said, "Okay. I'll go over everything with Al. I think we'll ship this rebuild back to the factory. We just got a brand new one in; we'll drop that one in the Princess. She needs to be right. We can't count on you being lucky all the time, though God knows you've been lucky so far."

"Damn it, Ed J.!" C.S. said as they rode the jeep to the hall to eat, "You're a complete demolition team all by yourself. But lucky! Damn lucky! Glad you pulled out of this one too."

After chow and the toast to Les Holmner, Ed found Soupy Campbell in the bar to thank him for chasing the 109s off his tail.

"Any time, Ol' Friend. I just happened to be in the right place at the right time. Anyway, we did more than chase them. Les nailed one before he crashed. I got the other."

"Well, I'm mighty glad you were in that place at that time."

"Man! You sure looked vulnerable. You were easy picking for them for a few seconds. What the hell happened, anyway?"

Ed described it to Soupy and the other pilots who had gathered around. "Keep this up, and we'll start calling you 'Lucky' instead of 'Balloon Killer' or 'Caruso,' the way we did at Maxwell," Grant said. He had just joined the group around Ed. "Lucky Eddy! Sounds pretty good, doesn't it?"

"Fits all right," C.S. said. "Might jinx you, though. I hear calling someone 'Lucky' can bring him bad luck. Buy you a drink, Ed?"

"Sure thing. Thanks for not using that knickname; I don't need a jinx." He raised his glass and said, "Here's to Princess Pat. She misbehaved a little bit, but she brought me home."

Chuck joined the group. "She did more than bring you home! Even though she was crippled, she let you get a couple of those guys. So, right, here's to her."

"Yeah," Ed said, and turned away.

Chuck caught up with him going up the stairs. "Hey, friend. What's the matter? You should feel good! That was damn good flying and great shooting. What's the problem?"

"I don't want to talk about it, okay?"

"Sure, but I . . ."

"Let's drop it, all right? Just drop it. Let's talk about something else."

"Sure, Sure. Whatever you say." Without further conversation, they continued up to their room.

Ed had been fingering the red spot on his chin, and when they were in the room he asked Chuck, "What's this thing look like to you, Chuck? Doc thinks it's an ingrown hair. He wants to look at it if it gets any bigger."

"I noticed it downstairs. Thought maybe it was from your oxygen mask rubbing you there. It looks pretty red and swollen. Did it bother you with your mask on?"

"Didn't notice until I held my mask up to call in for landing clearance. Yeh, it hurt a little then."

"Now I see it in the light in here, it looks pretty red. Better see Doc about it."

"Think I'll wait and see how it is in the morning. I have a bottle of rubbing alcohol—I'll put some on before I go to bed.

"It's your chin, Buddy. If it starts swelling much more, you sure won't be able to wear your mask. Doc'll be sure to ground you if that happens."

"I'll wait 'til morning; maybe it'll go away. Anyway, I don't even know if I'll have an airplane to fly tomorrow. If there's a mission, that is."

When Ed got up the next morning, his entire chin was swollen and throbbing. After breakfast, which he had trouble eating, he went to see the flight surgeon. "That's some chin you have there, Ed," the major said. "Let's have a look." He felt it gently. Ed jumped with every touch. "Pretty sore, is it?"

"Sure is, Doc. I don't mind if you don't touch it any more. What is it, anyway?"

"Looks like a boil, and a bad one. I'm going to have to ground you—you can't wear your mask with that. You have a little fever, too. How do you feel?"

"Okay. A little off, but okay. What can you do about it? I don't want to be grounded."

"I'll give you some aspirin. Take one every four hours today. It'll keep your temperature down, and blunt the pain. We may have to wait a couple of days before I can lance it. With these things, you have to let nature take her course. When it's ready, we'll open it and clean it out. Come in again tomorrow morning. If there's any change in it, or if you feel sick, come in right away. Meanwhile, you can't fly. You're grounded."

"Okay, Doc. Thanks," and he walked dejectedly back to the hall. "They can call me 'lucky,' but everything seems to be going against me right now," he thought. He felt grotesque with his whole chin swollen, and the dark stubble of his beard showing through the red, where he was too sore to shave.

"What'd Doc say?" Chuck asked as Ed stepped into their room. "Sure looks like hell this morning."

"Thanks, Ol' Boy," Ed responded. "Feels that way too. He grounded me. Thinks it's a boil—has to wait 'til it's ripe; then he'll lance it. Anything on for today?"

"Nothing yet. C.S. thinks there won't be. Saw Tom Moore downstairs—he said to tell you they're putting a new engine, not a rebuilt one, in Princess Pat. So, you're grounded, and so is she."

"Isn't that sweet," Ed said sarcastically. "Both of us out of action at once. That's good about the new engine. Hope it's right this time—it's no fun being a sitting target with bandits all around. Good thing Soupy happened to be right there."

"Sure was. I saw what was happening, but I couldn't get there from where I was," Chuck said. "I was too far in front of you. I think I'll check with Ops (Operations) and see if anything's coming up today. You take it easy, okay?"

"Right. I'm okay. See you later." He sat in the best armchair by the window and tried to read, but his mind kept wandering. He recalled the sinking feeling he'd had when the other members of his flight surged ahead and he was alone. He felt again the terrible vulnerability when the call came about the bandits on his tail. Then the enormous relief at Soupy's reassuring words. His mind leaped then to his own firing at the enemy planes, but he pushed this away, not wanting to think about it. He tried again to read, but the concern about his own involvement in the war's slaughter kept coming back. He told himself, "It's what I have to do. It's why I'm here. If I don't do it to them, they'll do it to me. Or, worse yet, they'll get the bombers. I will not think about it!" and he forced himself to concentrate on his book.

The aspirin helped, but Ed did not feel well the rest of the day. He took a little walk, enjoying the spring warming, the milder weather. As he turned toward the hall, he saw Grant coming toward him. "Hi," he greeted him.

"Some chin you've got there, Buddy. How's it feel?" Grant asked.

"Damn sore, and I feel rotten. How're you?"

"Okay. Thought you might want to go for a bike ride—it's a nice day. No missions. But I guess you don't feel like it."

"You're right. It'd be a great day for it, but I really don't feel up to it. Whatever's causing this thing on my chin must be bothering my whole system. I never get sick, but I sure don't feel right today. I'm grounded anyway; Doc probably wouldn't approve of my flying around on a bike either."

"See you later, then. I'm going to ride out a little bit into the country," Grant said, and hurried toward the bike rack at the side of the hall.

When Ed got up the next morning after a restless night, his lower jaw was puffed on both sides and his chin looked worse than ever, and it hurt even if not touched. He didn't even try to shave. A cup of coffee is all he had before heading for Doc's office. Doc was busy with "sick call," so Ed had to wait. He'd taken two aspirins with his coffee, and they started to work, reducing the pain, but not the throbbing.

His turn came and he stepped into Doc's office. "By damn, that's blossoming into a real beauty," Doc said. "Let's have a look at it." He peered closely at Ed's chin, but realizing how sore it must be, did not touch it. "No longer a simple boil, Ed. You now have a carbuncle."

"What does that mean?"

"Well, a boil has only one core; a carbuncle has several. It takes longer to be ready to lance, and it gets bigger and much sorer. It can make you feel quite ill. It leaves a large wound after lancing and cleaning it out, and it takes longer to heal."

"Is this one ready for cutting yet?" Ed asked, anxious to get it over with.

"Afraid not. Another two days, I'd guess. When we do open it, we'll use sulfa on it, and put in a gauze drain, so it can heal right, not leaving much of a scar. It'll be five days or a week after we open it before you can fly. The dressing will be bulky, even after the swelling subsides. You won't be able to put your mask on."

"That'll be a week or ten days I'll be grounded, Doc. I'll go crazy on the ground that long while all the other guys are flying. Isn't there any way we can hurry it up?" Ed pleaded.

"Sorry, my friend, but no. Some things you can hurry; this is not one of them. Maybe C.S. can give you something to keep you busy on the ground," Doc said.

"Oh, thanks a lot, just what I need! A desk job of some kind. No thanks."

"Sorry. You'll want to keep busy with something. I'll look at it again tomorrow. Take care of yourself."

"Thanks, Doc, see you then." He left even more depressed than when he had come.

After noon chow, C.S. called Ed aside. "Doc told me your situation. He also said that we'll have an opening in our Rest and Rehabilitation schedule; thinks you'd be a good candidate while you're healing after he operates on your carbuncle. I agree with him. You've been under a lot of stress lately—I'm going to recommend you for a one-week stay on the Farm."

"I'm going through more stress not being able to fly than anything else—I don't need time at the Flak Farm! Give it to one of the guys with more time in," Ed said, angrily.

"We could do that. But you'll be off flying anyway. And the Farm is really a good deal—been there myself. Beautiful country down in Dover. A giant keg of beer always on tap, you just help yourself, no pressure. No analysts bugging you. Relax and do whatever you want. They have organized activities if you want them, but you don't have to participate. You can sleep, or read, or write, whatever you want. My week was great. I think you ought to go. When you come back, Moore'll have Princess in top shape, ready to go. You'll fit right back in. What do you say?"

"Well, you make it sound pretty good. It isn't the first step to a Section Eight, is it?"

"Don't be stupid, Ed J., There's nothing about you or in your records to say you're crazy or a nut case. You can't fly for a little while, and we have an opening on the R&R farm. You're over halfway to ending a tour in combat hours, so it makes sense for you to go."

"Okay, C.S. I'll go, but I doubt if I'll enjoy it."

"Good. I'll check with Doc and have Colonel Morrison get the orders cut, so you can leave as soon as Doc says you can go."

"Thanks, C.S. . . . I think," Ed said, as he headed upstairs. By the time he got into his bunk that evening, his chin, while still tender to the touch and swollen, no longer throbbed, and he felt that he no longer had a temperature. He had the best night's sleep he'd had for several days. Right after breakfast he went to see the flight surgeon.

"It's ready. Ripened real fast," Doc said after examining Ed's chin. "Move over here," and he indicated a black leather reclining chair, just like a dentist's chair. He put a white towel under Ed's chin, then he lowered the chair-back so Ed was semi-reclining. Doc placed another towel under Ed's head, then pulled a stool over beside the operating chair. He washed his hands carefully and removed a small tray of instruments from a sterilizer. Gauze and cotton were placed on the towel on Ed's chest.

"Now, Ed, I'm going to numb this area, so you should feel a little pressure, but no pain. If I hurt you, say so, and I'll numb it more. He sprayed a solution on Ed's chin, making it feel cool at first, then go numb. With a piece of cotton he swabbed antiseptic over the entire area. It smelled like iodine to Ed. He lifted a small lancette from the tray, and made two incisions in the form of a cross. He poured antiseptic directly on the opening, then took surgical tweezers in one hand and a flat-bladed instrument in the other, and proceeded to clean all the yellow matter out of the carbuncle. Next, he poured more antiseptic into the entire opening and waited for it to evaporate. He opened a packet of Sulfa powder and sprinkled it into the wound. With a pair of sterilized scissors, he cut a small strip of gauze, one end of which he placed in the wound.

"That will allow the area to heal slowly, from the edges to the center, minimizing scarring." Next, with gauze and adhesive tape, he fashioned a bulky bandage and taped it down. "This won't stay in place too well with your whiskers sticking out, so use your fingertips to press the tape tighter as you feel it loosening. You'll be a little sore when the numbness wears off, but no real pain. You still have aspirin, don't you?"

"Yes," Ed replied.

"Good. Tomorrow morning, carefully remove the bandage and shave as close to the incision as you can. Then come and see me; I'll put a new dressing on. You can leave for the Farm tomorrow afternoon. Okay?"

"Okay, Doc, thanks. I'm still not crazy about the Flak Farm, but it's okay. See you tomorrow," and Ed returned to the hall.

Everyone he met on his way had some wise remark, "Hey, there's our wounded hero!" "They giving you a Purple Heart for that? They should." "Hear you earned a trip to the Funny Farm. Think they'll let you out?"

Each time Ed started to reply, or to laugh, he felt the bandage start to come loose, and he had to press in on the tape. This kept him from returning the banter, leading one of his friends to say, "What a relief! He can't talk. Say anything you want, guys—he can't answer back." So it went, all the way to his room. It was about to continue there, but he held up his hand, and Chuck and Dick Slade—a recent replacement pilot—instead of ribbing him, said, "Feel better, Ed? Hell of a bandage! And you smell like a laboratory! Doc satisfied now?"

Ed sat down, and holding the tape in place, told them all about it. "Going to miss you, Buddy," Chuck said. "Never had a better element leader; I'll be glad when you're back."

"Thanks," Ed answered, "I hate the whole idea. Who needs it!"

"Jim Burton told me he had a great time at the Farm. Said a pub down the road is a hangout for RAF Spit pilots. He got to know some of them, had a good time swapping stories. So look on the bright side," Chuck said.

"Roger, Blue Leader. Wilco," Ed responded.

"All right, all right!" Chuck snapped. "Hey! If you don't tell them why you're wearing a bandage, everybody'll think you were wounded in combat. You'll get special treatment. Everybody'll want to buy you a drink. Good deal, huh?"

"Yeah," Ed said, dropping his eyes to the floor.

"Oh, oh. Guess I touched a raw nerve. Just kidding, Pal."

"It's okay. I just thought that would cheapen the guys who really have been wounded—or killed."

"Yeah. Bad joke. Sorry."

"Okay. I just had a flashback to men faking war injuries and begging on Pittsburgh streets during the Depression. I always hated it, but I guess they were desperate. Made it worse for the ones who really were wounded vets," Ed said, carefully holding the dressing in place. "Guess I'd better take some aspirin. This thing is starting to ache."

Dick jumped to his feet. "Where are they? I'll get them for you," he said.

"You don't have to do that," Ed said. "There, on the table. Thanks."

Chuck had gone to the bathroom and brought back a cup of water. "Thanks to you, too," Ed said, taking the water and washing down the aspirin. "You must be getting me ready for invalid treatment at the F.F. I could get used to this."

"Better not," Chuck said. "You won't get it when you get back. We'll work your ass off. No more goofing off for you."

Ed managed to get a bath, but most of the morning he spent taking the jibes and needling of the other members of the group. Finally, they left on a mission right after lunch, so there was no one around to make jokes at his expense. Loneliness was his problem then, until the others returned from what they said was another milk-run. Even so, he envied them and wanted to hear all about it.

"Easy trip," Chuck told him. "No action. 24s hit a railroad marshalling yard in France. Not even much flak, except at the coast."

The next morning Ed removed the tape and bandage. It came off easily because it had never adhered very well, although there was some sticking at the incision. He shaved carefully, then put on a small gauze bandage Doc had given him. Without the bulky dressing, he was able to eat a big breakfast without any trouble, except for a little soreness.

"Looks good, Ed," Doc said. "I want to replace the drain, and the big dressing again, to keep it in place. I've prepared a packet of gauze and tape, plus a small bottle of iodine for you to take with you. Some cotton swabs too. Keep the big dressing on for today and tomorrow. It'll loosen up, but keep it on. Day after tomorrow, remove it carefully. If it looks okay, carefully remove the gauze drain, and swab in some iodine. It'll sting, but it's good to prevent infection. Stick on one of the gauze patches with tape. If it looks bad—inflamed or pussy—ask to see a doctor down there. It looks good, though, and should be all right. How do you feel?"

"Feel like flying, Doc, but okay. This thing ached last night so I took aspirin. That helped. A little sore this morning, but not bad. I had no trouble eating."

"Good. Have a good week of R&R, and don't even think about flying. Stop in to see me when you get back, okay? Oh, here are your sulfa pills for while you're gone. Don't want to mess up the big experiment. So long, Ed."

"'Bye, Doc," Ed said, and returned to his room to pack a duffel bag for his week's exile. While he was doing that, Dick Slade came in.

"I'll be flying you down in the Stinson," Dick said.

"What! They expect me to put my life in the hands of a rookie? They really do want to get rid of me, or are they nuts?" Ed said, jokingly.

"Matter of fact," Dick responded, "they picked me because I have more hours in light aircraft than most of the guys have in 51s. I was a civilian pilot for three years before I signed up. So, relax. If you're a good boy, I might let you take the stick when we just have straight-and-level to do. Think you can handle that?"

"Hey, that'd be great. Of course I can handle it. Thanks, Dick. You might be an all right guy after all," Ed said. He had hoped to fly down himself, but someone had to bring the Stinson back. Since no one else from the group was at the Farm, someone had to go along. Dick was a good choice.

True to his word, once in the air and on course, Dick said, "Here, Ed, take over."

Ed, in the co-pilot seat, took the stick, After P-40s and P-51s, the little Stinson seemed unbelievably light and underpowered. It took him a minute to adjust to the feel of the plane; then he just relaxed and held her on course, straight-and-level. "It's not bad," he said. "You'd better land her, though. I don't have enough time in this kind of bird; I'd probably have trouble getting her down. Wouldn't that be embarrassing for a couple of Air Corps guys landing at an RAF base?"

"Okay, Ed. We're just about five miles out. I'll take her now," Dick said.

"You've got her," and Ed released the stick.

They were cleared to land after three Spitfires landed in formation. Ed was impressed with Dick's coolness as he spoke with the Tower and came in for a gentle, precise touchdown. They taxied to where an RAF man was waving them in. Ed got out and thanked Dick, telling him to take care of himself. He also complimented him on his handling of the Stinson, and wished him good flying. Dick waved him off, and taxied out for his take-off.

Ed turned to return the RAF corporal's salute. "Jeep'll be here in a minute to pick you up, Sir," the corporal said, just as Ed spotted a jeep coming between two hangars.

"Lieutenant Thorne?" asked the driver, a slim, ash-blonde young lady in a fitted blue skirt and jacket. When he said that he was, she said, "Welcome, Sir. Stow your bag in the back and climb in; I'll take you to the Farm." Ed got in, and she took off on a fast, quick-turning trip that had him grabbing the hold bar at the side of his seat. She flashed him a smile after a particularly sharp turn, and he could tell by the glint in her eyes that she was out to show him women could drive as well as men.

They raced up a small rise faster than necessary, he thought, and as they topped it and started down the other side, he felt himself rise momentarily out of his seat. Now she braked hard, and he pitched forward. If he had not put his hands out to the top of the metal dashboard, his head would have hit the windshield. She swung into a narrow, tree-lined lane, and again flashed the smile. There was no mistaking the glint in her eyes, but this time it seemed to say, "I know you're going to make a play for me. We'll see how far you get." He noted that she was not pretty, but with her blonde hair, blue eyes, full wide mouth, and straight, slightly large nose, very attractive, especially when she smiled. When not smiling, her face was serious, and slightly stern looking. "I wonder what her interests are," he thought, "and why she seemed to challenge me, a stranger?"

Now, scattering gravel, she braked to a stop in front of a mansion—more impressive and much more elegant than Wretham Hall, but not as large. Well-tended flower gardens and shrubs surrounded the building and the gravelled courtyard in front of it. "Forgot to introduce myself, Lieutenant," the driver said. "I'm Jane Morgan. I'm the assistant director here. Bring your bag. I'll get you signed in and show you your room."

The high-ceilinged, oak-panelled reception area managed to look stately and welcoming at the same time. A pert, dark-haired English young lady clerk had him sign a large registry book, then asked him if he had any special needs, perhaps for his wound. Ed was embarrassed by the reference to his "wound," and for a moment was tempted to let them assume that it was that. This seemed to him dishonest, so he said, "Ladies, I have a confession to make; I don't want to fly under false colors. This is not a combat wound. I'm embarrassed to say it, but I had a huge boil on my chin."

There was a pause as the two ladies looked at each other, then broke into laughter. Holding his bandage in place with his fingers, Ed joined in their laughter, relieved that he had told them the truth. Jane said, "That's a relief! I was afraid you'd had half your chin shot away; I'm glad for you. Now, come on. I'll take you to your room." She was obviously more relaxed in her attitude toward him now, and he was glad. Walking together down a hallway to his first-floor room, Jane said, "You know, you could have let us all think you were wounded. Everybody would have treated you like a hero."

"I suppose so," Ed said, "but I've seen too many guys blown out of the sky to fake something like that. Any glory belongs to them; I'd just as soon not be injured in combat."

"Good, Ed. By the way, we don't pay any attention to rank here. We use first names, and the main thing is to relax and enjoy your time here," She opened the door to a bright, sunny room and said, "Here you are, Ed. There's an hour before eating time. Feel free to look around, relax here in your room, or come down to the lounge. There's also a recreation room downstairs. There are no rules or schedules, except for meals. Usually there are snacks available any time, but meals are served on a regular basis. I'll leave you here. See you later."

"Thanks, Jane," Ed said, as she walked briskly down the hall. He put his extra socks, underwear, and shirts in the dresser, stripped off his "pinks" and his blouse, hanging them in the closet, then put an his OD trousers, which he had put into his duffel bag at the last moment. He opened the other door of his room and found a bathroom, obviously shared with the occupant of the adjoining room. He relieved himself, rinsed his face, and inspected the dressing on his chin. He added a strip of adhesive tape, hoping that would help to hold it in place.

He turned toward his room just as the other door to the bathroom opened. "Thought I heard someone in here. Hi, I'm Jeff Granger. You just get here?"

"Yeah," Ed said, and introduced himself. They shook hands. "Take some flak on the chin?" Granger asked.

"Naw, looks that way, doesn't it? Nothing that dramatic. I had a big boil on my chin. Couldn't wear my oxygen mask, so the Doc grounded me. Since I couldn't fly, they sent me down here," Ed said. "I'll replace this bulky bandage with a smaller one tomorrow. Be glad to get it off."

"Sure looked like you took a shot on the chin; glad you didn't. Looks uncomfortable, all right. I'm in B-24s. You?"

"51s, at East Wretham."

"Little friend, eh? Always glad to see you guys. Good to meet you. See you later," and he turned back to his own door. Then, facing around again, "By the way, there's a big keg of beer open, just outside of the Rec Room. See you there later."

"Right, thanks," Ed said, and went into his room, where he glanced at the books and magazines on a stand between the bed and a lounge chair. The chair had a reading lamp beside it. He left his room and went down the hall. The lounge was easy to find, just off the reception hall. He entered the large room, panelled in oak like the reception hall, and furnished with heavy, comfortable-looking chairs and sofas. Bookcases loaded with books lined one wall; a large fireplace with a log fire burning in it dominated the opposite wall. Two massive French doors opened on a stone-paved terrace, from which steps led down to a garden. Beyond the garden were woodlands, and a bridle path led into the woods. Two men were playing chess and a third was reading near the fireplace. The chess players looked up, and one said, "Hello," and went back to their game. The reader introduced himself as Carl, and said, "There's a large keg of beer out on the terrace. We can draw a glass any time we want. Want one now?"

Ed said, "Sounds good," and he followed Carl out to the terrace. The keg was on its side on a stand, and mugs were hanging on pegs beside it. Carl drew a glass and handed it to Ed, then drew one for himself. "Well, as they say here, 'cheers," and he touched his glass to Ed's. It wasn't Guinness, but it was good. Carl and Ed sat on the low stone wall that extended from the steps to the wall of the mansion, giving a semi-enclosed feeling to the terrace. The air was cool, but the sun felt warm, so they drank their beer and chatted there, not needing to go inside.

Carl, a P-47 pilot, had been shot down over France and had been rescued by two underground fighters. They were able to get him on a fishing boat, which returned him to England. He had baled out and landed safely and uninjured.

"Pure luck," he said, "I could just as easily have been killed." Chimes sounded, and Carl said, "Chow time. Bring your beer with you, if you want to. This is my last day here. Tomorrow I'll be back with my buddies."

The meal was served to the twenty men who seated themselves at tables placed in no set pattern around the pleasant, light-blue dining room, brightened by light from large windows looking out on a flower garden with woods beyond. Jane moved about among the tables as the men ate, joining in conversations and laughter, seeming to enjoy being the only woman among so many young men.

After eating, Ed went out to explore the woods. He hadn't gone far when Carl caught up with him. "You know, Ed, right now we're the only two fighter pilots here?"

"No, I didn't know that."

"Yeah. Seems the bomb boys need R&R more than we do."

"I'm not surprised," Ed said. "I'd go out of my head completely if I had to sit up there straight-and-level the way they do on their bomb runs. That's got to be hell."

"No doubt about it," Carl replied.

Ed asked about Carl's experiences with the French, and enjoyed hearing about them. They spent a couple of hours wandering about, then returned. Outside Ed's room, Carl said, "Hey. There's a pub right down the road where some RAF Spitfire pilots get together every night. I've been talking with them. This'll be my last night. Want to go along?"

"I'd like that," Ed said.

Back in his room, Ed got into the shower. As he got his face wet, the dressing became looser and looser. Finally, he gave it a little tug, and it came off in his hand. With his other hand, he reached up and felt the gauze drain. It was very loose, so he took it off too, and tossed the entire mess into the wastebasket. Very carefully, he soaped and rinsed the entire area. He dried and looked in the mirror. The swelling was all gone, except for a little puffiness around the incision. That area was a little red, too, but there was no indication of infection, and most of the tenderness was gone. He took out the iodine and swabbed the entire area, trying to keep the antiseptic from flowing too far from the critical area.

Very carefully, he shaved right up to the incision, being cautious not to knick any part of it. After rinsing, he swabbed more antiseptic on. After it had dried, he taped on one of the small gauze patches Doc had given him. With clean socks and underwear, and the big bandage gone, and he felt like a new man.

He went down to the dining room to an excellent dinner of roast beef and a dish new to him—Yorkshire pudding. With dessert finished, Jane announced a "sing-song" in the lounge, indicating that the young English clerk-receptionist was an excellent singer and song leader. Most of the men cheered and went to the lounge, but Ed and Carl slipped out to go to the pub. Ed, not wishing to be charged with being out of uniform, went to his room and put on his tie and regular uniform as well as his peaked cap. Carl did the same, and they headed out.

The small pub was crowded, the fireplace bright with burning coal. Carl greeted his RAF friends and introduced Ed. They got a pint each and seated themselves at the table. After the usual parry-and-thrust ribbing, all in good humor, Ed said, "The Spit was my first love among fighters. Just before we got into the war, I was about to apply to the RCAF. I'm happy with Mustangs, but I still have a yen for the Spit." This led to rapid exchanges of opinion about the two airplanes' capabilities and faults, as well as a few comments about the Canadian fliers being a wild lot, but good.

Then one RAF Leftenant said, "If you really want to have a go at a Spitfire, we might be able to accomodate you."

"I'd jump at the chance; could you?" Ed asked.

The one who had made the offer put his head together with the others. After a few minutes of discussion, he looked at Ed and said, "Could you get away from the mansion early morn? Say 06:30?"

Ed looked at Carl, who said, "Why not? We aren't restricted, and there are no guards."

Feeling the beginning of excitement, Ed said, "Yes, yes!"

"Day after tomorrow, 06:30, be in the courtyard. We'll pick you up. We'll have a Spit all warmed up and ready for you. There's no traffic at our base in the early hours, and only one in the Tower, half-asleep. We'll strap you in, and you take it from there. Does that suit you?"

"Does it!" Ed exclaimed. "As you fellows say, 'good show!' I'll be ready." For the next hour, the RAF pilots briefed Ed on the Spitfire, her characteristics, her stalling speed, torque pull and take-off speed. Then they all left the pub, with the Englishmen bidding fond farewells to Carl. After saying goodbye to Ed, and cautioning him not to talk to anybody about the plan, they piled into a Morris Minor and left.

The sing-song was over when Ed and Carl got back to the mansion. Since neither one was interested in more beer, they said goodnight and went to their rooms. Delighted with the prospect of flying a Spit, and no longer bothered by the cumbersome bandage, Ed had no trouble falling asleep.

After breakfast, Jane and Ed, along with six others, saw Carl off, after which Jane took them to see the owner of the estate playing jai alai in a building which he had had built for that purpose. None of the fliers had even heard of the game, let alone seen it. The court was a gym-sized room, with hardwood floors and walls. Each of the four walls had a slanted ledge about six or eight feet up from the floor. The two players had a racquet strapped to one wrist, curved and shaped to catch and cradle the ball, then give it tremendous velocity as the player hurled the ball against the floor, any wall, the slanted edge, wherever he could to make the other player fail to catch it and hurl it in his turn.

The players had to be in great physical condition, because they had to race continuously up and down and across the floor, trying to get to the ball, catch it, then hurl it so the opponent couldn't get it. It was exciting to watch, but none of the fliers accepted the owner's invitation to give it a try.

Ed spent the afternoon playing ping-pong and snooker with the other guests, then drinking beer on the terrace with them. In the evening, he went alone to the pub to meet his new RAF friends and to confirm the arrangements. "All set," they said. "See you at 06:30." After a pint with them, he returned to the mansion, where he read until he was ready for bed.

Up and ready to go by 06:00, he was able to get a cup of coffee in the dining room before he went out to the courtyard.

Precisely at 06:30, two of his British friends drove up in the Morris. Ed got into the back seat, and they took off for the Spitfire base. The sun was not yet up, but it was clear daylight, with no fog and very little mist. They drove to the base and down the wide tarmac in front of the hangars, then on to a dispersal point concealed by trees, near the edge of the field farthest from the Control Tower.

"All right, Ed. You see the windsock? The wind is coming from the west; that's the far side of the field. The runway is just a few yards from here, and the east end is just a bit beyond. Just taxi down there and take off." This was told to him as his friends got him strapped in and oriented to the basic switches and controls and instruments. They were all standard, although the layout was different from the usual American one. The last thing they showed him was the wheels-up lever, and they insisted that he find it without looking.

"Right, Ol' Boy. She's all preflighted and warmed up. Crank her and take her away; just don't rack her up."

"Shouldn't I call the Tower for clearance? I don't feel right about that," Ed said.

"God, no! You'd blow the whole show. Our chaps often take off early like this without clearing. Get on!"

Ed started the engine with no problem, and at a signal from one of his friends, taxied out and toward the eastern end of the runway. When he got there, he stopped and checked the mags, enjoying the sound and feel of the Rolls Royce engine. He moved to the center of the runway. When he got there, he stopped to take another look and feel for the wheel-lever, then released the brakes and started to add throttle for his take-off.

At that moment, a red light flashed from the Tower, pointing right at him. He was tempted to ignore it, but a crisp voice came over his earphones, "Will the pilot in the Spitfire at the east end of runway 365 please hold position and identify himself, over?"

Sensing that the show was over, Ed responded, "Lieutenant Thorne, 0-817132, over."

"My God! A Yank. Return to your dispersal area and report to the Tower, please. Over and out."

Ed swung the plane around in disappointment and disgust at being so close and still not getting off the ground. He taxied back to his starting point, parked and shut down. Dejection showing in every move, and in his face, he climbed out. "I have to report to the Tower," he told his friends.

"Bloody bad show."

"Rotten luck."

"Ruddy bastard in the Tower!"

His friends commiserated. He thanked them, saying that he'd buy them drinks at the pub in the evening, then got in the Morris for a ride to the Tower.

"Will you fellows be in trouble?" he asked.

"Of course not. The Top might say a few words to us, but he's a grand chap. He'll cause no trouble, not for us or you."

Ed climbed to the Tower. The flying officer who was in charge said, "Sorry, old man, but we can't let that happen, you know. If anything happened, there'd be bloody hell to pay. Hope you understand."

"I do, but I am disappointed," Ed said. "The Spit has always been my dream airplane."

"A worthy and noble sentiment, but we just can't give you a ride without a great deal of negotiation between your top people and ours. Sorry."

"Okay, at least I got to sit in one and taxi her."

"How was it?"

"Great! I still want to fly her; thanks anyway, and goodbye." He thought he ought to get going before some less-forgiving officer showed up. He ran down the steps, and his friends drove him to the mansion. There, he invited them in for breakfast, and they accepted. He checked with Jane, and she was delighted to welcome the RAF men.

"Some digs," said Gregg, Ed's favorite of the Englishmen.

"Oh well," Ed replied. "You should see our quarters at East Wretham," putting them on a little. "The U.S. Army takes good care of its fliers."

"They do that," Gregg replied. "Well, so long as you take care of that daylight bombing, we don't mind."

Breakfast was accompanied by the same kind of banter that they carried on in the pub at night. Other guests came by their table to meet the RAF men and to make them welcome.

"Let me show you the lounge and the terrace," Ed said, as they finished breakfast.

"We should get back."

"It'll only take a couple of minutes." Ed led them into the lounge, then out onto the terrace. They were impressed, but they had to go.

"Sorry it didn't work out, chappy," Gregg said. "See you tonight. Remember, you're buying."

"Right, I'll be there. And thanks again for trying."

Let down about the Spitfire-flying, Ed spent the rest of the morning in his room reading and writing letters. After lunch, Jane organized a trip to visit the ruins of an ancient Norman castle, dating from the early Twelfth Century. Ed found this interesting, and he spent nearly three hours poking around among the rock remnants of walls and archways, trying to imagine the activities there when it was peopled by the conquerors of England in that remote time. Another hour was spent viewing a Roman wall and viaduct, after which they returned to the mansion for a beer, and then to wash up for dinner. After dinner, there was a sing-song, and Ed participated this time, finding pleasure in singing with the group. Unfortunately, from his point of view, Jane was near enough to him to hear his voice among the others.

Between songs Jane said, "We have a voice among us. Let's see if we can persuade Ed to sing something for us," and she started to clap. The others joined in.

"Okay," Ed said. "But it's your fault; you asked for it." Jane, who was not a bad pianist, was looking through the music stacked on top of the piano. Ed looked at the several she had pulled out. Among them was "Without A Song," in a key that he could manage, so they agreed on that. He sang, and the applause was long and loud. He was pleased, so he said, "One more, then." Jane had pulled out "O Sole Mio" in the key of G, the key in which he had always sung it. This was an equally big hit, and the listeners wanted more, but Ed said, "I'm out of condition for this," and begged off.

A few more songs by the entire group ended with "Good Night, Ladies." The evening was cool, but not cold, and a half-moon was shining brightly. Away from the moon, the stars were brilliant. Everybody went out on the terrace for beer. The inevitable questions about his singing were asked, and Ed answered them as well as he could. Jane, standing right next to Ed, asked if he had considered getting into Special Services as a singer instead of being a combat pilot. "No, I've always wanted to fly, and I wanted to be directly involved in stopping what the Nazis are doing."

This led to a general, often contentious, discussion of the war, what it means, who's going to gain by it, and the effectiveness of the air war. Somebody raised the question of when the long-anticipated invasion of France would take place. Several men said they thought that increasing U.S. and British activity, especially along the Channel, might mean something big was coming. All present expressed a wish that it would happen soon. Some wondered what part the Eighth Air Force would play, and some voiced concern about making mistakes and dropping their bombs on friends instead of enemies when the battle line, once established on the continent, began to move.

During this discussion, Ed was conscious of Jane's arm brushing against his. It felt good, so he moved slightly so that his arm touched hers more firmly. She did not move away. As the crowd thinned, he leaned over and said softly in her ear, "It's a beautiful night, and early. Would you like to take a walk out in the woods?"

She turned to look right into his eyes, then said, barely audibly, "Let me get my jacket, then, okay."

Ed was pleased, and he finished his beer, while Jane went inside to get her jacket. He considered Jane a nice lady, so he didn't have anything exceptional in mind—just a pleasant walk and some talking about home and family. There had not been many opportunities to be in the company of attractive, pleasant girls since coming to England.

Jane returned and said, "There's a well-marked path off to the left. It should be quite clear in this amount of moonlight." After they had passed beyond the light coming from the mansion, she slipped her arm through his. "You really have a lovely voice, and it's obvious that you have done a lot of singing in public. Thanks for doing it."

"Actually, I'm pretty rusty. But thanks." They turned a bend in the path, and Jane said, "Here. Isn't this nice." It was a sizeable pond with a marble bench at its side. "We can sit here for a little bit, if you like. Sometimes I need a little time away from so many men to take care of, so I sneak off here."

"It's beautiful," Ed said, as they sat side by side on the bench, "but maybe you'd rather be alone," hoping that she would say no.

She did say no, and snuggled a little closer. He put his arm around her and she pressed closer. This was much more than he had expected, or even hoped for. Touched by the moonlight, her face looked striking—even the nose was made to look softer, and somehow smaller. He leaned over and gently kissed her hair. She turned toward him, and again looked into his eyes. She moved her face closer, and he kissed her mouth. She responded, and pressed closer to him. He put both arms around her, and she put hers around his neck. They had a long kiss, both obviously enjoying it. They were responding to each other, and he wondered if she wanted to go farther. His question was answered when she hugged him harder, then pulled away.

"Don't get any ideas, Ed. This is as far as I go. I won't get deeply involved with someone who goes into combat over and over. I really like you, but in a few days you'll be gone, and I'll never see you again."

"Right, I understand. I think you're swell, but I don't try to make it with every girl I meet. It's great, though, to hold you and kiss you."

"I like it, too," she said, "but I think we'd better get back," and she stood, straightening her jacket.

Ed got up, and they started to walk back up the path. She slipped her hand into his, and said, "Don't hate me, I'm not a tease. But I just can't get involved over here."

"Everything's fine, Jane. We did more than I dreamed we would, and I understand. It's always the woman who gets hurt when the guy has his fun and takes off. You're a sweetheart. Nothing's changed, except that we know each other a little bit better."

The remaining days of Ed's R&R passed in a leisurely way, and although he found himself relaxing and resting, he was anxious to get back with his squadron. All that was left of the carbuncle was a tiny scab, and he felt fit and ready to fly. At last his departure day arrived and he said goodbye to his friends and gave Jane a hug, which she returned. She then drove him to the RAF field. Dick was right on time with the Stinson, and what turned out to be Ed's only visit to the Flak Farm was over. He waved a final goodbye to Jane, and he was off to East Wretham.

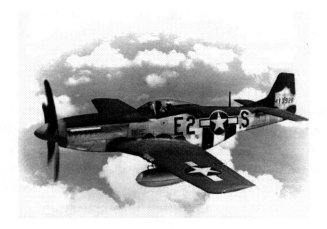

25

Back at the hall, Ed had time for a quick bath before going down for noon chow. "Glad to see you back, Ed. How was it down there?" Chuck asked when he stepped into his room.

"It was all right, but I sure missed flying. What's been going on here?" Ed asked.

"Mostly routine stuff," Chuck replied. "We had a really early trip this morning. Most of the guys are sacking out right now."

Ed looked and saw inert bodies in the other bunks. Chuck was the only one up. "Nearly got off in a Spitfire, but they caught me at the last minute before take-off. I'll tell you about it later; I want to take a bath before lunch."

"Okay," Chuck said. "C.S. tells me the Princess is ready to go. You'll probably want to take her up for a check ride, maybe this afternoon."

"Right, I do want to. And this time she's going as high as I can get her. I don't want her conking-out at altitude again," Ed said at the door with towel and clean clothes in his hands. He finished his bath and returned in time to go down to lunch with Chuck.

C.S. saw them come into the dining room and he went up to Ed and said, "Hello, First Lieutenant Edward J."

"You got that wrong, C.S. Just second lieutenant."

"Not any more. Congratulations, your promotion came through while you were away. Maybe if I go to the Flak Farm again I'll make lieutenant colonel," C.S. said, and he shook hands with Ed. "Drinks are on me, after dinner tonight."

"Okay, you bet. Thanks. I didn't even know if you'd want me back, and I find out I'm promoted. Wow!" Ed said.

"You had it coming," Chuck said.

Ed turned to him, "You knew this, didn't you? And you didn't say anything. Some friend!"

"Hey. It's the squadron CO's prerogative. C.S. had to tell you, not me," Chuck responded.

"Oh, by the way," C.S. said, "here's an old pair of silver bars I had lying around. You can use them until your next promotion. Then I want them back."

"Same ones I just returned to you?" Chuck asked.

"Same ones," C.S. said. "At least a dozen guys have used them; sort of a tradition in the squadron."

"Thanks, C.S. I'll put one on right now," Ed said. With Chuck's help, he removed the gold bar, replacing it with the silver one, on the side of his shirt collar opposite the Air Corps wings-and-propellor insignia.

After lunch all the pilots assembled in the bar to view films taken when they fired their guns, if they flicked the camera switch as required when ready to fire. The films served two purposes. First, it showed how accurate or inaccurate their firing had been. The pilots could learn from this. Second, it confirmed any hits they had made, so they could get credit for them. Each bit of film had the pilot's number preceding it.

Various comments were made as the pilots watched their pictures: "I sure blew that one." "Yeah! Got him!" "What a waste of ammunition." "Look at that guy trying to get away!" "What happened there?" "I'm embarrassed by that one."

After the viewing, Colonel Macon had a few comments, and the show was over. Back in the room, Chuck said to Ed, "I didn't see any of your film this time. How come? I know you fired your guns; in fact, I saw you get at least two bandits. What's going on?"

"I don't want to talk about it," Ed said.

"You have to switch on your cameras, you know. Did you forget?"

Showing irritation, Ed said, "Of course I know that. I said I don't want to talk about it!"

"Okay I heard you. Strange, though."

"Lay off, Chuck."

"Right. I'll drop it."

Changing the subject, Ed said, "C.S. said he'd buy drinks tonight. Then I'll buy a round. Don't forget to be there."

"Okay."

"I'm going to see if I can get cleared to take Princess up. Man, I hope she's okay. See you," and Ed left the room.

She was more than okay—she was perfect. The new Rolls Royce engine started quickly and ticked over steadily and evenly as Ed taxied to the end of the runway. Mags and manifold pressure checked out. Delighted to be flying again, and in his own airplane, he took off. Spiraling upward, he repeatedly advanced and retracted the throttle to full-power and back at various altitudes. At 10,000 feet, the supercharger came on—right on time—with the consequent surge of power. He turned on his oxygen. At 30,000 he put her through her paces: at full throttle and reduced throttle, in sharp turns, in dives, in climbs. Everything checked out perfectly. Then, flying straight-and-level, he shoved the throttle full forward as he had done when the other engine had failed him in enemy territory. The power was there, the response was immediate.

Descending, he gave her a workout at 25,000, 20,000, and on down at 5,000 feet intervals. No hitch, no glitch, no hesitation or balking. She was smoothly responsive to his every demand. Easy turns, tight turns, full-throttle, half-throttle, no throttle; climbing turns, diving turns, inverted turns. "I love you, Princess!" he exclaimed, and called for clearance to land. Before landing, he made a fast pass over the center of the field and did a slow roll, indicating that he and Princess were victorious over their troubles. Then he did a tight spiral approach and a good landing.

"She's great, Al," he said, after parking and shutting her down. "Never better—Perfect! We're both ready to go."

"No problems at all, Sir?"

"Not even a hint of a problem, Al. She's combat-ready."

"That's great news, Sir. Major Moore'll be glad. He really fussed over this airplane; wanted her to be right for you."

"Well, she's right, all right. I'll tell him so," Ed said, and added, "Wait a minute. You said 'Major Moore.'"

"Right, Sir. His promotion came through. I see you're wearing silver bars now."

"Yeah, Major Irvine lent me these. They're a tradition in the squadron., I have to give them back when—if—I get the next promotion."

"I know, Sir, I've seen them before. Congratulations. We all knew you'd be getting a promotion. Us ground jockeys can usually tell, and we knew you'd be moving up."

"That's enough brown-nosing, Al. You can put Princes to bed for today."

"Sure thing, Sir. Oh, Sir," he added as Ed turned away. "Have you heard any rumors?"

Ed turned back, "Rumors about what, Al?"

"Well, we keep hearing on the grapevine that something big is coming up."

"Haven't heard anything specific, but everybody's expecting something about an invasion. But we've been hearing that ever since I got over here."

"Yes, Sir. But there seems to be more of it around lately."

"Well, Al, we'll know it when it happens. Here's the jeep. See you later," and he climbed into the jeep to go to find Tom Moore to report on the test-flight.

Moore was pleased to get Ed's positive report. They congratulated each other on their promotions. Ed went on to the hall to clean up and find Grant before evening chow.

He found him just finishing a ping-pong game. "Hi, Ol' Buddy," Grant said. "I see you joined the silver-bar bunch, too."

"Yeah," Ed responded. "I don't know how you got yours, but I got mine by messing up three airplanes and spending time at the Flak Farm."

"Yeah I know. How was it? Welcome back."

"It was okay. Better than I expected," and he told Grant about the Farm, and especially about the Spitfire episode.

"You always did want to fly one of those, didn't you?" Grant asked.

"Yep. And I came close. It's a good-feeling ship even on the ground. For a minute there, I thought I was actually going to fly her. Well, you can't win 'em all. How are things with you?" Ed asked.

"Doing okay. Mostly routine stuff. We've had a few bandits, but no biggies since Berlin. So you haven't missed much. The Germans must be holding back for something," Grant said.

"For what?" Ed asked. "Have you heard anything?"

"The usual stuff, but more of it," Grant replied.

"That's what Al said," Ed said, "and the same stuff was floating around down on the Farm."

"Did the RAF guys know anything?"

"Never mentioned it, if they did. Chow time, let's go eat."

C.S. intercepted Ed as they entered the dining room. "Hi, Flight Leader Edward J.," he said.

Surprised, Ed said, "Wrong again, C.S. I'm just an element leader."

"Not now, you aren't. We had no choice. Too many of our good men have finished their tours and are being sent back to the States. And as you know, we've lost some. So we're scraping the bottom of the barrel for leaders. We found you there."

"Oh, thanks a lot, C.S."

"Just kidding, Ed. You're the right guy for the job, okay?"

"Sure, boss. Thanks. Trouble will be for the other three to keep up with Princess—she's sure an eager goer now."

"They'll keep up. You are, as of now, White Flight Leader."

"Roger, C.S. Thanks. I'll do my best."

"Okay, let's eat."

Briefing was early the next morning. They escorted bombers along the coast of France, where bombs were dropped on coastal installations. Flak was heavy, but no bandits appeared. The mission was repeated in the afternoon, with the same lack of enemy fighter response.

For the next two weeks, the group flew one or two missions every day. Some were deep bombing raids, and often they repeated the escort mission along the French coast. These always seemed to be done twice a day, when they were scheduled. No enemy fighters appeared on any of the coastal strikes, but they had some skirmishes on several of the deeper missions. Princess did her job to perfection, no matter what that job was.

Spring, with its beautiful weather sometimes interrupted by storms or heavy overcast, continued through May and into June. One morning during the first week of June, another early briefing was called. "Another coastal escort mission, I guess," Ed said, as he and the others gathered for the briefing.

It turned out, though, that the colonel's briefing was different this time. "We will patrol along the coast of France," he said, "specifically in the area known as Normandy," and he pointed to the area on the map. "Our job will be to intercept and destroy any and all enemy aircraft we sight in our patrol area. We are to fly to the limit of our endurance, then return to base, refuel, and return to our patrol area. We will continue through the day, until visibility is reduced to the point where we can no longer spot enemy aircraft."

A murmur of excitement went through the assembled pilots, then quickly subsided as the weather and intelligence briefing continued. "Sure as hell, something's up," Chuck said on their way out. "Hey, I'm sorry to lose you out of my flight, but congrats, Flight Leader."

Ed jumped from the jeep at his dispersal location and hurried toward Princess. He stopped and stared, then saw Al grinning at him. Alternating broad black-and-white stripes that had not been there before encircled the fuselage midway between the cockpit and the vertical stabilizer, and identical stripes were on the top and bottom of each wing, centered between the star-in-a-circle and where the wing joined the fuselage.

"They got us out of bed at midnight, Sir. Every one of our birds had to have these stripes in time for today's mission."

"Well, I'll be!" Ed said. "For easier identification of our aircraft, I guess. Probably every Allied plane will have them. Must be expecting a lot of action today."

"Got to be something big, Sir. The grapevine was extra busy all night. You could hear the guys talking all around the field all night, while we were putting on these stripes."

"We'll soon know, Al. We'll be flying all day along the east side of the Channel. Whatever happens, we'll see it."

"Congratulations, Sir. I understand you're now Red Leader."

"Thanks, Al. It's White Leader, though. The Major is still Red Leader. Princess all set? I'd better get out there and act like a leader."

"All ready, Sir. She checked out perfect this morning. All warmed up for you. Good flying, Sir."

Ed cranked up and headed to the downwind end of the field. The other three members of his flight fell in behind him. As they stopped to check their mags, Red Flight started its take-off run. Ed led his flight onto the field, and when all were in place, leaned forward and gunned his engine. They were halfway down the field as Red Flight cleared the trees at the end of the runway.

Climbing straight out on a heading just a little east of south, the group formed up along the east coast of England; then made a small adjustment eastward, and then south again over the open water—first the North Sea, then the Channel. As they entered the Channel area, they saw a scattering of small patrol boats, then an increasing number of boats the farther south they flew. Then they could see clouds of smoke rising, seemingly right up from the water. Getting closer, they saw an astonishing array of vessels of every size, from mighty battleships and cruisers standing broadside off the Normandy coast, down to tiny landing craft making their way to that same coast. An armada of thousands of ships were launching salvo after salvo at what were assumed to be enemy installations, fortifications, and gun emplacements.

Ed's group would patrol all day. Above the incredible concentration of armed might, seeing hundreds of Allied aircraft of every description—all showing the black and white stripes—only a handful of enemy planes appeared in the group's sector, and they seemed more interested in simply showing a potential threat than engaging in action. They came in from high altitude, diving to pick up enormous speed, making quick, swooping passes toward the invaders, then disappearing to the east. Ed and his friends had little chance at them, although the group did manage to destroy several who dove through their formation, which gave the 51 pilots a chance to pursue them, overtake them, and shoot them down. Mohair Leader—the colonel—had cautioned all the pilots during briefing that their primary mission was to patrol, so unless the enemy mounted a massive aerial assault, they were to maintain their formation. When a few German fighters came close, just two or three 51s would be sent after them; the remainder were to stay in position.

Twenty minutes after the group got into its patrol area, some five-hundred yards in from the coastline, Ed looked toward the Channel and saw waves of landing craft heading for the Normandy beach. Three of them were coming right at the stretch of shoreline just opposite where the group was flying back and forth above the bluffs and hillocks that lined the eastern edge of the beach. Ed looked down and saw a concrete barricade on top of the bluff. He could see eight men manning two machine guns and what appeared to be a rapid-fire small cannon—probably twenty-millimeter. He could see the barrels pointing directly at the part of the beach toward which the three landing craft were aiming to drop the front ramp and unload the men crowded in the craft.

He had a horrible vision of what was about to happen, and pushed his transmit button. "Tinplate White Leader to Tinplate Leader." Not waiting for C.S. to respond, he went on. "Request permission to strafe the gun emplacement just off to our left."

Before C.S. could respond, Ed heard, "Tinplate White Leader, this is Mohair. Hold your position. Repeat, hold your position."

"But, Sir," Ed said, knowing that he had no right to do so, could not keep quiet. "Don't you see what's going to happen? Those guys will be massa . . ."

"Tinplate White Leader, you're out of order. Get off the air!"

"Oh God! Oh God!" Ed said to himself. "Don't let the slaughter happen. Please." He was tempted to go down anyway. But the training in obeying orders had worked. Sick at what he could see was going to happen, he held his position.

Wave after wave of landing craft lodged against the bottom of the Channel, yards from the actual beach, and hundreds of doll-like figures spewed out of the fronts of the craft, fighting their way, too slowly, much too slowly, through the breakers and up on to the shore. The horror he had visualized became reality. The shore guns opened up. Not believing what he was seeing, Ed cried as he saw bodies explode, others crumble — not even getting to the shore. Others made it out of the water, only to be cut down by withering fire from the shore guns.

The firing from bunkers and barricades was unceasing and deadly. The landing men were defenseless, with no shelter, no way to escape the merciless fire, vulnerable. Sickened by what he was forced to watch, without being able to help the men below, Ed cried out, "Oh, God! Make it stop! Make it stop!" But it did not stop. The unprotected men were helpless. If they paused to attempt to return the fire, they were even easier targets. Their only hope was to keep running, zig-zagging, burdened with their equipment, until a few reached the inadequate shelter at the base of the bluffs. Once there, a few brave men could claw their way up to lob hand grenades at the gunners above them. Slowly, painfully, with incredible sacrifice, the invaders silenced gun after gun. Hour after hour passed before the beach was secured.

What had sickened Ed from the vantage point of his group's assigned area was endlessly repeated for the entire length of the beach. Vomit rose in his throat, and he swallowed it. When they returned to base for refueling, he jumped out of his plane, ran to the edge of the dispersal area, and let the vomit flow. He was pale and clammy all over. Al, understanding, looked away and did not speak.

Ed did not speak either. He knew that if he tried to talk about what he had seen, he would break down and cry right there. He wasn't sure, if that happened, that he could go back over. Still pale, he clamped his mouth shut and climbed in to return. This far from the unbelievable scenes he had watched, he thought, "All the years of planning and training, all the massing of equipment, all the organizing and spying, all the reconnaisance, and it looks like a debacle. The invasion looks like a failure. Can those few making it up the bluffs turn it around, or is all the slaughter for nothing? And why couldn't we, right there on the scene, be allowed to help?"

Sandwiches and coffee had been brought to the dispersal area, but Ed was too sick to have any. Before starting up, he had been able to ask Al the date. "June six, Sir," Al had replied.

Back patrolling, he could see that progress had been made. More and more men had made it to the bluffs, and many were now climbing up. Medics were helping those wounded on the beaches. Shelling from the ships continued and men were still pouring in. Not nearly so many were being gunned down now, and masses of equipment were being landed. It looked as if the invasion might be successful after all. Ed was more optimistic, but still deeply disturbed at the terrible cost of the success. He knew that a long, tough road had still to be traveled before the forces of Naziism would be wiped out. The conflict that had been gnawing at him for months now, between his revulsion at the deeds of the Hitler-led Germans, and his horror at the bloody price the Allies were paying to stop those deeds, was intensified by what he had witnessed, "How can we all behave so savagely?" he repeatedly asked himself.

On the second landing for fuel, Ed was able to eat a sandwich and drink some coffee. This picked him up and, although he was tired, as were the others, he suppressed his feelings. Wanting to do his part, even though it seemed ineffectual, he led his flight back to the battle scene in a mechanical way. This time, things in their sector were quieter, much more organized. There was not the chaos and sense of directionless futility that had marked the earlier forays. It was twilight when the group headed home for the third and last time of the day.

Dinnertime was quiet. The men seemed stunned by what they had seen. Very few had anything to say. Only two or three went into the bar after eating. Ed, tired as he was, felt the need for solitude, peace. He walked out into the trees behind the hall. A soft breeze stirred the leaves and made the small branches sway. He walked until he came to a small glade where he could see the stars. The sky seemed vast and unbelievably peaceful. He sat on the trunk of a fallen tree and gazed upward.

"Oh, God," he murmured, "what are we doing here? What is it all about? Why do we kill each other? Is there no other way?" There was no answer from the limitless sky, but as he gazed at the unperturbed stars, a measure of peace came over him. "I don't understand," he said, "but I guess I never will. We ought to be able to do better than we do. Maybe we can't solve our own problems — maybe we need some guidance or help. What we and they are doing to each other can't be right! It can't be right for all these men to die — young, promising men, on both sides. What a waste! But I don't know the answer."

For a long time he sat there. Then, utterly weary, but somewhat cleansed, he walked back to the hall and went to bed.

For the next several days, the group did some escort work, but was also called upon for patrol missions. Looking down on Normandy as the days passed, it became increasingly clear that the invasion would not be stopped. The little footholds the Allies had bought so dearly expanded and advanced slowly. More men and supplies flooded in. More and more territory came under Allied Military Control. Everybody seemed certain that, although much more fighting had yet to be done, this was the beginning of the end for the Nazis.

Ed made several attempts to talk to various of the pilots in the group about his feelings concerning the cost of young lives to accomplish what they were doing. Everyone, even those he liked and respected the most, in effect responded in the same way: "It's the price we have to pay, and it's our job. Put it out of your mind; don't think about it." Chuck, more sympathetic, had only the suggestion that Ed talk to one of the chaplains. He did. The chaplain's response was, "We're doing God's work, fighting evil. If it were not God's will, we would not be winning the war. God's will be done." Ed left the chaplain's office wondering if all victories in all history's wars were God's will, even those in which seemingly evil men won.

Ed recognized that all his friends, in the interests of their own sanity, must be suppressing their feelings, refusing to think about the ugly side of what was happening. When someone did think about it, and speak about it, the danger of being forced to confront what they did not want to face was met by rationalizing, usually dismissing the matter with some pat phrase, along with some fervid assertion about patriotism. Gradually, in the face of this Ed began to adopt the same way of living with the horror. He reached the realization that it was necessary to do so to keep from a mental/emotional breakdown. While this provided him with a survival technique, it did not dispel his haunting dilemma: The forces of Hitler were doing evil things. They must be stopped. But in order to stop them, *we* have to do terrible things.

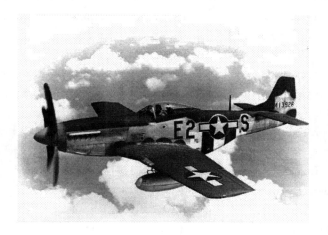

26

Now as summer moved toward fall, the group returned to mostly long-range escort missions, Many were milk-runs, but some were anything but. When they encountered enemy fighters now, the bandits usually came at them in large numbers, and fought with a ferocity that seemed to come from desperation. The result was wild dogfights that filled the sky in every direction. It seemed to Ed and his fellow fliers that the Germans realized that not only did the Allies now control the skies, but that they were well on their way to total domination of the skies. The attacks seemed like last, desperate attempts to prevent that domination.

On one of the milk-run missions, Ed spotted an airplane at eleven o'clock, a little lower than he was. It was unlike any plane he'd seen before. He called Tinplate Leader, "This is Tinplate White Leader. There is an odd-looking aircraft at about eleven o'clock, low. Shall I check it out, over?"

"Roger, White Leader. Take your flight over and see what it is. We'll watch you. Out."

Since all members of the squadron would have heard that exchange, Ed did not have to call his flight members. He simply broke off from the larger formation and headed toward the bogey, with his flight members following him.

As they got closer—close enough to see what it looked like, but not yet in firing range—Ed saw that it had no propellor. It had what appeared to be a round hole in its tail, and rudder on top of the fuselage, rather than as a coninuation of the fuselage. They would soon be within firing range, and Ed switched on his guns. The German insignia on the plane was now clearly visible.

What was perplexing was that the airplane did not either turn to meet them, or take evasive action. It was as though the pilot chose to ignore them. Very close now to having the bandit in range, Ed got it in his gunsight, centering on the round hole in its tail. Ed's finger began to tighten on the trigger. Abruptly, yellow smoke shot out of that hole. The nose of the airplane came up, and with incredible speed it climbed out of range. To Ed, it seemed to be in a vertical climb.

"Tinplate Leader," Ed called. "Were you watching? Over."

"Roger, White Leader. What the hell was it? Over."

"Beats me! I was just about to fire on her, then she was gone—I've never seen anything take off so fast. No way we could match that speed."

"Roger, White Leader. Return to formation. Out."

The remainder of the mission brought no further sightings of the unusual plane, nor any other enemy action. At debriefing, Ed reported what they had seen. The intelligence officer questioned him to get all the details he could, taking careful notes. He thanked Ed, then went over and had a quiet conversation with Colonel Macon.

The colonel stepped back to the front of the room, and everyone stopped talking. "Our intelligence people," he said, "have had some reports—from the other side—of an experimental fighter plane the Germans are developing. It is, evidently, potentially a very effective aircraft, with great speed and outstanding climbing ability. It does not have an internal combustion engine and prop, as conventional airplanes do. Instead, it uses what is called 'jet propulsion.' You may have read articles about this in engineering or scientific publications. As far as our intelligence people know, this sighting today is the first one reported. The yellow smoke that Ed saw is typical, and it results from the fuel it burns. It is probably peroxide-based. Those of us who saw it take off when Ed got close could see what a threat it could be if Germany ever gets it into production. We'll probably be hearing more about it. That is all. Dismissed."

All through noon chow the dining room was buzzing with excited talk about the new plane. The talk continued in the bar after lunch.

No mission was called for the remainder of the day, so Ed and Grant went for a bike ride. This one was shorter than the first one they had taken. It was a mild September day, but it was evident that colder weather was on the way, and they didn't know how many more chances they would have to ride out into the country.

After some five miles up and down hills, they pulled over and sat on a low stone wall in the sun to rest and talk. Ed said, "You know, Ol' Buddy, I'm moving in on enough hours to complete my first tour. How about you?"

"I'm not as far along as you. Remember, I was sick there for a while. Doc thought I was going to have pneumonia. I lost a little over three weeks," Grant responded.

"Yeah, I remember that," Ed said. "You wanted sack time more than you wanted combat time, so you convinced Doc that you were sick. Too bad you couldn't go to the Flak Farm."

"Doc wanted to keep me under observation, so I had to stay here. I never did get down to that resort."

"Well, anyway, you haven't forgotten what we agreed to when we first joined the group, have you?"

"You mean about completing a tour here, then after leave back home volunteering for another tour, but in the Pacific?"

"Right. You haven't forgotten. We still on for that?"

"I'm not sure we can be. You'll be done a couple of weeks before me."

"Yeah, I know. But I've been talking to C.S. He thinks we can work something out so I can stay on while you finish up. That is, if you still want to do it."

"Sure I do. I'm ready for it. So, yeah, if you and C.S. can work it out, great."

"Okay. I'll check with C.S. again and let you know. What say we head back? It's getting chilly."

"Yeah, let's go," and they rode home.

The conversation at dinner was still dominated by talk about the new German fighter. Grant, who had learned about jet propulsion in engineering school, explained how it worked. "It's basically a tube, open at each end. Somewhere in the tube are jets which inject fuel into the tube while air enters at the front end. The fuel mixture is ignited, and blows out the rear end. This provides the thrust to propel the craft forward. So, it's called 'jet propulsion.' Theoretically, since the faster it moves through the air, the more air comes in the front, the more thrust is developed as the mixture shoots out the back. So, the faster it goes, the faster it goes! Obviously, there are factors that limit its speed. Things like friction, resistance, structural weaknesses, and so on. But as we saw today, any country that perfects such a system would produce an airplane that would make all the prop-driven ones obsolete."

As Grant talked, more and more of the diners stopped talking to listen to him. When he finished, applause broke out, and various men said, "Way to go, Grant," and "It's starting to make sense to me now."

"Nice little lecture, Ol' Buddy,' Ed said, as they settled in the bar after dinner. "I guess there's something to be said for college after all. I think I get the picture, but I have some questions," and they continued to talk. Others gathered around, and the discussion went on until midnight. Then everybody went to bed, knowing there would be flying to do the next day.

Ed had trouble getting to sleep even though it was late. His conflicting feelings, his persistent dilemma, was unusually strong. He tried to keep his thoughts on it down by focusing on music he had heard before leaving home for the Air Corps. Nothing worked until he had the vivid auditory memory of one of the last Metropolitan Opera broadcasts he'd listened to just before leaving. It was a new production of Verdi's "Otello," based on Shakespeare's great tragic play, "Othello." It was the company's revival of the opera, after years of hiatus. The title role was sung by the great Italian tenor, Giovanni Martinelli, who had refused to undertake the role until he was in his fifties. He had brought to it an intense, emotionally committed interpretation, which won him great new acclaim, even though his voice was no longer functioning in the way it had in his previous roles. To Ed this slightly ragged voice gave a sense of vulnerability to the performance that, far from detracting from it, intensified it. He could hear it now, in his imagination, with the same overwhelming feeling he had had at the time of the broadcast. The other two major roles were sung by the noted soprano, Elizabeth Rethberg as Desdemona, and the reigning baritone of the company, Lawrence Tibbet, as Iago. Both complemented Martinelli's performance with their own memorable ones. The recalled sounds of this searing performance took Ed's mind totally off of the moral dilemma, and he fell asleep as Otello sang the last tragic notes after killing Desdemona and committing suicide.

The following day there was another film-viewing session. Again, there was no film with Ed's number on it. This time after the viewing, both Chuck and C.S. cornered Ed in the bar. "What the hell's going on, Ed? I've seen you shoot down enemy planes. Why don't we see any film of yours?" Chuck demanded.

"Yeah, Ed," C.S. said. "I know you get some kills. We need it on film to get you credit. You know you'll never be an ace if you don't get your kills on the record."

They kept pressing him. Finally, Ed said, "All right. It's because those aren't just airplanes we're shooting down. There are men in those planes. Young guys, just like us. 'Kids' is the right word for it, C.S. The Germans are putting kids in their planes! It was bad enough when they were men, but now, God help us, they're kids! Younger than us! I do it because it's my job. If we don't do our job, the evil that Hitler stands for might win. So I do it. But I don't want CREDIT for it. Stuff your credit! I don't think everybody has to see it my way, but it's the way I see it. So, let it rest, okay?"

"Hey," Chuck said, "I'm sorry, Pal, I won't mention it again."

"Right," C.S. added, "most of us don't even think of that. Yeah, I'll lay off too. Good man, Edward J. We just couldn't figure out why you had no pictures. So, you don't *forget* to switch on your camera. You don't *want* it on, right?"

"Right. Now, can we talk about something else," Ed said, feeling relief that he had at last said it to someone. "And do me a favor, will you? Keep this to yourselves."

"Will do," C.S. said, and Chuck agreed.

C.S. left for a meeting with the colonel and the other squadron leaders. Chuck and Ed stayed on in the bar, but they were subdued—Ed because of what he'd finally had to say to get Chuck and C.S. to stop interrogating him about the films, and Chuck because he'd heard it. Their thoughts were turned inward.

Now with the invasion referred to by everybody as "D-day" well under way, every brief-ing included specific information about the "bomb-line" with special emphasis on the area designated for the day's mission. This was necessary to keep the Allied airplanes from bomb-ing or strafing their own men. It was not a simple matter to keep the information up-to-date, as the movement of the Allied forces was not at an even, steady pace. There were thrusts and counter-thrusts, advances and retreats on both sides. By now, it was clear that the beach-heads of Normandy had developed into a huge wedge, advancing eastward, but also expand-ing north and south. Actually, it could no longer be pictured as a wedge, but rather as a long, jagged line, some sections stalled for days, others moving rapidly forward, with the uneve-ness that results when powerful forces opposing each other struggle mightily to advance against each other or, failing that, use all their power to impede the progress of each other.

Each time the Allied forces took and secured a major city or area, it was announced at the start of the briefing for that day's mission. All the pilots would cheer at the news. One morn-ing the news was announced that Ghent, a major city in Belgium, had been secured. This brought forth an especially loud cheer because the group had strafed a major airport near that city several times. Brussels had been taken some while previously, and taking Ghent was another major achievement.

By this time, a major technical development had been provided to all Eighth Air Force fighter pilots. It was called a "pressure suit," and it consisted of a pair of long trousers with attached suspenders, to be worn over the pilots' regular flying clothes. The trousers functioned to put pressure on the legs and lower bodies of the fliers to keep their blood from rushing from their upper bodies, and especially their heads, when they pulled out of fast dives or made very tight turns at speed.

When a pilot pulls out of a fast dive, either in pursuit of a bandit or after a dive-bombing run, the gravity force is multiplied. This is called "Gs," for G-force. So, coming out of such a dive, a pilot might pull five or six "Gs" — five or six times the normal force of gravity. The problem is that pulling that kind of G-force draws the blood down and away from his brain. The result can be partial or total blackout, causing the pilot to lose control of his airplane. So he may, and often does, crash. The standard way to prevent this was to lean forward and yell, forcing the blood to stay up by countering the force of gravity. It was crude, and not always effective. Even when effective, it took the pilot's attention away from what he was doing just when he needed most to be paying attention.

The G-suit was designed to counteract this condition, and to make it unnecesary for the pilot to bend over and scream. It worked on compressed air, and the control worked in response to the Gs being pulled: the more Gs, the more air pressure was pumped into the G-suit, and the more pressure the suit put on the legs and lower body of the pilot. It worked, although it did nothing to increase the comfort of the pilot.

In fact, there was a serious problem for the pilots when they started wearing G-suits. Using the "Pilot Relief Tube" for urination in flight was extremely difficult *without* the G-suit. With it on, doing so was impossible. Often, therefore, in addition to the agony of dinghy-butt, a pilot would suffer the agony of needing desperately to relieve himself, and having no way to do so except for the unacceptable alternative of wetting himself.

The day that the securing of Ghent and its airport was announced, the briefing was unusually long. This resulted in a shorter than usual time between briefing and take-off. Ed, along with some others, skipped the usual last-minute visit to the latrine, since as flight leader he had to be promptly ready for take-off.

A long mission, escorting 17s to Nuremberg, was their job that day. Except for the usual flak, it was a milk-run. No enemy fighters were seen, even that deep in enemy territory. By the time the group was scheduled to leave the bombers, not far from Frankfurt, Ed's bladder felt ready to explode. As planned during briefing, the group had spread out, with each flight to make its own way back to base. Ed was in agony as he led his flight across the Belgian border. He had already used every technique he could, such as not thinking about it—an impossibility due to the pain—and trying to squeeze the muscles of his urinary tract tight. He'd fumbled with the Pilot Relief Tube, but with his G-suit on, using it was impossible.

Ghent was just ahead. He could see the large airport with transport planes landing and taking off. "White Leader to White Number Two. I have to take care of something here. Take over and lead the flight home," he said on the radio. Then he pulled out of the formation and turned directly to the airport. He saw the windsock and the landing pattern being used. A C-47 was starting its approach, but it was far from the edge of the field. Ed knew he could cut in ahead of the C-47, land, and clear the runway well before the C-47 touched down. He pulled around in front of the C-47, lined up with the runway, and rocked his wings in apology to the transport's pilot.

He made a good, fast landing, rolled almost to a stop, turned off the runway onto grass, set the brakes, climbed out, and relieved himself. Just then a jeep driven by a WAAC raced at him. He finished, climbed in, waved to the WAAC—who appeared to be laughing—taxied back to the end of the runway and took off. He passed well over the C-47, which was now at the far end of the runway, safely on the ground. Much relieved, he flew on to his home base, fully expecting to be reprimanded for his unauthorized stop. To his surprise, nothing was said to him about it. When he told the others why he had stopped and what he had done, there was a big laugh. Even the colonel could not help laughing.

As Allied forces continued their advance eastward, fighting all the way, the group continued its missions. It was clear that the U.S. and English air forces dominated the air space all over Europe. In spite of this, the Nazis continued to put up significant numbers of fighters to attack Allied bombers and fighters, but they no longer had enough planes to cover all targets on any day. Their strategy now was to concentrate all the fighters they could muster in one or two areas. On one escort mission late in August, Ed's group was attacked by a swarm of FW-190s and ME-109s. In the fighting, as Ed and his wingman were closing in on a 190, another 190 broke away from its attack on the bombers and came directly at Ed from his right side. The bandit had a slight altitude advantage over Ed, and lowering his nose while turning to his right, he was able to get in a good deflection shot. Three of his slugs hit Princess Pat in the tail, damaging Ed's rudder control in such a way that his ability to turn left was reduced. Ed's wingman went after the 190 and got it. Ed called his Number Three and told him to take over; then he headed for home.

Seeing heavy cloud cover not far to the west, Ed went straight for it. There he'd be relatively safe from enemy planes, who were always on the lookout for lone, crippled Allied planes.

Once in the clouds, he took a heading of 270 degrees, knowing that that would take him across the Channel and over some part of England. Flying straight was not a problem, nor was making right turns. But going left was. He could not get the left rudder bar to move enough to give him very much of a turn. The torque of the engine helped. He used it as much as he could.

After flying due west for the amount of time he calculated would take him to England, he started to let down in a right spiral to break through the solid overcast in order to get himself oriented, and determine what heading to take to get home. He broke out of the clouds and at that moment anti-aircraft fire began to pop around him. "I can't still be over enemy territory," he said to himself. He made evasive moves to the right, changing altitude and turning continuously. Glancing down, he could see that he was over a large city. He looked ahead and saw a vertical cable extending upward into the clouds. He avoided it, then saw another one. The flak continued. Now it dawned on him that he had blundered into the air space over London, and that the cables were tethering barrage balloons, put there to prevent enemy aircraft from coming into that air space. As far as the gunners on the ground could tell, he might very well be a German about to attack the city.

Instead of attempting to climb back into the clouds since that would slow him — making him a better target for the gunners — he went into a zig-zagging dive, increasing his speed. His leftward zigs were not very good, but he managed to avoid the firing, which seemed half-hearted, probably due to the gunner recognizing that his was not a German plane. He dodged around a few more cables, then was out of the area. Maintaining an altitude of 1,000 feet, well below the clouds, he flew toward E. Wretham. Familiar landmarks told him he was nearing home. Circling the field to the right, he called the Tower, telling them of his problem, then saying, "I will come in in a rectangular pattern, making only right turns." Clearance to land was given immediately, and he got in with no trouble; he used right rudder and left brake to keep straight once his wheels were on the ground. The left-pulling torque minimized use of the brake.

After parking, Ed told Al of the problem, went in for debriefing, and then on to the hall. Al found that one of the German slugs had bent some metal in such a way that the left rudder cable was binding, causing the turning problem. It was easily repaired, and Princess was ready to go again.

Near the end of September, Ed completed the hours for his first combat tour. Grant still needed more hours to complete his. C.S. arranged things so Ed could fly missions on a voluntary basis. Whenever he wanted to go, he would schedule him. Otherwise, his time was his own to do whatever he wished. At first, he enjoyed his new freedom. He used the time to visit Cambridge and London, and to try to locate friends from cadet days at other bases in England. After a week of this, though, he began missing flying with the others, so he began to sign up for most of the group's trips.

Meanwhile, C.S. was given a month's leave. He returned to the States. His replacement, Major Stuart, had no combat experience, but he was an excellent pilot who had been instructing at the Training Command. The men liked him, but of course they missed C.S.

From Major Stuart's point of view, it was unfortunate that in all the missions on which he led the squadron through October, no enemy fighters were encountered. He was greatly worried that he'd be going back to Training Command without having fired his guns. He did not like this, and all the other pilots knew it. He mentioned it frequently, but the others didn't see that they could do anything about it. It was the luck of the draw.

November came, clear and cold. On the fourth day of the month, the group was scheduled to escort B-17s to Muenster. After briefing, when the pilots had put on their G-suits, Mae Wests, and backpack parachutes, Major Stuart pulled Ed aside and said, "Damn it, Ed, Major Irvine'll be back soon, and I'll have to go back to the States without ever firing my guns. I don't want to do that!"

"I understand that," Ed responded. "Maybe we'll have some action today."

"Not if it's like every mission I've been on so far. It's been milk-run after milk-run."

"That's the way it goes sometimes. But we know the Germans still have the capability of putting planes in the air. We just haven't been in the right place lately. You never know when they'll hit you. Could happen today or tomorrow; I guess we'll just have to wait and see what turns up.'"

"I'm running out of time; I'd like to make something happen."

"What do you mean?"

Pulling Ed farther away from the others, the major lowered his voice. "I'd like for you and me to pull out of formation after we leave the bombers, and look for targets of opportunity. Something we can strafe. We can tell our flights that we'll be leaving them. Tell them before we take off. What do you say?"

"What do I say! I say that's always fun, Sir. But you know Wing Command has a standing order against doing that unless they authorize it."

"I know, Ed, but let's do it anyway. It may be my only chance to shoot at something besides a practice target. Anyway, you've finished your tour; you're here voluntarily now. So what do you say?"

"My having finished a tour won't make any difference if we are called up on charges! You've got me worried, Major. So what I say is, you're my CO."

"You mean, if I tell you to do it, you'll do it?"

"Yes, Sir. I obey orders from anyone with authority to give me orders. You order me to do it, I'll do it."

"Okay, I'm ordering it. When you see me leave my flight, you break off too."

"Okay," Ed said, and they left for their planes. "Hi, Sir," Al greeted him. "Princess is all set for you." "Good, Al, thanks. I think she'll have a good workout today."

"You've given her a lot of those, Sir. You've got more combat hours than most."

"Princess has been great. You've kept her in great shape."

"Except for that one time when she poured out oil, Sir."

"That was no fault of yours, Al. We just got a bad rebuild job on that engine. When we got the new engine, she was fine. I'm beginning to wonder if I've been in combat too long. I don't even know what the date is today."

"I'm not sure either, Sir. Let me check the maintenance record on Princess. Here it is. Today is the 4th."

"Thanks, Al. November 4th, 1944. Well, I better get going. See you later," and Ed cranked up Princess and taxied out to lead his flight in take-off.

As Major Stuart had feared, the mission did turn out to be a milk-run. The group left the bombers well east of the Zeiter Zee, and Ed saw his CO leave his flight. Ed had arranged for his Number Three to take over, so he broke off and followed Major Stuart heading south. Increasing his speed, Ed pulled even with the major, but about an eighth of a mile away. They were at about 18,000 feet, both watching the skies for enemy fighters while scanning the land below for possible targets to strafe. Ed checked his well-marked map to be sure they were beyond the bomb-line. Anything that might be of use to enemy forces would be a suitable and legitimate target. Ed did not agree with the view that even livestock—cows, sheep, pigs, chickens—should be destroyed because they provided food for the armies of Hitler's Third Reich. Ed had avoided such targets after his first few choo-choos because, he reasoned, the civilians needed that food, even though some of it would likely become provisions for the enemy's forces.

With so many missions behind him, and because the group had not encountered enemy planes with any frequency lately, Ed had become casual—too casual—about flying over enemy territory. He simply followed Stuart's lead, not paying sufficient attention to altitude or to the terrain below them.

Now headed in a southeasterly direction, and not having noticed that they had dropped down to 15,000 feet, he felt a little hitch in his engine. It was turning over fine, and all his gauges read in the okay area, but there was some little feeling of something not being right in the engine. Thoughtlessly, he stopped being as watchful as he should have been. He stopped paying full attention to the sky and ground, even the altitude at which they were flying. As the most experienced of the two pilots, he had a special responsibility to be extra alert. But casually—as if over England, not enemy territory—he put his head down and forward toward the instrument panel, trying to hear more clearly the sound of his engine. He added and reduced throttle and changed the mixture control while watching his gauges, as if he were on a test run.

He stayed that way too long. Abruptly, flak explosions surrounded him. Beginning evasive moves, he glanced at his altimeter: 10,000 feet! What a mistake! In a diving turn to the left, he glanced down and saw that he was in as bad a place as it was possible to be: directly over a large German aerodrome. In spite of his maneuvers, his engine was hit. It stopped and would not restart. He prepared to bail out, then he was hit by shell fragments, which knocked him unconscious.

Major Stuart saw Ed's canopy fly off and Princess roll over and start to lose altitude. No sign of Ed or of his parachute appeared. "Come on, Ed!" the major yelled. But Ed's plane continued toward earth, disappearing into the mist. No sign of Ed or a chute. Once clear of the space over the aerodrome, Stuart dove toward the area where he estimated Ed's ship should be. He saw no sign of it, of a parachute, or of Ed. "No way he got out, and no place to land. Sorry!"

In the bar after debriefing, Major Stuart toasted Ed. "I hope he survived, but I doubt it. A good man—one of the best I've known. It was typical of him that after finishing a tour, he volunteered to fly more missions. This was one of them. May he fly with angels." There was a prolonged silence as all the pilots raised their glasses in salute, and downed their drinks.

PRISONER OF WAR

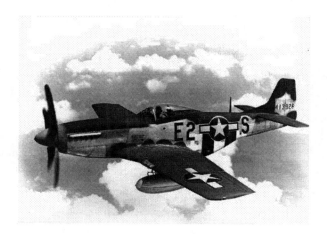

27

When Ed came to, he was in the sidecar of a German motorcycle, driven by a German soldier of the Wehrmacht. They were stopped at a railroad siding beside a baggage car which had been converted to a canteen. The driver was speaking to two uniformed young ladies. They responded by giving him two cups of hot ersatz coffee and two slices of rough black bread. The soldier-driver returned to the motorcycle and held out one cup and a slice of bread to Ed. Feeling very hungry, but also very woozy, Ed took the cup and the bread and put them in front of him on the metal top of the sidecar. Using both of his shaking hands, Ed tried to get the cup to his lips. Every part of him seemed to hurt. On the first try, he hit his chin with the cup. Pain shot through the chin, and he spilled some of the coffee down his front. With further pain, he lifted the slice of bread and gently bit off a bite. Chewing was too painful, so he let the bread dissolve in his mouth; then, with more discomfort, he swallowed it. Trying again, he was able to sip some of the hot coffee. Now he became aware that night had fallen. This accounted for his being hungry enough that the rough bread and false coffee tasted good. The night was cold, and the hot liquid felt good going down.

The German soldier reached for Ed's cup. Having no idea what the German word for 'more' was, Ed pulled the cup back, shaking his head and pointing into the cup. The soldier shrugged, not understanding. Ed pantomimed pouring into the cup. Now the soldier grinned and grunted, "Nein," and snatched the cup, returning it to the young ladies in the railroad car.

When the driver returned to the motorcycle, Ed put his hands between his legs and said, "Pissen," hoping this word would mean something to the German. The soldier laughed. "Ja," he said, and indicated that Ed should get out and do it. The German went to a tree and relieved himself as well.

Now Ed found that any effort to move sent jolts of pain through his back, his pelvic area, his legs, neck, and jaws. He made several efforts to get up and out, without success. The German finished at the tree. Turning, he saw Ed's efforts. Stepping to the sidecar, he put his hands under Ed's armpits and hoisted him up and out. Unable to put one foot in front of the other, Ed leaned his back against the sidecar, opened his fly, and relieved himself.

Finished, he started to turn back to the sidecar when a wave of pain swept over him, and his surroundings seemed to swirl around him. He gripped the sidecar to keep from falling.

"Was?" the German said as he caught Ed's arm, "Kommen Zie." With that, he again hoisted Ed up and onto the edge of the sidecar. Fighting unconsciousness, Ed forced his legs around and over the rear part of the car, then into the opening. Then, with another horrific jolt of pain, he slid down onto the seat, where he immediately blacked out.

When consciousness returned, the soldier and another man—who turned out to be a policeman—were lifting him, not very gently, out of the sidecar. One on each side they carried him, feet dragging, into a building and down a flight of stone steps, along a dank corridor, and into a jail cell. As they entered the building, Ed looked up and saw "Rhine" carved into the stone arch above the entrance.

The door was closed and locked behind Ed, and he was alone, standing, steadying himself with a hand against the cold stone wall beside the door.

A faint light from the corridor came through a barred opening above the door. Looking around, he saw that there was no bed or bunk of any kind. No chair, stool, or table; just the bare stone floor. At one end he could discern a pit of some sort. Using the wall to support himself, he inched his way toward the pit, thinking it might be some sort of bed. When he was closer, he could see straw in the pit. For a moment he thought that it might be a bed, but when he got closer, the smell rising from the straw made it clear that it was some sort of toilet, not a bed. With his right shoulder against the wall he urinated on the straw; then inched his way to the opposite end of the cell to get away from the smell.

Feeling light-headed and hurting all over, he put his back against the corner of the two walls and slowly eased himself into a sitting position on the floor, leaning back against the wall. He wondered what time of night it was. Looking at his left wrist for the first time, he saw that his watch had been removed and that his sleeve was stiff with blood, apparently from a scabbed wound on his wrist. Fearful that everything had been stripped from him, he felt for his dog tags. Relieved, he felt them on the chain around his neck. The silver identifi-cation bracelet that Pat had sent him was gone, as were the coins and keys he had had in his pockets. His dog tags and his wings, still pinned on his shirt, were all that he'd been left with. Then he found that his collar insignia, silver bar, and Air Corps insignia were still there. Even his .45 automatic was gone, along with his sunglasses, helmet, mask, gauntlets, everything. "I wonder what happened to Princess?" he thought.

Fortunately, his captors had left his torn and bloody flight jacket on him, for there was no heat in the cell. Lonely, cold, and in pain, he folded his arms over his chest, trying to hug his own body heat to himself. He fell again into unconsciousness.

When he came to again, he could see daylight through a barred window high up on the wall opposite the door. He heard voices speaking in German, and faces appeared at the win-dow. Word had apparently gotten around the village that an American prisoner was being held in the jail, for new faces appeared at the window as others left. Some of the people pointed at him and laughed; others gave angry looks and made obscene gestures at him, while a few spat into the cell. "No wonder it's so cold in here," he thought. "No glass in the window."

If anything, he was hurting even more now than he had been the preceding evening. With great pain, he used the two walls and managed to raise himself to a standing position, then made his way to the straw pit to relieve himself. Just as he finished, the door swung open and a uniformed guard put a mug of tea—with another slice of the brown bread rest-ing on top of it—on the floor beside the door. He left, locking the door behind himself.

Ed inched himself past the door and the cup and bread, back to his corner, where he again lowered himself to the floor.

Using his hands on the floor, he was able to move back to the cup and bread. The tea was hot, and he was grateful. The bread had a thin spreading of margerine on it. In spite of the pain that biting and swallowing gave him, he devoured both.

"What will they do with me now?" he wondered. "And will I ever get any medical atten-tion?" He heard the cell door being unlocked, and two Wehrmacht soldiers came in. One of them said something in German. Since he did not understand, Ed made no response. The second soldier then said the same thing, louder and slower, making hand motions that seemed to mean "get up." Ed started his slow, painful rising process, sliding his back against the wall. He got no help from the Germans, but finally he was standing and leaning against the wall.

One soldier stepped through the door, saying, "Kommen!" while motioning for Ed to follow. Ed inched his way to the door and leaned on the jamb. The soldier behind him pushed him to hurry him. If the one in the corridor had not caught him, he would have fallen face down. Now they seemed to understand that Ed could not walk, so they took hold of him and half-carried, half-dragged him through the corridor, up the stone steps, and through the entrance to the street. A military truck was at the curb, with what he later learned was a charcoal burner mounted on the front. He was to learn that the Germans, lacking adequate petroleum supplies, had developed methods of using a variety of fuels for civilian and behind-the-lines military purposes to conserve gasoline for their military actions.

A crowd of townspeople had gathered on the sidewalk, most of them giving Ed unfriendly glares, and several wagging fingers at him. Several started to gather spit in their mouths to spit in his direction, but the soldiers spoke sharply to them and they moved back, making a pathway to the curb. Some of the bystanders poked Ed with their fingers as the guards helped him toward the truck. One especially irate woman snatched at one of the tears in his jacket, tearing it further. Again one of the guards barked at the civilians, and they moved farther back. The Wehrmacht men hoisted him up to the bed of the truck, where he ended on his hands and knees. He dragged himself forward, away from the open rear of the truck, and managed to work his way to a sitting position on one of the side benches. He was grateful that the canvas cover hid him from the crowd of civilians and hoped that it would keep the cold air from freezing him once they were underway.

One guard climbed into the truck and the other closed the tailgate. The one inside closed and secured the canvas at the rear, then sat on the bench opposite Ed, resting his rifle between his knees. Reaching into a pocket, he brought out a small cardboard box of cigarettes and a packet of matches. In what Ed thought was a great gesture of friendliness, he held out the packet to Ed. It was such a friendly act that Ed was tempted to accept a cigarette, even though he didn't smoke, just to show his gratitude. Instead he smiled, which caused his lips and jaws to hurt, and used two of the few German words he knew, "Nein, danke."

The German shrugged, gave him a half-smile and said, "Bitte," then lit his own cigarette, leaning back with his eyes half closed, and exhaled slowly.

Now the truck's engine clattered loudly and they moved with a jerk, forcing Ed to put both hands on the bench to avoid being thrown off. He wondered why a full-sized truck should be used to transport a single prisoner. This question was answered about ten minutes later, when the truck came to a stop and the guard opened the rear canvas flap to let twenty-four more noisy Wehrmacht soldiers climb aboard. They crowded onto the benches, and Ed found himself with rough uniform sleeves over muscular arms pressing painfully against his own arms. Although uncomfortable, the body heat produced by the warmly clad newcomers made him warm for his first conscious moment since coming to in the motorcycle.

One German, sitting directly opposite Ed, stared at him for a few moments, then, apparently having a little English, asked, "Flier?"

Ed nodded and said, "Ja."

Looking surprised, the soldier said, "Sprechen Sie Deutsch?" "Nein," Ed said, shaking his head. "British?" the soldier asked. Ed shook his head too hard and winced as pain stabbed in his neck. He felt sweat prickle on his head. For a moment he thought he would pass out, but his vision cleared and he was all right.

"Amelican?" the "r" came out as "l."

"Ja," Ed replied, holding his head steady.

The man then spoke rapid German to the others. Some laughed, while others just glared at Ed. "I'll be in trouble if these guys get nasty," he thought.

Ed's guard snapped out a few words, and the soldiers paid no more attention to Ed. They talked to each other as the truck rumbled on.

After about an hour, the truck stopped again, and Ed could hear a brief exchange between the driver and someone outside the truck. After moving a short distance forward, the truck stopped. All the soldiers jumped or climbed out. Ed's guard stood in front of him. "Scheisen? Pissen?" he asked. Ed nodded. When some of the soldiers returned, the guard spoke to them, and two helped Ed out of the truck and into a latrine. Since he had not had a chance for a bowel movement since the morning before, back at the base, he was pleased to see a row of stools in the clean, antiseptic-smelling latrine. He relieved himself, used the harsh toilet paper, flushed, and was again assisted back into the truck and to his seat. Half of the soldiers did not return, so he assumed they had been assigned to duty at this place, which was obviously a military base.

Another hour went by; now the interior of the truck became much too warm. The sun was beating down on the canvas cover, adding to the heat of the bodies. Not sure he could get his jacket on again if he managed to take it off, Ed decided just to unzip it. One of the men opened the rear canvas, and this helped. After a few minutes more, the truck stopped again. All the soldiers started to leave, but once again the guard spoke, and two remained to help Ed out. He was put on a bench outside a neatly painted, sizeable wooden building. The soldiers went in, leaving Ed and the two guards on the bench.

After a wait of about five minutes, the two guards helped Ed into the building and seated him and themselves at a small table away from the long tables at which all the soldiers from the truck, as well as many others, were eating. "Essen?" one of the guards asked.

"Ja," Ed said, starting to nod vigorously, then stopped as the pain shot through his neck, jaws, and shoulders. Soon three plates, cups, knives, forks, and spoons were brought. Each plate held boiled potatoes, sauerkraut—with what looked like pieces of bacon mixed in—and two slices of the black bread; each cup was full of ersatz coffee. Famished, and half afraid his plate would be snatched away, Ed accepted the pain and crammed the food into his mouth as fast as he could, sipping the hot coffee to help him get the food down. He thought no meal had ever tasted better. As he finished, he noticed that he had been served exactly the same things and amounts as the guards and the rest of the soldiers, and he was grateful.

When they finished, the two guards helped Ed out and across the street to a latrine, where all three used the urinals. Outside again, the guards put Ed into the rear seat of a black four-door sedan, with one guard beside him and the other in the front beside the driver. He saw no insignia, but the car looked to him like an American Cheverolet, 1938 or 1939 vintage. He was feeling good about his treatment so far, and wondered how long it would last. Only the lack of medical attention bothered him. Just as the car started to move a wave of pain more intense than the earlier ones came over him and he passed out with his head on the seat back.

When he came back to consciousness he found that he had slumped to his right, and his head was against the door's window. It was an extremely uncomfortable position. Although the intense pain he had felt just before losing consciousness had subsided, everything else seemed to be hurting more than before. "I've got to pass out in a better position," he thought wryly, as he painfully straightened up.

The Chevy pulled up in front of what looked like a tiny military outpost. It consisted of a small office building, an even smaller building with a barred window on one side, and just beyond that an outhouse. The guard from the front seat went into the small office, then came out with what Ed thought looked like an officer, who unlocked and opened the small building with the barred window.

Ed was locked in the tiny building. Except for a three-legged stool, and being smaller, this cell was like the one he had occupied in Rhine. This one had wooden walls and floor. There was the smelly, straw-filled pit. He made his way to the stool and eased himself onto it as the last of the day's sun shone through the bars of the window. "Looks like another cold, sitting-up night," he thought dismally.

He slept fitfully with continuing pain, at times waking without being sure whether he had been unconscious or asleep. Everything seemed blurred together. The one constant was pain. Added to his general muscular and skeletal pain, he now became aware of a sharp, throbbing pain in his left thumb. He was unaware of when it was done, or by whom, but the thumb had been tightly bound with adhesive tape. He held the thumb to his nose and sniffed. It smelled very rank. "I don't know what's the matter with it," he thought, "but I don't think the tight tape is good for it, whatever it is." Dim light was coming through the window from a night-light outside the office door. By shifting his position, he was able to get enough light on his aching thumb to find the end of the tape. Gritting his teeth, he pulled the tape loose, unwound it, and exposed his thumb.

What he saw, and smelled, was a putrid mass of blood and pus where the thumbnail should have been. Evidently the nail had been torn off when whatever happened to him after he lost consciousness in the air happened, injuring the thumb. Apparently no antiseptic had been applied, just the tight taping, probably because the injury was bleeding. Now it was badly infected. "Don't know when, if ever, anybody is going to give this any attention, but certainly air will be better for it than the tape. If they ever take me to another latrine with running water, I'll at least wash it off. It feels better without the tape." He fell asleep, wondering if anybody in his group, or more importantly back home, knew he was alive.

Bright morning had already come when the door opened, and the inevitable cup of tea and piece of bread were put down beside the door. After making his way to the pit and relieving himself, he returned to the cup and bread. He could not walk in the normal way, but he had found by experimenting that he could move to either side by keeping his feet together and turning the toes to the side, then the heels, and by alternating toes and heels, he could, with a minimum of extra pain, get from place to place. He used this technique first to get to the pit, then back to his breakfast. Sliding his back down the wall, he sat on the floor and ate and drank his bread and tea.

Soon after the mug was removed, one of his guards came, opened the door, and said, "Kommen mit mir." Ed struggled to his feet and using his new technique, moved through the doorway. "Gut," the guard grunted, then added, "Nebengebäude," and pointed to the outhouse. Ed made his way to the hut, used it, and then as he stepped out, he saw two nuns coming up the road pulling a child's coaster wagon.

When the two nuns came up to the little cluster of buildings, they spoke with the guard. Ed guessed one nun to be about fifty years of age, and the other perhaps twenty-five. The older one turned to Ed and said in halting English, "Bad hurt? Need hospital? Ve take zie."

Ed replied, "Yes, Sister. I'm hurt. A hospital would be good. But I can't walk. How would I get there?"

The nun smiled, pointing to the wagon, "Ve dake, ookay?"

Ed laughed, even though it hurt, and said, "Ooky, ma'am."

The sisters turned the wagon around so it headed down the rough road, then with one on each side of him, eased him into a sitting position on the wagon, with his legs sticking out over the pull handle in front. In spite of their care, the ride down the rough road was painful for their passenger. He had to grip the sides of the wagon to keep from either falling off to one side, or falling back, with his back jarring against the hard lip of the wagon. Soon they were down and off the rough road and onto the smoother street of the village. There the going was much easier and smoother.

Pulling and pushing—the older one breathing heavily—the nuns took Ed up a hill to a small two-story tan brick building, and in through the front door. A tall, slender man of about forty, looking and acting very much like a doctor, met them in the lobby. After conferring with the nuns, the doctor said in passable English, "The sisters want to have you x-rayed. They will take you to the x-ray room."

Down the corridor they went, and Ed was assisted onto a medical table, where an x-ray machine was placed above him. It was on tracks, and they moved it several times over his abdomen and chest. Then the nuns turned him over on his stomach, and did the same thing with the machine over his back.

They helped him back onto the wagon. They thanked the doctor, then retraced their route to the little outpost. Ed said, "Danke schön" to the sisters, and went to his cell. "You jerk," he said to himself after the sisters had left, "why didn't you think of asking them to put something on your thumb?" He never heard anything more from the doctor, the nuns, or the hospital. He suspected that no pictures were actually taken with the machine, and that in case there was an investigation, the Germans could say that he had had medical attention. He was grateful for the efforts of the sisters, but the entire undertaking had done nothing for his painful injuries. Nonetheless, it was good to be outside, not under guard.

Not long after the nuns left, Ed passed out in his cell. Fortunately, he was sitting on the floor, or his injuries might have been made more serious by the fall. He came to at the sound of the door opening. A bowl of soup, made with a green, leafy vegetable that looked a lot like cattle fodder and a few pieces of potato was put down. It was hot, and, in spite of its looks, it tasted good. With it was another slice of the black bread and a cup of tea. He gulped all of it down, then sat on the stool in the corner to try to figure out where he was and where he might be taken. He also continued to wonder why he was not getting any meaningful medical attention. He had, after all, been in a civilian hospital, and no effort was made at treatment.

He dozed on the stool, wishing he had something to read or a radio to listen to. Or better yet, someone to talk to. When he woke up, he could tell by the fading sunlight and the cooling air that the day was nearly over. "Another miserable night on this hard, cold floor," he thought. Once again the door opened, and a cup of tea and two slices of black bread were placed inside. He ate and drank all of it.

After relieving himself in the smelly pit, he slid down in his corner and, exhausted, fell asleep. It seemed to him that he had just fallen asleep when the door opened, and his guard barked, "Aufwachen, Amerikanischer! Kommen!" He used the stool to boost himself to his feet. Through the open door he could see the blackness of night, and as he moved himself slowly out toward a waiting truck, the faint sound of a bell came from the direction of the village where the hospital was. He counted twelve strokes. At the tailgate of the truck he stopped, and the two guards hoisted him up and in. Just as before, one guard climbed in and closed the canvas flap at the rear; the other slammed the tailgate into place, stomped around the truck, and climbed into the cab.

Some ten minutes later, the truck stopped. Grumbling voices, speaking what could only be cursing and complaining, grew louder, and eighteen Wehrmacht soldiers climbed in and seated themselves, still muttering curses. With eighteen instead of the previous twenty-four, there was less crowding, but also less body heat. Ed felt as if the cold penetrated to the core of his being. These German soldiers, with their greatcoats, boots, gloves, and earmuffs on their hats, seemed to be feeling the cold. So Ed was not surprised that he, wearing only his torn flight jacket, with no hat of any kind and no gloves, felt almost frozen.

Just as he was beginning to feel some of the heat from the other men take the edge off the cold, and to appreciateiate it, sirens sounded and the truck came to a halt. All of the Wehrmacht men—except one of Ed's guards—jumped out and got into the ditch at the side of the road. The siren, obviously an air raid warning, continued to wail. The rear flap had been left open, so Ed shuffled to the rear of the truck and looked out. He could hear but could not see what had to be heavy bombers. "Has to be the RAF," he thought. "Come on you guys, let 'em have it!"

Now powerful searchlights began to beam upward, playing this way and that, then finding and fixing on the bombers, following them. Flak guns began to boom, with echoing booms in the sky, as their shells exploded around the airplanes. Parachute flares were dropped, lighting up the entire countryside, including the truck in which Ed stood in excitement, and his guard trembled in fear.

In the light of the flares, Ed could see the bombs dropping from the airplanes. The earth shook as the bombs began to detonate at what Ed estimated was no more than a half-mile away. He began to see the glow of fires started by the bombs. In his excitement, he began to cheer out loud. "Go, you Brits! Give' em hell! Blast 'em off the . . ." He stopped when the guard raised his rifle with the butt aimed right at Ed's head. "Okay, okay, I'll be quiet," he said. The guard lowered his gun.

The show was over. The flares faded out, and the sound of the bombers was soon gone. Whatever the target had been, it was now in flames, lighting up the sky. As the Germans climbed back into the truck, Ed's guard moved and sat next to him. The soldiers were cursing again, and some of them were looking angrily at Ed. The guard obviously saw it as his duty to protect his prisoner. Ed felt what was close to affection for the man, the only possible ally he had in this setting of animosity.

As the truck rolled on, stopping now and again to drop off four of the soldiers, tensions decreased and Ed felt safer than he had before, although he still appreciated his guard's presence beside him. Shortly after the last of the soldiers left the truck, Ed felt the truck again come to a stop. He heard voices up front. The rear flap and tailgate were opened, and the guard said, "Kommen!" and climbed out. Ed sat at the end of the truck bed and his two guards hoisted him down.

They led him into what was apparently a field hospital—a primitive one. A powerful stench met them at the door. Ed almost vomited. The room was dimly lit, but he could see rows of bunks with men, all with bandages, and some with arms or legs held up by pulley ropes. Most of the stench was coming from a man who had, evidently, been wounded in the kidneys. This hospital was clearly not equipped to do any repair work on him. He was suspended in a hammock-like contraption, with an opening through which discharge from his kidneys dripped into a bucket. He was moaning almost continuously, as were ten or so others. Medical corpsmen were moving about, doing what they could for the moaning men. To Ed, it was a nightmare of sights and sounds and smells, a phantasmagora of misery. "Hope they aren't going to put me in here," Ed said to himself. "I'd rather have no treatment at all than stay here."

It was soon clear that he was not there as a patient, but only to be given a bunk. He hoped it was only for one night. A bunk to sleep on was welcome though, even in this gruesome place. He was asleep as soon as his head hit the pillow. In the morning, he could see by the patients' uniforms and the sounds of those well enough to talk, that this was not a hospital for Germans, but for enemies of Germany. Now he was truly worried that he might be kept in this inadequate facility for treatment.

As he expected, an orderly brought him the usual slice of bread and cup, but this time it was not tea. Instead, it was ersatz coffee, just like he had had in the motorcycle sidecar. It was hot, and it tasted good, but he was still hungry after finishing it.

When the orderly returned to take his cup, Ed attempted to show him his thumb, hoping he would put something on it to halt the infection. The orderly shook his head vigorously, and hurried away.

His guards came and got him and took him out of the building to a small toilet where, he was glad to see, there was a single faucet of running water. After using the toilet, he washed his thumb as well as he could, and let it air dry.

His guards came and got him and put him into a small military vehicle, a German version of the American jeep. One guard sat in front with the driver; the other with Ed in the rear. The day's trip was not very long. At midafternoon they pulled into a tidy, clean military-looking post. A high fence with barbed wire at the top surrounded the entire post. All around the fence were elevated guard stands at intervals. In each stand was a guard with a sub-machine gun. The gate was guarded too, and had to be opened by armed guards before the jeep could pass through.

After helping Ed out of the jeep and up three steps, the guards opened a door, stepped into an office, then snapped to attention and gave the Nazi salute plus a "Heil Hitler" to a Wehrmacht officer, who returned the salute. Ed made his way into the office while his guards said some German words to the officer, handing him some papers. The officer read the papers quickly, then dismissed the two guards, who smiled at Ed as they passed him, one giving him a surreptitious thumbs-up sign. Then they were gone, and Ed was alone with the officer. The officer spoke to Ed in fair, though accented, English, saying, "Zit down, Leutenant. Vat iss your name?"

"Lieutenant Thorne, Edward J.," Ed answered, and the officer wrote it down in a ledger book.

"Und your zerial number, Leutenant?" Ed gave it to him, and he added it to what he had written in the book. "Now, Leutenant, haf you identivication dags?" Ed pulled his dog tags out from under his shirt and jacket so the officer could see them. He came around the desk, put on glasses, and peered at the tags. "Ja, gut," he said. "Now, Leutenant Toren," he continued, resuming his seat behind the desk, "I am Hauptmann Zimmerman, commandant of dis vork camp. You vill be here for zeveral dayss. Ve vill put you in ein ach—a bunk in ze vorkers haus, yust dere, trough dat door. Zo lonk ass you behafe yourzelf, you vill shtay dere. If you mizbehafe, ve haff anudder blaze for you, untershtandt?"

"Yes, Sir," Ed replied. "What is this place?"

"De rule iss no quvestions! Put, I vill answer you. Ve are not bad beoble, as your bro-baganda zays. Diss iss a blace for vorkers from die Nederlandts. Dey vork on der varm, making crops for die Tird Reich, undt der Fuhrer. Dey are zafe undt comvordable here. Ve are gut do dem, ven dey behafe," the Hauptmann said. Standing, he turned to a door near his desk and said, "Kommen."

In a long, clean, well-lighted room, Ed saw two rows of bunks, all neatly made, with lockers between the bunks against the wall. The hauptmann led Ed halfway down the row, consulted a sheet of paper, and pointing toward a bunk said, "Here, Diss iss for you."

Ed would have been delighted to have any bunk, but here was one for him in a warm room, with clean pillow and sheets, plus blankets. It was a dream come true. "Thank you, Captain," he said, and sat on the bunk. He was pleased to find it firm.

"Make yoursself gomfortable, Leutenant. Ven de vorkers come, vun off dem vill brink you food," and he marched back to his office. Ed stretched out and fell asleep.

A cool touch on his forehead wakened him and startled, he looked up to see a half-dozen young ladies standing on both sides of his bunk. One of them had her hand on his forehead. When the hauptmann had spoken of "vorkers," Ed had assumed that the workers would be men. It had not occurred to him that they might be women. He tried to sit up, and one woman on each side helped him. He swung his legs over the side of the bed and sat on the edge.

One of the smiling young women put a tray on his lap. On it was a bowl of potatoes and vegetables, with small bits of meat mixed in, along with two thick pieces of black bread spread with margerine, and a cup of tea. He said "Danke," and went to work on the food. All the young ladies laughed and giggled watching him eat. One reached out to touch the stubble of beard on his face. They all giggled and he smiled, painfully, at them. They all seemed to be talking at once, and to him it was gibberish. More young women came in, all crowding around this strange-looking foreigner on one of their bunks. He thought it was bizarre, too, but he did not intend to complain.

Out of the chatter, one or two recognizable words seemed to be repeated at various times. One was something like Americaniche; another sounded like flieger, or fliegend, which he knew from the Wagnerian opera, "Der Fliegende Hollander," meaning flying or flier. Another word said many times seemed to be kriegsgefangener. When he had finished the last swallow of tea and the last bite of bread, the same young woman took the tray away. He decided to try to communicate with these pleasant young women. "Kriegsgefangener? Was ist das?" he asked, hoping his poor attempt at German would be understood.

They looked at each other, then nodded, pointing their fingers at themselves and saying, "Kriegsgefangener." Ed interpreted that to mean they were whatever the word meant, so he made fists with both hands and crossed his wrists as if they were tied, and held them up. "Ja, ja, Kriegesfangen," they said, pointing to him and themselves. To himself, he said, "I guess it means prisoner of war."

Now a somewhat older woman who seemed to have some authority came over from where she had been sitting on a bunk. The others moved aside to allow her to come to the side of Ed's bunk. She spoke slowly, looking for words. "Ja, Mein Herr. Kriegsgefangener iss prisoner. Ve iss prisoners; ve must vork for Die Deutschlanders. Vou iss prisoner alzo. You schlaffen—um, zleep—hier die nacht, ja?"

"Thank you," Ed said. "Where do you come from?"

"Die Nederland, Amsterdam," she replied.

"How long a prisoner?"

She pointed to herself and held up four fingers. "Fur years. Dos udders, ein, schwei, drei," as she pointed to the other ladies. Then to herself again, "fur."

Ed shook his head. "Four years away from your home! That is sad."

She must have understood because she nodded, and her eyes filled with tears.

"Soon Deutschland will be kaput," Ed said. The older lady told the others what he had said. Now several of them had tears, but they all nodded and smiled. "Ja, ja. Deutschland kaput!" they chorused. Now a Wehrmacht soldier, wearing stripes on his sleeve, came in. "Was ist loas!" he said roughly. "Raus! komi" and all the ladies filed out into the other room.

Before long, Ed could hear male voices mixing in with the female ones. Later, there was singing, "They've learned to make the best of their situation," he thought.

Now, sitting alone, not hungry or cold, a vague thought that had flitted through his mind off and on for several days began to crystallize. "It is the duty of a prisoner of war to attempt to escape. If that is not possible, it is his duty to cause the enemy trouble, to harrass him." Something of that sort he had read, or it had been told to him. Now he could see that the window at the end of the barracks opposite the door to the office had no bars.

He struggled to his feet, and using his sideways technique, moved to the window. "Don't know what I'll do if I get out," he thought, "but I have to try." When he got to the window, he found that it was not nailed shut, as he feared, nor even latched. He pulled up on the lower sash, and it moved, not easily, but noisily. He inched it up until he had it open as far as it would go. Using both hands, he hoisted his right leg over the sill. He bent forward to get his head and upper body through.

At that moment, the door opened. One of the young women came into the room, leaving the door open. Seeing Ed halfway out the window, she let out an involuntary "Oh!"

Hearing her exclamation, two of the guards rushed through the doorway. Seeing what was happening, they shouted, "Haldt!" drawing their pistols as they ran to where Ed was.

They grabbed his arms and pulled him back in, then half dragged him to his bunk where they sat him down, not very gently. One of the young ladies ran to the window and closed it.

The hauptmann had been sent for. He hurried in. After speaking to the two guards, he turned to Ed. "Stupidt! Stupidt! Stupidt! Now ve cannot haff you stay in here. Stupidt! If vou gott oudt die vindow, vou vould be shodt! Stupidt!" Turning to the guards, he gave rapid orders. They grabbed Ed, pulled him out of the barracks, and dragged him to a separate small building. The door was unlocked and open, and Ed was pushed in, falling on his knees on the hard floor. One of the guards threw his jacket in after him.

The little room was just like the last cell he had occupied. He sighed. "Well, I blew it! Not only didn't escape, but I sure didn't cause the Germans any trouble, either. Well, at least I didn't get shot." He pulled on his jacket and got ready for another freezing night on the hard, cold floor. "Could have been in that warm room with all those nice Dutch girls. You're a schmuck, Ed. As der hauptmann said, I'm 'Stupidt!'"

An older Wehrmacht guard, perhaps fifty-five or sixty, came to the glassless window. He seemed to know some English words—enough to say, "Hello, Yank. All right?"

"I'm cold," Ed said. The guard looked blank. Ed repeated the word while squeezing his arms across his chest and hunching his shoulders, "cold!"

"Ja. Coldt," the guard said. Then, looking around, he put his face close to the bars and whispered, "Deutschland Kaput! Kaput."

Ed said, "Ja," and nodded.

The German backed away, said, "Gute nacht," and went on his rounds.

"It doesn't help me any but I guess some of them know they're done for. Right now, I'd rather have a blanket than that bit of information." He relieved himself in the straw pit and settled in a corner to try to sleep. Some of his pains had begun to fade, so he felt better than he had since his unintended visit to Germany. He was still unable to walk, and couldn't manage stairs without help, except by sitting down and raising himself one step at a time on his seat. Thinking of the Dutch ladies who had been torn away from their families and forced to work under guard, and wondering how much longer the Nazis would be able to fight, he dozed off. His uncomfortable sleep was fitful. At times he thought he would welcome unconsciousness, but now that he wanted it, it did not come.

At length he did sleep, only to be awakened by the sound of the cell door opening. The inevitable cup of tea and piece of black bread was put down. He got to it and devoured it. The day was sunless, gray, and very cold. Ed moved about his cell as much as he could to try to generate some warmth. It helped.

A different guard, younger than the other—about forty-five, he guessed—looked in the window. No words, just a nasty stare. The guard turned away, muttering what Ed thought was "Schweinhundt." That this is what he said was confirmed, as each time he passed the window he said the same thing. "Well, I've been called worse than a "swine-dog," Ed thought, and continued his efforts at exercise.

At what he estimated should be around noon, the older guard came on duty. His first time past the window, he said, "Guten tag," and kept on his way. Later, he came up to the window, looking carefully around, and handed Ed something wrapped in newspaper. The guard put his finger to his lips, signaling that Ed should not say anything. After opening the paper, Ed held a cooked soup bone with fragments of meat clinging to it. He mouthed "Danke schön" to the guard, who grinned, nodded, and left the window.

"Bless him," Ed thought. "He really risked a lot to do that." He gnawed, licked, and sucked at the bone, getting every bit of grease and fragment of meat off. Finally satisfied that there was no more, he wiped his hands on the paper and wrapped up the bone. "I always knew that all Germans could not be as bad as the movies and newsreels make them look," he thought. "This proves it. He's even in uniform, and look at the risk he took to do something good for the enemy!"

The day dragged on, and another freezing night came. Ed was settling down in his corner to sleep when he heard a vehicle drive up and German voices speaking. He pulled himself up to the window to see what was going on. Whatever it was, it was around the corner and out of his sight. Then he heard two distinctly American voices. "Where in hell is this?" one said.

Another one answered, "Only God knows."

Ed yelled, "Hey, Americans! Who are you? I'm a P-51 pilot in solitary."

The first voice said, "Hi, I'm out of P-47s, and this guy's from a B-17."

He was interrupted by the German voices; then Ed heard the barracks door open and close. No more yelled conversation. "What a relief to hear some Americans," Ed said to himself. "At least I know I'm not the only one here." At that point, the friendly guard came to the window. "Zwell, Yankees. You go domorrow," then he went on his way.

Even though he was excited, Ed soon fell asleep. The morning tea and bread was delivered, and he gulped it down. The friendly German came to the window again, and indicated that Ed should give him the paper and bone. The guard slipped it into his greatcoat pocket and disappeared. After a short time, the guard was back at the window. "You go dis tag, Yankee," and he carefully pushed a loaf of black bread through the bars. With thanks, Ed put the loaf under his jacket, "Wiedersehen," the guard said. "Go mit Gott!" Ed thanked him again, and put his hand through the bars. The guard shook it vigorously, and left.

About an hour passed. Ed picked bites off the loaf of bread, and chewed each one carefully before swallowing it. It was dry, and without something to wash it down, he had trouble getting it down. He heard a vehicle pull up and stop; then the engine was shut off. Soon he heard German voices giving orders, then an American saying, "Okay, okay, Kraut. Don't push, I'm going."

"Hope they don't forget me," Ed thought. Then he yelled, "Hey, P-47! Don't go without me!"

"Okay, 51. But I'm not driving." Then he said, "Hey, Jerry, the other American. What about him?"

Next Ed heard the hauptmann's voice say, "Der stupidt one? Ve vill not vorgedt him, ve vant him oudt off here!"

In a moment Ed's door opened and he moved out. "Jesus! What the hell happened to you?" the larger of the two Americans asked. "Did these krauts do that to you?"

"No, I was pretty shot up. I've been touring Germany for about two weeks. No shower, no shave, no medical attention. You look pretty good," Ed replied.

"Yeah. We both got hit on the same raid. Yesterday. We both bailed out. Not a scratch. The krauts saw us coming down and captured us immediately. I'm Jerry Singletary."

"Ed Thorne," and he took Jerry's hand.

"This is Billy Button. He was a tailgunner on one of the 17s hit in the raid." Ed shook hands with Billy.

Hauptmann Zimmermann said to Jerry and Billy, "Help your comrade. He cannot valk or climb. Helpt him!"

Jerry and Billy went to Ed's sides, and Ed, happy to be in touch with Americans at last, threw both his arms up and over their shoulders, partly in embrace, partly for their help. This pulled his jacket up, and the loaf of bread fell to the ground. The hauptmann snapped, "Ach! Wass ist?" and kicked the bread into the ditch. "Ha! Stupidt! Ve treat you gut, undt you schteal from uz! Stupidt. Ve vill pe gladt ven vou are gone. Go! Go! Go! You are American gangster! Ja, Gangster! Schwein!"

Billy and Jerry helped Ed to the station wagon waiting at the steps of the workers' barracks. They pushed Ed into the third seat and Billy started to climb in with him, but a guard said, "Nein!" and prevented him getting in. Instead, one guard got in beside Ed. Billy was then directed into the second seat, and moved all the way over. Next, the other guard got in, and then Jerry. They were off, not knowing where.

About an hour-and-a-half later, the wagon pulled into a sizeable city. Some vehicles, but mostly pedestrians, crowded the streets and sidewalks. Ed noticed considerable bomb damage as they moved slowly along. Soon the wagon drew up to what was obviously a railway station. They all got out of the wagon, and the Americans were escorted into the station. The guards seated Ed and his new companions on a bench. One guard sat on a bench facing them; the other went through a door marked "(something) Meister."

Soon that guard returned, and the two seated themselves at a table, facing the three prisoners. They placed their briefcases on the table, exchanged a few words, and then the other one got up and left. Shortly he returned, carrying two mugs of beer. They opened their briefcases and pulled out cheese, salami, and bread, pieces of which they cut off with their sheath knives and ate, washing down each bite with a mouthful of the beer.

As the three Americans sat with watering mouths, watching the guards eat, civilians passing by would stare at them or make humorous remarks and laugh. Several of them pointed menacing fingers at them, spat on the floor, and stomped away. At one point a group of seventeen- or eighteen-year-olds stopped in front of them, making threatening gestures and spitting out what could only be obscenities at them. One of the guards wiped his mouth with the back of his hand and shouted at them. The boys hurried on their way.

"Can't blame them," Ed said. "We've been bombing hell out of their country."

"Yeah," Billy agreed. "And we'll keep on doing it' til the crazy bastards give up."

Agreeing, Jerry added, "Good thing we have the guards. If some of these krauts started something, they'd tear us to pieces."

More passengers came into the waiting room, most of them giving the three Americans the same dirty looks and gestures. Hearing the train coming, the guards closed their briefcases and signaled the Americans to get up. They stepped out onto the platform and were immediately surrounded by civilians taunting, cursing, and spitting at them. Finally the two guards raised their rifles and yelled something. The crowd backed off.

The train sputtered, hissed, and banged to a stop, and a uniformed trainman waved the crowd back so passengers could get off the train. Then, spotting the guards and their prisoners, he restrained the crowd while they boarded and took over an empty compartment. No one else was admitted by the guards. There were two bench seats—one facing to the front of the train; the other to the rear. The guards put Jerry on the window end of the front-facing seat, one guard next, and Ed on the end near the door to the corridor. The second guard and Billy had the other bench to themselves, with the guard nearest the door.

They heard a short toot on the whistle, followed by a whistle from a trainman on the platform, and the train moved smoothly forward. Ed, in his excitement at hearing American voices and in anticipation of being moved away from the work camp, had forgotten to make a final use of the straw-pit toilet in his cell. Now he needed relief. As the train got up to speed, he said to the guard beside him, "Pissen?"

Looking disgusted, the guard said, "Gott in himmell" then "ja," and pointed toward the front of the train. The corridor outside the compartment was crowded with people, mostly civilians, but with a uniform here and there.

Ed hoisted himself from his seat, slid the door open, and shuffled out. There was a handrail along the outer wall of the corridor, but Ed could not use it due to the crowd of passengers holding on to it. He bumped into people as he labored to make progress toward the toilet. He staggered as the train swerved in a turn; he would have fallen if there had not been so many others there. Abruptly, a young, blond, neatly uniformed Luftwaffe officer stepped in front of him, blocking his way.

"Oh-oh," Ed thought, "I'm in trouble now!"

"American?" the young German asked, pleasantly.

"Ja," Ed replied.

"Fliegender?"

"Ja."

"Bombers?" He clearly articulated the middle 'b,' unlike Americans, who say 'bommers.'

"Nein."

"Jaegers?"

"Ja," Ed said, assuming this meant 'fighters.'

"Gut, Ich ben jaeger fliegender," and he pointed to the wings on his tunic breast,

"Ja," Ed. said, "pissen!" and made the appropriate gesture.

"Ahl Korn," and he led Ed through the crowd, making a path for him. When they reached the toilet door, he opened and held it for Ed, who hurried in as rapidly as he could. "As long as I'm here," he said to himself, "I might as well sheissen as well as pissen," and laughed as he did so.

Much relieved, he opened the door, and there was the German pilot, with two companions, one of whom spoke fair English. With him as translator, the three of them talked. They were impressed when he informed them that he flew P-51s. "Ach! The Mustang! We know it well. A fine aircraft," they said through the translator. They were ME-109 pilots, and Ed spoke to them of his respect for their airplane. But they said the problem now is fuel. They couldn't get enough, and what they got was poor quality.

Through the translator, they apologized to Ed for his not being given medical attention, or a chance to bathe and shave. "You are being taken to Frankfurt," they told him. "It is a big interrogation center. Der Fuhrer has ordered that no prisoners be given medical attention until they have been interrogated. After interrogation, you will get good medical attention and clean-up facilities. When you are well, we're sorry, but you will be taken to a prisoner-of-war camp."

Just then one of Ed's guards stepped out of the compartment, gave a piercing whistle, and yelled, "American kommen hier!"

The four German pilots laughed and said, "You'd better go. Don't get the Wehrmacht mad at you," then they shook hands and led Ed back to his compartment.

The guard who had called him was behind him. The other was looking at him with a look of amazement on his face. Neither saw Billy give him a signal, pointing to his seat. Ed looked and sat down quickly on what Billy had pointed to. It was the guard's sheath knife. Evidently he had failed to snap the strap that held the handle against the sheath, and it had worked loose and fallen to the seat.

Ed was pleased to get something belonging to a German soldier, in partial compensation for all that they had taken from him, and just to have something—some possession to call his own, since he had nothing. As the train rolled on, he carefully inched the knife up between his legs and into a tear in the outer fabric of his flight jacket. When that was accomplished without the guards seeing what he was doing, he smiled across at Billy, who grinned a broad grin in return. They had accomplished something, small as it was.

By the station clock it was 16:00 when they arrived at a station with signs proclaiming it was "Frankfurt." Ed told Jerry and Billy what the German pilots had said. "Now," Jerry said, "we'll see what happens."

The guards kept them in the compartment until all the other passengers had left, then they took them off the train and along a long platform to where a small bus stood. It was painted the blue-gray of the Luftwaffe. The three were surprised to see that the bus was nearly full of American and British fliers—all, like themselves, prisoners. Ed's two guards handed papers to a Luftwaffe officer after saluting; then they left. In addition to the officer, two armed guards and the driver were in Luftwaffe uniforms. Ed was helped aboard by Billy and Jerry, and the bus moved out.

After some forty-five minutes of maneuvering through the bomb-damaged town—some streets were impassable—the bus was in open country. Before long, it turned in to a compound with several imposing buildings. Up a drive the bus went, then around to the rear of a stark-looking concrete building with a few barred windows. It was isolated from the other buildings. The passengers were hurried out and through a door, then into a large room lined with benches in precise rows for its entire length.

The prisoners were ordered into places and told to remain standing in front of the benches. A P.A. system crackled into life, and an accented voice speaking understandable English said, "You are now at Luftwaffe Interrogation Center and Hospital at Frankfurt. You are prisoners of war, protected by the Geneva Conventions. The Third Reich will abide by those conventions. You will be well-treated as long as you cause no trouble and obey regulations and orders. Punishment will be severe and swift for those who get out of line. Now, strip, leave your clothes on the benches, and go to the showers as directed by the guards. After that, towel off with the towels provided by the Third Reich, then return and put on your clothes."

Along with the others, but more slowly because of his injuries—causing grunted complaints from the nearest guard—Ed stripped and stacked his clothes on a bench with his jacket on the bottom. He shuffled to the shower room, grateful for the abundant hot water, although, because he was late getting in, it was turned off before he had had enough to rinse well. He picked up a large gray towel from a stack and dried, feeling clean for the first time in days. Finished, he shuffled back to his clothes, and wishing he had clean ones, put on his dirty underwear, shirt, and trousers. Then he seated himself on the bench opposite where his jacket was to put on his socks and shoes.

"Hurry up!" came over the P.A. "You will be taken to cells to await interrogation. Food will be brought to your cells. Those who need medical attention will get it after interrogation, if you cooperate."

Ed was hoisting himself to his feet when a fellow prisoner standing beside Ed's jacket, wanting to be helpful, said, "Here you go, Buddy," scooping up the jacket and tossing it to him. Ed grabbed at it desperately, but the knife fell to the floor with a clatter. Two guards were beside him instantly. One put his foot on the knife; the other snatched the jacket and went through the pockets, feeling all around the sleeves and lining of the jacket. He had a look of distaste at having to handle the torn, filthy, blood-caked thing. Satisfied that there was nothing more concealed in it, he gave it back to Ed. The other one picked up the knife, and Ed watched sadly as his "revenge" weapon disappeared out the door.

Double doors swung open and all the prisoners were herded through them. Ed shuffled along at the end, with one guard repeating "Schnell! Schnell!" Ed did his best, and hurting from the effort, was put in a cell. The solid, metal-clad door was slammed to and bolted from the outside. He was happy to see a bunk fastened to the wall, even though it held only a thin mattress. He had not lost consciousness for several days, but now he felt faint, so he lowered himself to the bunk and blacked out immediately.

When he came to, he was soaked with sweat. The cell was like an oven. "I wanted to get away from the cold," he said to himself, "but not *this* far away." He wondered if something was wrong with the heating system, as the temperature still seemed to be rising. He was having trouble breathing and moving; even rolling onto his side seemed like an enormous effort. Nausea swept over him. If there'd been anything in his stomach, he was sure it would have come up. All he did was a dry retching, which tore at all the hurting parts of his body. His head hurt, his eyes seemed to be scorching, and every breath he took felt like flame in his lungs. He tried to yell for help, but no sound came out.

He knew he was on the verge of unconsciousness, but somewhere deep inside him, he sensed that if he lost consciousness he would never wake up. His instinct for survival forced him to fight to keep from passing out. He forced himself to think about home, family, Pat, friends, music, even the cold he had suffered while in various cells on his way to this place. Anything to hang onto consciousness. He felt that he was fighting for his life, even when at times he was delirious.

Despite his efforts, his grip on consciousness began to slip. All the images in his mind began to dim. Amazingly, he suddenly felt cool air beginning to flow over him. "God! I'm hallucinating," he thought. But the cool air continued, and it revived him. As the pain left his eyes, he looked up to see where the air was coming from and saw a vent in the ceiling. Out of that vent flowed the life-saving cool air. Now his breathing became easier, and the racking pain slowly subsided. No more feeling of losing his hold on consciousness or sanity. He was able to sit up. He spoke aloud to see if his voice would work. It did.

Looking around, he saw a tiny window high up near the ceiling; he also noticed a peep-hole, covered from the outside, in the door at about eye-level. The cool air continued to flow, and his sweat-soaked clothes began to chill him. He shivered. To get out of the direct flow of cold air, he struggled to his feet and moved around. Getting out of the stream of air helped, but the room temperature was dropping rapidly. His shivering became violent, more like spasms than ordinary shivering.

He attempted to pull up the mattress, thinking he could wrap it around himself, but it was secured to the bunk, impossible to move. The cold increased and he desperately, painfully, moved his arms about and stamped his feet to try to generate heat. He fantasized about warmth and clear, sun-filled skies. Images of a warm bed and an open fire floated through his head. He was sure he could feel the heat from the sun, the warm bed, the fire. At that moment, he collapsed on the floor.

The cell door banging open aroused him. In a daze, he looked up from the floor. A tall push trolley cart, with shelves from top to bottom, stood at his door. A man dressed in Luftwaffe-colored coveralls was sliding a tray from one of the shelves. Using the bed for support, Ed struggled to his feet, then sat on the bed. He had no idea how long he had been unconscious. There was no hint of excessive heat or cold in the cell; he felt comfortable, but confused.

"Goodt evening, Sir," the man said with a German accent, as he put the tray on Ed's lap. It was stainless steel and had compartments, each containing food, and an end compartment holding a spoon, a fork, and a table knife.

"Vhy shouldt you sleep on de floor, Sir?" the German asked pleasantly. "You vouldt be petter on de punk."

"Yeah. I would," Ed replied. "But I passed out trying to keep from freezing."

"Freezink, Sir? How couldt you pe freezink? De temperature iss normal in here."

"It is now. But it was very cold before. And before that it was so hot I couldn't stand it."

The German looked at Ed as if he were not quite right in the head, and said, "Put dat iss impossible, Sir. De demperature iss regulated. Itd iss kept between zixty-eight und zeventy degreess, Farenheit, I tink you use in America."

Afraid the tray would be taken away before he could eat the food, Ed began to devour the potatoes, cabbage, and small pieces of boiled beef. Also on the tray was a piece of black bread, a small bit of honey, and a cup of tea. The guard said, "Dake your dime, Sir. I gome back for de dray," and he left, closing and bolting the door. Ed relaxed somewhat and ate more slowly, enjoying the taste of the real food. Spreading honey on the bread, he thought, "Best meal I've had in Hitler's Germany," and sipped the tea.

He put the tray on the floor and stretched out on the bunk. The cell door opened and the attendant came in to pick up the tray. "Vere you injured in the head, Sir?" he asked.

"I was banged around, yes. I was knocked out by flak. Why?" Ed replied.

"Your ztrange dalk apout de demperature here madte me vonder."

"What do you mean? You think I made it up?"

"You must haff dreamed itd. Or imachined itd."

"No, it happened. First extreme heat, then extreme cold. I felt it, until I collapsed."

"Put, it iss imbossible, Sir. De demperature iss zentrally controlledt. If itd habbenedt in your cell, it vouldt haff habbenedt in de odders. None off your comradtes in de odder cells mendionedt anyting like dat. Perhaps you hadt a fantdasy."

"I don't think so. It was too real."

"All rightd, Sir. I haff to getd on mitt my vork. Dere iss a guardt in the gorridor. He vill dake you do de ladrine. Gut nightd, Sir," and he left the cell door remaining open.

Ed shuffled to the door and there was the guard, who walked beside Ed, then stopped and pointed his way into a doorless room. Ed went in and used the facilities, then was returned to his cell.

Lying down on the bunk, he recalled the hot-cold episode. "It was real. It happened. I didn't dream it. I was hot and cold," but a seed of doubt had been planted in his mind. He drifted off to sleep.

Suddenly, he was awake. Or dreamed that he was; he wasn't clear which, but it was hot again in the cell. There was no light, so he stared into the dark, so dark that he thought he could feel the blackness. Heat continued to wash over him, just as it had before, and the sweat poured out as it had before. What the attendant had said worked on his mind. "Maybe I *am* dreaming this," he thought. "Dreams can be real, like they're really happening." He felt his clothes. They were wet to his touch. "This is real! This is real!" he repeated, but his mind was whirling; nothing seemed solid. He gripped the sides of the bunk, trying to stop the whirling. He wished he would pass out, but it didn't happen. He seemed to hang onto the verge of unconsciousness, aware of what was happening but unable to control it, to do anything about it.

Now the cold air replaced the hot. For a few moments it felt good, then the shivering started. Colder and colder, then at last — oblivion.

When consciousness returned, the darkness was gone, and the temperature was again normal. His clothes were damp, as they would be if he had had a night sweat. He felt wrung out, as if he had spent the night having bad dreams. "What's happening to me?" he wondered. "Have I gone off my rocker? Can't I tell the real from the unreal anymore? Is that German right? Did my brain suffer damage? Is that why I've been passing out at times?"

A guard opened the door and signaled for Ed to come out, then accompanied him to the latrine. After relieving himself he threw cold water on his face, trying to clear his head. Back in his cell, he was brought two pieces of black bread spread with honey, and a cup of tea. It was brought by a different attendant, but he asked the same question, "How are you, Sir?"

"Well, I guess I'm okay, now that the temperature is back to normal."

"Vhat do you mean, Sir? Back to normal?"

"Oh, you know," Ed replied, "not going from hot to freezing cold."

The attendant looked sympathetically at Ed and shook his head. "Vell, Sir, nopadty elze nodiced idt. I'm sure de demperature in here vas normal."

Angrily, Ed said, "You think I'm nuts, don't you? You think bumps to my head have me all screwed up, don't you?"

"Vell, Sir, I am nodt qualivied to zay. Put zomedimes injured fliers do haff broblemss."

"Yeah, sure they do! What's next? Do I start banging my head on the wall? Maybe you don't exist either. Maybe I'm fantasizing you and this tea and bread! You know what I think? I think that's bullshit! You guys are doing this to me."

"It's not for me to say," the German said, picking up the empty cup. Then just as he was closing the door he added, "You must haff heardt of paranoia, Sir," and the door closed.

"Paranoia," Ed thought. "That's when you think people are doing things to you. *Out to get you.* Well, could be, but I don't think so. They are doing something to me. Oh, oh! That does sound like paranoia!" This preyed on his mind. "If a guy is paranoid, I guess he believes what he thinks is happening is really happening. No! Dammit! I know what was happening to me! Or do I? I sure wish I had somebody I could talk to, somebody I could trust. These Germans are too slick for me. They've already got me wondering if I know which end is up. What did they call this? 'Interrogation Center.' Yeah, this must be some kind of softening up process before interrogation."

Lying on the bunk, he tried to think of other things, but his thoughts kept returning to the nagging question, "Am I out of my mind? Is this real or am I dreaming?" Then an even more frightening thought came to him. "If I am mentally damaged, will it be permanent?" Then he sat up. "They're good. But all I'm going to tell them is my name, rank, and serial number, no matter what they do to me. Do to me? Is that paranoia? All right, stop it! There's nothing wrong with you. They just want you to think there is. Who are 'they'? Why, they're the Germans, the enemy. That's real. I'm their prisoner. That's real. This is a cell. That's real. I'm here, and I'm real. Okay, hang on to that. Name, rank and serial number. That's all I'm supposed to give them, and all they're supposed to ask. That's all they're going to get."

The door opened and a Luftwaffe sergeant said, "Lieutenant, come with me." He spoke American-sounding English. Ed shuffled to the door and followed the sergeant to the end of the corridor, where the Sergeant opened another door and showed Ed to a chair in front of a desk. Ed sat down, and the sergeant seated himself on the other side of the desk, facing Ed. "Well, Lieutenant, I'm Sergeant Mueller. You look very bad, Sir, I think you need medical treatment."

"It's about time," Ed said. "You've had me for two weeks without any kind of treatment."

"Oh, not quite, Lieutenant. Your papers indicate that you were taken to a hospital for x-rays, and you spent a night in a field hospital."

"That's a joke, Sergeant. Even if they actually took x-rays, nobody did anything, or told me anything. It's true, I spent a night in the poorest excuse for a hospital I've ever seen. Nobody looked at me. It was just a night in a bunk among moaning, groaning prisoners. Don't make me laugh." To himself he said, "You're talking too much. That's what this guy wants to do—get you talking, then he'll slip in some questions, and you'll be so involved with the conversation, you'll answer him. So, shut up!"

"Yes, Lieutenant. Your bombing raids have made it difficult for us to provide proper facilities everywhere to treat your wounded. Here, however, you will be given the best medical treatment."

"Yeah? When?"

"When your interrogation is completed. If you cooperate. If you do not, well, our medical staff has a very heavy load. It may take a long time to get you in, if you do not cooperate. Do you understand?"

"Sure. Now, Sergeant, I'm going to tell you exactly what I am required to tell you, and no more. I am First Lieutenant Edward J. Thorne, and my serial number is 0-817132."

"I understand, Lieutenant. By the way, have you ever been in Chicago? I used to live there."

Ed almost bit on that bait, but caught himself just in time. He just stared at the sergeant.

"I attended the University of Chicago," the sergeant continued. "They had an excellent German Studies program there. Where did you go to college, Lieutenant?"

Ed pressed his lips together, and just watched the sergeant.

"What are you afraid of, Lieutenant? This is just a friendly conversation. What harm can it do?"

"I've given you my name, rank and serial number, Sergeant. That's all I have to say."

"Afraid of us awful Nazis, Lieutenant? That we will read something into anything you say, forcing you to betray your country's secrets? Is that it, Lieutenant? Am I one of the 'they' you fantasize about? Are you, perhaps, a little paranoid, Lieutenant?"

There was that word again. "These guys are slick," Ed thought. "They work together—first the attendants, and now this hotshot sergeant. Bet he's really SS, or Nazi intelligence, maybe even Gestapo. Smooth. Don't give him anything."

"Have you been having trouble sleeping? That's one of the signs, you know. How about bad dreams? Have you dreamed you are being persecuted? Like the Jews, with their protests and crying! Do you think we are trying to damage your mentality?"

Remaining silent, but seething inside, Ed thought, "That's exactly what you bastards are doing! You and the attendants, you're all in on it. Very slick. You've got guts, even mentioning the 'Jews'! But it won't work."

"Now, Lieutenant, you really are in bad shape. You need the attention of our excellent medical staff, including a psychiatrist. I think you especially need the psychiatrist. You can have what you need. Just answer a few simple questions. All right?"

Ed said nothing.

Now, the sergeant's tone changed. Speaking sharply, he asked, "How many pilots in your squadron?"

No response.

"How many have you lost this month?" the sergeant demanded. No response. Showing anger, the sergeant shouted, "Do you have trouble getting replacement pilots? Answer me!"

Ed sat mute.

Now, another change in the sergeant's tone and manner. "You may not know this, Lieutenant," he said, "but Der Fuhrer will soon unleash secret weapons. This will turn the tide! We will be victorious!"

Almost biting on that one, Ed had to tighten his lips.

"You know, Lieutenant, when we have won the war, we will treat our friends very well. Prisoners who cooperate with us will be our friends. Those who do not will have to take the consequences. Be smart, Lieutenant; cooperate."

To himself, Ed said, "You'r bluffing, Jerry. The last I heard, our invasion was going very well, and we were advancing everywhere. Sell your propaganda to somebody else."

"What recent change in command did your squadron have?"

Nothing from Ed.

"How about yourself, Lieutenant? Did you not have enough combat time to qualify for a leave? Did they force you to keep on flying? And now look what has happened."

Surprised that the sergeant should know about his combat time, Ed wanted to say something, especially about the idea that he had been forced to continue flying after completing his tour. Instead, he spat out his name, rank and serial number, then clamped his mouth shut again.

"No reason to get angry, Lieutenant. I am, really, your friend. You know, our Gestapo has interrogation methods that work on even the toughest people. Compared to that, I am your friend! I think you should cooperate."

"Man! He's giving you the works," Ed said to himself. "You're protected by the Geneva Conventions on treatment of prisoners of war. Don't tell him anything."

Changing tactics again, the sergeant said, "Lieutenant, I really wish you'd discuss Chicago with me. I have fond memories of my time there. Come on, loosen up. What harm could it do?"

Ed thought, "Yeah. I've been briefed on this trap. You get me talking, and I'll let something slip. Forget it, Nazi!"

This game of cat-and-mouse went on, with Ed saying nothing more. Finally, the sergeant stood and said, "All right, Lieutenant. That's all for now. I hope you have a pleasant night in your cell."

Ed couldn't be sure, but he thought there was a hint of sarcasm in the sergeant's voice. Ignoring the hand held out to him, he shuffled out and, accompanied by the guard, returned to his cell.

Noon chow brought to his cell was three slices of black bread, which he was starting to like, and a piece of cheese, along with a mug of tea. It was brought by the same attendant who had brought last evening's meal. "Vell, Lieutenant, did the sergeant easse you mindt aboudt your vantasies and hallucinations?"

"Oh, sure. I know I just made up all that stuff about heat and cold. You nice people would never do anything like that. It was all in my mind."

Missing Ed's sarcasm, the German said, "Gut. You should gedt along very vell, den. Maype yust a demporary condition."

Ed had to laugh. "You mean there's hope for me?"

"I'm sure you will be all right. Especially after our excellent doctors see you," and he left. The guard was at the door, and he accompanied Ed to the latrine.

Back on his bunk, Ed thought about the interrogation process. He did not feel that he had outwitted the sergeant, but he was confident that he'd given nothing away. He dropped off. Dreams came. First he dreamed he was chained to the wall of a dank, ill-smelling cell. He could hear screams of other prisoners being tortured. He felt terror, believing that whatever caused the others to scream would soon happen to him. Then the dream changed, and he felt the heat increasing in his cell. He dreamed he was beginning to sweat. In his dream he was going through what he had gone through the day and night before. He jerked awake. He felt his clothes. No wetness. But the dream had seemed real. Had he, after all, dreamed the heat and cold of the previous times? The confusion of reality and dream came over him again; this time the uncertainty was more apparent to him. "Are they right? Did I dream all of it?"

The door opening to let the attendant bring in his food was a relief to him. "How iss your vantasy liffe, Sir?" the attendant asked.

"Fine and dandy. It all seems very real," Ed said, deciding not to discuss the matter with the German. He was certain that whatever he said would be reported. "What gourmet meal have you brought me this time?"

"Gut you are veeling petter, Sir. Beans, botatoes, a little bork, und breadt und tea. De Thirdt Reich veeds its brisoners vell," and he went out the door. Ed ate the food; then as usual, went to the latrine accompanied by a guard.

Since he had slept during the afternoon, he did not feel sleepy after his visit to the toilet. He scooted himself back on the bunk, leaning his back against the wall, and allowed his thoughts to wander. In the interests of maintaining his sanity, he tried to work through a chronology of events since returning to consciousness in the sidecar. The major result of this was that, even though he had had periods of unconsciousness, all of his conscious moments had been rational. He had seen, felt, smelled and tasted things as they were. They were not exaggerated or magnified. They were not fantasized. It seemed to him, then, that it was unlikely that here, in a comparatively stable environment, he would suddenly start to fantasize about the heat and cold he had experienced the preceding afternoon and night. "They may think they can convince me that I've gone off my rocker, but I don't think I have." He felt better for having again reached this conclusion. He was aware, though, that mentally unstable people do not usually think there is anything wrong with them. This continued to trouble him.

Restless from the lack of physical activity, he got to his feet, and using his sideways movement technique, moved back and forth the length of the cell. Not unexpectedly, the temperature began to change. Unlike the preceding day, when the room got hot, then cold, this time he felt the temperature dropping first. He knew he was feeling the change, not imagining it. Now he stood directly under the vent from which the cool air was flowing. Standing still and listening intently, he could hear a motor running quietly. "Aha!" if there's a motor running, it has to be turned on somewhere, by somebody. And there has to be a compressor of some kind to make the cold air. Trying to make me believe I'm nuts! Or worse, drive me nuts. Okay, Jerry, bring on your cold air and your hot air. I'm ready.

His bravado didn't keep him from feeling the cold, but it did help him to stay in touch with reality. The cold came and went, and the heat followed. Then the cycle was repeated. Having survived it once, he knew he could survive it again, especially since his questions about his sanity had been resolved in his own mind. When it was over, he slept peacefully until his breakfast came.

Immediately after breakfast, Sergeant Meuller came for him and led him to his office. "Well, Lieutenant, did you sleep well? Any more dreams or fantasies of hot and cold?"

"Slept just fine, Sergeant. As to fantasies, well, none at all," Ed responded.

"None at all!" The sergeant seemed startled, but he quickly covered it up. "That is remarkable, after all your distress of yesterday. This must prove to you that, as I said yesterday, you were fantasizing."

"All it proves, Sergeant, is that I know the difference between what is real and what is imagined."

"Hmmm. Very good, Lieutenant. Now, I have some questions for you. Please keep in mind that we want to give you medical treatment, but we can't if you don't cooperate."

"I seem to recall your saying something like that. Well, if you have questions, fire away."

For the next twenty minutes Mueller asked questions, often re-phrasing the same questions, feigning interest in Ed's experiences, background, interests, trying to engage him in conversation. Feeling good that he had resolved for himself the question of his own mental stability, Ed either said nothing, or repeated his name, rank and serial number.

Abruptly, and seeming annoyed, the sergeant stood. "Well, Lieutenant, since you are not cooperating, I will turn you over to the captain. I warn you, if you don't cooperate with him, you will remain in your cell indefinitely." Then, losing some of his professional detachment, he added, "And you can rot there as far as I am concerned!"

Ed was pleased that he had disrupted the cool sergeant's composure at least a little bit. He followed the now stiff-legged, ramrod-straight sergeant across the corridor to a larger office. Seated at a desk was a small, balding, ferret-faced soldier. When Sergeant Meuller stepped into the office, he came to attention. Meuller spoke to him in rapid, crisp German, and handed him a folder of papers. The soldier remained standing until the sergeant marched out of the office, then seated himself to pick up a telephone. He spoke a few German words, cradled the phone, picked up the folder, and leaving Ed standing at the desk, went quickly through another door.

Back in a few seconds, the soldier indicated that Ed should sit in a chair near the desk. Some five minutes passed, then a buzzer sounded on the desk, and the soldier sprang to his feet, saying, "Kommen, Leutenant." Ed pushed himself to his feet and, in his crab-like movement, followed the soldier to the door. The soldier opened the door on to an elegantly furnished, large paneled office. A tall, dark-haired man rose behind a leather-topped desk, came around extending his hand, and said, "Ah, Lieutenant Thorne. Do come in," as if he were greeting an old acquaintance. Ed shook his hand and said, "Captain," as he looked this German over.

Ed was reminded of the way Nazi officers were represented in Hollywood movies: Polished boots, immaculate uniform, stiffly erect, cold eyes above an ingratiating smile. The only thing missing was the monocle. On the desk, on top of the folder, was a pair of dark, shell-framed glasses.

"Please sit down, Lieutenant. I see you have difficulty moving. We must get you medical care." The voice was resonant, smooth, with an excellent British accent. No hint of German. The German picked up a pack of Chesterfield cigarettes and offered one to Ed.

"No thanks," Ed said.

"Mind if I do?" the hauptmann said, and not waiting for Ed to answer, fitted one to a long black and silver holder, lighting the cigarette with a matching lighter. "I'm Captain Immermann. Lieutenant, I am pleased to meet you." The manner was easy, conversational, friendly. "I see you were based in England. I spent five years there. At Oxford, actually. Lovely country."

Ed nodded, not wanting to get into a conversation with this smooth character. "What an actor," he thought. "Con man is more like it. He could sell ice cubes to Eskimos. I'll have to be careful; he's slicker than the sergeant, I'll bet."

"Would you care to tell me a little bit about yourself, Lieutenant? Your background? What you did as a civilian? Where you went to college?"

"No, Sir," Ed replied.

"What harm could it do? Your life and interests would be of no value to us, I am only interested as a person, in you as a person. What harm? What part of America do you come from? You sound northern. Perhaps Ohio?"

"Captain, you know all I am permitted to tell you is my name, rank and serial number. And that is all you're supposed to ask me. You already have those."

"Oh, come now, Lieutenant. That's rubbish, and you know it! Nobody pays any attention to that any more."

"Maybe not, but I have nothing more to say."

"You know, Lieutenant, every American I have ever had in here has talked freely about himself. Unlike the stubborn British. Why not you? You should welcome a friendly chat, after having no one to talk to for so long. Let me get you a cup of coffee. Cream? Sugar?"

"Just black, Sir. Thank you."

The captain pressed a button, and the soldier appeared from the outer office, stiffly at attention. After the captain spoke to him, he saluted and disappeared. "You see, Lieutenant, you did answer a question. It could not possibly do any harm."

"What ques . . ." Ed started to ask, then realized that he'd answered the question about coffee. "This guy is really sharp," he thought. "Okay, no more answers about anything."

The door opened and the soldier entered, carrying a silver tray with china cups and saucers, a silver coffee urn, cream and sugar containers, and silver spoons. As the soldier left, the captain poured coffee for Ed and himself, adding cream and sugar to his own, but not to Ed's, then sat back in his highbacked leather chair and looked keenly at Ed. He sipped his coffee, lit another cigarette, and as the smoke curled up past his face, he continued to study Ed's face. After making sure that the captain had swallowed some of the coffee, Ed sipped his own. A pleasant surprise! It was real coffee, and excellent.

Ed grew uncomfortable under the German's gaze. As the steady stare continued, he shifted uneasily in his chair. "What the hell is he looking at?" Ed thought, passing his hand over the rough stubble of his beard and his unkempt hair. "Another part of his technique, I guess."

At last the captain spoke. Softly, slowly, as if pondering a question of great moment, he said, "What does a young American, twenty-two or twenty-three at most, think about? What are his interests?"

The accuracy of the guess at his age made Ed think, "My twenty-fifth birthday is this month; I forgot." Then, to the German, "Sir, what date is today?"

"Why, it's November fifteenth. Why?"

Ed started to answer, "It's my . . ." and cut himself off. To himself, he said, "Don't fall for his tricks. Watch it!"

"Your birthday, is it? Well, now, happy birthday to you, Lieutenant. If we had a cake, it would be what? Twenty-three candles?" Ed was silent. "Yes," the captain continued, "twenty-three seems right." He sipped his coffee and drew on his cigarette, letting the smoke slowly out of his mouth, studying Ed's face for another minute. "Lieutenant, you have a very sensitive face under that scraggly beard. It responds to everything I say. Even if you don't speak, your face says everything. I can read it clearly. Now, what would your interests be? Flying, of course. Reading, I'm sure. Girls? Of course! That is universal at your age." He smiled his ingratiating, slightly condescending, smile. He flicked ashes into the ornate ashtray on his desk, "Art? No. Poetry? Perhaps. Writing? Doesn't seem right. Photography? No. Theatre? Ah! I see a reaction, not large, but there on your face. Hmmm . . . Acting? Some, but not intense. Ah! Music! I can see it. Music! I should have guessed. Violin? Piano? Oboe? No. What then? Opera? Yes! I see the response. Singing! That's it, isn't it?"

Ed sat still, saying nothing.

The captain went on quietly, as though giving every word serious thought. "Wagner? No, you haven't the build for it. Verdi, then, perhaps? Ah yes. Puccini! I can see it, that's it. We have that in common. Tosca, Boheme, Butterfly. Beautiful! But best of all his last opera, Turandot. Not very popular in America, but well-loved here. Magnificent! He must have listened carefully to our Wagner before working on that. Well, Lieutenant, surely we can talk about opera. No secrets there."

Ed felt a strong urge to go ahead and talk about opera and singers with this apparently knowledgeable German. He fought down the urge, saying, "No, Sir. My name is Thorne, Edward J., Serial Number 0-817132. I am a First Lieutenant in the U.S. Army Air Corps."

"Too bad, Lieutenant. And foolish. I should like very much for us to sit here, like civilized people from different countries, sipping excellent coffee, and exchanging views on opera and our favorite singers. I wager you are fond of the Swedish tenor, Jussi Bjoerling. He is marvelous, isn't he? And has there ever been a Wagnerian tenor like Melchior? Not German, but just the same, his Denmark is basically Germanic."

Almost biting on this tempting lead, Ed caught himself, clamped his mouth shut, and said nothing.

Abruptly, the captain leaned forward, stubbed his cigarette out, looked directly and intently into Ed's eyes, and in a totally different tone of voice, said loudly, "Lieutenant, you are wasting time. I must know your group and squadron, your commanding officer, and how many pilots and planes you have lost in the last month!"

The change was so complete, and the voice so imperious, that it caught Ed off guard, and he started to answer as if responding to an order. Then, catching himself, he repeated his name, rank and serial number.

"Fool!" the German said. "Do you think we don't know all this?" Then, softening, returning to his kinder tone and attitude, "It doesn't matter, Lieutenant. We have all the information we need about your outfit," and he pressed a button again, causing the soldier to appear. The captain snapped out German words to the soldier, who left, then returned with a loose-leaf volume the size of a telephone book.

Taking the book and opening it, the captain placed it in front of Ed. "Look, Lieutenant. See the numbers at the top of the first page?" The numbers were in regular Arabic numerals, not written in German, so Ed easily read them. "Those numbers represent your group and squadron, as you can see. Look at these," pointing to more numbers. "See? P-51s, and the number following that represents the number of P-51s currently in your group—fifty. See also, Stinson—one. Turn the page to your squadron number. There you see all the names, with Major C.S. Irvine—referred to affectionately as 'Chicken Shit,'" the German translated the words into English. "Yes, we even know that, and the name of his temporary replacement. Do you see it? And your name, the date you were shot down by our anti-aircraft gunners when you so foolishly flew over one of our closely protected airfields. Foolish indeed! That is why you are here now. Examine the book. You can figure out enough of it to see that our sources of information are very good. We have similar records of every Allied group and squadron in Europe and Britain. The little you could have told me would have been inconsequential. After all, you are only a lieutenant, not likely to have much information of consequence. But we could have had a pleasant talk about opera."

Ed sensed a note of genuine regret in the captain's voice. "Tough, Nazi, but I'm glad I wasted your time," Ed thought, as he turned over the pages of the book, astonished at the detail. Even menus for the meals served at the hall! The name of the local boy who brought newspapers to the base! "Incredible," he thought. "Our intelligence people are right. The Germans must have informers everywhere."

He closed the book and said, "Thank you, Captain. Very interesting. You know, of course, that we have similar information about your people."

"Certainly. Every country engages in this sort of thing. It is a necessary part of military operations. Well, Lieutenant Thorne, I've enjoyed our little chat, even though it was almost totally one-sided. Oh, by the way, has anyone told you what happened to you after you were hit by our anti-aircraft fire?"

"No, Sir. I have no idea. The last I knew, I was knocked unconscious just as I got ready to bail out."

"You are entitled to know, Lieutenant. I will step out of my official role as Interrogation Officer, and show you that when we are not obeying or giving orders, as we must do in our official capacities, we Germans are just like other human beings. Even though you did not give me any information, I will tell you what happened to you, without demanding anything in return."

"Thank you, Captain. I appreciate that."

"God was with you, Lieutenant," the captain said, surprising Ed, because he had been taught that all Nazis were atheists. "Our ground forces found you and your leader flying alone. Very foolishly, you came over one of our major airdromes, and at an altitude where our guns could easily reach you. They sighted you, tracked you, then opened fire. They scored hits on you almost at once. They saw you trying to keep your aircraft going, then saw your canopy fly off. They expected to see a parachute, but none appeared. Your plane continued downward, but seemed to be out of control. Next, they saw it roll over into an inverted position, continuing downward, though not as fast as before. It did a little half-circle, then plunged into a forest, still upside down. There was no smoke or other indication of fire.

"Vehicles and men were dispatched to the spot where you entered the forest. The men saw a group of farmers carrying pitchforks, and some with shotguns. The soldiers drove them away. As the men approached the place where your plane should be, they saw no sign of you or your plane on the ground. They got out of their trucks and searched the area, finding nothing.

"One of the men looked up and saw your airplane upside down, lodged in the tops of trees. Fortunately, they were pine trees, so your crash was eased. You could still not be seen, nor could they find any sign that you had fallen out, or climbed out and reached the ground.

"Two men were ordered to climb the trees closest to the cockpit. They did so. One called down that you were there, jammed down in the cockpit, partly under the instrument panel, in the area where the rudder bars are, You were not moving or responding to their calls or their shaking of you. Ladders were sent for and brought. Men climbed up with ropes, which they secured under your arms. Then with great effort, standing on the ladders, they were able to dislodge you, then lower you with the ropes.

"On the ground, two of our medics examined you. You were not moving. You were bloody from wounds on the shoulder, chin, head, and left wrist and thumb, but your pulse was strong. The bleeding had stopped by coagulation, so they lifted you into one of the trucks. Meanwhile, the enraged civilians had surged forward, screaming, "Kill him! Kill him! He has bombed and strafed us. Give him to us!" The soldiers held them at bay and left, taking you with them. At their base, you were loaded into a motorcycle sidecar, and sent on the journey that brought you here. I think you know the rest of the story."

"Yes, Sir, I do. Thank you. Nobody will believe me when I tell them this story. I can't believe it myself."

"It's true, Lieutenant. It is all in our official report. Now, Lieutenant, you will be returned to your cell. After lunch, you will be taken to the hospital for care and recovery. You will be surprised at how good the accomodations and treatment will be. When the doctors decide you are ready, you will be sent to a Stalag Luft, a prison camp for Air Corps captives. You are, of course, a Prisoner of War. I hope God continues to be good to you. Goodbye," and he shook Ed's hand.

"Goodbye, Captain, and thank you," Ed said as he shuffled out, still amazed at what he had been told.

Back in his cell, Ed felt good. He'd heard so many stories about Nazi interrogation techniques that he'd expected a terrible ordeal. It had turned out quite different from that. He was confident that he had not added to the Germans' knowledge about his group. And in spite of all the threats about no medical attention if he did not cooperate, he hadn't cooperated, but was going to get medical care anyway. "Things are looking up," he thought. "I'll be in the hospital this afternoon. If the hauptmanri wasn't lying, it should be pretty nice."

He thought about what Hauptmann Immermann had told him: how he had crashed into pine trees; the plane not burning; how they had pulled him out and lowered him; his being unconscious; being placed in a motorcycle sidecar. It all fit with what he remembered just before he was knocked unconscious in Princess Pat, and what he remembered about coming to. "An amazing story," he said to himself. "It must be true. Immermann would have no reason to lie to me about it. He's right, God was good to me."

He tried to relax on the bunk, but now he was too keyed up. Thoughts, ideas, recollections, hopes, worries, raced through his mind. Relaxation was impossible. What would the doctors find when they examined him? Would he get better? Would he be crippled? Would his lapses in consciousness continue? What kind of treatment would it be? What would the prison camp be like? What had Immermann called it? "Stalag Luft." He knew "luft" referred to flying or flight, or air, so "stalag" must mean either prison or camp.

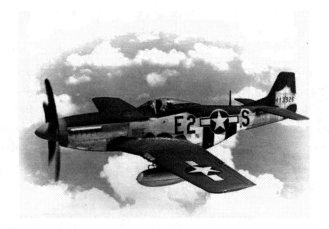

28

It semed that hours passed before the cell door opened and his food was brought in, then hours more before two guards came to remove him from the cell. In his excitement, he started out the door without his jacket. Just as one of the guards was closing the door, he turned around and said, "Wait!" Whether or not the guard understood the word, he waited, and Ed went back in and snatched his jacket from the bunk.

The guards walked him out of the building, across a roadway, and into another building. Just inside, another guard sat at a small desk. One of Ed's escorting guards handed papers to the seated guard, who said a few words, and the two left. "Sit down, Lieutenant," the receiving guard said in quite acceptable English. "You are First Lieutenant Edward J. Thorne, Serial No. 0-817132?" Ed nodded. "369th Fighter Squadron, 359th Fighter Group, flying P-51 Mustangs?" Ed did not respond. "All right, Lieutenant. Sign your name right here," and he pointed to a line at the bottom of the sheet of paper he put in front of Ed. Much more than his name, rank and serial number was printed on the page, but it was in German, so Ed could not read it.

"I'm not required to sign anything," Ed said. "According to the Geneva Conventions, I've done all I'm required to do. For all I know, signing this, which I can't read, could be like signing some sort of confession. I will not sign!"

The guard laughed. "Another stubborn American! Your interrogation is over, Lieutenant. This is a hospital. What I asked you to sign is an admission form, nothing else. It is for our records."

Ed replied, "Then you don't need my signature. And why the extra information? All you need is my name, rank and serial number."

"All right, Lieutenant. It is not important." He stamped the form, and pushed a button on the side of his desk.

In a moment a young man in a white jacket, wearing RAF blue trousers and black British military shoes, came through a door and said, "Another Yank, eh, Heinrich?" in a definite British accent. He picked up the stamped paper and to Ed said, "Come along, Leftenant. We'll get you properly situated."

Ed stood and started to shuffle after the Englishman. "Having trouble walking, are you? Well, we'll take care of that directly." Ed shuffled through the door the Englishman held open and entered a small reception room from which stretched a long, spotless, well-lit corridor. White-coated men moved briskly up and down the corridor, in and out of several doors that opened off the corridor.

"Here we are, Leftenant," his guide said to Ed, wheeling a wheelchair out to him. "Have a seat in this and let me get a bit of information from you," and he started to fill out a form, getting Ed's name, rank and serial number from the sheet he'd taken from the guard. Next, he asked questions about his condition, starting with the date when he was shot down and captured and what wounds or injuries he had sustained. He also wanted to know what, if any, medical treatment he had had. As Ed answered the questions, the attendant filled out the form.

The wheelchair was the most comfortable seat Ed had sat in since being taken prisoner. In the atmosphere of order and calm that he sensed in this busy, clean place, and the friendly, concerned attitude of the English attendant, he relaxed and talked freely as the attendant asked for details about pain, lack of mobility, discomfort . . . suddenly he froze as the attendant asked, "Is the information here accurate about your group and squadron?"

As he just stared at the attendant, saying nothing, he was thinking, "Is this bastard one of them? Or is he working with them? Is he an informer?"

The attendant looked up when Ed stopped answering his questions. He smiled at the look on Ed's face. "I understand, Leftenant. You're wondering if I'm collaborating with the enemy, right? Well, rest easy. I'm not. This medical facility is staffed and run by loyal British prisoners who happen to have some medical background. We are not doctors. The Germans send in doctors, including highly skilled specialists, on a weekly basis. We British provide only medical information to the Germans; no intelligence of any kind. I asked you if this information is accurate so we can inform the International Red Cross of your whereabouts and condition. We will not provide it to the Germans, so relax. We are on the same side."

What the man said made sense, and it was very convincing. Ed said, "Okay, yes."

"Goodo," the attendant said. "The Red Cross will notify your family, as well as your group, about your being a POW. Chances are that the preliminary report about you was, 'Missing in Action, Presumed Dead.' Your family will be greatly relieved, I should think, to receive a more accurate report. Now, let's get you to an examination room."

Ed was wheeled a short distance down the corridor and into a small, immaculately clean examination room containing an examination table, white metal stools on wheels, and sterilizer cabinets with probes, lights, magnifying glasses, small hammers, tweezers, and other medical implements.

He was asked to strip down to his shorts, and then helped onto the table. Another white-coated Englishman wearing a stethoscope around his neck came in. He read the form the other one had filled out, then turned to Ed, saying, "Hello, Leftenant. I'm Jerry Sanderson. I'm going to prod, push, pull and twist your limbs, neck and spine. If at any time you feel pain, say so immediately. Right?" Ed nodded, and Sanderson proceeded to do just as he said he would. He found many sensitive spots, and Ed responded vocally each time he found one. Each time, Sanderson checked that spot more thoroughly, trying to locate the problem more precisely. Then he would say something to the other attendant, who would write it down on the form.

When the examination was finished, Ed was helped into a hospital gown and back to his wheelchair. "You are badly banged up," Sanderson said. "Your legs, buttocks, back and rib cage are badly bruised. You have sensitive points all along your spine, as well as in your abdomen and pelvic area. You have several cracked ribs; fortunately none apparently punctured a lung. I can't tell with certainty about internal injuries to your abdomen, but I think it is just a matter of deep bruises and contusions, which are clearly giving you a great deal of pain. I am certain that your pelvis is broken, and you may have a chipped bone at the left hip joint. Your spine, neck, head, eyes, nose, lungs, all seem good but badly bruised.

"You already know that you have injuries, probably from shell fragments, to your head, chin, left wrist, and left shoulder, plus the deep cut and loss of the nail on your left thumb. We will clean and apply antiseptic to the surface injuries. They will, if kept clean, heal themselves. Now, in your report you indicate that you have had decreasingly frequent periods of unconsciousness blackouts. It is likely that these resulted from concussion. Most of what you need, so far as I can determine, is good food, warmth, cleanliness, and bed rest. You will get all of that here.

"This completes my preliminary examination. Tomorrow Dr. Chador will see you, He is a world-renowned Hungarian orthopoedic surgeon. The Germans lend him to us once a week; tomorrow is his day here. He will examine your pelvic area and spine, and see if my diagnosis is accurate. If your spells of blackout continue, we will have an internist check you. All right, Leftenant?"

"All right, of course. You didn't find anything very serious, then?" Ed asked.

"Nothing I could find. You have such extensive internal and external contusions and bruises, that I'm sure every move you have had to make since your capture has been painful. With time, everything will heal, including your pelvis. If none of the visiting doctors find anything else, what you will need is some bed rest and no strenuous activity. You will have both here."

"Thank you very much," Ed said, "I'm relieved. I've had all sorts of worries about what was causing me so much trouble."

The other attendant said, "Take your belt off, and take out anything you have in your pockets. We'll put your clothes in the laundry; just wear the gown until you're discharged from here." He moved Ed out of the examination room and down the corridor. "By the way, you'll want a bath and a shave. The Red Cross has provided us with kits containing a shaving outfit, cigarettes, some 'Kriegie' cards for writing home, chewing gum, things of that sort. We'll go in here to the ward, and I'll introduce you and show you your bed. The bath and toilets are right off the ward. You can use them as soon as you like, and any time you like. I think you need that, right?"

"Right," and Ed was wheeled into a large room full of beds, some with traction equipment but most without. Men were lying or sitting on almost all of the beds, some with bandages over their entire faces, with openings just for their eyes and mouths. Others wore casts and slings. Crutches or canes stood near some of the beds. It looked like what it was—a casualty ward of a hospital.

"This is Leftenant Ed Thorne," the attendant announced. "P-51 pilot. Been transported about the country for nearly two weeks. Now he's here. Banged up, but all right. Needs a bath and a shave, though."

A chorus of voices sang out, "Hullo, Ed." "Hi chum." "Yeah, Buddy." Some British, some American, and at least one Australian. "We're all 'kriegies' here, Ed," one voice said. "You'll fit right in; you're among friends. No 'goons' here."

Ed shook hands all around, placed his jacket and belt on the bed he was assigned, and went with the attendant to get his Red Cross kit. With that in hand, he went to the shower. The hot water and soap felt good, and he scrubbed hard from head to toes, leaning against the wall of the shower stall so he could reach everything, even though stretching hurt him. He was less concerned about the pain now, since the examination seemed to indicate that there was nothing serious wrong with him.

With the towel around him, he got out the Gillette safety razor and put in a blade. Making lather with soap, he pulled and scraped at his now long bristles until he was clean-shaven, though with several knicks. He put on the hospital gown again, gathered his things, and made his way back to his bed.

All the American and British airmen who were not confined to their beds were sitting or standing around his bed. As Ed approached, they all began to sing, "For he's a jolly good fellow." Ed, already feeling better knowing his injuries were not serious, and having showered and shaved, felt warm and welcome, and felt his eyes moistening. He had survived, and now, though a prisoner, was with comrades. They crowded around, asking questions about his treatment, how long since he'd been shot down, how the interrogation went, and so on. Ed answered the questions as well as he could, then mentioned the heat-and-cold in his cell.

One of the British men said, "Oh, that's the famous hot-and-cold treatment. Everybody gets it, some more than others. Then they try to break you down mentally by telling you you've been imagining things, or dreaming. Some men fall for it. Most don't."

"So I didn't fantacize it, eh? Good—I figured it out. Thanks for confirming it for me."

It was good to be back with friends. They told him of the excellent care they were being given, including good food and good medical care. There was a steady flow of good-natured insults and jibes between the Americans and the British. Jokes were told, and stories about flying, about combat engagements, about three-day passes to London, were related. Recent events in the invasion, how far the Allied forces had advanced, and the casualties both sides were sustaining were talked about. Some heavy-handed comments were made back and forth about the adequacies, or lack of them, of various British and American generals, such as Montgomery and Patton. Many songs were sung, including one about "kriegies," to the tune of "Oh, Tannenbaum."

Ed noted that word again, and when the song was done, he asked, "What is a 'kriegie'?"

"That's what you are, Ed," one Englishman replied.

"Okay, but what does it mean?"

The Englishman said, "It's short for the German word for Prisoners of War, 'Kriegsgefangener.' 'Krieg' means 'war.' The rest means 'prisoner.' It's what we are. We're all 'kriegies.' Nobody wants to try to wrap his tongue around the longer word, so we all just say 'kriegies'. It's a bloody rotten language, with almost as many unpronounceable words as bloody Welsh!"

"One ruddy minute, there, my Limey friend," a short, red-faced man spoke up. "Welsh is musical and poetic, unlike your stiff Limey language! It is Gaelic, and lovely to hear."

This led to some good-humored exchanges about endless, unpronounceable Welsh words with multiple consonants and no vowels. And so the afternoon went, until food trays were brought in, at which point every man went to his own bed. Ed found that the food was as good as he had been told. This meal was roast beef, potatoes and gravy, carrots and peas, milk, bread and butter, coffee and custard for dessert. He wondered how the Germans could provide such fare for prisoners, and why they should.

His new friends told him they understood that most of the food came from Switzerland, sent in by the International Red Cross. The Germans supplied only the bare necessities—potatoes and bread. An American captain, George Butler, who had been shot down and placed in a kriegie camp, had escaped, and then was wounded and recaptured, said, "Enjoy it while you can. You won't get anything like this in POW camp."

After dinner, most of the men read, played cards, or wrote letters on the small forms provided by the Red Cross. Some had quiet conversations with others, among them Ed and

George Butler, who, it turned out, was from Butler, Pennsylvania. He was also a P-51 pilot who had been shot down on a strafing mission in support of American troops just east of the Belgian-German border.

The ward grew quiet as most of the men went to sleep early. Ed was glad, because the day had been a tiring one. Just before he dropped off to sleep, he thought, "So far being a POW is not as bad as I expected. I wonder how long that will last."

Morning brought the Hungarian doctor, who examined Ed and confirmed the medic's diagnosis. "Rest," he said, in a heavily accented English. "No strenuous activity, Everything will heal itself. Do not attempt to walk normally for a week. Then try slowly, gently. All will heal and you will walk good. Like nothing happened. You had a concussion, but no lasting effect. You might faint a few more times, but soon that will pass too."

Ed thanked him, but he waved it off, saying, "Noddink," and went on to other patients. Ed felt better than he had since he'd been shot down. His back ached, and he still had pains everywhere, but they were less acute. Sudden or excess movement involving his rib cage produced sharp pain, so he avoided such movements. His ribs and pelvis would heal, the doctor had said, so he was no longer concerned. He was amazed at how different the world looked today than it had yesterday. "How lucky can I get," he thought. "Either I have more Irish blood in me than I thought I had, or it is so strong that the famous 'luck of the Irish' dominates my life. I hope it continues. Funny, my parents always played down the Irish part of our heritage. Didn't even talk about it. I learned about it by accident. Now I'm glad of the Irish in me, and, when I get back home, I'm going to do some research on it. What I've seen of the Irish in this war makes me proud."

He spent much of the rest of the day with George, who had made it his responsibility to chat every day with all the men who were confined to their beds. Ed went with him, and he heard enough stories to fill several volumes. He wondered how many of those stories would appear in print after the war. In the course of his conversations with George, he learned that he, too, was part Irish. Seeing George's kindness and consideration in talking with the bed-ridden patients—some of them badly wounded, some with their faces dreadfully burned—Ed's pride in his own Irish heritage grew.

He also discovered that the British medics had a radio. During the day it was tuned to German stations, which seemed either to broadcast music or propaganda all the time. But at night the medics tuned in the BBC Overseas Services. From those broadcasts they got what they all thought was more objective news than they could get from the German broadcasts. The Germans did not permit this practice, but the medics had learned how to carry on surreptitiously, with a spy-and-signal system to alert those listening to the BBC when a guard or other German was coming.

From these BBC broadcasts they heard night after night of Allied advances to the east, and Russian advances to the west; of the hundreds of German troops surrendering; of the collapse of Italy; of great strides being made in the Pacific, driving tenacious Japanese forces out of island and mainland jungles; of bombing attacks on Japanese strongholds, and even on Japan itself. They heard reports — mostly good, but some bad — about generals Patton, Bradley, Wainwright, Montgomery, and of course, Eisenhower and MacArthur. They heard about Churchill-Roosevelt-Stalin meetings. They learned of DeGaulle's return to Paris after the tumultuous liberation of that city, with French people throwing flowers at American troops as they entered the city, kissing them, handing them bottles of wine.

The tides of war had definitely turned favorable for the Allies on all fronts. They heard reports of the evolving plans for an international successor to the League of Nations, tentatively called the United Nations. They also heard reports of conflicting views of different leaders — military and civilian — on what demands should be made of the Axis nations in order to establish peace. Every bit of news was significant to all of the kriegies, and the medics saw to it that all of it was spread to all the patients. The abundance of good news was slightly mitigated by stories of a massive build-up of German forces in the northwest sector, likely for a last, desperate counter-assault. Not even this, which the kriegies discounted as having minimal chance of success, could lessen the euphoria brought on by the good news. Important to both Ed and George were the continuing reports of the Allied air forces' domination of the skies all over Europe. Bombers and fighters were penetrating almost at will everywhere. Things sounded so good that many of the kriegies started thinking they might never have to go to a POW camp — that they might be liberated right here.

Later in the day Ed was taken to a small room, where a German civilian snapped a picture of him. The attendant who had wheeled Ed to the room said, "This is part of the record. It is for identification. It will be pasted on a card with your name, rank and serial number on it. The card will be put in your file, which will be sent with you to your prison camp."

A week passed. Each day Ed felt less pain, and he was able to move better. He began to try a few tentative steps. He was able to move one foot in front of the other. He felt some pain at the first dozen steps, but everything seemed to be working. He walked a little, then sat down to rest. He did this off and on through the morning and after lunch. At 16:00 the Hungarian doctor visited the ward.

He checked his bed-ridden patients first, suggesting a new cast here, a change in tension there, an adjustment or removal of suspending equipment for someone else. Next, he looked at his ambulatory patients. When he asked Ed how he was, Ed said, "Much better, Doctor. I can walk now; want to see me?" The doctor nodded, so Ed walked ten steps away and back.

"Gud!" the doctor said. He had Ed lie on his bed, then he watched Ed's face as he pushed on his legs. Next, he used the heel of his hand to pound on each of Ed's heels, still watching Ed's face. Only when he pulled and twisted his legs did Ed wince. Coming to the side of the bed, the doctor probed, rather painfully for Ed, around the pelvic area, then around the rib cage. His fingers were strong, and he probed enough that Ed thought he was going to undo the healing that had taken place. But then he stopped and said, "Healink nizely. You should haf nod much more droubles. Anudder veek, und ve vill releaze you." Then he went on to other patients.

Ed was both glad and sad. Glad because he was healing. Sad because being released meant leaving the pleasant surroundings of the hospital, and more importantly his new friends. "Well, some of them will probably be released too. I wonder what kriegie camp will be like."

The next week passed much too quickly. Ed spent a lot of time with George, who told him a great deal about life in his former Stalag Luft. "But you will have to experience it before you can really know what it's like," he said. Ed felt that he'd heard enough that he wouldn't be too surprised by anything when he got there.

After the evening meal on the last day before leaving, Ed and the forty-nine others who were to be trasported to Stalag Lufts went about the hospital shaking hands, embracing, and saying goodbye to those who were staying. It was especially hard for Ed to say goodbye to George Butler, whose stomach wound had not healed enough to allow him to leave. In fact, over the last week, George had taken a bad turn, losing his appetite, running a fever, and lacking energy. The medics and doctors were concerned about his lack of response to treatment. He had been doing well during Ed's first week there, but then he began to decline.

"Hang in there, George. I expect to have you show up at my kriegie camp before long. I'm going to miss you, Buddy," Ed said.

"Don't hold your breath, Ed," George responded. "I'm not sure I'm going to make it. Something's wrong in here, and they don't seem to be able to do anything about it."

"Come on, George. You're going to make it! You're young and strong. Just a little bullet in the gut. You'll pull through," and Ed put his arms round George, hugging him. George returned the hug, but it was without much energy.

"Good luck, Ed. Good knowing you, but for too short a time. I don't advise trying to escape. Our troops are coming this way. They'll liberate all kriegies who are left when they get here."

"So long, George. See you later," Ed said, but he sensed a despair in George that hadn't been there before.

The departees were lined up and their names checked off on a list. As they were moved out into a corridor, they were stopped at a desk just outside the door. A German non-com was seated there. As each kriegie stopped in front of him, he looked at the prisoner's face, compared it with the photo on a card, then passed him on. As Ed stood there, the guard at the door was called back into the corridor. The German behind the desk looked all around, then placing his hand palm down over the card with Ed's picture on it, he closed his fingers over the picture so it came loose from the card. He put the photo down on the desktop, and let Ed pick it up. It was hard to believe, but here was another act of kindness by one of his captors. And once again, it was done at considerable risk to the one doing it. Ed had learned enough from George about how helpful an identification picture could be to a POW who might want to try to escape. He slipped the picture into his trousers pocket and moved on.

At the next table, each kriegie was issued a heavy GI overcoat and an OD knitted watch cap. Then they waited for the German guards, who would take them wherever they were to go next. As they waited, the medics walked along the line, shaking hands and saying good-bye to their former patients. One of them, Arnold, who had been especially helpful to Ed his first days there, stopped to speak to him.

"George doesn't know it yet," he said, "but when the doctors opened up his abdomen to repair the damage done by the bullet, they found cancer in an advanced stage. He's not going to make it—not because of the bullet, but because of the cancer."

"My God!" Ed exlaimed. "I've got to go back and see him again. This is terrible!"

Just then the guards arrived, and with much order-giving, shouting and pushing, they moved the prisoners out the doors to a railroad platform. All along the platform were identical doors, each one opening onto a tiny cubicle with a single bunk in it. Each prisoner was put into a cubicle, and the door was slammed shut and locked. Ed's cubicle, like the others, was unlighted and cold. "Poor George," he thought, as he pulled on the overcoat and rolled the watch cap down over his ears, "He must suspect something like that, and that's why he's so down. God! I wish I could be with him. It was a short friendship, but I really liked the guy. What a rotten break!"

He found the cot had a hard mattress and a single, gray woolen blanket on it. As night came on, the temperature dropped, so he laid down fully dressed and pulled the blanket over him. His last thoughts before drifting off to sleep were of George.

Sounds of a train chugging to a stop woke him; he was shivering with the cold. Guards opened the cubicle doors and let the prisoners out. They moved them all to the end of the platform, and directed them to urinate over the edge. They all needed to do so, so there was quite a deposit of steaming urine made there.

The train was a short one. Instead of coaches with passenger compartments, this train had two ancient cars with rough benches for the prisoners to sit on. Twenty-five of the men were herded into each car. German Red Cross ladies came aboard, and each man was given a thick slice of black bread and a cup of hot ersatz coffee. When they had collected the cups, the ladies left—to the kriegies' regret. A whistle blew and the train moved off.

Judging by the position of the sun, Ed concluded that they were going east. The car was drafty and unheated; fortunately, some warmth accumulated from the body heat of the prisoners.

The day wore on, and the train continued its slow way eastward. The men leaned on each other for warmth. At one point the train stopped in a tunnel and remained there for two hours. "Jaeger strafing!" one of the guards said, imitating a diving airplane with his hand and making a staccato noise to indicate machine gun fire.

When the train emerged from the tunnel, day had turned to evening. They were in hilly country now, and as darkness fell they passed through a small city. A mile or so on, the train stopped. The guards opened the car doors and stepped out onto a platform. They ordered the prisoners out and lined them up along the platform, where the officer in charge counted them. He then gave orders to the guards, who moved the prisoners in single file through a gate opened in a high chainlink fence with barbed wire at the top. Inside the high fence was more barbed wire, then a single steel wire at about knee height, which stretched into the distance along a well-trampled earthen walkway some twenty feet wide. Bordering the walkway were gray-painted wooden barracks. Outside the high fence were towers topped by roofed platforms, with walls that looked to be about three-and-a-half feet high. Between the low walls and the edges of the roofs could be seen, on each platform, the upper bodies of two armed guards and two machine guns trained on the walkway and the barracks buildings. Searchlights played over the entire compound. All the barracks were dark, but faces could be seen at the windows of the nearer ones. No prisoners were to be seen outside of the barracks.

The new prisoners were halted, and the gate was secured behind them. The officer in charge read off their names, and a number with each name. As a name and number was read, a guard would take the prisoner to a barracks, lead him inside, then open an inner door to a room, where he would be left.

When Ed's turn came and the barracks door was opened, he saw a dimly-lit corridor stretching to the far end of the building. No furniture of any kind could be seen in the corridor, nor any people. Closed doors faced the corridor from each side. His guard took him to a door halfway down the hall, where he knocked. The door opened onto a room dimly lit by a single bulb suspended from the ceiling. The windows were covered with blackout cloths. Six doubledeck bunks, several chairs and benches, a small table, and eleven men filled the room — overfilled it.

"Hullo, Yank," a clearly British voice said as Ed stepped in, "I'm Art Loveland."

Another British voice said, "Oh, God! Not another Yank!"

Ed shook the hand Art extended to him and said, "I'm Ed Thorne."

"Pay no attention to Andrew; Scots are like that," Art said, and he introduced Ed to the others. "Take off your heavy coat. We've just brewed up. Have a cuppa tea." Pointing to a lower bunk, Art continued, "There's your place."

Ed put his coat and hat on the bunk, took the cup Art offered, and sat on a bench near a tiny, obviously homemade stove that was burning coal, giving off good heat.

"Did they feed you, Ed?" Art asked.

"Not a bite since early morning."

"Well here, then. Have a bit of bread, and here's some butter in this tin, thanks to the Red Cross." Ed was grateful for the black bread and butter, and the hot tea. The others — five Americans counting himself, and seven British — all made him feel welcome, even Andrew, although he was quite reserved. They all questioned him about how and where he was captured, where he was based, what he flew, where he lived in the States, and so on. They were eager for news about the war, and about things in England and the U.S.

As the conversation continued, with all but Art and Ed staying on their bunks, he learned that this Stalag had been established early in the war, that it was well-run, that the prisoners were allocated food rations and a coal ration by the room. Then it was up to the occupants of each room to decide how to use the fuel and prepare, serve, and eat the food. The Red Cross parcels were supposed to be one per week per prisoner, but at this point, they were down to one-half per week. The policy in the room was to divide the cigarettes, D-bars, chewing gum, razor blades, and other such items evenly among the men in the room. Food items such as corned beef, soluble coffee, tea, sugar, powdered milk, biscuits, cereal, prunes and raisins were communal property to be used to prepare meals — along with the bread, potatoes, and occasional bits of meat or canisters of cattle-fodder soup supplied by the Germans.

He also learned that there was an active bartering program, and that cigarettes, D-bars, and chewing gum were excellent bartering items. Blackout rules were strictly enforced, with violators confined for a time in the "cooler," an unheated, unlit isolation cell. Other offenses were punished by time there too. Until recently, recaptured escapees were put in the cooler but lately the Germans had been shooting some escapees. Lights-out was at 22:00. As all this was being explained, the lights went out, and Ed and Art felt their way to their beds. Art adjusted the stove before he climbed into his bunk.

Just then, Ed remembered that he hadn't used a toilet since early morning, He spoke to the darkness, "Men, what chance is there of my getting to a toilet? It's been since early morning."

Art's voice came out of the darkness, "Righto. Come along," and he led Ed out the door into the corridor, where the dim bulb still gave its faint light. They went to the far end of the hall and turned left. Another dim light lit a latrine containing urinals and stalls; Ed went into a stall and sat. Art used a urinal, then said, "Can you find your way back to the room?"

"Sure can," Ed answered.

Art started to leave, then stepped back in and said, "Under no circumstances open the outside door. It's a good way to get shot, or attacked by roaming patrol dogs. We're allowed out of our rooms after lights-out only to use the latrine. See you later."

Ed made his way back to the room, where he left the door open, allowing enough of the dim light in so he could locate his bunk. Then, closing the door, he found his bed, removed his shoes, spread his overcoat over the single, thin blanket, and slipped into bed. His sleep was deep and uninterrupted.

Morning was announced by someone shouting in the hall, ""On appel!" Ed opened his eyes to see Art getting the coal fire started while all the others scrambled out of their beds and into their overcoats and hats. "What's going on?" he asked as he followed suit.

Sid, one of the Englishmen, said, "Sorry, old boy, we should have warned you. The goons have to count us to make sure no one has flown away during the night. It's bloody cold out there. Wear your heavy coat and your hat—we never know how long we'll have to stand to."

Ed followed the others out. On the frozen walkway in front of the line of barracks, prisoners lined up in four ranks, all shivering, and many only half awake. Armed guards stood in front and behind the ranks. Silence prevailed. Although the prisoners did not stand at attention, no one talked.

Now in the silence, boots could be heard striking the frozen clay in brisk march-time. Around the corner at the end of the row of barracks and past the end of the ranks of prisoners strode a single German officer, followed by four more officers, all in perfect step. The leading officer, walking as someone accustomed to command, wore a beautiful, dark leather greatcoat, the lower edge of which reached to a point midway between his knees and his feet. Below the hem could be seen his highly polished black boots. On his head he wore a high-crowned peak cap. The other four officers also wore leather coats, boots, and caps; less perfect-looking than the leader's.

The commanding officer placed himself opposite the center of the prisoners' formation, and just a pace in front of the single wire Ed had noticed the previous evening. The leader spoke, and the four officers spaced themselves two paces in front of their leader, and at equal intervals in front of the formation. Four guards took position at one end of the formation and on command from the leader—repeated by the four officers—each of the guards began counting one rank of prisoners.

As the guards finished their counting and reported to the four officers, more guards—one from each of the other barracks—also reported to the four officers. The officers then reported to the commanding officer, who said, "Sehr Gut." Then in crisp English, "Good morning, gentlemen. I hope you slept well. The counting is complete, and all are present. You are dismissed." The prisoners broke ranks and hurried into the barracks.

When Ed got back to his room, he saw that the fire Art had started before falling out for the head-count was burning well, but a bit smokily. Art adjusted the door of the little stove, and the smoke stopped. He watched Art put a coffeepot full of water on top of the stove and spoon in powdered coffee. Next, he cut slices of black bread and placed them on the flat top of the stove in front of the coffeepot. As the slices got toasted, he put them on tin plates, and Sid spread them with margerine, topped with a little honey, then passed the plates to the roommates. Meanwhile, Ted, one of the Americans, poured hot coffee into cups and passed them around. When the others had all been served, Art, Sid, and Ted served themselves. There was a wooden table at which all twelve could sit; a tight fit with five on benches on each side and two on stools at the ends. Several of the men, however, chose to sit on their bunks. There was enough coffee for refills for those who wanted them, and breakfast also included a vitamin C pill for each. These, Art told Ed, came in the Red Cross parcels.

Ed and Jack Burns, another of the Americans, were on cleanup, so they washed the cups, plates, knives, and spoons, putting them on shelves behind the stove. Several of the men returned to their bunks for more sleep, or to read by the light coming in through the uncovered windows. The blackout curtains were pulled back by the first one up each morning. This, it turned out, was usually Art. Others headed for the latrine to relieve themselves and to wash and shave. Ed joined them, and found that shaving with cold water was not much different from shaving with hot. When he got back to the room, Art said, "Let's go outside. I'll tell you more about this camp, and introduce you to the 'circuit.'"

The circuit was the hard-packed walkway Ed had seen the previous evening. It played a big part in kriegie life. Everybody walked the circuit every day. Some of the prisoners spent most of their time on it. It provided relief from the crowded rooms, and a chance for two or three to talk without having to include everybody in the conversation. Life stories, goals, plans, hopes, were shared. Sometimes arguments and disagreements were resolved. On rare occasions, fights broke out when problems could not be resolved. Escape plans were made and discussed in detail, and secrets were revealed to best buddies. In addition, a brisk walk several times around the circuit provided excellent exercise in the cold air, getting the blood moving and boosting the spirits. Without the socializing and humanizing effect the circuit provided, it is likely there would have been many more cases of men going "round the bend." And the prolonged confinement and restraint plus rigid discipline did drive some prisoners to suffer that mental-emotional breakdown.

The entire stalag was divided into compounds. Each compound was a square fenced-in area of multiple prisoner barracks, a shower building, a washhouse where prisoners could wash dishes, and several support buildings where German guards lived or supplies were stored. On every side of every compound, dividing adjoining compounds from one another and surrounding the stalag, were high guard stands along the fence. Kriegies were not permitted to go from one compound to another.

In Ed's compound, to his surprise, was a theater building built by the kriegies out of large wooden crates in which supplies, recreational equipment, musical instruments, and the like had been shipped in by the Salvation Army and the Red Cross and other charitable organizations. That was in the early years.

"The Germans are less tolerant now, and they no longer have the transport to bring things in for us. That is, of course, due to our destructive bombing and strafing. I mean, yours and ours. Our round-the-clock bombardment has devastated their roads, bridges, trains and tracks, and their manufacturing base. They are scarcely able to supply their own people and troops, let alone us."

The circuit followed the lines of the fence, going around all the barracks and other buildings, and just inside the single wire. The two walked briskly in the cold air as they talked. Ed was bothered some by the fast pace, but didn't want to admit it. Although it was uncomfortable, he thought it might be good for his bones and muscles. He did find it invigorating. "I'll show you the theater later on," Art said. "Notice the single wire stretched all around the circuit?" Art continued. "That's called the 'warning wire.' Don't get too close to it, and above all, don't touch it, step on it, or jump over it. The space between it and the high fence there, with all the barbed wire—that's what we call 'dead man's land.' The guards have standing orders to shoot anyone going inside the warning wire and they do it! They used to play games with us, but not any more. They've tightened down in every way."

As they walked and talked, more and more kriegies appeared on the circuit—singly, in twos, threes, occasionally fours—all walking in the same counter-clockwise direction. It was not crowded, but it was busy. "We have an ongoing educational program with courses in French and German, mathematics, literature, sketching, and writing, all taught by prisoners with expertise in various areas."

"Art," Ed said, "you've mentioned the 'early years' of the war, and of this camp. How long have you been here? Or is that a touchy subject?"

"Not at all. Do you remember Dunkirk?" Art replied.

"Yes. When was that? '39?" Ed said. Then realizing what Art meant, he went on, "God! No! You haven't been in here ever since then!"

"I have indeed. Quite a few of the other RAF types as well. Actually, it was 1940."

Still shocked, Ed said, "How have you stood it?"

"Oh, we cope. We keep busy. You'll see. It's become a way of life for us. But God willing, it'll be over soon."

"That's incredible! You must have had a lot go round the bend," Ed said, disbelief and admiration mixed in his voice.

"A few, especially at first, but not many. Most of us settled in and made the most of the situation. We planned escapes—some were done successfully—supported each other, kept active. Mail was much easier early on. We all corresponded with home regularly, and our families sent us personal parcels. We coped."

They walked a complete circuit before either spoke again, each lost in his own thoughts. Art was the first to restart the conversation. "By the way, Ed, this is strictly an officers' stalag. Only officers of the RAF and U.S. Air Corps. What you call 'enlisted men,' and we call 'the ranks,' are taken to other prison camps. The Germans are allowed by International Rules of War to require them to work. But not us. We have to find our own ways to keep busy, to keep from going bonkers. You'd best do the same. The ones who just lie around day after day are the ones who have the greatest trouble coping. We've learned that it's best to keep active."

"Sounds like a good idea; I'll get involved in something," Ed said. "I can't imagine just doing nothing all the time."

"Some manage to do just that, but not many. Just about everyone is involved in something, even if only elaborate escape plans. Some chaps work at that all the time. And some do it, too. They actually escape."

"You've actually had successful escapes?" Ed asked.

"Ah, yes. Quite a few over the years. We've actually gotten letters from escapees after they're safely at home. On that point, we've an efficient and elaborate intelligence system in our compound, and we coordinate with the other compounds. Part of that system is an 'escape committee.' Anyone planning an escape is supposed to clear the plan with the committee. If they approve, then assistance is provided for the attempt, as well as advice on the plan. Those who make an attempt without approval get no help and no support. We'll talk more about all this later. Right now, I have to get off to the theater for a rehearsal."

"Rehearsal? For what?" Ed asked.

Turning to leave the circuit, Art said, "We're preparing 'Messiah' for Christmas. Like to come along?"

"You bet I would," Ed replied. "Lead on."

As they approached the theater building, Ed noticed kriegies sitting or standing, singly or in pairs, at locations around the building. They gave the impression of just loafing about in the bright sunshine, or casually chatting. But he also noticed that they seemed to be looking alertly around all the time.

"Part of the intelligence system," Art said. "I'll tell you more about it later." He rapped two times, paused, then rapped once more. The door was opened from inside.

"Hullo, Art. Who's this? One of the new ones?" a British kriegie asked. Art introduced Ed, and they went in. The theater surprised Ed. It looked as if it would seat three or four hundred. There was a raised stage in front, and space for an orchestra in front of the stage. Music stands, chairs, and instruments were standing or leaning in the orchestra pit, but no players. There was a parlor organ in the pit at about the center, and a man was seated at the organ, pumping the pedals and going over passages of Handel's music.

On stage, standing around and talking to one another, were about sixty men. When Art stepped onto the stage, the men moved into four ranks in a semicircle. Art took a position in front of them, with a music stand in front of him. The organist stopped his playing and Art said, "All right. Good morning. Let's start our warm-up." Then turning his head to look around at the organist, he said, "An 'A' please, George." The organ sounded the note.

"Basses," Art said. "Humming, please," and a low humming started, then as Art moved his arms apart, it grew louder. He signalled, and the low humming stopped. "Tenors," and the same procedure on a higher pitch ensued, followed by "Altos," and "Sopranos." "Good," Art said. "Now, all together," and the four pitches of a chord were hummed, crescendoed, then de-crescendoed, and stopped. "Now on *ah*." Art was enlarging and diminishing the sound, listening and pointing to one section or another, asking for more or less, or indicating someone was off pitch. The singers took their breath in staggered timing, so the sound was continuous. Finally satisfied, Art said, "Worthy Is The Lamb." Now the organ gave the key, and the glorious opening chords of one of Ed's favorite parts of "Messiah" rang out vigorously, beautifully. He listened and was moved.

Art made some comments, then said, "Let's try that again. It's coming along nicely. Ready!" Again the beautiful sounds came, and Ed, remembering the tenor part, began to sing along. Hearing him, Art turned his head and nodded, so Ed continued, but now at full voice. The piece ended and Art said, "Relax for a minute," and came off the stage to speak to Ed.

"You have a fine voice, Ed. Are you a singer? I think you are."

Ed replied, "Well, yes. I did some professional singing before I enlisted. Out of shape now, and it hurts some to sing, but it also feels good. It's been a long time."

"You're trained, then? I thought so. And a tenor! We don't have a tenor soloist. Stay after rehearsal, and we'll talk." He returned to the stage to continue the rehearsal. He worked the singers hard, insisting on precise diction, exact pitch, perfect time, and the intonation he wanted. At last satisfied that they were on the right track, he took them through the entire chorus, then said, "We have a month to polish it. That will do for now. Let's have a go at 'Since By Man Came Death,'" and he worked them on this just as he had on "Worthy." Finally, he said, "Thank you, Gentlemen. That's all for today," and the chorus members left. "Can you stay, George?" he asked the organist.

"Righto, Art. I've no place to go."

"Thanks. Ed, this is George Boling—he's an excellent organist. He gets much more out of this little instrument than we have a right to expect. This is Ed Thorne, George. He has had professional training and experience and, remarkably, is a tenor."

"We need that," George said, shaking Ed's hand. "Now Ed, have you ever done the tenor solos of 'Messiah?'" Ed said that he had.

"Could we hear a bit?"

"Well, I'm out of shape. Haven't done any singing for several years. If you'll make allowances for that, I'll try 'Comfort Ye.'"

"Perfect. George?" Art said.

"Right," George said, and started the measured, quiet introductory chords.

"Comfort ye. Comfort ye, my people," Ed sang, and it felt good. He finished, and Art came up to him. "That was lovely, Ed," he said. "What a fine voice. Can you do 'Every Valley?'"

"I'd better not tackle that right now; better stop while I'm ahead. I'd need to do a lot of work on that. But if you want me to take part in 'Messiah,' I'm willing."

"Want you!" George exclaimed. "You're a Godsend! Isn't he Art?"

"He certainly is. Welome, Ed. Thrice welcome. You will fill a real gap for us. Yes, we'd love to have you. I'd like the others to hear you. It would give them a real boost. Could you do 'Comfort,' and one other tomorrow? It would be at 10:00 in the morning."

"All right," Ed replied. "I could probably do 'Behold and See.' Would that be okay?"

"Marvelous! Here, take a score with you. Refresh your memory," Art said. "Study it a little bit and see what solos you'd like to do. Look at the soprano solos, too. All right?"

"You're not serious."

"Indeed I am," Art said. "We need someone to sing at least some of the soprano solos."

"Okay, I'll see what I can do," Ed said, and left with the book. Elated that he would be involved in a major musical undertaking, something he could enjoy and contribute to and keep himself busy as well, he did two circuits before returning to the room. Art was already there, and had evidently told the others about the new soloist. They all asked him about his singing experiences, and said they were glad he would be doing the solos.

While that was going on, Art—who seemed to be the room leader as well as chief cook and fire-builder—with Sid's help, was supplementing the German-supplied "cattle fodder" soup with potatoes and buillion. The buillion was from Red Cross parcels; the potatoes provided by the Germans. The soup alone had little flavor, but with the additions, it was reasonably palatable, as long as it was hot.

The midday meal was the main one of the day. This day it consisted of the soup, black bread, coffee, and a pudding cake made of crumbled biscuits, softened with powdered milk and water, partially sweetened with sugar, and topped with marmalade. The biscuits, sugar, powdered milk and marmalade were from Red Cross parcels. These items were hoarded by the members of the room instead of being devoured as soon as the parcels arrived. This made it possible for Art and Sid, who, as Ed was to discover, were culinary magicians, consistently to make remarkable and varied meals from the minimum materials available.

After lunch, Art was off to take care of a class he was teaching, then a security meeting, and he had another meeting to attend in the evening, so Ed and Sid walked the circuit. "Art seems to be a busy guy," Ed said.

"Hell of a chap," Sid said. "He's been here since '40. Knows all the ropes. He's involved in everything important, not just in this compound, but in the others too. A doer."

"I can see that already. He sure knows how to handle the choir," Ed said.

"He should that. Did he not tell you of his background?"

"No, nothing."

"Just like him! Have you heard of Sir Adrian Boldt?"

"Yes. Isn't he conductor of one of the major English symphony orchestras? London Symphony, isn't it?"

"Exactly. Well, Art worked under him. He was assistant choral director of the symphony. Except for the war, I've no doubt he'd be the choral director," Sid said.

"No kidding! No wonder he knows what he's doing. I could tell he was good, but I didn't know that."

"He's well regarded in English music."

"I'm impressed. I look forward to talking with him some more."

"Not a lot of chance for that. He's a busy man, doesn't much care to sit around chatting. He'd rather be doing than talking."

Ed was to find this to be true as he got to know Art better. But at the next morning's rehearsal, where Ed met bass soloist John Casson, baritone Glenn Andrews, and the members of the chorus, Art showed no sign of being hurried or harried. Art, along with all the others, expressed gratitude that they now had a tenor soloist.

Before starting the choral rehearsal, Art asked Ed if he would do "Comfort Ye" for the chorus and John and Glenn. Ed did, and when he ended, they broke out in spontaneous applause. Ed did an exxagerated bow, and said "Thank you."

"Care to try 'Every Valley?" Art asked.

"Not today," Ed replied. "I'd like to go through 'Behold,' but we can wait 'til after."

"I don't think the chaps would mind if you did it now," Art said. "What say, men?" They all said good; hear, hear; or yes.

Because he had always considered this one of the more moving passages in 'Messiah,' Ed sang it with great feeling. The response from the chorus and the other two soloists was even more enthusiastic. John Casson who, Ed later learned, was a member of the well-known English acting family, was especially complimentary, saying that that was the best he'd ever heard it sung. Ed was sure that this was because in this relatively culturally deprived setting, he hadn't heard it at all.

Next, Art took the chorus through "Worthy Is The Lamb" twice, and to Ed it sounded marvelous. After that, John and Glenn sang their solos. Ed was impressed with both. John boomed out "The Trumpet Shall Sound" with a large, full bass voice. Glenn, a lighter, more flexible baritone with equally excellent quality, sang "He Was Despised." The chorus applauded both of them, and Ed told each how great they sounded. The rehearsal ended with everybody joining in a vigorous "Hallelujah Chorus."

After dismissing the chorus, John and Glenn, Art sat down beside Ed to tell him more about the "Escape Committee" and the camp intelligence system, including a secret radio receiver which kept them informed of how the war was progressing. He told him about "ferrets"—Germans who wore blue coveralls and soft shoes, whose job it was to sneak under the barracks or into the attics and listen to prisoners' conversations, to try to get information about escape plans or espionage efforts.

"The circuit is important for avoiding ferrets. Many important discussions are carried on during walks around the circuit.

"But we also have observers posted all over the compound, so we know where every ferret is, and every guard. Because of this, important strategy meetings can be held in our rooms, and the Escape Committee can hear and discuss escape plans. And of course the radio monitors have to be warned too. Sometimes we have discussions to mislead the goons, knowing a ferret is listening. We use this to camouflage real activities sometimes. It leads them to watch out for the wrong thing while the real thing is going on.

"In the next day or so, I'll take you around and show you our 'Print Shop,' where we have experts forging German identity and work papers to help approved escapes. I will also show you our 'Tailor Shop,' where real ingenious work is done in making civilian clothes and shoes out of military ones, including dyeing. These fellows are good. All of this has to be done surreptitiously, so you can see why our lookouts have to be alert."

Ed was amazed to hear all this, and said so.

"But," Art said, "I've saved the best for last. Sit tight for a minute, while I check on something." When he returned, he said, "Now, Ed, look around this building. Tell me what you see. Look carefully, walk around and examine everything. If you spot anything unusual, anything that seems out of place, or odd-looking, tell me."

Ed started with the stage, and the tiny wings on either side. He looked at the minimal curtains and pullies and lines. He paid particular attention to the stage floor, looking for signs of an opening, a trap door, a removable section. He found nothing. Next came the orchestra pit. Again, he found nothing. Looking at the audience seats, and under them at the wood floor, nothing appeared wrong or unusual. Finally, he examined the coal burning heating stove near the rear wall. To minimize the danger of fire, the wooden floor had not been installed where the stove stood. It was on loose, neatly raked earth, and it was burning, giving out excellent heat. He looked under it, around it, and above it. He examined the area around the metal chimney pipe, which passed through the roof.

He returned to where Art was leaning against the front edge of the stage. "I don't know what I was supposed to be looking for, but everything looked perfectly normal to me."

"That's good. We would be unhappy if you spotted anything. Come with me," Art said. Ed followed him as he went to one of the side doors, where he spoke to a kriegie who was lounging on the steps, sketching on a pad. "All clear, Sam?" Art asked. Without even looking up, Sam gave a barely perceptible nod, and Art closed the door.

"Over here, now," Art said, and went quickly to the stove. There he bent down and moved the shaker handle up and, grasping the stove by its two front legs, pushed it to his left. Ed was surprised to see the stove move easily, as if on a pivot, pushing a small mound of loose dirt ahead of it while the loose dirt under it moved with it. The smoke pipe seemed centered on the pivot point, with the lower part turning noiselessly inside the upper. As the dirt-covered base moved, Ed could see a square opening directly under the base. Art reached down and flipped a switch. Lights came on and Ed could see a tunnel running from one side of the opening.

"Get down on your knees and take a good look," Art told him, and he did so. He saw a long, lighted tunnel, with cross-beams and supporting uprights spaced evenly along its length. There were miniature tracks, and a few yards from the opening, a box rested on wheels, which fit the tracks. A rope stretched from the far end of the box down the tunnel, and another was coiled at the base of the opening.

Art switched off the light and said, "All right, get up. We can't keep this open too long. Push on the legs, and let's close it." Ed did so, then Art raked the soil around, obliterating all traces of movement and their foot and hand prints.

"Fantastic," Ed said.

"Let's get on out," Art said, just as the lounging kriegie could be heard whistling, "God Save the King."

"That's the signal that a goon's headed this way. Let's go!" They left by the other door as Art switched out the lights. They joined the others walking the circuit.

"Some tunnel!" Ed said, when they were at a spot where no one was near. "Looks like a big project."

"It is. Well-engineered, too. The work goes slowly. Only three men can be down there at any one time. One is digging at the far end, and two handle the cart. Digging has to be slow so no noise is transmitted above the dig. But a major problem is getting rid of the dirt."

"I can see that," Ed said. "You can't just make a pile of dirt beside the stove, or outside the building. What do you do with it?"

"I'll explain," Art replied. "But, first, we don't speak of this as a tunnel. It is called the project. Now then, the ones in the project are moles. Those who distribute the dirt are squirrels. They have holes in the side pocket of their trousers, or their overcoats in cold weather. With dirt in each hand, they walk the circuit, letting a few crumbs fall as they walk. The crumbs are walked on by others on the circuit, becoming part of the earth."

"Clever," Ed said. "I can see why progress has to be slow."

"Yes, and the same ones can't keep going in for more and coming out. That would be too obvious. So, you see, we have to have lots of squirrels. Also, there has to be some legitimate reason for people to be in the theater. Rehearsals for the choir, the orchestra, or a play are good cover. The members can leave one at a time, or all at once. Of course, if they leave all together, they can't all function as squirrels.

"Again, it would be too obvious if forty or fifty men left the theater all at once, all with their hands in their pockets, and all going directly to the circuit."

"Sounds like you've thought of everything."

"Not quite. We have not solved the ventilation problem. Work on the project has to be done with the stove over the opening, with three men inside. The air gets bad quite quickly. We've had some close calls.

"Suppose three men are in working, and have been for thirty minutes, which is about the maximum. But before they can be got out, a goon comes into the theater. Those above have to go on rehearsing or building scenery—whatever they may be there for—until the goon leaves. Meanwhile, nothing can be done about those in the project."

"That's scary!" Ed said. "Three men may be slowly suffocating. Everybody knows it, but they can't do anything about it. Have you actually lost anyone?"

"No, thank God! I'm not sure we'd go that far. We'd reveal the project rather than lose three men."

"I'm glad to hear that! How close have you come?"

"Much too close. The worst one I was involved in was last year about this time. We do 'Messiah' every year, just as we will this year. I was rehearsing the chorus while three men were in the project loading the cart so the squirrels in the chorus would have stuff to distribute. Time was up for them to be below. Two men were about to move the stove to get them out when the signal came that a goon was approaching. The two men came back to the stage and we went on with the rehearsal. Sure enough, the goon came in. Usually, they stay only a minute or two. It was a cold day, and the stove was giving off good heat, so the goon sat down to listen to the singing while he got warm. He stayed on, and I was getting worried.

"When we were ten minutes over time, I decided we had to take a chance. I said to the choir, 'You sound very good up on the stage. Now, I want to hear how you sound from the back of the theater. Take your places back there, and we'll do the Hallelujah Chorus.' They all knew the situation, so they hurried back and stood in front of the stove. Fortunately, the goon stayed where he was. While we sang the music good and loud, two men moved the stove, and three more voices joined the singing. We continued singing until I saw the heads of the two who had moved the stove reappear in the back line of the choir. This told me that everything was in order, so I continued to the end of the Hallelujah, then told them they sounded good from the back, too, and had them return to the stage. The three moles told me, loudly, that they had classes to get to, so they left the building. The goon left while the choir was re-assembling on the stage."

"What a close call that was!" Ed said. "Both the danger the goon might find out about the project, and the worry about the moles below. Must have had you sweating."

"I did a bit, right enough. We all did, but we couldn't let the three chaps suffocate, could we?"

"No, but . . ." Ed stopped short. "Real quick thinking on your part, Art."

"Not actually, I'd the plan in mind for months. Bit of luck that it worked out."

A few days later, Art took Ed to the Print Shop and the Tailor Shop. The documents turned out in the one, and the civilian-looking clothes by the other, were astonishing. "These guys are geniuses," Ed said, as he looked at work papers, travel permits, identification papers, passes, and tickets of various sorts, and then everything from farm workers' rough clothing to well-tailored business suits.

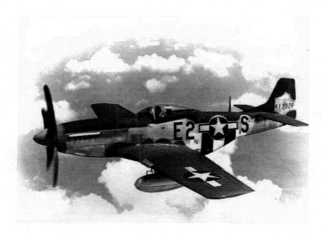

29

Real winter set in as Christmas approached. The BBC broadcast, monitored on the secret radio, reported on the extra hardship troops in the field were suffering due to the extreme cold. "The coldest weather in Germany for over a hundred years," was what they were saying. "With no let-up in sight." The guards were bothered by the cold, but they did not have to stay out in it day after day, night after night, as combat troops did. Nor did the prisoners. It was imposssible to keep the barracks rooms warm, but the kriegies were protected from the wind. The little homemade stoves took the edge off the cold during the day, and nights were spent sleeping with overcoats on over jackets in addition to every other thing they could wear.

There was not enough coal supplied to keep the fires going at night. Just before Christmas, the Germans reduced the coal ration even more. So in Ed's room, someone would crawl out of bed before the others and get a fire started. By the time roll call was over, the coffee water would be hot for the freezing men. The fire would be kept going long enough to make a hot breakfast out of whatever was available.

When Ed arrived at the stalag, Art was the one who started the fire every morning. He did so voluntarily. Ed, who had always been an early riser, started getting up too and assisting by fanning or whatever was needed to get the fire going. He watched carefully how Art went about it, then offered to take over the responsibility so Art could stay in bed longer if he wanted to. Art said, "No need to do that, Ed. I don't mind doing it." But Ed insisted, so Art agreed to let him try his hand.

For the first few days of Ed's fire-starting, the room was filled with smoke. He hadn't yet gotten the knack of controlling the door opening and the damper. Some of the roommates complained but Art said, "He'll get better at it. Anyway, the smoke is warming." So Ed continued starting the morning fire. He did improve, but he never got as good as Art, who had been doing it for years. When anyone complained too vigorously, Art would say, "Do you want to take over?" and the complaining would stop.

Fortunately, the coal ration for the theater was not reduced, so rehearsals went on in relatively good comfort. Ed was now doing most of the soprano solos as well as the tenor ones. Art worked with him, especially on "Every Valley," and he felt more confident as rehearsals went on.

News of Allied successes in overcoming German forces continued to come from the BBC. All the kriegies were feeling confident. Then one night, Dec. 16, a new, unexpected, massive German offensive in the west was reported. This very powerful, all-out operation seemed to catch the Allies by surprise, and the Germans were having great success in pushing the Allies back. It became known as the "Battle of the Bulge." As the news spread out over the camp, kriegies who had been thinking liberation was near—perhaps as early as Christmas—now grew disheartened. From the reports, they knew that liberation was not going to be in a matter of days, but ,of months.

Now, to add to the gloom, the kriegie intelligence people began to warn that it looked as if a massive movement of the prisoners was being planned by the Germans. They were all alerted to sleep fully clothed, which most of them were already doing, and to start saving D-bars, cereal, raisins, prunes, biscuits—anything that was highly nutritious and could be made a part of "iron rations," a highly concentrated, easily concealed and carried food. It had been developed for escapees to take with them. Each kriegie was to save a little of his Red Cross parcel share to make his own iron ration. This was an extra hardship, since the already too-small ration had been cut in half recently by the Germans.

About a week before Christmas, Ed was walking the circuit alone. Art joined him, saying nothing. Ed looked at him and saw that his face was pale and his mouth clamped shut, with his lips compressed in a straight line. Obviously, something was wrong. Not wanting to intrude, Ed kept quiet for one complete circuit. Then, worried about Art, who rarely showed his feelings, he asked, "What's wrong, Art? Want to talk about it?"

Uncharacteristically, Art did not respond. After they had walked another half lap, Art said through tight lips, "You've heard nothing?"

"About what?" Ed responded.

"You haven't heard about last night? Nothing?"

"I don't know what you're talking about, Art."

They walked a few more steps and Art said, with his expression still grim, "It's good you didn't hear anything. That means our security was good. Do you remember that I was out of the room for two hours last night?"

"I sure do. You said you were having a special rehearsal for the chorus."

"Right. And you wanted to go along, but I told you that wouldn't be a good idea."

"Yeah, I couldn't understand that. I was a little bit irritated about it."

"I knew you were, but I couldn't let you go along. The 'special rehearsal' was a cover for the great escape."

"You mean through the project?"

"Yes, that's exactly what I mean. After all of our work, our planning, we finally put the final stage into operation. If the news of the Allied advances had continued good, we might never have gone on with it. But the word about the big German offensive triggered a strong reaction among those scheduled to break out, so the Committee decided to go on it."

"That's great!" Ed said. "Aren't you excited? How many got out?" Then, seeing that Art's face was still grim, he asked, "What's wrong? What happened?"

Art took a deep breath and said, "What happened is that fifty-seven got out, but the goons were waiting for them! They knew about it, Ed! My God, out of fifty-seven only three got away. Thirty were shot trying to run away. All the others were brought back in and thrown in the cooler."

"God!" Ed exclaimed. "But why did so many keep climbing out after the first ones were caught?"

"The damned bloody goons stayed out of sight until all fifty-seven were out, and then they closed in on them." Art caught his breath in a half-sob. "God, Ed! We thought we might lose a few. That's an acceptable risk, but so many! Somebody had to break security; somebody talked. Damn him to hell, whoever he is! If we find him out, he's a dead man!"

Ed had never seen Art so emotional. He put his arm over Art's shoulder, but he didn't know what to say to him. After another two laps in silence, Art said, "Sorry, old man, I didn't mean to go off like that."

"Don't be stupid, Art. You had plenty of reason. What happens now?"

"Hard to know. The goons will probably have an inquiry, and our intelligence committee certainly will. But it's over. Rotten luck for the poor chaps so close to liberation. The committee members are all devastated. The attempt was approved."

"It sure wasn't the committee's fault. The guys wanted to go. It seemed the right thing to do."

"That's true. But it's tough to swallow anyway. Well, it's behind us, but it won't be easily forgotten."

"Come on, Art. You've been through so much! Don't let this one more thing, which was no fault of yours, get you."

"I won't. Too much to do. I'm going to put it out of my mind. Rehearsal will be as usual this afternoon. It will be tough, but we have to carry on."

Art went to a meeting of the intelligence committee, and Ed did two more laps, then went into the room. Rehearsal that afternoon was hard for everybody, but they all tried not to let the tragedy of the preceding night hurt their performance.

The evening roll call kept all of the kriegies standing in the piercing cold for over an hour as the commandant harangued them in German, with a translator repeating everything in English. This was something of an insult, since everybody knew that the commandant spoke quite good English.

Christmas came, and after standing in the bitter cold for the morning head-count, the twelve roommates came back into the room, which was smoky as usual from Ed's fire. Meager gifts were exchanged. Each one gave each of the others something he had hoarded for days: a couple of cigarettes, a stick or two of chewing gum, a piece of a D-bar, or some other such bit. In the non-kriegie world such small items would have been insignificant. But here they carried a great deal of weight because they meant that the giver had made a large sacrifice in resisting eating or using or bartering this item he now gave to his roommates. Ed found himself close to tears as they embraced each other, all trying to be merry as they wished one another "Merry Christmas."

Breakfast was a treat. Art and Sid had somehow bartered for enough tins of Vienna Sausages, which occasionally showed up in Red Cross parcels, and powdered eggs, to give each one in the room a meal of two slices of kriegie bread with marmalade, powdered eggs and a sausage, a few spoonfuls of stewed prunes and apricots, and hot coffee.

After breakfast, Ed and Art went to the theater to light the fire and arrange benches on the stage for the chorus and chairs for the soloists. Then they walked the circuit, sharing their hopes and ambitions for after liberation. "You'll be pursuing a singing career, of course," Art said to Ed.

"I don't know, Art," Ed replied. "I've been doing a lot of thinking about that. I'm not at all sure any more that that's what I want to do."

Art stopped walking and stared at Ed. "But you must! You have a talent. You must use it."

"Thanks, Art, but I'm twenty-five. I've lost three years of singing. Anyway, I was having voice problems before I left home. I'd have to find a new teacher—a truly competent one—and start over to rebuild my voice and learn better technique. A singing career in the States is tough enough, but with a late start and voice problems to work out, it could be impossible."

They resumed walking. "Listen Ed, I have heard no sign of voice problems in what you've been doing for us. Are you sure this isn't imaginary?"

"My voice has had lots of rest, so it seems fresh. And what I've been doing here has been enjoyable—not too demanding. Back home, I'd have to work a lot more and a lot harder to get anywhere. I couldn't work just a little bit every day, as we've been doing here."

"If you think it wouldn't work out for you in the States, come to England. We produce very few really fine tenor soloists. For some reason, we do better with basses and baritones, and of course, sopranos, but not tenors. We have excellent vocal coaches. I can almost guarantee success for you in my country."

"You're being kind, Art. Since you are a professional musician, I take what you say seriously. But I seem to have lost my motivation to pursue a singing career."

"Oh, come, now!" Art burst out. "I can tell by what you put into your singing that you love it. What do you mean, 'lost your motivation?'"

"I do enjoy singing, Art. I'll keep on singing for my own pleasure, no matter what else I do. I'm not awfully clear on what I mean. I've tried to figure it out since I've been here. The circuit is a great place to work things out in your mind. It's not been clear what I want to do, but it has something to do with the war, and the stupidity of humanity going to war and destroying each other. Not finding, in fact, not even *trying* to find, other ways of solving problems. We're getting so efficient at killing each other, I doubt we can survive another war after this one. We have to find another way! I don't think a singing career, even if I could have a successful one, would contribute much to solving that problem."

"But, Ed, old fellow, bringing enjoyment and pleasure to others is a great contribution; it enriches, it helps to humanize."

"I know that, Art, and I believe it. All the arts help to quell the animal in all of us. And artists have always been on the cutting edge of reform and revolution. But it isn't enough. Look at Germany! With all her great composers, musicians, poets, great artists! Yet misled by Hitler, they have engaged in the most organized and efficient dehumanizing and demeaning actions since the Roman Empire and its treatment of early Christians. I don't know what it will be, but I'm looking for some way to contribute directly to peaceful ways of solving problems. Wars are too easily started, and too increasingly destructive. All they seem to produce is more conflict, not solutions to humanity's problems. There must be some way we can stop relying on war to resolve differences. War is too efficient in destruction, and totally inefficient in solving problems. I want to find some way, even a small way, to contribute to preventing further wars."

"I'm amazed," Art said. "From the first time you sang for us at rehearsals, I've said to myself, 'This man will go far as a singer.' I've assumed that you would pursue a singing career. Now I find that there is something deeper and more far-reaching in you. I think that must be part of what makes your singing so rich. There is a lot more in you that is a part of your singing. Are you sure you don't want to bring this to the world?"

"No, Art, I'm not sure. I'm just trying to figure it out. You're the first person I've even mentioned this to."

"You haven't reached a decision yet, then? We must talk more. Don't close your mind to a singing career, will you?"

"Okay, Art. I appreciate your listening, and I would like to talk more. Talk some more! That's it! That may be the very thing I'm looking for. People all over the world must TALK to each other! If we don't talk to each other, we can't work together to solve our problems. This conversation with you has helped me at least get some direction in my thinking. Wouldn't it be great if all the people in the world would learn to talk to the rest of the people of the world? I mean, DEMAND that their leaders talk to other leaders, sincerely and honestly, not walk out as soon as there is a disagreement, but stay there and talk! Not go home and start preparing to fight!

"Just talking for talk's sake, or for show, won't solve problems. But talking honestly and openly, with a commitment to keep on talking, could. We need to communicate! Maybe this is where I can contribute." Ed grew more and more energetic and walked faster and faster.

"Slow down, Ed. Walking faster won't solve any problems, either," Art said. "What you're saying is important. Communication is a vital necessity, and an important area, all right. But we've had the League of Nations since WWI, and here we are in WWII!"

"But what we haven't had, Art, is a commitment by everybody to try to understand each other—what the problems are, what needs to be done, how to help each other. To keep talking until understanding is achieved, and some agreement reached. It seems to me that we have meetings where each participant is trying to further his own interests, not to solve the world's problems, or prevent those unsolved problems from carrying us into war."

"We will talk again, Ed. Right now, we'd better get back for our noon snack. We can't be late for our own 'Messiah' performance."

"You're right. Let's go." After toast and tea, Art and Ed went to the latrine to wash up and shave. Ed had no tie to wear with his uniform shirt, so Sid lent him a black one. All members of the chorus and the soloists wore shirts and ties; Art the same.

There were to be three performances to accomodate all who wanted to attend, including the German commandant and his staff, the guards—who rotated duties in order to attend different performances—and almost all of the kriegies. Forty-five minutes before the first performance, Art took the chorus and soloists through a warm-up.

At performance time, with the little theater crowded, all seats taken and all the back and side spaces jammed with standees, George played the organ introduction. Ed, having the first solo, then stood. He felt nervous as the introductory music came from the organ, then a great surge of emotion flooded through him. His voice responded to the emotion as he started "Comfort Ye." The words seemed appropriate to this audience of prisoners, and to the Germans as well, on this holy day. "Comfort ye! Comfort ye, my people, saith your God, saith your God." Ed felt this as he never had felt it before. He looked out on the eager faces and saw eyes glittering, as he felt his own were. He poured himself into the music and words, feeling his soul emptying itself of anger, frustration, and fear. He sensed the listeners giving back everything he gave. They and he seemed to merge into one, giving comfort to one another, then hope, as Ed went on to "Every Valley." His voice felt sure and true, and the music seemed to have a momentum of its own, with his part effortless—he was just an instrument of the music. It was a new experience for him. He felt awed and exalted. "The crooked straight, and the rough places plain" rolled out of his mouth, repeated, and it was over.

The entire audience rose, their faces lifted, and they stood in silence for a few moments, as though they and Ed had shared an experience that they weren't quite ready to have end. Even the commandant and the other Germans stood. No one applauded, as if they all were afraid it would break the spell. Art turned to direct the chorus. Ed saw that Art's eyes were gleaming as he nodded to Ed.

This inspiring start set the tone for the entire performance. Soloists and chorus poured out Handel's music and the familiar texts with energy and vivacity, with marvelous tone and shading, and the chorus responded to Art's every sign keenly and fully.

When Ed got to "Behold and see if there be any sorrow like unto His sorrow," the intensity and momentum was so great that he felt light-headed at first. But he let it have its way with him, trusting. The effect on him was magical, and he felt the response again from the audience.

Art had decided to put the "Hallelujah Chorus" at the end because of its celebratory tone and uplifting spirit. He invited the listeners to join in and they did, lustily, no holding back, so the theater rocked as everybody let loose his feelings and hopes in that famous chorus. When the final "Hallelujah" came, the last syllable was held an extra measure as Art extended his arms upward to hold, then stop, the singing. The listeners, already standing, began applauding, stamping feet and cheering. It went on for several minutes, with chorus and soloists and leader all applauding back to the audience. At last, the happy crowd left, and the singers went out for a breath of air and to find a latrine.

Art came to Ed, took his hand in both of his, looked deeply into his eyes, and said, "Ed, that was magical. You exposed your whole soul, and everybody was moved. That was singing at its best."

Ed thanked Art. He felt drained. He knew that in about an hour there would be another performance. He needed a quiet place where he could be alone. The theater had emptied. Even Art had gone back to the room for a cup of tea. After sitting for a few minutes in a front row seat, Ed realized that other kriegies would likely come in, or a guard would check the place. He had to find a place where he would not be disturbed. He remembered the small wings on each side of the stage. He went to the stage-right one, pulled a chair into a corner and sat. He forced himself to relax. As the minutes passed, the feeling of depletion decreased, and new energy began to flow. A feeling of accomplishment came over him, and he began to think of the next performance. By the time the chorus members began to drift back in, he was "up" for the next presentation.

Art came in, soloists and chorus took their places, and the warming-up was done. The doors were opened and the house filled to capacity again. The organ started and once again Handel's music poured forth. This performance, and the third, were excellent, but neither one reached the peak of the first one. Ed was sure that that was unrepeatable. He and the other participants were pleased with what they accomplished, and both audiences were moved and applauded vigorously, but the extra feeling of being over the top was reserved for that magical first "Messiah."

Back in the room they found that Sid, who had attended the first performance, had gone ahead preparing the dinner that he and Art had planned. Potatoes were cooked and ready for mashing. Canned carrots and peas were warming on the stove. Somehow the Germans had secured enough beef to give each room a piece large enough for every prisoner to have a few bites. As important as the few bites were, the aroma of the meat cooking was even more important. It wasn't turkey or goose, but it was a smell that the prisoners had not had in a long time. Now Chet, the most reserved of the RAF men, sprang his big surprise on the others. For months, he had hoarded a few raisins out of his rations and had bartered for some sugar. With these items, plus water, he had secretly made a jar full of "Kriegie Brew." It had fermented in a corner under his bed. Now he pulled the jar from its hiding place, filled each man's cup, and said, "Merry Christmas, everybody." They all responded with "Hear, hear!" It was like vintage wine to the kriegies, and they proposed toast after toast, mainly to liberation, or to the Allies, to families and friends back home, to each other. The brew was potent, and the first cups increased the already festive mood. They sipped, toasted, and sang carols for this brief time, forgetting cold, limited food, lack of freedom, and the loss of friends in the recent ill-fated escape attempt. Art and Sid together announced that dinner was ready.

Chet refilled each cup. Andrew MacPherson said a heartfelt grace, to which the others said "Amen," and they all sat down. Art and Sid filled each plate with an equal portion of the prepared food. Chet, usually taciturn, surprised everybody by saying, "Good food. Large porsh per pers," which set them all to laughing, and they all fell to. Silence fell as they ate, each one lost for a few moments in his own thoughts. Ed was not the only one at the table who had trouble swallowing for a short time, as he choked up with thoughts of freedom and what it meant, of other Christmases, and of how lucky he was to be alive and here with this group of men.

As the last of the main course disappeared, and Art and Sid served steaming portions of a delicious plum pudding made with prunes and black bread, along with coffee, the spirit of conviviality returned. More singing followed dinner, and Chet shared the last of his brew.

Just before lights-out, all the kriegies from all the rooms in the barracks crowded into the central corridor, milling about, shaking hands, and wishing their fellow prisoners "Merry Christmas." Someone started "Silent Night," and everybody joined in. Much quieter now, they all went back into their rooms. Ed and his roommates finished off the brew remaining in their cups and got into their bunks just as the lights went out. "Given the circumstances," Ed thought as he drifted off to sleep, "this was a great Christmas."

As far as the Germans were concerned, the Christmas spirit did not extend to the next morning. Too early, "Aufwachen!" sounded through the building, and with groans and many

"Oh my aching heads," the kriegies fell out to stand, many unsteadily, in line to be counted. The head-count took an extra long time because guards had to roust out some prisoners who had fallen back to sleep. Feet numbed with the cold, and many with aching heads, the kriegies were finally dismissed and they rushed to their rooms or to the latrine.

Ed and his roommates found that the room felt as cold as the outdoors, so everybody but Ed got back into bed. Ed got a tiny fire started, with only a little smoke in the room. He gradually fed in additional bits of coal and, huddling close to the stove, he warmed himself. This was the first time he had ever seen Art go back to bed. "He deserves it," he thought. "He's got to be exhausted."

Now, with the fire doing well, Ed put water into the coffeepot for the morning brew. As the temperature rose slightly in the room, and the smell of coffee began to reach them, the others yawned, moaned and groaned. Then, one at a time, they stretched and dragged themselves out of bed. Each one, after returning from the latrine, helped himself to a cup of coffee, then joined Ed near the stove. Remarkably, only two had reddened eyes and complained of headaches.

So the day after Christmas, 1944, began. After breakfast, Ed and Art walked the circuit. Just as they had for a week, they heard heavy guns booming to the east—miles away. Art recalled Ed's inspired singing and said, "It gave inspiration to all of us. We all performed over our heads."

"I did too, in that first performance," Ed said. "It felt wonderful, but I was really drained after that one. It took me a while to get up for the second performance."

"And you did, too. The extra special edge of the first one wasn't there, but you did excellent work in the other two. They were comparable to the best I've heard in years of doing—and learning—'Messiah.'"

They walked a full lap in silence, then Art said, "Have you thought any more about your future?"

"Yes, I have, Art. Nothing's changed. I'm not going to try for a singing career," Ed replied.

"I had thought that yesterday's performance might have changed you're mind. Can you give that up?"

"Yes. Yes I can. I don't mean I won't do any more singing; of course I will. But not as a career."

"You know, I meant what I said the other day. About coming to England. After what you did yesterday, I'm more certain than ever that you would have a great success in my country. At least consider that prospect."

"I have, Art. And thanks. But this other thing has burned its way into me. I'm sure I can't solve the world's problems, and I won't be able to bring about a revolution in our thinking so that we will declare peace, not war. But I can find a way to contribute toward that end."

"Well, of course, it's your decision. I'll be sorry that the music world will not have you. It will be a loss."

"Ah, come on Art! There are hundreds of talented singers out there; I'm not that good!"

"You could be. It's true—there are many people with talent, potentially good singers. What concerns me is that not many of them ever touch what you did yesterday. That superb linking up of singer and listeners. That is the mark of greatness. Only a few have it."

"Come off it, Art! It was a flawed performance, and you know it. Flattery will get you nowhere."

"It isn't flattery! It's true, your performance was not perfect. Not every note was exactly right. But that is not what I'm talking about. It was the CONNECTION you made with your listeners. That was palpable. It was alive and electric. Only the great ones have that."

"Okay, Art. There was something powerful going on there. But that—that first performance—that was an exception. How often does that happen? It didn't even happen in the second and third performances."

"That's true. It doesn't happen all the time with any artist. But for the great ones, the potential is there. That's what counts. It can happen with them. It never happens with the others. It happened with you, so it is there. It's a rare and precious thing. Paderewski, an undeniably great artist on the piano, sometimes missed notes, but the potential was there in every performance. The audience always sensed it, even when he wasn't at his best. And with him, more than with lesser pianists, the connection often happened. It is that that makes the difference between a performer and an artist."

"Well, thanks again, Art. I appreciate what you're saying, but I'm no Paderewski, and I know it. I never saw Caruso in person, but I understand he often connected with his listeners too. But I'm no Caruso. I know it, and I think you know it too."

"No, you aren't. But, the potential is there. Everything else can be learned—voice technique, musicianship, note-accuracy—everything. Everything but that extra ingredient. That is either there or it isn't. It can't be learned. It is an inherent part of the person. That is what you have, and that is what I regret seeing wasted."

Ed was moved, humbled, and quieted by this from an excellent musician and a man he admired. He said nothing further, and they walked in silence for another lap, each one absorbed in his own thoughts and feelings. Then Art went to the theater to gather the music and see that everything was in order. Ed continued to walk, his thoughts interrupted every minute or so by a "Well done, old boy," or a "Great yesterday," or "Nice going, Ed," as other walkers overtook him. At one point, as he passed near the guarded gate, the commandant stopped him. "That vas good, Lieutenent. Wery good. Tank you," and he walked back through the gate.

After three more laps, Ed went to his room. Chet, the silent one, invited him to a game of checkers. Of course, he called it "draughts," and Ed agreed. It was a silent game, and he was glad. He did not want to talk, and as usual, neither did Chet.

FORCED MARCH
AND
LIBERATION

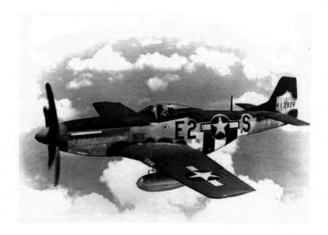

30

Following Christmas, the days dragged by. Daytimes were frigid, nightimes worse. Wind from the northeast stung the eyes and stiffened the face. It made circuit-walking difficult, but the men covered their faces with scarves, handkerchiefs, or rags, and walked. They all knew the danger of staying in their rooms hour after hour, day after day, or the even greater danger of staying in bed to keep warm. So they—almost all of them—forced themselves out on to the circuit every day, at least once, sometimes two or three times a day.

January came. Although it seemed to the men impossible for the temperature to drop more, it did. Now their desperate turns around the circuit were no longer describable as walking. Rather, they moved in a sort of stiff-legged trot, occasionally breaking into a clumsy run, to get the blood moving. Conversation became next to impossible on the circuit, so those who wanted to talk sought out spots where they would not feel the full force of the wind, speak for two or three minutes, then move on. Then they would stop again a little bit later to talk again, only for a couple of minutes. It was simply too cold to stand still.

According to the BBC, the Bulge battles continued, with the superior forces and supplies the Allies could throw into the fight slowly forcing the Germans to retreat. But it was bitter—the killing and the cold was nearly unbearable for both sides.

Allied forces were still too far west from the stalag for the kriegies to hear their guns.

Guns from the east, however, were heard more and more clearly, especially when the wind shifted more to that direction. The sound was both encouraging and threatening to the prisoners. Encouraging because it meant that the Russians were advancing. Threatening because the Germans were desperately afraid of being captured by the Russians. Stories abounded about what Russian soldiers did to German captives. This being the case, the kriegies were fearful that the Germans would panic and either slaughter the kriegies, which most thought unlikely, or drive them out in a forced march westward in the bitter winter weather. So the advancing Russian guns were a source of both hope and fear for the kriegies. It dominated most conversations and the thinking of most of the men. Some also wondered what the "Russkies" might do intentionally, or in fighting the Germans, to the prisoners in the stalag.

Red Cross parcel portions were cut even more now, and the men desperately hoarded what little they could to make their "iron rations." In their hunger, they fought the temptation to eat what they had. Some gave in and ate theirs.

On the fifteenth of January, quite abruptly, the wind diminished. But at the same time, temperatures went down a few more degrees. Coal rations were extremely low, so it was not possible to have a fire in Ed's room more than an hour in the morning and an hour in the evening. Fortunately, the Germans were now issuing already-cooked potatoes instead of raw ones, for the kriegies could never have cooked them. They were fortunate if they could heat water for tea or instant coffee—or just to drink as hot water.

On the seventeenth, the Russian guns sounded very close. An alert was passed from the kriegie intelligence committee to all the prisoners to have everything ready for a sudden move—sleep in clothes, including shoes and overcoats, and have string or rope or belts ready to tie up blankets in a roll with their most important possessions in the roll. Be sure to have some sort of head covering, preferably one that could be pulled over the ears; have iron rations and a cup or can at hand for drinking water and/or food. Everyone was nervous as night fell on that date. Nothing happened.

The next day, most of the prisoners relaxed a little bit, thinking perhaps nothing was going to happen. They went to bed early the night of the eighteenth to try to make up for sleep they had lost the night before. Ed was deep in sleep the moment he closed his eyes. When the shouts of "Raus!" and "Wecken, schweinhunts!" and "Schnell! Schnell, mach schnell!" echoed through the barracks, it seemed to him a long struggle up from oblivion to consciousness.

Now a very close voice was saying, "My God! It's 01:04 in the morning! What the hell are they doing!" Then he recognized Art's voice saying, "This is it! They're moving us out. Get moving, everybody! Get your things together. They won't go easy on us. They'll be nervous and trigger-happy. Let's move!"

Before Art was finished, Ed was out of bed and had his blanket roll around his neck, and the white stocking cap someone had given him pulled on and down over his ears. He rushed to the latrine and stood in line with the others to use the toilet. He shivered as the penetrating cold that had prevailed for the last few days seemed to cut right through his overcoat and clothes—even through his skin.

Everybody seemed to be talking at once. "Looks like they picked the goddam coldest night of the year to haul our asses out of here!" "Where you think they'll take us?" "Don't know. Somewhere west of here." "What'll it be, Chum? Lorries, buses, or will they jam us into a train?" "What the hell are you talking about? We're gonna walk!" "God! We'll die in this cold!" "They can't do that. It's against the Geneva Conventions!" "Are you kidding? They said 'fuck the Conventions!' a long time ago." "He's right! There'll be no rides for us. They don't have the transport to carry us, even if they wanted to."

Now the tense, insistent German voice ordered all the kriegies outside, and the British voice that called them out every morning sounded over the babble, "On appel! Everybody out! On appel!"

Out they went, each set of prisoners lining up as they did every morning for roll call in front of their barracks. Flood lights were shining down from every guard tower around Ed's compound, and he could see that the same was true in the adjoining compounds. There was no sign of the commandant. His underlings carried out the headcount. The counters made their reports. Now a voice speaking in heavily accented English came over speakers Ed had never heard used before, echoing through the frigid air. "Attention, prisoners off de Tird Reich! Ve must moof you vrom here to a zaffer blace to der vest. You must opey de commandts off der guards. You muzt schtay in line und maindain order, ve vill moof qvickly. Any brisoner who valls oudt of vormation vill be consideredt dryink do essgape, undt vill be shodt. Die Conwentions permit diss. Red Gross barcels vill be issued ass you bass trough de gate. De column must ztay to de right zide off de roadt at all dimes, zo our lorries carryink guards can bass by. Das ist all!"

This not very comforting message in English was followed by some German words, which one kriegie translated as, "Guards! Move the prisoners out according to the evacuation plan."

Since Ed's compound was the closest one to the main gate, his was the first ordered out. Each barracks group was moved in order. They started at a brisk walk, but this did not satisfy the guards, who yelled over and over, now and again adding emphasis by discharging a few rounds into the air from their automatic rifles, "Schnell! Schnell! Mach schnell!" By the time Ed and his roommates passed through the main gate, they were doing a fast trot. The method of "distributing" the food parcels was for the coverall-clad Germans—the "ferrets"—to throw them at the kriegies as they hurried to the main gate. Ferrets were not known for their love of the prisoners, so some of them hurled the boxes unnecessarily hard. In spite of this, and of the prodding of the guards, most of the prisoners managed to catch and hang on to one, or scoop up a dropped one as they passed by. As soon as Ed's group got through the gate and onto the road, the guards began to prod them even more, often supplementing their verbal urgings with rifle-butts, constantly ordering them to move faster.

The kriegies ran. As they ran, they tore open the parcels and removed the most important items—the food—stuffing it into pockets or into their blanket rolls. The cartons and the rest of the contents were strewn along the roadway.

In spite of the cold, Ed soon found himself sweating from the forced running. "This might be what keeps us alive," he thought. "But how long can we keep it up?" They ran for fifteen minutes, which then became thirty, then forty-five, an hour. Ed's legs ached, and his side hurt. The not-quite healed areas of his back were hurting badly. There were groans and breathless complaints from all the prisoners, but no one let up in the running. Several times Ed thought he'd have to drop out, but periodic bursts of gunfire and an occasional body lying inert on the road as he passed made him hang on. Chet, on his right, had a watch. "God!" he gasped. "An hour and a half! I've got to stop!"

Barely able to get the words out, Ed said, "No! You can't! They've got to give us a break. Hang on!"

After five minutes more of painful running, Chet's feet dragging with every step, Ed hanging on to his arm, trying feebly to keep him from falling, the Germans called a halt. The prisoners simply sank to the ground where they were, groaning. It turned out to be a fifteen-minute break, so as the kriegies slowly recovered and their breathing came easier, they stood and relieved themselves on the road.

After the first five minutes of the break had passed, the prisoners felt the cold penetrating them again as their bodies' exercise-generated heat dissipated. They had unbuttoned their coats as the running made them too warm, and now they began to shiver, buttoning up again. They hoped the Germans would pass out some ersatz coffee, or at least hot water, but nothing came. Ed and many others opened the small bottles of soluble coffee they'd kept from the parcels and put a few grains in their mouths. This made their mouths drier, so they gave that up. Someone suggested chewing gum to stimulate more saliva, so those who had kept their packs opened them, and some shared with those who had not. It helped.

By the end of the fifteen minutes, the kriegies were so cold that they welcomed the order to move on. A chorus of moans and groans arose as tired, aching muscles were again called upon to work. Any hope that the Germans would let them walk, not run, was quickly given up as "Mach Schnell!" was shouted and guns were discharged to get the column moving again. They fell into a fast trot, not quite up to the initial speed when they had left the Stalag. The first few moments were agonizing but as the muscles warmed again that pain diminished, soon to be replaced by the pain of labored breathing.

The German guards did not have to run or trot to keep up. They walked. Trucks were kept busy picking up guards from the rear and relaying them ahead of the column, where they started walking again as the prisoners trotted past them. It seemed that the Third Reich did not expect their "supermen" to keep up with their ill-fed, ill-clothed, injured prisoners.

As the second hour of trotting went by, Ed found that his body was adjusting to the demands he put upon it. His breathing became less strenuous, and his legs seemed to have gone into an automatic mode. He was less conscious of how tired they were. He was glad that he had walked regularly and briskly on the circuit. His back continued to hurt, but his side did not. He said to Chet, "How're you doing?"

"For some reason I'm not so bad," Chet answered. "Guess you can adjust to almost anything. Quite warm, isn't it?"

"Right," Ed replied. "Don't know where we're going, but we'll make it!" He noticed that the number of gunfire bursts had decreased. "Everybody still alive must be adjusting to it," he thought. "Man! What you can do when you have to!"

Now that the first big extended push was over, a pattern became apparent. They would trot for an hour, rest fifteen minutes, trot an hour, rest, and so on. As the sky began to turn gray, Ed could see more and more of the column ahead of him. He was able to see that many of the kriegies were helping others who were having trouble. If one stumbled, seemed about to fall or give up, two beside him would put arms around him and help him to keep going. Two others would have someone by the hands or wrists, forcing him to keep his feet going, or in some cases, dragging him along. Seeing this, Ed felt his respect for his fellow prisoners grow. Even when their own survival was in doubt, they helped others.

During the night the bedraggled column had passed through several tiny villages. Each time some villagers peered at them from their windows, and a few even opened their doors to look. Now, in the brightening daylight, they saw that they were entering a larger town. Some guards had evidently driven ahead and alerted the townspeople, because as the column moved down the main street, residents came to the side of the road with pitchers of steaming hot water. Seeing this, each prisoner who could do so got out a cup or can, which he held out to be filled with the hot water as they passed by. Fortunately, the German guards had slowed the column to a walk, or most of the hot water would have spilled on coat sleeves or fallen to the street.

Chet had a cup, which he got filled. Ed had one too, but he had tied it up in his blanket roll. Seeing this, Chet fished out of his pocket a clean soup can. Holding it out to Ed he said, "Here, old boy. Use this." Ed thanked him and held out the can. When it was filled, he had to snatch his stocking cap off of his head to hold the can without burning his fingers. He reciprocated by giving Chet some of his soluble coffee. "Rather have tea, wot?" Chet said. "But this will do nicely. Thanks."

The hot water/coffee and a nibble of iron ration was breakfast. As they left the town, everybody's morale seemed to be higher, even though they were forced into the trot again. All along the column the kriegies were beginning to talk as they trotted along. The sentences were short because breath was needed for trotting, but the talk was a sure sign that the prisoners now felt they could handle whatever the goons imposed on them.

Noon came and went as the pattern of an hour of trotting and fifteen minutes of rest continued. Snow began to fall, light at first, and gradually getting heavier. At 15:00 the prisoners were herded into an enormous farmyard surrounded by a farmhouse, a huge barn, and other farm sheds and buildings. The snow was no longer falling, and what had accumulated on the ground was soon trampled by the men. There were several fires burning—each one with several pots suspended above it or resting on the ground close to the fire.

Word was passed that they would remain at this place until dawn the next day. Kriegies were assigned to distribute boiled potatoes and hot water to their fellow prisoners. Everybody fished out a bowl or plate of some kind, his cup or can and—those who had it—soluble coffee or tea. A few had salt, and even fewer had kept cans of margerine or butter from the parcels. Art and Sid had packed salt from the room's supply, and they passed that around to the roommates. A loaf of bread was distributed to each twelve men. Potatoes, a chunk of bread, coffee, and a few raisins or prunes seemed like a banquet to the tired, hungry men.

Temporary outhouses had been set up—each a slit trench with a bench over it and a crude shed around it. As the kriegies finished eating and rinsing their utensils in the remaining hot water, the outhouses were kept busy. Groups of men stood or squatted everywhere, talking and some laughing. Spirits were remarkably good.

As daylight faded and snow started to fall again, the guards began to herd the prisoners into the barn and other buildings. The barn was a three-story affair, full of straw and hay. As the men filed in, guards directed the first ones to the top floor. As that floor became filled with kriegies lying side by side on or in the hay, the guards directed the next ones to the second story.

Sid pulled Ed aside as they approached the barn door. "Want to try sleeping out here?" he asked. "We could share our blankets and help keep each other warm."

"Do you think they'd let us?" Ed responded.

"If you want to, let's try and see." There was a lean-to on one side of the barn, and the ground there was dry. Ed and Sid put one blanket on the ground, and still wearing their overcoats, hats and shoes, they stretched out on the one blanket and pulled the other one over themselves. It seemed that it would work, so they settled down to sleep. A guard spotted them and stomped over. "Nein! Nein!" he shouted. "Insidt! All insidt! Raus!" They gave up their plan and found space in the hay on the ground floor with the others. Silence fell quickly as the weary men dropped off to sleep.

Gray was just starting to show in the eastern sky when the guards shouted them awake. Now their muscles felt like fire as they gathered their things and went to line up at the outhouses. Hot water and more bread was distributed, and the kriegies, groaning and grumbling, mixed their soluble coffee and ate and drank.

Word was passed around that they would move out in five minutes, so everybody scrambled to get his blanket-roll ready for the road. The snow had stopped during the night, leaving some four inches on the ground. Ed said to his friends as they finished packing, "Either I'm adjusting to the cold, or it's warmer this morning." They agreed that it was warmer. This seemed to be confirmed when the Germans moved them out without making them run or even trot. They were allowed to walk. No one complained about this. For two more days and parts of the nights, they walked. The sound of Russian guns had faded away behind them.

The next morning the Germans started separating the kriegies. At first, Ed couldn't tell if it was just a numerical division—half of them into each group, or what. When the guards got to his group it was clear, and it was painful: the British were separated from the Americans and Canadians. No time was allowed for goodbyes. They were herded into two groups, friends shouting hurried goodbyes and good luck to each other as the division was made.

Then the two columns started to move, with the British continuing to the west and the Americans and Canadians branching off onto a road heading south. "God! I'm going to miss those guys. Especially Art. Wonder if we'll ever see them again," Ed said to Sandy Billings, one of his American roomates.

That day followed the pattern of the preceding ones, except that the walking periods were two hours between rests, and bread and hot water were distributed at noon. That evening after the usual potatoes, bread, and coffee, they were again herded into a barn. During the evening meal, each of Ed's American roommates had found other friends—members of their bomber crews, or their fighter squadrons—and had joined up with them. This left Ed alone. He shrugged it off. He would miss the companionship, but felt he could handle it. Just as he entered the barn and was looking for a place to settle down, a voice called, "Hey, Ed! Over here." He looked and saw a man he didn't recognize signaling him to come.

When he got closer he thought, "I know this guy, but who is he?" Just as he came up to him, it dawned on him that it was Bill Schmidt. He grabbed his hand, saying, "I don't believe it! Primary and ol' Dan'l Boone."

"Sure was," Bill replied. "Then the S.S. Argentina. Been a while. Glad to see you, Ed. Had no idea you were a kriegie too. You haven't changed too much. I spotted you as soon as you came in."

"You look good, Bill. I couldn't tell who it was until I got close to you," Ed said.

"Must be this makeshift outfit I'm wearing. All your kriegie buddies leave you?"

"Yeah. They all seemed to find former crew members or fighter friends. Thought I was left in the lurch."

"Want to join up with us?"

"Sure do, if you'll have me."

"Not a problem. Hey, guys, this is my old friend from way back in Primary—Ed Thorne. Ed, these are our crew members from our B-17, rest its soul," and he introduced each one by name: Bud, Jim, Kip. "The others went to GI kriegie camps." After shaking hands, Ed said, "Bill, I don't want to intrude. You're a close-knit group. Maybe you don't need another one."

"Bullshit! What say, guys? You want to let this 'little friend' cruise along with us?"

They all said sure, no problem, so Ed dropped his blanket roll in an open space on the straw and sat, relieved to be part of a group again.

"Bill called you 'little friend,'" Bud said. "What did you fly?"

"Fifty-ones," Ed answered.

"Never got to fly Spits, eh?" Bill asked. "I remember you talking about that in Preflight and Primary."

"I came close," Ed replied. "I sat in one, cranked her up and taxied out to the runway. But the Tower stopped me. What about the rest of your crew?"

"Everybody got down okay. We were separated. You know, they weren't officers, so they had to go to another stalag."

"Yeah. That stupid rule! We're all Americans, but both the Germans and our Air Corps have that rule. It's always 'officers and men.' I suppose there's some reason for it, but it always has struck me as odd for a democratic society to have that kind of class separation in its armed forces," Ed said. "Anyway, it's lucky you all made it. The way I saw you big friends getting blasted over the target evey mission, I didn't see how any of you survived. That must have been rough. I wouldn't want to do that."

"Oh, yeah. It was rough. We were scared shitless every mission," Jim said. "But that was our job, so we did it."

"You sure did. That's what I call guts!" Ed said.

Bill said, "I don't know about that. We prayed a lot, I do know that. Especially long trips, like Berlin. Those were rough ones. We flew the first daylight American raid on Berlin."

"You did!" Ed exclaimed. "So did I. We escorted on that one."

"Hell you say," Kip put in. "I remember how glad we were to see those Mustangs all around us. Of course we were always glad to see our 'little friends' on every mission. Not that you could do anything about the flak, but you sure helped get rid of the bandits!"

"God!" Bill yelled. "Maybe we had a reunion in the sky over the big B, Ed. What color noses did your outfit have?"

"Green."

"I remember greens. You covered us on lots of trips," Jim said. "Hot damn!"

"I do too," Bill said. "I don't want to push this too far. But did you have a name on your ship?"

"Sure did. She was 'Princess Pat,'" Ed answered.

"Jesus H.!" Bill exploded. "Big and fancy, painted right up on the cowl? I saw you lots of times! Yeah! That name stood out like a hooker at a tea party. I can see her right now."

"Wait a minute, Bill," Ed said, laughing at the comparison. "Princess was no hooker."

"No offense, Ed. We called fighters 'whores' because they were in and out so fast. You know, 'quickies—bam, bam, thank you ma'm.' We had to have a sustained relationship with the target. You guys flitted around to one after another. Like hookers."

"I get it," Ed said. "And you made your 'johns' pay, right?"

"Yep," Kip added. "If they hooked up with us, they paid for it!"

"So," Ed continued, "you gave them your love in explosive bursts of passion, right? And it cost them so much they were ruined."

"That's right. I was the bombardier, so I delivered the love messages," Jim responded.

"So, Bill, we had our first reunion over enemy territory without knowing it. Now we're having a second one in enemy territory. How about that!" Ed said.

"I'd rather have had my reunions after we're all safe back home," replied Bill.

"Yeah, we all would," they all agreed. Tired, they snuggled down in the straw, pulling their blankets over them, and slept until the inevitable early dawn awakening by the Germans' voices with their "Raus! Raus! Wecken Zie!"

At noon on the third day after the separation from their RAF friends, the kriegies were herded into a large railroad yard. A long train of aged boxcars—the small European type—stood by a platform. The guards counted the kriegies as they mounted the platform, arbitrarily separating them into groups to be loaded into the boxcars. It was Ed's misfortune that he was at the end of his group of new friends. He was cut off from them. He tried to force his way on to go with them, but two guards stepped in front of him and roughly shoved him back. He wound up in a car packed with stangers.

As each car was loaded, the sliding doors were slammed shut and barred from the outside. There were so many crowded into each car that no one could lie down. By crowding together, jostling one another, they all managed to sit on the floor, elbows and knees poking into everyone. Dirty, damp clothes and unbathed bodies combined to make the air fetid. After the door was shut, the smell became overpowering. Ed, like the others, had trouble breathing. They all tried to keep their mouths shut, breathing shallowly through their noses. Nobody spoke except to utter a curse as someone's foot or elbow got in the wrong place on somebody else.

After a wait that seemed much longer than the hour it actually was, harsh German voices shouted orders, a whistle blew a long note and, with a jerk, the train began to move. This threw the prisoners against each other, bringing more irritated curses and annoyed "Watch it!" and "Get off me!" exclamations. As the train picked up speed, air came in through cracks and holes in the sides of the car, and breathing became easier. The incoming air was cold, so some of those seated near cracks and holes tried to cover them to avoid the frigid air. This brought protests from the others.

"What the hell do you expect us to do? We're freezing! You want to trade places? No? Well, shut your fucking mouth then." Those nearest the openings did what they could to keep the cold air off themselves. By this time, everybody in the car had grown accustomed to the rotten air and was breathing normally. Men began to talk to each other. Most of them were with their buddies. Ed felt very much like an outsider. He listened, but didn't say anything. Nobody bothered to say anything to him. He was sitting with nothing to lean on, and his back was hurting. Any time he tried to shift his position, he'd bump someone and he'd get bumped or shoved back. He envied those around him, pressing in on him, all seeming to be with friends. Most of them had worked out ways of sitting so their backs were against each other, giving each other support.

Hours passed. There came a lull in the talk. Not an actual stop, but a few moments when there was less sound. Into this relative quiet, a voice not far from Ed asked, "Any of you guys know anything about what the Nazis have been doing to Jews?"

Nobody else responded, so Ed, partly because he hadn't had any chance to talk since boarding the train, said, "I know a little bit. Pretty bad, concentration camps. Forced labor. Starvation. Working them to death. Surgical experiments without anaesthetic. Electrical stimulation of brain and nerves. Floggings. Torture to see how much a human can stand before dying. Prying out gold fillings. Sexual abuse of young girls and boys. I read about some of it before we got into the war. It was a main reason why I signed up."

"You didn't mention gas chambers," the voice came back.

"I never heard of them," Ed said. "What about them?"

"We heard about it on our radio, just after Christmas. From BBC. They're using what they call 'The Final Solution' to the Jewish problem." All other talk had stopped now.

"What do you mean, 'final solution?'" someone called out, followed by a chorus of "Yeah. What're you talking about?"

"I'm not sure it's true. I have trouble believing it, even about the Nazis. But that's what they reported."

"What?" "What did they report?" "What did they say about gas chambers?" "Come on!"

"Okay, okay. I just wanted to say that it's really hard to believe. They said the Nazis were sending thousands of Jews into what they call 'shower rooms.' Trouble is, they aren't shower rooms at all. They pack them in, lock and seal the doors, then shoot poison gas in on them. Then they haul out the bodies and incinerate them. I'm telling you, it's just a report. I can't believe it's true."

"It better not be true!" "Those bastards!" "I wouldn't put it past the sons-of-bitches!" "I think I'm going to be sick!" came out in a babble from all the kriegies. Then quiet came as each in his own way tried to deal with this new horror.

After a few minutes, a voice from a corner said, "You said 'by the thousands.' There must be millions of Jews in Germany, Austria, Poland—all the countries the Nazis have taken over. How do they get them to the gas chambers?"

Ed said, "We know they've been rounding them up for years. But just to put them in concentration camps and make forced laborers of them. But if they're trying to make a 'Final Solution,' that must mean killing all of them."

"Yeah. How do they get millions of them to the chambers?"

"That's the part I didn't want to tell you," said the original voice. "It probably doesn't mean anything."

"You son-of-a-bitch! Don't hold out on us. What didn't you want to tell us?"

"Okay. You asked for it. The Nazis are hauling the Jews to extermination centers in freight trains. Jamming them into boxcars!"

Total stunned silence followed this. Then a gasped, "Oh my God!" and a "God, no!" A voice whispered, "Is that why they separated us from the British?" "Yeah," someone else said. "The British are probably on their way home! And where are we going?" "Yeah, maybe we'll be part of their goddam 'final solution' too." "Yeah. Sweet revenge on us because we whipped their asses. They've got to hate us!" "Yeah. They have the facilities, and we're being transported, God knows where, just like the Jews."

Hysteria was beginning to take over as more and more voices joined in the clamor. Now a gray-haired man who had been sitting quietly in a corner, not far from Ed, pushed himself to his feet. He was tall, and his hat had a colonel's eagle pinned to its front. "Now, you bastards shut up and calm down," he said. "What we've just been told may or may not be true. Rumors always get reported as fact in wartime. I'm not saying it isn't true. I'm just saying that we don't know. And even if it is true about the Jews, it has nothing to do with us. We are Prisoners of War! We're protected by international rules."

"Yeah, Colonel. But how come we're jammed into this freight car? Just like the Jews."

"Use your head!" the colonel said. "It's the only kind of transport the Germans have left. Did you expect a luxury train? Just be glad we aren't being forced to walk all these miles. There's no way on God's green earth they're going to exterminate all the POWs they have. Think of the retribution that would come down on them!"

Other voices now spoke up, saying, "You're right, Colonel." "That makes sense." "Good!"

As quiet settled in again, Ed started to hum "Aloutte." A man to the side of him said, "Come on. Sing it," and Ed opened up. The whole car joined in, responding to the song. When he had exhausted all the variations he could think of, he started "Into the Air, Army Air Corps," and all the voices joined in. Next, someone else started "Off We Go, Into the Wild Blue Yonder," and they shouted that out too. For the next two hours, they sang and joked and ribbed each other and laughed. Morale was high. This continued until the train ground to a halt.

The doors were opened and the kriegies jumped out, finding themselves on a railraod siding near a foot-bridge spanning the tracks. A crowd of German civilians gathered on the bridge, looking down on the prisoners as they squatted with pants down to relieve themselves. "Shit on Germany!" one of the kriegies shouted, and others picked it up. It felt good to shout out this bit of defiance and just to be out of the stinking, cramped cars. Some of the Germans hooted, pointed, and laughed at them. Others spat and cursed. Several yelled, "Jugen!" Though the cool air felt good, that word, German for "Jews," sent a shiver down many spines among the kriegies.

As the sun set, blue-coveralled Germans brought loaves of bread and large pots of ersatz coffee. The kriegies tore off chunks of bread, and held out their cups and cans for coffee. It was far from gourmet food, but they devoured it. As before, Ed was astonished at the resilience and the spirit of his fellow prisoners, as well as his own. "What a bunch of guys," he thought.

Each man had left his bundle or his blanket roll at his place in the car, so when they were prodded and pushed back into what they now called "the cattle car," each one returned to his place. Ed was still without support. He felt less isolated since the singing, but his back pain had been only slightly eased by being out of the car. Before long, the pain was intense enough that he did not see how he could stand it. Every little sway or bump of the car sent an extra strong pulse of pain through him. He was certain that he could not stay in his unsupported sitting position all night; he would pass out.

Directly behind him were the stretched out legs of four men, two on each side, each of the men with a back-leaning buddy. They were there when Ed was put into the car. He twisted around and said to the men, "My back got pretty banged up when I was shot down. It's giving me hell right now. I don't see any way I'll get through the night without passing out. I've got to get some easing of my back. Would you guys be willing to raise your legs and let me lie down, and then just put your legs on top of me?" The four men looked at each other, nodded, and pulled their knees up to their chins, making enough space so Ed could lie down with his back flat on the floor.

As soon as the strain on the muscles of his back was eased, the pain started to lessen. He thanked the men. "Okay," one of them said, "but we won't be able to keep our legs pulled up like this very long."

Ed said, "Right. I know that. When you're ready, put them on top of me. I'm in your space, and I appreciate it. So don't hesitate when you have to put your legs out."

As the train rattled on, and the prisoners could see through the cracks that it was dark out, first one, then another of the four men had to stretch his legs out on top of Ed. It wasn't comfortable, but it was better for Ed than sitting up. The last two legs had no place to go but across Ed's face. He was surprised at how heavy they were. The added weight pressed him against the rough floor, but he could breathe, and his back was feeling much better.

Gradually, the talking in the cattle car stopped and everybody fell asleep. Like the others, Ed was exhausted, so even pressed down by his "blanket" of legs, he too fell into a deep sleep. When he came awake, he had a moment of panic, not knowing why he couldn't move or see, but then he realized where he was. The sleep had refreshed him and he wanted to sit up. Since none of the legs over him moved, he guessed that the four owners of those legs were still sleeping. Not wanting to disturb them, he stayed quiet and still, not very comfortable, but not in much pain either.

When he felt the train slowing, the legs stirred. He said, "Hey, guys, will you let me up now?" The men yawned and stretched, and drew up their legs. Ed pushed himself up to his sitting position as the train came to a stop. The door screeched open and the kriegies got out. This time there was no bridge over the tracks or German spectators as the prisoners relieved themselves at the side of the tracks. Beside the tracks was a clear strip about ten feet wide, then a fence, beyond which stretched a meadow. No people and no cattle were in sight. Only the guards and kriegies.

Now as the kriegies moved about the bare strip, stretching and shaking their legs, coveralled Germans began to get out of a coach near the engine, bringing pots of coffee and more of the black bread. Ed tore a chunk of bread off the loaf held out to him and recalled what the prisoners told him about that bread when it first arrived at the stalag. "It's made of sawdust," they said. He'd been skeptical, but one of the Americans, Andy Sipple, confirmed it. "When I was first captured," he said, "they didn't know I was an officer, so I was put in a prisoner work camp. We worked in a giant bakery, making this kind of bread. The batter was about three-quarters fine ground sawdust, the rest was wheat flour, plus a little salt and soda." Art had assured Ed that it was nutritious, that wood contained a lot of glucose—just like regular flour. Andy then mentioned that, not knowing the bread would be going to prisoners, they used to spit and piss into the batter every chance they got, thinking it was used to feed Germans.

"It's all right," Art had said. "The baking sterilizes it. We've never had anybody get sick from the bread."

Ed had said, "It sure tastes good when you're hungry. I'll try to forget what Andy said." It certainly tasted good now, as did the coffee. Equally good was the relief from the pain of sitting unsupported, and from the smell of the cattle car. This day the sun shone, and the air was feeling warmer. Heavy coats were unbuttoned and opened. Many kriegies took them off, carrying them over arms or shoulders as they chewed the bread, washing it down with the coffee. A few lit cigarettes from the Red Cross parcels.

Ed caught glimpses of Kip standing beside the cattle car in front of his. He made his way toward him, but was stopped by the gun-bearing guard at the gap between the cars. "Hey, Kip!" he called. Kip saw him and yelled, "Hi, Ed! How's it going? Hey, Bill. There's Ed," and Bill appeared beside Kip. They called questions and answers back and forth until the guards herded them back into the cars.

Evening brought another stop, this time in a large railroad marshalling yard, not far from what appeared to be a good-sized city. The meal, in addition to bread and coffee, included boiled potatoes. The hungry men ate skins and all, even the bruised and rotten parts. Word circulated that the city they could see was Nürnberg. "What difference does it make?" a kriegle said after Ed passed the word to him. "None, I guess," Ed replied, "except that it's pretty far south of Sagan, where we were before. Shouldn't be so cold."

"Yeah, so? If it isn't cold, it'll be something else. This goddam country is one big shithouse as far as I'm concerned," the disgruntled man said.

"Sure, you're right," Ed responded. "But if I have to live in a shithouse, I prefer a warm one to a cold one," and he walked away.

When they were again loaded into the cattle cars, the sun had set and twilight had fallen. The train started, stopped, backed, then moved forward again. It continued the forward movement, but never picked up much speed. Ed was just trying to prepare himself for another painful night when the train came to a full stop. It had been only forty-five minutes since it started after the last break. The door was opened, and he saw a flood-lit platform, and beyond that, high chain-link fences and barbed wire. Farther on he could see dark and dirty-looking barracks buildings.

"Raus! Aus mit!" the guards were shouting. The kriegies grabbed their bundles and stepped out onto the platform. More guards stood at intervals along the platform. The evening chill had replaced the warmer daytime temperature.

With many barked orders, the guards lined up the prisoners in a column of twos, then started counting them. Next, the column was turned to face left and directed down a short stairway at the end of the platform. Ed watched until he thought no guard was looking his way, and slipped out of line and up to where Bill and the others were. He made it, and stepped in beside Bud, who had no one beside him. "All right," Bud said quietly. "Good to see you."

"Not as good as it is to see you guys," Ed said. Now the column was moving through a gateway, in which only one of the two gates had been opened. They were being counted again as they passed in through the gate. As he looked at the bleak, unpainted and dirty buildings, a chill thought of the gas chambers caused Ed to shiver. He felt better when he saw that those in front of him were being directed into barracks buildings— each one dimly lit by bare, hanging lightbulbs. The guards didn't notice, or didn't care, that he had moved into a group to which he had not been assigned.

When Ed stepped into the building he and his friends were directed to, he saw wooden bunks stacked floor to ceiling, with insufficient head room between the layers for a man to sit up. Only in a lying position could a person be on one of the bunks. The building was divided into bays, separated by wooden pillars. Each bay held twenty-four bunks, in stacks of four. Ed and his four friends claimed bunks in a bay about at the middle of the building. Along the outer wall of the bay was a rough wooden bench, about table height, and wooden sitting benches fastened to the floor beside it. The place was filthy, but dry. On the bunks were ticking mattresses filled with what felt like straw, and each bunk had a gray German Army blanket on it.

"Well, men," Bill said. "I guess this is our new home. It doesn't meet the standards of the one we left, but it beats hell out of that running and walking, and, by a long shot, that cattle car. I saw some big coal bins out there, near the gate, and there are, I guess, half-a-dozen pot-belly stoves along the aisle here. If the goons bring us coal, we can be reasonably warm, and cook too. If we have anything to cook. How do you like it?"

"Why, Bill, it's perfectly lovely," Ed said. "Thank you for bringing us to this beautiful resort hotel. By the way, did anybody see a latrine?"

"I smelled one," Bud answered. "Seemed to be coming from a little building a few yards from the entrance to our suite. Looks like one latrine for each two barracks."

"I'm going to check it out. Ask the waiter to hold dinner 'til I get back, please," Ed said.

"Okay, jerk. We had dinner back in the railroad yard. Did you miss it?" Kip said. "Wait a sec, I'll go with you. You might get lost, since you were a fighter pilot." He pulled on his coat, and they went to find the latrine. It was right where Bud had said it was. They found a deep trough that emptied into a pipe on one side of the small building, and a row of holes in a wide wooden plank over the smelly, water-filled trough. The water seemed to be moving sluggishly into the pipe, toward some unknown destination, beyond the last building in the row. Each sat on one of the holes, sighing with relief at not having to squat to move their bowels.

"To quote a great philosopher of old," Ed said, "nothing is so pleasing to the human mind and body as sexual intercourse, or complete evacuation of the bowels."

"Oh, my God!" Kip exclaimed, "no paper."

"All is well," Ed said. "As the same philosopher said, or was it a Boy Scout, 'be prepared; always carry with you something to read.'" He pulled an old paperback book out of his coat pocket. "Here, have some literary wipe," and he handed the book to Kip. "Do not go beyond page one-fifty, since that's as far as I've read. Please return to sender."

Word came around that a ration of coal would be issued for each stove, and Bill and Ed went to get theirs. They had to identify which bay in which barracks, so Ed went back and figured out the German, which translated to "Bay 3, Barracks B." The German in charge carefully noted that in a large account book, and they were issued a bucket of coal, a bucket of potatoes, and two loaves of black bread.

When they got back to the bay, Ed said to all the men, his four friends, and the eleven others who had some of the other bunks in the bay, "Guys, we had potatoes and bread about an hour ago. What do you say we start a fire, heat some water for soluble coffee, then individually have snacks out of our personal hoards. That way, we can save the potatoes and bread for tomorrow?"

All agreed, so using some trash they found lying around in the building, and a few sticks picked up outside, they got a fire going. One man among the other eleven had a pan large enough to heat water, and the "feast" in celebration of their new home was underway. For most of them, it was coffee and a cracker or biscuit, and a small bite of iron ration for those who had any left. All the stoves were lit; although this did not overcome the chill in the entire building, everybody could get near enough to a stove to be comfortable without his overcoat on. Nobody knew how long the bucket of coal was supposed to last, so they used only enough to heat the water, then let the coals burn themselves out. That was sufficient, and they were all happy.

"We can make it here," Bill said, and everybody agreed. Nobody had slept well in the cattle cars, so as the coals died away, they all had trouble staying awake. When cold began to overcome the heat of the stove, they drifted to their bunks. Some put their overcoats on, but most spread their blankets over the German blankets, and rolled up their coats for pillows. Sleep was quick to come for everybody.

It was daylight when Ed awoke. There had been no call to fall out for roll call. It turned out that they were to be spared that annoyance. Bill and the others were awake, but not ready to get up. Ed found himself scratching everywhere. Itchy all over. He quickly threw back the blanket and crawled out. There were fleas crawling all over the woolen blankets. "Oh no," he groaned. "You guys itchy?"

"Now that you mention it, yeah," someone said, and others joined in with, "Yeah! I sure am."

"Well, check it out, campers. I've got giant fleas crawling all over my bed. We've been bitten while we slept." All the others slid out of their bunks and uttered various profanities as they saw the ugly critters they'd slept with. "At least they seemed to stay in the bed," Ed said. "I don't feel or see any on me. But they sure are everywhere in the bunk."

"What the hell do we do now?" Bill wondered.

Kip replied, "Maybe if we ask the goons real nice, they'll spray the place."

"Sure they will," Bud said. "We all know how concerned they are for our welfare! They love us."

"That was a joke, son," Kip said with an edge on his voice.

"Oh. Sorry, Kip. The fleas drained my sense of humor," Bud responded. "Anybody have any ideas?"

Ed saw the sun shining outside. "About all we can do is haul our blankets outside. Maybe the critters don't like the sun," he said.

"Yeah," Bill agreed. "At least there we can get a better look at what we're dealing with."

All five pulled their blankets off the bunks and, holding them away from their bodies, rushed outside with them. Between their barracks and the next one, and behind the latrine, was a large outcropping of rock. The sun and wind had cleared the snow from it. They spread the blankets out on the rocks and looked closely at them.

"These things are bigger than the fleas I've seen on dogs and cats," Jim said.

Ed said, "They sure are. Different color, too. Sort of brown and purple. Our pets always had little black ones."

"Look," Jim added, as he poked one with his finger. "They don't jump like our fleas back home."

Ed tried one with his finger. "You're right, Jim. Real fleas jump like crazy. They're hard to catch. We can catch these things."

"And what do we do with them, Ol' Buddy?" Bill asked.

"Well, how about a flea circus?" Ed suggested. "We could train them. Give us something to do."

This brought laughter from the entire group, and Ed could see that their sense of humor was intact. He went on, "We could train them, put on shows. Charge a slice of bread, or a stick of gum admission."

Now the laughter turned derisive, and Bill said, "Ol' Pal, you're just as much a whacko as you used to be. I'm not interested in trying to train fleas. Got any better ideas?"

"Kill them," Ed said. "When I caught fleas at home, I had to crush them between my two thumbnails. Just squeezing them between fingers didn't faze them."

"Yack!" Bill exclaimed.

Without any difficulty, Kip caught one of the fleas between his thumb and forefinger. "See, they don't jump," he said. "Easy to catch." He put the bug on the rock, picked up a small stone and crushed it.

A kriegie hurrying past with a pot called out, "Hey! The goons are handing out hot water. Don't have to use our coal to heat our own."

Bill rushed in to get the banged-up cooking pot he and his friends had clung to for the whole march, and joined the crowd lining up at the door of what turned out to be a cookhouse. The line moved swiftly, so soon he was back with the hot water. "Let's leave our blankets out here and go have coffee and bread. We can talk about what to do about the fleas while we eat."

The others agreed, but Jim said, "What if somebody grabs our blankets?"

Ed responded, "We can see them through the window. Nobody'd want them anyway. Let's go." So they went to their bay and breakfasted, keeping an eye on the blankets through the dirty window. Kip used an old German newspaper he had found to wipe some of the dirt off the window.

Bill and Bud had kept little jars of marmalade from their parcels. Bill said, "Bud, save yours for later. We can use mine first. Now watch it Jim! I know you have a sweet tooth, but just spread it thin. God knows when we'll get any more, so eat it slowly."

Ed had most of a package of prunes left, so he passed out one to each of his friends. "Five at a time, they won't last long. Make them last, and save the pits. We can crack them open and get the kernel out. Almost like almonds when they're dried."

While they ate, they saw others carrying out their blankets and spreading them. Many kriegies seemed to have decided that they would just live with the fleas, so the rock area was not overcrowded. When breakfast was over, they rinsed the dishes and put things away. While he was sliding things under the bottom bunk, Ed looked at the mattress. "Hey," he said, "the fleas don't like the mattress. I don't see any on it." The others rushed over and examined their own mattresses. They found that Ed was right. While the blankets were loaded with fleas, there were none to be seen on the mattresses.

"Guess they like the wool," Bill said. "At least we don't have to haul the mattresses out."

Together they went to the latrine. Bill had a paperback book, just as Ed had. They shared them with the others, using pages as toilet paper. "Okay," Bill said, "I'll share this, but don't go past page fifty-nine. I'm just reading sixty." They all laughed as they went out and returned to their blankets.

Ed demonstrated how to catch a flea, then crush it between thumbnails, which was quicker and easier than Kip's method of using a small stone. They were all disgusted, but it seemed the only way to cut down on the flea problem, so they all got to work on their blankets.

"Say, don't fleas carry diseases?" Kip asked.

Ed had read something about this somewhere. "Yeah, they can, if they bite a rat or something that's infected, then bite you, they can."

"What kind of disease?" Kip wanted to know.

Ed said, "I'm not sure, but I think I read that typhus was one and, yeah, I'm pretty sure plague was mentioned, too."

"Let's kill these little pests."

"God, yes! It's them or us," Bill said, and they all worked harder on the distasteful job. This became a daily chore, since the fleas multiplied rapidly, and tended to migrate from bunk to bunk.

When they had destroyed all the fleas they could find, they returned the blankets to their bunks, and Ed and Bill walked around the camp, finding men they had known back at Sagan, reminiscing about Maxwell and Bennettsville. "I heard you brown-nosed yourself to the top of the cadet corps," Bill said.

"No brown-nosing involved," Ed retorted. "They just recognized an outstanding cadet when they saw one. Anyway, we talked about this on the ship coming over. What about you, little man?"

"Did we? I forgot. Well, I didn't go for that stuff. I kept my nose clean and my head down, so nobody noticed me."

Bill answered, "Not too hard for you to keep your head down. It's just naturally lower than everybody else's."

"Yeah, I know. But I sure flew the B-17. No problems doing that."

"You liked it, eh?"

"What I always wanted. Had a great crew, too. Sure hope the rest of them are okay in enlisted mens' camps. We'll have a great reunion when we're all liberated. You fighter pilots can't imagine how close a bomber crew gets flying together in combat. It's a real family!"

"I can see that. But you can't imagine how free you are alone in a fighter. Even in formation, you are pretty much on your own. You don't have anybody else in the ship to worry about. You cover the other guys' tails, and you know they're covering yours, but you're still on your own. And when you break out of the formation, man! The freedom you feel is indescribable. It's you and your airplane, and you get to be a part of each other. You know what she can do, and you know she'll do it when you ask her to. I even found myself talking to Princess! You ever talk to your 17?"

"Not really, with a crew, there's always somebody talking on the intercom. Not much chance to talk to the airplane. But what a beautiful bird she was! And complex. A thousand things had to work right for her to operate. And they did! She was reliable and efficient. And

EDWARD J. THORNE

fast, and armed to the teeth. Fifty-calibres sticking out all over her. I wouldn't be surprised if heavy American bomber gunners shot down more enemy planes than all our fighters did."

Ed said, "I doubt it, but you could be right. You know, I had only four fifties, and they were pointed ahead of me. They were fixed in place—I could only shoot at something in front of me. Couldn't shoot behind or to the side, or above or below. In order to get my sights on a target, I had to aim the airplane at it. What I was flying was a gun platform. I aimed the guns by aiming the platform."

"I never thought of it like that," Bill said. "But that's right, isn't it?"

"Yep. If a 109 came up beside me and flew like my wingman, I couldn't do a thing to him. But of course, he couldn't do anything to me either. We'd each have to try to out-maneuver the other. I'd be trying to trick him, and he'd be trying to trick me. Each one trying to get on the tail of the other, or far enough to one side to turn toward him and aim his guns where he would be when his bullets got there. Called a deflection shot, remember? Just like skeet shooting, which you hated. Remember, you can't hit the clay pigeon by shooting at it. You have to shoot where it will be."

"God! You're right. I hated that," Bill said. "Maybe that's why I didn't want to fly fighters. Yeah. I remember about deflection shots. They were tough. Always had to shoot at empty air, and hope the target got in front of your shot."

"That's right, Bill. Now, complicate that with two other factors. In skeet shooting, the target is moving, but you are standing still. You move the gun, but you are standing in one spot. When one fighter is trying to get another one, they are both moving, and moving fast. And the target doesn't just move in a straight line. It is changing directions and angles and altitude all the time. So the fighter trying to get a shot at it has to be doing the same thing. You rarely get a simple deflection shot, as you do in skeet.

"The other factor is that in skeet, you're shooting buckshot, so a whole lot of bee-bees are launched at the clay pigeon. Only one has to hit it, and it is destroyed. The fighter has no buckshot. It fires solid bullets. Of course, the bullets are coming out of four barrels, in Princess, anyway. Later models of the fifty-one had six. And they keep coming, as long as you squeeze the trigger and your ammunition lasts. But you can't just keep firing and spray the other plane with bullets, like a garden hose. You don't have that much time. Mostly, you fire a short burst, and he's out of your gunsight. I should mention another factor, too, although you already know it. That is, the other guy is doing his best to get shots off at you, too. No clay target ever shot back at a skeet shooter."

"I don't know how any of you guys, on either side, ever shot each other down."

"It takes skill, and a lot of luck. It's a crazy business. When a couple dozen of theirs mix it up with a couple dozen of ours, it's really wild up there. You're trying to to keep the other guys from getting a shot at you while you try to get a shot at them. At the same time, you're trying to keep an eye out for your buddies, in case a bandit is getting on one of them. It's crazy. That's when the blue yonder is really wild! Let's change the subject, okay?"

475

"Sure," Bill said. "How were things going with, what's her name? Pat, before you became a guest of the Third Reich?"

"Far as I know, okay. We were writing back and forth," Ed replied.

"Did you see her on your leave before you came over?"

"Matter of fact, I didn't. She was away at college, in Tennessee. I'm not sure I would have contacted her anyway. I was sure when we did get together the old sparks would still be there—at least I hoped so. But knowing that I'd be going overseas, I didn't want to get anything going. You know, we didn't have any guarantees that we'd get back. Anyway, I liked having the feeling that we had a future together. Better to keep that dream while I was away."

"Yeah, I know. I felt the same way. And I guess we both came close to buying it, didn't we?"

"We sure did. If I'm lucky, Pat will still be available when I get back. Then we'll see."

Days went by, each one very much like the one before. The kriegies discovered that this dirty, ugly stalag had in previous years been a Hitler Youth training camp. They were sure that it had not been in its present deplorable condition then.

Ed and his friends never got their beds entirely free of fleas, but they kept them at a bearable level by persisting in their daily flea extermination. This camp had none of the amenities that the one at Sagan had. Ed's little group made the best of the situation. They did calesthenics, ran around the camp, played tag and king-of-the-hill on the rock outcroppings, and told each other stories. This was both to avoid boredom, and to keep themselves fit for whatever the goons might have in store for them next.

Food was extremely limited. The Germans continued to provide rations of boiled potatoes and bread, with an occasional "treat" in the form of cattle-fodder soup. No Red Cross parcels appeared, so the kriegies carefully hoarded the little they had left of what they had brought with them. Soluble coffee, which every kriegie had taken from the parcels that had been thrown at them as they left Sagan, was the only real treat they had left after a few weeks at Nürnberg. As time went on, Ed and his companions began to cut down on how much coffee they allowed themselves. At first, they made it weaker, then they cut back from three or four cups a day to two, then to one to start the day. For lunch and dinner, they drank hot water. As temperatures began to rise with spring approaching, the coal ration was reduced, so they became experts at making a few lumps last. Staying warm became less and less a problem.

Staying reasonably clean, however, became a serious problem. Only once were they taken to a shower room where they were provided with soap and a few minutes of hot water. At Sagan, they recalled nostalgically, they were allowed showers weekly. This single shower, the first and only one they had had since leaving Sagan, was welcome, and they made the most of it. The rest of the time, they washed themselves the best they could with cold water and—while it lasted—bits of soap.

March brought two things to the kriegies. One was windy, wet weather. The other was another forced march. No running this time. Rain and wind were a problem, but it was not extremely cold, as it had been on the previous march. Staying warm, even in damp clothes, was not a serious problem. Rain was not continuous, so in the intervals between showers, the prisoners' clothes dried as they walked. At times the sun shone, and this helped the drying. They were moving southeast. Combined with the onset of spring, the movement southward raised the daily temperature significantly. Nights were still quite cool. The krie-gies began carrying their overcoats, needing them at night. However, after several days, they found that the nights, too, were warming, so they began abandoning their coats by the way-side. They were quickly snatched up by farmers and villagers who watched the bedraggled prisoners slowly streaming by.

Word was passed along from an Air Corps brigadier general, the senior officer among the prisoners, not to attempt any escapes. Two reasons for this were given. First, if a prisoner was caught by civilians, he would almost certainly be hanged on the nearest tree. The Ger-mans were desperate and angry. Second, Allied forces were advancing. This meant that the German lines were falling back, and an escaped prisoner would have little chance of getting through the German lines and safely into Allied hands. "Let our forces come to us," was the message. "They will liberate us."

The guards, apparently fearful of reprisals once the inevitable liberation of the prisoners and their own capture took place, were less watchful and less brutal—no prisoners were shot on this march—even though krieges were sneaking out of line and stealing food from farms, or getting away at night to do the same after they had been herded into barns to sleep.

One night, Ed and Bill spotted a chicken strutting and pecking not far from the barn. Like experienced undercover agents, they slipped out of the barn, staying low and close to the side of the building, and sneaked up on the chicken. Ed took his stocking cap off and, with more luck than skill, got it over the chicken's head and held it tight so it couldn't squawk. Meanwhile, Bill strangled it. They weren't sure what they would do with it, but they were proud of their exploit.

Bud, a farm boy, took over. He had concealed a knife when they had been rushed out of Sagan, and he got it out now. Taking the dead chicken outside, close to the side of the barn, he decapitated it and removed its legs and "innards." He told Bill and Ed to get the cooking pot and fill it with water. Two German guards had a small fire going to keep them warm through the night. Jim, who knew a little of the German language, went with Bud to take the chicken to the guards. With his limited German and a lot of sign language, he made a deal with the guards. "Let us cook the chicken on your fire, and we'll share it with you." Finally, the Germans got it, and they laughed and nodded, saying "Ja."

Bud stuck the chicken on a stick and burned off the feathers. Then they put the chicken in the pot, and got it to boil. The five stood around the fire with the guards, savoring the smell of the cooking chicken. They carried on a limited conversation with the guards. Over and over, the guards said, "Deutschland Kaput! Deutschland Kaput!" Looking around to make sure that no other German was near, one of them whispered, "Der Fuhrer Kaput!" Then, rather nervously, he walked a few paces away as if pretending he had had nothing to do with what he had said.

Kip brought out their tin plates and forks, plus some salt, a small amount of which he put in the pot. The Germans had their mess kits with them, so they got them out. One of them put a pot of ersatz coffee on to heat. Soon Bud declared the chicken ready, and the seven of them split it up, then sat or leaned on a fence to enjoy the late night feast of stolen chicken and false coffee.

Pleased with their successful exploit, and delighted with the tasty, extra food, the five returned to the barn. Just as they entered, the general stood with his prized bagpipe under his arm, and roared, "Attention!" The kriegies started to get to their feet, but the general said that he only wanted their attention so he could make an announcement. "Gentlemen," he said, "the German officers in charge have asked me to ask you, since many of you have been out stealing food, not to take the farmers' seed potatoes."

This brought shouts of, "You're kidding!" "Why the hell not?" "If they won't give us food, we're going to steal it."

"All right, all right! Quiet down, men," the general continued. "I know, and I understand. I'm with you on that. And the next ones who come home with a chicken, I hope you invite me to join you. God! That smelled good! We nearly died smelling that. We almost came out and raided the bastards who had that chicken!"

"Free enterprise, Pal," Bill retorted. "Get off your ass and go scrounge up a chicken for yourself, if you want one. We had to give some to the guards to pay for using their fire. Barely enough to go around."

Ed was sure the general would turn on Bill for this bit of insubordination, but the general went on. "Now, listen up. The Germans are doing the best they can to feed us. There isn't much left in this country. And you all know what we've done to their transportation and factories. But the point about the seed potatoes is this: if we steal them, once we occupy the country—and that isn't far off—they won't be able to feed themselves at all. That means that we will have to ship in food—a lot more than we'll be shipping in anyway. So they are begging us not to take their seed potatoes."

"What if we do, General?" someone called out.

"You'll do it at your own risk. The guards have been instructed to shoot anyone caught stealing potatoes. They mean business about this. I'm not sure, but I don't think the Geneva Conventions protect us when we steal. So they're asking us to cooperate. But it's more than a request. That is all. Carry on!"

As the days passed, the weather grew warmer. The disorderly column of bedraggled prisoners walked on, looking more like a parade of hoboes than marching military men. Laughing, Ed said to Bill, "We don't look much like the cadets we were at Maxwell Field, do we?

Remember how sharp our formations were? How precisely we moved in our parades? Our white gloves, polished brass and shoes, glistening sabres? And look at us now."

"God, yes!" Bill replied. "What would our tac officers say if they could see us now?"

"I don't know," Kip commented, "but we'd sure have to walk off a lot of gigs for improper uniforms!"

"Hell, man! We've walked enough miles to cover all the gigs of all the cadets who ever went to Maxwell," Bud added. "I joined the goddam Air Corps so I wouldn't have to slog through rain and snow and mud. And here I am slogging through rain and mud. But, thank God, no more snow!"

Conversation went on all along the column, with kriegies exchanging stories about experiences as cadets and officers, combat flying, their civilian lives, and hopes and dreams after liberation. This made the time and the miles pass more quickly. Periodically, Ed noticed, conversation would slack off and even stop altogether, as if a silent order had been given. Each man turned his thoughts inward, quietly hoping—perhaps praying—for survival; for liberation; for a safe return to home, family, friends, sweethearts. During such times, he could hear the irregular sound of thousands of feet moving—without the cadence of marching, but with a sort of ragged rhythm of its own underlying the rumbling of the stomachs of those close by. All this was accented with the inevitable farts generated by kriegie bread.

With warmer weather, the walking men began to sweat more. The smell of unwashed bodies and dirty clothes, combined with the smell of "natural gas" being released by someone with every step, made an odorous miasma that surrounded them as long as they walked. It was so much a part of them that, unless they consciously paid attention to it, they weren't aware of it. Ed was certain that a stranger approaching this odd formation would find the smell overpowering. "You know how someone used to have to walk ahead of lepers, yelling 'unclean,' to warn others to stay away?" he said to his friends. "Well, we need somebody to go ahead yelling, 'smelly, smelly!'" This brought a laugh. He added, "We could call ourselves the 'Smelly Squadron.'"

"How about the 'Bathless Brigade?'" Jim suggested. "Stinking Soldiers?" Bill offered.

Kip suggested, "Fetid Fliers."

Humor, crude or not, obvious or subtle, planned or spontaneous, helped keep morale up. Morale also was boosted by the massive formations of American bombers they frequently saw high above, accompanied by fighters. Once, a few minutes after seeing one such formation, Kip yelled, "Look! There's a fighter coming this way!"

The entire column stopped and stared. Coming just above the treetops from their right, Ed recognized a P-51. The plane zoomed right over Ed's part of the column, then roared off out of sight to the left. A moment later, they saw it climbing and banking to its left. They watched it straighten out and fly well past the end of their column, then turn and come right up the road at them. The guards jumped off the road and hit the dirt. Their example was followed by the prisoners. All but Ed. "That's sure to make him think we're enemy troops!" he yelled. He stood in the middle of the road and waved his arms as the 51 roared toward him. Fortunately, the pilot did not open fire, or Ed would have been blown apart. As the plane sped on, climbing, its wings rocked in greeting. Now the other kriegies came out of the ditch cheering and yelling.

"You're a damn fool!" Bill said to Ed. "I figured you'd buy it for sure."

"I figured all our guys were briefed to watch out for columns of POWs like ours, and not to fire on them. Anyway, would a fellow fighter pilot shoot at me?" Ed responded.

"You're so full of shit I can't believe it," Bill said.

Kip said, "He can't be full of shit. Haven't you smelled him farting it out all day?"

"Just like everybody else," Ed laughed. "We're the 'farting formation,' remember?"

The experience had been scary, but now they knew their whereabouts were known. On several occasions after that, American planes came low over the kriegie column, but none quite so low or so menacing as that first P-51. Each one would circle, then rock his wings, and head off to the west. All the prisoners would wave and cheer. They knew they were being observed. They were not forgotten. This meant that friendly forces would know where they were on the road, and when and where they would be when they finally got there.

It was not long before the kriegies, too, knew where they would be. One rainy day in April, they were herded into a vast fenced and barbed-wire enclosure, with guard stands positioned all around the perimeter. A huge throng of prisoners crowded around the area inside the entrance gate. "Welcome to Mooseburg, the asshole of the world!" was shouted to them as they moved in. Some of the welcoming mob recognized friends among the new-comers, and pulled them out of the pack to shake their hands or embrace them.

Mooseburg was in the Silesian sector of Germany, with rolling hills surrounding it. It was the final concentration center for Nazi-held POWs. Thousands of Americans and French, along with some Hindus from India, were gathered here to await liberation. To Ed's disappointment there were no RAF men here. It seemed that all the British prisoners were gathered at some other concentration location.

Here the barracks were not partitioned into rooms as they had been at Sagan, nor arranged in bays as at Nürnberg. Instead, they were just open spaces jammed with indi-vidual bunks. Each man's bunk was his domain, and that was good, but the arrangement did not make for any group or "family" feeling. Everyone was surrounded by hundreds of others. But Ed felt that each one was alone and on his own.

After claiming a bunk in the building to which he was assigned, Ed sloshed around part of the camp and found a few people he had known previously, including several from his fighter group. He greeted them happily, but none were men he'd been particularly close to. He and Bill, Kip, Bud, and Jim kept in touch, walking around together or visiting each other's bunks. But it wasn't the same as when they shared the same bay at Nürnberg, and it was a far cry from the fraternal feeling engendered by the room-sharing at Sagan.

Food rations were very skimpy. A few boiled potatoes, a little bread, and some hot water was distributed to each prisoner each day. Everybody in each barracks had to line up each morning to get his rations for the day. Everybody resented this, but nobody missed the morning's lineup. Since there were no cooking facilities for use by the prisoners, and no coal supplied to them, they were totally dependent on the goons for cooking their potatoes, as well as providing them, and for the hot water.

Like most of the prisoners who had arrived with him, Ed had some soluble coffee left. This made the hot water into a treat while it lasted. He rationed the coffee out to himself very carefully. Also, he carried that little bottle, and his remaining meager bit of iron ration with him any time he left his bunk. He wasn't aware of any stealing going on, but he knew that out of the thousands of men collected here, inevitably some would not be able to resist pilfering something as precious as coffee or iron ration. "Extreme hunger tends to minimize the civilizing effects of conscience," he thought philosophically and a bit pompously. "Oh well," he said to himself, "epigrams tend to be pompous as well as trite. Especially home-made ones not spouted by famous thinkers."

There were real latrines, as well as showers in buildings located near the barracks. After the crude toilets and absence of showers at Nürnberg and on the road, these were welcome, and were used a great deal. Ed's first shower was, to him, real luxury, even though he had only a thin piece of soap that someone had left, and even though the hot water ran out before he finished. After a few days, he found that the best time to shower was late at night—midnight or after. At that time, he found, he was often the only one using the showers, and the hot water was plentiful. Since the kriegies were not restricted to the barracks at night, he started to make the late night his time to enjoy showers. He had no towel, but he found an old khaki shirt someone had thrown away. He took it in with him for his first shower and washed it out under the water. For that shower, he used his own shirt for a towel, putting his flight jacket on over his bare skin. After drying and dressing, he washed his own shirt in one of the wash basins and hung both shirts on nails in the wall near his bunk. The next day they were dry. He put his own shirt on and kept the other for a towel.

Here at Mooseburg, Ed found, the guards were lax. They seemed to know that the war was almost over and that they would soon be prisoners themselves, so they didn't bother to enforce the rules. In fact, most of them began talking back and forth with the prisoners—as much as their poor English and the prisoners' limited German allowed. Many prisoners took advantage of the laxness to find or make openings in the fence and get out to wander around the countryside. Some ignored the general's warning and went farther, not coming back. There was no way of knowing what happened to them.

The senior Allied officers, including the "Bagpipe General," sent out word to discourage escapes, or attempts, or too much wandering outside the fence. They did not forbid it—which they would be unable to enforce anyway—but they said, "We know of no German underground in this area to help you out there. We do know that civilians have hung some escapees, beaten others to death, and shot some. We also want to warn you that there is a barracks of SS troops outside the fence. These are 'never-say-die' bastards. They know what is going to happen to them when our forces get here. They will shoot any prisoner they see out there. We advise all to stay inside the fences until our forces get here."

Mooseburg was a miserable place. More so even than Nürnberg had been. As food rations grew smaller, the prisoners' preoccupation with food grew greater. Getting your share of the daily dole was the most important activity. Malnutrition was rampant, with starvation a constant threat never far from their thoughts. Everybody seemed to fantasize about food, including what they would get when they were liberated and, beyond that, when they got home. Steak, roast chicken, barbecue, spaghetti, roast beef, were all high on various wishlists. For some reason, since he had never had it, Ed often fantasized about a chilled concoction made up of a layer of vanilla wafers embedded in custard with slices of bananas on top.

Each time Ed stood in line for his daily rations, he, like all the others, had to decide what to do with it: gobble it all down, then wait twenty-four hungry hours for the next allotment; drink the hot water and eat a few bites of bread, maybe one small potato, and save the rest for later in the day; or save out a little each day to build up a hoard so at some point he could gorge himself, relatively speaking? He decided that he would limit himself to one-half slice of bread and all the hot water for breakfast; one whole slice of bread, tap water, and both his potatoes for lunch; and the last one-half slice of bread and tap water, plus a tiny nibble of his nearly exhausted iron ration, for supper. This way, he found, he was always hungry, but never agonizingly so. Also, this gave him something to look forward to all through the day. The nights, of course, were quite bad. At night he tried to keep busy, wandering slowly around the camp, not hurrying because that burned up too much energy/food, and talking with other kriegies. Then after midnight, he rewarded himself with a slow, comfortable shower.

Next to food, their greatest preoccupation was liberation. They wondered when it would happen, by whom, and what would transpire afterwards. Some of the speculation was wild, ranging from the SS troops surrounding the prisoners and shooting all of them when the liberating forces got near, to Army men sneaking in at night and distributing weapons to all the kriegies so they could join in the fighting. The reality, when at last it came, was not like any of their speculation.

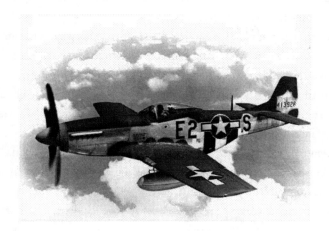

31

Liberation came in phases. The first was exciting but disappointing, in that it did not involve American soldiers armed to the teeth, coming in waves over the hills, shooting as they came.

"Hey! There's a jeep coming down the hill!" "Where?" "Right there!" "Yeah, I see it now." "Jesus! It has an American flag and a white flag on it!" Now a second crowd gathered around the first to see the jeep. "Looks like an enlisted man driving, and an officer passenger." The jeep pulled up to the gate. Ed saw that the driver was a sergeant and the passenger was a major. The major got out and spoke in German to one of the gate guards, who saluted, then pointed to the commandant's office. After speaking to the driver, the major walked to the door of the office.

The commandant came out and exchanged salutes with the major. After a few moments of talk, the two went to the gate. The major got back into the jeep and the commandant gave orders to the guards, who opened the gate. In came the jeep. The prisoners, uncertain what was going on, wondered whether this was just two more prisoners or what. They made their way toward the jeep. The jeep proceeded to a place near one of the latrines, close to the center of the compound, where it stopped. By this time, every prisoner had left whatever he was doing and had joined the throng surrounding the jeep.

Now, the major stood up in the jeep. "Where is the senior Allied officer?" he asked. Not the heroic words the kriegies had hoped for.

"Right here, major," the Bagpipe General said, as he made his way to the jeep. He returned the major's salute. "Welcome to Mooseburg, better known as 'the asshole of the world.'" This brought laughs and a few cheers from the men. "This is your welcoming committee, major," and he pointed to the mob of kriegies. "Sorry, but most of us are out of uniform." A big laugh came from the mob, followed by a bigger one when he added, "If we'd known you were coming, we'd have had a banquet ready."

"Thank you, General. I don't have any food to offer you either." Groans came from the kriegies. "Do I have your permission, General, to say a few words to these men?"

"By all means, Major. Give us the word."

"Gentlemen, I'm Major Brady, of General Patton's staff." Cheers erupted at the mention of General Patton. When the cheers subsided, the major continued, "This is Sergeant Miller. We are the newest POWs here at Mooseburg. The general sent us here to join you as prisoners, in order to bring you some messages. First, liberation is near!" More cheers, this time prolonged. "I have to warn you: since there is a contingent of SS troops nearby, there will be some gunfire. When the first units of our forces come over that hill," he pointed to the hill he had just come down, "you must take cover. If you are inside, lie on the floor. If outside, hit the deck right where you are."

"How soon, Major?"

"Should be day after tomorrow."

"Any food?"

"I can't answer that. If General Patton has any supplies, I'm sure he'll get them to you. Otherwise, it won't be long that supplies start coming after liberation. The commandant tells me that he has very little in the warehouse. He will continue to disburse that as long as it lasts. Another thing—the commandant assures me that the regular guards will not resist. They will stay at their posts until our men order them down; then they will drop their weapons and climb down peaceably to be taken into custody."

He stepped out of the jeep and said, "I need to take a piss," and the general led him to the latrine. The sergeant followed in the jeep. That ended the first phase of the liberation. Disappointing, but promising bigger things to follow.

During that night and all the next day, sporadic gunfire could be heard from over the hills to the west and south at a distance but getting closer. For the most part it sounded like light arms, such as foot soldiers would carry. But now and again heavier booms could be heard, as would be made by guns mounted on tanks. No men or machines could be seen, but the sounds continued into the night, getting closer.

At dawn the next day there was no gunfire. Ed and Bill moved away from all the other kriegies and, by listening very intently, they thought they heard a distant rumbling, like powerful, heavy vehicles moving. The sound seemed to increase, then fade, then grow louder. They kept listening. Others joined them, all trying to keep quiet and listen. Now the sound grew even louder, and it seemed to be just beyond the close hills to the west. Bill looked at Ed, his eyes glittering, "They're almost here! It won't be long now."

Others were saying the same thing, shaking hands, thumping each others' backs. As their enthusiasm mounted, someone said, "Wait a minute! I can't hear it any more." A hush fell over the crowd. All the sounds had stopped. "What's going on?" Kip wondered.

Ed said, "I don't know. Maybe they're all in position for the final move over the hills and on to us. They must be waiting for orders to go on." The others agreed that must be it. It was now 09:30. Kriegies drifted off to latrines, or to finish breakfast, or stretch out on their bunks, waiting for something to happen. No matter what they did, they all had a feeling of expectancy — that tension that comes when you know something momentous is about to happen, but you are powerless to make it happen sooner. You have to wait.

Ed and his friends stayed out and continued to watch and wait. Jim asked Bill what time it was. Bill, the only one who still had a watch, replied, "10:56." They heard the sound of a heavy engine starting, then another, and in a few minutes, the sound they had heard earlier was on again, not far away.

"There's one coming!" Kip yelled. Everybody looked where he pointed. A tank was coming over the hill directly to the west, heading straight toward them. Only the fence stood between it and them. Coming slowly, another appeared on its left — it turned to parallel the fence, heading north. A third came over the hill fifty yards to the north of the first one, and stopped with its guns pointed at the SS barracks. The kriegies could see a fourth tank farther north, also pointing toward the SS building.

Now the first tank was at the fence. It did not stop. It kept coming, demolishing the fence and the barbed wire inside it, continuing toward the crowd of kriegies. They scattered out of its path. It advanced until it was right in the space between the fence and the nearest barracks. It turned so its guns pointed toward the SS building. The hatch on top of the tank opened, and a grinning head came out. "Good to see you, but take cover! There will be firing. Get away from here. Get inside or down. Do it now!" The head disappeared and the hatch was closed.

In the meantime, foot soldiers had come up behind the tanks outside the fence and dropped to prone positions, with their weapons trained on the SS barracks. A loud voice called, "All right, Nazi bastards! Come out with your hands on your heads, or we'll blow you to hell, where you belong!"

There was no response for about ten seconds, during which Ed looked up from his place under the barracks near the tank, and could see no guards in the nearest guard stand. "Must all be lying on the floor," he said to others on the ground around him.

Now there was a burst of gunfire from the SS building. This was followed by individual shots. The SS men were not going to give up. Answering fire from the prone GIs was deafening. "Nobody could survive that," Ed thought, as he watched holes appearing in every part of the barracks walls. But shots still came from inside. Now the door flew open and two black-uniformed men stepped out, firing their automatic weapons as they came. In a second, they were almost cut in two by answering fire. Shots were still coming from the barracks. The tank in front of Ed and his friends seemed to jump a little, as it fired its 75 mm. at the barracks. It was a direct hit at close range. The building erupted like a volcano, with pieces of wood and roofing material flying upwards, then arking to the ground. There were no more shots from the barracks. All shooting stopped. It was as quiet as it had been noisy.

Ed and his mates started to wriggle out from under the barracks. They wanted to stand up and cheer. The hatch on the tank opened a few inches, and the voice yelled, "Stay down! One or two may be playing possum. Stay down!" They did. Watching, they saw three GIs crouching, weapons ready, advancing on the ruined building. There was a movement in the rubble. All three opened fire. No more movement. The three soldiers advanced and probed the wreckage. "All clear!" one shouted.

Now the cheering started. All the goon guards left their weapons in the stands and climbed down, putting their hands on their heads as their feet touched the ground. They were searched, then hustled off over the hill by some of the GIs. Soon the tanks moved out, followed by the rest of the foot soldiers.

As if a silent command had been given, all of the kriegies headed for the remaining fence and began tearing it down. It was the hated symbol of their imprisonment. Some of them climbed into the guard towers, hoping to find souvenirs, or even abandoned weapons, perhaps a bit of food. They found that the GIs had been very efficient. There was nothing. Ed and his four friends, though, stayed in one to enjoy the view and the freedom to be there. In the eastern distance, they could see the tanks and GIs moving on to their next objective. Phase two of their liberation was over. It had been more exciting than phase one.

Everything had been carried out so efficiently and so quickly that it was barely noon when the last of the GIs and their tanks waved to the kriegies and disappeared while the kriegies cheered and shouted their thanks.

Before long, the Bagpipe General and the visiting major called the former prisoners together. After the cheers that greeted the major as he stood up in the jeep subsided, he said, "Gentlemen, it isn't official yet, but you are informally returned to Allied Military Control." Cheers. "Your senior officer, the general, is your commanding officer until further notice. His orders, and those of his staff—which he has already appointed—are to be obeyed. Military discipline is in effect as of this moment. Without it, disorder and chaos will reign. We cannot have that. You are to conduct yourselves as officers of your country's military. As soon as possible, an official administrative staff will be brought in. The general will then turn his command over to them. The general may want to make this an order, but my advice to you is to stay in or near the camp. There is a lot of danger out there. Don't risk it. Your return to proper facilities, good medical care, clean uniforms, and good food will be expedited. Your cooperation will help in moving things along. I thank you for your hospitality. The sergeant and I will now return to our unit. General, take over please."

The kriegies applauded and cheered as the jeep drove away. General Hughes introduced a colonel, three majors, and nearly a dozen captains as his administrative staff. "My orders are very few," he said. "Number One: Stay here, don't wander off. Number Two: Do not attempt to break into the warehouses. There is very little food there. I have appointed men to dispense rations, just as the Germans did. It won't be long until more and better food is brought in for us. We must make what is available last until then. There will be armed guards assigned to the warehouses. I apologize for that, but we have to make sure everybody gets his share, and that nobody gets more. Third: Do not try to destroy the buildings outside the camp. When military adminstrators arrive, they will need offices and desks for all the paperwork necessary to move us out as quickly and efficiently as possible. They can move right into those buildings and get right to work. That will be good for all of us. I ask your cooperation in all of this. Thanks." He walked away, and the kriegies went off to eat their small lunch rations. Morale was high, griping was minimal, and excited talk prevailed everywhere.

Phase Three started late that afternoon, when someone yelled, "Hey! Here comes a jeep!" A rush of kriegies hurried to where the gate had been as a jeep advanced between the commandant's office and the warehouse. On each side of the jeep, next to the headlights, a small flag was attached. One was an American flag. The other had three stars on it—a lieutenant general's flag. "Must be General Patton himself," Ed said.

"I doubt it," Bill said. "Why would he come here? He'd send someone else."

The jeep stopped at the warehouse, in front of the loading platform. A silver-haired man who had been sitting beside the driver put on a helmet. It had three stars across the front. A gasp went up from the kriegies. "My God! It's him!" someone exclaimed.

The man stood up and stepped out. Now there was no doubt about it. He wore riding britches, knee-high boots, and a shirt with rows of ribbons over the left pocket. His face was sun-exposure red-tan, and his back was ramrod straight. Holsters on each side carried pearl-handled revolvers. He went up the steps and onto the loading dock. The same major who had come into the camp several days earlier followed him onto the dock.

The major held up his hands for quiet, and said, "Gentlemen. General George S. Patton." A tremendous cheer went up from the throng of men. It went on and on. Finally, the general held up his hands and the cheering stopped.

For a few moments, in the expectant silence, the general said nothing, while he looked over the ragged mob. At last, his rugged, deeply seamed face broke into a smile, and he said, "Hello Kriegies! What in hell are you doing here?" This started the cheers again. Once again the general signaled quiet. "You're the worst looking mob of sons-of-bitches I've ever seen! Are you sure you bastards are military people? I guess you are. I see a bar here and there, and what look like uniform shirts and jackets. So I guess I'm in the right place. But you sure look awful! Are you hungry?"

"Yeah! Hell yes!"

"I hate to tell you this, but so are my men. So am I, matter of fact. Our supplies are way behind us. I have word, though, that supplies are on their way. Both from our military and from the International Red Cross. You'll get them as soon as they arrive. Now, who's in charge here? Where's General Hughes?"

"Right here, Sir," the Bagpipe General replied.

"Get the hell up here," Patton said.

General Hughes went up and saluted. Patton returned the salute, then embraced him. "Good to see you, General," he said, "but you sure have a scurvy-looking bunch of shitheads for troops. You don't look much better yourself!" Then, turning toward the jeep, he yelled, "Sergeant! Get that flag up here!" Then again to the crowd, "What the hell is that goddam Nazi flag still up there for? Get it down, and let's get a *real* flag up there!"

A kriegie, standing not far from Ed, called out, "Save your flag, General! We brought one with us." It was Martin Allain, who had carried the flag—sewn between two blankets—from his former POW camp and through the entire trip to Mooseburg. He and a friend climbed the pole and tore down the Nazi flag, dropping it to the ground, where kriegies trampled it, then kicked it on to those next to them. It was kicked and trampled until it was reduced to a dirty, unrecognizable rag. Patton called out to the guy with the flag, "Hold it a minute up there. To the throng he shouted, "Is there a bugler in the outfit?"

"Here, Sir," a kriegie said, holding up a trumpet.

"Get up here, Son. Let him through there." When he was on the platform, the general asked him if he could play "To the Colors." He said that he could. "All right, up there! When you're ready, unfurl the colors." To the trumpeter he said, "Okay, blow that horn."

The trumpet sounded the notes, the general snapped to attention and raised his right hand in salute, and the ragged kriegies did the same. All eyes were on the flag as it slowly caught the breeze, unfurling, showing its stripes and stars. Ed felt tears pressing behind his eyes. He held them back until he glanced up at General Patton and saw tears rolling down the rugged face. Then he let his own go. His were not the only ones. The flag flared out fully as the last notes faded away. The general dropped his hand to his side, and the mightiest cheer yet rolled up from the crowd. Many were dabbing at their eyes, unashamed.

The cheers died away. Ed started "Oh say can you see," and every voice joined in. He doubted that the "Star Spangled Banner" had ever had a lustier or more heart-felt rendition. It was impossible to hold back tears. Unashamedly, all the men turned to those around them, friends or not, and hugged them at the end of the song. Eyes shiny with tears and joy were everywhere. Little was said—speaking was too hard. The embraces said it all.

Finally, as things quieted down, General Patton blew his nose into his handerchief and said, "You people will be all right. God bless you." He shook hands with General Hughes and mounted the jeep. Like the cavalry man he considered himself to be in his heart-of-hearts, he rode away. Cheers followed until he was out of sight. This was the climactic conclusion of Phase Three.

A profound silence fell over the throng as each man dealt with his feelings. All remained where they were, uncertain what to do next. They were free but had no place to go. They were jubilant about their liberation, but their immediate circumstances had not changed.

Still on the platform, General Hughes raised his hands and bellowed for attention. "We're the lucky ones!" he shouted. "We lived through this friggin' air war!" Then quietly, solemnly, he raised his right hand in salute, saying, "I salute the thousands of our flying buddies who did not. Never forget them. Now they fly with angels."

359TH FIGHTER GROUP

HISTORY:
Constituted as 359th Fighter Group on 20 Dec 1942. Activated on 15 Jan 1943. Apparently not manned until Mar 1943. Moved to England in Oct 1943 and became part of Eighth AF. Entered combat in mid-Dec, after some of the pilots had already flown combat missions with another fighter group. Began operations with P-47s; converted to P-51s in Apr 1944. In combat Dec 1943–May 1945. Flew escort, patrol, strafing, dive-bombing, and weather-reconnaissance missions. At first, engaged primarily in escort activities to cover bombers that attacked airfields in France. Expanded area of operations in May 1944 to provide escort for bombers that struck rail centers in Germany and oil targets in Poland. Supported the invasion of Normandy (Jun 1944), patrolling the English Channel, escorting bombardment formations to the French coast, and dive-bombing and strafing bridges, locomotives, and rail lines near the battle area. During the period Jul 1944–Feb 1945, engaged chiefly in escorting bombers to oil refineries, marshalling yards, and other targets in such cities as Ludwigshafen, Stuttgart, Frankfurt, Berlin, Merseburg, and Brux. Received a DUC for operations over Germany on 11 Sep 1944 when the group protected a formation of heavy bombers against large numbers of enemy fighters. In addition to its escort duties, the group supported campaigns in France during Jul and Aug 1944, bombed enemy positions to support the airborne invasion of Holland in Sep, and participated in the Battle of the Bulge (Dec 1944–Jan 1945). Flew missions to support the assault across the Rhine in Mar 1945, and escorted medium bombers that attacked various communications targets, Feb–Apr 1945.
Returned to the US in Nov 1945. Inactivated on 10 Nov 1945.

SQUADRONS:
156th: 1950–1952
368th (later 165th): 1943–1945; 1950–1952
369th (later 167th): 1943–1945; 1950–1952
370th: 1943–1945

STATIONS:
Westover Field, Mass, 15 Jan 1943
Grenier Field, NH, 7 Apr 1943
Republic Field, NY, 11 Jul 1943
Westover Field, Mass, 23 Aug–2 Oct 1943
East Wretham, England, Oct 1943–Nov 1945
Camp Kilmer, NJ, 9–10 Nov 1945.
Standiford Mun Aprt, Ky, 10 Oct 1950
Godman AFB, Ky, c. 20 Oct 1950–15 Nov 1951
Manston RAF Station, England, 10 Dec 1951–10 Jul 1952

COMMANDERS:
Col Avelin P Tacon Jr, Jan 1943
Col John P Randolph, 12 Nov 1944
Lt Col Donald A Baccus, 8 Apr 1945
Lt Col Daniel D McKee, c. 16 Sep 1945–unknown
Col Philip P Ardery, 10 Oct 1950
Lt Col William J Payne, 26 Oct 1950
Lt Col Chesley G Peterson, 20 Apr 1951
Lt Col Delynn E Anderson, 4 Aug 1951–Jul 1952

CAMPAIGNS:
Air Offensive, Europe; Normandy; Northern France; Rhineland; Ardennes-Alsace; Central Europe

DECORATIONS:
Distinguished Unit Citation: Germany, 11 Sep 1944